Sleep, Circadian Rhythms and Metabolism

Sleep, Circadian Rhythms and Metabolism

Editor: Robert Bennett

MURPHY & MOORE
www.murphy-moorepublishing.com

www.murphy-moorepublishing.com

MURPHY & MOORE

Cataloging-in-Publication Data

Sleep, circadian rhythms and metabolism / edited by Robert Bennett.
p. cm.
Includes bibliographical references and index.
ISBN 978-1-63987-500-9
1. Sleep. 2. Circadian rhythms. 3. Metabolism. 4. Psychophysiology. 5. Psychobiology. I. Bennett, Robert.
RA786 .S54 2022
613.794--dc23

Murphy & Moore Publishing,
1 Rockefeller Plaza,
New York City, NY 10020, USA

ISBN 978-1-63987-500-9 (Hardback)

Contents

Preface

The natural and internal process which maintains the sleep-wake cycle is termed as a circadian rhythm. It repeats every 24 hours. It is endogenous in nature and responds to the environment. Circadian rhythms are governed by the circadian clock and can be seen in various types of organisms such as animals, plants, cyanobacteria and fungi. The primary circadian clock within mammals is located within a specific collection of cells in the hypothalamus called the suprachiasmatic nucleus (SCN). Any disruption in the circadian rhythms causes metabolic dysregulation. Interactions have also been observed at cellular, molecular and neural scales. This book provides significant information of this discipline to help develop a good understanding of circadian rhythms and metabolism. From theories to research to practical applications, case studies related to all contemporary topics of relevance to this field have been included in it. The book is appropriate for students seeking detailed information in this area as well as for experts.

The information shared in this book is based on empirical researches made by veterans in this field of study. The elaborative information provided in this book will help the readers further their scope of knowledge leading to advancements in this field.

Finally, I would like to thank my fellow researchers who gave constructive feedback and my family members who supported me at every step of my research.

Editor

1

Factors Affecting Measurement of Salivary Cortisol and Secretory Immunoglobulin A in Field Studies of Athletes

Barry Thomas Pritchard[1], Warren Stanton[1], Roger Lord[2], Peter Petocz[3] and Gert-Jan Pepping[4]*

[1] *School of Physiotherapy, Australian Catholic University, Brisbane, QLD, Australia,* [2] *School of Science, Australian Catholic University, Brisbane, QLD, Australia,* [3] *Department of Statistics, Macquarie University, Sydney, NSW, Australia,* [4] *School of Exercise Science, Australian Catholic University, Brisbane, QLD, Australia*

Edited by:
Andries Kalsbeek,
Academic Medical Center,
Netherlands

Reviewed by:
Tamas Kozicz,
Radboud University Nijmegen,
Netherlands
Gábor B. Makara,
Institute of Experimental Medicine,
Hungary

****Correspondence:***
Barry Thomas Pritchard
barry.pritchard@acu.edu.au

Aims: Biological and lifestyle factors, such as daily rhythm, caffeine ingestion, recent infection, and antibiotic intake, have been shown to influence measurements of salivary cortisol (SC) and secretory immunoglobulin A (sIgA). Current methodology in unsynchronized, field-based biomarker studies does not take these effects into account. Moreover, very little is known about the combined effects of biological and lifestyle factors on SC and sIgA. This study supports development of a protocol for measuring biomarkers from saliva collected in field studies by examining the individual and combined effects of these factors on SC and sIgA.

Method: At three time points (start of the pre-season; start of playing season; and end of playing season), saliva samples were collected from the entire squad of 45 male players of an elite Australian Football club (mean age 22.8 ± 3.5 years). At each time, point daily rhythm and lifestyle factors were determined *via* a questionnaire, and concentrations of both SC and sIgA *via* an enzyme linked immuno-sorbent (ELISA) assay of saliva samples. In addition, player times to produce 0.5 mL of saliva were recorded.

Results: Analysis of covariance of the data across the three time points showed that daily rhythm had a more consistent effect than the lifestyle factors of caffeine ingestion, recent infection, and antibiotic intake on SC, but not on sIgA. Data for sIgA and SC concentrations were then adjusted for the effects of daily rhythm and lifestyle factors, and correlational analysis of the pooled data was used to examine the relative effects of these two sources of influence on sIgA and SC. With the exception of time to produce saliva, the biological measures of stress were affected by players' daily rhythms. When daily rhythm was taken into account the group of lifestyle factors did not have an additional effect.

Discussion: It is recommended that future studies measuring SC and sIgA make additional adjustments for the daily rhythm, in particular time since first sight of daylight, as small measurement errors of biomarkers can confound discrimination among study participants.

Keywords: stress, cortisol, sIgA, salivary immunoglobulin A, biomarkers, salivary cortisol, stress hormone, HPA axis

INTRODUCTION

Stress manifests by diverse etiologies with many undesirable health outcomes, including effects upon performance in sport, as well as other occupational and performance contexts. Major to minor health effects of stress have been reported (1), and in a sports environment, levels of stress have been linked to recovery time, burnout due to overtraining, muscle damage repair time, and susceptibility to infection (2–7).

Psychological and physiological stressors are important instigators of hypothalamus–pituitary–adrenal axis activation, which have downstream influence on parameters such as immunoglobulin levels and salivary cortisol (SC) concentrations in humans. For this reason, SC, and secretory immunoglobulin A (sIgA) are widely reported as biomarkers of stress (8). Previous studies of stress biomarkers have not adequately adjusted SC and sIgA for biological effects such as daily rhythm and lifestyle factors including caffeine ingestion, recent infection, and antibiotic intake (8, 9). For example, adjustment for daily rhythm is performed by collecting samples at similar times, but no studies could be identified that took into account daily rythym variation in participants' first seeing daylight after waking. To assist in the development of a protocol for measuring biomarkers from saliva collected in field studies, the aim of the current study was to investigate the combined effects of daily rhythm and lifestyle factors, specifically: caffeine ingestion, recent infection, and antibiotic intake, on SC and sIgA collected from a population of high performance athletes.

Cortisol and sIgA concentrations can be obtained *via* blood sampling, though the inherent risks associated with venipuncture are numerous (10). Previous research has shown that SC is a more robust measure of stress than serum cortisol because SC is a better measure of adrenal cortical function (11, 12). Saliva sample collection is non-invasive, more time efficient, and safer in field studies than blood collection. For this reason, saliva sample collection has become more widely used for measurement of SC and sIgA in the context of stress in research fields such as sports exercise physiology and biopsychology.

In terms of biological factors that affect measures of stress, daily rhythms have been reported to affect SC and sIgA concentrations and associated salivary flow rate (13). It is well understood that the first sight of daylight after waking initiates the circadian response although there is surprisingly little research available on daily rhythm variation within normal salivary flow rate over a 24-h period.

A number of lifestyle factors have been shown to confound measurement of SC and sIgA (8). In the current study of a homogenous group of elite athletes, we will focus on the most prevalent confounding influences of caffeine ingestion, recent infection, use of antibiotics, and recent surgery (14). Caffeine, a commonly ingested psychoactive agent found in coffee, tea, and energy drinks has been shown to elevate concentrations of SC (15). Ingestion of antibiotics and/or recent infection has been associated with an increased SC and sIgA production (16). An increase in sIgA occurs after antigenic stimulation *via* the humoral immunity response, which varies within individuals and type of antigen exposure. For example, influenza sIgA antibodies usually peak two weeks after stimulation in the majority of the population (17). Recent surgery has been shown to increase SC, likely as a stress response from the body to produce a higher prophylactic concentration of anti-inflammatory agent (14, 18, 19). Surprisingly, in many previous studies, the confounding effects of these lifestyle factors are not taken into account (20, 21).

When working with sports teams, it is often difficult to fit a testing protocol into their strict training regime. Players awake at different times of the morning, and often arrive at the athletic club to train in prearranged staggered groups. Dawes (22) showed that daily rhythms also affect the time taken to produce unstimulated saliva. This implies that measurement of SC, sIgA, and salivary flow rate should be standardized by regression to a common time point to adjust for the time differential since participants first saw daylight (22). A similar argument can be developed with regards to other factors that influence levels of SC and sIgA. It is likely that players have different levels of caffeine ingestion and rates of infection and antibiotic use, indicating a need to assess and adjust for these individual differences.

The development of reliable SC and sIgA quantification research methods for biomarker studies is imperative, to improve of the quality of studies of stress and the information used to assist medical care, coaching style, and player development of athletes. The rationale for this study was that a significant error may be introduced if measures are not adequately corrected for biological and lifestyle factors, in particular daily rhythm. The aim of this study, therefore, was to examine the effects of daily rhythm, caffeine ingestion, recent infection, and antibiotic intake on SC and sIgA concentrations. In particular, the study; (a) examined consistency in the effect of biological and lifestyle factors across three time points, and (b) compared the combined and separate effects of these factors.

MATERIALS AND METHODS

Sample

Participants in the study were a cohort of 46 elite male players from a club in the National Australian Football League, representing the entire training squad of the club. The study was approved by the Human Research Ethics Committee, Australian Catholic University (HREC ACU), and consent obtained from all research participants was both informed and written. The mean (±SD) age, height, and weight of the players was 22.8 ± 3.5 years, 187.9 ± 6.0 cm, and 88.3 ± 6.6 kg, respectively. Players' ages ranged from 19 to 31 years.

Procedures

Questionnaires were administered at three time points, the start of pre-season (T1), the start of the playing season (T2), and the end of the playing season (T3). Players provided information about demographic characteristics, recent injury history, time of first seeing daylight, caffeine ingestion before they arrived at the sports club, illness or infection in the past week, antibiotic ingestion in the past week, and surgery in the past month. Saliva samples were collected at each assessment time point.

Players arrived at the club in staggered groups of four. A sampling team of five experienced researchers were trained in the sampling procedure to ensure consistent technique. One member of the team was present at the point of entry to record arrival times and to ensure all players thoroughly rinsed their mouth with water. Players were requested to give a saliva sample 10 min after the rinse as per the immunoassay protocol (Salimetrics, Carlsbad, CA, USA).

Players were seated in a quiet room, where visual and verbal contact with other players was minimized. Research staff informed each player of the process required for passive saliva collection, and answered any participant questions. Unstimulated saliva was collected into a small pre-labeled Eppendorf tube *via* a straw, and the time taken to obtain 0.5 mL of saliva was recorded in seconds.

The saliva samples were immediately stored at approximately 4°C in a polystyrene container with ice, prior to transport and subsequent storage in the laboratory. The sample was de-identified by application of a laboratory number, sealed in a plastic snap lock bag, and chilled to prevent both microbial growth and protein degradation.

Within the testing laboratory, samples were split into two Eppendorf tubes to allow assay re-run if required. Labeled saliva samples were frozen at −80°C within a secure, back-up powered ultra-low freezer within 4 h of collection. No additional preservatives such as sodium azide were added to the samples to exclude possible assay interference. Freezing saliva samples are known to precipitate mucins within the saliva samples so before assaying, samples were thawed, vortexed, and centrifuged at 1,500 g (@3,000 rpm) for 15 min as per ELISA protocol (Salimetrics, Carlsbad, CA, USA). The sIgA and SC ELISA assays were both read using a Biorad iMark microplate reader with a 450 nm filter (23).

ELISA Assays

To quantify the steroid hormone SC and sIgA proteins, saliva samples were taken and assayed using competitive ELISA kits from Salimetrics (Carlsbad, CA, USA) and used in accordance with the manufacturer's directions.

Adjustment for the Effects of Daily Rhythm on Cortisol and IgA Concentrations

Salivary cortisol and sIgA diurnal fluctuation data [taken from Ref. (24)] were used to adjust cortisol concentrations to a standardized time of first daylight response. First, originally measured participant concentrations of SC were transformed to square root nmol/L, which for the remainder will be referred to as the unadjusted cortisol concentration ($SC_{unadjusted}$). From the time of seeing first daylight for the individual participant and the diurnal cycle data presented by Hucklebridge et al. (24), an individual adjustment concentration value (SC_{adjust}) was obtained. To calculate the adjusted SC concentration since awakening (Daily Rhythm Adjusted: SC_{DRA}), the individual adjustment concentration was added to the $SC_{unadjusted}$. In short:

$$SC_{DRA} = SC_{unadjusted} + SC_{adjust} \tag{1}$$

The same process was followed for sIgA. As Hucklebridge et al. (24) described diurnal sIgA response in concentration values of μg/mL, no transformation of units was necessary for sIgA. The adjusted sIgA concentration since awakening (Daily Rhythm Adjusted: $sIgA_{DRA}$) was calculated as the sum of the unadjusted sIgA concentration ($sIgA_{unadjusted}$) and the individual adjustment concentration value ($sIgA_{adjust}$), calculated from the time since awakening for the individual participant and the diurnal cycle data presented by Hucklebridge et al. (24).

$$sIgA_{DRA} = sIgA_{unadjusted} + sIgA_{adjust} \tag{2}$$

Adjustment for the Effects of Lifestyle Factor on Cortisol and IgA Concentrations

Adjustment for the lifestyle factors was achieved by subjecting SC_{DRA} and $sIgA_{DRA}$ to regression analysis, to obtain the means and unstandardized residual variances. The residuals were then added to the respective means to calculate lifestyle adjusted SC_{DRA}^{LA} and $sIgA_{DRA}^{LA}$ with the effect of daily rhythm and lifestyle factors removed.

Statistical Analysis

Consistency of Factors across Time

Analysis of covariance (ANCOVA) with Type III sums of squares model (SPSS, version 22; www.spss.com) was used to examine the effects of the daily rhythm and lifestyle factors on the biomarker measures of stress at three separate times. The outcome measures were $SC_{unadjusted}$ and $sIgA_{unadjusted}$, and salivary flow rate. The concentrations of sIgA and cortisol were analyzed on a log scale in order to satisfy the distributional assumptions required for the analyses. Age, height, and weight were included as covariates in the analysis. The independent variables of interest were caffeine ingestion on the day of testing, infection in the past week, and use of antibiotics in the past week (all coded no or yes), as well as time since seeing daylight to collection of saliva (minutes), and time to produce 0.5 mL of saliva (seconds).

Relative Effects of Daily Rhythm and Lifestyle Factors

The data for the three time points were pooled ($n = 130$) to provide an average effect across time. Correlational analysis was used to assess the effect of daily rhythm and lifestyle factors on the unadjusted and the adjusted measures of SC and sIgA concentrations. Percentage change in the correlation was used to estimate the size of the confounding effect.

RESULTS

Consistency across Time

Among the 130 assessments across the three time periods, caffeine consumption before arriving at training occurred on 22.0% of occasions, an infection in the past week occurred on 31.8% of occasions, and use of antibiotics in the past week occurred on 24.2% of occasions. None of the players had recent surgery. There was consistency across time for the rate of caffeine consumption and use of antibiotics, but the rate of infection was higher on the third assessment day (51.2%) compared to other days (21.7 and 23.3% respectively; chi-square = 11.02, $p = 0.004$).

The ANCOVA results shown in **Table 1** indicate that the biological factors of "time since seeing daylight" and "time to

TABLE 1 | Factors related to concentrations of cortisol and immunoglobulin A in saliva.[a,b]

Measure	Time 1 (n = 44) start pre-season		Time 2 (n = 43) start season		Time 3 (n = 43) end season	
	F	p	F	p	F	p
$SC_{unadjusted}$						
Caffeine (today)	0.32	0.58	0.01	0.97	0.14	0.71
Infection or illness (last week)	0.36	0.55	0.39	0.54	0.03	0.86
Antibiotics (last week)	6.17	0.02*	0.14	0.71	0.98	0.33
Caffeine × infection	0.89	0.35	0.49	0.49	0.12	0.73
Caffeine × antibiotics	0.45	0.51	0.13	0.73	0.88	0.36
Infection × antibiotics	6.13	0.02*	0.12	0.74	0.52	0.48
Time since seeing daylight (min)	1.55	0.22	5.70	0.02*	4.88	0.04*
Time for saliva[c] (s)	8.36	0.01*	0.45	0.83	0.02	0.88
$sIgA_{unadjusted}$						
Caffeine (today)	0.01	0.99	0.09	0.77	1.09	0.30
Infection or illness (last week)	0.19	0.67	0.07	0.79	1.09	0.30
Antibiotics (last week)	2.32	0.14	0.41	0.53	0.27	0.61
Caffeine × infection	0.78	0.38	1.59	0.22	0.74	0.40
Caffeine × antibiotics	4.94	0.03*	0.15	0.70	0.24	0.63
Infection × antibiotics	4.62	0.04*	0.48	0.49	0.05	0.82
Time since seeing daylight (min)	0.03	0.87	0.09	0.77	0.16	0.69
Time for saliva[c] (s)	0.29	0.59	0.77	0.39	0.13	0.72

*[a]Adjusted for age, height and weight, *$p < 0.05$.*
[b]Lifestyle factors of caffeine, antibiotics, and infection coded "yes" or "no."
[c]Time to produce 0.5 mL of saliva.

produce 0.5 mL of saliva" were associated only with $SC_{unadjusted}$. The measure of daily rhythm (time since seeing daylight) was the only factor related to a biomarker at more than one time point. Some lifestyle factors were associated with $SC_{unadjusted}$ and $sIgA_{unadjusted}$ concentrations when players returned after the off-season (Time 1) but not after the pre-season or playing season.

Relative Effects of Biological and Lifestyle Factors on Measures of Stress

The Pearson correlation statistics shown in **Table 2** for the pooled data indicate the extent of change from adjusting SC and sIgA concentrations for the effects of saliva flow rate, daily rhythm, CAI (caffeine consumption, infection, antibiotic use), and the combination of these factors. The time to produce 0.5 mL of saliva was least affected by the daily rhythm (1%). SC and sIgA concentrations changed by 5% or more due to the daily rhythm (Column 1 of **Table 2**). The table values in Column 2 of **Table 2** indicate that after adjustment for daily rhythm, adjustment for lifestyle factors made little or no further difference to the magnitude of correlation. A descriptive comparison of the original and adjusted values used for analysis is provided in **Figure 1** and **Table 3**.

DISCUSSION

Biomarkers are commonly used as measures of physiological reactions to stress, of which SC and sIgA are highly regarded. In the present study, development of a procedure to measure biomarkers of stress in field studies was conducted with a homogenous sample of fulltime sportsmen. We studied Australian Football players in a single team, with similar levels of environmental stressors such as training regimes and competition match play, and similar levels of psychological pressure related to the competitiveness of playing professional football. This enabled us to investigate the effects of daily rhythm and lifestyle factors on SC and sIgA.

TABLE 2 | Correlations of biomarker measurements of stress (n = 130).

Measure (adjustment)	Units	Adjustment	
		Daily rhythm	Daily rhythm + lifestyle factors
Time for saliva[a,b]	s	0.99	0.99
SC	μg/dL	0.95	0.94
sIgA	μg/mL	0.93	0.93

Daily rhythm = adjusted for daily rhythm.
Lifestyle factors = caffeine (today), antibiotics (last week), infection (last week).
[a]Time = time to produce 0.5 mL of saliva.
[b]Time since first sight of daylight used to represent the daily rhythm.

Effects of Lifestyle Factors

A relationship between lifestyle factors and biomarkers of stress was evident when players returned after the off-season, but not during the training and playing seasons. This relationship was represented mostly by interaction effects, for example combined effects of infection and antibiotic use (**Table 1**). This may have been due to changes in the intensity of the athletes' training regime (8), or a change in prevalence of the lifestyle factors. In addition, changes in individual IgA antibody responses may be related to the particular type of infection, indicating a need for future studies to investigate the relationship between stress response and type of infection. The absence of an effect of caffeine intake may be due to regular caffeine consumption producing tolerance effects. Research has shown that tolerance to caffeine is related to a reduced cortisol response (15).

In the analysis of the pooled data (**Table 2**), the biological factor of daily rhythm was taken into account before the lifestyle factors, as it was more consistently associated with levels of biomarker concentrations across time. After adjustment for this biological factor, the lifestyle factors no longer affected the degree of association with SC and sIgA. These findings suggest that field studies may not need to adjust for these lifestyle factors. Confirmation of this could be obtained by a study of the effect of lifestyle factors on biomarker concentrations, when saliva samples are collected at the same time relative to first sight of daylight.

Effects of Daily Rhythm

Analysis of the biomarkers at three separate time points indicated that daily rhythm, measured as time of saliva collection relative to first sight of daylight, was not related to sIgA concentrations but was significantly associated with cortisol concentrations during the periods over the playing season. A proxy measure of the effect of daily rhythm—time since seeing daylight—was used and has potential validation in the first part of the analysis (results in **Table 1**) as there are no published biological studies reporting the effect of daily rhythm on production of saliva. In the second part of the analysis (**Table 2**), correlation analysis of the pooled data

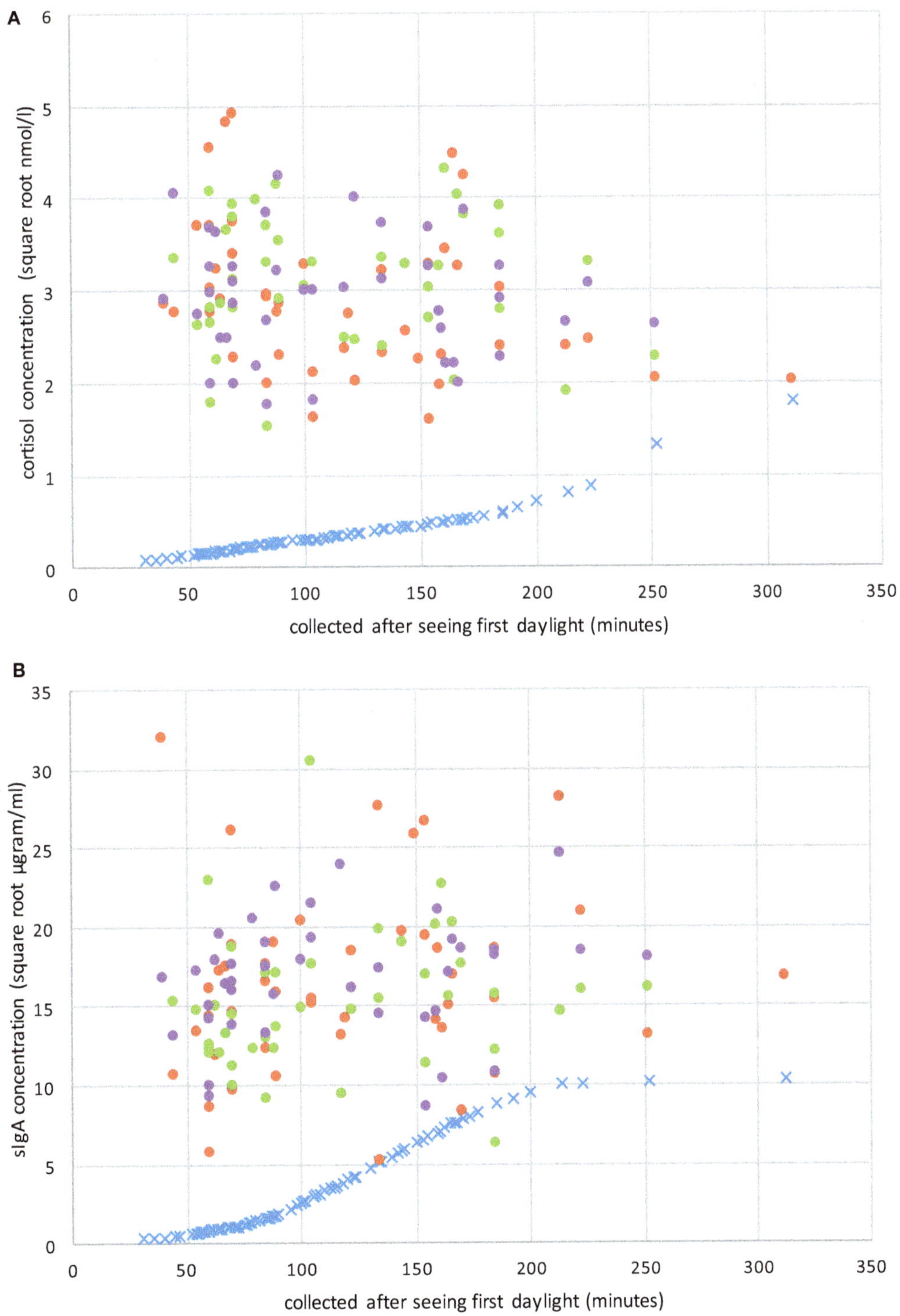

FIGURE 1 | Raw CS **(A)** and secretory immunoglobulin A (sIgA) **(B)** concentrations on the three sample periods (day 1 = solid red dots; day 2 = solid green dots; day 3 = solid purple dots), and the individual adjustment concentration value (blue "x") based on Hucklebridge et al. (24) as a function of when the sample was collected after seeing first daylight (in minutes).

indicated that the SC and sIgA were affected by daily rhythm with the exception of time to produce saliva (Column 1 of **Table 2**).

A measure of time from participants' first sight of morning daylight is simpler to apply to concentrations of stress biomarkers than transformations based on the non-linear effect of the diurnal cycle reported by Dawes (13) and Hucklebridge et al. (24). Although there is a high correlation between the linear measure of time, used in the first analysis, and the curvilinear measure of

TABLE 3 | Descriptive statistics of biomarker measurement of stress (n = 130).

Measure (adjustment)	Units	Mean	SD	Minimum	Maximum
Time	s	151.87	112.07	10.00	480.00
Time (daily rhythm)	s	167.56	112.63	15.45	487.50
Time (daily rhythm + lifestyle)	s	167.56	110.62	27.04	476.83
$SC_{unadjusted}$	μg/dL	0.34	0.16	0.08	0.86
SC_{DRA}	√nmol/L	3.30	0.68	1.84	5.10
SC_{DRA}^{LA}	μg/dL	3.30	0.68	1.87	5.08
$sIgA_{unadjusted}$	μg/mL	287.96	180.07	25.99	1,030.68
$sIgA_{DRA}$	√μg/mL	19.40	5.76	6.49	37.99
$sIgA_{DRA}^{LA}$	μg/mL	19.40	5.75	6.21	37.96

Time = time to produce 0.5 mL of saliva.
Lifestyle = Caffeine (today), antibiotics (last week), infection (last week).

daily rhythm used in the second analysis, it should be noted that use of the linear measure is associated with a small measurement error. On the other hand, the reported studies of the relationship between biomarkers and the circadian and diurnal cycle had small sample sizes and may also have contained measurement error. Further large sample and longitudinal studies are required to more accurately map the effect of daily rhythm on SC and sIgA.

The measure of time to produce a set amount of saliva production was found to be related to cortisol concentrations. Concentrations of cortisol are commonly reported to be independent of the rate of saliva production (Salimetrics Assay, Carlsbad, CA, USA). However, a measure of time to produce saliva could be an alternative biological measure of stress, as suggested by the results of Ref. (25). Further evidence of this relationship may provide a simpler, less invasive measure of stress than collection of saliva and should be investigated further as a proxy measure of stress.

Other Factors

It has been reported that gender affects susceptibility to stress and daily rhythms regarding salivary flow rate, sIgA, and SC release (26). These effects should be considered in future studies of female athletes. In addition, glucocorticosteroid administration by oral, intravenous, intramuscular, and rectal routes may affect assay concentrations of SC or sIgA. Other differences related to the measures of stress are likely to reflect changes in other factors such as training regimes, and warrant further controlled studies to examine the source of this variability.

CONCLUSION

Development of a protocol for accurate measurement of SC and sIgA should take into account the effects of daily rhythm. Obtaining research data from sports teams often requires unsynchronized access to a cohort of team members due to strict training regimes. The data from this study showed that adjustment of cortisol concentrations to account for an individual's daily rhythm is warranted. Staggered sampling times require adjustment of data to a common time point to standardize population biomarker data, in order to reduce measurement error and enable comparisons across measurements. Collection of saliva samples at the same time of day does not resolve this situation if there is variability in the time at which participants first saw daylight. Results of this study suggest that a significant percentage of variation within previous biomarker studies involving SC and sIgA concentrations could be attributed to these biological factors. It is highly recommended that all studies involving stress biomarkers adjust more rigorously for the effect of daily rhythm.

ETHICS STATEMENT

This study has been approved by the Human Research Ethics Committee at the Australian Catholic University. In the event that you have any complaint or concern, or if you have any query that the Investigator has not been able to satisfy, you may write to the Chair of the Human Research Ethics Committee care of the nearest branch of the Research Services Office.

AUTHOR CONTRIBUTIONS

BP: the original conception and design of the study, acquisition of data, assay procedure and analysis, drafting the research paper, editing and final approval of the version to be submitted. WS: conception and design of the study, acquisition of data, analysis and interpretation of data, design of the research paper, drafting, editing, and revising the paper critically for important intellectual content and final approval of the version to be submitted. RL: conception of the study, assay procedure and analysis, drafting the research paper, editing and final approval of the version to be submitted. PP: conception of the research paper, statistical analysis and interpretation of results, editing and revising the paper critically for important intellectual content and final approval of the version to be submitted. G-JP: conception and re-design of the research paper, interpretation of data, editing and revising the paper critically for important intellectual content and final approval of the version to be submitted.

ACKNOWLEDGMENTS

We wish to thank the coaching and medical staff at the football club for their assistance with administration and support. We also wish to thank the players for their participation in the study.

REFERENCES

1. Williams JM, Andersen MB. Psychosocial antecedents of sport injury: review and critique of the stress and injury model. *J Appl Sport Psychol* (1998) 10:5–25. doi:10.1080/10413209808406375
2. Hartwig TB, Naughton G, Searl J. Load, stress, and recovery in adolescent rugby union players during a competitive season. *J Sports Sci* (2009) 27:1087–94. doi:10.1080/02640410903096611
3. Krueger GP. Sustained work, fatigue, sleep loss and performance: a review of the issues. *Work Stress* (1989) 3:129–41. doi:10.1080/02678378908256939

4. Lac G, Maso F. Biological markers for the follow-up of athletes throughout the training season. *Pathol Biol (Paris)* (2004) 52:43–9. doi:10.1016/S0369-8114(03)00049-X
5. Maes M, Hendriks D, Van Gastel A, Demedts P, Wauters A, Neels H, et al. Effects of psychological stress on serum immunoglobulin, complement and acute phase protein concentrations in normal volunteers. *Psychoneuroendocrinology* (1997) 22:397–409. doi:10.1016/S0306-4530(97)00042-5
6. Neubauer O, Konig D, Wagner KH. Recovery after an Ironman triathlon: sustained inflammatory responses and muscular stress. *Eur J Appl Physiol* (2008) 104:417–26. doi:10.1007/s00421-008-0787-6
7. Neville V, Gleeson M, Folland JP. Salivary IgA as a risk factor for upper respiratory infections in elite professional athletes. *Med Sci Sports Exerc* (2008) 40:1228–36. doi:10.1249/MSS.0b013e31816be9c3
8. Hayes LD, Sculthorpe N, Cunniffe B, Grace F. Salivary testosterone and cortisol measurement in sports medicine: a narrative review and user's guide for researchers and practitioners. *Int J Sports Med* (2016) 37(13):1007–18. doi:10.1055/s-0042-105649
9. Bishop NC, Walker GJ, Scanlon GA, Richards S, Rogers E. Salivary IgA responses to prolonged intensive exercise following caffeine ingestion. *Med Sci Sports Exerc* (2006) 38:513–9. doi:10.1249/01.mss.0000187412.47477.ee
10. Sacar S, Turgut H, Kaleli I, Cevahir N, Asan A, Sacar M, et al. Poor hospital infection control practice in hand hygiene, glove utilization, and usage of tourniquets. *Am J Infect Control* (2006) 34:606–9. doi:10.1016/j.ajic.2006.02.006
11. Aardal E, Holm AC. Cortisol in saliva-reference ranges and relation to cortisol in serum. European journal of clinical chemistry and clinical biochemistry. *J Forum Eur Clin Chem Soc* (1995) 33:927–32.
12. Vining RF, McGinley RA, Maksvytis JJ, Ho KY. Salivary cortisol: a better measure of adrenal cortical function than serum cortisol. *Ann Clin Biochem* (1983) 20(Pt 6):329–35. doi:10.1177/000456328302000601
13. Dawes C. Circadian rhythms in human salivary flow rate and composition. *J Physiol* (1972) 220:529–45. doi:10.1113/jphysiol.1972.sp009721
14. Bjornsson GL, Thorsteinsson L, Gudmundsson KO, Jonsson H Jr, Gudmundsson S, Gudbjornsson B. Inflammatory cytokines in relation to adrenal response following total hip replacement. *Scand J Immunol* (2007) 65:99–105. doi:10.1111/j.1365-3083.2006.01872.x
15. Lovallo WR, Whitsett TL, al'Absi M, Sung BH, Vincent AS, Wilson MF. Caffeine stimulation of cortisol secretion across the waking hours in relation to caffeine intake levels. *Psychosom Med* (2005) 67:734–9. doi:10.1097/01.psy.0000181270.20036.06
16. Torpy DJ, Ho JT. Value of free cortisol measurement in systemic infection. *Horm Metab Res* (2007) 39:439–44. doi:10.1055/s-2007-980200
17. Cox RJ, Brokstad KA, Ogra P. Influenza virus: immunity and vaccination strategies. Comparison of the immune response to inactivated and live, attenuated influenza vaccines. *Scand J Immunol* (2004) 59:1–15. doi:10.1111/j.0300-9475.2004.01382.x
18. Di Padova F, Pozzi C, Tondre MJ, Tritapepe R. Selective and early increase of IL-1 inhibitors, IL-6 and cortisol after elective surgery. *Clin Exp Immunol* (1991) 85:137–42. doi:10.1111/j.1365-2249.1991.tb05694.x
19. Seeldrayers PA, Hoyle NR, Thomas DGT. Pre- and post-operative changes in serum immunoglobulin level in neurosurgical patients. *Acta Neurochir* (1984) 70:269–74. doi:10.1007/BF01406655
20. Kiess W, Meidert A, Dressendorfer RA, Schriever K, Kessler U, Kounig A, et al. Salivary cortisol levels throughout childhood and adolescence: relation with age, pubertal stage, and weight. *Pediatr Res* (1995) 37:502–6. doi:10.1203/00006450-199504000-00020
21. Smyth J, Ockenfels MC, Porter L, Kirschbaum C, Hellhammer DH, Stone AA. Stressors and mood measured on a momentary basis are associated with salivary cortisol secretion. *Psychoneuroendocrinology* (1998) 23:353–70. doi:10.1016/S0306-4530(98)00008-0
22. Dawes C. Circadian rhythms in the flow rate and composition of unstimulated and stimulated human submandibular saliva. *J Physiol* (1975) 244:535–48. doi:10.1113/jphysiol.1975.sp010811
23. Engvall E, Perlmann P. Enzyme-linked immunosorbent assay, Elisa. 3. Quantitation of specific antibodies by enzyme-labeled anti-immunoglobulin in antigen-coated tubes. *J Immunol* (1972) 109:129–35.
24. Hucklebridge F, Clow A, Evans P. The relationship between salivary secretory immunoglobulin A and cortisol: neuroendocrine response to awakening and the diurnal cycle. *Int J Psychophysiol* (1998) 31:69–76. doi:10.1016/S0167-8760(98)00042-7
25. Matos-Gomes N, Katsurayama M, Makimoto FH, Santana LLO, Paredes-Garcia E, Becker MADA, et al. Psychological stress and its influence on salivary flow rate, total protein concentration and IgA, IgG and IgM titers. *Neuroimmunomodulation* (2010) 17:396–404. doi:10.1159/000292064
26. Hellhammer DH, Wust S, Kudielka BM. Salivary cortisol as a biomarker in stress research. *Psychoneuroendocrinology* (2009) 34:163–71. doi:10.1016/j.psyneuen.2008.10.026

2

The RNA Helicase BELLE is Involved in Circadian Rhythmicity and in Transposons Regulation in *Drosophila melanogaster*

Paola Cusumano[1†], Milena Damulewicz[2†], Elena Carbognin[1†], Laura Caccin[1], Antonietta Puricella[3], Valeria Specchia[3], Maria Pia Bozzetti[3], Rodolfo Costa[1] and Gabriella M. Mazzotta[1]*

[1] Department of Biology, University of Padua, Padua, Italy, [2] Department of Cell Biology and Imaging, Jagiellonian University, Kraków, Poland, [3] Department of Biological and Environmental Sciences and Technologies, University of Salento, Lecce, Italy

Edited by:
Geoffrey A. Head,
Baker Heart and Diabetes Institute, Australia

Reviewed by:
Francesco Cappello,
Università degli Studi di Palermo, Italy
Joon (Kyungjoon) Lim,
La Trobe University, Australia

Correspondence:
Gabriella M. Mazzotta
gabriella.mazzotta@unipd.it

†These authors have contributed equally to this work

Circadian clocks control and synchronize biological rhythms of several behavioral and physiological phenomena in most, if not all, organisms. Rhythm generation relies on molecular auto-regulatory oscillations of interlocked transcriptional-translational feedback loops. Rhythmic clock-gene expression is at the base of rhythmic protein accumulation, though post-transcriptional and post-translational mechanisms have evolved to adjust and consolidate the proper pace of the clock. In *Drosophila*, BELLE, a conserved DEAD-box RNA helicase playing important roles in reproductive capacity, is involved in the small RNA-mediated regulation associated to the piRNA pathway. Here, we report that BELLE is implicated in the circadian rhythmicity and in the regulation of endogenous transposable elements (TEs) in both nervous system and gonads. We suggest that BELLE acts as important element in the piRNA-mediated regulation of the TEs and raise the hypothesis that this specific regulation could represent another level of post-transcriptional control adopted by the clock to ensure the proper rhythmicity.

Keywords: RNA helicase BELLE, *Drosophila*, post-transcriptional control, circadian clock, piRNA-mediated transposons regulation

INTRODUCTION

Circadian clocks have evolved in most, if not all, organisms to time their physiology and behavior to the most appropriate phases of the day–night cycles (Young and Kay, 2001; Dubruille and Emery, 2008; Peschel and Helfrich-Forster, 2011). They control and synchronize the biological rhythms of a vast array of behavioral and physiological phenomena, including visual sensitivity, hormone secretion, locomotion, hatching, eclosion, ecdysteroid synthesis, sperm release, gene expression, and sleep wake cycle (Sandrelli et al., 2008; Allada and Chung, 2010; Schiesari et al., 2011). Biological clocks are self-sustained in the absence of environmental cues. Rhythm generation occurs in single cells and is based on molecular auto-regulatory oscillations of interlocked transcriptional-translational feedback loops. In *Drosophila*, the transcription factors CLOCK (CLK) and CYCLE (CYC) activate, as heterodimer, the expression of the clock genes *period* (*per*) and *timeless* (*tim*). The correspondent proteins, PER and TIM, are post-translational regulated and eventually accumulate in the cytoplasm and enter the nucleus, where they ultimately inhibit their own transcription by repressing CLK-CYC activity. Two other interlocked feedback loops regulating the expression of the *Clock* gene and CLK/CYC mediated transcription, respectively, contribute to the robustness of the circadian oscillations (reviewed in Ozkaya and Rosato, 2012).

Rhythmic clock-gene expression is important to generate rhythmic protein accumulation; however, cycling protein levels do not depend only on cycling mRNAs but post-transcriptional and post-translational mechanisms have also evolved to adjust and consolidate the proper pace of the clock (Kojima et al., 2011). Among these, alternative splicing, mRNA nuclear export, polyadenilation, regulation of translation and degradation, play fundamental roles in the post-transcriptional regulation of circadian gene expression (Majercak et al., 1999, 2004; Collins et al., 2004; Boothroyd et al., 2007; Kojima et al., 2012; Huang et al., 2013; MacGregor et al., 2013; Robles et al., 2014; Montelli et al., 2015).

In recent years, a role for small, non-coding RNAs (miRNA) as post-transcriptional regulators of circadian rhythmicity in *Drosophila* has been also established. They regulate the proper development and maintenance of circadian rhythms acting either directly on the expression of clock genes or indirectly on signaling outputs (reviewed in Xue and Zhang, 2018).

Another class of small RNA, the piRNAs, has recently been associated to the age-dependent rhythmicity (Kuintzle et al., 2017). In particular, putative primary piRNA transcripts corresponding to transposons exhibit a *de novo* oscillation in old flies and circadian clock components appear to regulate these late rhythmicity (Kuintzle et al., 2017). piRNAs are small molecules protecting animal cells from the de-regulation of transposons and other repetitive genetic elements, preserving genome stability (Li et al., 2009; Thomson and Lin, 2009; Le Thomas et al., 2014). The piRNA biogenesis starts with the transcription of genomic clusters dispersed in the genome, producing the primary piRNA precursor transcripts (Brennecke et al., 2007). The piRNA pathway was first discovered in the gonads (Vagin et al., 2006; Aravin et al., 2007; Brennecke et al., 2007; Specchia et al., 2008, 2010, 2017; Specchia and Bozzetti, 2009; Bozzetti et al., 2015; Iwasaki et al., 2015; Sahin et al., 2016), but later it was observed in the nervous system of both *Drosophila* and mice (Lee et al., 2011; Perrat et al., 2013).

belle emerged in a screen for genes involved in the RNAi pathway: it binds to Ago1 and Ago2, involved in the small RNA-mediated regulation (Kim et al., 2005; Ulvila et al., 2006; Zhou et al., 2008). Very recently, a role of *belle* in the regulation on specific P-derived constructs in the ovary has been described (Lo et al., 2016), and therefore it is now considered a "bona fide" piRNA gene. *belle* encodes a DEAD-box RNA helicase: it is the closest paralog of *vasa* and plays roles in the reproductive system allowing fertility in *Drosophila melanogaster*. Like other members of the DEAD box family, Vasa and BELLE are supposed to have ATPase, RNA binding, and RNA unwinding activities (Liang et al., 1994; Sengoku et al., 2006). BELLE is essential for both male and female reproductive capacity and its function in gonads is conserved during evolution. It localizes at the perinuclear region, called "nuage," of the germ cells in male and female gonads (Johnstone et al., 2005; Kibanov et al., 2011), where the majority of key components regulating transposable elements (TEs) are located (Lim and Kai, 2007; Klattenhoff and Theurkauf, 2008; Kibanov et al., 2011; Nagao et al., 2011).

Here, we have identified for BELLE important roles as putative circadian clock component and regulator of TEs in brain and in gonads. These apparently unrelated functions suggest the hypothesis that BELLE might be a key element in small RNA (piRNA)-mediated regulation of the TEs and that this regulatory pathway is involved in circadian rhythmicity.

MATERIALS AND METHODS

Fly Strains

The following strains of *Drosophila melanogaster* were used: w^{1118}, *CantonS*, *yw;tim*-Gal4 (Emery et al., 1998), *UAS-belle*RNAi (VDRC #6299), *GMR*-Gal4 (BDSC #8440), *ninaE*-Gal4 (BDSC #1104), *repo*-Gal4 (BDSC #7415), *pdf*-Gal4 (BDSC #6900), *Eaat1*-Gal4 (BDSC #8849), *Lama*-Gal4 (BDSC #35543), per^0 (Smith and Konopka, 1981), *yw*;P{EPgy2}$bel^{EY08943}$ (BDSC #19945); P{PZ}$bel^{cap-1}ry^{506}$/TM3, ry^{RK} Sb^1 Ser^1 (BDSC #11778), *bel::GFP* (Morin et al., 2001) (Kyoto Stock Centre #*ZCL2696*), *UAS-CD8-GFP* (BDSC #5137). Co-IP was performed with *yw; tim-GAL4/+; UAS-HAcry/+* (Dissel et al., 2004). Flies were maintained on a standard cornmeal medium under LD 12:12 regime and at constant 23°C.

Co-immunoprecipitation, Mass Spectrometry Analysis, and Western Blot

Head extracts from overexpressing HACRY flies raised in 12:12 light:dark cycles and collected at Zeitgeber Time 24 (ZT24), before lights on, and after a 15-min light pulse were subjected to coimmunoprecipitation and Mass Spectrometry analysis as previously described (Mazzotta et al., 2013). Immunocomplexes were analyzed by Western blot using the following antibodies: rabbit polyclonal anti-BELLE (1:2000) (Johnstone et al., 2005) and mouse anti-HA (1:5000; Sigma Aldrich, St. Louis, MO, United States). Anti-rabbit IgG HRP (1:3000; BioRad Laboratories, Hercules, CA, United States) and anti-mouse IgG HRP (1:5000; Sigma Aldrich, St. Louis, MO, United States) were used as secondary antibodies.

RNA Extraction and qRT-PCR

RNA was extracted using the reagent Trizol (Invitrogen) as indicated in manufacturer's instructions. For the analysis of *belle* expression, around 50 heads from flies reared in LD cycles for at least 3 days and collected at the indicated time points were used. For the analysis of transposons 30 mg of male or female gonadal tissues or heads were used. 1 μg of total RNA was used as a template for oligonucleotide dT-primed reverse transcription using SuperScriptIII RNaseH-reverse transcriptase (Invitrogen), according to manufacturer's instructions. qRT-PCR was performed in the 7500 Real-TimePCR System (Applied Biosystem) using SYBR green (Celbio) according to the manufacturer's instruction. For quantification of the transcripts, we used the $2\Delta\Delta Ct$ method as previously reported

(Specchia et al., 2010). The primers used are listed in **Supplementary Table S1**.

Immunocytochemistry

For the analysis of BELLE localization, heads from 7 days old males were fixed in 4% paraformaldehyde in phosphate buffer saline (PBS; pH 7.4) for 4 h, then they were washed in PBS twice and cryoprotected by incubation in 12.5% sucrose for 10 min and in 25% sucrose at 4°C overnight. Material was embedded in Tissue-Tek, frozen in liquid nitrogen, and cryostat 20 μm sections were cut. The sections were washed in PBS for 30 min and five times in phosphate buffer (PB) with an addition of 0.2% Triton X-100 (PBT). After that, sections were incubated in 5% normal goat serum (NGS) with an addition of 0.5% bovine serum albumin (BSA) for 30 min first at room temperature, and then incubated with primary antibodies anti-REPO (mouse, 1:500, Hybridoma Bank), anti-Ebony (rabbit, 1:750, a gift from Dr. B. T. Hovemann, Ruhr Universität Bochum) and anti-GFP (rabbit, 1:1000, Novus Biologicals) for 24 h. Afterward, sections were washed six times in PBT/BSA, and blocked in 5% NGS for 45 min. After that, goat anti-mouse (conjugated with Cy3) and goat anti-rabbit (conjugated with Alexa 488) secondary antibodies (both 1:500, Jackson Immuno Research) were applied overnight in 4°C. Finally, sections were washed twice in BSA, six times in PBT, and twice in PBS. Then, cryosections were mounted in Vectashield medium (Vector) and examined with a Zeiss Meta 510 Laser Scanning Microscope. About 30 brains or cryosections were checked.

For the analysis of PER in clock-neurons, flies were synchronized by LD cycles at least for 3 days and then collected under LD or DD conditions at the indicated time points. Whole flies were quickly fixed for 2 h in PFA 4%. About 10–12 brains were dissected in PBS and then treated as previously described (Vanin et al., 2012). Average fluorescence values are reported.

Male and Female Fertility Analysis

One young male was mated to three control virgin females, and three virgin females were mated with three control males. Ten individual males and 30 females were tested for each genotype. After 4 days, the crosses were transferred to a fresh vial. The parental flies were removed from the last vial after an additional 4 days. The number of the adult progeny from each vial was counted.

Behavioral Analysis

Locomotor activity of individual flies was recorded for 3 days in LD and 7 days in DD using the Drosophila Activity Monitoring System (TriKinetics, Inc., Waltham, MA, United States). Data were collected every 5 min and then analyzed in 30 min bins using spectral analysis and autocorrelation (Zordan et al., 2007). Morning anticipations was detected fly-by-fly examining the activity mean of 3 days under LD conditions (Vanin et al., 2012) and the Morning Index was calculated as in Seluzicki et al. (2014).

Statistical Analyses

For comparisons between two measurements a two-tailed Student's t-test was used to show the significance level of the replicated experiments. Expression profile's significance was evaluated by non-parametric ANOVA, Kruskal–Wallis test (p-value < 0.05) whereas putative period and phase of oscillation were identified by RAIN non-parametric test for independent samples (adjusted p-value < 0.05) (Thaben and Westermark, 2014).

RESULTS

dCRY Interacts With the RNA Helicase BELLE

In an experiment aimed at the identification of new genes involved in the circadian machinery in *Drosophila*, a coimmunoprecipitation assay followed by mass spectrometry analysis was performed on transgenic flies overexpressing a hemagglutinin (HA)-tagged form of dCRY (HACRY) raised in 12:12 light:dark cycles and collected at Zeitgeber Time 24 (ZT24), before lights on, and after a 15-min light pulse (Mazzotta et al., 2013).

A ~85-kDa species was observed in the sample in the dark that was not present in the negative control (**Figure 1A**). This protein band was digested in-gel, and the peptide mixtures analyzed by liquid chromatography–mass spectrometry (LC-MS)/MS using an ESI-QTOF mass spectrometer (Wilm et al., 1996). Analysis of the MS/MS data using the MASCOT software yielded the identification of BELLE (**Supplementary Table S2**), a DEAD box RNA helicase involved in RNA metabolism at several levels (Linder and Jankowsky, 2011).

The presence of BELLE in the complex with HACRY was also confirmed by Western blot with an anti-BELLE antibody (Johnstone et al., 2005). By this procedure, BELLE was also detected after a 15 min of light pulse (**Figure 1B**). The same blot was hybridized also with an anti-HA antibody, in order to assess the specificity of the interaction (**Figure 1B**). The signal corresponding to BELLE was more intense in head collected in the dark; in fact after 15 min of light pulse the amount of BELLE was lower, in line with that of HACRY that decreased due to the well-known light-dependent degradation of CRY (Peschel et al., 2009).

The RNA Helicase BELLE Is Expressed in the Fly Brain

It is known that BELLE is expressed in germ cells throughout all developmental stages and in larval neurons (Johnstone et al., 2005; Rolls et al., 2007), but little information was available regarding its expression in the adult fly head.

In order to characterize BELLE expression in the fly brain, we performed an immunocytochemistry experiment on flies carrying a GFP exon trap in *belle* (*bel::GFP*) (Morin et al., 2001). Flies were maintained in standard light–dark conditions, brains were dissected and an anti-GFP antibody was used to detect BEL::GFP expression. We observed BELLE expression in clock neurons and in glial cells in the optic lobe, with a predominantly cytoplasmic localization (**Figures 2, 3**). In clock neurons, BELLE was expressed in either the small or the

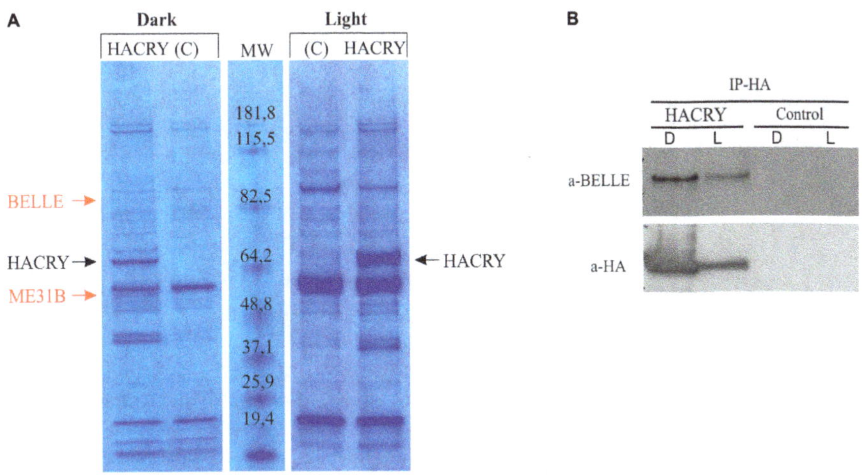

FIGURE 1 | dCRY interacts with BELLE. **(A)** Coomassie blue-stained gel of heads protein extracts coimmunoprecipitated with an anti-HA antibody. HACRY-overexpressing flies (HACRY, *yw;tim-GAL4/+; UASHAcry/+*) and relative controls (C, *yw;tim-GAL4*) were reared in 12:12 light: dark and collected in the dark (ZT24) and in the light (ZT24 + 15-min light pulse). Molecular masses of markers are indicated (BenchMark Pre-Stained Protein Ladder; Invitrogen). MW, molecular weight. Bands corresponding to HACRY are indicated in black, while stained proteins excised and characterized by mass spectrometry are indicated in red. **(B)** Co-immunoprecipitation and Western blot confirming the interaction between HACRY and BELLE in HACRY-overexpressing flies (HACRY, *yw;tim-GAL4/+; UASHAcry/+*). *tim-GAL4* flies were used as control. Heads were collected as in **(A)**. Membranes were probed with anti-BELLE and anti-HA antibodies.

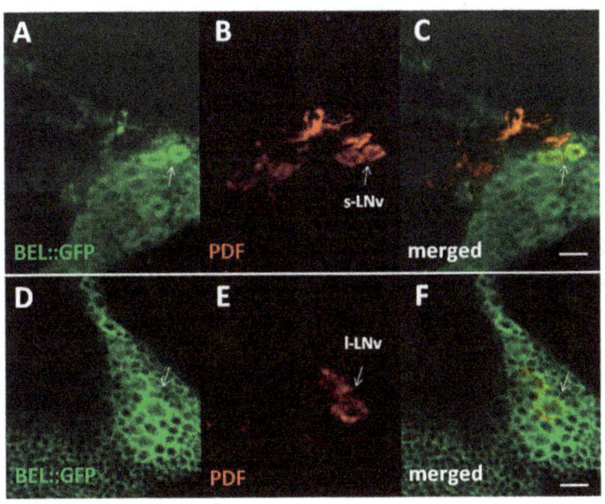

FIGURE 2 | BELLE localizes in the main pacemaker cells in the brain of *Drosophila melanogaster*. Confocal images of whole mount of adult brain expressing BELLE fused with green fluorescent protein (*bel::GFP*). Scale bar: 10 μm. **(A,D)** Anti-GFP immunostaining (BEL::GFP). **(B,E)** Anti-PDF was used to label PDF-expressing ventral lateral neurons. Depends on optical section small LNv (s-LNv) or large LNv (l-LNv) are visualized. **(C,F)** BEL::GFP and PDF immune staining co-localize in the area of LNv cell bodies.

large ventral lateral neurons (s-LNvs and l-LNvs respectively) (**Figure 2**), PDF-expressing cells that act in promoting and governing the circadian locomotor behavior. In glia we observed BELLE expression in the epithelial glia and a weak labeling also in the lamina (**Figures 3D–F**): position and shape of these GFP- labeled cells suggest they may be R1-R6 photoreceptor terminals (**Figures 3D–F**); however, anti-REPO staining showed glia cells nuclei at the top of each structure (**Figure 3G**). Observed columnar shape is also similar to anti-EBONY staining (**Figure 3H**), which is a marker for epithelial glia (Richard et al., 2002), suggesting that BELLE may be located in epithelial glia in the lamina. Moreover, we observed immunostaining for BEL::GFP also in giant inner chiasm glia, which connects the medulla with the lobula complex in the optic lobe (Kremer et al., 2017). In these cells, both BELLE and PER are expressed (**Supplementary Figure S1**).

Belle Expression Shows Circadian Features

In order to characterize the temporal expression of *belle*, mRNA and protein levels were analyzed during the 24 h. Wild-type flies $white^{1118}$ were synchronized by 12:12 LD cycles and collected every 3 h, either in LD regime or at the third day after being transferred to constant darkness (DD).

belle expression appeared to oscillate both in LD and in DD conditions. In particular, in LD cycles the level of differential expression during the 24 h was just below the limit of significance (Kruskal–Wallis p-value 0.06); nevertheless, the algorithm RAIN suggested the presence of a rhythmic expression pattern (adjusted p-value 2,61E-02) with a peak at ZT12 (**Figure 4A**). In constant darkness *belle* mRNA showed differential expression around the 24 h (Kruskal–Wallis p-value 0.03), and a peak at CT63 was identified (RAIN p-value 1,92E-05) (**Figure 4B**). These results are in line with a previous microarray study showing a peak of expression for *belle* at ZT17 (Claridge-Chang et al., 2001). In per^0 mutant, *belle* oscillation is maintained in LD cycles, although with a peak at ZT3 (Kruskal–Wallis p-value 0.02, RAIN p-value 4,91E-07) (**Figure 4A**), while it was lost in constant conditions (Kruskal–Wallis p-value 0.609) (**Figure 4B**).

The analysis of BELLE in fly heads by western blot showed no significant protein oscillation, neither in LD nor in DD (Kruskal–Wallis p-values 0.9 and 0.8, respectively) (**Supplementary

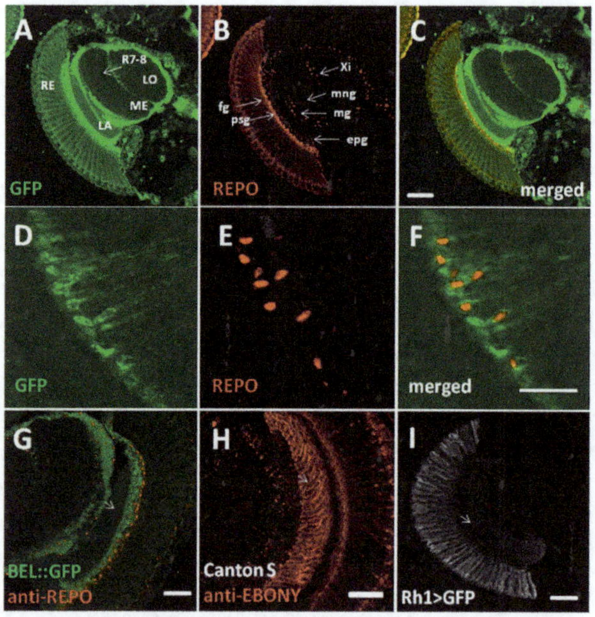

FIGURE 3 | BELLE localizes in the visual system of *Drosophila melanogaster*. Confocal images of horizontal cryosection of adult brain expressing BELLE fused with green fluorescent protein (*bel::GFP*). Anti-REPO was used to label all glia nuclei. **(A)** BEL::GFP signal is localized in the optic neuropils: lamina (LA), medulla (ME), and lobula (LO). Weak signal is visible in R7 and R8 photoreceptor terminals (R7-8) in the medulla. Signal in the retina (RE) is probably due to autofluorescence. **(B)** Anti-REPO staining allowed recognized different glia types: fenestrated glia (fg), pseudocartridge glia (psg), epithelial glia (epg), medulla glia (mg), marginal glia (mng), and inner chiasm glia (Xi). **(C)** Merged signal showed localization of BELLE in glial cells. Bar 50 μm. **(D–F)** Higher magnification of inner chiasm glia showed that BELLE is localized mostly in the cytoplasm. Bar 20 μm. **(G–I)** Localization of BELLE in the first optic neuropile, called lamina, analyzed on confocal images of horizontal cryosection of adult brain. Bar: 50 μm. **(G)** Anti-GFP and Anti-REPO immunostaining showing that BEL::GFP signal is higher in the distal lamina (close to retina), where interneurons cell bodies are located. Weak labeling is also visible across the lamina, forming regular columns. Glia nuclei staining overlaps with observed BELLE location, suggesting that this signal originates from epithelial glia. **(H)** Section of wild-type *CantonS* brain stained with anti-EBONY to label epithelial glial cells in the lamina and their specific columnar shape (see Richard et al., 2002). **(I)** Anti-GFP staining on section of Rh1 > GFP brains showing R1–R6 photoreceptors terminals in the lamina.

Information and Supplementary Figure S2). This result is in line with that obtained by co-immunoprecipitation (**Figure 1B**): the lower amount of BELLE pulled down in light compared to dark uniquely depends on the light-mediated degradation of CRY.

BELLE Affects Circadian Locomotor Activity

In order to unravel a possible involvement of *belle* in the generation of circadian rhythmicity in *Drosophila*, we depleted the expression of the gene by RNAi in both glia and clock neurons.

When we knocked down *belle* with the pan-glial driver *repo*-Gal4 (Awasaki and Ito, 2004) and *lama*-Gal4, a driver for glial precursor cells, lamina precursor cells and lamina neurons (Apitz and Salecker, 2016), we observed developmental lethality. The same result was obtained by KD in all canonical clock neurons and clock relevant glial cells expressing *timeless* (with a *tim*-Gal4) (Emery et al., 1998). This result is in agreement to what reported for the null allele of *belle* (Johnstone et al., 2005). When we depleted *belle* in PDF expressing neurons and a restricted subset of glial cells (with *pdf*-Gal4 and *Eaat1*-Gal4, respectively) (Renn et al., 1999; Rival et al., 2004), flies were viable and endogenous rhythmicity was not altered (**Table 1**); only a slight impairment in the morning anticipation of locomotor activity in LD was observed (**Table 2**). In contrast, RNAi against *belle* in the photoreceptor cells (*GMR*-Gal4 and *ninaE*-Gal4) did not affect either vitality or behavior (**Supplementary Table S3**).

We then decided to investigate a possible role for *belle* in the circadian machinery using two viable mutant lines generated by p-element insertion in the regulatory region (*belle* $^{cap-1}$ and *belle* ^{EY08943}) (Bellen et al., 2004). Flies were entrained for 3 days in light dark cycles at constant temperature (23°) followed by 7 days of constant darkness. Either mutant exhibited an impairment of the locomotor behavior (**Figure 5**): in LD conditions, both lines presented the canonical bimodal profile, but a severe loss of the morning anticipation of the locomotor activity was displayed (**Figure 5A** and **Table 3**). A high percentage of flies showed also an arrhythmic behavior in DD, although no defects were monitored concerning the period, which was comparable to wild-type (**Figure 5B** and **Table 4**).

Altered PER Cycling in Circadian Pacemaker Neurons in Belle Mutants

We performed PER staining on brains dissected every 4 h from flies collected under LD cycles and during the 5th day of DD conditions, in order to assess whether the impairment of the circadian locomotor activity of the *belle* mutants could be due to an altered PER cycling in the pacemaker neurons. PDF expressing cells were identified by co-staining for this peptide.

Mutant lines showed defects in some clusters of neurons. Under LD conditions, *belle* $^{cap-1}$ flies exhibited a significant reduction of oscillation amplitude in both s-LNvs and l-LNvs, particularly marked at ZT0 (**Figure 6**). Similarly, in constant darkness, a general decrease of PER staining was observed compared to wild-type, which was particularly enhanced during the subjective night/beginning of the subjective day (**Figure 7**). Quantification of PER levels indicated that the greatest effect occurs in the small PDF cells (s-LNvs) (**Figure 7**), those cells that normally show high PER expression and also govern the behavioral phenotype in constant conditions (Grima et al., 2004). Besides a decrease of its levels, in these cells the accumulation of PER is slow down, with a peak delayed of about 4 h with respect to control (**Figure 7**). In large PDF neurons (l-LNvs) PER cycling is dampened, similarly to control and in accordance to previous observations (Grima et al., 2004).

The *bel* ^{EY08943} mutant exhibited a less striking phenotype: a significant difference was observed in the PDF positive s-LNvs only in constant darkness, where the oscillation of PER was

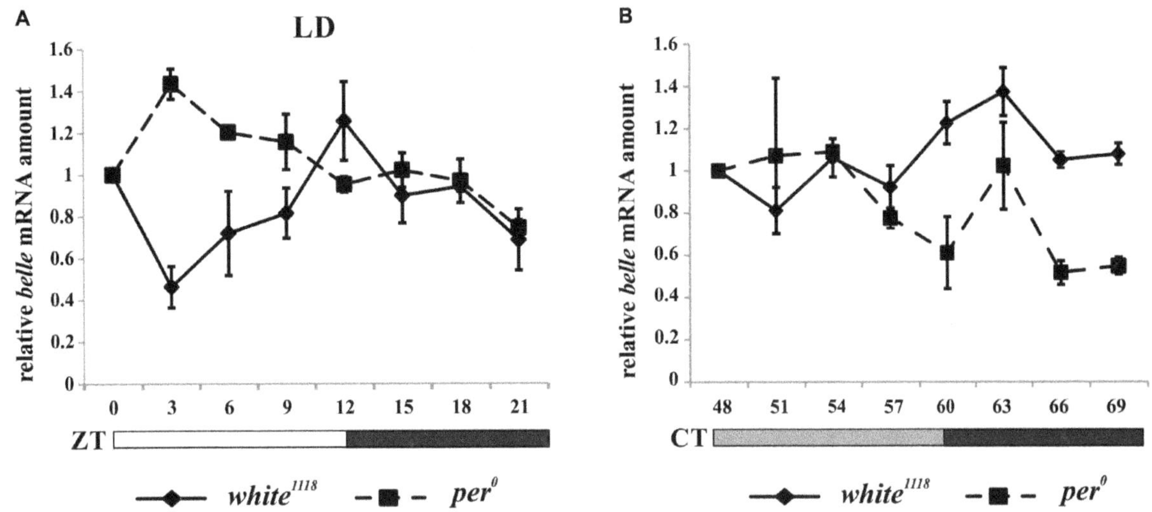

FIGURE 4 | *belle* mRNA expression shows circadian features. qRT-PCR on heads from *white*^{1118} and *per*^{0} flies reared in 12.12 LD **(A)** or over the third day in DD **(B)**. Relative abundance of *belle* mRNA was defined as a ratio with *rp49*. Values represent mean levels ± SEM of three biological replicates. The value corresponding to CT 54 in *per*^{0} flies represents mean level of two biological replicates.

TABLE 1 | Locomotor activity of *belle* Knock-Down flies under constant darkness (DD).

Genotype	N Tot	N Alive	N R	% R	τ		*SEM*
w;pdf-Gal4/+;UAS-RNAi-belle/+	63	55	48	87.27	24.95	±	0.12
w;Eaat-Gal4/+;UAS-RNAi-belle/+	32	31	27	87.10	24.01	±	0.07
w;pdf-Gal4/+	30	27	26	96.30	24.49	±	0.09
w;Eaat-Gal4/+	30	29	26	89.66	24.08	±	0.06
w;;UAS-RNAi-belle/+	47	39	33	84.62	23.96	±	0.07

R: rhythmic flies. The experiments were performed at 23°C.

TABLE 2 | Locomotor activity of *belle* Knock-Down flies in entrainment conditions (LD).

Genotype	MA (%)	EA (%)	MI		*SEM*	*N*
w;pdf-Gal4/+;UAS-RNAi-belle/+	54.55	92.73	0.069[a]	±	0.025	55
w;Eaat-Gal4/+;UAS-RNAi-belle/+	67.74	90.32	0.274	±	0.034	31
w;pdf-Gal4/+	74.05	100	0.141	±	0.038	27
w;Eaat-Gal4/+	86.21	100	0.254	±	0.038	29
w;;UAS-RNAi-belle/+	82.05	100	0.109	±	0.022	39

t-Test was performed. [a]: ns vs. w;pdf-Gal4/+and w;;UAS-RNAi-belle/+. MA: morning anticipation; EA: evening anticipation. MA and EA were detected, fly-by-fly, examining the bout of activity prior to light transitions. MI: Morning Index. The experiments were performed at 23°C.

4 h delayed compared to control (**Supplementary Figure S3**), similarly to what described in *bel*$^{cap-1}$ flies (see above).

Interestingly, both *belle* mutants were characterized by a reduction in the number of l-LNvs: a high percentage of brains, in fact, presented three neurons instead of the canonical four (83.93, 76.28, and 6.78% in *bel* $^{cap-1}$, *bel* ^{EY08943}, and *white* ^{1118}, respectively).

Belle Influences the Expression of Specific TEs in the Fly Heads and Gonads

As BELLE co-localizes with its paralog Vasa, a key component of the piRNA pathway-mediated regulation of the TEs, in ovaries and testes (Johnstone et al., 2005), we decided to further investigate about a possible involvement of *belle* in the piRNA-mediated regulation of TEs elements.

We analyzed the RNA expression of specific transposons in heads of adult *belle* ^{EY08943} and *belle* ^{cap1} flies. In *belle* ^{EY08943} two of them, *roo* and *blood*, showed a significant reduction in their expression compared to control (**Figure 8**, left panel). In addition, *R1* also exhibited a slight reduction in the RNA amount, though not significant. In *belle* $^{cap-1}$ the TE transcripts were greatly reduced, also compared to *belle* ^{EY08943}, and even *R1* exhibited a significant reduction compared to control (**Figure 8**, right panel). These results are in disagreement with other piRNA mutants, that normally show an increased amount of the TE transcripts (Vagin et al., 2006; Brennecke et al., 2007; Ghildiyal and Zamore, 2009;

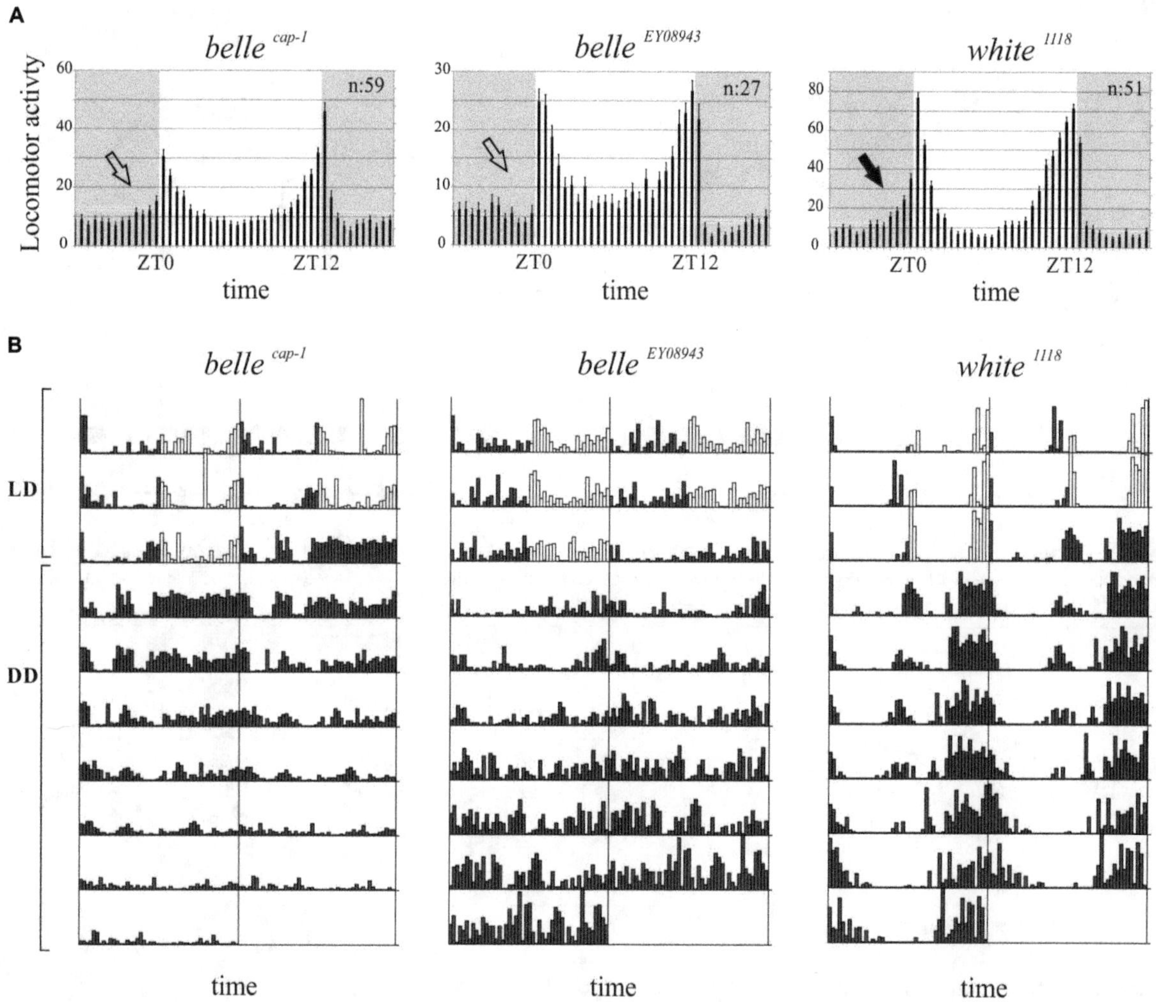

FIGURE 5 | BELLE affects circadian locomotor activity. **(A)** Activity means of flies over 3 days of LD cycles ± SEM. N: number of flies; gray boxes: dark phase. *Belle* mutants lost the morning anticipation (empty arrows) compared to control (black arrow). ZT0: lights-on, ZT12: lights-off. **(B)** Representative double-plotted locomotor activity of a single fly recorded for 3 days under LD and 7 days under DD conditions (gray bars: dark phase; white bars: light phase). LD: light–dark cycles; DD: constant darkness.

TABLE 3 | Locomotor activity of *belle* mutants in entrainment conditions (LD).

Genotype	MA (%)	EA (%)	MI		*SEM*	*N*
belle $^{cap-1\ a}$	42.37	81.36	0.022^a	±	0.033	59
belle $^{EY08943\ b}$	14.81	70.37	0.026^b	±	0.041	27
white ^{1118}	94.12	98.04	0.179	±	0.024	51

t-Test was performed. ^{a,b}*:* $p < 0.005$ *compared to white* ^{1118} *control. MA: morning anticipation; EA: evening anticipation. MA and EA were detected, fly-by-fly, examining the bout of activity prior to light transitions. MI: Morning Index. The experiments were performed at 23°C.*

TABLE 4 | Locomotor activity of *belle* mutants in constant darkness (DD).

Genotype	N Tot	N Alive	N R	% R	τ		*SEM*
belle $^{cap-1\ a}$	85	59	40	67.80	24.24	±	0.10
belle $^{EY08943\ b}$	46	27	8	29.63	24.36	±	0.25
white ^{1118}	54	51	45	88.24	24.44	±	0.12

R: rhythmic flies. The experiments were performed at 23°C.

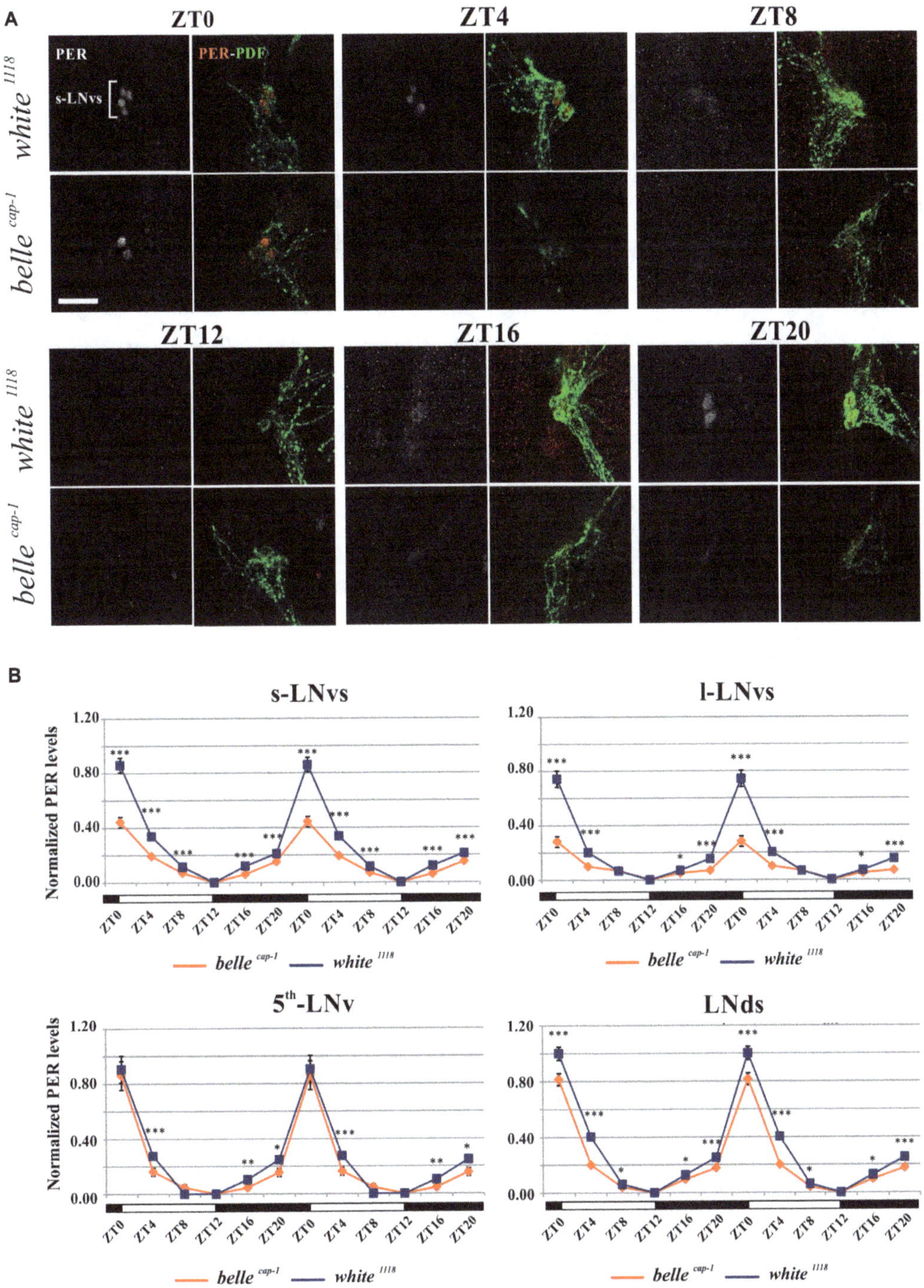

FIGURE 6 | Altered PER expression in *belle* $^{cap-1}$ mutant in entrainment conditions. PER oscillations in the clock Lateral Neurons of *belle* $^{cap-1}$ mutant flies in LD cycles. Flies were collected at the indicated time points after 3 days in LD and stained for PER and PDF. **(A)** Representative confocal stack images of PER staining in s-LNvs. *belle* $^{cap-1}$ mutants displayed lower PER expression in circadian pacemaker neurons, compared to control (*white* ^{1118}). Scale bar: 25 μm. **(B)** PER quantification in clock Lateral Neurons. Peak value was set to 1 and the rest of the values were normalized accordingly. Data are shown as double-plotted. *t*-Test: $^{***}p < 0.005$, $^{**}p < 0.01$, $^{*}p < 0.05$.

Khurana and Theurkauf, 2010; Specchia et al., 2010; Piacentini et al., 2014; Bozzetti et al., 2015). Nevertheless, based on our observations, a role for *belle* in the regulation of the TEs expression can still be hypothesized.

In order to better elucidate this involvement, we decided to investigate *belle* function in the gonads, where the role of the different components of the piRNA pathway is almost entirely known (Vagin et al., 2006; Brennecke et al., 2007;

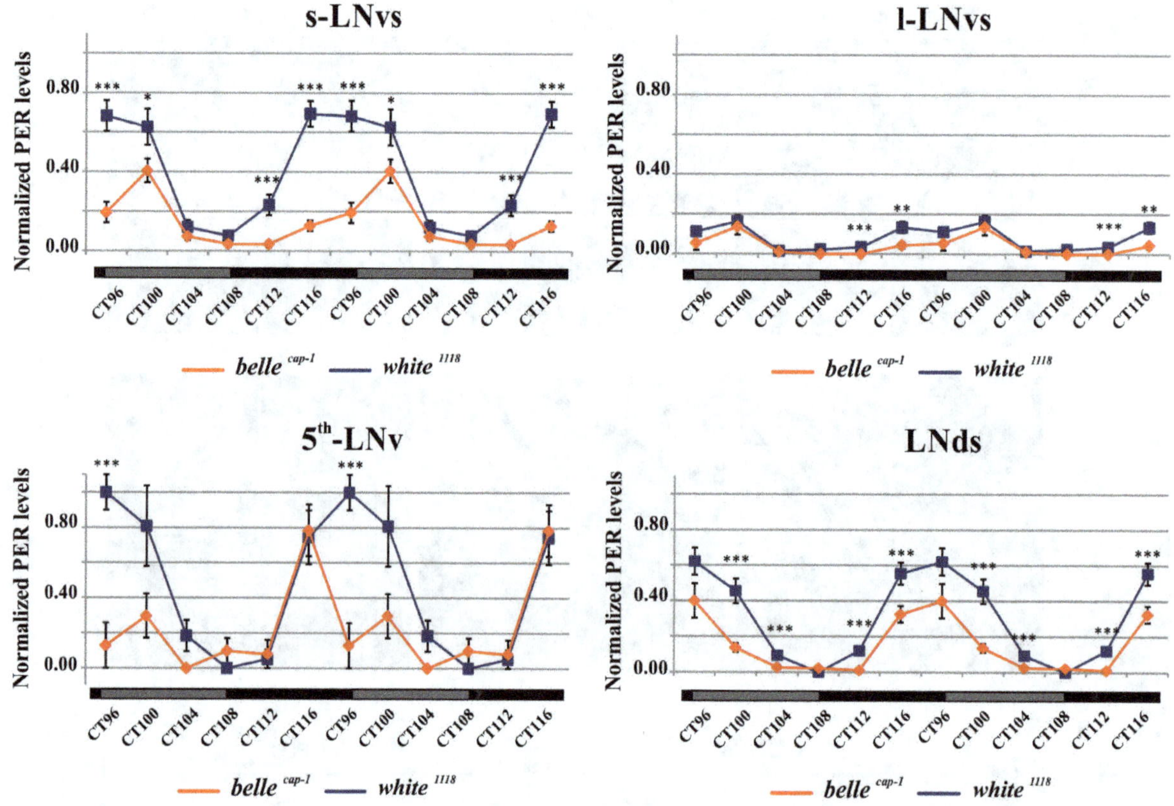

FIGURE 7 | Altered PER expression in *belle* $^{cap-1}$ mutant in constant conditions. PER quantifications in the clock Lateral Neurons of *belle* $^{cap-1}$ mutant flies in constant darkness. Flies were first entrained for 2 days in LD and then analyzed after 4 days of DD. Only arrhythmic flies were collected every 4 h and stained for PER expression during the 5th day of DD. Peak value was set to 1 and the rest of the values were normalized accordingly. Data are shown as double-plotted. *t*-Test: ***$p < 0.005$, **$p < 0.01$, *$p < 0.05$.

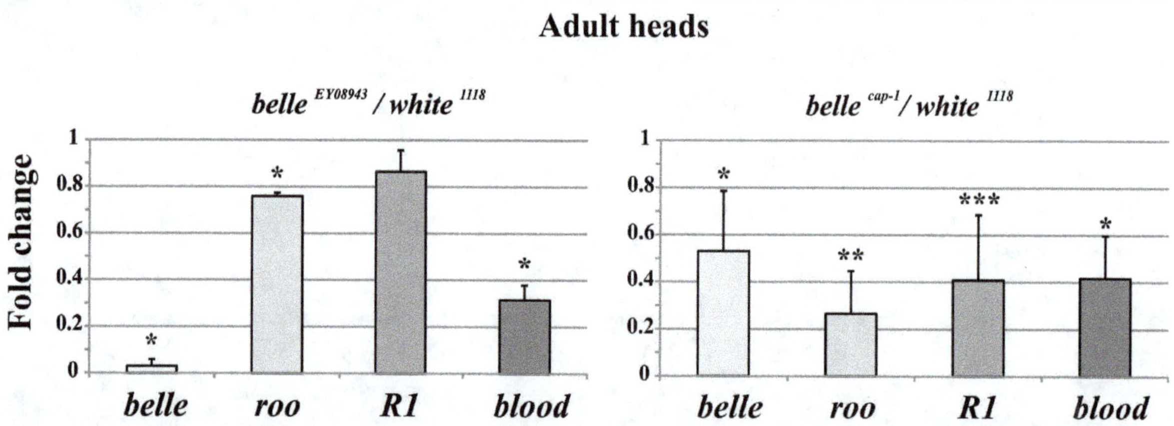

FIGURE 8 | Altered TEs expression in *belle* mutant heads. qRT-PCR on heads from *belle* ^{EY08943}, *belle* $^{cap-1}$, and *white* ^{1118} flies reared in 12:12 LD cycles and collected at ZT3. Represented are relative amount of *belle* and three transposable elements (TEs) (*roo, R1,* and *blood*) in *belle* ^{EY08943} **(A)** and in *belle* $^{cap-1}$ **(B)** compared to *white* ^{1118} control, to which an arbitrary value of 1 was assigned. Represented are mean ± SD of three biological replicates. ***$p < 0.005$, **$p < 0.01$, *$p < 0.05$.

Klattenhoff and Theurkauf, 2008; Li et al., 2009; Malone et al., 2009; Khurana and Theurkauf, 2010; Senti and Brennecke, 2010; Czech et al., 2013; Handler et al., 2013; Muerdter et al., 2013; Iwasaki et al., 2015). Our group has identified some key components of the piRNA pathway, like *aubergine, hsp83, dFmr1* (Specchia et al., 2008, 2010, 2017; Specchia and Bozzetti, 2009; Bozzetti et al., 2015) and demonstrated that TEs and repetitive sequences like *Stellate* are

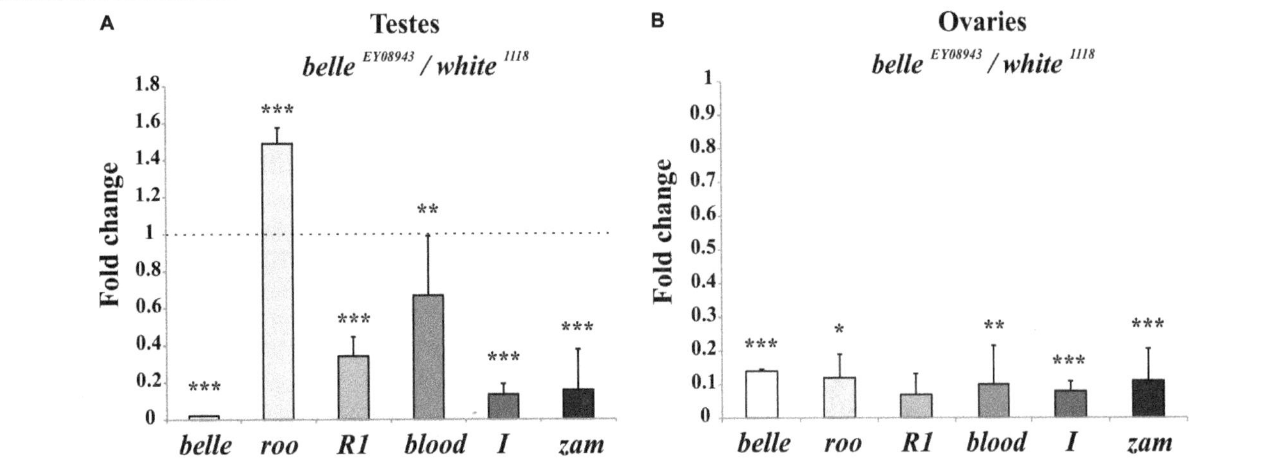

FIGURE 9 | Altered TEs expression in *belle* mutant gonads. qRT-PCR on ovaries **(A)** and testes **(B)** from *belle* ^{EY08943} and *white* ^{1118} flies reared in 12:12 LD cycles and collected at ZT3. Represented relative mRNA levels of *belle* and five TEs (*roo, R1, blood, I-element,* and *ZAM*) in *belle* ^{EY08943} compared to *white* ^{1118}, control, to which an arbitrary value of 1 was assigned. Represented are mean ± SD of three biological replicates. ***$p < 0.005$, **$p < 0.01$, *$p < 0.05$.

transcriptionally activated as a consequence of mutations in these piRNA genes (Aravin et al., 2001, 2003; Nishida et al., 2007; Specchia and Bozzetti, 2009; Bozzetti et al., 2012, 2015; Malone et al., 2015; Sahin et al., 2016).

We first tested the expression of some transposons in gonads: a dramatic reduction of transposons transcript was observed in ovaries from *belle* mutants in comparison to wild-type (**Figure 9B** and **Supplementary Figure S4**), similarly to what observed in heads. A similar reduction was also observed in *belle* ^{EY08943} testes, with the exception of *roo*, whose transcript increases in *belle* ^{EY08943} compared to control (**Figure 9A**).

We have also performed a fertility test, showing that mutant males are completely sterile with respect to controls (average progeny of 128), while females exhibit a severe reduction of fertility (average progeny of 6,6 in mutants with respect to 43,4 in control) (**Supplementary Figure S5**). This observation is in agreement to what reported for other alleles of *belle* (Johnstone et al., 2005).

DISCUSSION

Belle Is a Putative Circadian Clock Component

Aiming at finding new molecular component of the clock machinery in *Drosophila*, we have identified the DEAD-box RNA helicase BELLE as interactor of CRY. DEAD (Asp-Glu-Ala-Asp)-box RNA helicases are highly conserved proteins known to play central roles in essentially every stages of RNA metabolism, in both nucleus and cytoplasm (Linder and Fuller-Pace, 2013). BELLE has been implicated in splicing and translational regulation (Worringer et al., 2009; Ihry et al., 2012) and, more recently, in miRNA and siRNA pathways (Pek and Kai, 2011). It is essential for viability, organismal growth, and fertility (Johnstone et al., 2005).

The involvement of a RNA helicase in the circadian clock is not uncommon. In *Neurospora crassa*, in fact, two members of DEAD-box RNA helicase family play important roles in the circadian machinery: FRH (Frequency-interacting RNA Helicase), that regulates the stability of FREQUENCY (FRQ), thus acting on both negative and positive circadian feedback (Cheng et al., 2005; Guo et al., 2010; Shi et al., 2010; Lauinger et al., 2014), and PRD-1 (PERIOD-1), ortholog of human DDX5 and DDX17, specifically regulating circadian rhythmicity also in FRQ-less oscillators (Emerson et al., 2015; Adhvaryu et al., 2016).

BELLE has been extensively studied for its crucial role in the *Drosophila* gonads, where it is essential for viability and fertility (Johnstone et al., 2005; Kibanov et al., 2011). However the presence of BELLE has been reported also in *Drosophila* neurons, specifically in the neuronal cell body (Beckham et al., 2008), and proteomic data describe its expression in adult fly heads (Aradska et al., 2015).

We have depicted BELLE expression in both PDF expressing clock neurons and in the glial cells in the optic lobe. It is reported that adult glial cells contain a molecular clock and evidences about their role in the modulation of circadian rhythmicity are continuously accumulating (Siwicki et al., 1988; Zerr et al., 1990; Ewer et al., 1992; Pyza and Gorska-Andrzejak, 2004; Suh and Jackson, 2007; Damulewicz et al., 2013; Ng and Jackson, 2015; Ng et al., 2016). Nevertheless, the signaling between glia and the clock neurons that control the locomotor behavior is not yet fully understood. Many PER-expressing glial cells, such as epithelial glial, are located in proximity of clock neurons or their processes (Suh and Jackson, 2007), suggesting a direct communication. Epithelial glia affects rhythmic behavior also by regulating neurotransmitter metabolism through Ebony (Suh and Jackson, 2007). BELLE is mostly localized in the cytoplasm: this observation is in accordance with previous reports of a predominantly cytoplasmic distribution for BELLE in fly gonads (Johnstone et al., 2005) and its localization in cytoplasmic processing bodies (P-bodies), where it is supposed to act as translational repressor (Beckham et al., 2008). At the transcriptional level, we observed a clear daily rhythm for *belle* mRNA either in LD and DD; the phase of the oscillation is altered in per^0 flies in LD, while it is abolished in constant conditions, suggesting that the circadian clock controls the expression of this helicase.

These results are perfectly in line with previously reported observations: in fact, a microarray study showed a peak of expression for *belle* at ZT17 (Claridge-Chang et al., 2001) and, in a chromatin immunoprecipitation (ChIP) analysis, *belle* was found to be a direct target of CLK in fly heads (Abruzzi et al., 2011). The peak-time of *belle* mRNA in the late day/early night is in agreement with a direct control of CLOCK in the expression of this gene, since it is reported that CLK-CYC bind to E-box of their target genes in the late day (reviewed in Peschel and Helfrich-Forster, 2011).

The effect of down-regulation of *belle* in glia and in TIM-expressing cells, lethality and arrested growth at larval stage, respectively, is in agreement with previously reported observation (Johnstone et al., 2005). In fact, strong alleles of *belle* are zygotic lethal and larvae arrest their development at stage L1, which is prolonged up to 5 days (Johnstone et al., 2005). This larval growth arrest phenotype is common to other genes encoding for translation factors, such as elongation factors *elF4A* and *elF4E* (Galloni and Edgar, 1999; Lachance et al., 2002), for which a lethality was observed also when knocked down in TIM cells (Bradley et al., 2012). The down-regulation of *belle* in a restricted subset of clock neurons or glial cells resulted in the loss of the morning anticipation in about 60% of flies reared in entrainment conditions, suggesting a possible role for BELLE in the regulation of morning activity. This phenotype was much stronger in two viable allele of *belle*: in LD cycles, in fact, a high proportion of flies were devoid of morning anticipatory, further indicating that the small ventral lateral neurons, that constitute the morning oscillator (Grima et al., 2004), are affected in these flies. In constant conditions the percentage of rhythmic flies in the two *belle* mutants was significantly lower compared to wild-type, reinforcing the fact that the activity of lateral ventral neurons, that drive also the endogenous behavioral rhythmicity (Helfrich-Forster, 1998; Renn et al., 1999; Lin et al., 2004), are impaired by *belle* mutation.

We sought to analyze PER cycling in clock neurons of *belle* mutants, in order to determine whether an altered PER expression could account for the behavioral defects of these flies. In fact PER oscillation in circadian pacemaker neurons is a hallmark of a functioning molecular oscillator, and an impairment of LNvs activity results in a de-synchronization of PER cycling within different groups of circadian neurons (Renn et al., 1999; Peng et al., 2003; Lin et al., 2004).

Although with a different magnitude between the two mutants, a general decrease of PER staining was observed compared to control. In entrainment conditions, in *belle* $^{cap-1}$ flies the amplitude of PER oscillation was significantly reduced in both s-LNvs and l-LNvs, and the difference was particularly marked at ZT0. In constant conditions, s-LNvs displayed the stronger effect, with a PER reduction more pronounced at the end of subjected night/beginning of subjective day, when the protein is expressed at maximum levels. Moreover, in these cells the accumulation of PER was also slow down, reaching maximum levels about 4 h later than the control. The *belle* ^{EY08943} mutant exhibited a less striking phenotype: only in constant darkness PDF positive s-LNvs displayed a 4 h delay compared to control. Altered PER oscillation in PDF-positive LNvs may account for the defects in the morning anticipation of the locomotor activity of *belle* mutants. These flies did not display particular defects in PDF projections/arborizations, but a reduction in the number of large ventral lateral neurons (l-LNvs) was observed. The altered PER cycling in clock neurons is reminiscent of the phenotype observed in mutants for RNA binding proteins involved at different levels in the post-transcriptional regulation of circadian clock, such as the translational factors NAT1 (Bradley et al., 2012) and ATAXIN2 (ATX2) (Lim and Allada, 2013; Zhang et al., 2013). ATX-2 is a RNA-binding protein that very recently has been shown to sustain circadian behavior in *Drosophila* functioning as both activator and repressor of translation, and this switch is mediated by complex formation with two specific factors, LSM12 and ME31B/DDX6, respectively (Lim and Allada, 2013). *Lsm12* mutant flies exhibited a dampened PER cycling in circadian pacemaker neurons, that resulted in a lengthening of the locomotor activity period (Lee et al., 2017). ME31B is the homolog of human DDX6, a RNA helicase belonging to the same family of DEAD-box ATP-dependent helicase of BELLE, and flies in which the expression of this gene was depleted exhibit very poor rhythmicity (Lee et al., 2017). All these similarities led us to hypothesize that also BELLE could play a role in the post-transcriptional control of the circadian clock in *Drosophila*, probably in mechanisms in which the aforementioned factors are also involved. This idea is supported by the fact that we have found ME31B in our Co-IP and MS analysis in the same complex as BELLE in fly heads (**Figure 1** and **Supplementary Table S2**), and that the two proteins belongs to the same translational repression complex that in *Drosophila* embryo is responsible for both repression and degradation of non-localized *nanos* mRNA, in a mechanism that involves also the Piwi-interacting RNA (piRNA) machinery (Gotze et al., 2017).

BELLE Has a Role in the Regulation of the TEs in the Nervous System and in Gonads

BELLE has a well-studied role in the *Drosophila* gonads (Johnstone et al., 2005; Kibanov et al., 2011; Kotov et al., 2016). In this study we have observed that loss of *belle* function impinges on the expression of TEs either in the brain or in the gonads, with an impact on the fertility of both males and females. We have observed a reduction of the transposons' transcription in *belle* mutant, in comparison to wild-type; notably, other piRNA mutants normally exhibit an increased TEs' expression (Aravin et al., 2007; Specchia et al., 2008, 2017; Specchia and Bozzetti, 2009; Senti and Brennecke, 2010). This observation well-agrees with the recently reported data on the effect of *belle* mutants in the silencing of P-transposon-derived constructs in ovaries, depending on *de novo* piRNAs generated from the transgenes in the region of their insertion (Lo et al., 2016). Our data led us to infer that *belle* regulates the transposons probably *via* the piRNA-mediated pathway. This hypothesis is somehow supported by the fact that Vasa and Spindle-E, two members of the same DEAD box protein family, have a well-recognized role in the piRNA pathway in ovaries and testes, though their loss of function results in an up-regulation of TEs (Lasko, 2013; Iwasaki et al., 2015; Specchia et al., 2017), as opposite to that of *belle*. They also co-localize at the "nuage" of the germline where, Argonaute, Tudor and many other factors are also located for an efficient TE silencing (Lasko and Ashburner, 1990; Lim and Kai, 2007; Lasko, 2013; Bozzetti et al., 2015). However, in contrast to the majority of piRNA-related genes (Nishida et al., 2007; Specchia et al., 2008, 2010, 2017; Specchia and Bozzetti, 2009; Bozzetti et al., 2015; Sahin et al., 2016), *belle* seems not to be involved in the *crystal-Stellate* regulatory pathway, since mutant flies did not exhibited Stellate-made crystalline aggregates in the spermatocytes (**Supplementary Information and Supplementary Figure S6**). This observation well-agrees with the demonstration that *belle* ^{EY08943} mutant does not show an increase of RNA for TEs and repetitive sequences like *Stellate.*

A possible role of BELLE in the piRNA pathway is only starting to be elucidated: our experiments suggest that it might act in maintaining precise levels of TE RNAs, probably regulating the activity of other piRNA components.

The involvement of *belle* in both circadian rhythmicity and piRNA mediated transposon regulation suggests association between these two biological processes. This hypothesis is supported by indirect, though reasonable, observations.

First of all, circadian components have been linked to piRNA factors in the gonads. In fact, the mammalian CLOCK and BMAL1 transcription factors have been associated to the chromatoid body (CB) (Peruquetti et al., 2012), a cytoplasmic electron dense structure in the male germline with similarities to *Drosophila* polar granules and "nuage" of the germ cells (Grivna et al., 2006), where many components of different RNA metabolism pathways, like piRNAs, are located (Tanaka et al., 2000; Kotaja et al., 2006; Nagamori et al., 2011).

Secondly, a piRNA gene plays essential roles in neuronal development and circadian regulation. Our group has recently identified *dFmr1*, a gene with well-characterized functions in development of nervous system (Schenck et al., 2002; Napoli et al., 2008; Aitken and Lorsch, 2012; Doll and Broadie, 2016) and in regulation of circadian rhythmicity (Dockendorff et al., 2002; McBride et al., 2005; Santos et al., 2014), as a piRNA gene playing a crucial role in the gonads, where it ensures fertility and piRNA-regulated genome stability (Bozzetti et al., 2015; Specchia et al., 2017). Nevertheless, a role of this gene in the piRNA-mediated regulation in the nervous system has not been reported yet. *dFmr1* mutants display an altered rhythmicity in both eclosion and locomotor activity, due to an effect on the output factor CREB (cAMP response element binding protein) rather than the molecular oscillator (Dockendorff et al., 2002).

Third, circadian transposon regulation ensures genome integrity during aging. It is well-known that TEs activation induces an age-dependent loss of neuronal functions in *Drosophila* brain (Li et al., 2013). Very recently, a set of putative primary piRNA transcripts fully overlapping transposons in antisense were shown to display a clock-controlled *de novo* oscillation in old flies, raising the hypothesis that circadian piRNA expression could represent a new strategy adopted by the clock to preserve genome integrity during aging Kuintzle et al., 2017).

A clear involvement of the piRNA pathway in the circadian rhythmicity has not been demonstrated so far. However, we have described an emerging role of *belle* in both circadian rhythmicity and transposon regulation, that leads to the attractive hypothesis that piRNA-mediated regulation could be another level of post-transcriptional control adopted by the clock to ensure the proper rhythmicity.

AUTHOR CONTRIBUTIONS

RC, GMM, and MPB conceived and supervised the study. PC, MD, EC, LC, VS, and AP performed experiments and analyzed the data. PC, MD, GMM, RC, VS, and MPB discussed results and wrote the manuscript.

FUNDING

This work was funded by grants from: University of Padova to GMM (Grant No. CPDA099390/09) and PC ("Progetto Giovani 2010"_Grant GRIC101061), European Community (6th Framework Project EUCLOCK No. 018741), National Research Council of Italy and MIUR (EPIGEN Flagship Project - Subproject 4), INsecTIME Marie Curie Initial Training Network (Grant No. PITN-GA-2012-316790) to RC, TELETHON (Grant No. GG14181) to MPB, Polish National Science Centre (Narodowe Centrum Nauki, NCN _ Grant No. UMO-2014/15/D/NZ3/05207) to MD.

Stocks obtained from the Bloomington Drosophila Stock Center (NIH P40OD018537), Vienna Drosophila Resource Center (VDRC) and Kyoto Stock Centre were used in this study.

ACKNOWLEDGMENTS

We thank Moyra Mason (University of Padova) for her work on CoIP and MS; Federica Sandrelli (University of Padova) for her initial help with locomotor activity analysis; Alberto Biscontin (University of Padova) for help with statistical analyses; Prof. Paul Lasko (Department of Biology, McGill University, Montreal, QC, Canada) for anti-BELLE antibody.

REFERENCES

Abruzzi, K. C., Rodriguez, J., Menet, J. S., Desrochers, J., Zadina, A., Luo, W., et al. (2011). *Drosophila* CLOCK target gene characterization: implications for circadian tissue-specific gene expression. *Genes Dev.* 25, 2374–2386. doi: 10.1101/gad.174110.111

Adhvaryu, K., Firoozi, G., Motavaze, K., and Lakin-Thomas, P. (2016). PRD-1, a component of the circadian system of *Neurospora crassa*, is a member of the DEAD-box RNA Helicase family. *J. Biol. Rhythms* 31, 258–271. doi: 10.1177/0748730416639717

Aitken, C. E., and Lorsch, J. R. (2012). A mechanistic overview of translation initiation in eukaryotes. *Nat. Struct. Mol. Biol.* 19, 568–576. doi: 10.1038/nsmb.2303

Allada, R., and Chung, B. Y. (2010). Circadian organization of behavior and physiology in *Drosophila*. *Annu. Rev. Physiol.* 72, 605–624. doi: 10.1146/annurev-physiol-021909-135815

Apitz, H., and Salecker, I. (2016). Retinal determination genes coordinate neuroepithelial specification and neurogenesis modes in the *Drosophila* optic lobe. *Development* 143, 2431–2442. doi: 10.1242/dev.135004

Aradska, J., Bulat, T., Sialana, F. J., Birner-Gruenberger, R., Erich, B., and Lubec, G. (2015). Gel-free mass spectrometry analysis of *Drosophila melanogaster* heads. *Proteomics* 15, 3356–3360. doi: 10.1002/pmic.201500092

Aravin, A. A., Hannon, G. J., and Brennecke, J. (2007). The Piwi-piRNA pathway provides an adaptive defense in the transposon arms race. *Science* 318, 761–764. doi: 10.1126/science/.1146484

Aravin, A. A., Lagos-Quintana, M., Yalcin, A., Zavolan, M., Marks, D., Snyder, B., et al. (2003). The small RNA profile during *Drosophila melanogaster* development. *Dev. Cell* 5, 337Ű350. doi: 10.1016/S1534-5807(03)00228-4

Aravin, A. A., Naumova, N. M., Tulin, A. V., Vagin, V. V., Rozovsky, Y. M., and Gvozdev, V. A. (2001). Double-stranded RNA-mediated silencing of genomic tandem repeats and transposable elements in the D. melanogaster germline. *Curr. Biol.* 11, 1017–1027. doi: 10.1016/S0960-9822(01)00299-8

Awasaki, T., and Ito, K. (2004). Engulfing action of glial cells is required for programmed axon pruning during *Drosophila metamorphosis*. *Curr. Biol.* 14, 668–677. doi: 10.1016/j.cub.2004.04.001

Beckham, C., Hilliker, A., Cziko, A. M., Noueiry, A., Ramaswami, M., and Parker, R. (2008). The DEAD-box RNA helicase Ded1p affects and accumulates in *Saccharomyces cerevisiae* P-bodies. *Mol. Biol. Cell* 19, 984–993. doi: 10.1091/mbc.E07-09-0954

Bellen, H. J., Levis, R. W., Liao, G., He, Y., Carlson, J. W., Tsang, G., et al. (2004). The BDGP gene disruption project: single transposon insertions associated with 40% of *Drosophila* genes. *Genetics* 167, 761–781. doi: 10.1534/genetics.104.026427

Boothroyd, C. E., Wijnen, H., Naef, F., Saez, L., and Young, M. W. (2007). Integration of light and temperature in the regulation of circadian gene expression in *Drosophila*. *PLoS Genet.* 3:e54. doi: 10.1371/journal.pgen.0030054

Bozzetti, M. P., Fanti, L., Di Tommaso, S., Piacentini, L., Berloco, M., Tritto, P., et al. (2012). The "special" crystal-stellate system in *Drosophila melanogaster* reveals mechanisms underlying piRNA pathway-mediated canalization. *Gen. Res. Int.* 2012:324293. doi: 10.1155/2012/324293

Bozzetti, M. P., Specchia, V., Cattenoz, P. B., Laneve, P., Geusa, A., Sahin, H. B., et al. (2015). The *Drosophila* fragile X mental retardation protein participates in the piRNA pathway. *J. Cell Sci.* 128, 2070–2084. doi: 10.1242/jcs.161810

Bradley, S., Narayanan, S., and Rosbash, M. (2012). NAT1/DAP5/p97 and atypical translational control in the *Drosophila* circadian oscillator. *Genetics* 192, 943–957. doi: 10.1534/genetics.112.143248

Brennecke, J., Aravin, A. A., Stark, A., Dus, M., Kellis, M., Sachidanandam, R., et al. (2007). Discrete small RNA-generating loci as master regulators of transposon activity in *Drosophila*. *Cell* 128, 1089–1103. doi: 10.1016/j.cell.2007.01.043

Cheng, P., He, Q., Wang, L., and Liu, Y. (2005). Regulation of the Neurospora circadian clock by an RNA helicase. *Genes Dev.* 19, 234–241. doi: 10.1101/jad.1266805

Claridge-Chang, A., Wijnen, H., Naef, F., Boothroyd, C., Rajewsky, N., and Young, M. W. (2001). Circadian regulation of gene expression systems in the *Drosophila* head. *Neuron* 32, 657Ű671. doi: 10.1016/S0896-6273(01)00515-3

Collins, B. H., Rosato, E., and Kyriacou, C. P. (2004). Seasonal behavior in *Drosophila melanogaster* requires the photoreceptors, the circadian clock, and phospholipase C. *Proc. Natl. Acad. Sci. U.S.A.* 101, 1945–1950. doi: 10.1073/pnas.0308240100

Czech, B., Preall, J. B., McGinn, J., and Hannon, G. J. (2013). A transcriptome-wide RNAi screen in the *Drosophila* ovary reveals factors of the germline piRNA pathway. *Mol. Cell.* 50, 749–761. doi: 10.1016/j.molcel.2013.04.007

Damulewicz, M., Rosato, E., and Pyza, E. (2013). Circadian regulation of the Na+/K+-ATPase alpha subunit in the visual system is mediated by the pacemaker and by retina photoreceptors in *Drosophila melanogaster*. *PLoS One* 8:e73690. doi: 10.1371/journal.pone.0073690

Dissel, S., Codd, V., Fedic, R., Garner, K. J., Costa, R., Kyriacou, C. P., et al. (2004). A constitutively active cryptochrome in *Drosophila melanogaster*. *Nat. Neurosci.* 7, 834–840. doi: 10.1038/nn1285

Dockendorff, T. C., Su, H. S., McBride, S. M., Yang, Z., Choi, C. H., Siwicki, K. K., et al. (2002). *Drosophila* lacking dfmr1 activity show defects in circadian output and fail to maintain courtship interest. *Neuron* 34, 973–984. doi: 10.1016/S0896-6273(02)00724-9

Doll, C. A., and Broadie, K. (2016). Neuron class-specific requirements for fragile X mental retardation protein in critical period development of calcium signaling in learning and memory circuitry. *Neurobiol. Dis.* 89, 76–87. doi: 10.1016/j.nbd.2016.02.006

Dubruille, R., and Emery, P. (2008). A plastic clock: how circadian rhythms respond to environmental cues in *Drosophila*. *Mol. Neurobiol.* 38, 129–145. doi: 10.1007/s12035-008-8035-y

Emerson, J. M., Bartholomai, B. M., Ringelberg, C. S., Baker, S. E., Loros, J. J., and Dunlap, J. C. (2015). period-1 encodes an ATP-dependent RNA helicase that influences nutritional compensation of the Neurospora circadian clock. *Proc. Natl. Acad. Sci. U.S.A.* 112, 15707–15712. doi: 10.1073/pnas.1521918112

Emery, P., So, W. V., Kaneko, M., Hall, J. C., and Rosbash, M. (1998). CRY, a Drosophila clock and light-regulated cryptochrome, is a major contributor to circadian rhythm resetting and photosensitivity. *Cell* 95, 669–679. doi: 10.1016/S0092-8674(00)81637-2

Ewer, J., Frisch, B., Hamblen-Coyle, M. J., Rosbash, M., and Hall, J. C. (1992). Expression of the period clock gene within different cell types in the brain of *Drosophila* adults and mosaic analysis of these cells' influence on circadian behavioral rhythms. *J. Neurosci.* 12, 3321–3349. doi: 10.1523/JNEUROSCI.12-09-03321.1992

Galloni, M., and Edgar, B. A. (1999). Cell-autonomous and non-autonomous growth-defective mutants of *Drosophila* melanogaster. *Development* 126, 2365–2375.

Ghildiyal, M., and Zamore, P. D. (2009). Small silencing RNAs: an expanding universe. *Nat. Rev. Gen.* 10, 94–108. doi: 10.1038/nrg2504

Gotze, M., Dufourt, J., Ihling, C., Rammelt, C., Pierson, S., Sambrani, N., et al. (2017). Translational repression of the *Drosophila* nanos mRNA involves the RNA helicase Belle and RNA coating by Me31B and Trailer hitch. *RNA* 23, 1552–1568. doi: 10.1261/rna.062208.117

Grima, B., Chelot, E., Xia, R., and Rouyer, F. (2004). Morning and evening peaks of activity rely on different clock neurons of the *Drosophila* brain. *Nature* 431, 869–873. doi: 10.1038/nature02935

Grivna, S. T., Beyret, E., Wang, Z., and Lin, H. (2006). A novel class of small RNAs in mouse spermatogenic cells. *Genes Dev.* 20, 1709–1714. doi: 10.1101/gad.1434406

Guo, J., Cheng, P., and Liu, Y. (2010). Functional significance of FRH in regulating the phosphorylation and stability of Neurospora circadian clock protein FRQ. *J. Biol. Chem.* 285, 11508–11515. doi: 10.1074/jbc.M109.071688

Handler, D., Meixner, K., Pizka, M., Lauss, K., Schmied, C., Gruber, F. S., et al. (2013). The genetic makeup of the *Drosophila* piRNA pathway. *Mol. Cell* 50, 762–777. doi: 10.1016/j.molcel.2013.04.031

Helfrich-Forster, C. (1998). Robust circadian rhythmicity of Drosophila melanogaster requires the presence of lateral neurons: a brain-behavioral study of disconnected mutants. *J. Comp. Physiol. A* 182, 435–453. doi: 10.1007/s003590050192

Huang, Y., Ainsley, J. A., Reijmers, L. G., and Jackson, F. R. (2013). Translational profiling of clock cells reveals circadianly synchronized protein synthesis. *PLoS Biol.* 11:e1001703. doi: 10.1371/journal.pbio.1001703

Ihry, R. J., Sapiro, A. L., and Bashirullah, A. (2012). Translational control by the DEAD Box RNA helicase belle regulates ecdysone-triggered transcriptional cascades. *PLoS Genet.* 8:e1003085. doi: 10.1371/journal.pgen.1003085

Iwasaki, Y. W., Siomi, M. C., and Siomi, H. (2015). PIWI-interacting RNA: its biogenesis and functions. *Annu. Rev. Biochem.* 84, 405–433. doi: 10.1146/annurev-biochem-060614-034258

Johnstone, O., Deuring, R., Bock, R., Linder, P., Fuller, M. T., and Lasko, P. (2005). Belle is a *Drosophila* DEAD-box protein required for viability and in the germ line. *Dev. Biol.* 277, 92–101. doi: 10.1016/j.ydbio.2004.09.009

Khurana, J. S., and Theurkauf, W. (2010). piRNAs, transposon silencing, and *Drosophila* germline development. *J. Cell Biol.* 191, 905–913. doi: 10.1083/jcb.201006034

Kibanov, M. V., Egorova, K. S., Ryazansky, S. S., Sokolova, O. A., Kotov, A. A., Olenkina, O. M., et al. (2011). A novel organelle, the piNG-body, in the nuage of *Drosophila* male germ cells is associated with piRNA-mediated gene silencing. *Mol. Biol. Cell* 22, 3410–3419. doi: 10.1091/mbc.E11-02-0168

Kim, D. S., Gusti, V., Pillai, S. G., and Gaur, R. K. (2005). An artificial riboswitch for controlling pre-mRNA splicing. *RNA* 11, 1667–1677. doi: 10.1261/rna.2162205

Klattenhoff, C., and Theurkauf, W. (2008). Biogenesis and germline functions of piRNAs. *Development* 135, 3–9. doi: 10.1242/dev.006486

Kojima, S., Sher-Chen, E. L., and Green, C. B. (2012). Circadian control of mRNA polyadenylation dynamics regulates rhythmic protein expression. *Genes Dev.* 26, 2724–2736. doi: 10.1101/gad.208306.112

Kojima, S., Shingle, D. L., and Green, C. B. (2011). Post-transcriptional control of circadian rhythms. *J. Cell Sci.* 124, 311–320. doi: 10.1242/jcs.065771

Kotaja, N., Bhattacharyya, S. N., Jaskiewicz, L., Kimmins, S., Parvinen, M., Filipowicz, W., et al. (2006). The chromatoid body of male germ cells: similarity with processing bodies and presence of Dicer and microRNA pathway components. *Proc. Natl. Acad. Sci. U.S.A.* 103, 2647–2652. doi: 10.1073/pnas.0509333103

Kotov, A. A., Olenkina, O. M., Kibanov, M. V., and Olenina, L. V. (2016). RNA helicase Belle (DDX3) is essential for male germline stem cell maintenance and division in *Drosophila. Biochim. Biophys. Acta* 1863, 1093–1105. doi: 10.1016/j.bbamcr.2016.02.006

Kremer, M. C., Jung, C., Batelli, S., Rubin, G. M., and Gaul, U. (2017). The glia of the adult *Drosophila* nervous system. *Glia* 65, 606–638. doi: 10.1002/glia.23115

Kuintzle, R. C., Chow, E. S., Westby, T. N., Gvakharia, B. O., Giebultowicz, J. M., and Hendrix, D. A. (2017). Circadian deep sequencing reveals stress-response genes that adopt robust rhythmic expression during aging. *Nat. Commun.* 8:14529. doi: 10.1038/ncomms14529

Lachance, P. E., Miron, M., Raught, B., Sonenberg, N., and Lasko, P. (2002). Phosphorylation of eukaryotic translation initiation factor 4E is critical for growth. *Mol. Cell Biol.* 22, 1656–1663. doi: 10.1128/MCB.22.6.1656-1663.2002

Lasko, P. (2013). The DEAD-box helicase Vasa: evidence for a multiplicity of functions in RNA processes and developmental biology. *Biochim. Biophys. Acta* 1829, 810–816. doi: 10.1016/j.bbagrm.2013.04.005

Lasko, P. F., and Ashburner, M. (1990). Posterior localization of vasa protein correlates with, but is not sufficient for, pole cell development. *Genes Dev.* 4, 905–921. doi: 10.1101/gad.4.6.905

Lauinger, L., Diernfellner, A., Falk, S., and Brunner, M. (2014). The RNA helicase FRH is an ATP-dependent regulator of CK1a in the circadian clock of *Neurospora crassa. Nat. Commun.* 5:3598. doi: 10.1038/ncomms4598

Le Thomas, A., Toth, K. F., and Aravin, A. A. (2014). To be or not to be a piRNA: genomic origin and processing of piRNAs. *Genome Biol.* 15:204. doi: 10.1186/gb4154

Lee, E. J., Banerjee, S., Zhou, H., Jammalamadaka, A., Arcila, M., Manjunath, B. S., et al. (2011). Identification of piRNAs in the central nervous system. *RNA* 17, 1090–1099. doi: 10.1261/rna.2565011

Lee, J., Yoo, E., Lee, H., Park, K., Hur, J. H., and Lim, C. (2017). LSM12 and ME31B/DDX6 define distinct modes of posttranscriptional regulation by ATAXIN-2 protein complex in *Drosophila* circadian pacemaker neurons. *Mol. Cell* 66, 129–140.e7. doi: 10.1016/j.molcel.2017.03.004

Li, C., Vagin, V. V., Lee, S., Xu, J., Ma, S., Xi, H., et al. (2009). Collapse of germline piRNAs in the absence of Argonaute3 reveals somatic piRNAs in flies. *Cell* 137, 509–521. doi: 10.1016/j.cell.2009.04.027

Li, W., Cressy, M., Qin, H., Fulga, T., Van Vactor, D., and Dubnau, J. (2013). MicroRNA-276a functions in ellipsoid body and mushroom body neurons for naive and conditioned olfactory avoidance in *Drosophila. J. Neurosci.* 33, 5821–5833. doi: 10.1523/JNEUROSCI.4004-12.2013

Liang, L., Diehl-Jones, W., and Lasko, P. (1994). Localization of vasa protein to the Drosophila pole plasm is independent of its RNA-binding and helicase activities. *Development* 120, 1201–1211.

Lim, A. K., and Kai, T. (2007). Unique germ-line organelle, nuage, functions to repress selfish genetic elements in *Drosophila melanogaster. Proc. Natl. Acad. Sci. U.S.A.* 104, 6714–6719. doi: 10.1073/pnas.0701920104

Lim, C., and Allada, R. (2013). ATAXIN-2 activates PERIOD translation to sustain circadian rhythms in *Drosophila. Science* 340, 875–879. doi: 10.1126/science.1234785

Lin, Y., Stormo, G. D., and Taghert, P. H. (2004). The neuropeptide pigment-dispersing factor coordinates pacemaker interactions in the *Drosophila* circadian system. *J. Neurosci.* 24, 7951–7957. doi: 10.1523/JNEUROSCI.2370-04.2004

Linder, P., and Fuller-Pace, F. V. (2013). Looking back on the birth of DEAD-box RNA helicases. *Biochim. Biophys. Acta* 1829, 750–755. doi: 10.1016/j.bbagrm.2013.03.007

Linder, P., and Jankowsky, E. (2011). From unwinding to clamping - the DEAD box RNA helicase family. *Nat. Rev. Mol. Cell Biol.* 12, 505–516. doi: 10.1038/nrm3154

Lo, P. K., Huang, Y. C., Poulton, J. S., Leake, N., Palmer, W. H., Vera, D., et al. (2016). RNA helicase Belle/DDX3 regulates transgene expression in *Drosophila. Dev. Biol.* 412, 57–70. doi: 10.1016/j.ydbio.2016.02.014

MacGregor, D. R., Gould, P., Foreman, J., Griffiths, J., Bird, S., Page, R., et al. (2013). HIGH EXPRESSION OF OSMOTICALLY RESPONSIVE GENES1 is required for circadian periodicity through the promotion of nucleo-cytoplasmic mRNA export in Arabidopsis. *Plant Cell* 25, 4391–4404. doi: 10.1105/tpc.113.114959

Majercak, J., Chen, W. F., and Edery, I. (2004). Splicing of the period gene 3'-terminal intron is regulated by light, circadian clock factors, and phospholipase C. *Mol. Cell. Biol.* 24, 3359–3372. doi: 10.1128/MCB.24.8.3359-3372.2004

Majercak, J., Sidote, D., Hardin, P. E., and Edery, I. (1999). How a circadian clock adapts to seasonal decreases in temperature and day length. *Neuron* 24, 219–230. doi: 10.1016/S0896-6273(00)80834-X

Malone, C. D., Brennecke, J., Dus, M., Stark, A., McCombie, W. R., Sachidanandam, R., et al. (2009). Specialized piRNA pathways act in germline and somatic tissues of the *Drosophila* ovary. *Cell* 137, 522–535. doi: 10.1016/j.cell.2009.03.040

Malone, C. D., Lehmann, R., and Teixeira, F. K. (2015). The cellular basis of hybrid dysgenesis and stellate regulation in *Drosophila. Curr. Opin. Genet. Dev.* 34, 88–94. doi: 10.1016/j.gde.2015.09.003

Mazzotta, G., Rossi, A., Leonardi, E., Mason, M., Bertolucci, C., Caccin, L., et al. (2013). Fly cryptochrome and the visual system. *Proc. Natl. Acad. Sci. U.S.A.* 110, 6163–6168. doi: 10.1073/pnas.1212317110

McBride, S. M., Choi, C. H., Wang, Y., Liebelt, D., Braunstein, E., Ferreiro, D., et al. (2005). Pharmacological rescue of synaptic plasticity, courtship behavior, and mushroom body defects in a Drosophila model of fragile X syndrome. *Neuron* 45, 753–764. doi: 10.1016/j.neuron.2005.01.038

Montelli, S., Mazzotta, G., Vanin, S., Caccin, L., Corra, S., De Pitta, C., et al. (2015). period and timeless mRNA Splicing Profiles under Natural Conditions in Drosophila melanogaster. *J. Biol. Rhythms* 30, 217–227. doi: 10.1177/0748730415583575

Morin, X., Daneman, R., Zavortink, M., and Chia, W. (2001). A protein trap strategy to detect GFP-tagged proteins expressed from their endogenous loci in *Drosophila. Proc. Natl. Acad. Sci. U.S.A.* 98, 15050–15055. doi: 10.1073/pnas.261408198

Muerdter, F., Guzzardo, P. M., Gillis, J., Luo, Y., Yu, Y., Chen, C., et al. (2013). A genome-wide RNAi screen draws a genetic framework for transposon control and primary piRNA biogenesis in *Drosophila. Mol. Cell* 50, 736–748. doi: 10.1016/j.molcel.2013.04.006

Nagamori, I., Cruickshank, V. A., and Sassone-Corsi, P. (2011). Regulation of an RNA granule during spermatogenesis: acetylation of MVH in the chromatoid body of germ cells. *J. Cell Sci.* 124, 4346–4355. doi: 10.1242/jcs.096461

Nagao, A., Sato, K., Nishida, K. M., Siomi, H., and Siomi, M. C. (2011). Gender-specific hierarchy in nuage localization of PIWI-interacting RNA factors in *Drosophila. Front. Genet.* 2:55. doi: 10.3389/fgene.2011.00055

Napoli, I., Mercaldo, V., Boyl, P. P., Eleuteri, B., Zalfa, F., De Rubeis, S., et al. (2008). The fragile X syndrome protein represses activity-dependent translation through CYFIP1, a new 4E-BP. *Cell* 134, 1042–1054. doi: 10.1016/j.cell.2008.07.031

Ng, F. S., and Jackson, F. R. (2015). The ROP vesicle release factor is required in adult Drosophila glia for normal circadian behavior. *Front Cell Neurosci.* 9:256. doi: 10.3389/fncel.2015.00256

Ng, F. S., Sengupta, S., Huang, Y., Yu, A. M., You, S., Roberts, M. A., et al. (2016). TRAP-seq Profiling and RNAi-based genetic screens identify conserved glial genes required for adult *Drosophila* behavior. *Front. Mol. Neurosci.* 9:146. doi: 10.3389/fnmol.2016.00146

Nishida, K. M., Saito, K., Mori, T., Kawamura, Y., Nagami-Okada, T., Inagaki, S., et al. (2007). Gene silencing mechanisms mediated by aubergine piRNA complexes in *Drosophila* male gonad. *RNA* 13, 1911–1922. doi: 10.1261/rna.744307

Ozkaya, O., and Rosato, E. (2012). The circadian clock of the fly: a neurogenetics journey through time. *Adv. Genet.* 77, 79–123. doi: 10.1016/B978-0-12-387687-4.00004-0

Pek, J. W., and Kai, T. (2011). DEAD-box RNA helicase Belle/DDX3 and the RNA interference pathway promote mitotic chromosome segregation. *Proc. Natl. Acad. Sci. U.S.A.* 108, 12007–12012. doi: 10.1073/pnas.1106245108

Peng, Y., Stoleru, D., Levine, J. D., Hall, J. C., and Rosbash, M. (2003). *Drosophila* free-running rhythms require intercellular communication. *PLoS Biol.* 1:E13. doi: 10.1371/journal.pbio.0000013

Perrat, P. N., DasGupta, S., Wang, J., Theurkauf, W., Weng, Z., Rosbash, M., et al. (2013). Transposition-driven genomic heterogeneity in the *Drosophila* brain. *Science* 340, 91–95. doi: 10.1126/science.1231965

Peruquetti, R. L., de Mateo, S., and Sassone-Corsi, P. (2012). Circadian proteins CLOCK and BMAL1 in the chromatoid body, a RNA processing granule of male germ cells. *PLoS One* 7:e42695. doi: 10.1371/journal.pone.0042695

Peschel, N., Chen, K. F., Szabo, G., and Stanewsky, R. (2009). Light-dependent interactions between the *Drosophila* circadian clock factors cryptochrome, jetlag, and timeless. *Curr. Biol.* 19, 241–247. doi: 10.1016/j.cub.2008.12.042

Peschel, N., and Helfrich-Forster, C. (2011). Setting the clock–by nature: circadian rhythm in the fruitfly *Drosophila melanogaster. FEBS Lett.* 585, 1435–1442. doi: 10.1016/j.febslet.2011.02.028

Piacentini, L., Fanti, L., Specchia, V., Bozzetti, M. P., Berloco, M., Palumbo, G., et al. (2014). Transposons, environmental changes, and heritable induced phenotypic variability. *Chromosoma* 123, 345–354. doi: 10.1007/s00412-014-0464-y

Pyza, E., and Gorska-Andrzejak, J. (2004). Involvement of glial cells in rhythmic size changes in neurons of the housefly's visual system. *J. Neurobiol.* 59, 205–215. doi: 10.1002/neu.10307

Renn, S. C., Park, J. H., Rosbash, M., Hall, J. C., and Taghert, P. H. (1999). A pdf neuropeptide gene mutation and ablation of PDF neurons each cause severe abnormalities of behavioral circadian rhythms in Drosophila. *Cell* 99, 791–802. doi: 10.1016/S0092-8674(00)81676-1

Richard, A., Rybak, J., Stortkuhl, K., Meinertzhagen, I., and Hovemann, B. (2002). Ebony protein in the *Drosophila* nervous system: optic neuropile expression in glial cells. *J. Comp. Neurol.* 452, 93–102. doi: 10.1002/cne.10360

Rival, T., Soustelle, L., Strambi, C., Besson, M. T., Iché, M., and Birman, S. (2004). Decreasing glutamate buffering capacity triggers oxidative stress and neuropil degeneration in the *Drosophila* brain. *Curr. Biol.* 14, 599–605. doi: 10.1016/j.cub.2004.03.039

Robles, M. S., Cox, J., and Mann, M. (2014). In-vivo quantitative proteomics reveals a key contribution of post-transcriptional mechanisms to the circadian regulation of liver metabolism. *PLoS Genet.* 10:e1004047. doi: 10.1371/journal.pgen.1004047

Rolls, M. M., Satoh, D., Clyne, P. J., Henner, A. L., Uemura, T., and Doe, C. Q. (2007). Polarity and intracellular compartmentalization of Drosophila neurons. *Neural Dev.* 2:7. doi: 10.1186/1749-8104-2-7

Sahin, H. B., Karatas, O. F., Specchia, V., Tommaso, S. D., Diebold, C., Bozzetti, M. P., et al. (2016). Novel mutants of the aubergine gene. *Fly* 10, 81–90. doi: 10.1080/19336934.2016.1174355

Sandrelli, F., Costa, R., Kyriacou, C. P., and Rosato, E. (2008). Comparative analysis of circadian clock genes in insects. *Insect Mol. Biol.* 17, 447–463. doi: 10.1111/j.1365-2583.2008.00832.x

Santos, A. R., Kanellopoulos, A. K., and Bagni, C. (2014). Learning and behavioral deficits associated with the absence of the fragile X mental retardation protein: what a fly and mouse model can teach us. *Learn. Mem.* 21, 543–555. doi: 10.1101/lm.035956.114

Schenck, A., Van de Bor, V., Bardoni, B., and Giangrande, A. (2002). Novel features of dFMR1, the *Drosophila* orthologue of the fragile X mental retardation protein. *Neurobiol. Dis.* 11, 53–63. doi: 10.1006/nbdi.2002.0510

Schiesari, L., Kyriacou, C. P., and Costa, R. (2011). The hormonal and circadian basis for insect photoperiodic timing. *FEBS Lett.* 585, 1450–1460. doi: 10.1016/j.febslet.2011.02.026

Seluzicki, A., Flourakis, M., Kula-Eversole, E., Zhang, L., Kilman, V., and Allada, R. (2014). Dual PDF signaling pathways reset clocks via TIMELESS and acutely excite target neurons to control circadian behavior. *PLoS Biol.* 12:e1001810. doi: 10.1371/journal.pbio.1001810

Sengoku, T., Nureki, O., Nakamura, A., Kobayashi, S., and Yokoyama, S. (2006). Structural basis for RNA unwinding by the DEAD-box protein *Drosophila* Vasa. *Cell* 125, 287–300. doi: 10.1016/j.cell.2006.01.054

Senti, K. A., and Brennecke, J. (2010). The piRNA pathway: a fly's perspective on the guardian of the genome. *Trends Genet.* 26, 499–509. doi: 10.1016/j.tig.2010.08.007

Shi, M., Collett, M., Loros, J. J., and Dunlap, J. C. (2010). FRQ-interacting RNA helicase mediates negative and positive feedback in the Neurospora circadian clock. *Genetics* 184, 351–361. doi: 10.1534/genetics.109.111393

Siwicki, K. K., Eastman, C., Petersen, G., Rosbash, M., and Hall, J. C. (1988). Antibodies to the period gene product of *Drosophila* reveal diverse tissue distribution and rhythmic changes in the visual system. *Neuron* 1, 141–150. doi: 10.1016/0896-6273(88)90198-5

Smith, R. F., and Konopka, R. J. (1981). Circadian clock phenotypes of chromosome aberrations with a breakpoint at the per locus. *Mol. Gen. Genet.* 183, 243–251. doi: 10.1007/BF00270625

Specchia, V., Benna, C., Mazzotta, G. M., Piccin, A., Zordan, M. A., Costa, R., et al. (2008). aubergine gene overexpression in somatic tissues of aubergine(sting) mutants interferes with the RNAi pathway of a yellow hairpin dsRNA in *Drosophila melanogaster. Genetics* 178, 1271–1282. doi: 10.1534/genetics.107.078626

Specchia, V., and Bozzetti, M. P. (2009). Different aubergine alleles confirm the specificity of different RNAi pathways in *Drosophila melanogaster. Fly* 3, 170–172. doi: 10.4161/fly.8054

Specchia, V., D'Attis, S., Puricella, A., and Bozzetti, M. P. (2017). dFmr1 plays roles in small RNA pathways of *Drosophila melanogaster. Int. J. Mol. Sci.* 18:E1066. doi: 10.3390/ijms18051066

Specchia, V., Piacentini, L., Tritto, P., Fanti, L., D'Alessandro, R., Palumbo, G., et al. (2010). Hsp90 prevents phenotypic variation by suppressing the mutagenic activity of transposons. *Nature* 463, 662–665. doi: 10.1038/nature08739

Suh, J., and Jackson, F. R. (2007). *Drosophila* ebony activity is required in glia for the circadian regulation of locomotor activity. *Neuron* 55, 435–447. doi: 10.1016/j.neuron.2007.06.038

Tanaka, S. S., Toyooka, Y., Akasu, R., Katoh-Fukui, Y., Nakahara, Y., Suzuki, R., et al. (2000). The mouse homolog of *Drosophila* Vasa is required for the development of male germ cells. *Genes Dev.* 14, 841–853. doi: 10.1101/gad.14.7.841

Thaben, P. F., and Westermark, P. O. (2014). Detecting rhythms in time series with RAIN. *J. Biol. Rhythms* 29, 391–400. doi: 10.1177/07487304145530

Thomson, T., and Lin, H. (2009). The biogenesis and function of PIWI proteins and piRNAs: progress and prospect. *Annu. Rev. Cell Dev. Biol.* 25, 355–376. doi: 10.1146/annurev.cellbio.24.110707.175327

Ulvila, J., Parikka, M., Kleino, A., Sormunen, R., Ezekowitz, R. A., Kocks, C., et al. (2006). Double-stranded RNA is internalized by scavenger receptor-mediated endocytosis in Drosophila S2 cells. *J. Biol. Chem.* 281, 14370–14375. doi: 10.1074/jbc.M513868200

Vagin, V. V., Sigova, A., Li, C., Seitz, H., Gvozdev, V., and Zamore, P. D. (2006). A distinct small RNA pathway silences selfish genetic elements in the germline. *Science* 313, 320–324. doi: 10.1126/science.1129333

Vanin, S., Bhutani, S., Montelli, S., Menegazzi, P., Green, E. W., Pegoraro, M., et al. (2012). Unexpected features of *Drosophila* circadian behavioural rhythms under natural conditions. *Nature* 484, 371–375. doi: 10.1038/nature10991

Wilm, M., Shevchenko, A., Houthaeve, T., Breit, S., Schweigerer, L., Fotsis, T., et al. (1996). Femtomole sequencing of proteins from polyacrylamide gels by nano-electrospray mass spectrometry. *Nature* 379, 466–469. doi: 10.1038/379466a0

Worringer, K. A., Chu, F., and Panning, B. (2009). The zinc finger protein Zn72D and DEAD box helicase Belle interact and control maleless mRNA and protein levels. *BMC Mol. Biol.* 10:33. doi: 10.1186/1471-2199-10-33

Xue, Y., and Zhang, Y. (2018). Emerging roles for microRNA in the regulation of *Drosophila* circadian clock. *BMC Neurosci.* 19:1. doi: 10.1186/s12868-018-0401-8

Young, M. W., and Kay, S. A. (2001). Time zones: a comparative genetics of circadian clocks. *Nat. Rev. Genet.* 2, 702–715. doi: 10.1038/35088576

Zerr, D. M., Hall, J. C., Rosbash, M., and Siwicki, K. K. (1990). Circadian fluctuations of period protein immunoreactivity in the CNS and the visual system of *Drosophila*. *J. Neurosci.* 10, 2749–2762. doi: 10.1523/JNEUROSCI.10-08-02749.1990

Zhang, Y., Ling, J., Yuan, C., Dubruille, R., and Emery, P. (2013). A role for *Drosophila* ATX2 in activation of PER translation and circadian behavior. *Science* 340, 879–882. doi: 10.1126/science.1234746

Zhou, R., Hotta, I., Denli, A. M., Hong, P., Perrimon, N., and Hannon, G. J. (2008). Comparative analysis of argonaute-dependent small RNA pathways in *Drosophila*. *Mol. Cell.* 32, 592–599. doi: 10.1016/j.molcel.2008.10.018

Zordan, M. A., Benna, C., and Mazzotta, G. (2007). Monitoring and analyzing *Drosophila* circadian locomotor activity. *Methods Mol. Biol.* 362, 67–81. doi: 10.1007/978-1-59745-257-1_4

3

Fine-Tuning Circadian Rhythms: The Importance of *Bmal1* Expression in the Ventral Forebrain

Michihiro Mieda[1], Emi Hasegawa[1†], Nicoletta Kessaris[2] and Takeshi Sakurai[1†]*

[1] Department of Molecular Neuroscience and Integrative Physiology, Graduate School of Medical Sciences, Kanazawa University, Kanazawa, Japan, [2] Department of Cell and Developmental Biology, Wolfson Institute for Biomedical Research, University College London, London, UK

Edited by:
Etienne Challet,
CNRS UPR3212, University of Strasbourg, France

Reviewed by:
Andrew Coogan,
Swansea University, UK
Feillet Celine,
University of Nice Sophia Antipolis, France

***Correspondence:**
Michihiro Mieda
mieda@med.kanazawa-u.ac.jp

Although, the suprachiasmatic nucleus (SCN) of the hypothalamus acts as the central clock in mammals, the circadian expression of clock genes has been demonstrated not only in the SCN, but also in peripheral tissues and brain regions outside the SCN. However, the physiological roles of extra-SCN circadian clocks in the brain remain largely elusive. In response, we generated *Nkx2.1-Bmal1*$^{-/-}$ mice in which *Bmal1*, an essential clock component, was genetically deleted specifically in the ventral forebrain, including the preoptic area, nucleus of the diagonal band, and most of the hypothalamus except the SCN. In these mice, as expected, PER2::LUC oscillation was drastically attenuated in the explants of mediobasal hypothalamus, whereas it was maintained in those of the SCN. Although, *Nkx2.1-Bmal1*$^{-/-}$ mice were rhythmic and nocturnal, they showed altered patterns of locomotor activity during the night in a 12:12-h light:dark cycle and during subjective night in constant darkness. Control mice were more active during the first half than the second half of the dark phase or subjective night, whereas *Nkx2.1-Bmal1*$^{-/-}$ mice showed the opposite pattern of locomotor activity. Temporal patterns of sleep-wakefulness and feeding also changed accordingly. Such results suggest that along with mechanisms in the SCN, local *Bmal1*–dependent clocks in the ventral forebrain are critical for generating precise temporal patterns of circadian behaviors.

Keywords: bmal1, hypothalamus, *Nkx2.1*, circadian rhythm, sleep-wakefulness regulation, food intake

INTRODUCTION

The circadian oscillator in the suprachiasmatic nucleus (SCN) of the hypothalamus is the central pacemaker in mammals, orchestrating multiple circadian rhythms in organisms (Reppert and Weaver, 2002; Dibner et al., 2010). Each SCN cell has an individual cellular clock driven by autoregulatory transcriptional and translational feedback loops (TTFLs) of clock genes. Notably, such cellular clocks also appear in many peripheral tissues and brain regions outside the SCN (Balsalobre et al., 1998; Yamazaki et al., 2000; Yagita et al., 2001; Abe et al., 2002; Yoo et al., 2004; Guilding et al., 2009; Dibner et al., 2010). Cell type-specific manipulations of clock genes have clarified the roles of peripheral circadian clocks in a variety of tissues (McDearmon et al., 2006; Storch et al., 2007; Lamia et al., 2008; Westgate et al., 2008; Dibner et al., 2010; Marcheva et al., 2010; Sadacca et al., 2011; Fustin et al., 2012; Paschos et al., 2012; Nguyen et al., 2013; Gibbs et al., 2014; Jacobi et al., 2015; Xie et al., 2015; Dudek et al., 2016; Xu et al., 2016). By contrast, knowledge of the physiological roles of brain clocks in extra-SCN regions remains limited (Roybal et al., 2007; Mukherjee et al., 2010; Mieda and Sakurai, 2011; Spencer et al., 2013; Yu et al., 2014; Nakano et al., 2016; Orozco-Solis et al., 2016; Shimizu et al., 2016).

The hypothalamus plays a pivotal role in homeostasis and in controlling multiple bodily functions that exhibit circadian fluctuations, including sleep and wakefulness, body temperature, food intake, and autonomic nervous and endocrine systems. In addition, local brain clocks have been reported in multiple nuclei of the hypothalamus (Abe et al., 2002; Mieda et al., 2006; Guilding et al., 2009; Moriya et al., 2009; Yu et al., 2014; Orozco-Solis et al., 2016). Therefore, it is especially intriguing to pinpoint the roles of extra-SCN brain clocks in the hypothalamus.

To genetically dissect the roles of SCN and extra-SCN clocks, we used mice in which the expression of Cre recombinase was restricted to the hypothalamus outside the SCN. We focused on the developmental regulatory genes involved in the patterning of the neuroepithelium, which are often expressed in domains that give rise to certain brain regions and nuclei in adults. *Nkx2.1* is a good candidate because its expression affects a domain that generates the posteroventral hypothalamus, yet is devoid of the *Lhx1*-positive domain that differentiates into the SCN and its adjacent structures (Puelles and Rubenstein, 2003; Shimogori et al., 2010). Along with the neuroepithelial domain that gives rise to the posteroventral hypothalamus, *Nkx2.1* is also expressed developmentally in the medial ganglionic eminence (MGE) and anterior entopeduncular area (AEP) in the ventral forebrain, from which γ-aminobutyric acid (GABA) neurons originate and migrate into the cerebral cortex and basal ganglia, including the striatum and globus pallidus (Puelles and Rubenstein, 2003; Kessaris et al., 2006). The MGE and AEP also generate oligodendrocyte progenitors in developing cortical and subcortical structures, although those cells decline to a very small fraction of all oligodendrocytes in most parts of the adult forebrain (Kessaris et al., 2006).

In our study, we generated mice in which *Bmal1*, an essential transcription factor of the TTFL, was deleted specifically in cells marked by the developmental expression of *Nkx2.1*. We demonstrated that although the mice maintained nocturnality and a normal free-running period of behavioral rhythm driven by the intact SCN, the temporal patterns of their nocturnal locomotor activity, sleep-wakefulness cycle, and food intake were impaired.

METHODS

Animals

To generate *Nkx2.1-Bmal1*$^{-/-}$ mice (*Nkx2.1-Cre;Bmal1*$^{fl/-}$), *Nkx2.1-Cre* mice ($N > 7$ backcrossed to C57BL/6J; Kessaris et al., 2006) were mated with mice carrying a conditional *Bmal1* allele (*Bmal1*^{fl}; Storch et al., 2007) ($N > 7$ backcrossed to C57BL/6J, The Jackson Laboratory #007668), as well as with mice carrying a null *Bmal1* allele (*Bmal1*$^{-}$) generated from *Bmal1*^{fl} mice (Mieda and Sakurai, 2011). *Nkx2.1-Bmal1*$^{-/-}$ and control mice were further mated with *Per2::Luc* reporter mice (Yoo et al., 2004) in order to obtain *Nkx2.1-Bmal1*$^{-/-}$*;Per2::Luc* (*Nkx2.1-Cre;Bmal1*$^{fl/-}$*;Per2::Luc*) and Control;*Per2::Luc* (*Bmal1*$^{fl/-}$*;Per2::Luc*) mice. Mice were maintained under a strict 12-h light:dark (LD) cycle in a temperature- and humidity-controlled room and fed *ad libitum*. All experimental procedures involving animals were approved by the respective animal care and use committee of Kanazawa University and were in accordance with the guidelines of the National Institutes of Health.

Histological Study

To examine the specificity of Cre-mediated recombination, *Nkx2.1-Cre* mice were crossed with *Rosa26R-lacZ* reporter mice (Jackson Laboratory #003474) (Soriano, 1999). Animals were sacrificed by transcardial perfusion with PBS followed by 4% paraformaldehyde fixative. Serial coronal brain sections 30 μm thick were collected in four series, one of which was further stained by β-galactosidase enzymatic labeling as previously described (Kessaris et al., 2006). Immunostaining was performed as previously reported (Mieda et al., 2015) with rabbit anti-BMAL1 (Novus Biologicals, 1:10,000), biotinylated anti-rabbit antibody (Vector Labs, 1:500), and the Vectastain ABC kit (Vector Labs).

Bioluminescence Measurement

Male *Nkx2.1-Bmal1*$^{-/-}$*;Per2::Luc* ($n = 6$) and control;*Per2::Luc* mice (*Bmal1*$^{fl/-}$*;Per2::Luc*; $n = 5$), aged 17–19 weeks, were housed in LD before sampling. PER2::LUC bioluminescence in SCN tissue was measured with a photomultiplier tube (Atto, Kronos Dio) at 10-min intervals with an exposure time of 1 min. Coronal SCN slices of 300 μm were made with a vibratome (Leica, Vi1000S) at approximately ZT8–10. The SCN tissue was dissected at the midrostrocaudal region, and a paired SCN was cultured on a Millicell-CM culture insert (Millipore), as previously described (Mieda et al., 2015). Bilateral MBH explants containing the dorsomedial (DMH), ventromedial (VMH), and arcuate (Arc) nuclei of the hypothalamus, as well as the median eminence (ME) and pars tuberalis (PT) (Guilding et al., 2009) were cultured similarly to the SCN explant. Recorded values were detrended by subtracting 24-h moving average values and were smoothened with a 5-point moving average method. Because luminescence from the SCN of *Nkx2.1-Bmal1*$^{-/-}$*;Per2::Luc* mice was weak and its waveform was noisy, the middle of the time points crossing value 0 upward and downward were defined as acrophases, and the intervals between two adjacent acrophases were calculated for the periods. The average of periods of initial three cycles was calculated for each explant.

Measurements of Locomotor Activity and Food Intake

Male *Nkx2.1-Bmal1*$^{-/-}$ (*Nkx2.1-Cre;Bmal1*$^{fl/-}$; $n = 11$) and control (*Bmal1*$^{fl/-}$ and *Nkx2.1-Cre;Bmal1*$^{+/fl}$; $n = 8$ and 6, respectively) mice, aged 9–15 weeks, were housed individually in cages placed in a light-tight chamber with a light intensity of ~50 lux. Spontaneous locomotor activity and food intake were recorded by infrared motion sensors and food intake monitor (O'Hara) in 10-min bins. Actogram, activity profile, and χ^2 periodogram analyses were performed using ClockLab (Actimetrics). The free-running period was measured by periodogram for Days 5–21 in constant darkness (DD).

Sleep Recordings

This study used male *Nkx2.1-Bmal1*$^{-/-}$ (*Nkx2.1-Cre;Bmal1*$^{fl/-}$; $n = 4$) and control (*Bmal1*$^{fl/-}$ and *Nkx2.1-Cre;Bmal1*$^{+/fl}$; $n = 3$ for each genotype; i.e., 6 control mice in total) mice, aged 17–21 weeks. These mice were different from those used for measurements of locomotor activity and food intake. The implantation of an electroencephalogrammic (EEG) and electromyographic (EMG) electrode was performed as described previously (Sasaki et al., 2011). Following surgery, all animals were housed individually for a recovery period of at least 14 days, after which EEG-EMG recordings were performed on 3 consecutive days in LD. EEG-EMG data were analyzed as previously described (Sasaki et al., 2011).

Statistics

All results are expressed as the mean ± SEM. Comparisons between individuals were analyzed by a two-tailed Student's *t*-test. In Figure S1, an one-way repeated measure ANOVA was performed, followed by a Tukey-HSD *post-hoc* analysis. When appropriate, data were analyzed by a two-way repeated measure ANOVA, followed by a Tukey-HSD *post-hoc* test.

RESULTS

Cre-Mediated Recombination in the Hypothalamus of *Nkx2.1-Cre* Mice

According to the prosomeric model (Puelles and Rubenstein, 2003), the SCN and its adjacent areas develop from a field dorsal to the anterior basal floor of the secondary prosencephalon, which generates most areas of the hypothalamus and is delineated by the expression of the homeodomain transcription factor Nkx2.1. Therefore, we examined *Nkx2.1-Cre* mice (Kessaris et al., 2006) as a candidate Cre driver, in which Cre is expressed specifically in the hypothalamus but not the SCN. To localize cells with Cre-mediated recombination, *Nkx2.1-Cre* mice were crossed with *Rosa26R-lacZ* reporter mice, which expressed β-Galctosidase (βGal) after the Cre-mediated deletion of a *loxP*-flanked transcriptional blocker (Soriano, 1999). We mapped βGal+ cells in the entire brain of adult mice (**Figure 1**). Prominent βGal expression was observed in the medial septum, nucleus of the diagonal band (**Figure 1A**), medial preoptic area (**Figures 1B,G**), and most areas of the hypothalamus: the ventromedial (VMH), dorsomedial (DMH), arcuate (Arc) (**Figures 1D,J**), mammillary nuclei (MN) (**Figure 1E**), and the lateral hypothalamic area (LHA) at the rostrocaudal level of and posterior to the VMH (**Figure 1D**). Notably, the SCN, PVH, and adjacent regions were nearly devoid of βGal+ cells (**Figures 1C,I**). Moreover, βGal expression was detected in cells scattered in the cerebral cortex (**Figure 1K**), striatum, and globus pallidus (**Figure 1H**), which were likely GABAergic neurons originated from the Nkx2.1+ MGE and AEP. Such expression was entirely consistent with the developmental expression of Cre recombinase in *Nkx2.1-Cre* mice (Kessaris et al., 2006). We also detected several βGal+ cells in the dorsal raphe nucleus (**Figures 1F,L**). Altogether, *Nkx2.1-Cre* mice may be useful in revealing the roles of extra-SCN clocks in the hypothalamus.

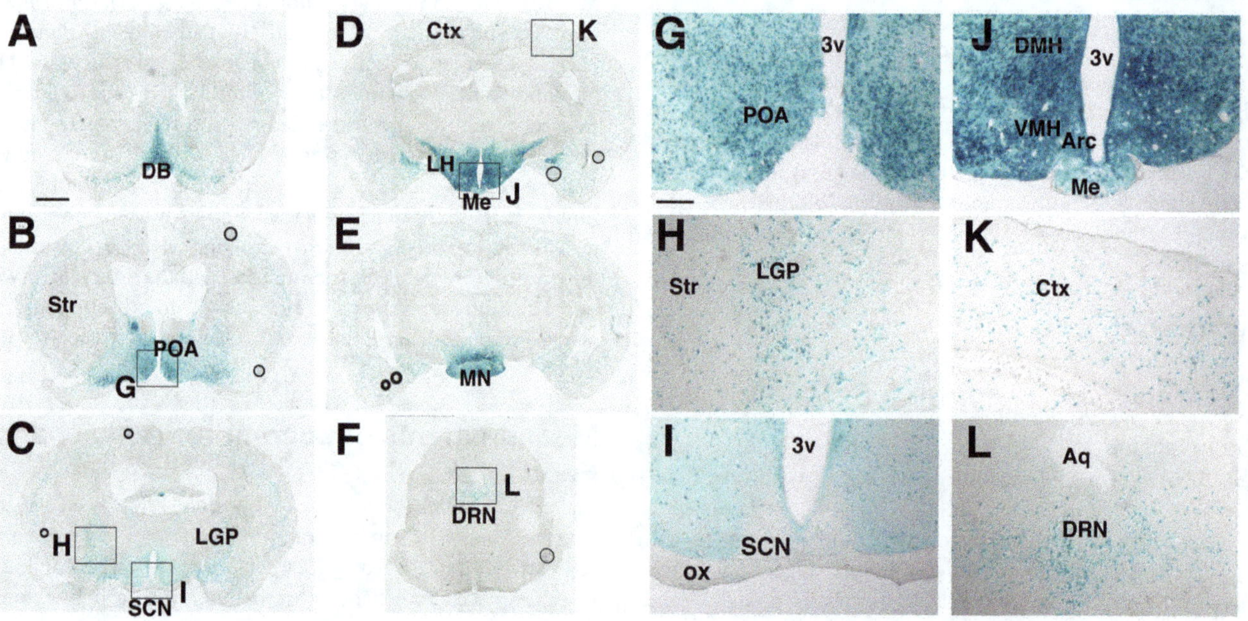

FIGURE 1 | Distribution of cells with Cre-mediated recombination in *Nkx2.1-Cre* mice crossed with *Rosa26R-lacZ* reporter mice. Coronal sections from the olfactory bulb to medulla were stained by β-galactosidase enzymatic labeling. **(A–F)** Representative images with positive cells. **(G–L)** Magnified images of regions in **(B–F)**. Scale bars, 1 mm for **(A–F)**; 200 μm for **(G–L)**. ac, anterior commissure; 3v, Arc, arcuate hypothalamic nucleus; Aq, aqueduct; Ctx, cerebral cortex; DB, diagonal band; DMH, dorsomedial hypothalamic nucleus; DRN, dorsal raphe nucleus; LGP, lateral globus pallidus; LH, lateral hypothalamus; Me, medial eminence; MN, mammillary nuclei; POA, preoptic area; SCN, suprachiasmatic nucleus; Str, striatum; VMH, ventromedial hypothalamic nucleus (Paxinos and Franklin, 2001).

PER2::LUC Oscillation Attenuated in the Mediobasal Hypothalamus of *Nkx2.1-Bmal1*$^{-/-}$ Mice

We generated mice without the *Bmal1* gene in the hypothalamus, except for in the SCN, by breeding *Nkx2.1-Cre* mice with mice carrying floxed *Bmal1* alleles (*Bmal1*^{fl}; Storch et al., 2007). To improve the efficiency of *Bmal1*^{fl} allele deletion, we generated *Nkx2.1-Cre;Bmal1*$^{fl/-}$ mice to have one floxed and one null allele of the *Bmal1* gene (Mieda and Sakurai, 2011), hereafter designated as *Nkx2.1-Bmal1*$^{-/-}$ mice. We first confirmed in these mice that BMAL1 expression was drastically reduced in the ventral forebrain, including the Arc, VMH, and the DMH, but not in the SCN and adjacent regions (**Figure 2A**). Before analyzing their behavior in detail, we further crossed *Nkx2.1-Cre* mice with mice carrying the PER2::LUC reporter (Yoo et al., 2004) to confirm *ex vivo* that circadian clocks in the mediobasal hypothalamus (MBH; Guilding et al., 2009) were functionally attenuated in *Nkx2.1-Bmal1*$^{-/-}$ mice. Coronal slices were prepared from adult mice, and PER2::LUC oscillation in the SCN of *Nkx2.1-Bmal1*$^{-/-}$ mice was similar to that of control mice (amplitude: 6002 ± 435 vs. 5872 ± 559, $p = 0.857$; **Figure 2B**). By contrast, PER2::LUC oscillation in the MBH of *Nkx2.1-Bmal1*$^{-/-}$ mice was far less robust and unstable with reduced amplitude (amplitude: 202 ± 24 vs. 482 ± 113, $p = 0.018$; **Figure 2C**). The values of period and first acrophase of PER2::LUC oscillation in control explants were similar to those reported previously in both the SCN and MBH (**Figures 2D–F**; Yoo et al., 2004; Guilding et al., 2009). Interestingly, the first acrophase of PER2::LUC oscillation in the MBH occurred earlier in *Nkx2.1-Bmal1*$^{-/-}$ mice than control mice. Thus, local circadian clocks in the MBH were severely impaired in *Nkx2.1-Bmal1*$^{-/-}$ mice, whereas the SCN central clock remained normal.

Altered Temporal Pattern of Nocturnal Locomotor Activity in *Nkx2.1-Bmal1*$^{-/-}$ Mice

We next measured the circadian rhythm of spontaneous locomotor activity in *Nkx2.1-Bmal1*$^{-/-}$ (*Nkx2.1-Cre;Bmal1*$^{fl/-}$) mice. We examined two strains of mice, *Bmal1*$^{fl/-}$ and *Nkx2.1-Cre;Bmal1*$^{+/fl}$, as control mice. All three lines demonstrated a clear nocturnal pattern of behavioral rhythm in LD (**Figure 3** and Figure S1). The free-running periods of behavioral rhythm in DD were similar between *Nkx2.1-Bmal1*$^{-/-}$ and two strains of control mice (**Figure 3C** and Figure S1C). However, the activity was substantially reduced in *Nkx2.1-Bmal1*$^{-/-}$ and *Nkx2.1-Cre;Bmal1*$^{+/fl}$ mice compared to that of *Bmal1*$^{fl/-}$ mice in LD (Figures S1A,E). We observed a similar attenuation of activity during the subjective night in those two strains free-running in DD (Figures S1A,D,E). Such results suggest that having the *Nkx2.1-Cre* allele caused a reduction of nocturnal activity regardless of the expression of *Bmal1*. Notably, the temporal pattern of nocturnal locomotor activity was clearly altered in *Nkx2.1-Bmal1*$^{-/-}$ mice compared to both control strains (Figure S1A). Such an alteration was more obvious when daily activity profiles were adjusted in accordance with activity levels (**Figure 3B** and Figure S1B). In both LD and DD, control mice were more active during the first than the second half of the dark phase or subjective night. By contrast, *Nkx2.1-Bmal1*$^{-/-}$ mice were more active during the second half of the dark phase or subjective night. The amplitude of the free-running rhythm of behavior, for which we calculated Qp values by periodogram analyses, was significantly lower in *Nkx2.1-Bmal1*$^{-/-}$ mice than in control mice (**Figure 3D** and Figure S1D). Thus, *Nkx2.1-Bmal1*$^{-/-}$ mice remained nocturnal, but did not maintain the precise temporal pattern of nocturnal activity. Because the function of SCN remained normal in those mice, peripheral circadian clocks in the extra-SCN hypothalamus might play a role in delineating the activity profile during the dark phase and subjective night.

Altered Temporal Sleep-Wakefulness Pattern Parallel to Locomotor Activity in *Nkx2.1-Bmal1*$^{-/-}$ Mice

We also examined whether the temporal pattern of daily sleep-wakefulness was altered in *Nkx2.1-Bmal1*$^{-/-}$ mice. As expected, *Nkx2.1-Bmal1*$^{-/-}$ mice remained nocturnal, but the hourly patterns of wakefulness, NREM sleep, and REM sleep were all altered similarly to that of locomotor activity (**Figure 4**). Time spent in wakefulness during 24-h of day or during the 12-h dark phase were significantly reduced (whole day: 722.1 ± 10.7 vs. 654.6 ± 21.8 m, $p = 0.015$; dark phase: 505.1 ± 7.8 vs. 455.0 ± 21.6 m, $p = 0.034$), while those in NREM sleep were significantly increased in *Nkx2.1-Bmal1*$^{-/-}$ mice (whole day: 642.3 ± 10.5 vs. 701.5 ± 25.9 m, $p = 0.041$; dark phase: 200.7 ± 7.5 vs. 249.4 ± 20.9 m, $p = 0.034$).

Altered Temporal Pattern of Nighttime Food Intake in *Nkx2.1-Bmal1*$^{-/-}$ Mice

We further examined the hourly food intake of *Nkx2.1-Bmal1*$^{-/-}$ mice. As with the patterns of locomotor activity and sleep-wakefulness, the temporal pattern of food intake during the dark phase was altered in *Nkx2.1-Bmal1*$^{-/-}$ mice (**Figure 5**). Daily food intake according to body weight did not differ between control and *Nkx2.1-Bmal1*$^{-/-}$ mice (0.119 ± 0.003 vs. 0.119 ± 0.004 g/g body weight, $p = 0.960$). Intriguingly, food intake in the light phase was significantly increased in *Nkx2.1-Bmal1*$^{-/-}$ mice compared to control mice (0.024 ± 0.002 vs. 0.017 ± 0.001 g/g body weight, $p = 0.002$), especially in the second half of the light phase. This increase might be correlated with a similar increase of locomotor activity in the latter half of the light phase (**Figure 3A**). As such, locomotor activity, sleep-wakefulness, and food intake demonstrated similar changes in their temporal patterns during the night in *Nkx2.1-Bmal1*$^{-/-}$ mice.

DISCUSSION

We demonstrated that the SCN central clock alone cannot precisely delineate the locomotor activity pattern in the dark phase. The SCN grants mice nocturnality and roughly determines when they are active, whereas *Bmal1*-dependent local clocks in

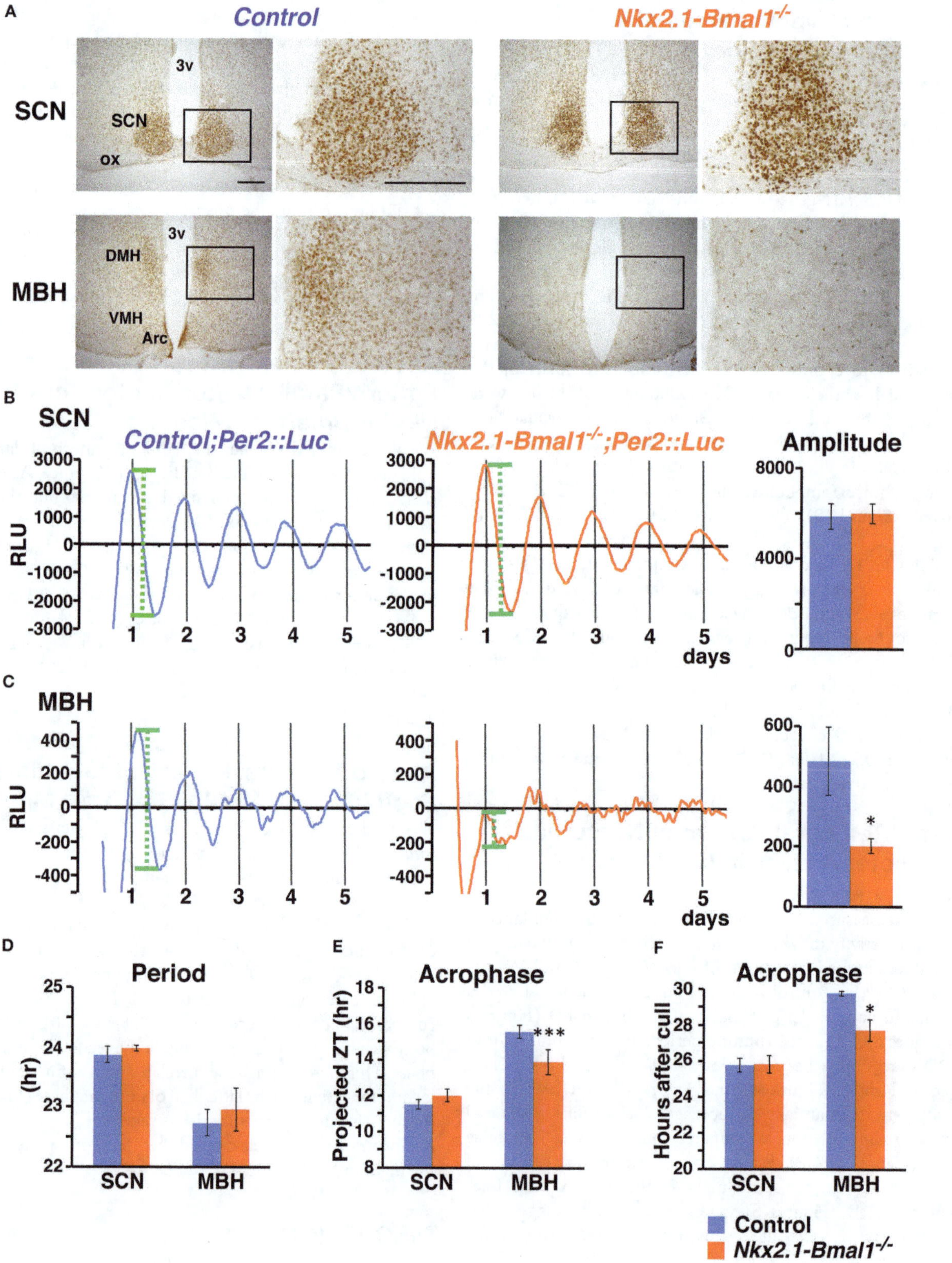

FIGURE 2 | PER2::LUC oscillation is attenuated in the mediobasal hypothalamus but not in the SCN of *Nkx2.1-Bmal1*$^{-/-}$ mice. (A) BMAL1 expression in the SCN and mediobasal hypothalamus (MBH) of control and *Nkx2.1-Bmal1*$^{-/-}$ mice. Coronal brain sections were immunostained for BMAL1. The locations of the

(Continued)

FIGURE 2 | Continued
magnified images are indicated by rectangles in the low-power images. Scale bars, 200 μm. **(B,C)** Representative circadian rhythm of PER2::LUC in slices of the SCN **(B)** and MBH **(C)** of control and *Nkx2.1-Bmal1*$^{-/-}$ mice housed in LD. Mean amplitudes of PER2::LUC oscillation are shown on the right. Definition of amplitude was demonstrated by green dotted lines in **(B,C)**. **(D–F)** Mean periods **(D)** and first acrophases **(E,F)** of PER2::LUC oscillation. Because PER2::LUC expression in the MBH was reported to be significantly correlated with time of cull (Guilding et al., 2009), the first acrophases were also expressed in hours after cull **(F)**. Two-way repeated measures ANOVAs revealed statistical significances in the effect of brain region for period [$F_{(1, 8)} = 17.16$, $p = 0.003$], in the effects of genotype [$F_{(1, 8)} = 619.19$, $p < 0.001$] and region [$F_{(1, 8)} = 230.96$, $p < 0.001$], as well as in the interaction between genotype and region [$F_{(1, 8)} = 339.05$, $p < 0.001$] for first acrophase (projected ZT), and in the effects of genotype [$F_{(1, 8)} = 6.92$, $p = 0.030$] and region [$F_{(1, 8)} = 22.27$, $p = 0.002$] for first acrophase (hours after cull). Values are mean ± SEM. *$p < 0.05$; ***$p < 0.001$; comparison between genotypes by a Tukey-HSD *post-hoc*. $n = 5$ for control;*Per2::Luc*, $n = 6$ for *Nkx2.1-Bmal1*$^{-/-}$;*Per2::Luc* mice.

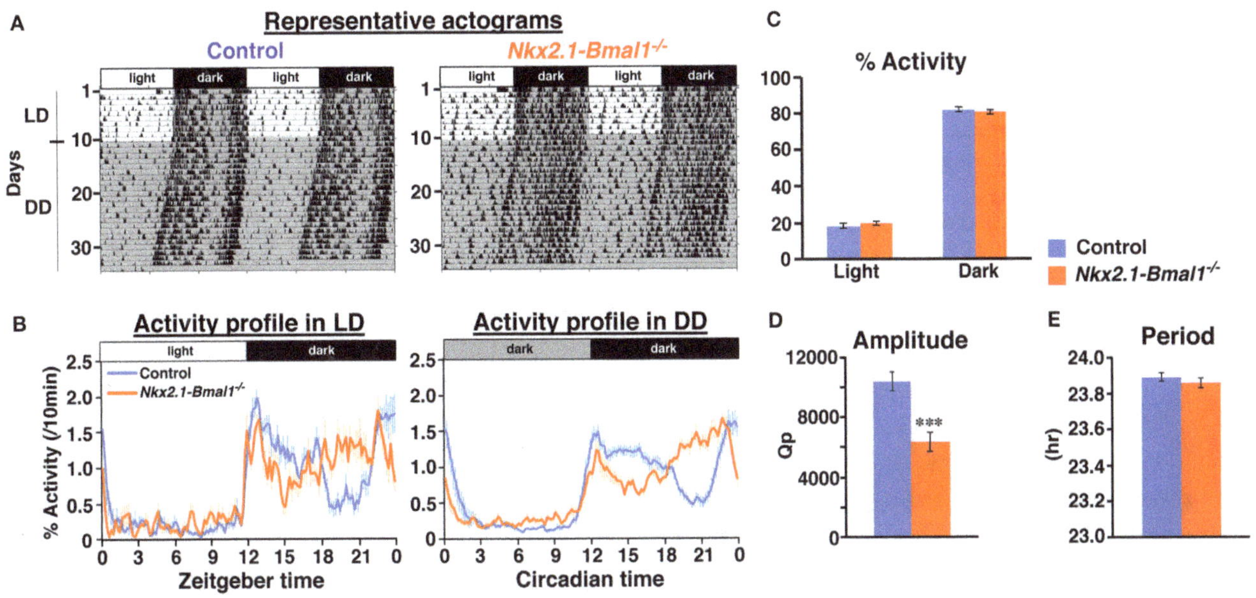

FIGURE 3 | Temporal pattern of nocturnal locomotor activity is altered in *Nkx2.1-Bmal1*$^{-/-}$. **(A)** Representative locomotor activity of control and *Nkx2.1-Bmal1*$^{-/-}$ mice. Animals were initially housed in 12:12-h light/dark (LD) conditions and later transferred to constant darkness (DD). Gray shading indicates when lights were off. **(B)** Daily profile of locomotor activity in LD or DD. Activity counts are expressed as percentage of daily total. **(C)** Relative activity during 12-h light phase (Light) and 12-h dark phase (Dark). No significant difference was detected between genotypes. **(D,E)** Mean free-running period and amplitude (Qp values of periodogram) in DD. Values for activity in DD were calculated for data on Days 5–19 in DD. Values are mean ± SEM. $n = 14$ for control, $n = 11$ for *Nkx2.1-Bmal1*$^{-/-}$ mice. ***$p < 0.001$ by a two-tailed Student's *t*-test.

regions defined by developmental *Nkx2.1-Cre* expression might fine-tune the temporal pattern of nocturnal activity.

A remarkable feature of *Nkx2.1-Cre* mice in our study was that Cre expression occurred in most of the hypothalamus, but not in the SCN or its adjacent areas. Such a feature made this Cre driver line suitable for studying local circadian clocks in the hypothalamus without affecting the central clock in the SCN. During development, the SCN and PVH originate from a region immediately dorsal to an area marked by the expression of *Nkx2.1* and that generates many hypothalamic structures, including the VMH, DMH, ARC, and MN (Puelles and Rubenstein, 2003; Shimogori et al., 2010). In addition to the hypothalamus, *Nkx2.1* is developmentally expressed in the AEP and MGE, from which inhibitory neurons in the cortex and basal ganglia originate (Puelles and Rubenstein, 2003; Kessaris et al., 2006). Therefore, the distribution of βGal+ cells in adult *Nkx2.1-Cre;Rosa26R-lacZ* mice matched well with developmental *Nkx2.1* expression, except for those in the DRN, which might be due to an ectopic expression of Cre in *Nkx2.1-Cre* mice (Puelles and Rubenstein, 2003; Kessaris et al., 2006; Shimogori et al., 2010).

In contrast to those addressing peripheral clocks in peripheral organs, a limited number of reports address what local brain clocks do in the regulation of behavior and physiology. Dudley et al. initially reported that the lack of NPAS2, a paralog of CLOCK expressed in the forebrain, altered temporal patterns of locomotor activity and sleep-wakefulness in the active phase, meaning that a brief break in circadian locomotor activity beginning midway through the active phase was attenuated (Dudley et al., 2003). Pioneered by McClung et al. the contribution of local clocks in the ventral tegmental area and nucleus accumbens, which constitute the mesolimbic dopaminergic pathway, in mood regulation has been well-characterized (McClung et al., 2005; Roybal et al., 2007; Mukherjee et al., 2010; Spencer et al., 2013; Chung et al., 2014). More recently, Shimizu et al. reported that the suprachiasmatic nucleus circadian oscillatory protein (SCOP) mediates the circadian regulation of long-term memory

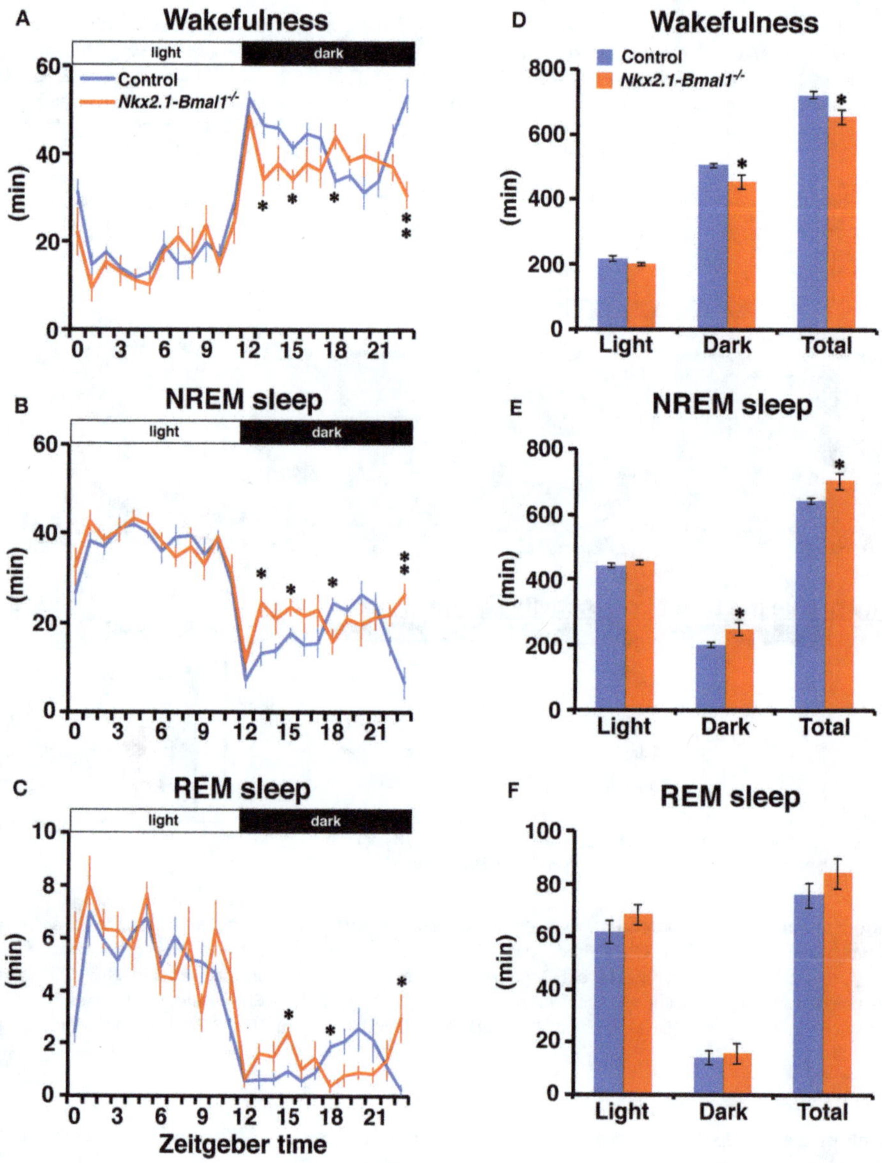

FIGURE 4 | Temporal pattern of sleep-wakefulness during the dark phase is altered in *Nkx2.1-Bmal1*$^{-/-}$ mice. (A–C) Hourly plots of time spent in wakefulness **(A)**, NREM sleep **(B)**, or REM sleep **(C)** in LD. **(D–F)** Time spent in wakefulness **(D)**, NREM sleep **(E)**, or REM sleep **(F)** during 12-h light phase (Light), 12-h dark phase (Dark), and 24-h day (Total). Values are mean ± SEM. $n = 6$ for control, $n = 4$ for *Nkx2.1-Bmal1*$^{-/-}$ mice. $^*p < 0.05$; $^{**}p < 0.01$ by a Tukey-HSD *post-hoc*. The *p*-values calculated by two-way repeated measures ANOVAs are: **(A)** the effect of genotype, $F_{(1,\ 184)} = 9.52$, $p = 0.015$; the effect of time, $F_{(23,\ 184)} = 31.71$, $p < 0.001$; and the interaction between genotype and time, $F_{(23,\ 184)} = 2.60$, $p < 0.001$; **(B)** $F_{(1,\ 184)} = 5.94$, $p = 0.041$; $F_{(23,\ 184)} = 29.30$, $p < 0.001$; $F_{(23,\ 184)} = 2.60$, $p < 0.001$; **(C)** $F_{(23,184)} = 24.36$, $p < 0.001$; $F_{(23,184)} = 2.26$, $p = 0.02$; **(D)** the effect of genotype, $F_{(1,\ 8)} = 9.52$, $p = 0.015$; the effect of time (Light vs. Dark), $F_{(1,\ 8)} = 559.33$, $p < 0.001$; and the interaction between genotype and time, $F_{(1,\ 8)} = 2.04$, $p = 0.191$; **(E)** $F_{(1,\ 8)} = 5.94$, $p = 0.041$; $F_{(1,\ 8)} = 567.63$, $p < 0.001$; $F_{(1,\ 8)} = 4.17$, $p = 0.075$; **(F)** $F_{(1,\ 8)} = 1.24$, $p = 0.299$; $F_{(1,\ 8)} = 155.87$, $p < 0.001$; $F_{(1,\ 8)} = 0.41$, $p = 0.538$.

formation by local clocks in the hippocampus (Shimizu et al., 2016), and Nakano et al., found that the same molecule regulates the circadian expression of anxiety-like behavior under the control of local clocks in the basolateral amygdala (Nakano et al., 2016). On another front, Yu et al. reported that *Bmal1*-dependent local clock in histaminergic neurons of tuberomammillary nucleus (TMN) regulate sleep architecture, likely via transcriptional control of the *histidine decarboxylase* gene, which encodes a histamine-synthesizing enzyme, but is not involved in regulating circadian rhythms (Yu et al., 2014). Furthermore, Orozco-Solis et al. revealed that the *Bmal1*-dependent local clock of VMH Sf1 neurons controls circadian energy expenditure through the rhythmic activation of BAT's metabolism, yet plays little role in delineating circadian activity and feeding rhythms (Orozco-Solis et al., 2016).

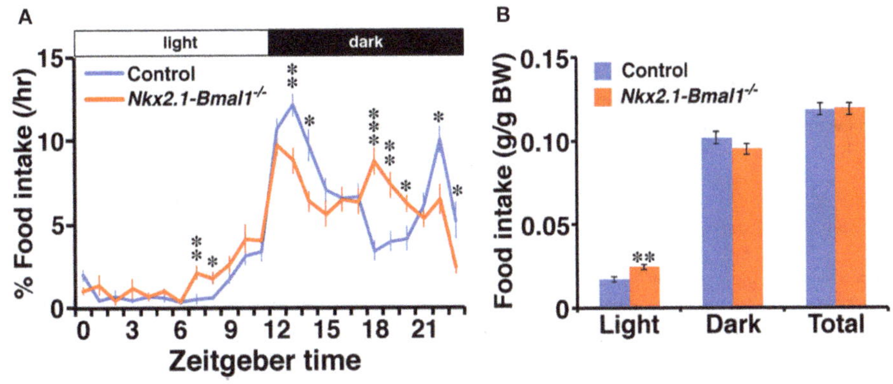

FIGURE 5 | Temporal pattern of food intake during the dark phase is altered in *Nkx2.1-Bmal1*$^{-/-}$ mice. (A) Hourly plots of food intake, expressed as percentage of daily total. **(B)** Food intake per body weight during 12-h light phase (Light), 12-h dark phase (Dark), and 24-h day (Total). Values are mean ± SEM. $n = 6$ for control, $n = 4$ for *Nkx2.1-Bmal1*$^{-/-}$ mice. *$p < 0.05$; **$p < 0.01$; ***$p < 0.001$ by a Tukey-HSD *post-hoc*. The *p*-values calculated by two-way repeated measures ANOVAs are: **(A)** the effect of genotype, $F_{(1, 529)} > 1000$, $p < 0.001$; the effect of time, $F_{(23, 529)} = 53.22$, $p < 0.001$; and the interaction between genotype and time, $F_{(23, 529)} = 5.65$, $p < 0.001$; **(B)** the effect of genotype, $F_{(1, 23)} = 0.003$, $p = 0.960$; the effect of time (Light vs. Dark), $F_{(1, 23)} = 559.33$, $p < 0.001$; and the interaction between genotype and time, $F_{(1, 23)} = 2.04$, $p = 0.026$.

It is notable that circadian rhythms of locomotor activity, sleep-wakefulness, and food intake were all altered in parallel in *Nkx2.1-Cre* mice. Hypothalamic areas originating from *Nkx2.1*-positive neuroepithelium include several nuclei and neurons implicated in the regulation of locomotor activity, sleep-wakefulness, and feeding. For instance, orexinergic neurons in the perifornical area and histaminergic neurons in the TMN are wake-active and promote wakefulness, while a population of GABAergic neurons in the POA is sleep-active and increases sleep (Mieda and Sakurai, 2009; Saper et al., 2010). The basal forebrain also contains multiple types of neurons that control sleep-wakefulness (Saper et al., 2010; Xu et al., 2015). The Arc, VMH, DMH, and LHA play important roles in the regulation of feeding and energy metabolism (Gautron et al., 2015). As mentioned previously, mice without *Bmal1* specifically in histaminergic or VMH Sf1 neurons showed phenotypes unlike those of *Nkx2.1-Bmal1*$^{-/-}$ mice (Yu et al., 2014; Orozco-Solis et al., 2016). Such observations suggest that *Bmal1*-dependent local clocks in histaminergic or Sf1 neurons are not solely responsible for altering nocturnal activity patterns in *Nkx2.1-Bmal1*$^{-/-}$ mice. Orexinergic neurons may be well-placed to regulate multiple rhythms consistently because these neurons have been suggested to control locomotor activity, wakefulness, and food intake cooperatively (Mieda and Sakurai, 2009). Alternatively, multiple local brain clocks may differentially fine-tune these three rhythms.

Although, *Bmal1* is the sole non-redundant factor of cellular clocks, the impairment caused by loss of *Bmal1* may not be necessarily due to disruption of clock function. Indeed, several defects observed in standard *Bmal1* knockout mice, such as reduced life span, fertility, and body weight, were not detected in inducible *Bmal1* knockout mice that expressed the gene during embryogenesis but not after birth (Yang et al., 2016). Because *Nkx2.1* is expressed in the neuroepithelium during embryogenesis, the possibility that the impairments of circadian rhythms in *Nkx2.1-Bmal1*$^{-/-}$ might reflect the function of *Bmal1* unrelated to the cellular clock cannot be excluded.

In conclusion, we demonstrated that *Bmal1*-dependent circadian clocks in the SCN and extra-SCN brain regions cooperate to delineate the precise daily patterns of locomotor activity, sleep-wakefulness, and food intake. However, the location of relevant local clocks remains unidentified and thus a task for future research.

AUTHOR CONTRIBUTIONS

MM conceived and performed experiments, wrote the manuscript, and secured funding. EH performed experiments. MM and NK provided resources. TS provided expertise and feedback.

ACKNOWLEDGMENTS

This study was supported in part by Grants-in-Aid for Scientific Research (B) (24390052 and 16H05120 to MM) and for Scientific Research on Innovative Areas (25126708, 16H01608 to MM and 15H01425 to TS) from JSPS; by the Cabinet Office, Government of Japan, through its "Funding Program for Next Generation World-Leading Researchers" (LS048 to TS); and by European Research Council (ERC) Starting Grant (207807 to NK). We thank for P. Soriano for the *Rosa26R-lacZ* reporter mice; C. J. Weitz for the *Bmal1*$^{fl/f}$ mouse; and J. Takahashi for the *Per2::Luc* reporter mouse.

REFERENCES

Abe, M., Herzog, E. D., Yamazaki, S., Straume, M., Tei, H., Sakaki, Y., et al. (2002). Circadian rhythms in isolated brain regions. *J. Neurosci.* 22, 350–356.

Balsalobre, A., Damiola, F., and Schibler, U. (1998). A serum shock induces circadian gene expression in mammalian tissue culture cells. *Cell* 93, 929–937. doi: 10.1016/S0092-8674(00)81199-X

Chung, S., Lee, E. J., Yun, S., Choe, H. K., Park, S. B., Son, H. J., et al. (2014). Impact of circadian nuclear receptor REV-ERBalpha on midbrain dopamine production and mood regulation. *Cell* 157, 858–868. doi: 10.1016/j.cell.2014.03.039

Dibner, C., Schibler, U., and Albrecht, U. (2010). The mammalian circadian timing system: organization and coordination of central and peripheral clocks. *Annu. Rev. Physiol.* 72, 517–549. doi: 10.1146/annurev-physiol-021909-135821

Dudek, M., Gossan, N., Yang, N., Im, H. J., Ruckshanthi, J. P., Yoshitane, H., et al. (2016). The chondrocyte clock gene Bmal1 controls cartilage homeostasis and integrity. *J. Clin. Invest.* 126, 365–376. doi: 10.1172/JCI82755

Dudley, C. A., Erbel-Sieler, C., Estill, S. J., Reick, M., Franken, P., Pitts, S., et al. (2003). Altered patterns of sleep and behavioral adaptability in NPAS2-deficient mice. *Science* 301, 379–383. doi: 10.1126/science.1082795

Fustin, J. M., Doi, M., Yamada, H., Komatsu, R., Shimba, S., and Okamura, H. (2012). Rhythmic nucleotide synthesis in the liver: temporal segregation of metabolites. *Cell Rep.* 1, 341–349. doi: 10.1016/j.celrep.2012.03.001

Gautron, L., Elmquist, J. K., and Williams, K. W. (2015). Neural control of energy balance: translating circuits to therapies. *Cell* 161, 133–145. doi: 10.1016/j.cell.2015.02.023

Gibbs, J., Ince, L., Matthews, L., Mei, J., Bell, T., Yang, N., et al. (2014). An epithelial circadian clock controls pulmonary inflammation and glucocorticoid action. *Nat. Med.* 20, 919–926. doi: 10.1038/nm.3599

Guilding, C., Hughes, A. T., Brown, T. M., Namvar, S., and Piggins, H. D. (2009). A riot of rhythms: neuronal and glial circadian oscillators in the mediobasal hypothalamus. *Mol. Brain* 2:28. doi: 10.1186/1756-6606-2-28

Jacobi, D., Liu, S., Burkewitz, K., Kory, N., Knudsen, N. H., Alexander, R. K., et al. (2015). Hepatic bmal1 regulates rhythmic mitochondrial dynamics and promotes metabolic fitness. *Cell Metab.* 22, 709–720. doi: 10.1016/j.cmet.2015.08.006

Kessaris, N., Fogarty, M., Iannarelli, P., Grist, M., Wegner, M., and Richardson, W. D. (2006). Competing waves of oligodendrocytes in the forebrain and postnatal elimination of an embryonic lineage. *Nat. Neurosci.* 9, 173–179. doi: 10.1038/nn1620

Lamia, K. A., Storch, K. F., and Weitz, C. J. (2008). Physiological significance of a peripheral tissue circadian clock. *Proc. Natl. Acad. Sci. U.S.A.* 105, 15172–15177. doi: 10.1073/pnas.0806717105

Marcheva, B., Ramsey, K. M., Buhr, E. D., Kobayashi, Y., Su, H., Ko, C. H., et al. (2010). Disruption of the clock components CLOCK and BMAL1 leads to hypoinsulinaemia and diabetes. *Nature* 466, 627–631. doi: 10.1038/nature09253

McClung, C. A., Sidiropoulou, K., Vitaterna, M., Takahashi, J. S., White, F. J., Cooper, D. C., et al. (2005). Regulation of dopaminergic transmission and cocaine reward by the Clock gene. *Proc. Natl. Acad. Sci. U.S.A.* 102, 9377–9381. doi: 10.1073/pnas.0503584102

McDearmon, E. L., Patel, K. N., Ko, C. H., Walisser, J. A., Schook, A. C., Chong, J. L., et al. (2006). Dissecting the functions of the mammalian clock protein BMAL1 by tissue-specific rescue in mice. *Science* 314, 1304–1308. doi: 10.1126/science.1132430

Mieda, M., Ono, D., Hasegawa, E., Okamoto, H., Honma, K., Honma, S., et al. (2015). Cellular clocks in AVP neurons of the SCN are critical for interneuronal coupling regulating circadian behavior rhythm. *Neuron* 85, 1103–1116. doi: 10.1016/j.neuron.2015.02.005

Mieda, M., and Sakurai, T. (2009). Integrative physiology of orexins and orexin receptors. *CNS Neurol. Disord. Drug Targets* 8, 281–295. doi: 10.2174/187152709788921663

Mieda, M., and Sakurai, T. (2011). Bmal1 in the nervous system is essential for normal adaptation of circadian locomotor activity and food intake to periodic feeding. *J. Neurosci.* 31, 15391–15396. doi: 10.1523/JNEUROSCI.2801-11.2011

Mieda, M., Williams, S. C., Richardson, J. A., Tanaka, K., and Yanagisawa, M. (2006). The dorsomedial hypothalamic nucleus as a putative food-entrainable circadian pacemaker. *Proc. Natl. Acad. Sci. U.S.A.* 103, 12150–12155. doi: 10.1073/pnas.0604189103

Moriya, T., Aida, R., Kudo, T., Akiyama, M., Doi, M., Hayasaka, N., et al. (2009). The dorsomedial hypothalamic nucleus is not necessary for food-anticipatory circadian rhythms of behavior, temperature or clock gene expression in mice. *Eur. J. Neurosci.* 29, 1447–1460. doi: 10.1111/j.1460-9568.2009.06697.x

Mukherjee, S., Coque, L., Cao, J. L., Kumar, J., Chakravarty, S., Asaithamby, A., et al. (2010). Knockdown of Clock in the ventral tegmental area through RNA interference results in a mixed state of mania and depression-like behavior. *Biol. Psychiatry* 68, 503–511. doi: 10.1016/j.biopsych.2010.04.031

Nakano, J. J., Shimizu, K., Shimba, S., and Fukada, Y. (2016). SCOP/PHLPP1beta in the basolateral amygdala regulates circadian expression of mouse anxiety-like behavior. *Sci. Rep.* 6:33500. doi: 10.1038/srep33500

Nguyen, K. D., Fentress, S. J., Qiu, Y., Yun, K., Cox, J. S., and Chawla, A. (2013). Circadian gene Bmal1 regulates diurnal oscillations of Ly6C(hi) inflammatory monocytes. *Science* 341, 1483–1488. doi: 10.1126/science.1240636

Orozco-Solis, R., Aguilar-Arnal, L., Murakami, M., Peruquetti, R., Ramadori, G., Coppari, R., et al. (2016). The circadian clock in the ventromedial hypothalamus controls cyclic energy expenditure. *Cell Metab.* 23, 467–478. doi: 10.1016/j.cmet.2016.02.003

Paschos, G. K., Ibrahim, S., Song, W. L., Kunieda, T., Grant, G., Reyes, T. M., et al. (2012). Obesity in mice with adipocyte-specific deletion of clock component Arntl. *Nat. Med.* 18, 1768–1777. doi: 10.1038/nm.2979

Paxinos, G., and Franklin, K. B. (2001). *The Mouse Brain in Stereotaxic Coordinates.* San Diego, CA: Academic Press.

Puelles, L., and Rubenstein, J. L. (2003). Forebrain gene expression domains and the evolving prosomeric model. *Trends Neurosci.* 26, 469–476. doi: 10.1016/S0166-2236(03)00234-0

Reppert, S. M., and Weaver, D. R. (2002). Coordination of circadian timing in mammals. *Nature* 418, 935–941. doi: 10.1038/nature00965

Roybal, K., Theobold, D., Graham, A., DiNieri, J. A., Russo, S. J., Krishnan, V., et al. (2007). Mania-like behavior induced by disruption of CLOCK. *Proc. Natl. Acad. Sci. U.S.A.* 104, 6406–6411. doi: 10.1073/pnas.0609625104

Sadacca, L. A., Lamia, K. A., deLemos, A. S., Blum, B., and Weitz, C. J. (2011). An intrinsic circadian clock of the pancreas is required for normal insulin release and glucose homeostasis in mice. *Diabetologia* 54, 120–124. doi: 10.1007/s00125-010-1920-8

Saper, C. B., Fuller, P. M., Pedersen, N. P., Lu, J., and Scammell, T. E. (2010). Sleep state switching. *Neuron* 68, 1023–1042. doi: 10.1016/j.neuron.2010.11.032

Sasaki, K., Suzuki, M., Mieda, M., Tsujino, N., Roth, B., and Sakurai, T. (2011). Pharmacogenetic modulation of orexin neurons alters sleep/wakefulness states in mice. *PLoS ONE* 6:e20360. doi: 10.1371/journal.pone.0020360

Shimizu, K., Kobayashi, Y., Nakatsuji, E., Yamazaki, M., Shimba, S., Sakimura, K., et al. (2016). SCOP/PHLPP1[β] mediates circadian regulation of long-term recognition memory. *Nat. Commun.* 7:12926. doi: 10.1038/ncomms12926

Shimogori, T., Lee, D. A., Miranda-Angulo, A., Yang, Y., Wang, H., Jiang, L., et al. (2010). A genomic atlas of mouse hypothalamic development. *Nat. Neurosci.* 13, 767–775. doi: 10.1038/nn.2545

Soriano, P. (1999). Generalized lacZ expression with the ROSA26 Cre reporter strain. *Nat. Genet.* 21, 70–71. doi: 10.1038/5007

Spencer, S., Falcon, E., Kumar, J., Krishnan, V., Mukherjee, S., Birnbaum, S. G., et al. (2013). Circadian genes Period 1 and Period 2 in the nucleus accumbens regulate anxiety-related behavior. *Eur. J. Neurosci.* 37, 242–250. doi: 10.1111/ejn.12010

Storch, K. F., Paz, C., Signorovitch, J., Raviola, E., Pawlyk, B., Li, T., et al. (2007). Intrinsic circadian clock of the mammalian retina: importance for retinal processing of visual information. *Cell* 130, 730–741. doi: 10.1016/j.cell.2007.06.045

Westgate, E. J., Cheng, Y., Reilly, D. F., Price, T. S., Walisser, J. A., Bradfield, C. A., et al. (2008). Genetic components of the circadian clock regulate thrombogenesis *in vivo*. *Circulation* 117, 2087–2095. doi: 10.1161/CIRCULATIONAHA.107.739227

Xie, Z., Su, W., Liu, S., Zhao, G., Esser, K., Schroder, E. A., et al. (2015). Smooth-muscle BMAL1 participates in blood pressure circadian rhythm regulation. *J. Clin. Invest.* 125, 324–336. doi: 10.1172/JCI76881

Xu, C., Ochi, H., Fukuda, T., Sato, S., Sunamura, S., Takarada, T., et al. (2016). Circadian clock regulates bone resorption in mice. *J. Bone Miner. Res.* 31, 1344–1355. doi: 10.1002/jbmr.2803

Xu, M., Chung, S., Zhang, S., Zhong, P., Ma, C., Chang, W. C., et al. (2015). Basal forebrain circuit for sleep-wake control. *Nat. Neurosci.* 18, 1641–1647. doi: 10.1038/nn.4143

Yagita, K., Tamanini, F., van Der Horst, G. T., and Okamura, H. (2001). Molecular mechanisms of the biological clock in cultured fibroblasts. *Science* 292, 278–281. doi: 10.1126/science.1059542

Yamazaki, S., Numano, R., Abe, M., Hida, A., Takahashi, R., Ueda, M., et al. (2000). Resetting central and peripheral circadian oscillators in transgenic rats. *Science* 288, 682–685. doi: 10.1126/science.288.54 66.682

Yang, G., Chen, L., Grant, G. R., Paschos, G., Song, W. L., Musiek, E. S., et al. (2016). Timing of expression of the core clock gene Bmal1 influences its effects on aging and survival. *Sci. Transl. Med.* 8, 324ra316. doi: 10.1126/scitranslmed.aad 3305

Yoo, S. H., Yamazaki, S., Lowrey, P. L., Shimomura, K., Ko, C. H., Buhr, E. D., et al. (2004). PERIOD2::LUCIFERASE real-time reporting of circadian dynamics reveals persistent circadian oscillations in mouse peripheral tissues. *Proc. Natl. Acad. Sci. U.S.A.* 101, 5339–5346. doi: 10.1073/pnas.0308709101

Yu, X., Zecharia, A., Zhang, Z., Yang, Q., Yustos, R., Jager, P., et al. (2014). Circadian factor BMAL1 in histaminergic neurons regulates sleep architecture. *Curr. Biol.* 24, 2838–2844. doi: 10.1016/j.cub.2014.10.019

4

Desynchronization of Circadian Clocks in Cancer: A Metabolic and Epigenetic Connection

Kiran Padmanabhan[1,2]* *and Marc Billaud*[3]

[1]*"Molecular and Epigenetic Regulation of Biological Clocks", Université de Lyon, Institut de Génomique Fonctionnelle de Lyon, CNRS UMR 5242, École Normale Supérieure de Lyon, Université Claude Bernard Lyon 1, Lyon, France,* [2]*INSERM, Paris, France,* [3]*"Clinical and Experimental Model of Lymphomagenesis", Université de Lyon, Université Claude Bernard Lyon 1, INSERM 1052, CNRS 5286, Centre Léon Bérard, Centre de recherche en cancérologie de Lyon, Lyon, France*

Edited by:
Etienne Challet, UPR3212 Institut des Neurosciences Cellulaires et Intégratives (INCI), France

Reviewed by:
Masao Doi, Kyoto University, Japan
Feillet Celine, University of Nice Sophia Antipolis, France

Correspondence:
Kiran Padmanabhan
kiran.padmanabhan@ens-lyon.fr

Circadian clocks are innate oscillators that drive daily rhythms in metabolism, physiology, and behavior. 24-h rhythms in gene expression, driven by core clock transcription factors, reflect the epigenetic state of the cell, which in turn is dictated by the metabolic environment. Cancer cells alter their metabolic state and gene expression and therefore are likely to tweak circadian clock function in their favor. Over the past decade, we have witnessed an extraordinary increase in systems-level studies that suggest intricate mechanistic links between the cellular metabolome and the circadian epigenome. In parallel, reprogramming of cellular clock function in cancers is increasingly evident and the role of clock genes in the development of hematological tumors, as well as their pathophysiological effects on tissues distal to the tumor, has been described. Furthermore, the interplay between components of the circadian clock, metabolic enzymes, and oncogenes is starting to be better understood, such as the close association between overexpression of the Myc oncogene and perturbation of circadian and metabolic rhythms, thus opening new avenues to treat cancers. This review article explores current knowledge on the circadian metabolome and the molecular pathways they control, with a focus on their involvement in the development of hematopoietic malignancies.

Keywords: circadian clocks, epigenetics, metabolomics, hematological malignancies, AMPK-MYC-SIRT axis

CIRCADIAN CLOCKS

Circadian clocks are ubiquitous timers that synchronize physiology, metabolism, and behavior with the solar day. Cell-autonomous circadian oscillators drive daily rhythms in gene expression and protein function and help to build and maintain a homeostatic relationship with the external environment. Over two decades of genetic and proteomic screens have helped identify many molecular components of the circadian clock that seems to be conserved across species (1). In mammals, the master clock resides in the suprachiasmatic nucleus (SCN) within the hypothalamus. However, circadian clocks are not just restricted to the brain but instead are present virtually in all peripheral tissues and cells (2). Circadian phenomena emerge from self-sustained cellular clocks in these individual tissues and are globally sensitive to environmental rhythms in light and temperature and to social phenomena such as work, physical activity, and feeding behavior. SCN clocks keep track of external time mainly *via* photic cues from the retina and downstream neurohumoral pathways then synchronize oscillators in other brain nuclei as well as peripheral tissues (3). While the photoperiod serves as the dominant time-setting cue (*Zeitgeber, time giver*), time of food intake and daily rhythms in temperature are also important Zeitgebers. Food intake timing has physiological impact on sleep-activity rhythms, hormonal cycles, glucose homeostasis, and lipid metabolism and is deeply linked to organismal metabolic state (4). Consequences of modern lifestyle, such as excess light exposure at night, improper sleep schedules, high-fat diets, and intermittent feeding schedules, have a significant impact on normal circadian rhythms and its regulation of physiology and human health. Large sections of the human population that experience such desynchronous environments—night shift workers or regular long distance travelers, for example—display metabolic imbalances, with higher incidences of obesity and higher risks for cardiovascular disease and cancer (5, 6). In this review, we will highlight the cross talk between the cellular metabolic state and the circadian oscillator, in normal as well as in malignant conditions.

Within mammalian cells, a BMAL1:CLOCK transcription factor heterodimer drives the expression of the repressor complex component genes *PER* and *CRY*, which assemble into a ~1 MDa complex with other proteins to repress BMAL1:CLOCK function on chromatin (7–9). This negative feedback inhibits new *PER* and *CRY* synthesis. Eventually PER and CRY protein concentrations decline *via* turnover, resulting in the termination of negative feedback and reinitiation of a new molecular cycle. The negative feedback loop operates in almost all cells and tissues to generate stable, self-sustaining molecular rhythms with an intrinsic period close to 24 h. BMAL1:CLOCK *via* recruitment to promoter E-box elements (CACGTT) drives the rhythmic transcription of an additional 10–15% of expressed genes—the so-called clock-controlled genes (CCGs) (1, 10–13). A second regulatory loop comprising orphan nuclear receptors acts to stabilize the core oscillator. REV-ERBα, a nuclear hormone receptor under circadian transcriptional control, competes with retinoic acid-related orphan receptor alpha (RORα) to bind response elements (ROREs) in the *BMAL1* promoter. RORs activate transcription of *BMAL1*, whereas REVERBs represses it, effectively buffering BMAL1 levels and thereby stabilizing circadian transcription in individual cells (14). These pathways eventually impinge on regulation of rhythmic behavior and metabolism (15). These *cis*-acting elements, the E-boxes and ROREs, together help to promote precisely phased circadian transcription of clock output genes throughout the genome. The past few years have expanded the output pathways beyond the coding genome to a large fraction of the non-coding genome as well as the metabolome (10, 13, 16).

CIRCADIAN EPIGENETIC REGULATION AND METABOLIC CONTROL

Studies over the past decade have clearly shown that epigenetic control plays a central role in circadian gene expression rhythms (17, 18). The mechanisms include methylation, acetylation, and other covalent modifications of histones, methylation of DNA itself, and posttranscriptional regulation of coding and non-coding RNA reviewed in great detail elsewhere (19, 20).

Genome-wide chromatin immunoprecipitation-deep sequencing analyses (ChIP-Seq) have demonstrated widespread epigenetic modifications that coincide with RNA PolII recruitment and rhythmic transcription in mammalian tissues (10, 13). A variety of enzymes that acetylate or methylate histones or conversely deacetylate or demethylate them have been found to interact with the core clock machinery (20). CLOCK itself was found to harbor histone H3 acetyltransferase activity targeting the H3K9 and H3K14 residues (21). Interestingly, CLOCK can trans-acetylate its binding partner BMAL1 (22).

The acetylation of cellular proteins (histones and non-histone proteins) depends on availability of acetyl-coA, the metabolite that provides the acetyl moiety. Nuclear and cytosolic acetyl-coA levels are controlled by a synthetase (acetyl-CoA synthetase, AceCS1) as well as ATP-citrate lyase (23). Cellular acetate levels also depend on the feeding state of the animal, the gut microbiome, as well as the activity of histone deacetylases (HDACs)—a class of proteins that play a critical role in transcriptional control. The class III HDAC SIRT1 drives circadian oscillations in acetyl-CoA levels by deacetylating and activating AceCS1, and impacts several metabolic pathways including autophagy (24).

Unlike class I and II HDACs, the activity of the class III HDACs (e.g., SIRT1, SIRT6) depends on yet another metabolite—NAD. A series of reports initially identified a crucial role for nicotinamide adenine dinucleotide (NAD^+) in clock control and later went on to describe the role of NAD-dependent deacetylases, SIRT1 and SIRT6 circadian physiology (25–32). The levels of nicotinamide adenine nucleotide (NAD^+), an essential co-factor for these Sirtuins, shows robust 24-h rhythms (31). SIRTs consume NAD for their activity and generate nicotinamide adenine mononucleotide (NAM), which acts as a product inhibitor for this enzymatic reaction (33). In the salvage pathway, NAM is converted *via* a mononucleotide intermediate (NMN) back to NAD by mononucleotide adenylyltransferases. NMN formation is regulated by NAMPT whose expression is under circadian control, thus ultimately resulting in circadian oscillations in NAD synthesis (34). Direct regulation of the NAMPT pathway also occurs *via* the AMP-activated kinase (AMPK) pathway, which senses AMP/ATP ratio and is key in adapting energetic supply to the nutrient demands of cells facing situations of metabolic stress. AMPK regulates the levels of NAD^+ by increasing NAMPT expression and thus activates SIRT1 pathway (35, 36).

SIRT1 eventually drives rhythmic deacetylation of histone H3, BMAL1, and PER2 (26). Specific loss of SIRT1 in murine livers indicates that along with SIRT6, it contributes to genomic partitioning of circadian transcription (28). Meanwhile, AMPK can integrate metabolic cues to modulate the clock circuitry and the circadian remodeling of chromatin. AMPK promotes the degradation of the circadian repressors CRY1 and PER2 (37, 38) while it activates SIRT1 (35, 36).

Thus, not only do epigenetic pathways depend on the oscillating metabolome but synthesis and salvage pathways that generate these metabolites are also regulated by cell-autonomous clocks. In this regard, the Sirtuins (along with its regulators such as the AMPK pathway) seem to be central to the modulation of the circadian epigenome and likely culprits in metabolic disorders stemming from clock dysfunction.

CIRCADIAN REGULATION OF THE METABOLOME

Cellular metabolites not only influence cellular state but also are a direct readout of the biochemical activity of a cell. Unlike transcriptomic or epigenomic methods, metabolomic approaches allow for a global quantitative assessment of endogenous metabolites within a biologic system, thus reflecting changes in cellular phenotype. Clocks regulate multiple aspects of animal metabolism and "systems" approaches have revealed widespread cross talk between 24hr rhythms and metabolic pathways. Accordingly, a recent study revealed that 50% of mouse liver metabolites are circadian (39). Sleep deprivation in animal models strongly impact glucose and energy metabolism (40–43). By comparing wild-type and *Clock*$^{-/-}$ mice, Eckel-Mahan and coworkers demonstrated that the diurnal metabolome and rhythms in enzymes controlling pyrimidine salvage pathway, Kreb's cycle and lipid metabolism are controlled by environmental signals. *Clock* mutant mice, in contrast, show very few rhythmic metabolites (44). Ultimately, the timing of food intake and nutritional richness seem to underlie many physiological consequences of the circadian metabolome. High-fat diets lead to widespread reorganization of metabolic pathways, reduction in BMAL1:CLOCK recruitment *via* misregulation of the PPARγ pathway (18). Time-restricted feeding was shown to promote healthy physiology, robust circadian rhythms, and protects against obesity and metabolic consequences of a high-fat diet (45, 46). Of late, the role of the gut microbiota as a mediator of nutritional state to set tissue clocks has been extensively reported (47–50).

CANCER METABOLISM: THE CASE OF BLOOD TUMORS

When malignancy arises, these homeostatic mechanisms are clearly lost or altered, as the energy needs of a cancer cell are vastly different. Tumor development is coincident with massive genomic and metabolic reprogramming with fundamental changes to epigenetic state. One of the earliest described metabolic hallmarks of tumors was an elevated glycolytic rate even in the presence of sufficient oxygen. This so-called Warburg effect or aerobic glycolysis is now known to constitute an adaptation of malignant cells to their nutrient-poor microenvironment in order to optimize the uptake of these nutrients to synthesize macromolecules needed for their survival and proliferation (51, 52). Tumors reprogram their metabolism to ensure a steady supply of metabolites to generate new biomass. Thus, malignancy is coincident with elevated aerobic glycolysis, increased lipogenesis needed for membrane production, fatty acid oxidation, and a dependency on methionine synthesis—pathways that clearly display diurnal or circadian rhythms. Hematological malignancies account for nearly 10% of clinical diagnoses of all cancers and their metabolic signature has been reviewed recently in depth (53). Nearly 30 metabolites were found to be differentially expressed in acute lymphoid leukemia (ALL) patients, glycerophospholipid metabolism in particular seemed to be linked to the development and disease progression. In acute myeloid leukemia (AML), UDP-D-glucose, a glycogenic precursor, was found to be persistently upregulated (54). Chronic lymphocytic leukemia (CLL) patients on the other hand showed high levels of pyruvate and glutamate in their blood. Myelodysplastic syndromes following therapy were correlated with alterations in the metabolism of aspartate, alanine, dicarboxylate, glyoxylate, and phenylalanine (55). Given the widespread circadian influence on the metabolite levels, care needs to be taken in interpretation of tumor metabolome data and circadian biomarkers could potentially be used to normalize noise in these studies (56, 57).

CLOCK GENES AND CIRCADIAN MISREGULATION IN HEMATOPOIETIC MALIGNANCIES

Not surprisingly, core clock gene dysfunction has been implicated in many hematological malignancies. Diffuse large B-cell lymphoma (DLBCL), ALL, and AML display promoter hypermethylation at the *BMAL1* gene. The CCAAT/enhancer binding protein alpha (C/EBPalpha) regulates the expression of *PER2* and depletion of BMAL1 in unmethylated cells promotes tumor growth while its reintroduction in tumor cells slowed down growth in colony assays and nude mice (58). The mixed-lineage leukemia genes MLL1 and MLL3 are CCGs that regulate recruitment of BMAL1:CLOCK to chromatin by controlling promoter histone methylations and furthermore epigenetically regulate the function of many downstream target genes rhythmically over 24 h (59–61). In CLL patients, CRY1 expression or a *CRY1:PER2* expression ratio could isolate subgroups of patients and help prognosis (62). PER2 was found to be reduced in lymphoma and AML patient samples while overexpression of PER2 led to cell cycle arrest and loss of clonogenicity (63). In a small study, newly diagnosed chronic myeloid leukemia (CML) patients showed disruption in daily core clock gene expression patterns, which were then partially reversed in those that displayed cytogenetic and molecular response to imatinib treatment (64). The tumor suppressor PML has been shown to directly interact with PER2 and regulate its nuclear localization (65). Double *PML/PER* knockout mice showed changes in circadian behavior implying a reciprocal role for PML in clock function (66). While most studies point to an oncogenic role for clock mutations, there are exceptions. Recently, Puram et al. described how BMAL1:CLOCK are essential transcription factors in a murine model of AML with a well-defined leukemia stem cell population (67). Disruption of the canonical clock pathway in this study surprisingly produced antileukemic effects and impaired proliferation, increased differentiation, and a depletion of LSCs. Thus, while it is evident that clock genes play a role in hematological malignancies, whether they promote or hamper tumor growth is not clear. Indeed, the effectors of the core clock machinery might also display non-circadian functions, which would be involved in the cancer development, as exemplified by BMAL1 function during early development (68). A potential link and a resolution to this apparent dilemma could lie in a series of recent studies that have explored the role of the oncogene MYC in circadian clocks.

MYC—A POTENTIAL LINK BETWEEN HEMATOLOGICAL MALIGNANCIES AND CLOCKS

MYC, a helix-loop-helix leucine zipper transcription factor, was originally identified as the genetic target of the t(8;14)(q24;q32) chromosome translocation in Burkitt lymphoma (69). *MYC* expression is deregulated in a wide array of cancers and is generally associated with poor prognosis. Decades of work in cancer biology has linked Myc activation to the loss of cell cycle regulation, in the activation of the p53 pathway *via* inhibition of MDM2-mediated degradation and in promoting pro-apoptotic pathways *via* the induction of BIM-BAX-BAK cascade in mitochondria (69). In lymphomas, MYC affects the metabolome, by stimulating glycolysis and glutaminolysis (70). Increased *MYC* expression in normal cells can drive both enhanced cellular proliferation and also conversely lead to upregulation of pro-apoptotic pathways, reflecting a need for tight regulation of its expression in normal cells.

MYC and BMAL1:CLOCK bind to identical DNA cis-elements and much like the latter, MYC is thought to regulate the transcription of 10–15% of genes in the human genome. Its misexpression and activation in cancer cells is thought to lead to large-scale transcriptomic effects. At high oncogenic levels, MYC potentially could bind and compete for BMAL1:CLOCK E-boxes and disrupt circadian transcription. Instead, Shostak et al. found that overexpression of *MYC* has little effect on transcription of *Per* and *Cry* genes. High levels of MYC *via* the assembly of a repressive MYC–MIZ1 complex led to the downregulation of BMAL1 and CLOCK expression and lowered protein levels (71). Another study linked the loss of BMAL1 expression to the MYC-driven upregulation of REV-ERBα and REV-ERBβ, secondary oscillator loop components that dampen BMAL1 expression (72). BMAL1 levels correlate inversely with that of MYC protein in nearly 100 human lymphomas (71). Together these studies point to two different means by which Myc impacts circadian clock dynamics. A study from Tyler Jacks' group offered further support for a circadian link to Myc function—wherein either physiologic disruption of clocks (using a jetlag protocol) or genetic loss of central clock components led to increased *c-MYC* expression, loss of metabolic homeostasis, and increased proliferation in a lung adenocarcinoma model (73). c-MYC expression can be regulated by E-boxes in its own promoter and by core clock proteins (74, 75). Additionally, it can also be regulated at the posttranslational level (76), with a very recent study indicating that the circadian repressor protein CRY2 targets MYC for degradation *via* the F-box protein FBXW7 (77). Thus, a negative cross talk between the MYC pathway and circadian oscillator is likely to exist in cancer cells.

Could SIRT1 then be the link between circadian clock dysfunction and Myc-driven cancers? Intriguingly, several studies have explored the cross talk between the SIRT1 and MYC pathways with some reports indicating a positive feedback between the two pathways (78). A c-MYC-related network that enhances SIRT1 protein expression in human AML LSCs was found to contribute to leukemic stem cell maintenance (79). In some instances, increased expression of c-MYC leads to increase in SIRT1 protein, NAD, and NAMPT mRNA and additionally leads to SIRT1 activation by sequestering the inhibitory protein deleted in breast cancer 1 (80). SIRT1 in turn stabilizes MYC levels and promotes its transcriptional activity. NAMPT thus is a target of both BMAL1:CLOCK and oncogenic MYC in Myc-driven cancers. While a series of studies have shown a positive feedback loop existing between MYC and SIRT1 function in cells, one report indicated negative feedback between these two pathways (81). The contrasting data might result from variable SIRT1 protein levels in cells. SIRT1 dosage was shown to be critical in the regulation of Myc, with non-overlapping results obtained upon either heterozygous or homozygous deletion of the SIRT1 gene (82). In the study by Ren et al., heterozygous deletion of *SIRT1* induced c-MYC expression, enhancing glutamine metabolism and subsequent proliferation and malignancy, while SIRT1 homozygous deletion triggered apoptosis and reduced cancer formation. The impact on cellular clocks under these distinct and opposing states of SIRT1 expression and MYC function however remains to be explored.

Finally, much like MYC, AMPK functions as a conditional tumor suppressor and as a contextual oncogene—thus, a dysfunction of the LKB1/AMPK signaling pathway could rewire the circadian epigenome and rhythmic gene expression to contribute eventually to cancer development. AMPK functions in parallel with MYC (83) and it is a therapeutic target in several hematopoietic malignancies including AML (84), ALL (85), CLL (86), lymphomas (87, 88), and MM (89). Moreover, Metformin, a known activator of AMPK, modulates the metabolic rhythms generated by the circadian clock (90). It will thus be relevant to explore whether the antitumor effects of pharmacological agents targeting AMPK depend on their ability to normalize daily

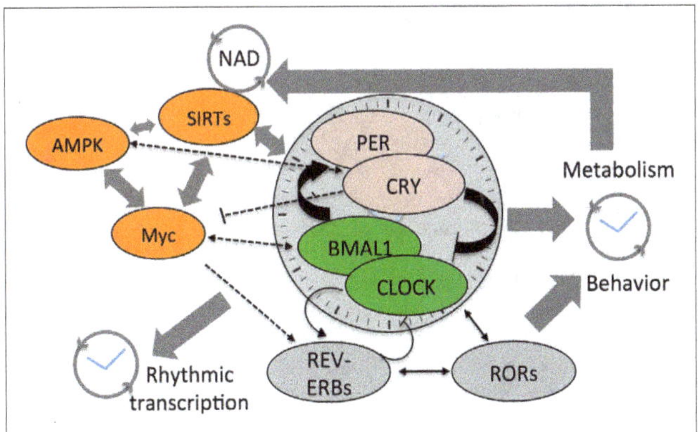

FIGURE 1 | Cartoon depicts the cross talk between various components of the core clock mechanism and the stabilizing loops (Rev-erbs and RORs) that drive daily system-wide rhythms in gene expression and metabolites. Also shown are the three core-metabolic sensing pathways—AMP-activated kinase (AMPK), Myc, and SIRTs. NAD+ feedsback to control the clock by regulating the function of class III histone deacetylases—the Sirtuins. The SIRTs and core clock components regulate Myc expression that competes with BMAL1:CLOCK on transcription targets sites and also drives Rev-erb expression. Colored components within the cartoon highlight the factors linked to hematological malignancies such as acute myeloid leukemia, chronic myeloid leukemia, and diffuse large B-cell lymphoma.

rhythms through the synchronization of the clock involving the reshaping of the circadian chromatin landscape and the regulation of the MYC-SIRT1 axis.

SUMMARY

Circadian architecture regulates cellular metabolic state (see **Figure 1**). Far from being an unidirectional regulatory event, circadian transcription that drives oscillations in small metabolites is in turn affected by the abundance of these small molecules. While homeostasis with the environment ensures a regular rhythm in metabolite levels, perturbations that arise from modern lifestyles have now all been shown to alter rhythmic pathways. Many malignancies of hematological origin, which account for nearly 10% of clinical diagnoses of all cancers, display altered clock function and parallel widespread metabolic arrhythmia. MYC is either amplified or shows misexpression in at least 50% of all cancers and a majority of human leukemia and lymphoma cases (91) and SIRT1 is implicated in similar hematological malignancies (92, 93). These results suggest that disruption of circadian clocks in blood cancers might be more widespread than currently appreciated. Circadian metabolomic screens, when integrated with transcriptomics and epigenomics may thus provide a more comprehensive understanding of the complex biology associated with tumorigenesis and malignant transformation.

AUTHOR CONTRIBUTIONS

KP conceived, drafted, and prepared the manuscript along with MB.

REFERENCES

1. Takahashi JS. Transcriptional architecture of the mammalian circadian clock. *Nat Rev Genet* (2017) 18:164–79. doi:10.1038/nrg.2016.150
2. Schibler U, Ripperger J, Brown SA. Peripheral circadian oscillators in mammals: time and food. *J Biol Rhythms* (2003) 18:250–60. doi:10.1177/0748730403018003007
3. Dibner C, Schibler U, Albrecht U. The mammalian circadian timing system: organization and coordination of central and peripheral clocks. *Annu Rev Physiol* (2010) 72:517–49. doi:10.1146/annurev-physiol-021909-135821
4. Froy O. Circadian aspects of energy metabolism and aging. *Ageing Res Rev* (2013) 12:931–40. doi:10.1016/j.arr.2013.09.002
5. Schernhammer ES, Laden F, Speizer FE, Willett WC, Hunter DJ, Kawachi I, et al. Rotating night shifts and risk of breast cancer in women participating in the nurses' health study. *J Natl Cancer Inst* (2001) 93:1563–8. doi:10.1093/jnci/93.20.1563
6. Haus EL, Smolensky MH. Shift work and cancer risk: potential mechanistic roles of circadian disruption, light at night, and sleep deprivation. *Sleep Med Rev* (2013) 17:273–84. doi:10.1016/j.smrv.2012.08.003
7. Duong HA, Robles MS, Knutti D, Weitz CJ. A molecular mechanism for circadian clock negative feedback. *Science* (2011) 332:1436–9. doi:10.1126/science.1196766
8. Gekakis N, Staknis D, Nguyen HB, Davis FC, Wilsbacher LD, King DP, et al. Role of the CLOCK protein in the mammalian circadian mechanism. *Science* (1998) 280:1564–9. doi:10.1126/science.280.5369.1564
9. Kume K, Zylka MJ, Sriram S, Shearman LP, Weaver DR, Jin X, et al. mCRY1 and mCRY2 are essential components of the negative limb of the circadian clock feedback loop. *Cell* (1999) 98:193–205. doi:10.1016/S0092-8674(00)81014-4
10. Koike N, Yoo SH, Huang HC, Kumar V, Lee C, Kim TK, et al. Transcriptional architecture and chromatin landscape of the core circadian clock in mammals. *Science* (2012) 338:349–54. doi:10.1126/science.1226339
11. Panda S, Antoch MP, Miller BH, Su AI, Schook AB, Straume M, et al. Coordinated transcription of key pathways in the mouse by the circadian clock. *Cell* (2002) 109:307–20. doi:10.1016/S0092-8674(02)00722-5
12. Storch KF, Lipan O, Leykin I, Viswanathan N, Davis FC, Wong WH, et al. Extensive and divergent circadian gene expression in liver and heart. *Nature* (2002) 417:78–83. doi:10.1038/nature744
13. Vollmers C, Schmitz RJ, Nathanson J, Yeo G, Ecker JR, Panda S. Circadian oscillations of protein-coding and regulatory RNAs in a highly dynamic mammalian liver epigenome. *Cell Metab* (2012) 16:833–45. doi:10.1016/j.cmet.2012.11.004
14. Guillaumond F, Dardente H, Giguere V, Cermakian N. Differential control of Bmal1 circadian transcription by REV-ERB and ROR nuclear receptors. *J Biol Rhythms* (2005) 20:391–403. doi:10.1177/0748730405277232
15. Cho H, Zhao X, Hatori M, Yu RT, Barish GD, Lam MT, et al. Regulation of circadian behaviour and metabolism by REV-ERB-alpha and REV-ERB-beta. *Nature* (2012) 485:123–7. doi:10.1038/nature11048
16. Menet JS, Rodriguez J, Abruzzi KC, Rosbash M. Nascent-seq reveals novel features of mouse circadian transcriptional regulation. *Elife* (2012) 1:e00011. doi:10.7554/eLife.00011
17. Eckel-Mahan K, Sassone-Corsi P. Epigenetic regulation of the molecular clockwork. *Prog Mol Biol Transl Sci* (2013) 119:29–50. doi:10.1016/B978-0-12-396971-2.00002-6
18. Eckel-Mahan KL, Patel VR, de Mateo S, Orozco-Solis R, Ceglia NJ, Sahar S, et al. Reprogramming of the circadian clock by nutritional challenge. *Cell* (2013) 155:1464–78. doi:10.1016/j.cell.2013.11.034
19. Ripperger JA, Merrow M. Perfect timing: epigenetic regulation of the circadian clock. *FEBS Lett* (2011) 585:1406–11. doi:10.1016/j.febslet.2011.04.047
20. Aguilar-Arnal L, Sassone-Corsi P. Chromatin landscape and circadian dynamics: spatial and temporal organization of clock transcription. *Proc Natl Acad Sci U S A* (2015) 112(22):6863–70. doi:10.1073/pnas.1411264111
21. Doi M, Hirayama J, Sassone-Corsi P. Circadian regulator CLOCK is a histone acetyltransferase. *Cell* (2006) 125:497–508. doi:10.1016/j.cell.2006.03.033
22. Hirayama J, Cho S, Sassone-Corsi P. Circadian control by the reduction/oxidation pathway: catalase represses light-dependent clock gene expression in the zebrafish. *Proc Natl Acad Sci U S A* (2007) 104:15747–52. doi:10.1073/pnas.0705614104
23. Yang XJ, Seto E. Lysine acetylation: codified crosstalk with other post-translational modifications. *Mol Cell* (2008) 31:449–61. doi:10.1016/j.molcel.2008.07.002
24. Sahar S, Masubuchi S, Eckel-Mahan K, Vollmer S, Galla L, Ceglia N, et al. Circadian control of fatty acid elongation by SIRT1 protein-mediated deacetylation of acetyl-coenzyme A synthetase 1. *J Biol Chem* (2014) 289:6091–7. doi:10.1074/jbc.M113.537191
25. Aguilar-Arnal L, Katada S, Orozco-Solis R, Sassone-Corsi P. NAD(+)-SIRT1 control of H3K4 trimethylation through circadian deacetylation of MLL1. *Nat Struct Mol Biol* (2015) 22:312–8. doi:10.1038/nsmb.2990
26. Asher G, Gatfield D, Stratmann M, Reinke H, Dibner C, Kreppel F, et al. SIRT1 regulates circadian clock gene expression through PER2 deacetylation. *Cell* (2008) 134:317–28. doi:10.1016/j.cell.2008.06.050
27. Chang HC, Guarente L. SIRT1 mediates central circadian control in the SCN by a mechanism that decays with aging. *Cell* (2013) 153:1448–60. doi:10.1016/j.cell.2013.05.027
28. Masri S, Rigor P, Cervantes M, Ceglia N, Sebastian C, Xiao C, et al. Partitioning circadian transcription by SIRT6 leads to segregated control of cellular metabolism. *Cell* (2014) 158:659–72. doi:10.1016/j.cell.2014.06.050
29. Masri S, Sassone-Corsi P. Sirtuins and the circadian clock: bridging chromatin and metabolism. *Sci Signal* (2014) 7:re6. doi:10.1126/scisignal.2005685
30. Nakahata Y, Kaluzova M, Grimaldi B, Sahar S, Hirayama J, Chen D, et al. The NAD+-dependent deacetylase SIRT1 modulates CLOCK-mediated chromatin remodeling and circadian control. *Cell* (2008) 134:329–40. doi:10.1016/j.cell.2008.07.002

31. Ramsey KM, Yoshino J, Brace CS, Abrassart D, Kobayashi Y, Marcheva B, et al. Circadian clock feedback cycle through NAMPT-mediated NAD+ biosynthesis. *Science* (2009) 324:651–4. doi:10.1126/science.1171641
32. Peek CB, Affinati AH, Ramsey KM, Kuo HY, Yu W, Sena LA, et al. Circadian clock NAD+ cycle drives mitochondrial oxidative metabolism in mice. *Science* (2013) 342:1243417. doi:10.1126/science.1243417
33. Magni G, Amici A, Emanuelli M, Orsomando G, Raffaelli N, Ruggieri S. Enzymology of NAD+ homeostasis in man. *Cell Mol Life Sci* (2004) 61:19–34. doi:10.1007/s00018-003-3161-1
34. Nakahata Y, Sahar S, Astarita G, Kaluzova M, Sassone-Corsi P. Circadian control of the NAD+ salvage pathway by CLOCK-SIRT1. *Science* (2009) 324:654–7. doi:10.1126/science.1170803
35. Fulco M, Cen Y, Zhao P, Hoffman EP, McBurney MW, Sauve AA, et al. Glucose restriction inhibits skeletal myoblast differentiation by activating SIRT1 through AMPK-mediated regulation of NAMPT. *Dev Cell* (2008) 14:661–73. doi:10.1016/j.devcel.2008.02.004
36. Canto C, Gerhart-Hines Z, Feige JN, Lagouge M, Noriega L, Milne JC, et al. AMPK regulates energy expenditure by modulating NAD+ metabolism and SIRT1 activity. *Nature* (2009) 458:1056–60. doi:10.1038/nature07813
37. Lamia KA, Sachdeva UM, DiTacchio L, Williams EC, Alvarez JG, Egan DF, et al. AMPK regulates the circadian clock by cryptochrome phosphorylation and degradation. *Science* (2009) 326:437–40. doi:10.1126/science.1172156
38. Um JH, Yang S, Yamazaki S, Kang H, Viollet B, Foretz M, et al. Activation of 5′-AMP-activated kinase with diabetes drug metformin induces casein kinase Iepsilon (CKIepsilon)-dependent degradation of clock protein mPer2. *J Biol Chem* (2007) 282:20794–8. doi:10.1074/jbc.C700070200
39. Krishnaiah SY, Wu G, Altman BJ, Growe J, Rhoades SD, Coldren F, et al. Clock regulation of metabolites reveals coupling between transcription and metabolism. *Cell Metab* (2017) 25:961–74.e4. doi:10.1016/j.cmet.2017.04.023
40. Jha PK, Foppen E, Kalsbeek A, Challet E. Sleep restriction acutely impairs glucose tolerance in rats. *Physiol Rep* (2016) 4:e12839. doi:10.14814/phy2.12839
41. Kumar Jha P, Challet E, Kalsbeek A. Circadian rhythms in glucose and lipid metabolism in nocturnal and diurnal mammals. *Mol Cell Endocrinol* (2015) 418(Pt 1):74–88. doi:10.1016/j.mce.2015.01.024
42. Copinschi G, Leproult R, Spiegel K. The important role of sleep in metabolism. *Front Horm Res* (2014) 42:59–72. doi:10.1159/000358858
43. Zarrinpar A, Chaix A, Panda S. Daily eating patterns and their impact on health and disease. *Trends Endocrinol Metab* (2016) 27:69–83. doi:10.1016/j.tem.2015.11.007
44. Eckel-Mahan KL, Patel VR, Mohney RP, Vignola KS, Baldi P, Sassone-Corsi P. Coordination of the transcriptome and metabolome by the circadian clock. *Proc Natl Acad Sci U S A* (2012) 109:5541–6. doi:10.1073/pnas.1118726109
45. Hatori M, Vollmers C, Zarrinpar A, DiTacchio L, Bushong EA, Gill S, et al. Time-restricted feeding without reducing caloric intake prevents metabolic diseases in mice fed a high-fat diet. *Cell Metab* (2012) 15:848–60. doi:10.1016/j.cmet.2012.04.019
46. Hatori M, Panda S. Response of peripheral rhythms to the timing of food intake. *Methods Enzymol* (2015) 552:145–61. doi:10.1016/bs.mie.2014.10.027
47. Thaiss CA, Levy M, Korem T, Dohnalova L, Shapiro H, Jaitin DA, et al. Microbiota diurnal rhythmicity programs host transcriptome oscillations. *Cell* (2016) 167:1495–1510e12. doi:10.1016/j.cell.2016.11.003
48. Liang X, Bushman FD, FitzGerald GA. Rhythmicity of the intestinal microbiota is regulated by gender and the host circadian clock. *Proc Natl Acad Sci U S A* (2015) 112:10479–84. doi:10.1073/pnas.1501305112
49. Asher G, Sassone-Corsi P. Time for food: the intimate interplay between nutrition, metabolism, and the circadian clock. *Cell* (2015) 161:84–92. doi:10.1016/j.cell.2015.03.015
50. Mukherji A, Kobiita A, Ye T, Chambon P. Homeostasis in intestinal epithelium is orchestrated by the circadian clock and microbiota cues transduced by TLRs. *Cell* (2013) 153:812–27. doi:10.1016/j.cell.2013.04.020
51. Potter M, Newport E, Morten KJ. The Warburg effect: 80 years on. *Biochem Soc Trans* (2016) 44:1499–505. doi:10.1042/BST20160094
52. Liberti MV, Locasale JW. The Warburg effect: how does it benefit cancer cells? *Trends Biochem Sci* (2016) 41:211–8. doi:10.1016/j.tibs.2015.12.001
53. Allegra A, Innao V, Gerace D, Bianco O, Musolino C. The metabolomic signature of hematologic malignancies. *Leuk Res* (2016) 49:22–35. doi:10.1016/j.leukres.2016.08.002
54. Bhanot H, Reddy MM, Nonami A, Weisberg EL, Bonal D, Kirschmeier PT, et al. Pathological glycogenesis through glycogen synthase 1 and suppression of excessive AMP kinase activity in myeloid leukemia cells. *Leukemia* (2015) 29:1555–63. doi:10.1038/leu.2015.46
55. Cano KE, Li L, Bhatia S, Bhatia R, Forman SJ, Chen Y. NMR-based metabolomic analysis of the molecular pathogenesis of therapy-related myelodysplasia/acute myeloid leukemia. *J Proteome Res* (2011) 10:2873–81. doi:10.1021/pr200200y
56. Laing EE, Moller-Levet CS, Poh N, Santhi N, Archer SN, Dijk DJ. Blood transcriptome based biomarkers for human circadian phase. *Elife* (2017) 6:e20214. doi:10.7554/eLife.20214
57. Kasukawa T, Sugimoto M, Hida A, Minami Y, Mori M, Honma S, et al. Human blood metabolite timetable indicates internal body time. *Proc Natl Acad Sci U S A* (2012) 109:15036–41. doi:10.1073/pnas.1207768109
58. Taniguchi H, Fernandez AF, Setien F, Ropero S, Ballestar E, Villanueva A, et al. Epigenetic inactivation of the circadian clock gene BMAL1 in hematologic malignancies. *Cancer Res* (2009) 69:8447–54. doi:10.1158/0008-5472.CAN-09-0551
59. Kim DH, Rhee JC, Yeo S, Shen R, Lee SK, Lee JW, et al. Crucial roles of mixed-lineage leukemia 3 and 4 as epigenetic switches of the hepatic circadian clock controlling bile acid homeostasis in mice. *Hepatology* (2015) 61:1012–23. doi:10.1002/hep.27578
60. Valekunja UK, Edgar RS, Oklejewicz M, van der Horst GT, O'Neill JS, Tamanini F, et al. Histone methyltransferase MLL3 contributes to genome-scale circadian transcription. *Proc Natl Acad Sci U S A* (2013) 110:1554–9. doi:10.1073/pnas.1214168110
61. Katada S, Sassone-Corsi P. The histone methyltransferase MLL1 permits the oscillation of circadian gene expression. *Nat Struct Mol Biol* (2010) 17:1414–21. doi:10.1038/nsmb.1961
62. Eisele L, Prinz R, Klein-Hitpass L, Nuckel H, Lowinski K, Thomale J, et al. Combined PER2 and CRY1 expression predicts outcome in chronic lymphocytic leukemia. *Eur J Haematol* (2009) 83:320–7. doi:10.1111/j.1600-0609.2009.01287.x
63. Gery S, Koeffler HP. Per2 is a C/EBP target gene implicated in myeloid leukemia. *Integr Cancer Ther* (2009) 8:317–20. doi:10.1177/1534735409352084
64. Yang MY, Yang WC, Lin PM, Hsu JF, Hsiao HH, Liu YC, et al. Altered expression of circadian clock genes in human chronic myeloid leukemia. *J Biol Rhythms* (2011) 26:136–48. doi:10.1177/0748730410395527
65. Miki T, Xu Z, Chen-Goodspeed M, Liu M, Van Oort-Jansen A, Rea MA, et al. PML regulates PER2 nuclear localization and circadian function. *EMBO J* (2012) 31:1427–39. doi:10.1038/emboj.2012.1
66. Miki T, Chen-Goodspeed M, Zhao Z, Lee CC. Circadian behavior of mice deficient in PER1/PML or PER2/PML. *J Circadian Rhythms* (2013) 11:9. doi:10.1186/1740-3391-11-9
67. Puram RV, Kowalczyk MS, de Boer CG, Schneider RK, Miller PG, McConkey M, et al. Core circadian clock genes regulate leukemia stem cells in AML. *Cell* (2016) 165:303–16. doi:10.1016/j.cell.2016.03.015
68. Yang G, Chen L, Grant GR, Paschos G, Song WL, Musiek ES, et al. Timing of expression of the core clock gene Bmal1 influences its effects on aging and survival. *Sci Transl Med* (2016) 8:324ra16. doi:10.1126/scitranslmed.aad3305
69. Ott G. Impact of MYC on malignant behavior. *Hematology Am Soc Hematol Educ Program* (2014) 2014:100–6. doi:10.1182/asheducation-2014.1.100
70. Le A, Lane AN, Hamaker M, Bose S, Gouw A, Barbi J, et al. Glucose-independent glutamine metabolism via TCA cycling for proliferation and survival in B cells. *Cell Metab* (2012) 15:110–21. doi:10.1016/j.cmet.2011.12.009
71. Shostak A, Ruppert B, Ha N, Bruns P, Toprak UH, Project IM-S, et al. MYC/MIZ1-dependent gene repression inversely coordinates the circadian clock with cell cycle and proliferation. *Nat Commun* (2016) 7:11807. doi:10.1038/ncomms11807
72. Altman BJ, Hsieh AL, Sengupta A, Krishnanaiah SY, Stine ZE, Walton ZE, et al. MYC disrupts the circadian clock and metabolism in cancer cells. *Cell Metab* (2015) 22:1009–19. doi:10.1016/j.cmet.2015.09.003
73. Papagiannakopoulos T, Bauer MR, Davidson SM, Heimann M, Subbaraj L, Bhutkar A, et al. Circadian rhythm disruption promotes lung tumorigenesis. *Cell Metab* (2016) 24:324–31. doi:10.1016/j.cmet.2016.07.001
74. Fu L, Pelicano H, Liu J, Huang P, Lee C. The circadian gene Period2 plays an important role in tumor suppression and DNA damage response in vivo. *Cell* (2002) 111:41–50. doi:10.1016/S0092-8674(02)01223-0

75. Fu L, Patel MS, Bradley A, Wagner EF, Karsenty G. The molecular clock mediates leptin-regulated bone formation. *Cell* (2005) 122:803–15. doi:10.1016/j.cell.2005.06.028
76. Repouskou A, Prombona A. c-MYC targets the central oscillator gene Per1 and is regulated by the circadian clock at the post-transcriptional level. *Biochim Biophys Acta* (2016) 1859:541–52. doi:10.1016/j.bbagrm.2016.02.001
77. Huber AL, Papp SJ, Chan AB, Henriksson E, Jordan SD, Kriebs A, et al. CRY2 and FBXL3 cooperatively degrade c-MYC. *Mol Cell* (2016) 64:774–89. doi:10.1016/j.molcel.2016.10.012
78. Menssen A, Hermeking H. c-MYC and SIRT1 locked in a vicious cycle. *Oncotarget* (2012) 3:112–3. doi:10.18632/oncotarget.440
79. Li L, Osdal T, Ho Y, Chun S, McDonald T, Agarwal P, et al. SIRT1 activation by a c-MYC oncogenic network promotes the maintenance and drug resistance of human FLT3-ITD acute myeloid leukemia stem cells. *Cell Stem Cell* (2014) 15:431–46. doi:10.1016/j.stem.2014.08.001
80. Menssen A, Hydbring P, Kapelle K, Vervoorts J, Diebold J, Luscher B, et al. The c-MYC oncoprotein, the NAMPT enzyme, the SIRT1-inhibitor DBC1, and the SIRT1 deacetylase form a positive feedback loop. *Proc Natl Acad Sci U S A* (2012) 109:E187–96. doi:10.1073/pnas.1105304109
81. Yuan J, Minter-Dykhouse K, Lou Z. A c-Myc-SIRT1 feedback loop regulates cell growth and transformation. *J Cell Biol* (2009) 185:203–11. doi:10.1083/jcb.200809167
82. Ren NS, Ji M, Tokar EJ, Busch EL, Xu X, Lewis D, et al. Haploinsufficiency of SIRT1 enhances glutamine metabolism and promotes cancer development. *Curr Biol* (2017) 27:483–94. doi:10.1016/j.cub.2016.12.047
83. Haikala HM, Anttila JM, Klefstrom J. MYC and AMPK-save energy or die! *Front Cell Dev Biol* (2017) 5:38. doi:10.3389/fcell.2017.00038
84. Sujobert P, Poulain L, Paubelle E, Zylbersztejn F, Grenier A, Lambert M, et al. Co-activation of AMPK and mTORC1 induces cytotoxicity in acute myeloid leukemia. *Cell Rep* (2015) 11:1446–57. doi:10.1016/j.celrep.2015.04.063
85. Sengupta TK, Leclerc GM, Hsieh-Kinser TT, Leclerc GJ, Singh I, Barredo JC. Cytotoxic effect of 5-aminoimidazole-4-carboxamide-1-beta-4-ribofuranoside (AICAR) on childhood acute lymphoblastic leukemia (ALL) cells: implication for targeted therapy. *Mol Cancer* (2007) 6:46. doi:10.1186/1476-4598-6-46
86. Santidrian AF, Gonzalez-Girones DM, Iglesias-Serret D, Coll-Mulet L, Cosialls AM, de Frias M, et al. AICAR induces apoptosis independently of AMPK and p53 through up-regulation of the BH3-only proteins BIM and NOXA in chronic lymphocytic leukemia cells. *Blood* (2010) 116:3023–32. doi:10.1182/blood-2010-05-283960
87. Drakos E, Atsaves V, Li J, Leventaki V, Andreeff M, Medeiros LJ, et al. Stabilization and activation of p53 downregulates mTOR signaling through AMPK in mantle cell lymphoma. *Leukemia* (2009) 23:784–90. doi:10.1038/leu.2008.348
88. Campas C, Santidrian AF, Domingo A, Gil J. Acadesine induces apoptosis in B cells from mantle cell lymphoma and splenic marginal zone lymphoma. *Leukemia* (2005) 19:292–4. doi:10.1038/sj.leu.2403593
89. Baumann P, Mandl-Weber S, Emmerich B, Straka C, Schmidmaier R. Activation of adenosine monophosphate activated protein kinase inhibits growth of multiple myeloma cells. *Exp Cell Res* (2007) 313:3592–603. doi:10.1016/j.yexcr.2007.06.020
90. Barnea M, Haviv L, Gutman R, Chapnik N, Madar Z, Froy O. Metformin affects the circadian clock and metabolic rhythms in a tissue-specific manner. *Biochim Biophys Acta* (2012) 1822:1796–806. doi:10.1016/j.bbadis.2012.08.005
91. Delgado MD, Leon J. Myc roles in hematopoiesis and leukemia. *Genes Cancer* (2010) 1:605–16. doi:10.1177/1947601910377495
92. Li L, Bhatia R. Role of SIRT1 in the growth and regulation of normal hematopoietic and leukemia stem cells. *Curr Opin Hematol* (2015) 22:324–9. doi:10.1097/MOH.0000000000000152
93. Yuan H, Su L, Chen WY. The emerging and diverse roles of sirtuins in cancer: a clinical perspective. *Onco Targets Ther* (2013) 6:1399–416. doi:10.2147/OTT.S37750

5

Glial Cells in the Genesis and Regulation of Circadian Rhythms

Donají Chi-Castañeda [1,2] *and Arturo Ortega* [1*]

[1] *Laboratorio de Neurotoxicología, Departamento de Toxicología, Centro de Investigación y de Estudios Avanzados del Instituto Politécnico Nacional, Ciudad de Mexico, Mexico,* [2] *Soluciones para un México Verde S.A. de C.V., Ciudad de Mexico, Mexico*

Edited by:
Jolanta Górska-Andrzejak, Jagiellonian University, Poland

Reviewed by:
Maurizio De Pittà, University of Chicago, United States
Eddy A. Van Der Zee, University of Groningen, Netherlands

***Correspondence:**
Arturo Ortega
arortega@cinvestav.mx

Circadian rhythms are biological oscillations with a period of ~24 h. These rhythms are orchestrated by a circadian timekeeper in the suprachiasmatic nucleus of the hypothalamus, the circadian "*master clock,*" which exactly adjusts clock outputs to solar time via photic synchronization. At the molecular level, circadian rhythms are generated by the interaction of positive and negative feedback loops of transcriptional and translational processes of the so-called "*clock genes.*" A large number of clock genes encode numerous proteins that regulate their own transcription and that of other genes, collectively known as "*clock-controlled genes.*" In addition to the sleep/wake cycle, many cellular processes are regulated by circadian rhythms, including synaptic plasticity in which an exquisite interplay between neurons and glial cells takes place. In particular, there is compelling evidence suggesting that glial cells participate in and regulate synaptic plasticity in a circadian fashion, possibly representing the missing cellular and physiological link between circadian rhythms with learning and cognition processes. Here we review recent studies in support of this hypothesis, focusing on the interplay between glial cells, synaptic plasticity, and circadian rhythmogenesis.

Keywords: circadian rhythms, clock genes, glial oscillators, learning, memory, plasticity

INTRODUCTION

Most light-sensitive organisms have an internal timekeeping mechanism to anticipate daily changes associated with the transition of day to night that is commonly known as "circadian clock". In 1959, Halberg denominated "circadian rhythms" the biological rhythms that have a period of ~24 h (Halberg, 1959). These rhythms regulate a large number of physiological and behavioral functions in vertebrates, such as hormone secretion, body temperature, metabolism, and even memory processes. The sleep-wake cycle is one the most studied rhythms (Schibler and Sassone-Corsi, 2002; Stratmann and Schibler, 2006; Walker and Stickgold, 2006).

Sleep is a highly conserved process (Hartse, 2011), and several hypotheses support the notion that sleep supersedes learning and memory, possibly through the control of synaptic plasticity (Benington and Frank, 2003; Frank and Benington, 2006; Frank, 2011; Fellin et al., 2012; Frank and Cantera, 2014; De Pittà et al., 2016). Synaptic plasticity refers to the biochemical processes by which synaptic strength changes in an activity-dependent fashion. These cellular cascades are a combination of post-translational modifications that change neural activity, and also result in the reshaping of synaptic terminals (Lohmann and Kessels, 2014). Depending on its temporal course, synaptic plasticity is distinguished into three classes: (1) short-term plasticity, that occurs in the milliseconds to minutes range, and includes the modulation of neurotransmitter release, and depends on post-translational modifications via phosphorylation, ubiquitination, and several other molecular processes (Bliss and Collingridge, 1993; Martin et al., 2000); (2) long-term plasticity, such as long-term potentiation (LTP) and depression (LTD), which may last from hours to months and is represented by cellular changes involving modification of the cellular protein repertoire that may require changes in transcriptional activity and are strictly dependent on protein synthesis (Martin et al., 2000); (3) homeostatic plasticity, which is the result of a variety of molecular and cellular events that shape neuronal circuits, continuously occurs in parallel with other plasticity phenomena and is thought to prevent runaway of neural activity by excessive excitation (Turrigiano, 2011).

Various studies have shown that disruptions of circadian rhythms alter synaptic plasticity and thus, learning and memory, including spatial and place learning and trace fear memory (Winocur and Hasher, 2004; Van der Zee et al., 2008; Wang et al., 2009; Jilg et al., 2010; Kondratova et al., 2010). Based on these studies, it has been suggested that a functional circadian clock is required for optimal learning and memory formation and consolidation (Becker-Weimann et al., 2004; Eckel-Mahan and Storm, 2009). The neural correlates and the mechanisms underpinning these clocks remain largely unknown. In the past two decades, the notion that brain function exclusively relies on neuronal signaling has been challenged by evidence that glial cells work in coordination with neurons, to regulate neurotransmission (Araque et al., 1999). These regulatory events occur through a set of molecular mechanisms that control neurotransmitter recycling (Danbolt et al., 2016), energy requirements (Newman et al., 2011; Suzuki et al., 2011), and eventually sleep homeostasis (Halassa et al., 2009b). This often involves, but is not limited to, the secretion of neuroactive molecules (or "gliotransmitters") in an activity-dependent manner which target synaptic terminals modulating synaptic transmission (Bergles et al., 1997; Haydon, 2001; Lin and Bergles, 2004; Fellin et al., 2006; Perea et al., 2009).

Interestingly, astrocytes which are the most common glial cells in the cortex, have also been implicated in the circadian control of synaptic plasticity (Lavialle and Servière, 1993; Du et al., 2005; Lavialle et al., 2011; Hayashi et al., 2013a,b), suggesting a possible non-neuronal, glial candidate for the regulation of circadian rhythms that control learning and memory processes. This review focuses on this hypothesis, further elaborating on the possible clinical implications associated with disruptions of glial-mediated pathways on circadian rhythms related to high brain function.

CIRCADIAN CLOCKS AND THEIR MOLECULAR/GENETIC BASES

Mammalian circadian clocks are hierarchically organized by a *"master clock"* in the suprachiasmatic nucleus (SCN) of the anterior hypothalamus. This clock coordinates independent peripheral clocks (Reppert and Weaver, 2002; Lowrey and Takahashi, 2004). At the molecular level, all of these clocks are the result of a translation-based, interconnected feedback loops in which the transcription factors Brain and Muscle ARNT-Like Protein 1 (BMAL1) and Circadian Locomotor Output Cycles Kaput (CLOCK) form heterodimers that regulate the circadian expression of *Cryptochrome* (*Cry*) and *Period* (*Per;* Dunlap, 1999; Reppert and Weaver, 2001), whose products lead to the inhibition of their own transcription. Additionally, an accessory regulatory loop involves the regulation of *Bmal1* transcription by the coordinated action of the orphan nuclear receptors *Reverse erb α* (*Rev-erbα*, repressor) and *Retinoid-related orphan receptor-α* (*Rorα*, activator) through the binding to the evolutionarily conserved nucleotide sequence [A/T]A[A/T]NT[A/G]GGTCA present in the promoter region of *Bmal1* (Dunlap, 1999; Harmer et al., 2001; Reppert and Weaver, 2001; Preitner et al., 2002).

Significantly, a large number of circadian transcription factors not only regulate their own transcription, but also the expression of numerous other *"clock-controlled genes"* (CCGs) (Dunlap, 1999; Reppert and Weaver, 2001) whose protein products are not essential for the core clock mechanism itself. Among the genes that are part of the CCGs, various enzymes are included, like *phosphoenolpyruvate carboxykinase, glycogen phosphorylase,* and *glucose-6-phosphatase* (Panda et al., 2002); ion channels, like cGMP-gated cation channels, various voltage-gated calcium and potassium channels, the Na^+/K^+*-ATPase*, and a long-opening cation channel (Ko et al., 2009); peptides, such as *arginine-vasopressin* (*Avp*; Jin et al., 1999) and *D element-binding protein* (*DBP*; Le Martelot et al., 2009). In fact, cells rhythmically synthesize about 10% of their transcripts, including those involved in neuronal signaling and synaptic plasticity (Panda et al., 2002; Lowrey and Takahashi, 2004).

CIRCADIAN CLOCKS, SLEEP, AND THEIR INVOLVEMENT IN SYNAPTIC PLASTICITY

In recent years, numerous reports of *in vitro* and *in vivo* studies, have suggested an essential functional role of sleep in synaptic plasticity (Frank, 2011; Fellin et al., 2012). Accordingly, sleep has been proposed to strengthen, stabilize, or weaken synapses (Benington and Frank, 2003; Frank and Benington, 2006; Frank and Cantera, 2014). The molecular basis of these synaptic changes and whether sleep is necessary for their occurrence remain largely unknown. While sleep is the result of a combination of circadian rhythms and homeostatic mechanisms (Frank and Cantera, 2014), a clear causal connection between circadian clocks, sleep homeostasis, and synaptic plasticity has not been demonstrated.

In this context, it is noteworthy that the recycling of glutamate (Glu) is regulated by clock components, strongly suggesting a functional interplay between circadian rhythms and excitatory synaptic transmission (Beaulé et al., 2009). In fact, glial glutamate transporters are regulated by clock genes having a significant impact in the dynamic, activity-dependent metabolic coupling of glial cells with glutamatergic neurons. This glia/neuron interplay is mediated by the glutamate/glutamine cycle and the astrocyte/neuron/lactate shuttle (Martínez-Lozada and Ortega, 2015). In the same vein, taking into consideration the major role of Glu as the most abundant excitatory transmitter and its role in the molecular models of synaptic plasticity, like LTP and LTD, it is tempting to speculate that another molecular loop between clock genes' expression and glia/neuron coupling via the glutamatergic tripartite synapses control synaptic plasticity at the immediate, mediate and long-term ranges (Flores-Méndez et al., 2016).

GLIAL REGULATION OF SYNAPTIC PLASTICITY

Astrocytes

Beyond their recognized role in synapse development and neurodegeneration, astrocytes provide a delicate ensheathment of synapses in the mature brain (Chao et al., 2002; Theodosis et al., 2008). It is well-established that the degree of astrocytic ensheathing greatly changes with the brain area, hinting local specialization. In the hippocampus for example, a single astrocyte is in close proximity to few hundreds dendrites of different neurons, but can ensheathe up to several hundred thousands synapses (Bushong et al., 2002; Halassa et al., 2007; Agulhon et al., 2008). Such morphological arrangement provides the structural substrate for tight functional interactions between astrocytes and neurons (Saab et al., 2012; Bernardinelli et al., 2014).

Astrocytes are also recognized for their role in clearance of neurotransmitters, such as Glu and gamma-aminobutyric acid (GABA), from the synaptic cleft. Perisynaptic astrocytes processes are indeed enriched in transporters that guarantee rapid and efficient removal of the released neurotransmitters (Anderson and Swanson, 2000; Conti et al., 2004). Interestingly, the regulation of the kinetics and the extent of neurotransmitter clearance by astrocytes have been related to synaptic plasticity insofar as they both affect the degree of postsynaptic activation and desensitization (Tzingounis and Wadiche, 2007). Moreover, through the release of a variety of neuroactive molecules, such as Glu, D-serine, adenosine triphosphate (ATP), adenosine, GABA, tumor necrosis factor-α (TNFα), prostaglandins, proteins and peptides, astrocytes are capable of regulating synaptic transmission and plasticity (Halassa and Haydon, 2010; Araque et al., 2014). These neuroactive molecules activate extrasynaptic metabotropic and ionotropic receptors, modifying neurotransmitter release and regulating short-term plasticity and synaptic efficacy (Parpura et al., 1994; Araque et al., 1998a,b, 2014; Halassa et al., 2009a; Halassa and Haydon, 2010).

Increasing evidence indicates that astrocytes could be involved in the synchronization of cortical firing. Cortical circuits for sensory integration are known to display transient synchrony of neuronal ensembles (Harris et al., 2003; Haider and McCormick, 2009). The hallmark of this synchronized activity is the alternation of UP states—i.e., episodes of persistent neuronal firing lasting few milliseconds—and DOWN states—i.e., episodes of neuronal hyperpolarization (Steriade et al., 2001; Brecht and Sakmann, 2002; Cossart et al., 2003; Kenet et al., 2003). UP and DOWN states are common in a wide range of conditions, including quiescent wakefulness (Gentet et al., 2010), anesthesia (Steriade et al., 1993; Ramaswamy and Muller, 2015), and sleep itself (Massimini and Amzica, 2001). Moreover, astrocytes have been implicated in UP state genesis through the release of D-serine, adenosine and ATP (Fellin et al., 2009, 2012; Halassa et al., 2009b; Poskanzer and Yuste, 2011, 2016). Interestingly, gliotransmission has been proposed to operate on different time scales (Fellin et al., 2012). According to the Hill and Tononi's model of sleep and in agreement with the modulation cortical UP and DOWN states, Fellin and colleagues have demonstrated that the depolarizing effect of NMDA receptors currents preserves the UP state (Hill and Tononi, 2004; Fellin et al., 2012). Such a role for NMDA receptors is thought to be dependent on the availability of glia-released D-serine (Fellin et al., 2012), again demonstrating a prominent role of glia/neuron coupling.

Oligodendrocytes

Oligodendrocytes projections wrap neuronal axons forming the myelin sheaths in the central nervous system (CNS). These myelin sheaths insulate the fibers, and help them to carry the nerve impulses. Interestingly, myelin can influence conduction velocity of the electrical impulse by regulating the axon diameter, thickness of the myelin sheath, the number and spacing of nodes of Ranvier, and nodal structure and molecular composition of ion channels in the node and paranodal region (Berthold et al., 1983; Wurtz and Ellisman, 1986; Baker and Stryker, 1990; Carr and Konishi, 1990; Dupree et al., 2004). Taking this into a consideration, it has been shown that myelin specific proteins, including Nogo-A (Chen et al., 2000; GrandPré et al., 2000), myelin-associated glycoprotein (MAG; McKerracher et al., 1994) and oligodendrocyte-myelin glycoprotein (OMgp; Wang et al., 2002; Huang et al., 2005), inhibit directly axon sprouting and synaptogenesis and constrain nervous system plasticity. This finding indicates the participation of myelin in learning, memory, and cognition.

Microglia

These glial cells are part of the brain's immune system and are mainly involved in the phagocytosis of foreign matter and cellular wastes of the CNS (Aloisi, 2001). Moreover, during postnatal development and adaptation to novel environments, microglia has a critical role in synaptic remodeling through the elimination of synapses and axon terminals. Additionally, increasing evidence points out that microglia could regulate synaptic plasticity and neurotransmission through the release of gliotransmitters (Batchelor et al., 1999, 2002; Zhong et al., 2010; Harry and Kraft, 2012; Sierra et al., 2013), as well as an increase hippocampal LTP and NMDA receptor-mediated responses via the secretion of glycine (Thomson et al., 1989; Abe et al., 1990; Hayashi et al., 2006). During neuroinflammation, microglia is capable to regulate excitatory neurotransmission by the rapid production of small amounts of ATP, that in turn, recruit astrocytes to augment ATP formation and Glu exocytosis enhancing synaptic transmission via metabotropic Glu receptors (Pascual et al., 2012). In fact, several reports reveal that some of the established astrocytic functions are regulated by the upstream activation of microglia (Ben Achour and Pascual, 2010; Pascual et al., 2012).

CIRCADIAN MODULATION OF THE SYNAPTIC PLASTICITY IN GLIAL CELLS

Since 1978, it has been demonstrated that diverse cognitive processes are regulated by the circadian clocks in a phase-specific manner (Monk and Folkard, 1978). Particularly, in long-term memories generated in diverse learning paradigms, a role for the endogenous circadian clock has been reported both in vertebrates and invertebrates (Rudy and Pugh, 1998; Valentinuzzi et al., 2004; Rawashdeh et al., 2007). However, the circadian modulation of short-term memory formation has been almost impossible to prove. In this section, we summarize the evidence that involves different glial cells in processes of synaptic plasticity regulated by circadian generators.

Astrocytes

Gliotransmission is the process by which astrocytes interact with nearby neurons via the release of transmitters, like ATP and Glu (Haydon, 2001; Perea et al., 2009; Parpura and Zorec, 2010). Remarkably, ATP has been linked to modulation of LTP but also of synaptic depression (Gordon et al., 2005; Pascual et al., 2005; Bains and Oliet, 2007). *In vivo*, an astrocyte-dependent rhythmic ATP release is present in the SCN. Although the mechanisms responsible for these ATP oscillations are unknown, calcium-dependent signaling seems to be involved (Womac et al., 2009). Subsequently, it was shown that astrocytes display daily extracellular ATP oscillations that depend on the clock genes (*Clock*, *Per*, and *Bmal1*) and in inositol triphosphate (IP_3) signaling, indicating that extracellular ATP levels increase at a specific time of day and suggest a clock-induced increase in energy metabolism and glial activity, which participate in sleep-wake changes in the brain and in control synaptic transmission (Marpegan et al., 2011).

To date, there is no report demonstrating that the circadian clock regulates Glu release. In contrast, accumulating evidence indicates that the glutamate/aspartate transporter (*Glast*) gene expression and protein levels exhibit a diurnal rhythm in a light/dark 12/12 h cycle (Spanagel et al., 2005). These findings are consistent with the absence of rhythmicity of GLAST in the *Per2* mutant mice, pointing out the presence of a circadian control (Spanagel et al., 2005). Later on, using cultured cortical astrocytes from *Clock* mutant animals, it was observed a marked decrease in *Glast* mRNA and protein levels, proposing that glial Glu uptake activity is a function of the clock genes: *Clock*, *Npas2*, and *Per2* (Beaulé et al., 2009). Specifically, the dependence related to CLOCK and NPAS2 may be due to their involvement in *Glast* transcription, or in GLAST stability and/or localization (Danbolt, 2001). It is important to mention that no conclusive evidence has been shown for a circadian-dependent change in Glu uptake, suggesting a non-circadian role for clock proteins in *Glast* transcription or *Glast* mRNA translation and/or stability (Beaulé et al., 2009). However, it is clear that the regulation and precise function of this transporter is very important to guarantee an efficient glutamatergic neurotransmission. A failure in synaptic Glu clearance is neurotoxic due to a hyperactivation of postsynaptic Glu receptors resulting in the phenomena known as excitotoxicity, which is implicated in most of neurodegenerative diseases (McEntee and Crook, 1993; Domingues et al., 2010; Gegelashvili and Bjerrum, 2014).

In the adult brain, the distribution of the specific astrocyte marker, glial fibrillary acidic protein (GFAP), has been reported to peak during daily rhythms in the SCN (Lavialle and Servière, 1993). Furthermore, it has been demonstrated that this peak also prevails in constant darkness (Lavialle and Servière, 1993; Moriya et al., 2000), strongly suggesting that these rhythms are essential and independent of environmental light. Although the function of circadian fluctuations of GFAP immunoreactivity is unknown, it has been observed that mice lacking the *gfap* gene show reduced eyeblink training and impaired LTD in the cerebellum (Shibuki et al., 1996), suggesting that this protein plays a role in the regulation of neuronal functions.

CNS excitatory synapses are extremely dynamic structures that show stabilization in response to learning and memory process. These synapses are surrounded by intricate astrocytic processes denominated perisynaptic astrocytic processes (PAPs; Iino et al., 2001; Hirrlinger et al., 2004; Nishida and Okabe, 2007). It has been described in primary cultured astrocytes that ezrin (an actin-binding protein) is required for filopodia formation and motility of PAPs, such motility can be induced by Glu via activation of metabotropic Glu receptors 3 and 5 (Lavialle et al., 2011). Moreover, changes in glutamatergic circadian activity in the hamster SCN are in synchrony with changes in ezrin immunoreactivity which is consistent with Glu-induced perisynaptic glial motility (Lavialle et al., 2011). These results suggest that ezrin is essential for Glu-induced PAPs plasticity that could be regulated by circadian system.

On the other hand, the brain fatty-acid binding protein (FABP7) localizes in astrocytes and neuronal cell precursors in the mature brain, and presents a high binding affinity to long chain fatty acids whose effects on brain function include development, emotion, learning, and memory (Yamamoto et al., 1987; Jensen et al., 1996; Wainwright et al., 1997; Moriguchi et al., 2000; Takeuchi et al., 2003). Gerstner and colleagues demonstrated in adult murine brain that levels of *Fabp7* mRNA oscillate over a 24 h period in brain areas that participate in daily activity and sleep like the hypothalamus, the tuberomammilary nucleus, the pons and the *locus coeruleus*. In these areas, *Fabp7* diminish in the dark phase and increase instead in the light phase (Gerstner et al., 2006, 2008). In contrast with its mRNA levels, FABP7 levels are higher during the dark phase (Gerstner et al., 2008), indicating that expression of this protein is delayed by 12 h with regards to its mRNA. More recently, the same group demonstrated that FABP7 is specifically augmented in the perisynaptic compartment of fine astrocytic processes that surround synapses. Furthermore, CPEB-mediated cytoplasmic polyadenylation controls the diurnally regulated *Fabp7* mRNA levels (Gerstner et al., 2012). Accordingly, in plasticity terms, targeting of *Fabp7* and CPEB-mediated polyadenylation could participate in controlling astrocytic process extension, although it is unknown if variations in synaptic plasticity and/or neuronal activity modify polyadenylation and trafficking of *Fabp7* mRNA resulting in morphological modifications of the astrocytic processes (Gerstner et al., 2012). In addition, variations in cycle-dependent memory formation and synaptic plasticity could regulate the circadian variations in subcellular trafficking and localization of *Fabp7* mRNA in hippocampal tripartite synapses (Gerstner et al., 2009, 2012).

Oligodendrocytes

To date, there is no evidence that oligodendrocytes have an internal circadian clock; however, it has been reported that oligodendrocytes precursor cells (OPCs) proliferation in the hippocampus could be regulated by clock genes (Matsumoto et al., 2011). It should be noted that OPCs proliferation itself could modulate the synaptic plasticity of the hippocampus in response to neuronal activity, thus circadian proliferation of these cells could regulate hippocampal function. Particularly, the OPCs give rise to mature oligodendrocytes, and are thought to be a constitutive reservoir of oligodendrocytes that replace damaged myelin (Levine et al., 1993) or add *de novo* myelination (McCarthy and Leblond, 1988). Interestingly, *myelin proteolipid protein* (*plp*), a myelin-specific gene, is regulated by *Clock* (Du et al., 2005), suggesting that the circadian clock controls myelin formation.

Microglia

Microglial cells constantly retract and extend their processes to sense their local environment contributing to the maintenance of healthy neuronal circuits (Kirchhoff, 2013). There is evidence that an intrinsic molecular clock exists in cortical microglia which controls diurnal morphological changes of its processes, and whereby these cells regulate the sleep-wake cycle-dependent changes in synaptic strength (Hayashi et al., 2013a,b). In line with these findings, it has been reported that the microglia-specific lysosomal cysteine protease Cathepsin S (CatS) exhibits a circadian expression in cortical microglia. The expression of CatS is involved in diurnal variations of synaptic strength in cortical neurons via the proteolytic modification of the perineuronal environment. However, disruptions in CatS lead to hyperlocomotor activity and to the deletion of the diurnal variations in spine density and synaptic activity of these cortical neurons as a consequence of the failure to downscale synaptic strength during sleep (Hayashi et al., 2013a). Since downscaling of synaptic strength is required for the acquisition and consolidation of novel information upon awakening, it is evident that dysfunction of the microglial intrinsic circadian clock is involved in neuropsychiatric disorders based on sleep disturbance, including depression and cognitive impairment (Bhattacharjee, 2007; Hayashi et al., 2014).

On the other hand, microglial cells express ATP receptors of the P2X (P2XR, ligand-gated ion-channel receptor) and P2Y subtypes (P2YR, G protein-coupled receptor). ATP released by glial cells during neuronal activity is then, capable to influence synaptic transmission. In fact in microglial cells, ATP increases the number their branch points, extension of their processes and morphological complexity (Fontainhas et al., 2011). Specifically, it has been demonstrated that the degree of microglial process extension is controlled by microglial $P2Y_{12}Rs$ (Haynes et al., 2006). Moreover, Hayashi and colleagues reported that microglial $P2Y_{12}Rs$ present circadian oscillations regardless that microglia would be isolated under constant darkness conditions (Hayashi et al., 2013b). Interestingly, inhibition of these purinergic receptors disrupts the rhythmic patterns of synaptic strength or spine density, while upregulated $P2Y_{12}Rs$ during the dark phase results in extension of the microglial processes that are partially retracted during the light phase resulting in a decrease of synaptic strength or spine density (Hayashi et al., 2013b). In the same fashion of CatS disruptions, dysfunctions in microglia-synapse interactions participate in neuropsychiatric disorders (Bhattacharjee, 2007; Hayashi et al., 2014).

Concerning P2X purinergic receptors, Nakazato and coworkers demonstrated that ATP selectively promotes the expression of the protein and mRNA of *Per1* through the activation of P2X7R in microglial cells (Nakazato et al., 2011). While the outcome of this upregulation is not completely clear, it has been reported that *Per* is not only crucial for long-term memory formation (LTM), but overexpression of this gene also enhances memory formation (Sakai et al., 2004). Taken together these evidences suggest that *Per* has an important function in the regulation of circadian synaptic plasticity in microglia.

Additionally, several reports indicate that ATP promotes microglial cells to secrete several signaling molecules, like interleukin-1 beta (IL-1β), TNFα, and plasminogen (Inoue et al., 1998; Hide et al., 2000; Sanz and Di Virgilio, 2000; Suzuki et al., 2004); which are involved in the modulation of synaptic transmission and plasticity (Ikegaya et al., 2003; Becker et al., 2013; Liu et al., 2014). Finally, it should be noted that microglia display rhythmic fluctuations in the gene expression of these mediators (Fonken et al., 2015).

CLINICAL IMPLICATIONS

Although synaptic dysfunction is the cellular basis of most mental illnesses, disturbance of the circadian clock system and dysfunctions of glial cells are likely to be involved in diverse brain pathologies. Up to now, only few studies, summarized in **Table 1**, provide a link between brain disorders, circadian rhythm dysfunction and glial physiology. For example, a study using $Per2^{Brdm1}$ mutant mice demonstrated that a nonfunctional *Per2* results in a hyperglutamatergic state due to a reduced GLAST expression and as a consequence, Glu uptake by astrocyte is diminished (Spanagel et al., 2005). Accordingly, one could expect that a reduction of astrocytic Glu uptake would be related to severe pathophysiological implications as shown in several disease models, including multiple sclerosis, Alzheimer's, and Huntington diseases (Domingues et al., 2010). Additionally, several studies related to proteins that are involved in the regulation of the astrocytic processes extension that surround synapses, like ezrin and FABP7, have shown that dysfunctions in these proteins lead to impairment in processes, like development, learning, memory, and emotion (Lavialle et al., 2011; Gerstner et al., 2012).

The fact that microglia exhibits circadian rhythmicity, such as oscillating expression patterns of clock genes that regulate the expression of $P2Y_{12}R$ and of the CatS protease suggests that alteration of these two factors disrupts the rhythmic patterns of synaptic strength and spine density (Hayashi et al., 2013a,b).

TABLE 1 | Clock-controlled genes (CCG) and their implications in brain pathologies.

CCG	Preparation	Pathological implications	References
ASTROCYTES			
ATP	Cortical astrocyte cultures	Disruptions in sleep-wake changes in the brain and in control synaptic transmission.	Marpegan et al., 2011
GLAST	*Per2* mutant mice	Dysregulation in the Glu uptake process.	Spanagel et al., 2005
GFAP	GFAP mutant mice	Impaired LTD in the cerebellum, as well as reduced eyeblink conditioning.	Shibuki et al., 1996
Ezrin	Primary astrocytes cultures	Alterations in the Glu-induced PAPs plasticity.	Lavialle et al., 2011
FABP7	Primary mouse astrocyte culture	Dysregulation of astrocytic processes extension.	Gerstner et al., 2012
OLIGODENDROCYTES			
OPCs	Mouse hippocampus slices	Alterations in synaptic plasticity for the hippocampal function.	Matsumoto et al., 2011
MICROGLIA			
CatS	CatS$^{-/-}$ mice	Neurological disorders by disruption of the circadian oscillation patterns of synaptic strength and spine density in cortical neurons.	Hayashi et al., 2013a
$P2Y_{12}R$	Cortical microglia cultures	Neurological disorders by disruption of the rhythmic patterns of synaptic strength or spine density.	Hayashi et al., 2013b
P2X7R	Cultured murine microglia and BV-2 cells	Downregulates *Per1* mRNA expression.	Nakazato et al., 2011
		Reduces the number of processes in microglial cells as a result of cellular activation.	

ATP, Adenosine triphosphate; CatS, cathepsin S; FABP7, brain-type fatty acid binding protein; GFAP, glial fibrillary acidic protein; GLAST, Glu/aspartate transporter; LTD, long-term depression; OPCs, oligodendrocytes precursor cells; P2X7R, P2X7 receptor; $P2Y_{12}R$, $P2Y_{12}$ receptor; PAPs, perisynaptic astrocytic processes.

In this context, healthy brain synaptic homeostasis depends on microglia-synapse interactions controlled by the intrinsic microglial clock, so the dysfunction of this clock most probably leads to neuropsychiatric disorders, like depression and cognitive deficits (Bhattacharjee, 2007; Hayashi et al., 2014).

Finally, it has been demonstrated that sleep disturbances are involved with multiple negative effects on human physiology, including neuronal dysfunction (Joo et al., 2013), mood disturbances (Dinges et al., 1997), cognitive impairments (Lo et al., 2012), and disruption to circadian rhythmicity (Möller-Levet et al., 2013).

CONCLUSIONS

Glial cells have long been regarded as simple supportive cells of neuronal function. However, in recent years, several reports have demonstrated the involvement glial cells in diverse processes required for proper brain function, including contribution to the regulation of the synaptic plasticity. Taking into consideration that clock genes modify glial Glu transporters and, by these means, control the strength and continuity of the major excitatory system, their role in higher brain functions is likely of a high relevance. Accordingly, specific alterations of the circadian system are related to various diseases in which glutamatergic transmission is impaired. Additionally, dysfunction of astrocyte-neuron signaling plays a critical role in the pathology of most of the neurodegenerative diseases, such as Alzheimer, Parkinson, and Huntington. Altogether, these findings make it clear that glial cells are an important tool to understand the circadian regulation of synaptic plasticity, both in the short and in the long terms. Certainly, characterization of the activity-dependent and clock-dependent changes in glial proteins repertoire will provide a major input to our understanding of the pivotal role of glial cells in higher brain functions.

AUTHOR CONTRIBUTIONS

DC-C gathered the relevant information, wrote the manuscript, as well as elaborated the table. AO reviewed and edited the final version of the manuscript.

FUNDING

The work in the lab is supported by grants from Conacyt-México (255087) and "Soluciones para un México Verde S.A. de C.V." to AO; DC-C is supported by SNI-Conacyt.

REFERENCES

Abe, K., Xie, F. J., Watanabe, Y., and Saito, H. (1990). Glycine facilitates induction of long-term potentiation of evoked potential in rat hippocampus. *Neurosci. Lett.* 117, 87–92. doi: 10.1016/0304-3940(90)90124-R

Agulhon, C., Petravicz, J., McMullen, A. B., Sweger, E. J., Minton, S. K., Taves, S. R., et al. (2008). What is the role of astrocyte calcium in neurophysiology? *Neuron* 59, 932–946. doi: 10.1016/j.neuron.2008.09.004

Aloisi, F. (2001). Immune function of microglia. *Glia* 36, 165–179. doi: 10.1002/glia.1106

Anderson, C. M., and Swanson, R. A. (2000). Astrocyte glutamate transport: review of properties, regulation, and physiological functions. *Glia* 32, 1–14. doi: 10.1002/1098-1136(200010)32:1<1::AID-GLIA10>3.0.CO;2-W

Araque, A., Carmignoto, G., Haydon, P. G., Oliet, S. H., Robitaille, R., and Volterra, A. (2014). Gliotransmitters travel in time and space. *Neuron* 81, 728–739. doi: 10.1016/j.neuron.2014.02.007

Araque, A., Parpura, V., Sanzgiri, R. P., and Haydon, P. G. (1998a). Glutamate-dependent astrocyte modulation of synaptic transmission between cultured hippocampal neurons. *Eur. J. Neurosci.* 10, 2129–2142.

Araque, A., Parpura, V., Sanzgiri, R. P., and Haydon, P. G. (1999). Tripartite synapses: glia, the unacknowledged partner. *Trends Neurosci.* 22, 208–215. doi: 10.1016/S0166-2236(98)01349-6

Araque, A., Sanzgiri, R. P., Parpura, V., and Haydon, P. G. (1998b). Calcium elevation in astrocytes causes an NMDA receptor-dependent increase in the frequency of miniature synaptic currents in cultured hippocampal neurons. *J. Neurosci.* 18, 6822–6829.

Bains, J. S., and Oliet, S. H. R. (2007). Glia: they make your memories stick! *Trends Neurosci.* 30, 417–424. doi: 10.1016/j.tins.2007.06.007

Baker, G. E., and Stryker, M. P. (1990). Retinofugal fibres change conduction velocity and diameter between the optic nerve and tract in ferrets. *Nature* 344, 342–345. doi: 10.1038/344342a0

Batchelor, P. E., Liberatore, G. T., Wong, J. Y., Porritt, M. J., Frerichs, F., Donnan, G. A., et al. (1999). Activated macrophages and microglia induce dopaminergic sprouting in the injured striatum and express brain-derived neurotrophic factor and glial cell line-derived neurotrophic factor. *J. Neurosci.* 19, 1708–1716.

Batchelor, P. E., Porritt, M. J., Martinello, P., Parish, C. L., Liberatore, G. T., Donnan, G. A., et al. (2002). Macrophages and microglia produce local trophic gradients that stimulate axonal sprouting toward but not beyond the wound edge. *Mol. Cell. Neurosci.* 21, 436–453. doi: 10.1006/mcne.2002.1185

Beaulé, C., Swanstrom, A., Leone, M. J., and Herzog, E. D. (2009). Circadian modulation of gene expression, but not glutamate uptake, in mouse and rat cortical astrocytes. *PLoS ONE* 4:e7476. doi: 10.1371/journal.pone.0007476

Becker, D., Zahn, N., Deller, T., and Vlachos, A. (2013). Tumor necrosis factor alpha maintains denervation-induced homeostatic synaptic plasticity of mouse dentate granule cells. *Front. Cell. Neurosci.* 7:257. doi: 10.3389/fncel.2013.00257

Becker-Weimann, S., Wolf, J., Herzel, H., and Kramer, A. (2004). Modeling feedback loops of the mammalian circadian oscillator. *Biophys. J.* 87, 3023–3034. doi: 10.1529/biophysj.104.040824

Ben Achour, S., and Pascual, O. (2010). Glia: the many ways to modulate synaptic plasticity. *Neurochem. Int.* 57, 440–445. doi: 10.1016/j.neuint.2010.02.013

Benington, J. H., and Frank, M. G. (2003). Cellular and molecular connections between sleep and synaptic plasticity. *Prog. Neurobiol.* 69, 71–101. doi: 10.1016/S0301-0082(03)00018-2

Bergles, D. E., Dzubay, J. A., and Jahr, C. E. (1997). Glutamate transporter currents in Bergmann glial cells follow the time course of extrasynaptic glutamate. *Proc. Natl. Acad. Sci. U.S.A.* 94, 14821–14825. doi: 10.1073/pnas.94.26.14821

Bernardinelli, Y., Muller, D., and Nikonenko, I. (2014). Astrocyte-synapse structural plasticity. *Neural Plast.* 2014, 1–13. doi: 10.1155/2014/232105

Berthold, C. H., Nilsson, I., and Rydmark, M. (1983). Axon diameter and myelin sheath thickness in nerve fibres of the ventral spinal root of the seventh lumbar nerve of the adult and developing cat. *J. Anat.* 136, 483–508.

Bhattacharjee, Y. (2007). Is internal timing key to mental health? *Science* 317, 1488–1490. doi: 10.1126/science.317.5844.1488

Bliss, T. V., and Collingridge, G. L. (1993). A synaptic model of memory: long-term potentiation in the hippocampus. *Nature* 361, 31–39. doi: 10.1038/361031a0

Brecht, M., and Sakmann, B. (2002). Dynamic representation of whisker deflection by synaptic potentials in spiny stellate and pyramidal cells in the barrels and septa of layer 4 rat somatosensory cortex. *J. Physiol.* 543, 49–70. doi: 10.1113/jphysiol.2002.018465

Bushong, E. A., Martone, M. E., Jones, Y. Z., and Ellisman, M. H. (2002). Protoplasmic astrocytes in CA1 stratum radiatum occupy separate anatomical domains. *J. Neurosci.* 22, 183–192.

Carr, C. E., and Konishi, M. (1990). A circuit for detection of interaural time differences in the brain stem of the barn owl. *J. Neurosci.* 10, 3227–3246.

Chao, T. I., Rickmann, J. R., and Wolff, J. R. (2002). "The synapse-astrocyte boundary: An anatomical basis for an integrative role of glia in synaptic transmission," in *The Tripartite Synapse: Glia in Synaptic Transmission*, eds A. Volterra, P. J. Magistretti, and P. G. Haydon (Oxford: Oxford University Press), 3–23.

Chen, M. S., Huber, A. B., van der Haar, M. E., Frank, M., Schnell, L., Spillmann, A. A., et al. (2000). Nogo-A is a myelin-associated neurite outgrowth inhibitor and an antigen for monoclonal antibody IN-1. *Nature* 403, 434–439. doi: 10.1038/35000219

Conti, F., Minelli, A., and Melone, M. (2004). GABA transporters in the mammalian cerebral cortex: localization, development and pathological implications. *Brain Res. Rev.* 45, 196–212. doi: 10.1016/j.brainresrev.2004.03.003

Cossart, R., Aronov, D., and Yuste, R. (2003). Attractor dynamics of network UP states in the neocortex. *Nature* 423, 283–288. doi: 10.1038/nature01614

Danbolt, N. C. (2001). Glutamate uptake. *Prog Neurobiol.* 65, 1–105. doi: 10.1016/S0301-0082(00)00067-8

Danbolt, N. C., Furness, D. N., and Zhou, Y. (2016). Neuronal vs glial glutamate uptake: resolving the conundrum. *Neurochem. Int.* 98, 29–45. doi: 10.1016/j.neuint.2016.05.009

De Pittà, M., Brunel, N., and Volterra, A. (2016). Astrocytes: Orchestrating synaptic plasticity? *Neuroscience* 323, 43–61. doi: 10.1016/j.neuroscience.2015.04.001

Dinges, D. F., Pack, F., Williams, K., Gillen, K. A., Powell, J. W., Ott, G. E., et al. (1997). Cumulative sleepiness, mood disturbance, and psychomotor vigilance performance decrements during a week of sleep restricted to 4-5 hours per night. *Sleep* 20, 267–277.

Domingues, A. M., Taylor, M., and Fern, R. (2010). Glia as transmitter sources and sensors in health and disease. *Neurochem. Int.* 57, 359–366. doi: 10.1016/j.neuint.2010.03.024

Du, Y. Z., Fan, S. J., Meng, Q. H., Wang, G. Q., and Tong, J. (2005). Circadian expression of clock and screening of clock-controlled genes in peripheral lymphocytes of rat. *Biochem. Biophys. Res. Commun.* 336, 1069–1073. doi: 10.1016/j.bbrc.2005.08.228

Dunlap, J. C. (1999). Molecular bases for circadian clocks. *Cell* 96, 271–290. doi: 10.1016/S0092-8674(00)80566-8

Dupree, J. L., Mason, J. L., Marcus, J. R., Stull, M., Levinson, R., Matsushima, G. K., et al. (2004). Oligodendrocytes assist in the maintenance of sodium channel clusters independent of the myelin sheath. *Neuron Glia Biol.* 1, 179–192. doi: 10.1017/S1740925X04000304

Eckel-Mahan, K. L., and Storm, D. R. (2009). Circadian rhythms and memory: not so simple as cogs and gears. *EMBO Rep.* 10, 584–591. doi: 10.1038/embor.2009.123

Fellin, T., Ellenbogen, J. M., De Pittà, M., Ben-Jacob, E., and Halassa, M. M. (2012). Astrocyte regulation of sleep circuits: experimental and modeling perspectives. *Front. Comput. Neurosci.* 6:65. doi: 10.3389/fncom.2012.00065

Fellin, T., Halassa, M. M., Terunuma, M., Succol, F., Takano, H., Frank, M., et al. (2009). Endogenous nonneuronal modulators of synaptic transmission control cortical slow oscillations *in vivo*. *Proc. Natl. Acad. Sci. U.S.A.* 106, 15037–15042. doi: 10.1073/pnas.0906419106

Fellin, T., Pascual, O., and Haydon, P. G. (2006). Astrocytes coordinate synaptic networks: balanced excitation and inhibition. *Physiology* 21, 208–215. doi: 10.1152/physiol.00161.2005

Flores-Méndez, M., Mendez-Flores, O. G., and Ortega, A. (2016). Glia plasma membrane transporters: key players in glutamatergic neurotransmission. *Neurochem. Int.* 98, 46–55. doi: 10.1016/j.neuint.2016.04.004

Fonken, L. K., Frank, M. G., Kitt, M. M., Barrientos, R. M., Watkins, L. R., and Maier, S. F. (2015). Microglia inflammatory responses are controlled by an intrinsic circadian clock. *Brain Behav. Immun.* 45, 171–179. doi: 10.1016/j.bbi.2014.11.009

Fontainhas, A. M., Wang, M., Liang, K. J., Chen, S., Mettu, P., Damani, M., et al. (2011). Microglial morphology and dynamic behavior is regulated by ionotropic glutamatergic and GABAergic neurotransmission. *PLoS ONE* 6:e15973. doi: 10.1371/journal.pone.0015973

Frank, M. G. (2011). Sleep and developmental plasticity not just for kids. *Prog. Brain Res.* 193, 221–232. doi: 10.1016/B978-0-444-53839-0.00014-4

Frank, M. G., and Benington, J. H. (2006). The role of sleep in memory consolidation and brain plasticity: dream or reality? *Neuroscience* 12, 477–488. doi: 10.1177/1073858406293552

Frank, M. G., and Cantera, R. (2014). Sleep, clocks, and synaptic plasticity. *Trends Neurosci.* 37, 491–501. doi: 10.1016/j.tins.2014.06.005

Gegelashvili, G., and Bjerrum, O. J. (2014). High-affinity glutamate transporters in chronic pain: an emerging therapeutic target. *J. Neurochem.* 131, 712–730. doi: 10.1111/jnc.12957

Gentet, L. J., Avermann, M., Matyas, F., Staiger, J. F., and Petersen, C. C. H. (2010). Membrane potential dynamics of GABAergic neurons in the barrel cortex of behaving mice. *Neuron* 65, 422–435. doi: 10.1016/j.neuron.2010.01.006

Gerstner, J. R., Bremer, Q. Z., Vander Heyden, W. M., LaVaute, T. M., Yin, J. C., and Landry, C. F. (2008). Brain fatty acid binding protein (Fabp7) is diurnally regulated in astrocytes and hippocampal granule cell precursors in adult rodent brain. *PLoS ONE* 3:e1631. doi: 10.1371/journal.pone.0001631

Gerstner, J. R., Lyons, L. C., Wright, K. P., Loh, D. H., Rawashdeh, O., Eckel-Mahan, K. L., et al. (2009). Cycling behavior and memory formation. *J. Neurosci.* 29, 12824–12830. doi: 10.1523/JNEUROSCI.3353-09.2009

Gerstner, J. R., Vander Heyden, W. M., LaVaute, T. M., and Landry, C. F. (2006). Profiles of novel diurnally regulated genes in mouse hypothalamus: expression analysis of the cysteine and histidine-rich domain-containing, zinc-binding protein 1, the fatty acid-binding protein 7 and the GTPase, ras-like family member 11b. *Neuroscience* 139, 1435–1448. doi: 10.1016/j.neuroscience.2006.01.020

Gerstner, J. R., Vanderheyden, W. M., LaVaute, T., Westmark, C. J., Rouhana, L., Pack, A. I., et al. (2012). Time of day regulates subcellular trafficking, tripartite synaptic localization, and polyadenylation of the astrocytic Fabp7 mRNA. *J. Neurosci.* 32, 1383–1394. doi: 10.1523/JNEUROSCI.3228-11.2012

Gordon, G. R., Baimoukhametova, D. V., Hewitt, S. A., Rajapaksha, W. R., Fisher, T. E., and Bains, J. S. (2005). Norepinephrine triggers release of glial ATP to increase postsynaptic efficacy. *Nat. Neurosci.* 8, 1078–1086. doi: 10.1038/nn1498

GrandPré, T., Nakamura, F., Vartanian, T., and Strittmatter, S. M. (2000). Identification of the Nogo inhibitor of axon regeneration as a Reticulon protein. *Nature* 403, 439–444. doi: 10.1038/35000226

Haider, B., and McCormick, D. A. (2009). Rapid neocortical dynamics: cellular and network mechanisms. *Neuron* 62, 171–189. doi: 10.1016/j.neuron.2009.04.008

Halassa, M. M., Fellin, T., and Haydon, P. G. (2009a). Tripartite synapses: roles for astrocytic purines in the control of synaptic physiology and behavior. *Neuropharmacology* 57, 343–346. doi: 10.1016/j.neuropharm.2009.06.031

Halassa, M. M., Fellin, T., Takano, H., Dong, J.-H., and Haydon, P. G. (2007). Synaptic islands defined by the territory of a single astrocyte. *J. Neurosci.* 27, 6473–6477. doi: 10.1523/JNEUROSCI.1419-07.2007

Halassa, M. M., Florian, C., Fellin, T., Munoz, J. R., Lee, S.-Y., Abel, T., et al. (2009b). Astrocytic modulation of sleep homeostasis and cognitive consequences of sleep loss. *Neuron* 61, 213–219. doi: 10.1016/j.neuron.2008.11.024

Halassa, M. M., and Haydon, P. G. (2010). Integrated brain circuits: astrocytic networks modulate neuronal activity and behavior. *Annu. Rev. Physiol.* 72, 335–355. doi: 10.1146/annurev-physiol-021909-135843

Halberg, F. (1959). Physiologic 24-hour periodicity; general and procedural considerations with reference to the adrenal cycle. *Int. Z. Vitaminforsch. Beih.* 10, 225–296.

Harmer, S. L., Panda, S., and Kay, S. A. (2001). Molecular bases of circadian rhythms. *Annu. Rev. Cell Dev. Biol.* 17, 215–253. doi: 10.1146/annurev.cellbio.17.1.215

Harris, K. D., Csicsvari, J., Hirase, H., Dragoi, G., and Buzsáki, G. (2003). Organization of cell assemblies in the hippocampus. *Nature* 424, 552–556. doi: 10.1038/nature01834

Harry, G. J., and Kraft, A. D. (2012). Microglia in the developing brain: a potential target with lifetime effects. *Neurotoxicology* 33, 191–206. doi: 10.1016/j.neuro.2012.01.012

Hartse, K. M. (2011). "The phylogeny of sleep," in *Handbook of Clinical Neurology, Vol. 98*, eds P. Montagna and S. Chokroverty (Amsterdam: Elsevier), 97–109.

Hayashi, Y., Ishibashi, H., Hashimoto, K., and Nakanishi, H. (2006). Potentiation of the NMDA receptor-mediated responses through the activation of the glycine site by microglia secreting soluble factors. *Glia* 53, 660–668. doi: 10.1002/glia.20322

Hayashi, Y., Koyanagi, S., Kusunose, N., Okada, R., Wu, Z., Tozaki-Saitoh, H., et al. (2013a). The intrinsic microglial molecular clock controls synaptic strength via the circadian expression of cathepsin S. *Sci. Rep.* 3:2744. doi:10.1038/srep02744

Hayashi, Y., Koyanagi, S., Kusunose, N., Takayama, F., Okada, R., Wu, Z., et al. (2013b). Diurnal spatial rearrangement of microglial processes through the rhythmic expression of P2Y12 receptors. *J. Neurol. Disord.* 1:120. doi: 10.4172/2329-6895.1000120

Hayashi, Y., Wu, Z., and Nakanishi, H. (2014). A possible link between microglial process dysfunction and neuropsychiatric disorders. *J. Neurol. Disord. Stroke* 2:1060.

Haydon, P. G. (2001). GLIA: listening and talking to the synapse. *Nat. Rev. Neurosci.* 2, 185–193. doi: 10.1038/35058528

Haynes, S. E., Hollopeter, G., Yang, G., Kurpius, D., Dailey, M. E., Gan, W.-B., et al. (2006). The P2Y12 receptor regulates microglial activation by extracellular nucleotides. *Nat. Neurosci.* 9, 1512–1519. doi: 10.1038/nn1805

Hide, I., Tanaka, M., Inoue, A., Nakajima, K., Kohsaka, S., Inoue, K., et al. (2000). Extracellular ATP triggers tumor necrosis factor-alpha release from rat microglia. *J. Neurochem.* 75, 965–972. doi: 10.1046/j.1471-4159.2000.0750965.x

Hill, S., and Tononi, G. (2004). Modeling sleep and wakefulness in the thalamocortical system. *J. Neurophysiol.* 93, 1671–1698. doi: 10.1152/jn.00915.2004

Hirrlinger, J., Hülsmann, S., and Kirchhoff, F. (2004). Astroglial processes show spontaneous motility at active synaptic terminals *in situ*. *Eur. J. Neurosci.* 20, 2235–2239. doi: 10.1111/j.1460-9568.2004.03689.x

Huang, J. K., Phillips, G. R., Roth, A. D., Pedraza, L., Shan, W., Belkaid, W., et al. (2005). Glial membranes at the node of Ranvier prevent neurite outgrowth. *Science* 310, 1813–1817. doi: 10.1126/science.1118313

Iino, M., Goto, K., Kakegawa, W., Okado, H., Sudo, M., Ishiuchi, S., et al. (2001). Glia-synapse interaction through Ca2+-permeable AMPA receptors in Bergmann glia. *Science* 292, 926–929. doi: 10.1126/science.1058827

Ikegaya, Y., Delcroix, I., Iwakura, Y., Matsuki, N., and Nishiyama, N. (2003). Interleukin-1beta abrogates long-term depression of hippocampal CA1 synaptic transmission. *Synapse* 47, 54–57. doi: 10.1002/syn.10154

Inoue, K., Nakajima, K., Morimoto, T., Kikuchi, Y., Koizumi, S., Illes, P., et al. (1998). ATP stimulation of Ca2+-dependent plasminogen release from cultured microglia. *Br. J. Pharmacol.* 123, 1304–1310. doi: 10.1038/sj.bjp.0701732

Jensen, C. L., Chen, H., Fraley, J. K., Anderson, R. E., and Heird, W. C. (1996). Biochemical effects of dietary linoleic/alpha-linolenic acid ratio in term infants. *Lipids* 31, 107–113. doi: 10.1007/BF02522419

Jilg, A., Lesny, S., Peruzki, N., Schwegler, H., Selbach, O., Dehghani, F., et al. (2010). Temporal dynamics of mouse hippocampal clock gene expression support memory processing. *Hippocampus* 20, 377–388. doi: 10.1002/hipo.20637

Jin, X., Shearman, L. P., Weaver, D. R., Zylka, M. J., de Vries, G. J., and Reppert, S. M. (1999). A molecular mechanism regulating rhythmic output from the suprachiasmatic circadian clock. *Cell* 96, 57–68. doi: 10.1016/S0092-8674(00)80959-9

Joo, E. Y., Noh, H. J., Kim, J.-S., Koo, D. L., Kim, D., Hwang, K. J., et al. (2013). Brain gray matter deficits in patients with chronic primary insomnia. *Sleep* 36, 999–1007. doi: 10.5665/sleep.2796

Kenet, T., Bibitchkov, D., Tsodyks, M., Grinvald, A., and Arieli, A. (2003). Spontaneously emerging cortical representations of visual attributes. *Nature* 425, 954–956. doi: 10.1038/nature02078

Kirchhoff, F. (2013). "Role of microglia in the normal brain," in *Neuroglia*, eds H. Kettenmann, and B. R. Ransom (New York, NY: Oxford University Press), 605–613.

Ko, G. Y., Shi, L., and Ko, M. L. (2009). Circadian regulation of ion channels and their functions. *J. Neurochem.* 110, 1150–1169. doi: 10.1111/j.1471-4159.2009.06223.x

Kondratova, A. A., Dubrovsky, Y. V., Antoch, M. P., and Kondratov, R. V. (2010). Circadian clock proteins control adaptation to novel environment and memory formation. *Aging* 2, 285–297. doi: 10.18632/aging.100142

Lavialle, M., Aumann, G., Anlauf, E., Pröls, F., Arpin, M., and Derouiche, A. (2011). Structural plasticity of perisynaptic astrocyte processes involves ezrin and metabotropic glutamate receptors. *Proc. Natl. Acad. Sci. U.S.A.* 108, 12915–12919. doi: 10.1073/pnas.1100957108

Lavialle, M., and Servière, J. (1993). Circadian fluctuations in GFAP distribution in the Syrian hamster suprachiasmatic nucleus. *Neuroreport* 4, 1243–1246. doi: 10.1097/00001756-199309000-00008

Le Martelot, G., Claudel, T., Gatfield, D., Schaad, O., Kornmann, B., Lo Sasso, G., et al. (2009). REV-ERBalpha participates in circadian SREBP signaling and bile acid homeostasis. *PLoS Biol* 7:e1000181. doi: 10.1371/journal.pbio.1000181

Levine, J. M., Stincone, F., and Lee, Y.-S. (1993). Development and differentiation of glial precursor cells in the rat cerebellum. *Glia* 7, 307–321. doi: 10.1002/glia.440070406

Lin, S.-C., and Bergles, D. E. (2004). Synaptic signaling between neurons and glia. *Glia* 47, 290–298. doi: 10.1002/glia.20060

Liu, Z., Li, Y., Qian, J., Cui, Y., and Chopp, M. (2014). Plasminogen deficiency causes reduced corticospinal axonal plasticity and functional recovery after stroke in mice. *PLoS ONE* 9:e94505. doi: 10.1371/journal.pone.0094505

Lo, J. C., Groeger, J. A., Santhi, N., Arbon, E. L., Lazar, A. S., Hasan, S., et al. (2012). Effects of partial and acute total sleep deprivation on performance across cognitive domains, individuals and circadian phase. *PLoS ONE* 7:e45987. doi: 10.1371/journal.pone.0045987

Lohmann, C., and Kessels, H. W. (2014). The developmental stages of synaptic plasticity. *J. Physiol.* 592, 13–31. doi: 10.1113/jphysiol.2012.235119

Lowrey, P. L., and Takahashi, J. S. (2004). Mammalian circadian biology: elucidating genome-wide levels of temporal organization. *Annu. Rev. Genomics Hum. Genet.* 5, 407–441. doi: 10.1146/annurev.genom.5.061903.175925

Marpegan, L., Swanstrom, A. E., Chung, K., Simon, T., Haydon, P. G., Khan, S. K., et al. (2011). Circadian regulation of ATP release in astrocytes. *J. Neurosci.* 31, 8342–8350. doi: 10.1523/JNEUROSCI.6537-10.2011

Martínez-Lozada, Z., and Ortega, A. (2015). Glutamatergic transmission: a matter of three. *Neural Plast.* 2015, 1–11. doi: 10.1155/2015/787396

Martin, S. J., Grimwood, P. D., and Morris, R. G. (2000). Synaptic plasticity and memory: an evaluation of the hypothesis. *Annu. Rev. Neurosci.* 23, 649–711. doi: 10.1146/annurev.neuro.23.1.649

Massimini, M., and Amzica, F. (2001). Extracellular calcium fluctuations and intracellular potentials in the cortex during the slow sleep oscillation. *J. Neurophysiol.* 85, 1346–1350. doi: 10.1152/jn.2001.85.3.1346

Matsumoto, Y., Tsunekawa, Y., Nomura, T., Suto, F., Matsumata, M., Tsuchiya, S., et al. (2011). Differential proliferation rhythm of neural progenitor and oligodendrocyte precursor cells in the young adult hippocampus. *PLoS ONE* 6:e27628. doi: 10.1371/journal.pone.0027628

McCarthy, G. F., and Leblond, C. P. (1988). Radioautographic evidence for slow astrocyte turnover and modest oligodendrocyte production in the corpus callosum of adult mice infused with 3H-thymidine. *J. Comp. Neurol.* 271, 589–603. doi: 10.1002/cne.902710409

McEntee, W. J., and Crook, T. H. (1993). Glutamate: its role in learning, memory, and the aging brain. *Psychopharmacology* 111, 391–401. doi: 10.1007/BF02253527

McKerracher, L., David, S., Jackson, D. L., Kottis, V., Dunn, R. J., and Braun, P. E. (1994). Identification of myelin-associated glycoprotein as a major myelin-derived inhibitor of neurite growth. *Neuron* 13, 805–811. doi: 10.1016/0896-6273(94)90247-X

Möller-Levet, C. S., Archer, S. N., Bucca, G., Laing, E. E., Slak, A., Kabiljo, R., et al. (2013). Effects of insufficient sleep on circadian rhythmicity and expression amplitude of the human blood transcriptome. *Proc. Natl. Acad. Sci. U.S.A.* 110, E1132–E1141. doi: 10.1073/pnas.1217154110

Monk, T. H., and Folkard, S. (1978). Concealed inefficiency of late-night study. *Nature* 273, 296–297. doi: 10.1038/273296a0

Moriguchi, T., Greiner, R. S., and Salem, N. (2000). Behavioral deficits associated with dietary induction of decreased brain docosahexaenoic acid concentration. *J. Neurochem.* 75, 2563–2573. doi: 10.1046/j.1471-4159.2000.0752563.x

Moriya, T., Yoshinobu, Y., Kouzu, Y., Katoh, A., Gomi, H., Ikeda, M., et al. (2000). Involvement of glial fibrillary acidic protein (GFAP) expressed in astroglial cells in circadian rhythm under constant lighting conditions in mice. *J. Neurosci. Res.* 60, 212–218. doi: 10.1002/(SICI)1097-4547(20000415)60:2<212::AID-JNR10>3.0.CO;2-P

Nakazato, R., Takarada, T., Yamamoto, T., Hotta, S., Hinoi, E., and Yoneda, Y. (2011). Selective upregulation of Per1 mRNA expression by ATP through activation of P2X7 purinergic receptors expressed in microglial cells. *J. Pharmacol. Sci.* 116, 350–361. doi: 10.1254/jphs.11069FP

Newman, L. A., Korol, D. L., and Gold, P. E. (2011). Lactate produced by glycogenolysis in astrocytes regulates memory processing. *PLoS ONE* 6:e28427. doi: 10.1371/journal.pone.0028427

Nishida, H., and Okabe, S. (2007). Direct astrocytic contacts regulate local maturation of dendritic spines. *J. Neurosci.* 27, 331–340. doi: 10.1523/JNEUROSCI.4466-06.2007

Panda, S., Antoch, M. P., Miller, B. H., Su, A. I., Schook, A. B., Straume, M., et al. (2002). Coordinated transcription of key pathways in the mouse by the circadian clock. *Cell* 109, 307–320. doi: 10.1016/S0092-8674(02)00722-5

Parpura, V., Basarsky, T. A., Liu, F., Jeftinija, K., Jeftinija, S., and Haydon, P. G. (1994). Glutamate-mediated astrocyte–neuron signalling. *Nature* 369, 744–747. doi: 10.1038/369744a0

Parpura, V., and Zorec, R. (2010). Gliotransmission: exocytotic release from astrocytes. *Brain Res. Rev.* 63, 83–92. doi: 10.1016/j.brainresrev.2009.11.008

Pascual, O., Ben Achour, S., Rostaing, P., Triller, A., and Bessis, A. (2012). Microglia activation triggers astrocyte-mediated modulation of excitatory neurotransmission. *Proc. Natl. Acad. Sci. U.S.A.* 109, E197–E205. doi: 10.1073/pnas.1111098109

Pascual, O., Casper, K. B., Kubera, C., Zhang, J., Revilla-Sanchez, R., Sul, J.-Y., et al. (2005). Astrocytic purinergic signaling coordinates synaptic networks. *Science* 310, 113–116. doi: 10.1126/science.1116916

Perea, G., Navarrete, M., and Araque, A. (2009). Tripartite synapses: astrocytes process and control synaptic information. *Trends Neurosci.* 32, 421–431. doi: 10.1016/j.tins.2009.05.001

Poskanzer, K. E., and Yuste, R. (2011). Astrocytic regulation of cortical UP states. *Proc. Natl. Acad. Sci. U.S.A.* 108, 18453–18458. doi: 10.1073/pnas.1112378108

Poskanzer, K. E., and Yuste, R. (2016). Astrocytes regulate cortical state switching *in vivo*. *Proc. Natl. Acad. Sci. U.S.A.* 113, E2675–E2684. doi: 10.1073/pnas.1520759113

Preitner, N., Damiola, F., Lopez-Molina, L., Zakany, J., Duboule, D., Albrecht, U., et al. (2002). The orphan nuclear receptor REV-ERBalpha controls circadian transcription within the positive limb of the mammalian circadian oscillator. *Cell* 110, 251–260. doi: 10.1016/S0092-8674(02)00825-5

Ramaswamy, S., and Muller, E. B. (2015). Cell-type specific modulation of neocortical UP and DOWN states. *Front. Cell. Neurosci.* 9:370. doi: 10.3389/fncel.2015.00370

Rawashdeh, O., de Borsetti, N. H., Roman, G., and Cahill, G. M. (2007). Melatonin suppresses nighttime memory formation in zebrafish. *Science* 318, 1144–1146. doi: 10.1126/science.1148564

Reppert, S. M., and Weaver, D. R. (2001). Molecular analysis of mammalian circadian rhythms. *Annu. Rev. Physiol.* 63, 647–676. doi: 10.1146/annurev.physiol.63.1.647

Reppert, S. M., and Weaver, D. R. (2002). Coordination of circadian timing in mammals. *Nature* 418, 935–941. doi: 10.1038/nature00965

Rudy, J. W., and Pugh, C. R. (1998). Time of conditioning selectively influences contextual fear conditioning: further support for a multiple-memory systems view of fear conditioning. *J. Exp. Psychol. Anim. Behav. Process.* 24, 316–324. doi: 10.1037/0097-7403.24.3.316

Saab, A. S., Neumeyer, A., Jahn, H. M., Cupido, A., Šimek, A. A. M., Boele, H.-J., et al. (2012). Bergmann glial AMPA receptors are required for fine motor coordination. *Science* 337, 749–753. doi: 10.1126/science.1221140

Sakai, T., Tamura, T., Kitamoto, T., and Kidokoro, Y. (2004). A clock gene, period, plays a key role in long-term memory formation in Drosophila. *Proc. Natl. Acad. Sci. U.S.A.* 101, 16058–16063. doi: 10.1073/pnas.0401472101

Sanz, J. M., and Di Virgilio, F. (2000). Kinetics and mechanism of ATP-dependent IL-1 beta release from microglial cells. *J. Immunol.* 164, 4893–4898. doi: 10.4049/jimmunol.164.9.4893

Schibler, U., and Sassone-Corsi, P. (2002). A web of circadian pacemakers. *Cell* 111, 919–922. doi: 10.1016/S0092-8674(02)01225-4

Shibuki, K., Gomi, H., Chen, L., Bao, S., Kim, J. J., Wakatsuki, H., et al. (1996). Deficient cerebellar long-term depression, impaired eyeblink conditioning, and normal motor coordination in GFAP mutant mice. *Neuron* 16, 587–599. doi: 10.1016/S0896-6273(00)80078-1

Sierra, A., Abiega, O., Shahraz, A., and Neumann, H. (2013). Janus-faced microglia: beneficial and detrimental consequences of microglial phagocytosis. *Front. Cell. Neurosci.* 7:6. doi: 10.3389/fncel.2013.00006

Spanagel, R., Pendyala, G., Abarca, C., Zghoul, T., Sanchis-Segura, C., Magnone, M. C., et al. (2005). The clock gene Per2 influences the glutamatergic system and modulates alcohol consumption. *Nat. Med.* 11, 35–42. doi: 10.1038/nm1163

Steriade, M., Nuñez, A., and Amzica, F. (1993). Intracellular analysis of relations between the slow (< 1 Hz) neocortical oscillation and other sleep rhythms of the electroencephalogram. *J. Neurosci.* 13, 3266–3283.

Steriade, M., Timofeev, I., and Grenier, F. (2001). Natural waking and sleep states: a view from inside neocortical neurons. *J. Neurophysiol.* 85, 1969–1985. doi: 10.1152/jn.2001.85.5.1969

Stratmann, M., and Schibler, U. (2006). Properties, entrainment, and physiological functions of mammalian peripheral oscillators. *J. Biol. Rhythms* 21, 494–506. doi: 10.1177/0748730406293889

Suzuki, A., Stern, S. A., Bozdagi, O., Huntley, G. W., Walker, R. H., Magistretti, P. J., et al. (2011). Astrocyte-neuron lactate transport is required for long-term memory formation. *Cell* 144, 810–823. doi: 10.1016/j.cell.2011.02.018

Suzuki, T., Hide, I., Ido, K., Kohsaka, S., Inoue, K., and Nakata, Y. (2004). Production and release of neuroprotective tumor necrosis factor by P2X7 receptor-activated microglia. *J. Neurosci.* 24, 1–7. doi: 10.1523/JNEUROSCI.3792-03.2004

Takeuchi, T., Iwanaga, M., and Harada, E. (2003). Possible regulatory mechanism of DHA-induced anti-stress reaction in rats. *Brain Res.* 964, 136–143. doi: 10.1016/S0006-8993(02)04113-6

Theodosis, D. T., Poulain, D. A., and Olliet, S. H. (2008). Activity-dependent structural and functional plasticity of astrocyte-neuron interactions. *Physiol. Rev.* 88, 983–1008. doi: 10.1152/physrev.00036.2007

Thomson, A. M., Walker, V. E., and Flynn, D. M. (1989). Glycine enhances NMDA-receptor mediated synaptic potentials in neocortical slices. *Nature* 338, 422–424. doi: 10.1038/338422a0

Turrigiano, G. (2011). Too many cooks? Intrinsic and synaptic homeostatic mechanisms in cortical circuit refinement. *Annu. Rev. Neurosci.* 34, 89–103. doi: 10.1146/annurev-neuro-060909-153238

Tzingounis, A. V., and Wadiche, J. I. (2007). Glutamate transporters: confining runaway excitation by shaping synaptic transmission. *Nat. Rev. Neurosci.* 8, 935–947. doi: 10.1038/nrn2274

Valentinuzzi, V. S., Menna-Barreto, L., and Xavier, G. F. (2004). Effect of circadian phase on performance of rats in the Morris water maze task. *J. Biol. Rhythms* 19, 312–324. doi: 10.1177/0748730404265688

Van der Zee, E. A., Havekes, R., Barf, R. P., Hut, R. A., Nijholt, I. M., Jacobs, E. H., et al. (2008). Circadian time-place learning in mice depends on Cry genes. *Curr. Biol.* 18, 844–848. doi: 10.1016/j.cub.2008.04.077

Wainwright, P. E., Xing, H. C., Mutsaers, L., McCutcheon, D., and Kyle, D. (1997). Arachidonic acid offsets the effects on mouse brain and behavior of a diet with a low (n-6):(n-3) ratio and very high levels of docosahexaenoic acid. *J. Nutr.* 127, 184–193.

Walker, M. P., and Stickgold, R. (2006). Sleep, memory, and plasticity. *Annu. Rev. Psychol.* 57, 139–166. doi: 10.1146/annurev.psych.56.091103.070307

Wang, K. C., Koprivica, V., Kim, J. A., Sivasankaran, R., Guo, Y., Neve, R. L., et al. (2002). Oligodendrocyte-myelin glycoprotein is a Nogo receptor ligand that inhibits neurite outgrowth. *Nature* 417, 941–944. doi: 10.1038/nature 00867

Wang, L. M.-C., Dragich, J. M., Kudo, T., Odom, I. H., Welsh, D. K., O'Dell, T. J., et al. (2009). Expression of the circadian clock gene Period2 in the hippocampus: possible implications for synaptic plasticity and learned behaviour. *ASN Neuro* 1:e00012. doi: 10.1042/AN20090020

Winocur, G., and Hasher, L. (2004). Age and time-of-day effects on learning and memory in a non-matching-to-sample test. *Neurobiol. Aging* 25, 1107–1115. doi: 10.1016/j.neurobiolaging.2003.10.005

Womac, A. D., Burkeen, J. F., Neuendorff, N., Earnest, D. J., and Zoran, M. J. (2009). Circadian rhythms of extracellular ATP accumulation in suprachiasmatic nucleus cells and cultured astrocytes. *Eur. J. Neurosci.* 30, 869–876. doi: 10.1111/j.1460-9568.2009.06874.x

Wurtz, C. C., and Ellisman, M. H. (1986). Alterations in the ultrastructure of peripheral nodes of Ranvier associated with repetitive action potential propagation. *J. Neurosci.* 6, 3133–3143.

Yamamoto, N., Saitoh, M., Moriuchi, A., Nomura, M., and Okuyama, H. (1987). Effect of dietary alpha-linolenate/linoleate balance on brain lipid compositions and learning ability of rats. *J. Lipid Res.* 28, 144–151.

Zhong, Y., Zhou, L.-J., Ren, W.-J., Xin, W.-J., Li, Y.-Y., Zhang, T., et al. (2010). The direction of synaptic plasticity mediated by C-fibers in spinal dorsal horn is decided by Src-family kinases in microglia: the role of tumor necrosis factor-α. *Brain Behav. Immun.* 24, 874–880. doi: 10.1016/j.bbi.2010.01.007

6

Diet-Induced Obesity and Circadian Disruption of Feeding Behavior

Aurea Blancas-Velazquez[1,2,3], *Jorge Mendoza*[1], *Alexandra N. Garcia*[2,3] and *Susanne E. la Fleur*[2,3]*

[1] *Institute of Cellular and Integrative Neurosciences, Centre National de la Recherche Scientifique UPR-3212, University of Strasbourg, Strasbourg, France,* [2] *Department of Endocrinology and Metabolism, Academic Medical Center, University of Amsterdam, Amsterdam, Netherlands,* [3] *Metabolism and Reward Group, Netherlands Institute for Neuroscience, Amsterdam, Netherlands*

Edited by:
Sebastien G. Bouret, University of Southern California, USA

Reviewed by:
Gina Leinninger, Michigan State University, USA
Shin Jae Lee, ETH Zurich, Switzerland
Zane B. Andrews, Monash University, Australia
Thierry Alquier, Université de Montréal & CRCHUM, Canada

***Correspondence:**
Susanne E. la Fleur
s.e.lafleur@amc.nl

Feeding behavior shows a rhythmic daily pattern, which in nocturnal rodents is observed mainly during the dark period. This rhythmicity is under the influence of the hypothalamic suprachiasmatic nucleus (SCN), the main biological clock. Nevertheless, various studies have shown that in rodent models of obesity, using high-energy diets, the general locomotor activity and feeding rhythms can be disrupted. Here, we review the data on the effects of diet-induced obesity (DIO) on locomotor activity and feeding patterns, as well as the effect on the brain sites within the neural circuitry involved in metabolic and rewarding feeding behavior. In general, DIO may alter locomotor activity by decreasing total activity. On the other hand, DIO largely alters eating patterns, producing increased overall ingestion and number of eating bouts that can extend to the resting period. Furthermore, within the hypothalamic areas, little effect has been reported on the molecular circadian mechanism in DIO animals with *ad libitum* hypercaloric diets and little or no data exist so far on its effects on the reward system areas. We further discuss the possibility of an uncoupling of metabolic and reward systems in DIO and highlight a gap of circadian and metabolic research that may help to better understand the implications of obesity.

Keywords: circadian, hypothalamus, reward, feeding, obesity, clock-genes, palatable, dopamine

INTRODUCTION

Biological rhythms are the cyclic variations of any biological process of a living organism. Rhythms with a ~24 h duration are called circadian, a word with Latin etymologies that means *circa* (around) and *dies* (day). Circadian rhythms are adaptive to the cyclic environment caused by the rotation of the earth on its own axis, where the most evident variation is the light-dark (LD) cycle, causing the day and night. General locomotor activity and food intake are two of the behavioral outputs of the endogenous circadian system which, in normal feeding and LD conditions, are coupled and synchronized to the activity period of the organism; predominantly during the day in humans and during the night in most rodents (Aschoff, 1981; Silver and LeSauter, 2008). Biological rhythms are not only displayed as a response to the environmental changes but they are inherently paced by a timekeeping system comprised of several organs, tissues, and brain nuclei called oscillators. The rhythmic properties of these oscillators can be observed, for instance, in the electrical activity of the cells, neurotransmitter and molecule synthesis and release, or gene expression. In natural conditions, these oscillators can be entrained by several external or environmental factors (such as the alternance of day-night, food availability, and/or temperature) that set the timing of their functions (Rensing and Ruoff, 2002; Challet, 2010). The main synchronizer or *zeitgeber* (ZT;

a German noun adopted to define a time-giver) is the solar time, which is able to pace the activity/inactivity cycles (in chronobiology ZT0 is used to indicate the start of the light period). Thus, activity cycles are entrained by photic signals that are received by the ganglion cells in the retina and transmitted via the optic tract to the hypothalamic suprachiasmatic nuclei (SCN; Albrecht, 2012). These nuclei, located bilaterally adjacent to the third ventricle and dorsal to the optical chiasm, are considered the main biological clock since its physical or genetic function ablation causes disorganized locomotor activity as well as disrupted eating and drinking rhythmic patterns (Stephan and Zucker, 1972; Albus et al., 2002).

Food ingestion, an essential part of energy balance, is controlled by two main processes in the brain: One that evaluates the quantity of the required energy intake and another that regulates the quality of the food including its hedonic properties (Berthoud and Morrison, 2008). The first system, in charge of the energy balance, resides in the hypothalamus, a central area that receives and sends information from and to the peripheral organs via neuronal and hormonal signals (Schwartz et al., 2000; Lenard and Berthoud, 2009). Whereas, the reward-limbic system processes the characteristics and quality of the food, reinforcing the preference for palatable/rewarding items, which in general contain high levels of sugar and/or fat (Avena et al., 2012). Nowadays, people have a large choice of food items, due to the relatively easy access to ultra-processed food. The exposure to food-enriched environment, together with social variables like education and socioeconomical status, determine the food choice made by an individual (Drewnowski and Specter, 2004). The obesity epidemic and the concomitant metabolic diseases are thus, partly caused by the overexposure to palatable food choices (Juul and Hemmingsson, 2015; Louzada et al., 2015). But the caloric consumption beyond homeostatic need does not fit into the energy homeostasis model. One hypothesis is that the exposure to an enriched food environment stimulates our visual, olfactory and gustatory senses, overriding the energy-balance system by means of over excitation of the reward system (Zheng et al., 2009). In obese humans, behavioral changes such as an increase in depressive symptoms and disruption of sleep patterns indicates a close relationship between the reward and circadian systems (Kudlow et al., 2013; Ulrich-lai et al., 2016). Moreover, the relationship between food intake and the circadian system is observed in people that are night-workers who are forced to change their normal activity rhythms which is associated with increased risk to develop obesity and metabolic diseases (Peplonska et al., 2015). Another situation that links circadian rhythms and food intake is the night eating syndrome in which people binge on food during the normal resting period consuming a big amount of calories coming from hypercaloric palatable foods (Gallant et al., 2012).

This review focuses on the data available from mice and rat models aiming to determine the effects of hyper caloric diets on the daily rhythms of locomotor activity and feeding behavior. Furthermore, we describe the current evidence how hyper caloric diets affect circadian properties of the homeostatic and reward systems.

CYCLES OF THE HOMEOSTATIC HYPOTHALAMIC CLOCK(S)

The hypothalamus is a brain center that integrates internal and external signals to produce vital behaviors such as eating. Within this region, several nuclei important for homeostatic regulation have been identified, including the SCN, the hypothalamic arcuate nuclei (ARC), ventromedial and dorsomedial hypothalamic nuclei (VMH and DMH), paraventricular nuclei (PVN), and lateral hypothalamic area (LH) (Schwartz et al., 2000; Gonnissen et al., 2013). These nuclei contain different cell populations that synthesize and release neuropeptides and neurotransmitters that are important for regulating food intake. Given the vital function of food ingestion, it is not surprising that redundant systems exist within the hypothalamus to ensure this important behavior continues. The presence of several orexigenic molecules in different areas such as neuropeptide Y (NPY) and agouti related peptide (AgRP) in the ARC and the melanin-concentrating hormone (MCH) and the hypocretines/orexin in the LH are evidence of the complex regulation of feeding. In the ARC two anorexigenic peptides pro-opiomelanocortins (POMC) and cocaine and amphetamine regulated transcript (CART) produce signals of satiety (Schwartz et al., 2000). The decrease of circulating glucose and nutrients as well as other hunger signals such as an empty stomach are sensed and processed by the brain to trigger feeding behavior (Berthoud and Morrison, 2008). In conditions where the organism ingests a nutritionally balanced diet (i.e., a laboratory chow diet) feeding behavior is arranged in a temporal manner, which is coupled with the activity period. Although the SCN is considered to be the main biological clock, there are also several organs and brain areas containing oscillatory properties and thus, they are known as peripheral circadian oscillators (Albrecht, 2012). In normal healthy conditions, these peripheral oscillators show different rhythmic features such as a variation in electrical activity, neurotransmitter release, and/or gene expression.

Neuronal Activity

The SCN cells show clear rhythmic electrical activity. In brain slices of hamsters, rats, and mice, electrophysiological experiments have revealed a rhythmic firing rate with higher levels during the light period (Gillette and Reppert, 1987; Shibata and Moore, 1988; Albus et al., 2002). Similarly, the ARC shows clear circadian firing rate even in the absence of the SCN input as evidenced with *ex-vivo* slice preparations (Guilding et al., 2009). In the DMH, although circadian rhythms are present, the amplitude of the oscillations is decreased and dampens faster than those observed in the ARC, whereas the VMH has no clear oscillation after tissue culture (Guilding et al., 2009). Nevertheless, another study in rats, recorded the electrical activity of the VMH *in-vivo,* finding a rhythmic activity with an acrophase (highest activity around the 24 h) in the dark period. Moreover, when the SCN was lesioned, the *in-vivo* rhythmicity of the VMH was blunted (Inouye, 1983). The fact that some nuclei show self-sustained rhythms (although in a lesser extent compared to the SCN), and some others are not able to oscillate in the absence of SCN signals is evidence of the hierarchic nature of the circadian system.

Diurnal Variation of Neurotransmitter Levels

Neuropeptides and neurotransmitters within the hypothalamus also show circadian rhythmicity. These oscillations can be observed in neuropeptides such as NPY, which has receptors located within hypothalamic nuclei, forebrain and cortex (Keen-rhinehart et al., 2010; Kash et al., 2015). In rats, the expression of both NPY and its receptor Y1R in the ARC and PVN are higher during the active period (Cohen et al., 2015). Interestingly, the NPY and its Y1R receptor were detected in the hippocampus and the basolateral amygdala but no clear day and night difference was observed (Cohen et al., 2015). In mice, gene expression of the AgRP, NPY (Stütz et al., 2007) and orexin (Stütz et al., 2007; Opperhuizen et al., 2016), molecules that increase appetite and decrease metabolism and energy expenditure, exhibit diurnal variation. Moreover, a clear time difference was also seen for MCH and the leptin receptor but not in the levels of POMC or CART (Stütz et al., 2007). A study using immunohistochemistry reported no day-night variation of orexin peptide in the hypothalamus of mice, however, c-fos co-localization with ORX cells was higher during the active period (Marston et al., 2008). Taken together, the evidence suggests that not all hypothalamic molecules implicated in the regulation of feeding and energy balance have the ability to oscillate. The contribution of a single variable in rhythmic behavior was assessed by interfereing with the function of the NPY receptor in the mediobasal hypothalamus. The ablation of NPY signaling in this hypothalamic area produced disturbed sleeping and feeding patterns; i.e., rats increased feeding during the light period (Wiater et al., 2011). Another approach was the use of viral gene transfer to overexpress NPY peptide in the LH and PVN. The overexpression of NPY in the LH but not in the PVN resulted in a reduced amplitude of locomotor activity and disruption of the diurnal eating pattern (Tiesjema et al., 2007). Thus, some alterations can be observed when the NPY rhythmicity is disturbed by constantly suppressing or over-expressing NPY. These studies demonstrate that disrupting the rhythm of one single molecule already disrupt a circadian behavioral rhythm. Further investigation is needed to understand why some molecules have a circadian variation and what implications these oscillations have on physiology.

Rhythmic Clock-Gene Expression

The molecular gene machinery can be observed in cells throughout the body and is comprised of several molecules that generate rhythms of transduction/translation with a ~24 h duration. In this oscillating mechanism *Bmal1* and *Clock* genes form part of the positive loop, which promotes the transcription of the Period (Per 1–3) and Cryptochrome (Cry 1–2) genes. The latter genes form the negative loop components, which in turn suppresses the activity of *Bmal1* and *Clock* dimer (Takahashi, 2015). These genes and their products are relevant molecules for building the circadian variations in physiology and behavior. *Per1* and *Per2* clock-proteins have been evaluated with immunohistochemistry in both the rat and mouse hypothalami at different time points of the day. A daily rhythmic expression of these proteins is found in the ARC, DMH, and VMH with higher levels at night (Verwey et al., 2007; Feillet et al., 2008). Another way of analyzing PER2 expression is with the *ex-vivo* bioluminescence technique, where the PER2 protein is coupled to a luciferase reporter, which allows the measurement of the photon emission produced when PER2 protein is expressed. Using this method, PER2 in the ARC and DMH of animals kept in light/dark (LD) and dark/dark (DD) conditions has been shown to oscillate even when these nuclei are isolated from the rest of the brain (Guilding et al., 2009; Hughes et al., 2011). Similar results have been found for PER1 bioluminescence in the PVN and LH with the acrophase during the night time (Abe et al., 2002). This technique has made it possible to describe rhythmic properties of clock-genes and their proteins in different brain areas. Moreover, the rhythm in the SCN is stronger than those of the peripheral oscillators which, when isolated, show lower amplitude and their oscillations dampen with a faster rate (Abe et al., 2002). As for the rhythmic expression of clock genes, the electrical activity varies in intensity depending on the brain nuclei (Guilding et al., 2009), but its functionality is not fully understood. Several experiments have demonstrated that the complete knockdown of clock-genes in the body alters physiology and behavior. For instance, the mutation of the *clock* gene includes loss of normal locomotor activity patterns as well as metabolic alterations and obesity (Rudic et al., 2004; Turek et al., 2005). The knockout of systemic *Per2* produces a phenotype that displays disrupted rhythmicity of locomotor activity in constant darkness (DD) conditions, as well as lower body weight and disrupted lipid metabolism (Zheng et al., 1999; Grimaldi et al., 2010). Although there is a large body of evidence that links the clock gene function to metabolic physiology, the implications of the rhythmic clock-gene expression within the different areas of the hypothalamus are still unclear. An attempt to determine the effect of a single clock-gene in a specific area was made within the hypothalamic tuberomammilar nucleus (TMN), an area that integrates inputs from the circadian and the sensory stimuli to modulate locomotion and arousal (Torrealba et al., 2012). When *Bmal1* is knocked down from the histaminergic cells in the TMN of mice their normal rhythmic levels of histamine are lost and they display fragmented sleep no changes in overall locomotor activity (Yu et al., 2014). This highlights the important role a single clock-gene can play in specific brain areas and functions. These findings lead to generate questions about which functions are controlled by each clock-gene in different brain areas.

THE CYCLES OF THE REWARD SYSTEM

The reward system comprises several nuclei as well as different neurotransmitters, with the mesolimbic dopaminergic pathway playing a central role. This circuit includes the ventral tegmental area (VTA), a nucleus containing dopaminergic cells that projects to the nucleus accumbens (NAc) and the cortex (Koob and Volkow, 2010). Other nuclei that send projections to the NAc are the amygdala and hippocampus, which are involved in the regulation of emotion and memory consolidation (Sesack and Grace, 2010). The bed nucleus of the stria terminalis (BNST) is known to densely project to the amygdala and is considered part of the extended amygdala, where the corticotropin-releasing factor, a neuropeptide involved in stress response, is a key signal (Kash et al., 2015; Daniel and Rainnie, 2016). The septum forms part of the limbic system, where it receives dopaminergic projections from the VTA and regulates affective behaviors (Mogenson et al., 1980; Sokolowski and Corbin, 2012). Beyond the classical mesolimbic dopaminergic circuitry, other structures integrate the wiring of the reward process such as the lateral hypothalamus (LH) and the habenula. The LH is part of the feeding behavior neurocircuitry and it is anatomically connected to the dopaminergic system which regulates motivation and arousal (Harris et al., 2005; Berthoud and Münzberg, 2011; Stuber and Wise, 2016). The habenula is an epithalamic area that can be divided into different sub regions: the medial and lateral part. The medial habenula (MHb) receives inhibitory and excitatory projections from the septum (Qin and Luo, 2009). The lateral habenula (LHb) sends excitatory glutamatergic projections to the tail of the VTA (Matsumoto and Hikosaka, 2007; Bianco and Wilson, 2009). Thus, the LHb is able to modulate dopamine release and it is involved in the processing of the reward-prediction error and negative motivational states (Proulx et al., 2014; Salaberry and Mendoza, 2016). The reward system is known to regulate the appetitive state of the organism by influencing the approach and intake of food. Recently, the function of the LH and the LHb have been shown to communicate and to modulate the control of motivational feeding (Stamatakis et al., 2016). Areas of the reward system have different cyclic properties that can be observed in neuronal activity, neurotransmitter release and gene expression.

Neuronal Activity

By using the neuronal activity marker c-fos, an immediate early gene, Baltazar et al. (2013) found that there is a day-night rhythm of neuronal activity in the rat PFC, NAc, and VTA, with higher levels during the night (Baltazar et al., 2013). A diurnal variation of c-Fos has also been observed in the LH and LHb, with the LH having higher levels during the night in mice (Marston et al., 2008) and the LHb during the daytime around ZT6 in rats (Chastrette et al., 1991; Xu et al., 2015). However, other studies have found in hamsters and also in mice higher levels of c-fos during the night time (2 h after lights off), compared to day time (2 h before lights off; Tavakoli-Nezhad, 2005; Tavakoli-Nezhad and Schwartz, 2006). The different results found for c-fos could be due to species differences and/or the time point of when the c-fos was evaluated. Despite these discrepancies, the findings point to the existence of rhythmic c-fos expression in the LHb. Another piece of evidence of direct neuronal activity comes from experiments using cellular multi-unit recordings, where a cyclic variation of electrical activity in the NAc and medial septum of hamsters has been measured *in-vivo* (Yamazaki et al., 1998). This observation has also been reported *in vitro* with LHb cells of mice, where the firing rate was found to peak during the latter part of the light period (Sakhi et al., 2014). In rats this activity has been evaluated in *in vivo* and *in vitro* with both showing the highest activity around ZT6 (Zhao and Rusak, 2005).

Diurnal Variation of Neurotransmitter Levels

As stated previously, the neuronal activity can vary throughout the day, and this oscillation might be reflected in the cyclic functions of other variables like the neurotransmitter production and/or release. Dopamine (DA), adrenaline, and noradrenaline (NA) are part of the catecholamine family of neurotransmitters in which tyrosine hydroxylase (TH) is the precursor of all (Squire et al., 2008). The dopaminergic system is highly oscillating, in mice higher levels of TH mRNA production in the VTA have been shown during the early resting period (Chung et al., 2014). Similar results have been found in rats, with higher protein expression of TH at ZT6, during the light period (Webb et al., 2009). Furthermore, not only the production, but also the release of DA is highly rhythmic during the LD cycle, within the dorsal striatum (DS) of rats (Smith et al., 1992; Paulson and Robinson, 1994; Ferris et al., 2014) as well as ventral striatum of rats and mice (Castañeda et al., 2004; Hampp et al., 2008; Hood et al., 2010). The endogenous rhythmicity of DA release in the NAc has also been observed in DD conditions where higher levels are observed during the active period of rats (Castañeda et al., 2004). The rhythmic dopaminergic activity in the mesolimbic system has been reviewed previously by Webb et al. (2015). The rhythmicity of adrenaline and NA, implicated in the activation of the fight or flight behavior in response to a threatening situation (Squire et al., 2008) has also been studied. Measured from the blood of human adults, a clear rhythmic pattern is present, showing the highest levels during the active period (Scheer et al., 2009).

Serotonin (5-HT) is another important neurotransmitter within the reward system, which is produced in the raphe nuclei and projects throughout the brain. It is involved in the regulation of mood, food intake, and circadian rhythms (Versteeg et al., 2015). The levels of 5-HT and its main metabolite, 5-HIAA, have been measured during different time points. Interestingly, when measuring 5-HIAA with microdialysis in the DS and NAc of rats there is a rhythm, which is synchronized to the LD cycle where the highest levels are observed during the night. Nevertheless, when the light condition is changed to constant light (LL), the rhythms of 5-HT and 5-HIAA in both DS and NAc are ablated whereas in the DD condition the rhythm is still present in the NAc but not in the DS (Castañeda et al., 2004). A different report on the diurnal levels of 5-HT assessed the variations in rats at six different time points but found no diurnal variation of this neurotransmitter in the anterior hypothalamus or the cortex (Cagampang et al., 1993). Nevertheless, studies using microdialysis to measure 5-HT levels in the SCN of rats (Cagampang et al., 1993) and hamsters (Dudley et al., 1998) have shown that there is clear rhythmicity though there are some differences between species. Rats show higher levels during the light period whereas levels are higher during the dark period in hamsters. Despite species differences, the results point toward a rhythmic function of 5-HT that varies across brain regions.

Rhythmic Clock-Gene Expression

The rhythmic variation of the function and activation of the reward system can also be extended to clock-genes, which are widely expressed in these areas. In the mesolimbic system including the NAc, the PFC, DS, BNST, and amygdala the genes *Per 1–3*, *Clock*, and *Npas2* oscillate in a circadian manner (Harbour et al., 2013; Webb et al., 2015). The habenula, which regulates mesolimbic dopaminergic release, also shows daily variations of the *Per2* gene and protein (Zhao et al., 2015). But when the BNST, NAc and VTA are isolated and cultured for *ex-vivo* bioluminescence recordings, no rhythmicity of PER1 is observed (Abe et al., 2002). Recently, a study assessing *ex-vivo* bioluminescence showed rhythmicity of PER2 in NAc cells (Logan et al., 2015), which differs from the findings for PER1. This may indicate that different molecules from the molecular clock-machinery might persist more than others, and thus be a stronger molecular timekeeper. Using the same technique, it has been shown that in the habenula PER2 also displays robust oscillations (Guilding et al., 2010). Taken together these results indicate that the reward system has several parameters that are able to oscillate, but further research is needed to understand the physiological repercussions of these diurnal and circadian variations. The circadian function of the reward system might be altered by external factors that stimulate and modify its function. One of these possible factors is food intake, especially the ingestion of highly rewarding food that facilitates the development of obesity.

INFLUENCE OF HIGHLY CALORIC INTAKE ON THE CIRCADIAN SYSTEM OUTPUT

Locomotor Activity

Feeding is generally coupled to the period of arousal and (locomotor) activity. In mice and rats, the highest locomotor activity is performed at night, although some bouts of activity are also present during the day-time. This activity pattern is observed when the animals are under normo-caloric feeding conditions. However, when rats and mice are offered a high caloric diet, the normal rhythm of locomotor activity is altered showing an overall decrease in the amount of activity during the night (Mendoza et al., 2008; Sherman et al., 2012; Pendergast et al., 2013; Sun et al., 2015). Moreover, some studies in mice have found that the activity during the daytime is also disrupted, generating spares activity throughout the light period resulting in a-rhythmic activity (Pendergast et al., 2013; Branecky et al., 2015). Nevertheless, these alterations are not observed through all the studies using a highly caloric diet (**Table 1**). Kosaka et al., didn't find differences in the amount of activity during the day on high-fat fed vs. normal chow-fed mice under LD conditions, but the behavioral recordings (actograms) resembles the disrupted behavior reported by Pendergast et al. (2013), Kohsaka et al. (2007). In DD conditions mice fed a hyper caloric diet increased the length of their activity period compared to the normo-caloric fed mice during the first week of diet exposure (Kohsaka et al., 2007; Mendoza et al., 2008). In addition to the locomotor activity changes, similar disturbances have been observed in sleep-wake physiology recorded in mice and rats. The electroencephalogram of the animals fed with a high-fat diet showed decreased awake time as well as wake fragmentation and more rapid eye movement (REM) and non-REM sleep episodes (Jenkins et al., 2006; Guan et al., 2008; Luppi et al., 2014). This highlights that, when they are present, the effects of the diet content on general activity might evolve together with changes in sleep patterns. Data presented in this section reflect the influence of the ingestion of a high-fat diet in a pellet over the disruption of the locomotor activity. However, high caloric diets that are not only high in fat but also offer free access to sugar did not clearly find an effect on general locomotion (la Fleur et al., 2007; Oosterman et al., 2015) suggesting that not only the highly caloric content but the quality of food influences the changes observed in behavior.

Eating Patterns

When rats and mice are fed with a highly-caloric diet, some disturbances can be observed in the locomotor activity, as reviewed in the previous section. Nevertheless, the main behavioral output that is largely affected by hypercaloric consumption is the feeding behavior. The first observation is a clear over ingestion of calories and secondly, a development of a fragmented feeding pattern where rats and mice fed with a single high-fat pellet eat in small but frequent bouts instead of consolidated large meals (Kohsaka et al., 2007; Pendergast et al., 2013; Branecky et al., 2015; Mifune et al., 2015). This eating pattern resembles human snacking behavior where the caloric intake does not only rely on the three meals but in the consumption of several snacks spared in the day and night-time. Because the food intake of animals with normo caloric regimen is rhythmic and well consolidated to the active period, a snacking pattern that extends to the normal resting period might reflect an alteration in circadian rhythmicity. Moreover, this snacking pattern might be influenced by the rewarding properties of the hyper caloric foods as shown by experimental models where the rats were able to choose among different food items. In a model of free choice High-Fat High-Sugar, the rats are free to eat their most preferred food among: chow food, a dish with fat, a bottle of water and a bottle of sugar offered *ad libitum*. As expected, the animals display an overall increased caloric consumption but interestingly, the snacking behavior is mainly observed from the bottle of sugar (la Fleur et al., 2014; Oosterman et al., 2015). In another experiment with food choices, two groups of rats were given access to normal chow food, together with either canola oil (low in saturated fatty acids) or butter (high saturated fatty acids). Although both groups developed a snacking pattern, the diurnal disruption was more evident in the group fed with butter (Hariri and Thibault, 2011). These are interesting observations since the rats with free food choices barely alter their day-night consumption of chow food, a fact that might indicate that the alteration in the rhythmic feeding is influenced by the palatability of food.

TABLE 1 | Effects of *ad libitum* highly caloric diets on rhythmic behavioral outputs and clock gene expression.

References	Locomotor activity	Eating patterns	Clock genes	Diet	Species
Branecky et al., 2015	>Amplitude	<Amplitude	*Ex-vivo* bioluminiscence Liver PER2 phase advanced	Pellet 45% kcal from fat	Male mice C57BL/6J::LUC
Sherman et al., 2012	Overall decrease	NR	qPCR Liver disrupted *Clock*, *Bmal1*, *Per2*, *Cry1*, *Cry2*	Pellet 42% kcal from fat	Male mice C57BL/6J
Sun et al., 2015	Overall decrease	NR	qPCR Liver *Clock*, *Bmal1* and *Per2* lost rhythm	Pellet 45% kcal from fat	Male mice C57BL/6J
Pendergast et al., 2013	Not a clear effect	<Feeding during day	PER2::Luc in the ARC complex. No change	45% kcal from fat	Male mice C57BL/6J::LUC
Mendoza et al., 2008	>Wheel running at night	NR	NR	53% kcal from fat	Male mice C57BL/6J
Kohsaka et al., 2007	No differences	<Feeding at day>Feeding at night	*Clock*, *Bmal1* and *Per2* qPCR, Hypothalamus No change. Fat tissue and liver > amplitude	45% kcal from fat	Male mice C57BL/6J
Guan et al., 2008	>Wake <Non REM sleep	NR	NR	59.3% kcal from fat	Male mice C57BL/6J
Jenkins et al., 2006	>Wakefulness and <NREMS	NR	NR	59.3% kcal from fat	Male mice C57BL/6J
Luppi et al., 2014	<REM and nREM sleep	NR	NR	35% fat	Male rat sprague-dawley
Oosterman et al., 2015	No differences	NR	NR	Fat and sugar choice. Average: 30.1% from fat 33.4% from sucrose	Male rat wistar
la Fleur et al., 2007	No change	NR	NR	37.4% from fat 14.8 from sucrose	Male rat wistar
Mifune et al., 2015	>Amplitude	<Kcal during day compared to chow fed group	NR	60% kcal from fat	Male rat sprague-dawly
Hariri and Thibault, 2011	NR	<Feeding at day specially from butter based pellet	NR	Pellet 65% kcal from either cannola oil or butter	Female rat sprague-dawley
Cunningham et al., 2016	>During night	>Meal events during the night	Hypothalamus qPCR in whole hypothalamic punches no effect >BMAL1 in DIO mice under DD	Pellet 60% kcal from fat, 16w	Male Mice C57BL/6J, Mice C57BL/6J::LUC
Wong et al., 2015	>At day and night with the corn oil enriched	NR	NR	40% kcal from fat in olive and corn oil enriched pellets	Female mice C57/Bl6
Jang et al., 2012	NR	<Feeding at day > Feeding at night	*Bmal1*, *Per2* and *Clock* in hypothalamus. No change	Pelllet 60% kcal from fat	Male mice C57BL/6N

NR, not reported.

Effects of Hyper Caloric Diets on Rhythmic Activity of the Homeostatic Neural System

When the body is challenged with a hyper caloric diet, fat stores rapidly increase, affecting the levels of circulating hormones such as leptin and corticosterone already within the first days on the diet (Buettner et al., 2007; Cano et al., 2008; la Fleur et al., 2010). Both leptin and corticosterone show diurnal rhythmity and have been described to be altered by high fat diets, mainly influencing the amplitude of the rhythm (Cha et al., 2000; Cano et al., 2008). Within the brain, NPY, 5-HT and DA are rhythmic-expressing molecules that are also affected in the obese state (Pritchet and Hajnal, 2011; Koopman et al., 2013; Gumbs et al., 2015). At the level of the clock gene expression, the hyper caloric diet largely alters clock gene expression in peripheral organs such as the liver and adipose tissue with varying effects depending on the energy content of the diet, the age and species of the animals used in the studies as well as the duration of the diet (Pendergast et al., 2013; Branecky et al., 2015; Wong et al., 2015; Cunningham et al., 2016). With regard to rhythmic expression of neuropeptides and clock-genes in the brain only few studies have focused on the effects of a diet-induced obesity (DIO). In mice, *Bmal1*, *Per2* and *Clock* gene expression have been assessed using qPCR in animals fed a normo-caloric and a hyper caloric diet, no differences were found within the hypothalamic area (Kohsaka et al., 2007; Jang et al., 2012). Moreover, PER2, expression, measured with *ex-vivo* bioluminescence, was not changed in the arcuate complex of mice fed with a hypocaloric diet vs. chow diet (Pendergast et al., 2013). When the hypothalamic structures were separately evaluated for *Per2* gene expression using qPCR, the high-fat diet did not exert an effect on the ARC or the DMH in DD conditions. A separate study showed, using *in situ* hybridization, decreased amplitude in expression of *Bmal1* in the SCN of DIO mice under DD conditions (Cunningham et al., 2016). In peripheral tissues such as the liver, remarkable changes caused by DIO can be observed in the clock gene expression. These changes include a PER2 phase advance in the liver of mice DIO mice, evidenced by bioluminescence (Branecky et al., 2015). Other changes include the blunted rhythmicity of Per2, Bmal1 and *clock* mRNA in the liver (Kohsaka et al., 2007; Sun et al., 2015) and white adipose tissue (Kohsaka et al., 2007). Taken together, the main findings are that the peripheral organ and peripheral circulating hormones are largely altered by a hypercaloric diet and obesity, but little to no effects of hyper caloric diets offered *ad libitum* are found on the hypothalamic clock-gene expression. One possibility is that the DIO state could be generating an uncoupling of hypothalamic and peripheral organ oscillators.

Effects of the Hyper Caloric Diets on Rhythmic Parameters in the Reward System

The exposure to a highly caloric diet can change locomotor activity and feeding patterns, but little is known about the clock gene expression in the reward related areas during a diet-induced obese state. So far, no studies have focused on the effects of an *ad libitum* hyper caloric diet on the clock-gene expression or other oscillatory properties of the reward system. Nevertheless, the influence of the pleasurable food on the behavioral rhythmic outputs has been evidenced with different experimental paradigms. During a palatable scheduled feeding experiments, a palatable treat is given daily at the same time during several days to animals fed with regular chow *ad libitum*. In this way, the rewarding properties of the food are dissociated from the metabolic needs. The behavioral outcomes from these studies done in both mice and rats, show that animals can entrain their behavior, developing an anticipatory general activity previous to the food (Mendoza et al., 2005; Angeles-Castellanos, 2008; Hsu et al., 2010; Gallardo et al., 2012; Merkestein et al., 2012). During this palatable food anticipation, the NAc, PFC and LH showed an increase in *Per1* (Angeles-Castellanos, 2008). In a similar study, *Per2* was unchanged in the BNST and amygdala of rats (Verwey et al., 2007), suggesting that the effects of palatable food under a scheduled feeding regimen depend on the clock-gene and brain area. The experiments discussed in this section used a palatable treat, given daily in a small amount that did not result in body weight gain and thus conclusions can only be drawn about palatable intake effects on the rhythmic

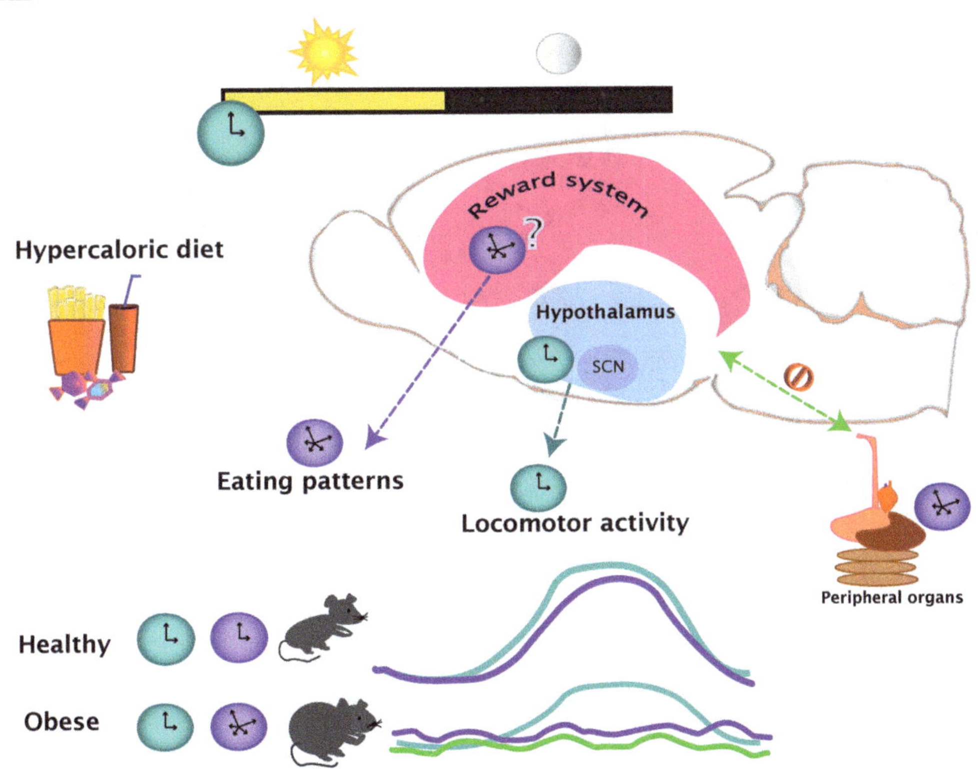

FIGURE 1 | The day-night cycles set the regular oscillations of eating (purple line) and locomotor activity (blue line), which are coupled during a healthy state. Intake of hypercaloric diets, leading in obesity, disrupts the eating daily patterns, producing small but frequent bouts of ingestion even during the normal resting period. The locomotor activity and eating pattern rhythms are uncoupled in an obese state. The effects of a hypercaloric diet over the rhythmicity of the reward system are unknown but as the evidence suggest that the rhythmicity in the hypothalamus is mainly unaffected (blue dotted line), the reward system might be influencing the disturbances of the daily eating patterns (purple dotted line). In the diet-induced obese state, the rhythmicity of the peripheral organs are altered (green line), causing an internal desynchrony of central and peripheral oscillators (green dotted line).

clock-gene expression in the reward system and not about DIO effects.

CONCLUSION

The effects of obesity in general physiology have been widely studied and a large amount of knowledge has been gathered about the changes within the brain produced by hyper caloric diets. Nevertheless, the changes in circadian outputs like locomotor activity and eating patterns are not reported in most of these studies. From the studies discussed in the present review, it appears that the access to a hyper caloric regime does not alter general locomotor activity to the same extent as the food intake rhythmicity. One possibility for this might be that the rhythmic locomotor output is more resistant to change due to the lack of effects in the SCN and in other hypothalamic areas, while the eating patterns guided by the food palatability might be changing together with the changes in the brain reward system (**Figure 1**). No conclusion can be drawn at this point due to the fact that the effects of a hyper caloric diet on the rhythmic brain parameters is inconclusive for the hypothalamus and non-existent for the nuclei from the reward system. At level of the brain, studies are region and system-specific, and therefore, the findings might differ due to varying methodological approaches. Nevertheless, a study looking at the broad spectrum of metabolomics and genomics supports the observations of altered gene expression in obesity (Eckel-Mahan et al., 2013). Showing how the relationship of the reward and metabolic systems integrate and intercommunicate with circadian function might be a step to gaining a better understand of the causes and consequences of obesity.

AUTHOR CONTRIBUTIONS

AB, JM, and Sl structured, designed, and wrote the content of the review. AG revised the content and edited the writing of the work.

REFERENCES

Abe, M., Herzog, E. D., Yamazaki, S., Straume, M., Tei, H., Sakaki, Y., et al. (2002). Circadian rhythms in isolated brain regions. *J. Neurosci.* 22, 350–356.

Albrecht, U. (2012). Timing to perfection: the biology of central and peripheral circadian clocks. *Neuron* 74, 246–260. doi: 10.1016/j.neuron.2012.04.006

Albus, H., Bonnefont, X., Chaves, I., Yasui, A., Doczy, J., van der Horst, G. T. J., et al. (2002). Cryptochrome-deficient mice lack circadian electrical activity in the suprachiasmatic nuclei. *Curr. Biol.* 12, 1130–1133. doi: 10.1016/S0960-9822(02)00923-5

Angeles-Castellanos, M. (2008). Expectancy for food or expectancy for chocolate reveals timing systems for metabolism and reward. *Neuroscience* 155, 297–307. doi: 10.1016/j.neuroscience.2008.06.001

Aschoff, J. (1981). "A survey on biological rhythms," in *Biological Rhythms*, ed J. Aschoff (New York, NY: Plenum Press), 3–10. doi: 10.1007/978-1-4615-6552-9_1

Avena, N. M., Bocarsly, M. E., and Hoebel, B. G. (2012). "Animal models of sugar and fat bingeing: relationship to food addiction and increased body weight," in *Psychiatric Disorders: Methods and Protocols, Methods in Molecular Biology*, ed F. H. Kobeissy (Totowa, NJ: Humana Press), 351–365.

Baltazar, R. M., Coolen, L. M., and Webb, I. C. (2013). Diurnal rhythms in neural activation in the mesolimbic reward system: critical role of the medial prefrontal cortex. *Eur. J. Neurosci.* 38, 2319–2327. doi: 10.1111/ejn.12224

Berthoud, H.-R., and Morrison, C. (2008). The brain, appetite, and obesity. *Annu. Rev. Psychol.* 59, 55–92. doi: 10.1146/annurev.psych.59.103006.093551

Berthoud, H.-R., and Münzberg, H. (2011). The lateral hypothalamus as integrator of metabolic and environmental needs: from electrical self-stimulation to opto-genetics. *Physiol. Behav.* 104, 29–39. doi: 10.1016/j.physbeh.2011.04.051

Bianco, I. H., and Wilson, S. W. (2009). The habenular nuclei: a conserved asymmetric relay station in the vertebrate brain. *Philos. Trans. R. Soc. B Biol. Sci.* 364, 1005–1020. doi: 10.1098/rstb.2008.0213

Branecky, K. L., Niswender, K. D., and Pendergast, J. S. (2015). Disruption of daily rhythms by high-fat diet is reversible. *PLoS ONE* 10:e0137970. doi: 10.1371/journal.pone.0137970

Buettner, R., Schölmerich, J., and Bollheimer, L. C. (2007). High-fat diets: modeling the metabolic disorders of human obesity in rodents. *Obesity* 15, 798–808. doi: 10.1038/oby.2007.608

Cagampang, F. R. A., Yamazaki, S., Otori, Y., and Inouye, S. I. T. (1993). Serotonin in the raphe nuclei–regulation by light and an endogenous pacemaker. *Neuroreport* 5, 49–52. doi: 10.1097/00001756-199310000-00012

Cano, P., Jiménez-Ortega, V., Larrad, Á., Toso, C. F. R., Cardinali, D. P., and Esquifino, A. I. (2008). Effect of a high-fat diet on 24-h pattern of circulating levels of prolactin, luteinizing hormone, testosterone, corticosterone, thyroid-stimulating hormone and glucose, and pineal melatonin content, in rats. *Endocrine* 33, 118–125. doi: 10.1007/s12020-008-9066-x

Castañeda, T. R., de Prado, B. M., Prieto, D., and Mora, F. (2004). Circadian rhythms of dopamine, glutamate and GABA in the striatum and nucleus accumbens of the awake rat: modulation by light. *J. Pineal. Res.* 36, 177–185. doi: 10.1046/j.1600-079X.2003.00114.x

Cha, M. C., Chou, C. J., and Boozer, C. N. (2000). High-fat diet feeding reduces the diurnal variation of plasma leptin concentration in rats. *Metabolism* 49, 503–507. doi: 10.1016/S0026-0495(00)80016-5

Challet, E. (2010). Interactions between light, mealtime and calorie restriction to control daily timing in mammals. *J. Comp. Physiol. B* 180, 631–644. doi: 10.1007/s00360-010-0451-4

Chastrette, N., Pfaff, D. W., and Gibbs R. B. (1991). Effects of daytime and nighttime stress on Fos-like immunoreactivity in the paraventricular nucleus of the hypothalamus, the habenula, and the posterior paraventricular nucleus of the thalamus. *Brain Res.* 563, 339–344. doi: 10.1016/0006-8993(91)91559-J

Chung, S., Lee, E. J., Yun, S., Choe, H. K., Park, S. B., Son, H. J., et al. (2014). Impact of circadian nuclear receptor REV-ERB? on midbrain dopamine production and mood regulation. *Cell* 157, 858–868. doi: 10.1016/j.cell.2014.03.039

Cohen, S., Vainer, E., Matar, M. A., Kozlovsky, N., Kaplan, Z., Zohar, J., et al. (2015). Diurnal fluctuations in HPA and neuropeptide Y-ergic systems underlie differences in vulnerability to traumatic stress responses at different zeitgeber times. *Neuropsychopharmacology* 40, 774–790. doi: 10.1038/npp.2014.257

Cunningham, P. S., Ahern, S. A., Smith, L. C., Carla, S., Santos, S., Wager, T. T., et al. (2016). Targeting of the circadian clock via CK1δ/ε to improve glucose homeostasis in obesity. *Nat. Publ. Gr.* 6:29983. doi: 10.1038/srep29983

Daniel, S. E., and Rainnie, D. G. (2016). Stress modulation of opposing circuits in the bed nucleus of the stria terminalis. *Neuropsychopharmacology* 41, 103–125. doi: 10.1038/npp.2015.178

Drewnowski, A. and Specter, S. E. (2004). Poverty and obesity: the role of energy density and energy costs. *Am. J. Clin. Nutr.* 79, 6–16.

Dudley, T. E., DiNardo, L. A., and Glass, J. D. (1998). Endogenous regulation of serotonin release in the hamster suprachiasmatic nucleus. *J. Neurosci.* 18, 5045–5052.

Eckel-Mahan, K. L., Patel, V. R., De Mateo, S., Orozco-Solis, R., Ceglia, N. J., Sahar, S., et al. (2013). Reprogramming of the circadian clock by nutritional challenge. *Cell* 155, 1464–1478. doi: 10.1016/j.cell.2013.11.034

Feillet, C. A., Mendoza, J., Albrecht, U., Pévet, P., and Challet, E. (2008). Forebrain oscillators ticking with different clock hands. *Mol. Cell. Neurosci.* 37, 209–221. doi: 10.1016/j.mcn.2007.09.010

Ferris, M. J., España, R. A., Locke, J. L., Konstantopoulos, J. K., Rose, J. H., Chen, R., et al. (2014). Dopamine transporters govern diurnal variation in extracellular dopamine tone. *Proc. Natl. Acad. Sci. U.S.A.* 111, E2751–E2759. doi: 10.1073/pnas.1407935111

Gallant, A. R., Lundgren, J., and Drapeau, V. (2012). The night-eating syndrome and obesity. *Obes. Rev.* 13, 528–536. doi: 10.1111/j.1467-789X.2011.00975.x

Gallardo, C. M., Gunapala, K. M., King, O. D., and Steele, A. D. (2012). Daily scheduled high fat meals moderately entrain behavioral anticipatory activity, body temperature, and hypothalamic c-Fos activation. *PLoS ONE* 7:e41161. doi: 10.1371/journal.pone.0041161

Gillette, M. U., and Reppert, S. M. (1987). The hypothalamic suprachiasmatic nuclei: circadian patterns of vasopressin secretion and neuronal activity in vitro. *Brain Res. Bull.* 19, 135–139. doi: 10.1016/0361-9230(87)90176-6

Gonnissen, H. K. J., Hulshof, T., and Westerterp-Plantenga, M. S. (2013). Chronobiology, endocrinology, and energy- and food-reward homeostasis. *Obes. Rev.* 14, 405–416. doi: 10.1111/obr.12019

Grimaldi, B., Bellet, M. M., Katada, S., Astarita, G., Hirayama, J., Amin, R. H., et al. (2010). PER2 controls lipid metabolism by direct regulation of PPARγ. *Cell Metab.* 12, 509–520. doi: 10.1016/j.cmet.2010.10.005

Guan, Z., Vgontzas, A. N., Bixler, E. O., and Fang, J. (2008). Sleep is increased by weight gain and decreased by weight loss in mice. *Sleep* 31, 627–633.

Guilding, C., Hughes, A. T. L., and Piggins, H. D. (2010). Circadian oscillators in the epithalamus. *Neuroscience* 169, 1630–1639. doi: 10.1016/j.neuroscience.2010.06.015

Guilding, C., Hughes, A. T. L., Brown, T. M., Namvar, S., and Piggins, H. D. (2009). A riot of rhythms: neuronal and glial circadian oscillators in the mediobasal hypothalamus. *Mol. Brain* 2:28. doi: 10.1186/1756-6606-2-28

Gumbs, M. C. R., van den Heuvel, J. K., and la Fleur, S. E. (2015). The effect of obesogenic diets on brain Neuropeptide, Y. *Physiol. Behav.* 162, 161–173. doi: 10.1016/j.physbeh.2016.04.049

Hampp, G., Ripperger, J. A., Houben, T., Schmutz, I., Blex, C., Perreau-Lenz, S., et al. (2008). Regulation of monoamine oxidase A by circadian-clock components implies clock influence on mood. *Curr. Biol.* 18, 678–683. doi: 10.1016/j.cub.2008.04.012

Harbour, V. L., Weigl, Y., Robinson, B., and Amir, S. (2013). Comprehensive mapping of regional expression of the clock protein PERIOD2 in rat forebrain across the 24-h Day. *PLoS ONE* 8:76391. doi: 10.1371/journal.pone.0076391

Hariri, N., and Thibault, L. (2011). Dietary obesity caused by a specific circadian eating pattern. *Chronobiol. Int.* 28, 216–228. doi: 10.3109/07420528.2010.548614

Harris, G. C., Wimmer, M., and Aston-Jones, G. (2005). A role for lateral hypothalamic orexin neurons in reward seeking. *Nature* 437, 556–559. doi: 10.1038/nature04071

Hood, S., Cassidy, P., Cossette, M.-P., Weigl, Y., Verwey, M., Robinson, B., et al. (2010). Endogenous dopamine regulates the rhythm of expression of the clock protein PER2 in the rat dorsal striatum via daily activation of D2 dopamine receptors. *J. Neurosci.* 30, 14046–14058. doi: 10.1523/JNEUROSCI.2128-10.2010

Hsu, C. T., Patton, D. F., Mistlberger, R. E., and Steele, A. D. (2010). Palatable meal anticipation in mice. *PLoS ONE* 5:e12903. doi: 10.1371/journal.pone.0012903

Hughes, A. T. L., Guilding, C., and Piggins, H. D. (2011). Neuropeptide signaling differentially affects phase maintenance and rhythm generation in SCN and extra-SCN circadian oscillators. *PLOS ONE* 6:e18926. doi: 10.1371/journal.pone.0018926

Inouye, S. I. T. (1983). Does the ventromedial hypothalamic nucleus contain a self-sustained circadian oscillator associated with periodic feedings? *Brain Res.* 279, 53–63. doi: 10.1016/0006-8993(83)90162-2

Jang, H., Lee, G., Kong, J., Choi, G., Park, Y. J., and Kim, J. B. (2012). Feeding period restriction alters the expression of peripheral circadian rhythm genes without changing body weight in mice. *PLoS ONE* 7:e49993. doi: 10.1371/journal.pone.0049993

Jenkins, J. B., Omori, T., Guan, Z., Vgontzas, A. N., Bixler, E. O., and Fang, J. (2006). Sleep is increased in mice with obesity induced by high-fat food. *Physiol. Behav.* 87, 255–262. doi: 10.1016/j.physbeh.2005.10.010

Juul, F., and Hemmingsson, E. (2015). Trends in consumption of ultra-processed foods and obesity in Sweden between 1960 and 2010. *Public Health Nutr.* 18, 3096–3107. doi: 10.1017/S1368980015000506

Kash, T. L., Pleil, K. E., Marcinkiewcz, C. A., Lowery-Gionta, E. G., Crowley, N., Mazzone, C., et al. (2015). Neuropeptide regulation of signaling and behavior in the BNST. *Mol. Cells* 38, 1–13. doi: 10.14348/molcells.2015.2261

Keen-rhinehart, E., Dailey, M. J., and Bartness, T. (2010). Physiological mechanisms for food-hoarding motivation in animals. *Philos. Trans. R. Soc. Lond. B Biol. Sci.* 961–975. doi: 10.1098/rstb.2009.0225

Kohsaka, A., Laposky, A. D., Ramsey, K. M., Estrada, C., Joshu, C., Kobayashi, Y., et al. (2007). High-fat diet disrupts behavioral and molecular circadian rhythms in mice. *Cell Metab.* 6, 414–421. doi: 10.1016/j.cmet.2007.09.006

Koob, G. F., and Volkow, N. D. (2010). Neurocircuitry of addiction. *Neuropsychopharmacology* 35, 217–238. doi: 10.1038/npp.2009.110

Koopman, K. E., Booij, J., Fliers, E., Serlie, M. J., and la Fleur, S. E. (2013). Diet-induced changes in the lean brain: hypercaloric high-fat-high-sugar snacking decreases serotonin transporters in the human hypothalamic region. *Mol. Metab.* 2, 417–422. doi: 10.1016/j.molmet.2013.07.006

Kudlow, P. A., Cha, D. S., Lam, R. W., and McIntyre, R. S. (2013). Sleep architecture variation: a mediator of metabolic disturbance in individuals with major depressive disorder. *Sleep Med.* 14, 943–949. doi: 10.1016/j.sleep.2013.04.017

la Fleur, S. E., Luijendijk, M. C. M., van der Zwaal, E. M., Brans, M. A., and Adan, R. A. (2014). The snacking rat as model of human obesity: effects of a free-choice high-fat high-sugar diet on meal patterns. *Int. J. Obes. (Lond.).* 38, 1–24. doi: 10.1038/ijo.2013.159

la Fleur, S. E., Vanderschuren, L. J., Luijendijk, M. C., Kloeze, B. M., Tiesjema, B., and Adan, R. A. (2007). A reciprocal interaction between food-motivated behavior and diet-induced obesity. *Int. J. Obes. (Lond.).* 31, 1286–1294. doi: 10.1038/sj.ijo.0803570

la Fleur, S. E., van Rozen, A. J., Luijendijk, M. C. M., Groeneweg, F., and Adan, R. A. (2010). A free-choice high-fat high-sugar diet induces changes in arcuate neuropeptide expression that support hyperphagia. *Int. J. Obes.* 34, 537–546. doi: 10.1038/ijo.2009.257

Lenard, N. R., and Berthoud, H. (2009). Central and peripheral regulation of food intake and physical activity: pathways and genes. *Obesity (Silver. Spring)* 16, S11–S22. doi: 10.1038/oby.2008.511

Logan, R. W., Edgar, N., Gillman, A. G., Hoffman, D., Zhu, X., and McClung, C. A. (2015). Chronic stress induces brain region-specific alterations of molecular rhythms that correlate with depression-like behavior in mice. *Biol. Psychiatry* 78, 249–258. doi: 10.1016/j.biopsych.2015.01.011

Louzada, M. L., Baraldi, L. G., Steele, E. M., Martins, A. P. B., Canella, D. S., Moubarac, J. C., et al. (2015). Consumption of ultra-processed foods and obesity in Brazilian adolescents and adults. *Prev. Med. (Baltim).* 81, 9–15. doi: 10.1016/j.ypmed.2015.07.018

Luppi, M., Cerri, M., Martelli, D., Tupone, D., Del Vecchio, F., Di Cristoforo, A., et al. (2014). Waking and sleeping in the rat made obese through a high-fat hypercaloric diet. *Behav. Brain Res.* 258, 145–152. doi: 10.1016/j.bbr.2013.10.014

Marston, O. J., Williams, R. H., Canal, M. M., Samuels, R. E., Upton, N., and Piggins, H. D. (2008). Circadian and dark-pulse activation of orexin/hypocretin neurons. *Mol. Brain* 1:19. doi: 10.1186/1756-6606-1-19

Matsumoto, M., and Hikosaka, O. (2007). Lateral habenula as a source of negative reward signals in dopamine neurons. *Nature* 447, 1111–1115. doi: 10.1038/nature05860

Mendoza, J., Angeles-Castellanos, M., and Escobar, C. (2005). Entrainment by a palatable meal induces food-anticipatory activity and c-Fos expression in reward-related areas of the brain. *Neuroscience* 133, 293–303. doi: 10.1016/j.neuroscience.2005.01.064

Mendoza, J., Pévet, P., and Challet, E. (2008). High-fat feeding alters the clock synchronization to light. *J. Physiol.* 586, 5901–5910. doi: 10.1113/jphysiol.2008.159566

Merkestein, M., Brans, M. A. D., Luijendijk, M. C. M., de Jong, J. W., Egecioglu, E., Dickson, S. L., et al. (2012). Ghrelin mediates anticipation to a palatable meal in rats. *Obesity* 20, 963–971. doi: 10.1038/oby.2011.389

Mifune, H., Tajiri, Y., Nishi, Y., Hara, K., Iwata, S., Tokubuchi, I., et al. (2015). Voluntary exercise contributed to an amelioration of abnormal feeding behavior, locomotor activity and ghrelin production concomitantly with a weight reduction in high fat diet-induced obese rats. *Peptides* 71, 49–55. doi: 10.1016/j.peptides.2015.06.007

Mogenson, G. J., Jones, D. L., and Yim, C. Y. (1980). From motivation to action: functional interface between the limbic system and the motor system. *Prog. Neurobiol.* 14, 69–97. doi: 10.1016/0301-0082(80)90018-0

Oosterman, J. E., Foppen, E., van der Spek, R., Fliers, E., Kalsbeek, A., and la Fleur, S. E. (2015). Timing of fat and liquid sugar intake alters substrate oxidation and food efficiency in male Wistar rats. *Chronobiol. Int.* 32, 289–298. doi: 10.3109/07420528.2014.971177

Opperhuizen, A.-L., Wang, D., Foppen, E., Jansen, R., Boudzovitch-Surovtseva, O., de Vries, J., et al. (2016). Feeding during the resting phase causes profound changes in physiology and desynchronization between liver and muscle rhythms of rats. *Eur. J. Neurosci.* 44, 2795–2806. doi: 10.1111/ejn.13377

Paulson, P. E., and Robinson, T. E. (1994). Relationship between circadian changes in spontaneous motor activity and dorsal versus ventral striatal dopamine neurotransmission assessed with on-line microdialysis. *Behav. Neurosci.* 108, 624–635. doi: 10.1037/0735-7044.108.3.624

Pendergast, J. S., Branecky, K. L., Yang, W., Ellacott, K. L. J., Niswender, K. D., and Yamazaki, S. (2013). High-fat diet acutely affects circadian organisation and eating behavior. *Eur. J. Neurosci.* 37, 1350–1356. doi: 10.1111/ejn.12133

Peplonska, B., Bukowska, A., and Sobala, W. (2015). Association of rotating night shift work with BMI and abdominal obesity among nurses and midwives. *PLoS ONE* 10, 1–13. doi: 10.1371/journal.pone.0133761

Pritchet, C. E., and Hajnal, A. (2011). Obesogenic diets may differentially alter dopamine control of sucrose and fructose intake in rats. *Physiol. Behav.* 104, 111–116. doi: 10.1016/j.physbeh.2011.04.048

Proulx, C. D., Hikosaka, O., and Malinow, R. (2014). Reward processing by the lateral habenula in normal and depressive behaviors. *Nat. Neurosci.* 17, 1146–1152. doi: 10.1038/nn.3779

Qin, C., and Luo, M. (2009). Neurochemical phenotypes of the afferent and efferent projections of the mouse medial habenula. *Neuroscience* 161, 827–837. doi: 10.1016/j.neuroscience.2009.03.085

Rensing, L., and Ruoff, P. (2002). Temperature effect on entrainment, phase shifting, and amplitude of circadian clocks and its molecular bases. *Chronobiol. Int.* 19, 807–864. doi: 10.1081/CBI-120014569

Rudic, R. D., McNamara, P., Curtis, A. M., Boston, R. C., Panda, S., Hogenesch, J. B., et al. (2004). BMAL1 and CLOCK, two essential components of the circadian clock, are involved in glucose homeostasis. *PLoS Biol.* 2:e377. doi: 10.1371/journal.pbio.0020377

Sakhi, K., Wegner, S., Belle, M. D. C., Howarth, M., Delagrange, P., Brown, T. M., et al. (2014). Intrinsic and extrinsic cues regulate the daily profile of mouse lateral habenula neuronal activity. *J. Physiol.* 592, 5025–5045. doi: 10.1113/jphysiol.2014.280065

Salaberry, N. L., and Mendoza, J. (2016). Insights into the role of the habenular circadian clock in addiction. *Front Psychiatry* 6:179. doi: 10.3389/fpsyt.2015.00179

Scheer, F. A. J. L., Hilton, M. F., Mantzoros, C. S., and Shea, S. A. (2009). Adverse metabolic and cardiovascular consequences of circadian misalignment. *Proc. Natl. Acad. Sci. U.S.A.* 106, 4453–4458. doi: 10.1073/pnas.0808180106

Schwartz, M. W., Woods, S. C., Porte, D., Seeley, R. J., and Baskin, D. G. (2000). Central nervous system control of food intake. *Nature* 404, 661–671. doi: 10.1038/35007534

Sesack, S. R., and Grace, A. A. (2010). Cortico-Basal Ganglia reward network: microcircuitry. *Neuropsychopharmacology* 35, 27–47. doi: 10.1038/npp.2009.93

Sherman, H., Genzer, Y., Cohen, R., Chapnik, N., Madar, Z., and Froy, O. (2012). Timed high-fat diet resets circadian metabolism and prevents obesity. *FASEB J.* 26, 3493–3502. doi: 10.1096/fj.12-208868

Shibata, S., and Moore, R. Y. (1988). Electrical and metabolic activity of suprachiasmatic nucleus neurons in hamster hypothalamic slices. *Brain Res.* 438, 374–378. doi: 10.1016/0006-8993(88)91367-4

Silver, R., and LeSauter, J. (2008). Circadian and homeostatic factors in arousal. *Ann. N.Y. Acad. Sci.* 1129, 263–274. doi: 10.1196/annals.1417.032

Smith, A. D., Olson, R. J., and Justice, J. B. (1992). Quantitative microdialysis of dopamine in the striatum: effect of circadian variation. *J. Neurosci. Methods* 44, 33–41. doi: 10.1016/0165-0270(92)90111-P

Sokolowski, K., and Corbin, J. G. (2012). Wired for behaviors: from development to function of innate limbic system circuitry. *Front. Mol. Neurosci.* 5:55. doi: 10.3389/fnmol.2012.00055

Squire, L. R., Bloom, F. E., Splitzer, N. C., du Lac, S., Ghosh, A., and Berg, D. (2008). "Chapter 7 neurotransmitters," in *Fundamental Neuroscience, 3rd Edn.*, eds L. Squire, D. Berg, F. E. Bloom, S. du Lac, A. Ghosh and N. Spitzer (Academic Press, Elsevier), 133–155.

Stamatakis, A. M., Van Swieten, M., Basiri, M. L., Blair, G. A., Kantak, P., and Stuber, G. D. (2016). Lateral hypothalamic area glutamatergic neurons and their projections to the lateral habenula regulate feeding and reward. *J. Neurosci.* 36, 302–311. doi: 10.1523/JNEUROSCI.1202-15.2016

Stephan, F. K., and Zucker, I. (1972). Circadian rhythms in drinking behavior and locomotor activity of rats are eliminated by hypothalamic lesions. *Proc. Natl. Acad. Sci.U.S.A.* 69, 1583–1586. doi: 10.1073/pnas.69.6.1583

Stuber, G. D., and Wise, R. A. (2016). Lateral hypothalamic circuits for feeding and reward. *Nat. Neurosci.* 19, 198–205. doi: 10.1038/nn.4220

Stütz, A. M., Staszkiewicz, J., Ptitsyn, A., and Argyropoulos, G. (2007). Circadian expression of genes regulating food intake. *Obesity (Silver. Spring)* 15, 607–615. doi: 10.1038/oby.2007.564

Sun, L., Wang, Y., Song, Y., Cheng, X. R., Xia, S., Rahman, M. R. T., et al. (2015). Resveratrol restores the circadian rhythmic disorder of lipid metabolism induced by high-fat diet in mice. *Biochem. Biophys. Res. Commun.* 458, 86–91. doi: 10.1016/j.bbrc.2015.01.072

Takahashi, J. S. (2015). Molecular components of the circadian clock in mammals. *Diabetes Obes. Metab.* 17, 6–11. doi: 10.1111/dom.12514

Tavakoli-Nezhad, M. (2005). C-fos expression in the brains of behaviorally "split" hamsters in constant light: calling attention to a dorsolateral region of the suprachiasmatic nucleus and the medial division of the lateral habenula. *J. Biol. Rhythms* 20, 419–429. doi: 10.1177/0748730405278443

Tavakoli-Nezhad, M., and Schwartz, W. J. (2006). Hamsters running on time: is the lateral habenula a part of the clock? *Chronobiol. Int.* 23, 217–224. doi: 10.1080/07420520500521947

Tiesjema, B., Adan, R. A., Luijendijk, M. C. M., Kalsbeek, A., and la Fleur, S. E. (2007). Differential effects of recombinant adeno-associated virus-mediated neuropeptide Y overexpression in the hypothalamic paraventricular nucleus and lateral hypothalamus on feeding behavior. *J. Neurosci.* 27, 14139–14146. doi: 10.1523/JNEUROSCI.3280-07.2007

Torrealba, F., Riveros, M. E., Contreras, M., and Valdes, J. L. (2012). Histamine and motivation. *Brain* 6, 1–14. doi: 10.3389/fnsys.2012.00051

Turek, F. W., Joshu, C., Kohsaka, A., Lin, E., Ivanova, G., McDearmon, E. L., et al. (2005). Obesity and metabolic syndrome in circadian clock mutant mice. *Science* 308, 1043–1045. doi: 10.1126/science.1108750

Ulrich-lai, Y. M., Fulton, S., Wilson, M., Petrovich, G., and Rinaman, L. (2016). Stress exposure, food intake, and emotional state. 18, 381–399. doi: 10.3109/10253890

Versteeg, R. I., Serlie, M. J., Kalsbeek, A., and la Fleur, S. E. (2015). Serotonin, a possible intermediate between disturbed circadian rhythms and metabolic disease. *Neuroscience* 301, 155–167. doi: 10.1016/j.neuroscience.2015.05.067

Verwey, M., Khoja, Z., Stewart, J., and Amir, S. (2007). Differential regulation of the expression of Period2 protein in the limbic forebrain and dorsomedial hypothalamus by daily limited access to highly palatable food in food-deprived and free-fed rats. *Neuroscience* 147, 277–285. doi: 10.1016/j.neuroscience.2007.04.044

Webb, I. C., Baltazar, R. M., Wang, X., Pitchers, K. K., Coolen, L. M., and Lehman, M. N. (2009). Diurnal variations in natural and drug reward, mesolimbic tyrosine hydroxylase, and clock gene expression in the male rat. *J. Biol. Rhythms* 24, 465–476. doi: 10.1177/0748730409346657

Webb, I. C., Lehman, M. N., and Coolen, L. M. (2015). Diurnal and circadian regulation of reward-related neurophysiology and behavior. *Physiol. Behav.* 143, 58–69. doi: 10.1016/j.physbeh.2015.02.034

Wiater, M. F., Mukherjee, S., Li, A. J., Dinh, T. T., Rooney, E. M., Simasko, S. M., et al. (2011). Circadian integration of sleep-wake and feeding requires NPY receptor-expressing neurons in the mediobasal hypothalamus. *Am. J. Physiol. Regul. Integr. Comp. Physiol.* 301, R1569–R1583. doi: 10.1152/ajpregu.00168.2011

Wong, C. K., Botta, A., Pither, J., Dai, C., Gibson, W. T., and Ghosh, S. (2015). A high-fat diet rich in corn oil reduces spontaneous locomotor activity and induces insulin resistance in mice. *J. Nutr. Biochem.* 26, 319–326. doi: 10.1016/j.jnutbio.2014.11.004

Xu, H., Zhang, C., and Zhao, H. (2015). Effect of Suprachiasmatic nucleus lesion on Period2 and C-fos expression in habenular nucleus. *Int. J. Chem.* 7, 163–169. doi: 10.5539/ijcv7n2p163

Yamazaki, S., Kerbeshian, M. C., Hocker, C. G., Block, G. D., and Menaker, M. (1998). Rhythmic properties of the hamster suprachiasmatic nucleus *in vivo*. *J. Neurosci.* 18, 10709–10723.

Yu, X., Zecharia, A., Zhang, Z., Yang, Q., Yustos, R., Jager, P., et al. (2014). Circadian factor BMAL1 in histaminergic neurons regulates sleep architecture. *Curr. Biol.* 24, 2838–2844. doi: 10.1016/j.cub.2014.10.019

Zhao, H., and Rusak, B. (2005). Circadian firing-rate rhythms and light responses of rat habenular nucleus neurons *in vivo* and *in vitro*. *Neuroscience* 132, 519–528. doi: 10.1016/j.neuroscience.2005.01.012

Zhao, Z., Xu, H., Liu, Y., Mu, L., Xiao, J., and Zhao, H. (2015). Diurnal expression of the per2 gene and protein in the lateral habenular nucleus. *Int. J. Mol. Sci.* 16, 16740–16749. doi: 10.3390/ijms160816740

Zheng, B., Larkin, D. W., Albrecht, U., Sun, Z. S., Sage, M., Eichele, G., et al. (1999). The mPer2 gene encodes a functional component of the mammalian circadian clock. *Nature* 400, 169–173. doi: 10.1038/22659

Zheng, N. H., Lenard, A., and Shin, H. B. (2009). Appetite control and energy balance regulation in the modern world: reward-driven brain overrides repletion signals. *Int. J. Obes.* 33, 3260–3268. doi: 10.1038/ijo.2009.65

7

Interactions of Circadian Rhythmicity, Stress and Orexigenic Neuropeptide Systems: Implications for Food Intake Control

Anna Blasiak[1], Andrew L. Gundlach[2,3], Grzegorz Hess[1,4] and Marian H. Lewandowski[1]*

[1] Department of Neurophysiology and Chronobiology, Institute of Zoology, Jagiellonian University, Krakow, Poland, [2] Neuropeptides Division, The Florey Institute of Neuroscience and Mental Health, Parkville, VIC, Australia, [3] Florey Department of Neuroscience and Mental Health, The University of Melbourne, Parkville, VIC, Australia, [4] Institute of Pharmacology, Polish Academy of Sciences, Krakow, Poland

Edited by:
Etienne Challet,
Institute of Cellular and Integrative Neurosciences (CNRS), France

Reviewed by:
Hugh D. Piggins,
University of Manchester, UK
Lily Yan,
Michigan State University, USA

Correspondence:
Anna Blasiak
anna.blasiak@uj.edu.pl

Many physiological processes fluctuate throughout the day/night and daily fluctuations are observed in brain and peripheral levels of several hormones, neuropeptides and transmitters. In turn, mediators under the "control" of the "master biological clock" reciprocally influence its function. Dysregulation in the rhythmicity of hormone release as well as hormone receptor sensitivity and availability in different tissues, is a common risk-factor for multiple clinical conditions, including psychiatric and metabolic disorders. At the same time circadian rhythms remain in a strong, reciprocal interaction with the hypothalamic-pituitary-adrenal (HPA) axis. Recent findings point to a role of circadian disturbances and excessive stress in the development of obesity and related food consumption and metabolism abnormalities, which constitute a major health problem worldwide. Appetite, food intake and energy balance are under the influence of several brain neuropeptides, including the orexigenic agouti-related peptide, neuropeptide Y, orexin, melanin-concentrating hormone and relaxin-3. Importantly, orexigenic neuropeptide neurons remain under the control of the circadian timing system and are highly sensitive to various stressors, therefore the potential neuronal mechanisms through which disturbances in the daily rhythmicity and stress-related mediator levels contribute to food intake abnormalities rely on reciprocal interactions between these elements.

Keywords: agouti-related peptide, circadian timing system, HPA-axis, neuropeptide Y, melanin-concentrating hormone, orexin, relaxin-3

INTRODUCTION

Circadian (~24 h) fluctuations of different components of the external environment, in particular light-dark conditions, shape animals' physiology and behavior for the optimal synchronization to the cyclical changes encountered. As a consequence of this influence, biological processes called circadian rhythms developed in most organisms (Vaze and Sharma, 2013). In mammals, circadian rhythms are shaped by the master circadian pacemaker, the suprachiasmatic nucleus (SCN), and secondary circadian clocks in brain and peripheral areas (Schibler et al., 2003; Mendoza and Challet, 2009). The SCN coordinates secondary clocks through neural and endocrine pathways, and glucocorticoids released from the adrenal cortex play a key role in the coordination of the circadian timing system (Balsalobre et al., 2000; Barclay et al., 2012). Importantly, mediators of the hypothalamic-pituitary-adrenal (HPA) axis, a key regulator of stress responses, directly and indirectly influence both the circadian timing system and brain centers responsible for food intake control (Dallman et al., 1995; Balsalobre et al., 2000; Segall et al., 2009; Nader et al., 2010).

In the industrialized world, chronic exposure to psychological stress, work/activity during late-night hours, and the introduction of artificial light and resultant sleep reduction, all lead to disturbances in the circadian rhythmicity in HPA-axis functioning (Stevens and Zhu, 2015; Koch et al., 2016). At the same time psychological stress and chronodisruption lead to disturbances in food intake-related processes (Kyrou et al., 2006; Antunes et al., 2010). Among other factors, food intake remains under the control of orexinergic neuropeptides, including agouti-related peptide, neuropeptide Y, orexin, melanin-concentrating hormone and relaxin-3, and the goal of this mini-review is to summarize current knowledge about mechanisms linking circadian rhythms, stress and orexigenic neuropeptides, which may underlie stress- and chronodisruption-induced food-intake abnormalities (**Figure 1**).

HPA-AXIS RHYTHMICITY AND THE CIRCADIAN TIMING SYSTEM—A MUTUAL RELATIONSHIP

The HPA-axis consists of the paraventricular nucleus (PVN), the anterior lobe of the pituitary gland, and the adrenal cortex. PVN neurons synthesize corticotrophin-releasing hormone (CRH) and arginine vasopressin (AVP), which stimulates secretion of adrenocorticotrophic hormone (ACTH) from the anterior pituitary and ACTH controls the release of glucocorticoids (GCs) from the adrenal cortex (Ulrich-Lai and Herman, 2009).

PVN neurons are under direct and indirect control of the SCN (Kalsbeek et al., 1992, 1996). Rhythmic release of neurotransmitters from SCN inputs to the PVN cause circadian oscillations in PVN activity (Tousson and Meissl, 2004) and daily fluctuations in CRH hnRNA and peptide levels (Owens et al., 1990; Girotti et al., 2009). ACTH plasma levels are driven by CRH secretion, but also remain under the control of the SCN (Cascio et al., 1987; Kalsbeek et al., 1996). Similarly GC release is controlled by the circadian master clock through neural control of CRH and ACTH release (Ulrich-Lai and Herman, 2009) and the autonomic innervation of the adrenal gland (Buijs et al., 1999). The rhythmic synthesis of corticosterone depends directly on the master clock, since destruction of the SCN abolishes this rhythmicity (Moore and Eichler, 1972).

Moreover, the adrenal gland has its own clock for circadian GC production (Son et al., 2008) and chronodisruption alters HPA-axis reactivity and plasma GC concentrations (Wu et al., 2008). Not surprisingly, disturbed cyclical functioning of the HPA-axis is implicated in many diseases (Chung et al., 2011). Notably, the activity of the HPA-axis exhibits ultradian rhythmicity and both ACTH and GC secretion is pulsatile in an hourly pattern (Spiga et al., 2011). Similarly to circadian fluctuations, the ultradian pattern of HPA-axis activity is crucial for proper stress responses (Sarabdjitsingh et al., 2010), however, unlike the circadian pattern, ultradian oscillations in GC secretion persist in SCN-lesioned animals and in constant light conditions (Waite et al., 2012). This uncoupling from daily rhythmicity indicates that pulsatile secretion of GC is not SCN-dependent and suggests its reliance on other oscillatory mechanisms.

Importantly, the HPA-axis reciprocally influences the circadian system. Rhythmic GC secretion synchronizes peripheral and central circadian oscillators (Balsalobre et al., 2000; Nader et al., 2010) and is crucial for the synchronization of intrinsic rhythmicity to external factors (Balsalobre et al., 2000). In the majority of tissues GCs affect the expression of clock-related genes, however GCs do not act within the SCN, where the concentration of GC-receptors is low/absent (Balsalobre et al., 2000; Pezuk et al., 2012).

Managing stress involves habituation, which provides appropriate stress coping and avoids harmful, chronic physiological consequences (Spyrka and Hess, 2010). Unfortunately, stressors that are unpredictable and experienced in high intensity lead to disruption of homeostasis, including altered circadian rhythmicity and disturbances in metabolism. One consequence of prolonged stress exposure for humans is overweight and obesity (Coccurello et al., 2009), now a major worldwide public health issue (World Health Organization, 2016). Despite increasing data concerning the reasons for and the mechanisms underlying this phenomenon, much is still to be learnt about the neuronal and humoral underpinnings of stress-induced overconsumption of food.

CENTRAL REGULATION OF FOOD INTAKE: THE INTERACTION OF OREXIGENIC NEUROPEPTIDE SIGNALING, STRESS AND CIRCADIAN RHYTHMICITY

Homeostatic regulation of food intake and energy expenditure relies on central and peripheral signals that are processed within brain centers and peripheral organs. Among many neurotransmitters involved in appetite control, centrally synthetized orexigenic neuropeptides are considered important mediators, and disturbances in their synthesis and/or signaling may contribute to malfunctioning of energy management. In the following sections, data regarding the mutual relationship between major central orexigenic neuropeptides systems, the stress-response axis and circadian systems are provided, indicating potential neuronal mechanisms involved in stress- and chronodisruption-mediated food-intake dysregulation.

Neuropeptide Y and Agouti-Related Peptide

The arcuate nucleus (ARC) of the hypothalamus is a key appetite regulatory center (Banks, 2010). It contains two major neuronal populations, one synthesizing orexigenic neuropeptide Y (NPY) and agouti-related peptide (AgRP), and a second

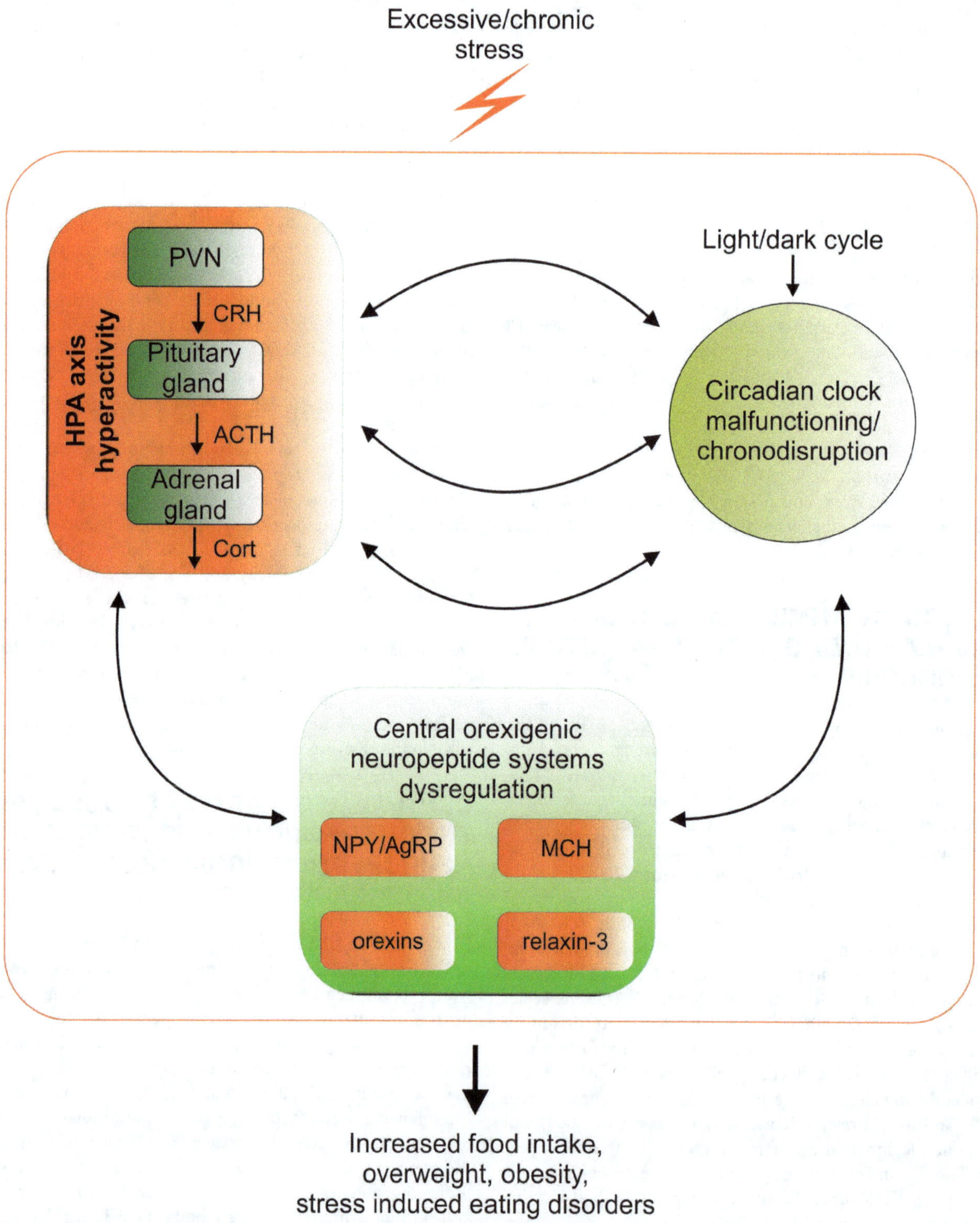

FIGURE 1 | Mutual relationship between the biological circadian clock, stress and orexigenic peptide systems. Circadian clock structures in the brain are under direct influence of the stress HPA-axis mediators: corticotropin-releasing hormone (CRH), adrenocorticotropic hormone (ACTH) and glucocorticoids (GCs), therefore excessive exposure to stress disrupts the circadian rhythmicity of the organism. Coincidently, chronic stress through excessive release of HPA mediators deregulates the synthesis and action of orexigenic brain peptides, which can lead to overconsumption of food, weight gain, obesity and stress-related eating disorders. The control of orexigenic peptide synthesis during prolonged stress exposure is dysregulated at several levels, since excessive stress disrupts circadian rhythmicity, which directly controls both neuropeptide release and HPA-axis function. The cycle of excessive stress influences on food intake-promoting peptide system activity and circadian clock structures is closed by the sensitivity of both HPA-axis and clock structures to orexigenic peptide system mediators.

expressing anorexigenic proopiomelanocortin and cocaine and amphetamine-regulated transcript (Benite-Ribeiro et al., 2016).

Acute and chronic icv NPY administration result in hyperphagia, obesity and changes in metabolism (Beck et al., 1992; Su et al., 2016). Fasting increases ARC levels of NPY and AgRP mRNA (Hahn et al., 1998; Kim et al., 2005) and compromised NPY release delays physiological food intake (Krashes et al., 2013). Central AgRP injections increase feeding (Kim et al., 2000) and fasting increases the expression of AgRP mRNA and peptide (Hahn et al., 1998; Liu et al., 2012). Finally, ablation of AgRP neurons result in acute anorexia (Gropp et al., 2005) and selective activation of AgRP neurons drives feeding behavior (Krashes et al., 2011).

Both NPY and AgRP synthesis are sensitive to HPA-axis mediators. NPY levels increase after exogenous GC treatment (Larsen et al., 1994) and immobilization increases NPY mRNA in the ARC (Conrad and McEwen, 2000). Importantly, prolonged elevations in GC levels lead to overconsumption of food through inhibition of CRH and stimulation of NPY expression (Kaye et al., 1990; Cavagnini et al., 2000).

Interestingly, although AgRP and NPY are co-expressed in the same neuron, their mRNA levels are differentially regulated by stressful events. For example, footshock stress increases NPY mRNA levels, but decreases AgRP mRNA levels (Kas et al., 2005). In rats, repeated footshock (for 14 days) increases ARC AgRP mRNA levels (Helmreich et al., 2005) and chronic (4 weeks) corticosterone treatment increases hypothalamic AgRP, but not NPY, mRNA (Sefton et al., 2016). Psychological stressors, such as restraint stress, reduce the number of AgRP-expressing neurons in the ARC after both acute and repeated exposure (Chagra et al., 2011), highlighting the importance of the duration and type of stressor. Stress hormones may directly act within the ARC, since AgRP-ARC neurons are directly innervated by PVN/CRH neurons, express CRH_1-receptors and CRH decreases their excitability (Kuperman et al., 2016). Similarly, GC-receptors are highly expressed in the ARC (Morimoto et al., 1996) and their activation stimulates NPY release (Yi et al., 2012) as well as NPY and AgRP gene expression (Shimizu et al., 2008).

At the same time ARC neurons innervate the PVN (Kuperman et al., 2016; Fenselau et al., 2017) and central NPY administration increases the level of CRH, ACTH and corticosterone (Alfalah and Michel, 2004). Moreover, NPY administration into the PVN stimulates food intake (Stanley and Leibowitz, 1985) and induces increased PVN neural activity (Fan et al., 2016); while sustained, viral-mediated overexpression of NPY within this structure results in obesity (Tiesjema et al., 2009). A bidirectional relationship between the HPA-axis and ARC may therefore constitute a positive feedback loop, underlying stress-induced food intake.

Importantly, ARC neuron activity is influenced by the circadian system; indirectly through HPA axis and through direct inputs from the SCN (Yi et al., 2006). Indeed, diurnal rhythm of ARC c-Fos expression (Jamali and Tramu, 1999) and enhancement of AgRP neuron activity during the active phase of the diurnal cycle was demonstrated (Krashes et al., 2013). Simultaneously, NPY/AgRP cells in the vmARC are essential for generating and maintaining circadian rhythms of *ad libitum* feeding (Li et al., 2012); and ARC lesions result in rest-activity disturbances (Wiater et al., 2011). Moreover, ARC NPY/AgRP circuits are crucial for the entrainment of activity by photic cues and entrainment of temperature by food (Wiater et al., 2013). Therefore, NPY/AgRP signaling is a key element of the feeding/energy homeostasis control system, through which stress and chronodisruption may influence food intake.

Orexins/Hypocretins and Melanin-Concentrating Hormone

Orexins/hypocretins are synthesized within the lateral hypothalamus (LH) (Peyron et al., 1998). Orexin neurons are involved in the control of a variety of homeostatic functions including feeding and energy expenditure (Date et al., 1999). When centrally or intraperitoneally injected, orexins stimulate food intake (Edwards et al., 1999). Fasting induces up-regulation of prepro-orexin mRNA levels (Sakurai et al., 1998), and increases the number of excitatory synapses on orexin neurons (Horvath and Gao, 2005). Chemogenetic activation of orexin neurons simultaneously increases locomotor activity and food intake (Inutsuka et al., 2014) and blockade of orexin receptors reduces food intake (Haynes et al., 2000) and binge eating behavior (Piccoli et al., 2012). Orexins are also necessary for arousal maintenance and orexins stimulate arousal-related behaviors (Hagan et al., 1999). A loss of orexin neurons leads to narcolepsy, but does not cause weight loss, and narcoleptic patients suffer abnormalities in energy metabolism and often obesity (Schuld et al., 2000). Similarly, in orexin-deficient mice, in addition to sleep/arousal cycle abnormalities, a lower level of spontaneous physical activity and obesity (regardless of hypophagia) have been described (Hara et al., 2001). Despite an orexigenic effect of acute orexin treatment, chronic icv orexin-A infusion does not lead to weight gain (Yamanaka et al., 1999). Moreover, recent findings reveal that orexin cells activity decreases after eating onset and their silencing leads to eating facilitation (González et al., 2016), which is in line with the obesity observed in orexin-deficient mice (Hara et al., 2001). However, the role of orexins in the maintenance of wakefulness during food searching and reward-related food consumption (Cason et al., 2010) highlights their importance in food intake control.

Orexin neurons are directly activated by CRH and stress (Winsky-Sommerer et al., 2004) and play a key role in stress-induced overconsumption of food (Piccoli et al., 2012), and reinstatement of alcohol- and drug-seeking behavior (Kastman et al., 2016; Schmeichel et al., 2016). The functional link between the HPA-axis and orexin neurons is reciprocal, since orexins evoke an induction of *c-fos* mRNA in the PVN, and an increase in plasma ACTH and corticosterone (Kuru et al., 2000). These pathways may be involved in stress-induced over-activation of orexin neurons, leading to reward-based binge eating behavior.

An accepted role of the orexin system is in the integration of circadian and metabolic influences to shape the arousal and nutritional states of the organism (Selbach and Haas, 2006). Orexins are essential for maintenance of the sleep-wake cycle (Kantor et al., 2009) and strong bidirectional neural connections exist between circadian and orexin systems. Chronodisruption may disturb orexin neuron functioning and disrupted orexin system activity may influence the circadian system. Orexin neurons receive both direct and indirect innervation from the SCN (Abrahamson et al., 2001; Deurveilher and Semba, 2005). Consequently, SCN-dependent circadian patterns are observed in brain orexin levels (Yoshida et al., 2001; Deboer et al., 2004; Zhang et al., 2004) and orexin neurons activation (Marston et al., 2008). On the other hand, SCN neurons are surrounded by orexin fibers and express orexin receptors (Belle et al., 2014). Orexins influence the activity of SCN neurons and are able to induce variable phase shifts in neonatal cultured SCN neurons and phase advances in organotypic brain slices (Klisch et al., 2009). In adult brain, orexins hyperpolarize SCN neurons and enhance the capacity of NPY to shift the phase of *Period1* gene expression in adult brain slices, without an ability to induce such phase shifts alone (Belle et al., 2014). Moreover, orexins modulate the activity of structures involved in non-photic circadian entrainment such as the intergeniculate leaflet (Pekala et al., 2011; Palus et al., 2015) and dorsal raphe nucleus (Kohlmeier et al., 2013).

Within the LH, orexin neurons are intermingled with cells synthesizing melanin-concentrating hormone (MCH) (Broberger et al., 1998). Icv injections of MCH increase food intake in satiated rats (Guesdon et al., 2009), MCH knockout mice are hyperactive and lean (Shimada et al., 1998), and fasting increases levels of MCH mRNA (Bertile et al., 2003). Notably, optogenetic activation of MCH neurons in mice induces sleep, but not food consumption (Konadhode et al., 2013). However, MCH signaling can promote motivational behaviors leading to overconsumption of highly-palatable, calorically-dense food (Georgescu et al., 2005) and is involved in stress-induced binge eating (Pankevich et al., 2010), as well as cocaine (Chung et al., 2009) and alcohol (Duncan et al., 2005; Karlsson et al., 2016a,b) consumption. The involvement of MCH in food intake in animals prompted investigation of potential therapeutic effects of MCH receptor (MCHR) antagonists as anti-obesity agents in humans, but currently no compounds have proceeded to Phase II studies (Macneil, 2013).

MCH synthesis is sensitive to stress, as footshock decreases MCH mRNA levels, an effect mimicked by adrenalectomy and counteracted by dexamethasone replacement (Presse et al., 1992). Chronic mild stress in mice increases MCH-receptor expression in hippocampus (Roy et al., 2007) and repeated restraint up-regulates MCH expression (Kim and Han, 2016). Moreover, treatment of hippocampal neurons with corticosterone *in vitro* increases MCH expression (Kim and Han, 2016). Therefore, MCH neurons constitute another substrate through which stressors can affect feeding behavior (Hervieu, 2003).

Similar to other orexigenic peptide systems, the relationship between MCH signaling and stress is reciprocal. Blockade of MCHR1 has strong anxiolytic and antidepressant effects (Borowsky et al., 2002; Smith et al., 2006) and MCHR1 knockout mice exhibit reduced depressive-like behavior (Roy et al., 2007). Furthermore, the mode of MCH action on the stress axis depends on the circadian time, since significant activation of the HPA-axis through activation of CRH neurons and subsequent stimulation of ACTH release were observed after icv MCH injections in the early light/inactive phase (Jezova et al., 1992). Similarly, icv MCH injections during the light phase lead to increased plasma corticosterone levels and anxiety-like behavior (Smith et al., 2006) and MCHR1 antagonists reverse the effect of chronic and acute stress in mice (Smith et al., 2009; Lee et al., 2011).

In the rat, MCH mRNA expression fluctuates in a circadian manner, with a low level during the light/inactive phase and a peak after the onset of the dark/active period (Bluet-Pajot et al., 1995). MCH is a strong sleep-inducing factor (Verret et al., 2003) and MCH neurons fire during REM sleep, in direct contrast to orexin neurons (Hassani et al., 2009). Direct innervation of the MCH neurons by SCN efferents (Abrahamson et al., 2001) allows for a direct influence of the circadian master clock on MCH levels. The potential feedback of MCH on circadian structures still needs to be verified, but the presence of MCH-receptors on SCN neurons (Chee et al., 2013), and reciprocal connections with neurons influencing circadian clock function, notably orexins neurons (Guan et al., 2002), supports the assumption of a reciprocal interaction of circadian and MCH systems.

The circadian clock control of MCH and orexins synthesis, key neuropeptides involved in stress-induced overconsumption of palatable food and drug-seeking behavior, imposes a need to monitor daily rhythmicity in studies where disturbances in reward-related behaviors are being examined.

Relaxin-3

The neuropeptide relaxin-3 is synthesized mainly in brainstem *nucleus incertus* (NI) neurons (Ma et al., 2007). Relaxin-3 is highly-conserved, with similarities in distribution between mammalian species, including non-human primate and human brain (Ma et al., 2016), which suggest conservation of its function. Relaxin-3 regulates a variety of physiological processes, including stress responses, motivated behaviors, learning and memory, and food intake (Ma et al., 2016).

An orexigenic effect of relaxin-3 was first described by McGowan et al. (2005) who demonstrated that relaxin-3 was "equipotent" with ghrelin and NPY following icv administration. Further studies confirmed an orexigenic action of relaxin-3 injections (Hida et al., 2006) with higher sensitivity of females to the orexigenic effects of relaxin-3 (Calvez et al., 2015, 2016a). An important site for the orexigenic action of relaxin-3 is the PVN, since intra-PVN injection of the peptide (McGowan et al., 2005, 2006), and virally-mediated secretion of relaxin-3 receptor (RXFP3) agonist within the PVN (Ganella et al., 2013) increases food intake and body weight in rats. The orexigenic action of RXFP3 activation likely involves inhibition of anorexigenic oxytocin (OT) and arginine vasopressin (AVP) synthesis, since a robust reduction in OT and AVP mRNA levels was observed in response to RXFP3 activation in the PVN (Ganella et al., 2013) and relaxin-3 has an inhibitory action on PVN OT and AVP neurons *in vitro* (Kania et al., 2017).

Neurons in the NI are highly sensitive to stress and increases in relaxin-3 mRNA, hnRNA and peptide were observed after both physical (Calvez et al., 2016b) and psychological stressors (Tanaka et al., 2005; Banerjee et al., 2010; Lenglos et al., 2013). Moreover, a majority of relaxin-3 neurons in NI and PAG express CRH_1-receptors and are excited by CRH injections *in vivo* and *in vitro* (Tanaka et al., 2005; Blasiak et al., 2013; Ma et al., 2013). The relaxin-3/RXFP3 system plays a role in stress-induced binge eating (Lenglos et al., 2013; Calvez et al., 2016b) and stress-induced reinstatement of alcohol seeking (Ryan et al., 2013; Kastman et al., 2016; Walker et al., 2016). Relaxin-3/RXFP3 signaling may reciprocally influence stress responses since icv injections of relaxin-3 in male rats result in increased *c-fos* and CRH mRNA expression in PVN neurons and increased plasma ACTH and corticosterone levels (Watanabe et al., 2011; McGowan et al., 2014; Lenglos et al., 2015). The overall data suggest an important role of relaxin-3 in mechanisms underlying stress influences on food intake related processes.

A growing body of evidence suggests a link between the relaxin-3 system and circadian-related processes and circadian clock structures. Relaxin-3 positive nerve fibers/terminals are present in the main neuronal structures of the circadian system; SCN, IGL and raphe nuclei (Ma et al., 2007) and *in vitro* relaxin-3 receptor activation alters the electrical activity of IGL neurons (Blasiak et al., 2013), which innervate the SCN. Relaxin-3 *and* RXFP3 knockout mice display reduced voluntary running wheel activity during the dark/active phase (Smith et al., 2012; Hosken et al., 2015) and activation of relaxin-3 receptors promotes arousal (Smith et al., 2013). Currently, there are no reports of a circadian rhythmicity in relaxin-3 levels, but sensitivity of relaxin-3 neurons to neuropeptides synthetized in a circadian manner, such as CRH and orexins (Blasiak et al., 2013, 2015) suggest that relaxin-3 expression and/or excitability of NI relaxin-3 neurons may vary over the 24-h cycle.

In conclusion, excessive and prolonged stress experienced on an everyday basis leads to circadian and metabolic disturbances, which constitute overweight and obesity risk factors (Kyrou et al., 2006; Antunes et al., 2010). Considerable experimental evidence indicates that the orexigenic neuropeptides, as critical regulators of energy homeostasis, are important elements of stress- and chronodisruption-induced malfunctioning of feeding behavior. Importantly, the circadian clock, HPA-axis and orexigenic neuropeptide systems display extensive crosstalk, and a better understanding of the mechanisms that control these mutual relationships is necessary for improving treatment strategies for food intake related disorders.

AUTHOR CONTRIBUTIONS

AB proposed the concept, reviewed the literature, and wrote the manuscript; ALG, GH, and MHL discussed the concept and revised the manuscript critically. All authors accepted the final version of the article.

REFERENCES

Abrahamson, E. E., Leak, R. K., and Moore, R. Y. (2001). The suprachiasmatic nucleus projects to posterior hypothalamic arousal systems. *Neuroreport* 12, 435–440. doi: 10.1097/00001756-200102120-00048

Alfalah, M., and Michel, M. C. (2004). *Neuropeptide Y and Related Peptides.* Berlin; New York, NY: Springer.

Antunes, L. C., Levandovski, R., Dantas, G., Caumo, W., and Hidalgo, M. P. (2010). Obesity and shift work: chronobiological aspects. *Nutrition Res Rev.* 23, 155–168. doi: 10.1017/S0954422410000016

Balsalobre, A., Brown, S. A., Marcacci, L., Tronche, F., Kellendonk, C., Reichardt, H. M., et al. (2000). Resetting of circadian time in peripheral tissues by glucocorticoid signaling. *Science* 289, 2344–2347. doi: 10.1126/science.289.5488.2344

Banerjee, A., Shen, P. J., Ma, S., Bathgate, R. A., and Gundlach, A. L. (2010). Swim stress excitation of nucleus incertus and rapid induction of relaxin-3 expression via CRF1 activation. *Neuropharmacology* 58, 145–155. doi: 10.1016/j.neuropharm.2009.06.019

Banks, W. A. (2010). Blood-brain barrier as a regulatory interface. *Forum Nutr.* 63, 102–110. doi: 10.1159/000264398

Barclay, J. L., Tsang, A. H., and Oster, H. (2012). Interaction of central and peripheral clocks in physiological regulation. *Prog. Brain Res.* 199, 163–181. doi: 10.1016/B978-0-444-59427-3.00030-7

Beck, B., Stricker-Krongrad, A., Nicolas, J. P., and Burlet, C. (1992). Chronic and continuous intracerebroventricular infusion of neuropeptide Y in Long-Evans rats mimics the feeding behaviour of obese Zucker rats. *Int. J. Obes. Relat. Metab. Disord.* 16, 295–302.

Belle, M. D., Hughes, A. T., Bechtold, D. A., Cunningham, P., Pierucci, M., Burdakov, D., et al. (2014). Acute suppressive and long-term phase modulation actions of orexin on the mammalian circadian clock. *J. Neurosci.* 34, 3607–3621. doi: 10.1523/JNEUROSCI.3388-13.2014

Benite-Ribeiro, S. A., Putt, D. A., Soares-Filho, M. C., and Santos, J. M. (2016). The link between hypothalamic epigenetic modifications and long-term feeding control. *Appetite* 107, 445–453. doi: 10.1016/j.appet.2016.08.111

Bertile, F., Oudart, H., Criscuolo, F., Maho, Y. L., and Raclot, T. (2003). Hypothalamic gene expression in long-term fasted rats: relationship with body fat. *Biochem. Biophys. Res. Commun.* 303, 1106–1113. doi: 10.1016/S0006-291X(03)00481-9

Blasiak, A., Blasiak, T., Lewandowski, M. H., Hossain, M. A., Wade, J. D., and Gundlach, A. L. (2013). Relaxin-3 innervation of the intergeniculate leaflet of the rat thalamus - neuronal tract-tracing and *in vitro* electrophysiological studies. *Eur. J. Neurosci.* 37, 1284–1294. doi: 10.1111/ejn.12155

Blasiak, A., Siwiec, M., Grabowiecka, A., Blasiak, T., Czerw, A., Blasiak, E., et al. (2015). Excitatory orexinergic innervation of rat nucleus incertus - Implications for ascending arousal, motivation and feeding control. *Neuropharmacology* 99, 432–447. doi: 10.1016/j.neuropharm.2015.08.014

Bluet-Pajot, M. T., Presse, F., Voko, Z., Hoeger, C., Mounier, F., Epelbaum, J., et al. (1995). Neuropeptide-E-I antagonizes the action of melanin-concentrating hormone on stress-induced release of adrenocorticotropin in the rat. *J. Neuroendocrinol.* 7, 297–303. doi: 10.1111/j.1365-2826.1995.tb00761.x

Borowsky, B., Durkin, M. M., Ogozalek, K., Marzabadi, M. R., DeLeon, J., Lagu, B., et al. (2002). Antidepressant, anxiolytic and anorectic effects of a melanin-concentrating hormone-1 receptor antagonist. *Nat. Med.* 8, 825–830. doi: 10.1038/nm0902-1039b

Broberger, C., De Lecea, L., Sutcliffe, J. G., and Hokfelt, T. (1998). Hypocretin/orexin- and melanin-concentrating hormone-expressing cells form distinct populations in the rodent lateral hypothalamus: relationship to the neuropeptide Y and agouti gene-related protein systems. *J. Comp. Neurol.* 402, 460–474

Buijs, R. M., Wortel, J., Van Heerikhuize, J. J., Feenstra, M. G., Ter Horst, G. J., Romijn, H. J., et al. (1999). Anatomical and functional demonstration of a multisynaptic suprachiasmatic nucleus adrenal (cortex) pathway. *Eur. J. Neurosci.* 11, 1535–1544. doi: 10.1046/j.1460-9568.1999.00575.x

Calvez, J., de Avila, C., Guèvremont, G., and Timofeeva, E. (2016a). Sex-specific effects of chronic administration of relaxin-3 on food intake, body weight and hypothalamo-pituitary-gonadal axis in rats. *J. Neuroendocrinol.* doi: 10.1111/jne.12439. [Epub ahead of print].

Calvez, J., de Avila, C., Matte, L. O., Guèvremont, G., Gundlach, A. L., and Timofeeva, E. (2016b). Role of relaxin-3/RXFP3 system in stress-induced binge-like eating in female rats. *Neuropharmacology* 102, 207–215. doi: 10.1016/j.neuropharm.2015.11.014

Calvez, J., Lenglos, C., de Avila, C., Guèvremont, G., and Timofeeva, E. (2015). Differential effects of central administration of relaxin-3 on food intake and hypothalamic neuropeptides in male and female rats. *Genes Brain Behav.* 14, 550–563. doi: 10.1111/gbb.12236

Cascio, C. S., Shinsako, J., and Dallman, M. F. (1987). The suprachiasmatic nuclei stimulate evening ACTH secretion in the rat. *Brain Res.* 423, 173–178. doi: 10.1016/0006-8993(87)90837-7

Cason, A. M., Smith, R. J., Tahsili-Fahadan, P., Moorman, D. E., Sartor, G. C., and Aston-Jones, G. (2010). Role of orexin/hypocretin in reward-seeking and addiction: implications for obesity. *Physiol. Behav.* 100, 419–428. doi: 10.1016/j.physbeh.2010.03.009

Cavagnini, F., Croci, M., Putignano, P., Petroni, M. L., and Invitti, C. (2000). Glucocorticoids and neuroendocrine function. *Int. J. Obes. Relat. Metab. Disord.* 24(Suppl. 2), S77–S79. doi: 10.1038/sj.ijo.0801284

Chagra, S. L., Zavala, J. K., Hall, M. V., and Gosselink, K. L. (2011). Acute and repeated restraint differentially activate orexigenic pathways in the rat hypothalamus. *Regul. Pept.* 167, 70–78. doi: 10.1016/j.regpep.2010.11.006

Chee, M. J., Pissios, P., and Maratos-Flier, E. (2013). Neurochemical characterization of neurons expressing melanin-concentrating hormone receptor 1 in the mouse hypothalamus. *J. Comp. Neurol.* 521, 2208–2234. doi: 10.1002/cne.23273

Chung, S., Hopf, F. W., Nagasaki, H., Li, C. Y., Belluzzi, J. D., Bonci, A., et al. (2009). The melanin-concentrating hormone system modulates cocaine reward. *Proc. Natl. Acad. Sci. U.S.A.* 106, 6772–6777. doi: 10.1073/pnas.0811331106

Chung, S., Son, G. H., and Kim, K. (2011). Circadian rhythm of adrenal glucocorticoid: its regulation and clinical implications. *Biochim. Biophys. Acta* 1812, 581–591. doi: 10.1016/j.bbadis.2011.02.003

Coccurello, R., D'Amato, F. R., and Moles, A. (2009). Chronic social stress, hedonism and vulnerability to obesity: lessons from rodents. *Neurosci. Biobehav. Rev.* 33, 537–550. doi: 10.1016/j.neubiorev.2008.05.018

Conrad, C. D., and McEwen, B. S. (2000). Acute stress increases neuropeptide Y mRNA within the arcuate nucleus and hilus of the dentate gyrus. *Mol Brain Res.* 79, 102–109. doi: 10.1016/S0169-328X(00)00105-4

Dallman, M. F., Akana, S. F., Strack, A. M., Hanson, E. S., and Sebastian, R. J. (1995). The neural network that regulates energy balance is responsive to glucocorticoids and insulin and also regulates HPA axis responsivity at a site proximal to CRF neurons. *Ann. N. Y. Acad. Sci.* 771, 730–742. doi: 10.1111/j.1749-6632.1995.tb44724.x

Date, Y., Ueta, Y., Yamashita, H., Yamaguchi, H., Matsukura, S., Kangawa, K., et al. (1999). Orexins, orexigenic hypothalamic peptides, interact with autonomic, neuroendocrine and neuroregulatory systems. *Proc. Natl. Acad. Sci. U.S.A.* 96, 748–753. doi: 10.1073/pnas.96.2.748

Deboer, T., Overeem, S., Visser, N. A., Duindam, H., Frolich, M., Lammers, G. J., et al. (2004). Convergence of circadian and sleep regulatory mechanisms on hypocretin-1. *Neuroscience* 129, 727–732. doi: 10.1016/j.neuroscience.2004.07.049

Deurveilher, S., and Semba, K. (2005). Indirect projections from the suprachiasmatic nucleus to major arousal-promoting cell groups in rat: implications for the circadian control of behavioural state. *Neuroscience* 130, 165–183. doi: 10.1016/j.neuroscience.2004.08.030

Duncan, E. A., Proulx, K., and Woods, S. C. (2005). Central administration of melanin-concentrating hormone increases alcohol and sucrose/quinine intake in rats. *Alcohol. Clin. Exp. Res.* 29, 958–964. doi: 10.1097/01.ALC.0000167741.42353.10

Edwards, C. M., Abusnana, S., Sunter, D., Murphy, K. G., Ghatei, M. A., and Bloom, S. R. (1999). The effect of the orexins on food intake: comparison with neuropeptide Y, melanin-concentrating hormone and galanin. *J. Endocrinol.* 160, R7–R12. doi: 10.1677/joe.0.160r007

Fan, S., Dakshinamoorthy, J., Kim, E. R., Xu, Y., Huang, C., and Tong, Q. (2016). An indirect action contributes to c-Fos induction in paraventricular hypothalamic nucleus by neuropeptide Y. *Sci. Rep.* 6:19980. doi: 10.1038/srep19980

Fenselau, H., Campbell, J. N., Verstegen, A. M., Madara, J. C., Xu, J., Shah, B. P., et al. (2017). A rapidly acting glutamatergic ARC→PVH satiety circuit postsynaptically regulated by alpha-MSH. *Nat. Neurosci.* 20, 42–45. doi: 10.1038/nn.4442

Ganella, D. E., Callander, G. E., Ma, S., Bye, C. R., Gundlach, A. L., and Bathgate, R. A. (2013). Modulation of feeding by chronic rAAV expression of a relaxin-3 peptide agonist in rat hypothalamus. *Gene Ther.* 20, 703–716. doi: 10.1038/gt.2012.83

Georgescu, D., Sears, R. M., Hommel, J. D., Barrot, M., Bolanos, C. A., Marsh, D. J., et al. (2005). The hypothalamic neuropeptide melanin-concentrating hormone acts in the nucleus accumbens to modulate feeding behavior and forced-swim performance. *J. Neurosci.* 25, 2933–2940. doi: 10.1523/JNEUROSCI.1714-04.2005

Girotti, M., Weinberg, M. S., and Spencer, R. L. (2009). Diurnal expression of functional and clock-related genes throughout the rat HPA axis: system-wide shifts in response to a restricted feeding schedule. *Am. J. Physiol. Endocrinol. Metab.* 296, E888–E897. doi: 10.1152/ajpendo.90946.2008

González, J. A., Jensen, L. T., Iordanidou, P., Strom, M., Fugger, L., and Burdakov, D. (2016). Inhibitory interplay between orexin neurons and eating. *Curr. Biol.* 26, 2486–2491. doi: 10.1016/j.cub.2016.07.013

Gropp, E., Shanabrough, M., Borok, E., Xu, A. W., Janoschek, R., Buch, T., et al. (2005). Agouti-related peptide-expressing neurons are mandatory for feeding. *Nat. Neurosci.* 8, 1289–1291. doi: 10.1038/nn1548

Guan, J. L., Uehara, K., Lu, S., Wang, Q. P., Funahashi, H., Sakurai, T., et al. (2002). Reciprocal synaptic relationships between orexin- and melanin-concentrating hormone-containing neurons in the rat lateral hypothalamus: a novel circuit implicated in feeding regulation. *Int. J. Obes. Relat. Metab. Disord.* 26, 1523–1532. doi: 10.1038/sj.ijo.0802155

Guesdon, B., Paradis, E., Samson, P., and Richard, D. (2009). Effects of intracerebroventricular and intra-accumbens melanin-concentrating hormone agonism on food intake and energy expenditure. *Am. J. Physiol. Regul. Integr. Comp. Physiol.* 296, R469–R475. doi: 10.1152/ajpregu.90556.2008

Hagan, J. J., Leslie, R. A., Patel, S., Evans, M. L., Wattam, T. A., Holmes, S., et al. (1999). Orexin A activates locus coeruleus cell firing and increases arousal in the rat. *Proc. Natl. Acad. Sci. U.S.A.* 96, 10911–10916. doi: 10.1073/pnas.96.19.10911

Hahn, T. M., Breininger, J. F., Baskin, D. G., and Schwartz, M. W. (1998). Coexpression of Agrp and NPY in fasting-activated hypothalamic neurons. *Nat. Neurosci.* 1, 271–272. doi: 10.1038/1082

Hara, J., Beuckmann, C. T., Nambu, T., Willie, J. T., Chemelli, R. M., Sinton, C. M., et al. (2001). Genetic ablation of orexin neurons in mice results in narcolepsy, hypophagia, and obesity. *Neuron* 30, 345–354. doi: 10.1016/S0896-6273(01)00293-8

Hassani, O. K., Lee, M. G., and Jones, B. E. (2009). Melanin-concentrating hormone neurons discharge in a reciprocal manner to orexin neurons across the sleep-wake cycle. *Proc. Natl. Acad. Sci. U.S.A.* 106, 2418–2422. doi: 10.1073/pnas.0811400106

Haynes, A. C., Jackson, B., Chapman, H., Tadayyon, M., Johns, A., Porter, R. A., et al. (2000). A selective orexin-1 receptor antagonist reduces food consumption in male and female rats. *Regul. Pept.* 96, 45–51. doi: 10.1016/S0167-0115(00)00199-3

Helmreich, D. L., Parfitt, D. B., Lu, X. Y., Akil, H., and Watson, S. J. (2005). Relation between the hypothalamic-pituitary-thyroid (HPT) axis and the hypothalamic-pituitary-adrenal (HPA) axis during repeated stress. *Neuroendocrinology* 81, 183–192. doi: 10.1159/000087001

Hervieu, G. (2003). Melanin-concentrating hormone functions in the nervous system: food intake and stress. *Expert Opin. Ther. Targets* 7, 495–511. doi: 10.1517/14728222.7.4.495

Hida, T., Takahashi, E., Shikata, K., Hirohashi, T., Sawai, T., Seiki, T., et al. (2006). Chronic intracerebroventricular administration of relaxin-3 increases body weight in rats. *J. Recept. Signal Transduct. Res.* 26, 147–158. doi: 10.1080/10799890600623373

Horvath, T. L., and Gao, X. B. (2005). Input organization and plasticity of hypocretin neurons: possible clues to obesity's association with insomnia. *Cell Metab.* 1, 279–286. doi: 10.1016/j.cmet.2005.03.003

Hosken, I. T., Sutton, S. W., Smith, C. M., and Gundlach, A. L. (2015). Relaxin-3 receptor (Rxfp3) gene knockout mice display reduced running wheel activity: implications for role of relaxin-3/RXFP3 signalling in sustained arousal. *Behav. Brain Res.* 278, 167–175. doi: 10.1016/j.bbr.2014.09.028

Inutsuka, A., Inui, A., Tabuchi, S., Tsunematsu, T., Lazarus, M., and Yamanaka, A. (2014). Concurrent and robust regulation of feeding behaviors and metabolism by orexin neurons. *Neuropharmacology* 85, 451–460. doi: 10.1016/j.neuropharm.2014.06.015

Jamali, K. A., and Tramu, G. (1999). Control of rat hypothalamic pro-opiomelanocortin neurons by a circadian clock that is entrained by the daily light-off signal. *Neuroscience* 93, 1051–1061. doi: 10.1016/S0306-4522(99)00208-0

Jezova, D., Bartanusz, V., Westergren, I., Johansson, B. B., Rivier, J., Vale, W., et al. (1992). Rat melanin-concentrating hormone stimulates adrenocorticotropin secretion: evidence for a site of action in brain regions protected by the blood-brain barrier. *Endocrinology* 130, 1024–1029.

Kalsbeek, A., Buijs, R. M., van Heerikhuize, J. J., Arts, M., and van der Woude, T. P. (1992). Vasopressin-containing neurons of the suprachiasmatic nuclei inhibit corticosterone release. *Brain Res.* 580, 62–67. doi: 10.1016/0006-8993(92)90927-2

Kalsbeek, A., van Heerikhuize, J. J., Wortel, J., and Buijs, R. M. (1996). A diurnal rhythm of stimulatory input to the hypothalamo-pituitary-adrenal system as revealed by timed intrahypothalamic administration of the vasopressin V1 antagonist. *J. Neurosci.* 16, 5555–5565.

Kania, A., Czerw, A., Grabowiecka, A., de Avila, C., Blasiak, T., Rajfur, Z., et al. (2017). Inhibition of oxytocin and vasopressin neuron activity in rat hypothalamic paraventricular nucleus by relaxin-3/RXFP3 signalling. *J. Physiol.* doi: 10.1113/jp273787. [Epub ahead of print].

Kantor, S., Mochizuki, T., Janisiewicz, A. M., Clark, E., Nishino, S., and Scammell, T. E. (2009). Orexin neurons are necessary for the circadian control of REM sleep. *Sleep* 32, 1127–1134. doi: 10.1093/sleep/32.9.1127

Karlsson, C., Aziz, A. M., Rehman, F., Pitcairn, C., Barchiesi, R., Barbier, E., et al. (2016a). Melanin-concentrating hormone and its MCH-1 receptor: relationship between effects on alcohol and caloric intake. *Alcohol. Clin. Exp. Res.* 40, 2199–2207. doi: 10.1111/acer.13181

Karlsson, C., Rehman, F., Damdazic, R., Atkins, A. L., Schank, J. R., Gehlert, D. R., et al. (2016b). The melanin-concentrating hormone-1 receptor modulates alcohol-induced reward and DARPP-32 phosphorylation. *Psychopharmacology* 233, 2355–2363. doi: 10.1007/s00213-016-4285-y

Kas, M. J., Bruijnzeel, A. W., Haanstra, J. R., Wiegant, V. M., and Adan, R. A. (2005). Differential regulation of agouti-related protein and neuropeptide Y in hypothalamic neurons following a stressful event. *J. Mol. Endocrinol.* 35, 159–164. doi: 10.1677/jme.1.01819

Kastman, H. E., Blasiak, A., Walker, L., Siwiec, M., Krstew, E. V., Gundlach, A. L., et al. (2016). Nucleus incertus Orexin2 receptors mediate alcohol seeking in rats. *Neuropharmacology* 110, 82–91. doi: 10.1016/j.neuropharm.2016.07.006

Kaye, W. H., Berrettini, W., Gwirtsman, H., and George, D. T. (1990). Altered cerebrospinal fluid neuropeptide Y and peptide YY immunoreactivity in anorexia and bulimia nervosa. *Arch. Gen. Psychiatry* 47, 548–556. doi: 10.1001/archpsyc.1990.01810180048008

Kim, H. J., Lee, J. H., Choi, S. H., Lee, Y. S., and Jahng, J. W. (2005). Fasting-induced increases of arcuate NPY mRNA and plasma corticosterone are blunted in the rat experienced neonatal maternal separation. *Neuropeptides* 39, 587–594. doi: 10.1016/j.npep.2005.09.003

Kim, M. S., Rossi, M., Abusnana, S., Sunter, D., Morgan, D. G., Small, C. J., et al. (2000). Hypothalamic localization of the feeding effect of agouti-related peptide and alpha-melanocyte-stimulating hormone. *Diabetes* 49, 177–182. doi: 10.2337/diabetes.49.2.177

Kim, T. K., and Han, P. L. (2016). Physical exercise counteracts stress-induced upregulation of melanin-concentrating hormone in the brain and stress-induced persisting anxiety-like behaviors. *Exp. Neurobiol.* 25, 163–173. doi: 10.5607/en.2016.25.4.163

Klisch, C., Inyushkin, A., Mordel, J., Karnas, D., Pevet, P., and Meissl, H. (2009). Orexin A modulates neuronal activity of the rodent suprachiasmatic nucleus *in vitro*. *Eur. J. Neurosci.* 30, 65–75. doi: 10.1111/j.1460-9568.2009.06794.x

Koch, C. E., Leinweber, B., Drengberg, B. C., Blaum, C., and Oster, H. (2016). Interaction between circadian rhythms and stress. *Neurobiol. Stress.* 6, 57–67. doi: 10.1016/j.ynstr.2016.09.001

Kohlmeier, K. A., Tyler, C. J., Kalogiannis, M., Ishibashi, M., Kristensen, M. P., Gumenchuk, I., et al. (2013). Differential actions of orexin receptors in brainstem cholinergic and monoaminergic neurons revealed by receptor knockouts: implications for orexinergic signaling in arousal and narcolepsy. *Front. Neurosci.* 7:246. doi: 10.3389/fnins.2013.00246

Konadhode, R. R., Pelluru, D., Blanco-Centurion, C., Zayachkivsky, A., Liu, M., Uhde, T., et al. (2013). Optogenetic stimulation of MCH neurons increases sleep. *J. Neurosci.* 33, 10257–10263. doi: 10.1523/JNEUROSCI.1225-13.2013

Krashes, M. J., Koda, S., Ye, C., Rogan, S. C., Adams, A. C., Cusher, D. S., et al. (2011). Rapid, reversible activation of AgRP neurons drives feeding behavior in mice. *J. Clin. Invest.* 121, 1424–1428. doi: 10.1172/JCI46229

Krashes, M. J., Shah, B. P., Koda, S., and Lowell, B. B. (2013). Rapid versus delayed stimulation of feeding by the endogenously released AgRP neuron mediators GABA, NPY, and AgRP. *Cell Metab.* 18, 588–595. doi: 10.1016/j.cmet.2013.09.009

Kuperman, Y., Weiss, M., Dine, J., Staikin, K., Golani, O., Ramot, A., et al. (2016). CRFR1 in AgRP neurons modulates sympathetic nervous system activity to adapt to cold stress and fasting. *Cell Metab.* 23, 1185–1199. doi: 10.1016/j.cmet.2016.04.017

Kuru, M., Ueta, Y., Serino, R., Nakazato, M., Yamamoto, Y., Shibuya, I., et al. (2000). Centrally administered orexin/hypocretin activates HPA axis in rats. *Neuroreport* 11, 1977–1980. doi: 10.1097/00001756-200006260-00034

Kyrou, I., Chrousos, G. P., and Tsigos, C. (2006). Stress, visceral obesity, and metabolic complications. *Ann. N. Y. Acad. Sci.* 1083, 77–110. doi: 10.1196/annals.1367.008

Larsen, P. J., Jessop, D. S., Chowdrey, H. S., Lightman, S. L., and Mikkelsen, J. D. (1994). Chronic administration of glucocorticoids directly upregulates prepro-neuropeptide Y and Y1-receptor mRNA levels in the arcuate nucleus of the rat. *J. Neuroendocrinol.* 6, 153–159. doi: 10.1111/j.1365-2826.1994.tb00566.x

Lee, C., Parks, G. S., and Civelli, O. (2011). Anxiolytic effects of the MCH1R antagonist TPI 1361-17. *J. Mol. Neurosci.* 43, 132–137. doi: 10.1007/s12031-010-9425-y

Lenglos, C., Calvez, J., and Timofeeva, E. (2015). Sex-specific effects of relaxin-3 on food intake and brain expression of corticotropin-releasing factor in rats. *Endocrinology* 156, 523–533. doi: 10.1210/en.2014-1743

Lenglos, C., Mitra, A., Guevremont, G., and Timofeeva, E. (2013). Sex differences in the effects of chronic stress and food restriction on body weight gain and brain expression of CRF and relaxin-3 in rats. *Genes Brain Behav.* 12, 370–387. doi: 10.1111/gbb.12028

Li, A. J., Wiater, M. F., Oostrom, M. T., Smith, B. R., Wang, Q., Dinh, T. T., et al. (2012). Leptin-sensitive neurons in the arcuate nuclei contribute to endogenous feeding rhythms. *Am. J. Physiol. Regul. Integr. Comp. Physiol.* 302, R1313–R1326. doi: 10.1152/ajpregu.00086.2012

Liu, T., Kong, D., Shah, B. P., Ye, C., Koda, S., Saunders, A., et al. (2012). Fasting activation of AgRP neurons requires NMDA receptors and involves spinogenesis and increased excitatory tone. *Neuron* 73, 511–522. doi: 10.1016/j.neuron.2011.11.027

Ma, S., Blasiak, A., Olucha-Bordonau, F. E., Verberne, A. J., and Gundlach, A. L. (2013). Heterogeneous responses of nucleus incertus neurons to corticotrophin-releasing factor and coherent activity with hippocampal theta rhythm in the rat. *J. Physiol.* 591, 3981–4001. doi: 10.1113/jphysiol.2013.254300

Ma, S., Bonaventure, P., Ferraro, T., Shen, P. J., Burazin, T. C., Bathgate, R. A., et al. (2007). Relaxin-3 in GABA projection neurons of nucleus incertus suggests widespread influence on forebrain circuits via G-protein-coupled receptor-135 in the rat. *Neuroscience.* 144, 165–190. doi: 10.1016/j.neuroscience.2006.08.072

Ma, S., Smith, C. M., Blasiak, A., and Gundlach, A. L. (2016). Distribution, physiology and pharmacology of relaxin-3/RXFP3 systems in brain. *Br. J. Pharmacol.* doi: 10.1111/bph.13659. [Epub ahead of print].

Macneil, D. J. (2013). The role of melanin-concentrating hormone and its receptors in energy homeostasis. *Front. Endocrinol. (Lausanne)* 4:49. doi: 10.3389/fendo.2013.00049

Marston, O. J., Williams, R. H., Canal, M. M., Samuels, R. E., Upton, N., and Piggins, H. D. (2008). Circadian and dark-pulse activation of orexin/hypocretin neurons. *Mol. Brain* 1:19. doi: 10.1186/1756-6606-1-19

McGowan, B. M., Minnion, J. S., Murphy, K. G., Roy, D., Stanley, S. A., Dhillo, W. S., et al. (2014). Relaxin-3 stimulates the neuro-endocrine stress axis via corticotrophin-releasing hormone. *J. Endocrinol.* 221, 337–346. doi: 10.1530/JOE-13-0603

McGowan, B. M., Stanley, S. A., Smith, K. L., Minnion, J. S., Donovan, J., Thompson, E. L., et al. (2006). Effects of acute and chronic relaxin-3 on food intake and energy expenditure in rats. *Regul. Pept.* 136, 72–77. doi: 10.1016/j.regpep.2006.04.009

McGowan, B. M., Stanley, S. A., Smith, K. L., White, N. E., Connolly, M. M., Thompson, E. L., et al. (2005). Central relaxin-3 administration causes hyperphagia in male Wistar rats. *Endocrinology* 146, 3295–3300. doi: 10.1210/en.2004-1532

Mendoza, J., and Challet, E. (2009). Brain clocks: from the suprachiasmatic nuclei to a cerebral network. *Neuroscientist* 15, 477–488. doi: 10.1177/1073858408327808

Moore, R. Y., and Eichler, V. B. (1972). Loss of a circadian adrenal corticosterone rhythm following suprachiasmatic lesions in the rat. *Brain Res.* 42, 201–206. doi: 10.1016/0006-8993(72)90054-6

Morimoto, M., Morita, N., Ozawa, H., Yokoyama, K., and Kawata, M. (1996). Distribution of glucocorticoid receptor immunoreactivity and mRNA in the rat brain: an immunohistochemical and *in situ* hybridization study. *Neurosci. Res.* 26, 235–269. doi: 10.1016/S0168-0102(96)01105-4

Nader, N., Chrousos, G. P., and Kino, T. (2010). Interactions of the circadian CLOCK system and the HPA axis. *Trends Endocrinol. Metab.* 21, 277–286. doi: 10.1016/j.tem.2009.12.011

Owens, M. J., Bartolome, J., Schanberg, S. M., and Nemeroff, C. B. (1990). Corticotropin-releasing factor concentrations exhibit an apparent diurnal rhythm in hypothalamic and extrahypothalamic brain regions: differential sensitivity to corticosterone. *Neuroendocrinology* 52, 626–631. doi: 10.1159/000125655

Palus, K., Chrobok, L., and Lewandowski, M. H. (2015). Orexins/hypocretins modulate the activity of NPY-positive and -negative neurons in the rat intergeniculate leaflet via OX1 and OX2 receptors. *Neuroscience* 300, 370–380. doi: 10.1016/j.neuroscience.2015.05.039

Pankevich, D. E., Teegarden, S. L., Hedin, A. D., Jensen, C. L., and Bale, T. L. (2010). Caloric restriction experience reprograms stress and orexigenic pathways and promotes binge eating. *J. Neurosci.* 30, 16399–16407. doi: 10.1523/JNEUROSCI.1955-10.2010

Pekala, D., Blasiak, T., Raastad, M., and Lewandowski, M. H. (2011). The influence of orexins on the firing rate and pattern of rat intergeniculate leaflet neurons–electrophysiological and immunohistological studies. *Eur. J. Neurosci.* 34, 1406–1418. doi: 10.1111/j.1460-9568.2011.07868.x

Peyron, C., Tighe, D. K., van den Pol, A. N., de Lecea, L., Heller, H. C., Sutcliffe, J. G., et al. (1998). Neurons containing hypocretin (orexin) project to multiple neuronal systems. *J. Neurosci.* 18, 9996–10015.

Pezuk, P., Mohawk, J. A., Wang, L. A., and Menaker, M. (2012). Glucocorticoids as entraining signals for peripheral circadian oscillators. *Endocrinology* 153, 4775–4783. doi: 10.1210/en.2012-1486

Piccoli, L., Micioni Di Bonaventura, M. V., Cifani, C., Costantini, V. J., Massagrande, M., Montanari, D., et al. (2012). Role of orexin-1 receptor mechanisms on compulsive food consumption in a model of binge eating in female rats. *Neuropsychopharmacology* 37, 1999–2011. doi: 10.1038/npp.2012.48

Presse, F., Hervieu, G., Imaki, T., Sawchenko, P. E., Vale, W., and Nahon, J. L. (1992). Rat melanin-concentrating hormone messenger ribonucleic acid expression: marked changes during development and after stress and glucocorticoid stimuli. *Endocrinology* 131, 1241–1250.

Roy, M., David, N., Cueva, M., and Giorgetti, M. (2007). A study of the involvement of melanin-concentrating hormone receptor 1 (MCHR1) in murine models of depression. *Biol. Psychiatry* 61, 174–180. doi: 10.1016/j.biopsych.2006.03.076

Ryan, P. J., Büchler, E., Shabanpoor, F., Hossain, M. A., Wade, J. D., Lawrence, A. J., et al. (2013). Central relaxin-3 receptor (RXFP3) activation decreases anxiety- and depressive-like behaviours in the rat. *Behav. Brain Res.* 244, 142–151. doi: 10.1016/j.bbr.2013.01.034

Sakurai, T., Amemiya, A., Ishii, M., Matsuzaki, I., Chemelli, R. M., Tanaka, H., et al. (1998). Orexins and orexin receptors: a family of hypothalamic neuropeptides and G protein-coupled receptors that regulate feeding behavior. *Cell* 92, 573–585. doi: 10.1016/S0092-8674(00)80949-6

Sarabdjitsingh, R. A., Conway-Campbell, B. L., Leggett, J. D., Waite, E. J., Meijer, O. C., de Kloet, E. R., et al. (2010). Stress responsiveness varies over the ultradian glucocorticoid cycle in a brain-region-specific manner. *Endocrinology* 151, 5369–5379. doi: 10.1210/en.2010-0832

Schibler, U., Ripperger, J., and Brown, S. A. (2003). Peripheral circadian oscillators in mammals: time and food. *J. Biol. Rhythms* 18, 250–260. doi: 10.1177/0748730403018003007

Schmeichel, B. E., Herman, M. A., Roberto, M., and Koob, G. F. (2016). Hypocretin neurotransmission within the central amygdala mediates escalated cocaine self-administration and stress-induced reinstatement in rats. *Biol. Psychiatry.* 81, 606–615. doi: 10.1016/j.biopsych.2016.06.010

Schuld, A., Hebebrand, J., Geller, F., and Pollmacher, T. (2000). Increased body-mass index in patients with narcolepsy. *Lancet* 355, 1274–1275. doi: 10.1016/S0140-6736(05)74704-8

Sefton, C., Harno, E., Davies, A., Small, H., Allen, T. J., Wray, J. R., et al. (2016). Elevated hypothalamic glucocorticoid levels are associated with obesity and hyperphagia in male mice. *Endocrinology* 157, 4257–4265. doi: 10.1210/en.2016-1571

Segall, L. A., Milet, A., Tronche, F., and Amir, S. (2009). Brain glucocorticoid receptors are necessary for the rhythmic expression of the clock protein, PERIOD2, in the central extended amygdala in mice. *Neurosci. Lett.* 457, 58–60. doi: 10.1016/j.neulet.2009.03.083

Selbach, O., and Haas, H. L. (2006). Hypocretins: the timing of sleep and waking. *Chronobiol. Int.* 23, 63–70. doi: 10.1080/07420520500545961

Shimada, M., Tritos, N. A., Lowell, B. B., Flier, J. S., and Maratos-Flier, E. (1998). Mice lacking melanin-concentrating hormone are hypophagic and lean. *Nature* 396, 670–674. doi: 10.1038/25341

Shimizu, H., Arima, H., Watanabe, M., Goto, M., Banno, R., Sato, I., et al. (2008). Glucocorticoids increase neuropeptide Y and agouti-related peptide gene expression via adenosine monophosphate-activated protein kinase signaling in the arcuate nucleus of rats. *Endocrinology* 149, 4544–4553. doi: 10.1210/en.2008-0229

Smith, C. M., Blasiak, A., Ganella, D. E., Chua, B. E., Layfield, S. L., Bathgate, R. A., et al. (2013). Viral-mediated delivery of an RXFP3 agonist into brain promotes arousal in mice. *Ital. J. Anat. Embryol.* 118, 42–46. doi: 10.13128/IJAE-13890

Smith, C. M., Hosken, I. T., Sutton, S. W., Lawrence, A. J., and Gundlach, A. L. (2012). Relaxin-3 null mutation mice display a circadian hypoactivity phenotype. *Genes Brain Behav.* 11, 94–104. doi: 10.1111/j.1601-183X.2011.00730.x

Smith, D. G., Davis, R. J., Rorick-Kehn, L., Morin, M., Witkin, J. M., McKinzie, D. L., et al. (2006). Melanin-concentrating hormone-1 receptor modulates neuroendocrine, behavioral, and corticolimbic neurochemical stress responses in mice. *Neuropsychopharmacology* 31, 1135–1145. doi: 10.1038/sj.npp.1300913

Smith, D. G., Hegde, L. G., Wolinsky, T. D., Miller, S., Papp, M., Ping, X., et al. (2009). The effects of stressful stimuli and hypothalamic-pituitary-adrenal axis activation are reversed by the melanin-concentrating hormone 1 receptor antagonist SNAP 94847 in rodents. *Behav. Brain Res.* 197, 284–291. doi: 10.1016/j.bbr.2008.08.026

Son, G. H., Chung, S., Choe, H. K., Kim, H. D., Baik, S. M., Lee, H., et al. (2008). Adrenal peripheral clock controls the autonomous circadian rhythm of glucocorticoid by causing rhythmic steroid production. *Proc. Natl. Acad. Sci. U.S.A.* 105, 20970–20975. doi: 10.1073/pnas.0806962106

Spiga, F., Waite, E. J., Liu, Y., Kershaw, Y. M., Aguilera, G., and Lightman, S. L. (2011). ACTH-dependent ultradian rhythm of corticosterone secretion. *Endocrinology* 152, 1448–1457. doi: 10.1210/en.2010-1209

Spyrka, J., and Hess, G. (2010). Repeated restraint-induced modulation of long-term potentiation in the dentate gyrus of the mouse. *Brain Res.* 1320, 28–33. doi: 10.1016/j.brainres.2010.01.031

Stanley, B. G., and Leibowitz, S. F. (1985). Neuropeptide Y injected in the paraventricular hypothalamus: a powerful stimulant of feeding behavior. *Proc. Natl. Acad. Sci. U.S.A.* 82, 3940–3943. doi: 10.1073/pnas.82.11.3940

Stevens, R. G., and Zhu, Y. (2015). Electric light, particularly at night, disrupts human circadian rhythmicity: is that a problem? *Philos. Trans. R. Soc. Lond. B. Biol. Sci.* 370, 1–9. doi: 10.1098/rstb.2014.0120

Su, Y., Foppen, E., Fliers, E., and Kalsbeek, A. (2016). Effects of Intracerebroventricular administration of neuropeptide Y on metabolic gene expression and energy metabolism in male rats. *Endocrinology* 157, 3070–3085. doi: 10.1210/en.2016-1083

Tanaka, M., Iijima, N., Miyamoto, Y., Fukusumi, S., Itoh, Y., Ozawa, H., et al. (2005). Neurons expressing relaxin 3/INSL 7 in the nucleus incertus respond to stress. *Eur. J. Neurosci.* 21, 1659–1670. doi: 10.1111/j.1460-9568.2005.03980.x

Tiesjema, B., la Fleur, S. E., Luijendijk, M. C., and Adan, R. A. (2009). Sustained NPY overexpression in the PVN results in obesity via temporarily increasing food intake. *Obesity (Silver Spring)* 17, 1448–1450. doi: 10.1038/oby.2008.670

Tousson, E., and Meissl, H. (2004). Suprachiasmatic nuclei grafts restore the circadian rhythm in the paraventricular nucleus of the hypothalamus. *J. Neurosci.* 24, 2983–2988. doi: 10.1523/JNEUROSCI.5044-03.2004

Ulrich-Lai, Y. M., and Herman, J. P. (2009). Neural regulation of endocrine and autonomic stress responses. *Nat. Rev. Neurosci.* 10, 397–409. doi: 10.1038/nrn2647

Vaze, K. M., and Sharma, V. K. (2013). On the adaptive significance of circadian clocks for their owners. *Chronobiol. Int.* 30, 413–433. doi: 10.3109/07420528.2012.754457

Verret, L., Goutagny, R., Fort, P., Cagnon, L., Salvert, D., Leger, L., et al. (2003). A role of melanin-concentrating hormone producing neurons in the central regulation of paradoxical sleep. *BMC Neurosci.* 4:19. doi: 10.1186/1471-2202-4-19

Waite, E. J., McKenna, M., Kershaw, Y., Walker, J. J., Cho, K., Piggins, H. D., et al. (2012). Ultradian corticosterone secretion is maintained in the absence of circadian cues. *Eur. J. Neurosci.* 36, 3142–3150. doi: 10.1111/j.1460-9568.2012.08213.x

Walker, L. C., Kastman, H. E., Koeleman, J. A., Smith, C. M., Perry, C. J., Krstew, E. V., et al. (2016). Nucleus incertus corticotrophin-releasing factor 1 receptor signalling regulates alcohol seeking in rats. *Addict. Biol.* doi: 10.1111/adb.12426. [Epub ahead of print].

Watanabe, Y., Miyamoto, Y., Matsuda, T., and Tanaka, M. (2011). Relaxin-3/INSL7 regulates the stress-response system in the rat hypothalamus. *J. Mol. Neurosci.* 43, 169–174. doi: 10.1007/s12031-010-9468-0

Wiater, M. F., Li, A. J., Dinh, T. T., Jansen, H. T., and Ritter, S. (2013). Leptin-sensitive neurons in the arcuate nucleus integrate activity and temperature circadian rhythms and anticipatory responses to food restriction. *Am. J. Physiol. Regul. Integr. Comp. Physiol.* 305, R949–R960. doi: 10.1152/ajpregu.00032.2013

Wiater, M. F., Mukherjee, S., Li, A. J., Dinh, T. T., Rooney, E. M., Simasko, S. M., et al. (2011). Circadian integration of sleep-wake and feeding requires NPY receptor-expressing neurons in the mediobasal hypothalamus. *Am. J. Physiol. Regul. Integr. Comp. Physiol.* 301, R1569–R1583. doi: 10.1152/ajpregu.00168.2011

Winsky-Sommerer, R., Yamanaka, A., Diano, S., Borok, E., Roberts, A. J., Sakurai, T., et al. (2004). Interaction between the corticotropin-releasing factor system and hypocretins (orexins): a novel circuit mediating stress response. *J. Neurosci.* 24, 11439–11448. doi: 10.1523/JNEUROSCI.3459-04.2004

World Health Organization (2016). *Obesity and Overweight.* [online] Available online at: http://www.who.int/mediacentre/factsheets/fs311/en/index.html

Wu, H., Zhao, Z., Stone, W. S., Huang, L., Zhuang, J., He, B., et al. (2008). Effects of sleep restriction periods on serum cortisol levels in healthy men. *Brain Res. Bull.* 77, 241–245. doi: 10.1016/j.brainresbull.2008.07.013

Yamanaka, A., Sakurai, T., Katsumoto, T., Yanagisawa, M., and Goto, K. (1999). Chronic intracerebroventricular administration of orexin-A to rats increases food intake in daytime, but has no effect on body weight. *Brain Res.* 849, 248–252. doi: 10.1016/S0006-8993(99)01905-8

Yi, C. X., Foppen, E., Abplanalp, W., Gao, Y., Alkemade, A., la Fleur, S. E., et al. (2012). Glucocorticoid signaling in the arcuate nucleus modulates hepatic insulin sensitivity. *Diabetes* 61, 339–345. doi: 10.2337/db11-1239

Yi, C. X., van der Vliet, J., Dai, J., Yin, G., Ru, L., and Buijs, R. M. (2006). Ventromedial arcuate nucleus communicates peripheral metabolic information to the suprachiasmatic nucleus. *Endocrinology* 147, 283–294. doi: 10.1210/en.2005-1051

Yoshida, Y., Fujiki, N., Nakajima, T., Ripley, B., Matsumura, H., Yoneda, H., et al. (2001). Fluctuation of extracellular hypocretin-1 (orexin A) levels in the rat in relation to the light-dark cycle and sleep-wake activities. *Eur. J. Neurosci.* 14, 1075–1081. doi: 10.1046/j.0953-816x.2001.01725.x

Zhang, S., Zeitzer, J. M., Yoshida, Y., Wisor, J. P., Nishino, S., Edgar, D. M., et al. (2004). Lesions of the suprachiasmatic nucleus eliminate the daily rhythm of hypocretin-1 release. *Sleep* 27, 619–627. doi: 10.1093/sleep/27.4.619

8

Rodent Models for the Analysis of Tissue Clock Function in Metabolic Rhythms Research

*Anthony H. Tsang[1,2], Mariana Astiz[1], Brinja Leinweber[1] and Henrik Oster[1]**

[1] Chronophysiology Group, Medical Department I, University of Lübeck, Lübeck, Germany, [2] Department of Clinical Biochemistry, Institute of Metabolic Science, University of Cambridge, Cambridge, UK

Edited by:
Andries Kalsbeek,
Academic Medical Center,
Netherlands

Reviewed by:
Michael T. Sellix,
University of Rochester School of Medicine and Dentistry, USA
David A. Bechtold,
University of Manchester, UK

Correspondence:
Henrik Oster
henrik.oster@uni-luebeck.de

The circadian timing system consists on a distributed network of cellular clocks that together coordinate 24-h rhythms of physiology and behavior. Clock function and metabolism are tightly coupled, from the cellular to the organismal level. Genetic and non-genetic approaches in rodents have been employed to study circadian clock function in the living organism. Due to the ubiquitous expression of clock genes and the intricate interaction between the circadian system and energy metabolism, genetic approaches targeting specific tissue clocks have been used to assess their contribution in systemic metabolic processes. However, special requirements regarding specificity and efficiency have to be met to allow for valid conclusions from such studies. In this review, we provide a brief summary of different approaches developed for dissecting tissue clock function in the metabolic context in rodents, compare their strengths and weaknesses, and suggest new strategies in assessing tissue clock output and the consequences of circadian clock disruption *in vivo*.

Keywords: clock genes, metabolism, gene targeting, *Bmal1*, conditional knockout, CRE-*loxP* system

INTRODUCTION

A network of cellular clocks adapts physiology and behavior to a 24-h rhythmic environment. Epidemiological evidence suggests a strong association between circadian rhythm disruption—e.g., in shift workers—and metabolic disorders (1). The development of genetic rodent models has been essential in deciphering the mechanisms linking clock dysfunction and the pathogenesis of metabolic diseases, highlighting the therapeutic potential of circadian rhythm manipulation in this context. Here, we provide a brief overview of the metabolic consequences of circadian disruption derived from rodent model studies and discuss potential and pitfalls of emerging genetic techniques in studying clock-metabolism crosstalk.

NON-GENETIC CIRCADIAN DISRUPTION MODELS

Early approaches describing the interplay between circadian clock function and metabolism were based on models of non-genetic circadian disruption (**Table 1**). Lesion experiments identified the suprachiasmatic nucleus (SCN) as the central circadian pacemaker (2, 3). In rats, SCN lesions abolish plasma rhythms of glucose, insulin (4), and leptin (5). In terms of general energy homeostasis, there are differences between studies that range from slight weight reductions (6) to no effect (5) and marked obesity (7). In the latter study on mice, increased weight is accompanied by hepatic insulin

TABLE 1 | Advantages and disadvantages of different clock targeting approaches in rodents.

Paradigm	Advantages	Disadvantages
Non-genetic clock disruption	• No gene targeting necessary • No developmental effects • At least partly reversible	• Non-specific (except for lesioning) and non-targeted (very broad intervention)
Classical (global) gene targeting	• High recombination efficiency	• No spatio-temporal control • Possible developmental effects • Irreversible and non-tunable
Conventional CRE-*loxP* gene targeting	• Relatively high recombination efficiency	• Relative tissue specificity • Possible developmental effects • Irreversible and non-tunable
Inducible CRE-*loxP* gene targeting	• Exclude developmental effects	• Relative tissue specificity • Irreversible and non-tunable • Reduced recombination efficiency
Chemogenetics	• Reversible, tunable, and good temporal control (depending on the pharmacokinetics of the drug used)	• Drug administration can interfere with the experiment • Poor tissue specificity (unless combined with the use of CRE-driver mice and/or viral transgene delivery)
Optogenetics	• Very good tissue specificity with implantation of light sources (when combined with the use of CRE-driver mice and/or viral transgene delivery) • Reversible, tunable, and excellent temporal resolution	• Phototoxicity for extended activation • Technically demanding and only few (mainly CNS) tissues are applicable in mammals

resistance. In sum, these studies illustrate that the SCN regulates metabolic hormones and tissue physiology either directly or *via* its control on food intake rhythms.

In an alternative paradigm, exposure to altered light regimens leads to disruption of behavioral circadian rhythms and energy metabolism. Mice exposed to bright day/dim night illumination lose their feeding rhythm along with reduced glucose tolerance and increased body weight (8). Constant light (LL)-exposed mice develop a higher body weight together with a profound loss in insulin sensitivity (7). In rats, LL exposure disrupts pancreatic beta cell clocks, correlating with reduced glucose-stimulated insulin secretion (9). In type-2 diabetes-prone rats, LL accelerates disease development due to a 50% reduction in beta cell mass (10). Most of these studies interpret their findings as a consequence of the disruptive effects of abnormal light exposure on SCN function. However, light can alter various centrally controlled functions such as mood and appetite independent of a clock effect (11, 12). Moreover, even though irregular light regimens are common for many animals and humans, there are only very few occasions where continuous light exposure above a certain threshold level may occur, making LL a highly artificial paradigm.

Several studies have outlined shift-working as a risk factor for the development of metabolic diseases (13), and various animal models have been developed to mimic this condition. Mice exposed to repeated 6-h advances of the light/dark (LD) cycle gain significantly more body weight than stable-LD controls (14). Interestingly, when mice are exposed to paradigms mimicking even more rapidly rotating weekly shift-work patterns, there is no or only a moderate effect on body weight (15). Sleep-restricting mice during their normal rest phase for 2 weeks leads to significant alterations in liver clock gene expression rhythms associated impaired pyruvate-stimulated gluconeogenesis, but no significant alterations in body weight (16). A similar approach in rats further yielded body weight increases and impaired glucose tolerance (17).

The mixed metabolic outcomes in the mentioned shift-work studies are likely directly related to the ability of the chosen paradigms to provoke food intake during the normal rest phase. Rest phase-restricted food access in mice promotes weight gain without increased energy intake (18). In line with that, while both the rapid-shift (15) and our sleep-restriction study in mice (16) showed no change in food intake rhythms, the 6-h shift model (14) and the rat sleep-restriction study (17) reported misaligned food intake. Considering the reciprocal interaction between energy intake and clock function, it has been speculated that epigenetic programming may be an important mechanism in the circadian regulation of energy metabolism—even across generations [reviewed in Ref. (19, 20)].

METABOLIC ALTERATIONS IN CONVENTIONAL CLOCK GENE MUTANT MICE

The development of clock gene mutant mouse models has provided a substantial tool to understand clock-metabolism interaction at the molecular level. Following the identification of *circadian locomotor output cycles kaput* (*Clock*) (21), further mammalian *clock genes* have been cloned and functionally characterized in corresponding mouse mutants (22–25). So far, brain and muscle ARNT-like 1 (BMAL1) has been identified as the only essential component of the molecular clockwork in mammals. Deletion of *Bmal1* in mice abolishes behavioral circadian rhythms in constant environmental conditions (25). Gene expression profiling experiments show that the rate-limiting steps of various metabolic pathways are subject to circadian regulation (26). *Bmal1* knockout (KO) mice show impaired glucose metabolism and insulin hypersensitivity (27, 28). At young age, they also gain weight more rapidly than wild-type littermates (28). Recently, an inducible global *Bmal1* KO mouse model has been developed. Unexpectedly, adult-onset *Bmal1* KOs do not suffer from many metabolic abnormalities described in the standard *Bmal1* KOs (29).

Mice expressing a dominant-negative CLOCK variant (CLOCK-Δ19) on a C57BL/6J genetic background display altered 24-h feeding patterns (30). *Clock-Δ19* mice are hyperphagic and show reduced energy expenditure. They also develop hyperglycemia, hyperlipidemia, hyperleptinemia, hypoinsulinemia, and increase in body weight and visceral adiposity under different diet conditions. These phenotypes may be partly explained by a reduced lipolytic capacity of white adipose tissue (31). By contrast, on an ICR genetic background, the same *Clock-Δ19* mutation leads to a reduction in body weight and impaired dietary lipid absorption, suggesting that the genetic background influences clock-metabolism interaction (32).

Inconsistent findings were also reported for the metabolic consequences of mutations in another clock gene, *Period (Per) 2*. *Per2*^{Brdm1} mutant mice (24) show hyperphagy, diet-induced obesity (33), hyperinsulinemia with altered insulin sensitivity, hypoglycemia, and low fasting hepatic glycogen content (34). By contrast, *Per2*^{ldc} mutants (35) show reduced adiposity, increased fatty acid oxidation, and hypotriglyceridemia (36), but are normoglycemic with improved clearance after glucose challenge (37). Of note, while genetic background may also play a role here, residual protein-coding transcripts have been detected in both mutants that may yield biologically active peptides (35, 38). Male, but not female, *Per1/2/3* triple mutants become obese under an HFD (39). A *Per3* KO alone has even stronger effects on male diet-induced weight gain, suggesting a genetic interaction of different *Per* genes in metabolic regulation (39).

Liver transcriptomic analyses from mice carrying *Rev-Erbα* loss- or gain-of-function alleles have identified it as a circadian regulator of cholesterol/lipid and bile acid homeostasis (40). In line with this, mice with adult-onset global loss of *Rev-Erbα/β* show deregulated glucose and lipid metabolism (41). Moreover, administration of REV-ERB agonists in mice induces body weight loss and decreased lipogenesis in liver and white adipose tissue, increased lipid and glucose oxidation in skeletal muscle, and elevated energy expenditure (42).

Together, these studies provide evidence that the circadian clock plays a fundamental role in energy homeostasis and that different clock components have specific functions in this context. However, because the mice used in these studies carry clock gene mutations in all tissues including the SCN, much like the non-genetic models discussed above, metabolic phenotypes may be confounded by systemic abnormalities such as altered sleep patterns, activity and feeding behaviors, or counteractive consequences of clock disruption in different tissues.

TISSUE CLOCK FUNCTION IN METABOLIC REGULATION

Several techniques have been developed to study the physiology of tissue circadian clocks (**Table 1**). *In vitro* experiments allow the study of tissue rhythms in the absence of external influences (43). However, such approaches have only limited potential for predicting the impact of tissue clock disruption on complex physiological processes such as energy metabolism. Transplantations have been used to study tissue clock function (44, 45). However, such techniques are highly invasive and only applicable for few tissues. Instead, conditional CRE-*loxP*-based gene targeting has been widely used for tissue-specific deletion of clock function *in vivo* (in most cases by targeting *Bmal1*) (46, 47). Here, we highlight some studies which have provided important insights into the contribution of different tissue clocks to metabolism.

Hepatocyte-specific deletion of *Bmal1* (L-Bmal1 KO) improves glucose tolerance—the opposite effect of a global *Bmal1* KO—which was attributed to reduced hepatic glucose export during the fasting phase *via* glucose transporter 2 (28). By contrast, mice with pancreatic beta cell-specific *Bmal1* deletion (P-Bmal1 KOs) show hyperglycemia and impaired glucose tolerance (48) due to decreased insulin exocytosis (49). Further, while mice with muscle-specific deletion of *Bmal1* (M-Bmal1 KO) show no significant change in systemic glucose regulation, impaired myocyte glucose uptake, and metabolism have been reported (50). Finally—and similar to global *Bmal1* KOs and *Clock-Δ19* mutants—mice with adipocyte-specific *Bmal1* deletion (A-*Bmal1* KOs) become obese (*ca.* 20% body weight) under HFD but not normal chow conditions. This phenotype correlates with misaligned food intake and blunted secretion rhythms of appetite-regulating polyunsaturated fatty acids from adipocytes (51).

Clock gene rhythms have been reported in central energy regulatory circuits (52). So far, few studies have addressed the biological function of specific brain clocks. With regard to metabolism, deletion of *Bmal1* in steroidogenic neurons of the ventromedial hypothalamus reduces sympathetic activation of thermogenesis in brown adipose tissue (53).

These few examples make clear that tissue-specific dissection of clock gene function has provided a much more detailed picture on how circadian clocks affect energy metabolism *in vivo*. Nevertheless, conclusions drawn from these experiments are often confounded by intrinsic drawbacks of the classical CRE-*loxP* system which novel genetic tools may help to overcome.

LIMITATIONS OF CLASSICAL GENETIC MODELS IN CHRONOBIOLOGY RESEARCH

Poor Specificity of the CRE Driver

In CRE-*loxP*-based gene targeting, the tissue-specific mutation is determined by the transcription dynamics of the CRE-expressing promoter. While this may not be such an issue for processes confined to specific tissues, for the ubiquitously active circadian system, this poses an important limitation: many allegedly *tissue-specific* promoters show varying amounts of off-target activity. For example, for two of the studies mentioned above, CRE drivers with off-target activities have been employed, namely *Fabp4-Cre* for A-*Bmal1* and *Pdx1-Cre* for P-*Bmal1* KOs. Critically, their expression in several metabolism-regulating circuits in the brain has been documented (54). Though the authors of these studies used different approaches to address this problem (such as supplementing *in vitro*/*ex vivo* data or repeating key experiments with another CRE driver), certain conclusions drawn from the *in vivo* metabolic experiments may still be ambiguous. Similarly, in the hypothalamic steroidogenic neuron *Bmal1* KO study, the *Sf1-Cre* line used may very likely affect steroidogenic cells in other tissues (53).

Developmental Compensation

Some CRE drivers are developmentally active and clock genes are known to be involved in early developmental processes (55). Therefore, some phenotypes observed in adult mice might reflect changes in developmental programs while others may be masked by compensatory responses. A strategy circumventing this issue is to employ an inducible version of CRE (T2-CRE), which is activated only when animals receive tamoxifen (56). This approach has been used to globally delete *Bmal1* and *Rev-erbα/β* (29, 41). In the M-*Bmal1* KO study discussed above, a muscle strength phenotype was only observed in mutants with conventional, but not inducible CRE deletion (50).

Incomplete Recombination

Due to variations in expression levels or epigenetic effects, CRE-mediated recombination frequently does not occur in all cells of the same tissue. This issue is further exaggerated with the T2-CRE system. Thus, the lack of certain phenotypes in tissue-specific mutants may stem from non-recombined cells sufficient to maintain tissue function. In the circadian clock context, this issue becomes critical in tissues of strong intercellular coupling such as the SCN. Our own approach to target SCN pacemaker function using a Syt10-Cre-driver line revealed that only with the highest CRE dosage ($Syt10^{Cre/Cre}$) and on a $Bmal1^{flox/del}$ background, recombination was sufficient to ablate behavioral rhythmicity (57).

The Non-Circadian Role of Individual Clock Genes

Many clock gene mutant studies fail to discern whether a phenotype is caused by altered clock rhythmicity or by loss of a specific clock component. For example, in the L-*Bmal1* KO study, the mutation not only abolishes the transcription rhythm of *Glut2*, but also dramatically downregulates its overall expression (28). The multifaceted phenotype of *Bmal1* KO mice suggests that this gene has important functions outside the circadian timekeeping system (58). Along this line, the monopolized use of *Bmal1* targeting for tissue-specific clock deletion further exacerbates this issue since some of the reported phenotypes may be caused by a loss of *Bmal1* rather than of the clockwork.

EMERGING GENETIC TECHNIQUES FOR CHRONOBIOLOGY RESEARCH

Some of the emerging novel genetic techniques may help to overcome the issues discussed above. Below we will highlight some methodologies that may help improving our understanding of the role of tissue clocks in complex physiological contexts.

Improving the Spatio-Temporal Resolution of Clock Gene Manipulation

Though pharmacologically inducible CRE systems bypass developmental effects, this strategy often compromises the recombination efficiency and complicates experimental designs (56). Moreover, the manipulation is irreversible, rendering it unsuitable for certain biological questions. As an alternative approach, chemogenetic manipulations such as tetracycline-based (i.e., Tet-ON/OFF) systems achieve anatomical specificity by expressing effectors under tissue-specific promoters, the activity of which depends on the presence/absence of an otherwise inert chemical (59, 60). These systems are reversible and have a very flexible space-time window for manipulations. For example, two complementary studies have established mouse lines expressing *Clock-Δ19* and *Rev-erbα* as clock disruptors in brain and liver, respectively, in a tetracycline-dependent manner, to elucidate the relative contribution of central and peripheral clocks to physiological rhythms (61, 62). This revealed that circadian expression rhythms of most rhythmic transcripts in the liver depend on local oscillators whereas 10% of the rhythmic transcripts (including *Per2*) are sustained by systemic signals.

Optogenetic techniques have recently been introduced in chronobiology research. Photic stimulation on channelrhodopsin-2-expressing SCN neurons results in phase-resetting of SCN firing and behavioral rhythms (63). Other optogenetic systems allow for photo-switchable control of specific cellular and molecular processes (64). Of note, one strategy employs modified photo-sensitive plant cryptochrome 2 clock proteins from *Arabidopsis* (64), which would allow to directly affect molecular clock function by light. In addition to high spatial control (by directing light exposure), optogenetics may benefit chronobiology research because of their supreme temporal resolution, e.g., in phase-resetting experiments.

While standard viral transgene delivery approaches using short tissue-specific promoters often fall short to confer sufficient specificity (65), this is circumvented by combining virus injections with CRE-driver mouse lines targeting transgene expression to specific cells and tissues (66). Viral approaches further benefit from high spatio-temporal control through injection time/sites and viral capsid serotypes. They, however, often suffer from somewhat reduced penetrance and technical variability (67). Viruses can be used in conjugation with chemogenetic or optogenetic manipulations to interrogate the role of circadian clock in metabolic regulation and other physiological systems with unprecedented spatio-temporal resolution.

Perspectives for Developing Animal Models That Can Dissociate Circadian and Non-Circadian Functions of Clock Genes

Clock gene knockdown/KO experiments often cannot distinguish between circadian (i.e., timing related) and non-circadian effects of a given mutation. This may to some extent be addressed by comparing phenotypes between mutants of different clock genes. However, because of the interactive nature of clock genes this may often not yield further insights. As an alternative approach, the direct modulation of circadian period length without abolishing clock function itself in a tissue-specific manner is achievable *via* manipulating period-determining genes such as casein kinase I ϵ (44). To some extent, this and other similar approaches still inevitably change clock protein levels and, thus, pleiotropic clock gene output.

An ideal animal model would be one with altered phasing of clock gene expression rhythms but unaffected overall clock protein abundance. Generating such model has become possible

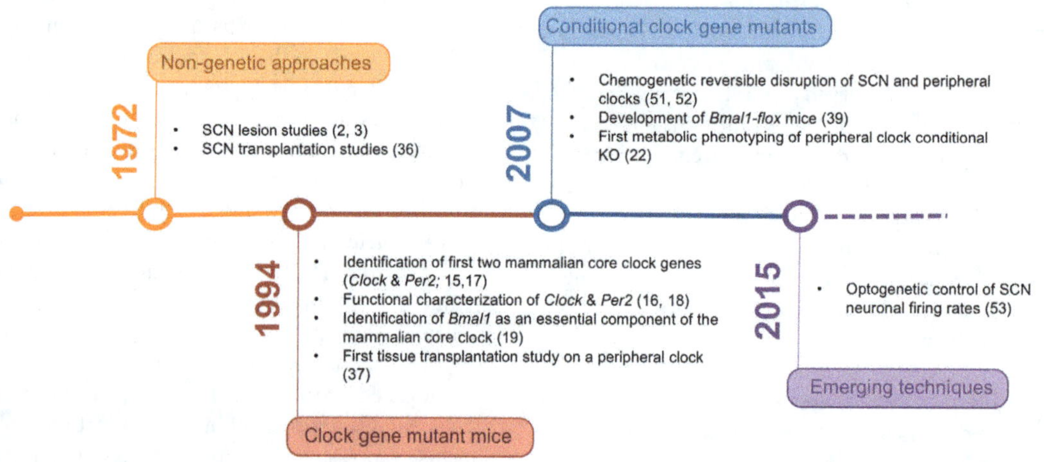

FIGURE 1 | **Timeline of the development of experimental rodent models and corresponding milestone papers in circadian tissue clock research.**

with recent developments in genome editing such as CRISPR and TALEN (68, 69). CRISPR techniques have been used to "cure" retinal degeneration models in rats (70, 71). Together with the expanding knowledge of the role of the cis-regulatory elements of clock genes in determining the phase of expression rhythms, such as the identification of the phase-determining intronic enhancer of *Cry1* (72), *in vivo* genome editing may allow to selectively manipulate clock gene phasing.

CONCLUSION

In the last decades, the tools for studying the mechanisms underlying organismal circadian timekeeping and its role in metabolic regulation have been constantly refined (**Figure 1**). The network structure of the circadian system represents an important challenge in this context, posing high demands on both tempo-spatial control and recombination efficiency in genetic experiments. Novel genetic approaches may help to overcome these issues and provide a clearer picture of the complex interaction of different tissue clocks in the regulation of energy metabolism.

AUTHOR CONTRIBUTIONS

AT, MA, BL, and HO discussed the concept, complied the literature, and wrote the paper.

REFERENCES

1. Gan Y, Yang C, Tong X, Sun H, Cong Y, Yin X, et al. Shift work and diabetes mellitus: a meta-analysis of observational studies. *Occup Environ Med* (2015) 72(1):72–8. doi:10.1136/oemed-2014-102150
2. Moore RY, Eichler VB. Loss of a circadian adrenal corticosterone rhythm following suprachiasmatic lesions in the rat. *Brain Res* (1972) 42(1):201–6. doi:10.1016/0006-8993(72)90054-6
3. Stephan FK, Zucker I. Circadian rhythms in drinking behavior and locomotor activity of rats are eliminated by hypothalamic lesions. *Proc Natl Acad Sci U S A* (1972) 69(6):1583–6. doi:10.1073/pnas.69.6.1583
4. Yamamoto H, Nagai K, Nakagawa H. Role of SCN in daily rhythms of plasma glucose, FFA, insulin and glucagon. *Chronobiol Int* (1987) 4(4):483–91. doi:10.3109/07420528709078539
5. Kalsbeek A, Fliers E, Romijn JA, La Fleur SE, Wortel J, Bakker O, et al. The suprachiasmatic nucleus generates the diurnal changes in plasma leptin levels. *Endocrinology* (2001) 142(6):2677–85. doi:10.1210/endo.142.6.8197
6. Ishikawa K, Shimazu T. Circadian rhythm of liver glycogen metabolism in rats: effects of hypothalamic lesions. *Am J Physiol* (1980) 238(1):E21–5.
7. Coomans CP, van den Berg SA, Lucassen EA, Houben T, Pronk AC, van der Spek RD, et al. The suprachiasmatic nucleus controls circadian energy metabolism and hepatic insulin sensitivity. *Diabetes* (2013) 62(4):1102–8. doi:10.2337/db12-0507
8. Fonken LK, Workman JL, Walton JC, Weil ZM, Morris JS, Haim A, et al. Light at night increases body mass by shifting the time of food intake. *Proc Natl Acad Sci U S A* (2010) 107(43):18664–9. doi:10.1073/pnas.1008734107
9. Qian J, Block GD, Colwell CS, Matveyenko AV. Consequences of exposure to light at night on the pancreatic islet circadian clock and function in rats. *Diabetes* (2013) 62(10):3469–78. doi:10.2337/db12-1543
10. Gale JE, Cox HI, Qian J, Block GD, Colwell CS, Matveyenko AV. Disruption of circadian rhythms accelerates development of diabetes through pancreatic beta-cell loss and dysfunction. *J Biol Rhythms* (2011) 26(5):423–33. doi:10.1177/0748730411416341
11. Krysta K, Krzystanek M, Janas-Kozik M, Krupka-Matuszczyk I. Bright light therapy in the treatment of childhood and adolescence depression, antepartum depression, and eating disorders. *J Neural Transm (Vienna)* (2012) 119(10):1167–72. doi:10.1007/s00702-012-0863-2
12. Al-Karawi D, Jubair L. Bright light therapy for nonseasonal depression: meta-analysis of clinical trials. *J Affect Disord* (2016) 198:64–71. doi:10.1016/j.jad.2016.03.016
13. Boivin DB, Tremblay GM, James FO. Working on atypical schedules. *Sleep Med* (2007) 8(6):578–89. doi:10.1016/j.sleep.2007.03.015
14. Oike H, Sakurai M, Ippoushi K, Kobori M. Time-fixed feeding prevents obesity induced by chronic advances of light/dark cycles in mouse models of jet-lag/shift work. *Biochem Biophys Res Commun* (2015) 465(3):556–61. doi:10.1016/j.bbrc.2015.08.059

15. McGowan NM, Coogan AN. Circadian and behavioural responses to shift work-like schedules of light/dark in the mouse. *J Mol Psychiatry* (2013) 1(1):7. doi:10.1186/2049-9256-1-7
16. Barclay JL, Husse J, Bode B, Naujokat N, Meyer-Kovac J, Schmid SM, et al. Circadian desynchrony promotes metabolic disruption in a mouse model of shiftwork. *PLoS One* (2012) 7(5):e37150. doi:10.1371/journal.pone.0037150
17. Salgado-Delgado RC, Saderi N, Basualdo Mdel C, Guerrero-Vargas NN, Escobar C, Buijs RM. Shift work or food intake during the rest phase promotes metabolic disruption and desynchrony of liver genes in male rats. *PLoS One* (2013) 8(4):e60052. doi:10.1371/journal.pone.0060052
18. Arble DM, Bass J, Laposky AD, Vitaterna MH, Turek FW. Circadian timing of food intake contributes to weight gain. *Obesity (Silver Spring)* (2009) 17(11):2100–2. doi:10.1038/oby.2009.264
19. Feng D, Lazar MA. Clocks, metabolism, and the epigenome. *Mol Cell* (2012) 47(2):158–67. doi:10.1016/j.molcel.2012.06.026
20. Katada S, Imhof A, Sassone-Corsi P. Connecting threads: epigenetics and metabolism. *Cell* (2012) 148(1–2):24–8. doi:10.1016/j.cell.2012.01.001
21. Vitaterna MH, King DP, Chang AM, Kornhauser JM, Lowrey PL, McDonald JD, et al. Mutagenesis and mapping of a mouse gene, Clock, essential for circadian behavior. *Science* (1994) 264(5159):719–25. doi:10.1126/science.8171325
22. Antoch MP, Song EJ, Chang AM, Vitaterna MH, Zhao Y, Wilsbacher LD, et al. Functional identification of the mouse circadian Clock gene by transgenic BAC rescue. *Cell* (1997) 89(4):655–67. doi:10.1016/S0092-8674(00)80246-9
23. Sun ZS, Albrecht U, Zhuchenko O, Bailey J, Eichele G, Lee CC. RIGUI, a putative mammalian ortholog of the *Drosophila* period gene. *Cell* (1997) 90(6):1003–11. doi:10.1016/S0092-8674(00)80366-9
24. Zheng B, Larkin DW, Albrecht U, Sun ZS, Sage M, Eichele G, et al. The mPer2 gene encodes a functional component of the mammalian circadian clock. *Nature* (1999) 400(6740):169–73. doi:10.1038/22118
25. Bunger MK, Wilsbacher LD, Moran SM, Clendenin C, Radcliffe LA, Hogenesch JB, et al. Mop3 is an essential component of the master circadian pacemaker in mammals. *Cell* (2000) 103(7):1009–17. doi:10.1016/S0092-8674(00)00205-1
26. Panda S, Antoch MP, Miller BH, Su AI, Schook AB, Straume M, et al. Coordinated transcription of key pathways in the mouse by the circadian clock. *Cell* (2002) 109(3):307–20. doi:10.1016/S0092-8674(02)00722-5
27. Rudic RD, McNamara P, Curtis AM, Boston RC, Panda S, Hogenesch JB, et al. BMAL1 and CLOCK, two essential components of the circadian clock, are involved in glucose homeostasis. *PLoS Biol* (2004) 2(11):e377. doi:10.1371/journal.pbio.0020377
28. Lamia KA, Storch KF, Weitz CJ. Physiological significance of a peripheral tissue circadian clock. *Proc Natl Acad Sci U S A* (2008) 105(39):15172–7. doi:10.1073/pnas.0806717105
29. Yang G, Chen L, Grant GR, Paschos G, Song WL, Musiek ES, et al. Timing of expression of the core clock gene Bmal1 influences its effects on aging and survival. *Sci Transl Med* (2016) 8(324):324ra316. doi:10.1126/scitranslmed.aad3305
30. Turek FW, Joshu C, Kohsaka A, Lin E, Ivanova G, McDearmon E, et al. Obesity and metabolic syndrome in circadian Clock mutant mice. *Science* (2005) 308(5724):1043–5. doi:10.1126/science.1108750
31. Shostak A, Meyer-Kovac J, Oster H. Circadian regulation of lipid mobilization in white adipose tissues. *Diabetes* (2013) 62(7):2195–203. doi:10.2337/db12-1449
32. Oishi K, Atsumi G, Sugiyama S, Kodomari I, Kasamatsu M, Machida K, et al. Disrupted fat absorption attenuates obesity induced by a high-fat diet in Clock mutant mice. *FEBS Lett* (2006) 580(1):127–30. doi:10.1016/j.febslet.2005.11.063
33. Yang S, Liu A, Weidenhammer A, Cooksey RC, McClain D, Kim MK, et al. The role of mPer2 clock gene in glucocorticoid and feeding rhythms. *Endocrinology* (2009) 150(5):2153–60. doi:10.1210/en.2008-0705
34. Carvas JM, Vukolic A, Yepuri G, Xiong Y, Popp K, Schmutz I, et al. Period2 gene mutant mice show compromised insulin-mediated endothelial nitric oxide release and altered glucose homeostasis. *Front Physiol* (2012) 3:337. doi:10.3389/fphys.2012.00337
35. Bae K, Jin X, Maywood ES, Hastings MH, Reppert SM, Weaver DR. Differential functions of mPer1, mPer2, and mPer3 in the SCN circadian clock. *Neuron* (2001) 30(2):525–36. doi:10.1016/S0896-6273(01)00302-6
36. Grimaldi B, Bellet MM, Katada S, Astarita G, Hirayama J, Amin RH, et al. PER2 controls lipid metabolism by direct regulation of PPARgamma. *Cell Metab* (2010) 12(5):509–20. doi:10.1016/j.cmet.2010.10.005
37. Bhatwadekar AD, Yan Y, Qi X, Thinschmidt JS, Neu MB, Li Calzi S, et al. Per2 mutation recapitulates the vascular phenotype of diabetes in the retina and bone marrow. *Diabetes* (2013) 62(1):273–82. doi:10.2337/db12-0172
38. Zheng B, Albrecht U, Kaasik K, Sage M, Lu W, Vaishnav S, et al. Nonredundant roles of the mPer1 and mPer2 genes in the mammalian circadian clock. *Cell* (2001) 105(5):683–94. doi:10.1016/S0092-8674(01)00380-4
39. Dallmann R, Weaver DR. Altered body mass regulation in male mPeriod mutant mice on high-fat diet. *Chronobiol Int* (2010) 27(6):1317–28. doi:10.3109/07420528.2010.489166
40. Le Martelot G, Claudel T, Gatfield D, Schaad O, Kornmann B, Lo Sasso G, et al. REV-ERBalpha participates in circadian SREBP signaling and bile acid homeostasis. *PLoS Biol* (2009) 7(9):e1000181. doi:10.1371/journal.pbio.1000181
41. Cho H, Zhao X, Hatori M, Yu RT, Barish GD, Lam MT, et al. Regulation of circadian behaviour and metabolism by REV-ERB-alpha and REV-ERB-beta. *Nature* (2012) 485(7396):123–7. doi:10.1038/nature11048
42. Solt LA, Wang Y, Banerjee S, Hughes T, Kojetin DJ, Lundasen T, et al. Regulation of circadian behaviour and metabolism by synthetic REV-ERB agonists. *Nature* (2012) 485(7396):62–8. doi:10.1038/nature11030
43. Yamaguchi S, Isejima H, Matsuo T, Okura R, Yagita K, Kobayashi M, et al. Synchronization of cellular clocks in the suprachiasmatic nucleus. *Science* (2003) 302(5649):1408–12. doi:10.1126/science.1089287
44. Ralph MR, Foster RG, Davis FC, Menaker M. Transplanted suprachiasmatic nucleus determines circadian period. *Science* (1990) 247(4945):975–8. doi:10.1126/science.2305266
45. Oster H, Damerow S, Kiessling S, Jakubcakova V, Abraham D, Tian J, et al. The circadian rhythm of glucocorticoids is regulated by a gating mechanism residing in the adrenal cortical clock. *Cell Metab* (2006) 4(2):163–73. doi:10.1016/j.cmet.2006.07.002
46. Gu H, Marth JD, Orban PC, Mossmann H, Rajewsky K. Deletion of a DNA polymerase beta gene segment in T cells using cell type-specific gene targeting. *Science* (1994) 265(5168):103–6. doi:10.1126/science.8016642
47. Storch KF, Paz C, Signorovitch J, Raviola E, Pawlyk B, Li T, et al. Intrinsic circadian clock of the mammalian retina: importance for retinal processing of visual information. *Cell* (2007) 130(4):730–41. doi:10.1016/j.cell.2007.06.045
48. Marcheva B, Ramsey KM, Buhr ED, Kobayashi Y, Su H, Ko CH, et al. Disruption of the clock components CLOCK and BMAL1 leads to hypoinsulinaemia and diabetes. *Nature* (2010) 466(7306):627–31. doi:10.1038/nature09253
49. Perelis M, Marcheva B, Ramsey KM, Schipma MJ, Hutchison AL, Taguchi A, et al. Pancreatic beta cell enhancers regulate rhythmic transcription of genes controlling insulin secretion. *Science* (2015) 350(6261):aac4250. doi:10.1126/science.aac4250
50. Dyar KA, Ciciliot S, Wright LE, Bienso RS, Tagliazucchi GM, Patel VR, et al. Muscle insulin sensitivity and glucose metabolism are controlled by the intrinsic muscle clock. *Mol Metab* (2014) 3(1):29–41. doi:10.1016/j.molmet.2013.10.005
51. Paschos GK, Ibrahim S, Song WL, Kunieda T, Grant G, Reyes TM, et al. Obesity in mice with adipocyte-specific deletion of clock component Arntl. *Nat Med* (2012) 18(12):1768–77. doi:10.1038/nm.2979
52. Piggins HD, Guilding C. The neural circadian system of mammals. *Essays Biochem* (2011) 49(1):1–17. doi:10.1042/bse0490001
53. Orozco-Solis R, Aguilar-Arnal L, Murakami M, Peruquetti R, Ramadori G, Coppari R, et al. The circadian clock in the ventromedial hypothalamus controls cyclic energy expenditure. *Cell Metab* (2016) 23(3):467–78. doi:10.1016/j.cmet.2016.02.003
54. Harno E, Cottrell EC, White A. Metabolic pitfalls of CNS Cre-based technology. *Cell Metab* (2013) 18(1):21–8. doi:10.1016/j.cmet.2013.05.019
55. Landgraf D, Koch CE, Oster H. Embryonic development of circadian clocks in the mammalian suprachiasmatic nuclei. *Front Neuroanat* (2014) 8:143. doi:10.3389/fnana.2014.00143
56. Leone DP, Genoud S, Atanasoski S, Grausenburger R, Berger P, Metzger D, et al. Tamoxifen-inducible glia-specific Cre mice for somatic mutagenesis in oligodendrocytes and Schwann cells. *Mol Cell Neurosci* (2003) 22(4):430–40. doi:10.1016/S1044-7431(03)00029-0
57. Husse J, Zhou X, Shostak A, Oster H, Eichele G. Synaptotagmin10-Cre, a driver to disrupt clock genes in the SCN. *J Biol Rhythms* (2011) 26(5):379–89. doi:10.1177/0748730411415363
58. Kondratov RV, Kondratova AA, Gorbacheva VY, Vykhovanets OV, Antoch MP. Early aging and age-related pathologies in mice deficient in BMAL1, the

core componentof the circadian clock. *Genes Dev* (2006) 20(14):1868–73. doi:10.1101/gad.1432206

59. Zhou X, Vink M, Klaver B, Berkhout B, Das AT. Optimization of the Tet-On system for regulated gene expression through viral evolution. *Gene Ther* (2006) 13(19):1382–90. doi:10.1038/sj.gt.3302780
60. Whissell PD, Tohyama S, Martin LJ. The use of DREADDs to deconstruct behavior. *Front Genet* (2016) 7:70. doi:10.3389/fgene.2016.00070
61. Hong HK, Chong JL, Song W, Song EJ, Jyawook AA, Schook AC, et al. Inducible and reversible Clock gene expression in brain using the tTA system for the study of circadian behavior. *PLoS Genet* (2007) 3(2):e33. doi:10.1371/journal.pgen.0030033
62. Kornmann B, Schaad O, Bujard H, Takahashi JS, Schibler U. System-driven and oscillator-dependent circadian transcription in mice with a conditionally active liver clock. *PLoS Biol* (2007) 5(2):e34. doi:10.1371/journal.pbio.0050034
63. Jones JR, Tackenberg MC, McMahon DG. Manipulating circadian clock neuron firing rate resets molecular circadian rhythms and behavior. *Nat Neurosci* (2015) 18(3):373–5. doi:10.1038/nn.3937
64. Tischer D, Weiner OD. Illuminating cell signalling with optogenetic tools. *Nat Rev Mol Cell Biol* (2014) 15(8):551–8. doi:10.1038/nrm3837
65. Nathanson JL, Jappelli R, Scheeff ED, Manning G, Obata K, Brenner S, et al. Short promoters in viral vectors drive selective expression in mammalian inhibitory neurons, but do not restrict activity to specific inhibitory cell-types. *Front Neural Circuits* (2009) 3:19. doi:10.3389/neuro.04.019.2009
66. Schnutgen F, Doerflinger N, Calleja C, Wendling O, Chambon P, Ghyselinck NB. A directional strategy for monitoring Cre-mediated recombination at the cellular level in the mouse. *Nat Biotechnol* (2003) 21(5):562–5. doi:10.1038/nbt811
67. Choudhury SR, Hudry E, Maguire CA, Sena-Esteves M, Breakefield XO, Grandi P. Viral vectors for therapy of neurologic diseases. *Neuropharmacology* (2016). doi:10.1016/j.neuropharm.2016.02.013
68. Carlson DF, Fahrenkrug SC, Hackett PB. Targeting DNA With Fingers and TALENs. *Mol Ther Nucleic Acids* (2012) 1:e3. doi:10.1038/mtna.2011.5
69. Doudna JA, Charpentier E. Genome editing. The new frontier of genome engineering with CRISPR-Cas9. *Science* (2014) 346(6213):1258096. doi:10.1126/science.1258096
70. Bakondi B, Lv W, Lu B, Jones MK, Tsai Y, Kim KJ, et al. In vivo CRISPR/Cas9 gene editing corrects retinal dystrophy in the S334ter-3 rat model of autosomal dominant retinitis pigmentosa. *Mol Ther* (2016) 24(3):556–63. doi:10.1038/mt.2015.220
71. Suzuki K, Tsunekawa Y, Hernandez-Benitez R, Wu J, Zhu J, Kim EJ, et al. In vivo genome editing via CRISPR/Cas9 mediated homology-independent targeted integration. *Nature* (2016) 540(7631):144–9. doi:10.1038/nature20565
72. Ukai-Tadenuma M, Yamada RG, Xu H, Ripperger JA, Liu AC, Ueda HR. Delay in feedback repression by cryptochrome 1 is required for circadian clock function. *Cell* (2011) 144(2):268–81. doi:10.1016/j.cell.2010.12.019

9

Restricted Feeding Schedules Modulate in a Different Manner the Expression of Clock Genes in Rat Hypothalamic Nuclei

*Leonardo D. De Araujo [1], Silvia L. Roa [2], Ana C. Bueno [3], Fernanda B. Coeli-Lacchini [2], Clarissa S. Martins [2], Ernane T. Uchoa [1], Jose Antunes-Rodrigues [1], Lucila L. Elias [1], Paula C. Elias [2], Ayrton C. Moreira [2] and Margaret De Castro [2]**

[1] Department of Physiology, University of Sao Paulo, Ribeirao Preto, Brazil, [2] Department of Internal Medicine, University of Sao Paulo, Ribeirao Preto, Brazil, [3] Department of Pediatrics of the Ribeirao Preto Medical School, University of Sao Paulo, Ribeirao Preto, Brazil

Edited by:
Adries Kalsbeek,
Academic Medical Center,
Netherlands

Reviewed by:
Virginie Tolle,
French Institute of Health and Medical Research (INSERM), France
Carolina Escobar,
Universidad Nacional Autónoma de México (UNAM), Mexico

Correspondence:
Margaret De Castro
castrom@fmrp.usp.br

Food access restriction is associated to changes in gene expression of the circadian clock system. However, there are only a few studies investigating the effects of non-photic synchronizers, such as food entrainment, on the expression of clock genes in the central oscillators. We hypothesized that different feeding restriction patterns could modulate the expression of clock genes in the suprachiasmatic nucleus (SCN) "master" clock and in extra-SCN oscillators such as the paraventricular (PVN) and arcuate (ARC) hypothalamic nuclei. *Wistar* rats were divided into four groups: Control group (CG; food available *ad libitum*), Restricted night-fed (RF-n; food access during 2 h at night), Restricted day-fed (RF-d; food access during 2 h at daytime), Day-fed (DF; food access during 12 h at daytime). After 21 days, rats were decapitated between ZT2-ZT3 (0800–0900 h); ZT11-ZT12 (1700–1800 h), or ZT17-18 (2300–2400 h). Plasma corticosterone was measured by radioimmunoassay (RIA). The expression of *Clock*, *Bmal1, Per1*, *Per2, Per3, Cry1, Cry2*, *Rev-erbα,* and *Rorα* were assessed in SCN, PVN, and ARC hypothalamic nuclei by RT-PCR and calculated by the $2^{[-\text{DeltaDeltaCT(Cyclethreshold)}]}(2^{-\Delta\Delta CT})$ method. Restricted food availability during few h led to decreased body weight in RF-n and RF-d groups compared to controls and DF group. We also observed an anticipatory corticosterone peak before food availability in RF-n and RF-d groups. Furthermore, the pattern of clock gene expression in response to RF-n, RF-d, and DF schedules was affected differently in the SCN, PVN, and ARC hypothalamic nuclei. In conclusion, the master oscillator in SCN as well as the oscillator in PVN and ARC, all brain areas involved in food intake, responds in a tissue-specific manner to feeding restriction.

Keywords: circadian oscillators, hypothalamic nuclei, food restriction, clock gene expression, corticosterone

INTRODUCTION

Physiological rhythms are regulated by neuronal hypothalamic circadian oscillators (Bass and Takahashi, 2010). Circadian oscillators are kept synchronized one with another and with environmental time by the suprachiasmatic nucleus (SCN), known as "master" clock in mammals. The SCN receives direct photic input from the retina, generates a pronounced circadian rhythm and in turn, synchronizes other subsidiary cellular oscillators (Reppert and Weaver, 2001).

In mammals, the mechanism of cell-autonomous circadian clock depends on two core clock genes, *Clock,* and *Bmal1*, which are transcriptional activators of an auto-regulatory negative feedback loop (Lowrey and Takahashi, 2004). These genes form a heterodimer that activates their target genes, *Period* (*Per*), and *Cryptochrome* (*Cry*), which form a repressor complex in the cytoplasm that returns to the nucleus and interacts with CLOCK-BMAL1 to inhibit their own transcription (Takahashi et al., 2008). *Bmal1* and *Clock* genes also increase the mRNA levels of *Rev-erbα* and *Rorα*, which compete for the binding to the retinoic acid-related orphan receptor response elements (ROREs) repressing or activating the expression of *Bmal1* (Green et al., 2008). Post-translational modifications also modulate these auto-regulatory loops (Lamia et al., 2009; Nakahata et al., 2009; Jang et al., 2012).

Glucocorticoid circadian secretion is modulated via CRH and ACTH periodic release under the SCN control (Dallman et al., 1978, 1993; Buijs et al., 2003; Fahrenkrug et al., 2008). Furthermore, the glucocorticoid release is also modulated by the central circadian clock system in a manner independent of the HPA axis, possibly due to altering the sensitivity of the adrenal cortex to ACTH through the autonomic nervous system (Ishida et al., 2005; Kalsbeek et al., 2006; Nader et al., 2010). In addition to the photoperiod, feeding time is a powerful Zeitgeber of the glucocorticoid circadian rhythm. Rats display an anticipatory peak of glucocorticoid, release 1–2 h before the availability of food (Krieger et al., 1977). This phenomenon seems to be dependent on a distinct food-entrainable hypothalamic oscillator (Stephan et al., 1979; Stephan, 2002). Indeed, glucocorticoids are required for meal-induced changes in the expression of hypothalamic neuropeptides (Uchoa et al., 2012). Paraventricular (PVN) and arcuate (ARC) nuclei have been implicated in the control of energy homeostasis and express orexigenic and anorexigenic peptides. PVN receives projections not only from satiety-related neurons from the nucleus of the solitary tract but also from ARC neurons indicating that the hypothalamus plays an important role in the integrative responses that control food intake (Schwartz et al., 2000).

Although SCN generates a circadian rhythm, the daily rhythm of food intake can also regulate other hypothalamic nuclei, such as PVN, ARC, dorsomedial (DMH), and ventromedial (VMH) nuclei. Previous studies tested the susceptibility of non-photic entrainment cues and demonstrated that restricting food availability with maintenance of photoperiod cues, is a strong Zeitgeber that changes only slightly SCN clock gene expression but can alter *Per1, Per2,* and *Bmal1* expression in the PVN, anterior pituitary, and adrenal tissue (Girotti et al., 2009). In addition, timed hypocaloric feeding was also able to synchronize the temporal organization of SCN clockwork (Caldelas et al., 2005). Moreover, restricted feeding schedules entrain oscillations of *Per1, Per2,* and *Bmal1* expression in different phases among various hypothalamic structures (Mieda et al., 2006; Verwey et al., 2007; Minana-Solis et al., 2009). Furthermore, peripheral clocks, particularly the liver, pancreas, kidney, and heart can be modulated by food restriction (Damiola et al., 2000; Le Minh et al., 2001; Stokkan et al., 2001; Green et al., 2008).

The majority of the studies on the effects of non-photic synchronizers, such as food entrainment, on the expression of clock genes in the hypothalamus used restriction feeding schedule with access to food restricted to a few hours daily during the light phase. In nocturnal animals, restricting feeding time to the dark does not seem to significantly alter the phase angle of the cyclic clock gene expression (Damiola et al., 2000). However, when food is offered only during the light phase, the expression of clock-related genes in the liver becomes inverted (Damiola et al., 2000; Le Minh et al., 2001). Moreover, food restriction, i.e., hypocaloric feeding, seems to cause changes not only in the temporal organization of peripheral oscillators, but also in the circadian SCN rhythm in rodents (Challet, 2007). Therefore, in this study, we investigate whether different restricted feeding schedules during the light phase or during the dark phase can alter clock gene expression in the SCN and other hypothalamic nuclei of rats despite the presence of photoperiodic cues.

MATERIALS AND METHODS

Animals and Experimental Design

This study was approved by the Animal Ethics Committee of the Ribeirao Preto Medical School of University of Sao Paulo, Brazil (Protocol n° 077/2011). Adult male *Wistar* rats weighing about 200 g, were housed for 5 days in individual cages with food and water *ad libitum*, under controlled conditions of temperature, humidity and on a 12:12 h light/dark (LD) cycle, with lights on at 0600 h (Zeitgeber time; ZT 0).

All animals were fed with standard chow. After 5 days of acclimation period, rats were divided into four groups with different dietary patterns for 21 days. Control group (CG, total number of 23 rats): food *ad libitum*, available at all the time; Restricted night-fed (RF-n, total number of 25 rats): access to food restricted to ZT12–ZT14 (1800–2000 h); Restricted day-fed (RF-d, total number of 27 rats): access to food restricted to ZT3–ZT5 (0900–1100 h); Day-fed (DF, total number of 21 rats): access to food from ZT0–ZT12 (0600–1800 h). Water was offered *ad libitum* to all groups. Food intake and body weight were determined every day throughout the experiment. On the 21th day, 6–10 rats were decapitated per time point between 0800 and 0900 h (ZT3), between 1700 and 1800 h (ZT11), or between 2300 and 2400 h (ZT17).

To avoid unspecific or stress-related elevations of corticosterone secretion, animals were handled by the same investigator during the experiment and on the last day animals were decapitated within 60 s. Trunk blood was immediately collected for corticosterone determination by RIA, as previously described (Castro et al., 1995). The assay sensitivity was 0.4 μg/dl, and the inter- and intra-assay variations were 4.8% and 6.7%, respectively. Animals of control group decapitated at ZT3, which showed plasma concentrations of corticosterone above 3 ug/dl were excluded because of undesirable stress condition, as previously published by our laboratory (Laguna-Abreu et al., 2005).

Brain was collected and flash-frozen in a dry ice-isopentene bath at −30°C and stored at −80°C until processing. SCN, PVN, and ARC hypothalamic nuclei were microdissected bilaterally by punch technique in a cryostat according to coordinates from −0.92 to −1.52 (600 μm thicknesses), −0.92 to −2.12 (1200 μm),

−2.12 to −3.62 (1500 μm) from the bregma (Paxinos, 1997), respectively, using a stainless steel punch needle of 1.0 mm in diameter for the SCN and 1.5 mm for other nuclei. Tissue samples were transferred to a microtube containing RNA later reagent (Ambion, USA) and stored at −80°C until RNA isolation.

RNA Isolation, cDNA Synthesis, and Amplification by Real-Time PCR

Total RNA was isolated from each micropunched hypothalamic tissue sample using TRIzol reagent (Life Technologies) according to the manufacturer's protocol. RNA concentrations were quantified by spectrometry (Nanodrop 2000, Thermo Fisher Scientific Inc., Waltham, MA, USA). RNA integrity was verified by measuring the 28/18S ratio, with an acceptable range of 1.6–2.0 and confirmed by 1.2% agarose gel electrophoresis. mRNA was reverse transcribed from 500 ng of total RNA using the High Capacity cDNA Reverse Transcription kit and MultiScribe® enzyme (Life Technologies).

For semi-quantitative Real-Time PCR (qPCR), TaqMan® assays (Life Technologies, Foster City, CA, USA) were used according to the manufacturer's recommendation using cDNA (diluted 1:5) as template. The specific probes and TaqMan® Gene Expression Assays IDs used were *Clock* (Rn00573120_m1), *Bmal1* (Rn00577590_m1), *Per1* (Rn01325256_m1), *Per2* (Rn01427704_m1), *Per3* (Rn00709499_m1), *Cry1* (Rn01503063_m1), *Cry2* (Rn00591457_m1) *Rev-erbα* (Rn01460662_m1), and *Rorα* (Rn01173769_m1) genes. Each PCR reaction was performed in duplicate. Water, instead of cDNA, was used as a negative control. Housekeeping genes, GAPDH (Rn99999916_s1), and ACTB (Rn00667869_m1), mRNA expression were analyzed for each cDNA sample. For each sample, the threshold cycle (Ct) was determined and normalized to the average of the two housekeeping genes (ΔCt = Ct Unknown − Ct Housekeeping genes). The determination of gene transcript levels in each sample was obtained by the $2^{-\Delta\Delta Ct}$ method (Livak and Schmittgen, 2001). The median value obtained to each sample of tissues from animals submitted to different dietary pattern was compared with the median value obtained from control rats decapitated at ZT3 (0900 h).

Statistical Analysis

Quantitative variables were expressed as mean and standard error (X ± SEM). Differences among morning, afternoon, and night values in the same feeding schedule or differences among rats of different groups at the same time were analyzed by non-parametric analysis of variance of Kruskal-Wallis with Dunn's *post-test*. Analyses were performed using the GraphPad Prism 5.0 (GraphPad, San Diego, CA). Statistical significance was considered at $P < 0.05$.

RESULTS

Body Weight and Food Intake

All groups presented similar body weight at the beginning of the experiment. After 21 days, decreased body weight ($P < 0.01$) was observed in RF-n (274.5 ± 59.3 g) and RF-d (250.0 ± 56.0 g) groups compared with CG (387.0 ± 49.1 g) and DF groups (379.5 ± 35.7 g); no difference was observed between RF-n and RF-d groups as well as between CG and DF groups (**Figure 1**). Similarly, daily food intake (g) and consequently lower caloric intake were observed ($p < 0.0001$) in RF-n (15.2 ± 3.0) and RF-d (14.3 ± 2.6) groups compared with CG (30.7 ± 3.8) and DF (25.0 ± 2.8) groups; no difference was observed between RF-n and RF-d groups as well as between CG and DF groups. Of note, even after normalization of food intake to body weight, RF-n and RF-d groups still presented smaller ingestion than CG and DF groups.

Plasma Corticosterone Levels

Figure 2 shows the plasma corticosterone levels (μg/dl) in CG, RF-d, RF-n, and DF groups at ZT3, ZT11, and ZT17. CG presented higher corticosterone levels at ZT11 (14.1 ± 8.0; $P < 0.01$) and ZT17 (12.9 ± 6.2; $P < 0.01$) compared with ZT3 (1.0 ± 0.6), with no difference between ZT11 and ZT17. The RF-n group showed higher corticosterone levels at ZT11 (20.7 ± 7.6, $P < 0.01$) compared with ZT3 (3.6 ± 2.6) and ZT17 (3.5 ± 2.6) with no difference between ZT3 and ZT17. On the other hand, RF-d group showed an inverted daily pattern of corticosterone secretion compared with CG and RF-n groups with higher levels at ZT3 (22.7 ± 6.2) compared with ZT11 (10.6 ± 5.7) and ZT17 (5.6 ± 3.3; $P = 0.0002$) with no difference between ZT11 and ZT17. The DF group showed higher corticosterone levels at ZT11 (11.6 ± 4.0, $P < 0.01$) compared with ZT3 (2.9 ± 1.6) and ZT17 (7.3 ± 3.3) with no difference either between ZT3 and ZT17 or between ZT11 and ZT17.

Gene Expression

The expression of clock genes in the SCN of CG, RF-n, RF-d, and DF groups at ZT3, ZT11, and ZT17 are presented in **Figure 3**. Differences among morning, afternoon, and night values in the same feeding schedule showed no difference in *Rev-erbα* expression among ZT3, ZT11, and ZT17 in any group. In CG, no differences were observed in the mRNA expression of *Clock, Bmal1, Per1, Per3, Cry1, Cry2,* and *Rorα* among ZT3, ZT11, and ZT17. In DF group, there were no differences in

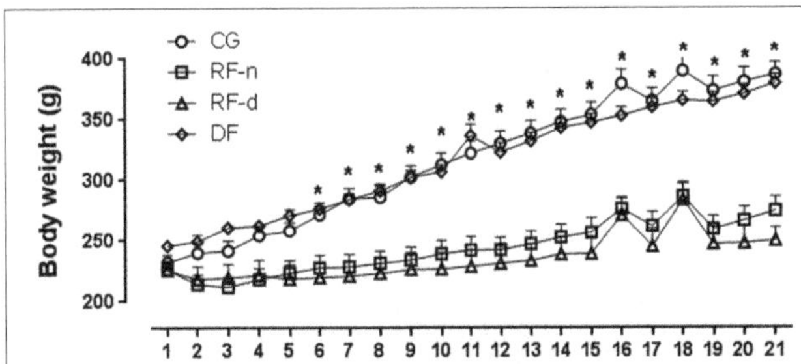

FIGURE 1 | Evolution of the body weight from Day 0–21 in the control group (circles) with food *ad libitum*, restricted night-fed group (RF-night, squares) with access to food restricted to ZT12 to ZT14 (1800–2000 h), restricted day-fed group (RF-day, triangles) with access to food restricted to ZT3 to ZT5 (0900–1100 h) and, restricted day-fed group (DF, diamonds) with access to food restricted to ZT0 to ZT12 (0600–1800 h). *N* = 6–10 rats per time point per group. ZT, Zeitgeber Time. Significant difference among ZTs within the same feeding condition: **P* < 0.05.

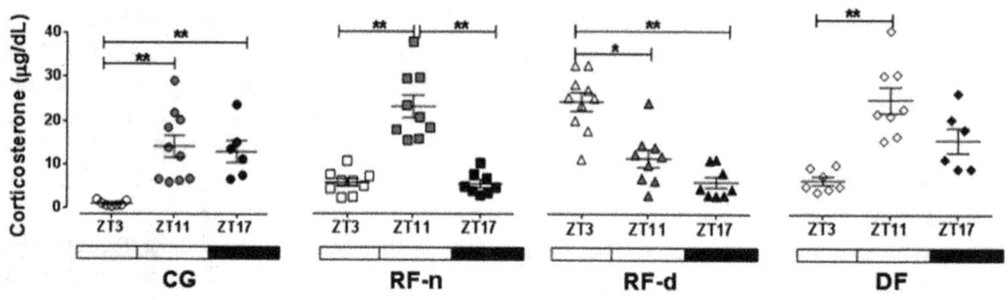

FIGURE 2 | Plasma corticosterone (μg/dl) in the control group (circles) with food *ad libitum*, restricted night-fed group (RF-night, squares) with access to food restricted to ZT12 to ZT14 (1800–2000 h), restricted day-fed group (RF-day, triangles) with access to food restricted to ZT3–ZT5 (0900–1100 h) and, restricted day-fed group (DF, diamonds) with access to food restricted to ZT0 to ZT12 (0600–1800 h) at ZT3, ZT11, and, ZT17 (black symbols), corresponding to 900, 1700, and 2300 h; respectively. $N = 6$–10 rats per time point per group. ZT, Zeitgeber Time. Significant difference among ZTs within the same feeding condition: $^{*}P < 0.05$, $^{**}P < 0.01$.

the expression of *Per3* and *Rorα* in any ZT, while higher gene expression were observed for *Clock* at ZT3 compared with ZT11 ($P = 0.02$), for *Bmal1* at ZT17 compared with ZT11 ($P = 0.01$), for *Cry1*, and *Cry2* at ZT17 compared with ZT3 ($P = 0.03$ and $P = 0.02$, respectively), and for *Per1* at ZT11 compared with ZT3 ($P = 0.02$). Regarding *Per2*, the highest expression was observed at ZT11 and the lowest at ZT17 in all groups ($P < 0.01$). The expression of *Clock, Per1,* and *Per3* genes did not show differences at ZT3, ZT11, and ZT17 in CG; however, in RF-d and RF-n groups, these genes presented higher expression in the morning and in the afternoon ($P < 0.01$). Compared with CG and RF-n groups, in which food access occurred without dissociation with the usual pattern of rat nocturnal activity, higher expression of *Bmal1* was observed at ZT11 ($P = 0.05$) in the RF-d group, while *Cry1* ($P < 0.01$), *Cry2* ($P = 0.01$), and *Rorα* at ZT3 and ZT11 ($P < 0.01$).

The expression of clock genes in the PVN of CG, RF-n, RF-d, and DF groups at ZT3, ZT11, and ZT17 are presented in **Figure 4**. Regarding differences among morning, afternoon, and night values in the same feeding schedule, we observed no differences in the expression of *Clock, Bmal1,* and *Cry1* genes at ZT3, ZT11, and ZT17 in any studied group. In the CG, higher *Per1* expression was observed in the afternoon (ZT11) and at night (ZT17) ($P < 0.01$), while higher expression of *Per2, Per3,* and *Rorα* ($P < 0.01$) were observed at night (ZT17). No different *Rev-erbα* expression was observed among the three different ZT points. In the RF-n group, the pattern of expression of *Per2* ($P < 0.01$), *Per3* ($P = 0.04$), and *Rorα* ($P < 0.01$) genes was similar to CG, with higher expression at night (ZT17), while *Per1* and *Cry2* diurnal variation observed in the CG was abolished in this group. In the RF-d group, there was no difference in the expression of the studied genes among ZT3, ZT11, and ZT17, with exception of *Rev-erbα*, which had higher expression at night (ZT17) ($P = 0.03$). DF group showed higher expression of *Rorα* and *Rev-erbα* at ZT3 compared with ZT17 ($P = 0.02$).

The expression of clock genes in the ARC of CG, RF-n, RF-d, and DF groups at ZT3, ZT11, and ZT17 are presented in **Figure 5**. No difference in *Bmal1* expression was observed among ZT3, ZT11, and ZT17 in any group. In the CG, *Cry1* expression was higher ($P = 0.02$) in the morning (ZT3), while *Clock, Per1, Per2, Per3, Cry2, Rev-erbα,* and *Rorα* ($P < 0.01$) showed higher expression at night (ZT17). Compared with CG, RF-n and RF-d groups showed similar pattern of expression of *Clock* ($P < 0.01$ and $P = 0.04$), *Per3* ($P < 0.01$ and $P < 0.01$), *Cry2* ($P < 0.01$ and $P < 0.01$), and *Rorα* ($P < 0.01$ and $P < 0.01$), while the pattern of expression of *Per2* and *Cry1* was lost. RF-n also had higher *Per1* expression at ZT17 ($P < 0.01$), while RF-d exhibited higher *Per1* expression at morning (ZT3) and at night (ZT17) ($P < 0.01$). RF-d group maintained the pattern of *Rev-erbα* expression observed in CG group, while RF-n lost this pattern. DF group presented higher expression of *Cry1* at ZT17 than at ZT3 and ZT11 ($P < 0.01$).

The Feeding Restriction Schedules and the Modulation of Temporal Relationship of Clock Gene Expression with Corticosterone Secretion

In the SCN of control animals, the higher *Per2* expression was concomitant with the higher corticosterone secretion while no relationship was observed regarding *Clock, Bmal1, Per1, Per3, Cry1, Cry2, Rev-erbα,* and *Rorα* genes. In the RF-n group, besides *Per2*, the expression of *Clock, Per1,* and *Per3* genes also exhibited higher expression coinciding with higher corticosterone secretion. The same pattern was observed for *Per1* and *Per3* in RF-d group, in which there was also a delay of the higher expression of *Clock, Bmal1, Per2, Cry1, Cry2,* and *Rorα* compared with the higher corticosterone secretion. On the other hand, in DF group the most interesting finding was the anticipatory higher expression of *Clock* and *Bmal1* regarding the corticosterone secretion.

In the PVN of control animals, the higher expression of *Per1, Per2, Per3, Cry2,* and *Rorα* were concomitant with the higher corticosterone secretion, while no relationship was observed regarding *Clock, Bmal1, Cry1,* and *Rev-erbα* genes. In the RF-n, the higher expression of *Per2, Per3,* and *Rorα* was delayed concerning the corticosterone secretion, while there was no relationship regarding the expression of *Clock, Bmal1, Per1, Cry1, Cry2,* and *Rev-erbα* genes. On the other hand, in the RF-d and DF groups, the majority of the studied genes lost

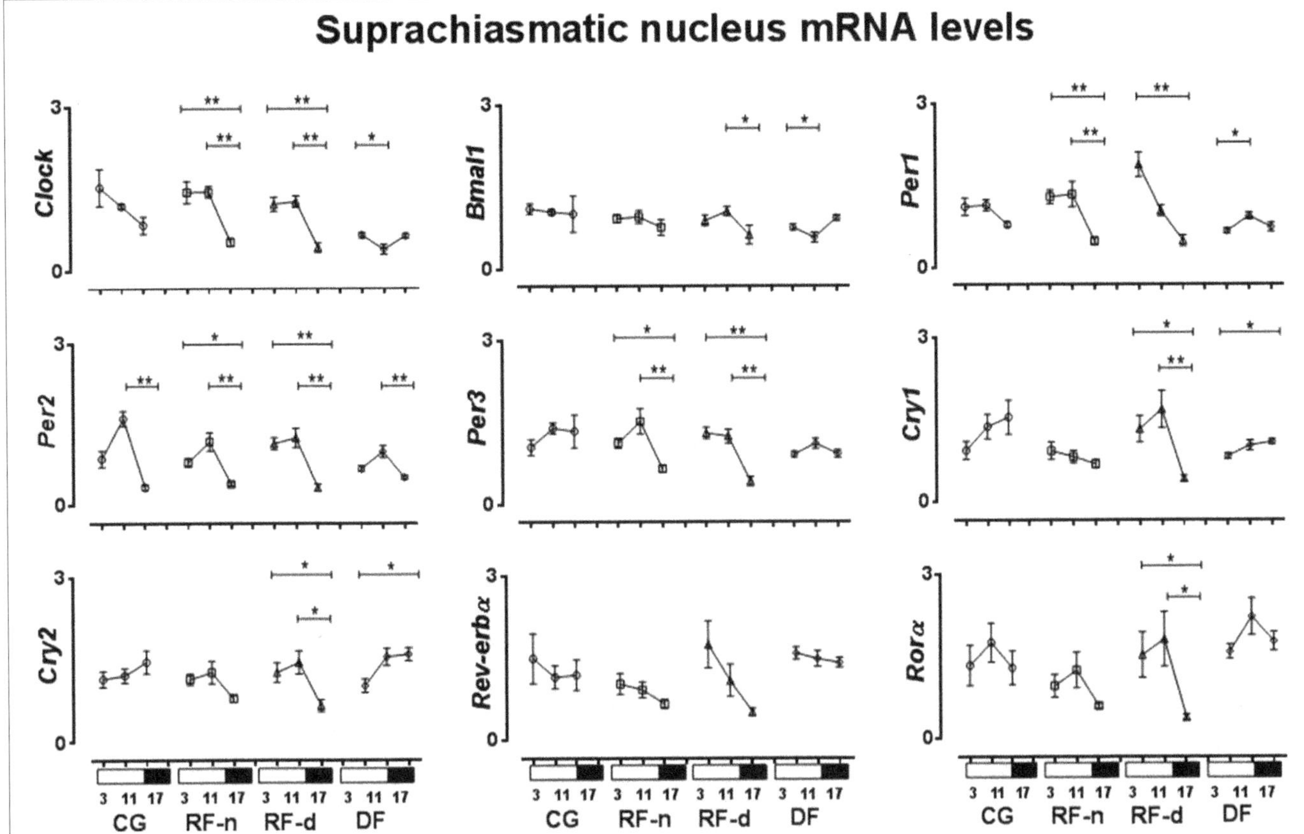

FIGURE 3 | Relative expression of clock genes in Suphrachiasmatic nucleus (SCN) in the control group, with food *ad libitum*; restricted night-fed group (RF-night), with access to food restricted to ZT12–ZT14 (1800–2000 h); restricted day-fed group (RF-day), with access to food restricted to ZT3–ZT5 (0900–1100 h); and day-fed group (DF), with access to food restricted to ZT0–ZT12 (0600–1800 h) at ZT3, ZT11, and ZT17, corresponding to 0900, 1700, and 2300 h; respectively. $N = 6$–10 rats per time point per group. ZT, Zeitgeber Time. Significant difference among ZTs within the same feeding condition: *$P < 0.05$, **$P < 0.01$.

their relationship with corticosterone secretion compared with the pattern observed in control and RF-n groups. Of note, in DF group, the higher expression of *Rorα* and *Rev-erbα* was anticipatory concerning corticosterone secretion.

In the ARC of control animals, while the higher expression of *Clock, Per1, Per2, Per3, Cry2, Rev-erbα*, and *Rorα* was coincident, the *Cry1* higher expression was anticipatory in relation to corticosterone secretion. No relationship was observed regarding *Bmal1* gene. On the other hand, in the RF-n and RF-d groups, there was a delay of the higher expression of *Clock, Per1, Per3, Cry2, Rev-erbα*, and *Rorα* compared with corticosterone secretion. No relationship was observed concerning *Bmal1, Cry1*, and *Per2* in RF-n group and *Rev-erbα* in RF-d group, respectively. Of note, in DF group, most of the genes lost the pattern of expression, also missing any relationship with corticosterone secretion.

DISCUSSION

In the present study, rats submitted to three different schedules of food restriction changed the diurnal pattern of *Per1, Per2*, and *Per3* expression in the SCN and in the extra-SCN oscillators—PVN and ARC nuclei—suggesting that non-photic cues can modulate the expression of clock genes, but not in a uniform way, throughout the hypothalamic nuclei. Furthermore, the corticosterone anticipatory peak was verified irrespective to the food timing access, except in the DF group. Altogether our data confirm that restricted feeding schedules can be an entrainment cue for glucocorticoid circadian variation.

The initial body weight of rats was similar in all groups, but at the end of the experiment, RF-d and RF-n groups showed lower weight as well as lower daily food intake than control and DF groups, similarly to studies using food restriction but with different duration of food access (Honma et al., 1983; Stephan and Becker, 1989; Stephan, 2002). In our study, the time of feeding in RF-d and RF-n groups was restricted by 2 h of food access leading to about 50% calorie intake restriction when compared with controls, suggesting that body weight could be determined primarily by the amount of energy intake and not by the time of feeding. Indeed, control and DF groups showed similar body weight. Arble et al. (2009) showed that mice fed during the 12-h light phase gained even more weight than mice fed on an equivalent amount of calories during the 12-h dark

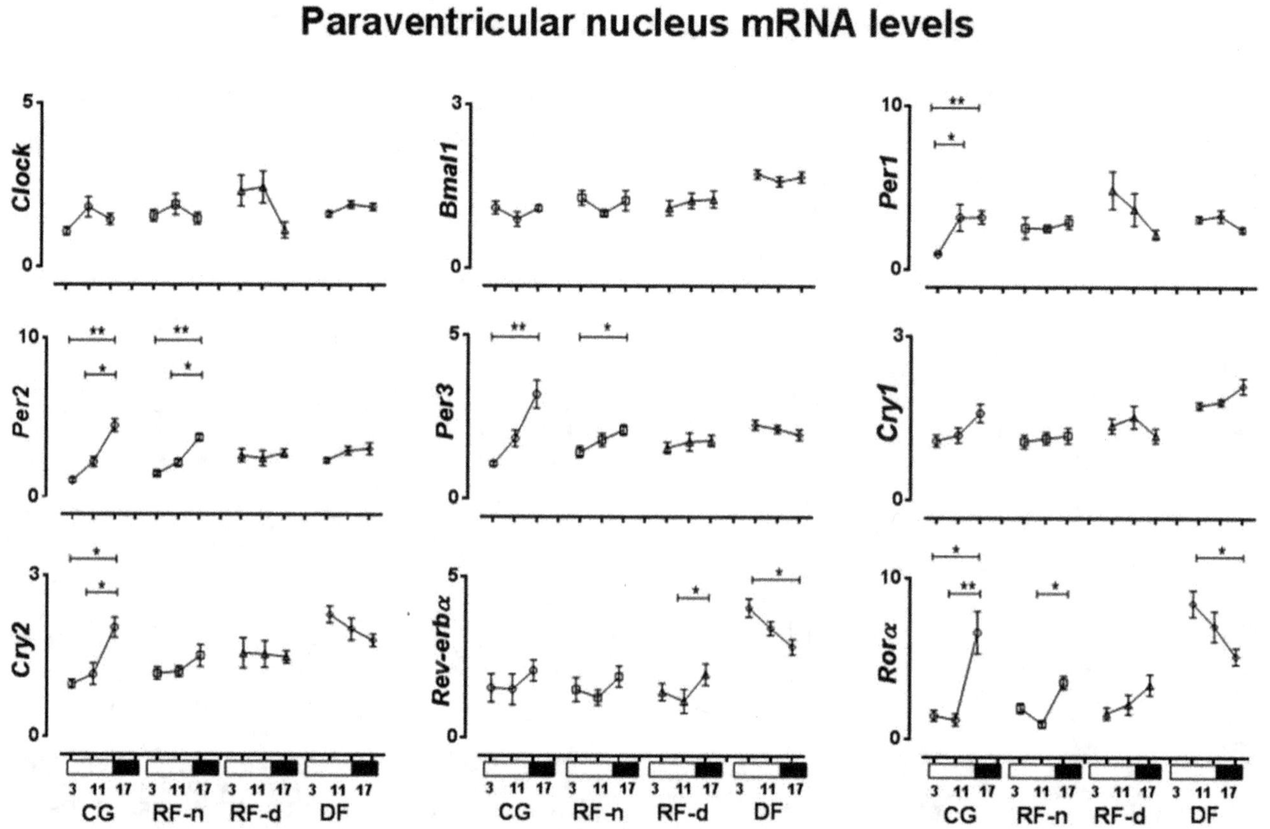

FIGURE 4 | Relative expression of clock genes in Paraventricular nucleus (PVN) in the control group, with food *ad libitum*; restricted night-fed group (RF-night), with access to food restricted to ZT12 to ZT14 (1800–2000 h); restricted day-fed group (RF-day), with access to food restricted to ZT3 to ZT5 (0900–1100 h); and day-fed group (DF), with access to food restricted to ZT0 to ZT12 (0600–1800 h) at ZT3, ZT11, and ZT17, corresponding to 0900, 1700, and 2300 h; respectively. $N = 6$–10 rats per time point per group. ZT, Zeitgeber Time. Significant difference among ZTs within the same feeding condition: $^*P < 0.05$, $^{**}P < 0.01$.

phase (Arble et al., 2009). Of note, in that study, differently from our study, mice were fed with high-fat diet during 6 weeks. Altogether, these data point out that a longer extent of daytime feeding would be necessary to achieve higher body weight.

Change in the daily eating pattern is considered a powerful Zeitgeber for the diurnal rhythm of glucocorticoids (Krieger, 1974; Leal and Moreira, 1996; Girotti et al., 2009). Higher corticosterone concentrations were observed in the control and RF-n groups at ZT11 than at ZT3, coincident with the onset of the nocturnal activity period of rats (Le Minh et al., 2001). On the other hand, RF-d group, which was allowed to eat only during 2 h in the morning, showed higher concentrations of corticosterone at ZT3 than at ZT11, inverting the rat corticosterone circadian pattern, as previously described (Krieger, 1974; Moreira and Krieger, 1982; Leal et al., 1995; Leal and Moreira, 1996). Of note, in the RF-n group, in which food access was restricted but occurred without dissociation with the pattern of rat nocturnal activity, we observed an entrainment of corticosterone peak coincident with food availability. Furthermore, the ZT3 and ZT11 time points allowed us to observe the well known anticipatory corticosterone peak before food availability during the light phase of the light/dark cycle (Oliveira et al., 1993; Le Minh et al., 2001). This finding was not observed in the DF group, which presented higher corticosterone levels at ZT11 as control and RF-n groups. Our data are in agreement with previous reports showing that anticipatory corticosterone peak did not happen when food availability occurs during longer intervals of the day (Honma et al., 1983; Belda et al., 2005). Probably, in this situation the photic cue continues as the main Zeitgeber.

In the SCN, all groups of restricted feeding schedules exhibited different patterns of the expression of *Clock* and *Per1* genes when compared to the control group, while the *Per3* gene expression was only modified in the RF-d and RF-n groups, characterized by an intense food deprivation (food availability restricted by 2 h). The expression of *Bmal1, Cry1,* and *Cry2* was only modified in the RF-d and DF groups, which food access occurred in dissociation with the pattern of rat nocturnal activity, presenting higher expression in the morning, and early evening. In contrast, a higher expression of *Per2* at ZT11 than at ZT17 was observed in all groups, thus the expression of this gene was

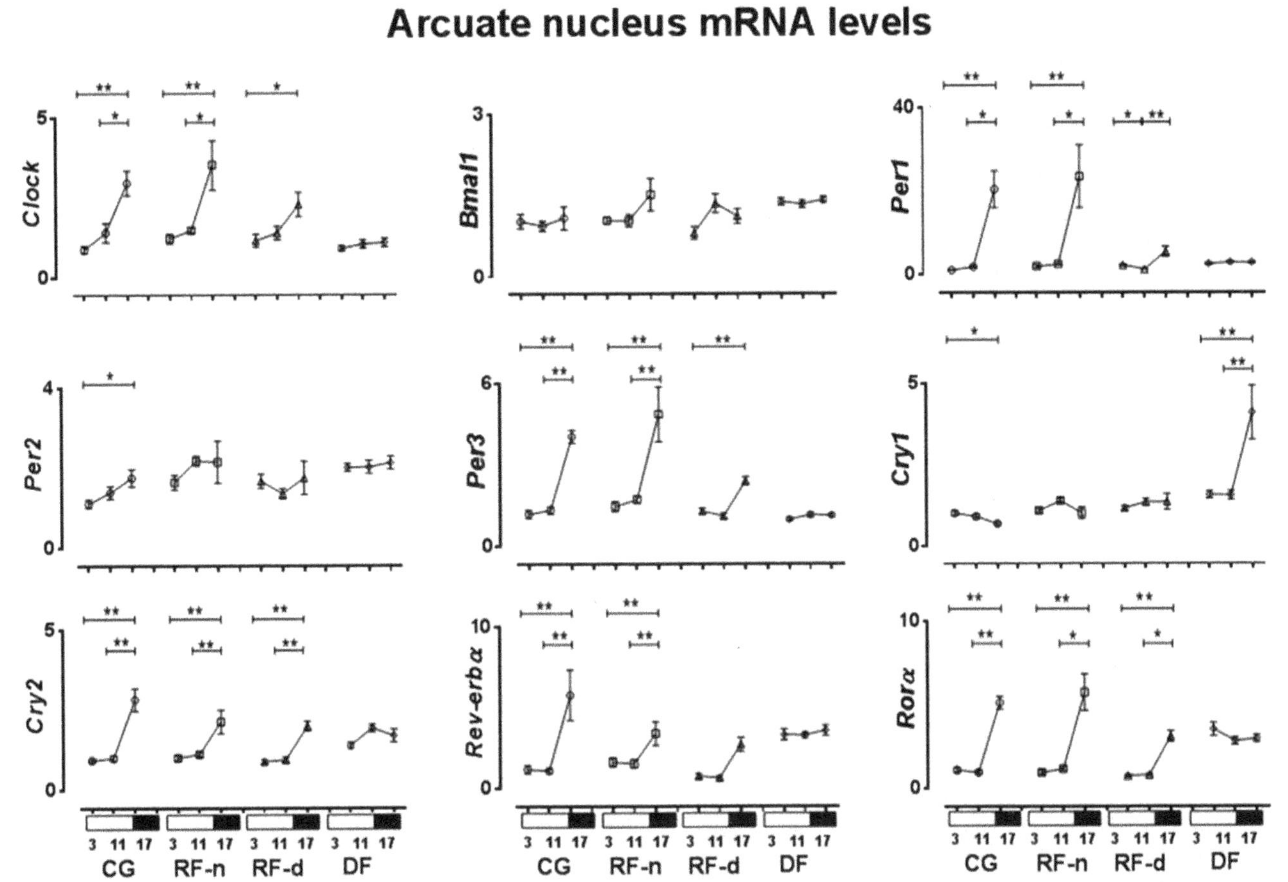

FIGURE 5 | Relative expression of clock genes in Arcuate nucleus (ARC) in the control group, with food *ad libitum*; restricted night-fed group (RF-night), with access to food restricted to ZT12–ZT14 (1800–2000 h); restricted day-fed group (RF-day), with access to food restricted to ZT3–ZT5 (0900–1100 h); and day-fed group (DF), with access to food restricted to ZT0–ZT12 (0600–1800 h) at ZT3, ZT11, and ZT17, corresponding to 0900, 1700, and 2300 h; respectively. $N = 6$–10 rats per time point per group. ZT, Zeitgeber Time. Significant difference among ZTs within the same feeding condition: $^*P < 0.05$, $^{**}P < 0.01$.

unchanged by variable food schedule. Our data demonstrated, in agreement with Caldelas et al. (2005) and Minana-Solis et al. (2009) but in contrast to others (Damiola et al., 2000; Hara et al., 2001; Wakamatsu et al., 2001; Verwey et al., 2007) that SCN is also affected by food entrainment. This controversial data can be explained mainly because of the period in which rats were food entrained in the different protocols, as well as by the duration of daily food access, which varied from 2 h, similar to our study, as long as 12 h as established by Damiola et al. (2000). Thus, time of the day as well as the duration of daily food access may modulate the SCN response, as previously suggested by Minana-Solis et al. (2009). Therefore, feeding cycle can be considered the dominant Zeitgeber for the clock gene expression not only in the peripheral but also in the central pacemakers.

We were not able to detect daily variations in the expression of clock genes in the SCN of the control group, except for *Per2*. Our protocol explored three time points only, which could be a possible limitation to properly study variations in circadian rhythm but it is still informative to understand the role of restricted feeding on the expression of clock genes in hypothalamic nuclei. However, in the PVN and ARC, higher expressions of *Per2, Per3,* and *Cry2* were observed synchronically at ZT17 in the dark period, whereas the other clock genes phased differently. In addition, different food schedules changed the expression of some clock genes in the SCN, PVN, and ARC, compared with CG. Thus, our data demonstrated that under *ad libitum* food access or under food restriction there are different phases in the clock gene expression between the SCN and extra-SCN nuclei as PVN and ARC hypothalamic nuclei.

Data on ARC and in other energy balance and feeding behavior related areas have shown that dietary restriction induces or increases the amplitude of the daily rhythms of *Per1* and *Per2* genes and their proteins (Mieda et al., 2006; Verwey et al., 2007; Angeles-Castellanos et al., 2008; Guilding et al., 2009). In addition, c-*fos*, *Per1*, *Per2*, and *Bmal1* rhythms were in antiphase with the respective SCN genes in the PVN in rats under food restriction, suggesting that extra-SCN neuronal clocks can be, but not always, expressed in antiphase from the SCN (Damiola et al.,

2000). Another study also showed that the daily food restriction did not lead to a uniform timing effect in clock gene expression in the different hypothalamic nuclei (Minana-Solis et al., 2009). Our data expand these findings since we studied a larger number of clock genes and three different food restriction schedules. Indeed, RF-n, RF-d, and DF groups also showed differential effects on the expression of clock genes, inducing phase alteration in some cases or keeping them unaffected in others. Of note, daily restricted feeding can produce food-entrainable oscillations in the cerebral cortex, hippocampus, striatum, pyriform cortex, and PVN even in SCN-lesioned animals (Wakamatsu et al., 2001). Thus, clock genes in extra-SCN oscillators do not respond to feeding schedules in a uniform manner, suggesting a tissue-specific regulation (Feillet et al., 2008; Minana-Solis et al., 2009).

Our data regarding the modulation of feeding restriction schedules on temporal relationship between clock gene expression and corticosterone secretion show that the most important changes were observed in RF-d and DF groups, in which conditions the eating pattern was not coincident with the onset of the nocturnal activity period, suggesting that a disruption in feeding cues may cause dissociation between gene expression and corticosterone secretion. This misalignment can explain night eating syndrome observed in humans, which is characterized by increased food consumption late in the day, in the evening, and in the night and has been linked to obesity and increased risk of metabolic syndrome (Nader et al., 2010).

In conclusion, our data show that feeding restriction schedules induce changes in the body weight, in the corticosterone circadian variation, and in the expression of the clock genes in hypothalamic nuclei, suggesting the ability of animals to predict, anticipate, and respond to food availability. The pattern of clock gene expression in response to RF-n, RF-d, and DF schedules was not affected uniformly, suggesting that the master oscillator in SCN as well as PVN and ARC, areas involved in energy homeostasis and homeostatic aspect of feeding, are regulated in a tissue-specific manner in response to feeding restriction, a non-photic cue, in order to entrain clock gene system.

AUTHOR CONTRIBUTIONS

LD: Conception and design of research, performed experiments, analyzed data, interpreted results of experiments, prepared figures, drafted manuscript, edited, and revised manuscript, approved final version of manuscript. SR: Performed experiments, interpreted results of experiments, prepared figures, revised manuscript and approved final version of manuscript. AB: Performed experiments, analyzed data and interpreted results of experiments. FC: Performed experiments, analyzed data and interpreted results of experiments. CM: Performed experiments, analyzed data and interpreted results of experiments, revised manuscript and approved final version of manuscript. EU: Conception and design of research, performed experiments and interpreted results of experiments. JA: Conception and design of research, revised manuscript, approved final version of manuscript. LE: Conception and design of research, revised manuscript, approved final version of manuscript. PE: Conception and design of research, revised manuscript, approved final version of manuscript. AM: Conception and design of research, analyzed data, interpreted results of experiments, edited and revised manuscript, approved final version of manuscript. MC: Conception and design of research, analyzed data, interpreted results of experiments, prepared figures, drafted manuscript, edited and revised manuscript, approved final version of manuscript. I certify that all authors had a substantial contribution to the manuscript.

ACKNOWLEDGMENTS

We thank Rogerio Zuliani, Jose Roberto Silva, Maria Valci dos Santos, and Rubens Fernando de Melo for their excellent technical assistance.

REFERENCES

Angeles-Castellanos, M., Salgado-Delgado, R., Rodriguez, K., Buijs, R. M., and Escobar, C. (2008). Expectancy for food or expectancy for chocolate reveals timing systems for metabolism and reward. *Neuroscience* 155, 297–307. doi: 10.1016/j.neuroscience.2008.06.001

Arble, D. M., Bass, J., Laposky, A. D., Vitaterna, M. H., and Turek, F. W. (2009). Circadian timing of food intake contributes to weight gain. *Obesity* 17, 2100–2102. doi: 10.1038/oby.2009.264

Bass, J., and Takahashi, J. S. (2010). Circadian integration of metabolism and energetics. *Science* 330, 1349–1354. doi: 10.1126/science.1195027

Belda, X., Ons, S., Carrasco, J., and Armario, A. (2005). The effects of chronic food restriction on hypothalamic-pituitary-adrenal activity depend on morning versus evening availability of food. *Pharmacol. Biochem. Behav.* 81, 41–46. doi: 10.1016/j.pbb.2005.02.009

Buijs, R. M., Van Eden, C. G., Goncharuk, V. D., and Kalsbeek, A. (2003). The biological clock tunes the organs of the body: timing by hormones and the autonomic nervous system. *J. Endocrinol.* 177, 17–26. doi: 10.1677/joe.0.1770017

Caldelas, I., Feillet, C. A., Dardente, H., Eclancher, F., Malan, A., Gourmelen, S., et al. (2005). Timed hypocaloric feeding and melatonin synchronize the suprachiasmatic clockwork in rats, but with opposite timing of behavioral output. *Eur. J. Neurosci.* 22, 921–929. doi: 10.1111/j.1460-9568.2005.04284.x

Castro, M., Figueiredo, F., and Moreira, A. C. (1995). Time-course of hypothalamic CRH and pituitary ACTH contents, and pituitary responsiveness to CRH stimulation after bilateral adrenalectomy. *Horm. Metab. Res.* 27, 10–15. doi: 10.1055/s-2007-979897

Challet, E. (2007). [Clock genes, circadian rhythms and food intake]. *Pathol. Biol.* 55, 176–177. doi: 10.1016/j.patbio.2006.12.005

Dallman, M. F., Engeland, W. C., Rose, J. C., Wilkinson, C. W., Shinsako, J., and Siedenburg, F. (1978). Nycthemeral rhythm in adrenal responsiveness to ACTH. *Am. J. Physiol.* 235, R210–R218.

Dallman, M. F., Strack, A. M., Akana, S. F., Bradbury, M. J., Hanson, E. S., Scribner, K. A., et al. (1993). Feast and famine: critical role of glucocorticoids with insulin in daily energy flow. *Front. Neuroendocrinol.* 14, 303–347. doi: 10.1006/frne.1993.1010

Damiola, F., Le Minh, N., Preitner, N., Kornmann, B., Fleury-Olela, F., and Schibler, U. (2000). Restricted feeding uncouples circadian oscillators in peripheral tissues from the central pacemaker in the suprachiasmatic nucleus. *Genes Dev.* 14, 2950–2961. doi: 10.1101/gad.183500

Fahrenkrug, J., Hannibal, J., and Georg, B. (2008). Diurnal rhythmicity of the canonical clock genes *Per1, Per2* and *Bmal1* in the rat adrenal gland is unaltered after hypophysectomy. *J. Neuroendocrinol.* 20, 323–329. doi: 10.1111/j.1365-2826.2008.01651.x

Feillet, C. A., Mendoza, J., Albrecht, U., Pévet, P., and Challet, E. (2008). Forebrain oscillators ticking with different clock hands. *Mol. Cell. Neurosci.* 37, 209–221. doi: 10.1016/j.mcn.2007.09.010

Girotti, M., Weinberg, M. S., and Spencer, R. L. (2009). Diurnal expression of functional and clock-related genes throughout the rat HPA axis: system-wide shifts in response to a restricted feeding schedule. *Am. J. Physiol. Endocrinol. Metab.* 296, E888–E897. doi: 10.1152/ajpendo.90946.2008

Green, C. B., Takahashi, J. S., and Bass, J. (2008). The meter of metabolism. *Cell* 134, 728–742. doi: 10.1016/j.cell.2008.08.022

Guilding, C., Hughes, A. T., Brown, T. M., Namvar, S., and Piggins, H. D. (2009). A riot of rhythms: neuronal and glial circadian oscillators in the mediobasal hypothalamus. *Mol. Brain* 2:28. doi: 10.1186/1756-6606-2-28

Hara, R., Wan, K., Wakamatsu, H., Aida, R., Moriya, T., Akiyama, M., et al. (2001). Restricted feeding entrains liver clock without participation of the suprachiasmatic nucleus. *Genes Cells* 6, 269–278. doi: 10.1046/j.1365-2443.2001.00419.x

Honma, K., Von Goetz, C., and Aschoff, J. (1983). Effects of restricted daily feeding on freerunning circadian rhythms in rats. *Physiol. Behav.* 30, 905–913. doi: 10.1016/0031-9384(83)90256-1

Ishida, A., Mutoh, T., Ueyama, T., Bando, H., Masubuchi, S., Nakahara, D., et al. (2005). Light activates the adrenal gland: timing of gene expression and glucocorticoid release. *Cell Metab.* 2, 297–307. doi: 10.1016/j.cmet.2005.09.009

Jang, H., Lee, G., Kong, J., Choi, G., Park, Y. J., and Kim, J. B. (2012). Feeding period restriction alters the expression of peripheral circadian rhythm genes without changing body weight in mice. *PLoS ONE* 7:e49993. doi: 10.1371/journal.pone.0049993

Kalsbeek, A., Palm, I. F., La Fleur, S. E., Scheer, F. A., Perreau-Lenz, S., Ruiter, M., et al. (2006). SCN outputs and the hypothalamic balance of life. *J. Biol. Rhythms* 21, 458–469. doi: 10.1177/0748730406293854

Krieger, D. T. (1974). Food and water restriction shifts corticosterone, temperature, activity and brain amine periodicity. *Endocrinology* 95, 1195–1201. doi: 10.1210/endo-95-5-1195

Krieger, D. T., Hauser, H., and Krey, L. C. (1977). Suprachiasmatic nuclear lesions do not abolish food-shifted circadian adrenal and temperature rhythmicity. *Science* 197, 398–399. doi: 10.1126/science.877566

Laguna-Abreu, M. T., Koenigkam-Santos, M., Colleta, A. M., Elias, P. C., Moreira, A. C., Antunes-Rodrigues, J., et al. (2005). Time course of vasopressin and oxytocin secretion after stress in adrenalectomized rats. *Horm. Metab. Res.* 37, 84–88. doi: 10.1055/s-2005-861159

Lamia, K. A., Sachdeva, U. M., Ditacchio, L., Williams, E. C., Alvarez, J. G., Egan, D. F., et al. (2009). AMPK regulates the circadian clock by cryptochrome phosphorylation and degradation. *Science* 326, 437–440. doi: 10.1126/science.1172156

Leal, A. M., Forsling, M. L., and Moreira, A. C. (1995). Diurnal variation of the pituitary-adrenal and AVP responses to stress in rats under food restriction. *Life Sci.* 56, 191–198. doi: 10.1016/0024-3205(94)00434-T

Leal, A. M., and Moreira, A. C. (1996). Feeding and the diurnal variation of the hypothalamic-pituitary-adrenal axis and its responses to CRH and ACTH in rats. *Neuroendocrinology* 64, 14–19. doi: 10.1159/000127092

Le Minh, N., Damiola, F., Tronche, F., Schütz, G., and Schibler, U. (2001). Glucocorticoid hormones inhibit food-induced phase-shifting of peripheral circadian oscillators. *EMBO J.* 20, 7128–7136. doi: 10.1093/emboj/20.24.7128

Livak, K. J., and Schmittgen, T. D. (2001). Analysis of relative gene expression data using real-time quantitative PCR and the $2^{-\Delta\Delta CT}$ method. *Methods* 25, 402–408. doi: 10.1006/meth.2001.1262

Lowrey, P. L., and Takahashi, J. S. (2004). Mammalian circadian biology: elucidating genome-wide levels of temporal organization. *Annu. Rev. Genomics Hum. Genet.* 5, 407–441. doi: 10.1146/annurev.genom.5.061903.175925

Mieda, M., Williams, S. C., Richardson, J. A., Tanaka, K., and Yanagisawa, M. (2006). The dorsomedial hypothalamic nucleus as a putative food-entrainable circadian pacemaker. *Proc. Natl. Acad. Sci. U.S.A.* 103, 12150–12155. doi: 10.1073/pnas.0604189103

Minana-Solis, M. C., Angeles-Castellanos, M., Feillet, C., Pevet, P., Challet, E., and Escobar, C. (2009). Differential effects of a restricted feeding schedule on clock-gene expression in the hypothalamus of the rat. *Chronobiol. Int.* 26, 808–820. doi: 10.1080/07420520903044240

Moreira, A. C., and Krieger, D. T. (1982). The effects of subdiaphragmatic vagotomy on circadian corticosterone rhythmicity in rats with continuous or restricted food access. *Physiol. Behav.* 28, 787–790. doi: 10.1016/0031-9384(82)90194-9

Nader, N., Chrousos, G. P., and Kino, T. (2010). Interactions of the circadian CLOCK system and the HPA axis. *Trends Endocrinol. Metab.* 21, 277–286. doi: 10.1016/j.tem.2009.12.011

Nakahata, Y., Sahar, S., Astarita, G., Kaluzova, M., and Sassone-Corsi, P. (2009). Circadian control of the NAD^+ salvage pathway by CLOCK-SIRT1. *Science* 324, 654–657. doi: 10.1126/science.1170803

Oliveira, M. H., Antunes-Rodrigues, J., Leal, A. M., Elias, L. L., and Moreira, A. C. (1993). Circadian variations of plasma atrial natriuretic peptide and corticosterone in rats with continuous or restricted access to food. *Life Sci.* 53, 1795–1801. doi: 10.1016/0024-3205(93)90487-N

Paxinos, G.,A. C. W. (1997). *The Rat Brain in Stereotaxic Cordinates.* London: Elsevier Inc.

Reppert, S. M., and Weaver, D. R. (2001). Molecular analysis of mammalian circadian rhythms. *Annu. Rev. Physiol.* 63, 647–676. doi: 10.1146/annurev.physiol.63.1.647

Schwartz, M. W., Woods, S. C., Porte, D. Jr., Seeley, R. J., and Baskin, D. G. (2000). Central nervous system control of food intake. *Nature* 404, 661–671. doi: 10.1038/35007534

Stephan, F. K. (2002). The "other" circadian system: food as a Zeitgeber. *J. Biol. Rhythms* 17, 284–292. doi: 10.1177/074873002129002591

Stephan, F. K., and Becker, G. (1989). Entrainment of anticipatory activity to various durations of food access. *Physiol. Behav.* 46, 731–741. doi: 10.1016/0031-9384(89)90359-4

Stephan, F. K., Swann, J. M., and Sisk, C. L. (1979). Entrainment of circadian rhythms by feeding schedules in rats with suprachiasmatic lesions. *Behav. Neural Biol.* 25, 545–554. doi: 10.1016/S0163-1047(79)90332-7

Stokkan, K. A., Yamazaki, S., Tei, H., Sakaki, Y., and Menaker, M. (2001). Entrainment of the circadian clock in the liver by feeding. *Science* 291, 490–493. doi: 10.1126/science.291.5503.490

Takahashi, J. S., Hong, H. K., Ko, C. H., and Mcdearmon, E. L. (2008). The genetics of mammalian circadian order and disorder: implications for physiology and disease. *Nat. Rev. Genet.* 9, 764–775. doi: 10.1038/nrg2430

Uchoa, E. T., Silva, L. E., de Castro, M., Antunes-Rodrigues, J., and Elias, L. L. (2012). Glucocorticoids are required for meal-induced changes in the expression of hypothalamic neuropeptides. *Neuropeptides* 46, 119–124. doi: 10.1016/j.npep.2012.02.002

Verwey, M., Khoja, Z., Stewart, J., and Amir, S. (2007). Differential regulation of the expression of Period2 protein in the limbic forebrain and dorsomedial hypothalamus by daily limited access to highly palatable food in food-deprived and free-fed rats. *Neuroscience* 147, 277–285. doi: 10.1016/j.neuroscience.2007.04.044

Wakamatsu, H., Yoshinobu, Y., Aida, R., Moriya, T., Akiyama, M., and Shibata, S. (2001). Restricted-feeding-induced anticipatory activity rhythm is associated with a phase-shift of the expression of *mPer1* and *mPer2* mRNA in the cerebral cortex and hippocampus but not in the suprachiasmatic nucleus of mice. *Eur. J. Neurosci.* 13, 1190–1196. doi: 10.1046/j.0953-816x.2001.01483.x

10

Amyloid-β–Induced Changes in Molecular Clock Properties and Cellular Bioenergetics

*Karen Schmitt[1,2], Amandine Grimm[1,2] and Anne Eckert[1,2]**

[1] *Neurobiology Lab for Brain Aging and Mental Health, Transfaculty Research Platform, Molecular and Cognitive Neuroscience, University of Basel, Basel, Switzerland,* [2] *Psychiatric University Clinics, University of Basel, Basel, Switzerland*

Edited by:
Etienne Challet,
Institute of Cellular and Integrative Neurosciences (CNRS), France

Reviewed by:
Michael Antle,
University of Calgary, Canada
Martin Sládek,
Institute of Physiology (CAS), Czechia

***Correspondence:**
Anne Eckert
anne.eckert@upkbs.ch

Ageing is an inevitable biological process that results in a progressive structural and functional decline, as well as biochemical alterations that altogether lead to reduced ability to adapt to environmental changes. As clock oscillations and clock-controlled rhythms are not resilient to the aging process, aging of the circadian system may also increase susceptibility to age-related pathologies such as Alzheimer's disease (AD). Besides the amyloid-beta protein (Aβ)-induced metabolic decline and neuronal toxicity in AD, numerous studies have demonstrated that the disruption of sleep and circadian rhythms is one of the common and earliest signs of the disease. In this study, we addressed the questions of whether Aβ contributes to an abnormal molecular circadian clock leading to a bioenergetic imbalance. For this purpose, we used different oscillator cellular models: human skin fibroblasts, human glioma cells, as well as mouse primary cortical and hippocampal neurons. We first evaluated the circadian period length, a molecular clock property, in the presence of different Aβ species. We report here that physiologically relevant $A\beta_{1-42}$ concentrations ranging from 10 to 500 nM induced an increase of the period length in human skin fibroblasts, human A172 glioma cells as well as in mouse primary neurons whereas the reverse control peptide $A\beta_{42-1}$, which is devoid of toxic action, did not influence the circadian period length within the same concentration range. To better understand the underlying mechanisms that are involved in the Aβ-related alterations of the circadian clock, we examined the cellular metabolic state in the human primary skin fibroblast model. Notably, under normal conditions, ATP levels displayed circadian oscillations, which correspond to the respective circadian pattern of mitochondrial respiration. In contrast, $A\beta_{1-42}$ treatment provoked a strong dampening in the metabolic oscillations of ATP levels as well as mitochondrial respiration and in addition, induced an increased oxidized state. Overall, we gain here new insights into the deleterious cycle involved in Aβ-induced decay of the circadian rhythms leading to metabolic deficits, which may contribute to the failure in mitochondrial energy metabolism associated with the pathogenesis of AD.

Keywords: Alzheimer's disease, amyloid-β, bioenergetic balance, energetic state, mitochondria

INTRODUCTION

Ageing leads to a functional deterioration of many brain systems, including the circadian clock, an internal time-keeping system that generates ~24-h rhythms in physiology and behavior. Healthy as well as pathological brain aging is associated with disturbances in both sleep-wake cycle and circadian rhythms (Froy, 2011; Kondratova and Kondratov, 2012; Musiek and Holtzman, 2016). Age-related circadian abnormalities have generally been considered as consequences of neurodegenerative processes. However, it has been recently implied that circadian disruptions can exacerbate the severity of several age-related neurodegenerative pathologies. AD is the most common neurodegenerative disorder among elderly individuals. It accounts for up to 80% of all dementia cases and ranks as the fourth leading cause of death among those above 65 years of age. Multiple clinical studies have demonstrated that the disruption of sleep and circadian rhythms is one of the common and earliest signs of AD. Thus, abnormalities in the circadian clock and in sleep quality worsen as the disease progresses (Hofman and Swaab, 2006; Wulff et al., 2010). Although this link between AD and circadian system is increasingly evident, the underlying mechanisms are still not well understood. Potential molecular mechanisms include the circadian control of physiological processes such as brain metabolism, amyloid-β (Aβ) metabolism, reactive oxygen species (ROS) homeostasis, hormone secretion, autophagy, and stem cell proliferation (Hastings et al., 2007; Kang et al., 2009; Lai et al., 2012; Eckel-Mahan and Sassone-Corsi, 2013). However, it remains mostly unclear if or how Aβ might lead to disruption of the circadian clock which, in turn, could exacerbate the neurodegenerative processes. As the underlying mechanisms of AD onset are still unknown, it is worth considering the core clock as a potential therapeutic target for the prevention of neurodegeneration.

Although the exact molecular nature of AD pathogenesis is still unclear and widely debated, a growing body of evidence supports mitochondrial dysfunction as a prominent and early, chronic oxidative stress-associated event that contributes to synaptic abnormalities and ultimately, selective neuronal degeneration in AD (Schmitt et al., 2012). The mitochondrial energy deficiency is a fundamental characteristic of the AD brain (Manczak et al., 2004) as well as of peripheral cells derived from AD patients (Gibson et al., 1998). Since cellular function relies heavily on this organelle, alterations to the mitochondrial function have severe consequences on neuronal activity and survival, which can, at least in part, contribute to the development of AD.

It is essential to better understand the underlying molecular mechanisms between the circadian network and the AD pathology, particularly in regards to Aβ-related mitochondrial alterations. In this study, we show evidence that Aβ (i) likely contributes to the circadian clock disruption in AD at the molecular level and (ii) impairs the circadian oscillations of the mitochondrial activity with regard to oxygen consumption and ATP generation. Our findings are consistent with the existence of a crosstalk between the clock and the mitochondrial network that maintains bioenergetic homeostasis in response to circadian metabolic changes as well as with the Aβ-related mitochondrial cascade hypothesis.

MATERIALS AND METHODS

Chemicals and Reagents

Dulbecco's-modified Eagle medium (DMEM), RPMI-1640 medium, fetal calf serum (FCS), penicillin/streptomycin, NAD^+, NADH, dihydrorhodamine 123 (DHR), HBSS, MTT [3-(4,5-Dimethylthiazol-2-yl)-2,5-diphenyltetrazolium bromide] and PES (phenazine ethosulfate) were from Sigma-Aldrich (St. Louis, MO, USA). Glutamax and DPBS were from Life Technologies (Waltham, MA, USA). XF Cell Mitostress kit was from Seahorse Bioscience (North Billerica, MA, USA). Horse serum (HS) was from Amimed, Bioconcept (Allschwil, Switzerland).

Cell Culture and Synchronization of the Circadian Rhythms

Isolated human skin fibroblasts from biopsies and glioma cell line A172 (gift from Dr Steven A. Brown) were cultured in DMEM/1% penicillin-streptomycin (v/v)/1% Glutamax (v/v) [DMEM complete (DMEMc)]/20% heat-inactivated FBS (v/v) (Pagani et al., 2011; Gaspar and Brown, 2015). Confluent cells were infected using mice Bmal1::luciferase lentivirus and were positively selected 3 days after infection. Mouse cortical and hippocampal neurons were prepared from E15 embryos according to the Swiss guidelines and were plated in poly-l-lysine-coated plates according to the instruction of the manufacturer (Lonza, Switzerland). After 7 days at 37°C, 50% of the medium was replaced with fresh medium every third day.

Prior to the assessment of circadian period length, cells were synchronized for 15 min at 37°C with 100 mM dexamethasone as described previously (Pagani et al., 2011), while prior to the measurement of nucleotide levels, mitochondrial reactive oxygen species (mROS) and oxygen consumption rate (OCR) in human primary fibroblast culture, serum shock treatment [DMEMc supplemented with 50% heat-inactivated horse serum (v/v)] was performed for 2 h at 37°C to synchronize the cells accordingly to a previously optimized method for these kind of experiments (Cooper, 2003; Rosner et al., 2013). For measurements of nucleotides levels and mitochondrial reactive oxygen species (mROS) levels, experiments were performed starting from 12 h post-synchronization time point and measured at 4 h intervals. For measurements of oxygen consumption, experiments were performed at 16 and 28 h post-shock.

Amyloid-Beta Peptide Preparation and Treatment

The different amyloid-beta (Aβ) fragments [$Aβ_{1-42}$; reverse peptide ($Aβ_{42-1}$); $Aβ_{1-40}$; N-terminal fragment ($Aβ_{1-28}$); C-terminal fragment ($Aβ_{34-42}$); shortest active peptide fragments ($Aβ_{25-35}$, $Aβ_{15-25}$)] (Bachem, Bubendorf, Switzerland) were rapidly dissolved in sterile PBS 1x, pH~7.4 (stock concentration 500 μM) and stored as aliquots at −80°C until needed. One day before treatment of cells with Aβ peptide fragments, 50 μM Aβ working solutions were prepared in PBS 1x, pH~7.4. After securing the caps with parafilm, the tubes were incubated on a table-top thermomixer (Eppendorf, Hamburg, Germany) at 1,000 rpm (~250 × g) at 37°C for 24 h in order to induce aggregation of the Aβ peptides into fibrils. For the circadian period length determination, after synchronization with dexamethasone (100 nM, 15 min at 37°C), fibroblasts were treated with 1, 10, 250, and 500 nM of Aβ in DMEM cell culture medium containing 1% penicillin-streptomycin (v/v)/1% Glutamax (v/v) (DMEMc)/10% FBS (v/v) for 5 days until analyzed. This experimental setting requesting a rather long incubation time over several days in aqueous medium, predicting the formation of insoluble fibrillar Aβ aggegrates and fibrils, did not allow to study the effects only of soluble Aβ species. Therefore, also in the following assays, the same Aβ preparations were used for the determination of nucleotides, ROS and oxygen consumption rate to mimic corresponding conditions of Aβ assembly and chronic toxicity. Thus, the cells were pre-treated with 500 nM pre-aggregated Aβ (the most effective concentration on bioenergetics readouts without cell death-inducing properties) in DMEM cell culture medium containing 1% penicillin-streptomycin (v/v)/1% Glutamax (v/v) [DMEM complete (DMEMc)]/20% heat-inactivated FBS (v/v) for 5 days. After the synchronization, cells were treated again with 500 nM Aβ in DMEM/1% penicillin-streptomycin (v/v)/1% Glutamax (v/v) (DMEMc)/2% FBS (v/v) up to 48 h to maintain the Aβ pressure on the synchronized cells.

Circadian Period Length Measurement

Human skin fibroblasts transfected with the lentiviral circadian reporter mice Bmal1::luciferase (Brown et al., 2005; Gaspar and Brown, 2015) were plated in single culture dishes (35 × 10 mm) at a cell density sufficient to reach 70–80% of confluency on the start day of recording of period length. After synchronization with dexamethasone (100 nM, 15 min at 37°C), cells were cultured in DMEM supplemented with 10% heat-inactivated FBS, 10 mM HEPES and 0.1 mM luciferin. For at least 5 days, the amount of produced light that is proportional to Bmal1 gene expression was measured using a Lumicycle instrument (Actimetrics). Data were analyzed with Lumicycle Analysis software (Lumicycle™, version 2.31, Actimetrics Software) and the period of oscillation was calculated by least-mean-squares fitting of dampened sine wave functions to the actual data as described previously (Pagani et al., 2011).

Nucleotides Measurements

The total ATP content from synchronized human skin fibroblasts was determined using a bioluminescence assay (ViaLighTM HT; Cambrex Bio Science, Walkersville, MD USA) according to the instruction of the manufacturer. Cells were plated in 8 replicates into a 96-wells cell culture plate at a cell density sufficient to reach 40–50% of confluency on the following day. The enzyme luciferase, which catalyzes the formation of light from ATP and luciferin was used. The emitted light is linearly related to the ATP concentration and is measured using a multilabel plate reader VictorX5 (Perkin Elmer).

To measure NAD^+ and NADH, the two molecules were separately extracted using an acid-base extraction method (HCL 0.1 mol/l–NAOH 0.1 mol/l). To determinate both NAD^+ and NADH, an assay was used that is based on passing the electron from ethanol through reduced pyridine nucleotides to MTT [3-(4,5-Dimethylthiazol-2-yl)-2,5-diphenyltetrazolium bromide] in a PES (phenazine ethosulfate)-coupled reaction resulting in the formation of a purple precipitate (formazan) that, once dissolved, can be quantified at 595 nm (VictorX5, Perkin Elmer).

Oxygen Consumption Rate (OCR)

The OCR was evaluated in synchronized fibroblasts as previously described (Invernizzi et al., 2012). Briefly, human skin fibroblasts were seeded at the density of 3×10^4 cells/100 μl per well on Seahorse Biosciences 24-well culture plates 1 day prior to the serum-shock synchronization. On the next day, cells were synchronized using serum shock (2 h at 37°C). Afterwards, the medium was exchanged to 500 μl of assay medium [glucose-free RPMI-1640 medium containing 2% FBS (v/v), 2 mM sodium pyruvate, pH~ 7.4]. Before to be placed in the Seahorse XF24 Analyzer, the microplates were equilibrated in a CO_2-free incubator at 37°C for 60 min. Then, the OCR allocated to basal respiration at 16 and 28 h after synchronization were recorded in real-time over 30 min.

Mitochondrial Reactive Oxygen Species (mROS) Determination

Total level of mROS was assessed using the fluorescent dye dihydrorhodamine 123 (DHR). Cells were plated in 8 replicates into a black 96-wells cell culture plate at a cell density sufficient to reach 40–50% of confluency on the day of the start of mROS recording. After synchronization, cells were loaded at the indicated time points with 10 μM of DHR for 15 min at room temperature in the dark on an orbital shaker. After washing twice with HBSS, DHR, which is oxidized to cationic rhodamine 123 that localizes within the mitochondria, exhibits a green fluorescence that was detected using the multilabel plate reader VictorX5 at 485 nm (excitation)/538 nm (emission). The intensity of fluorescence was proportional to mROS levels in mitochondria.

Statistical Analysis

Data were presented as mean ± S.D. Statistical analyses were performed using the GraphPad Prism software. The curves were generated by using a standard curve fit function in the GraphPad Prism software. For statistical comparisons, One-way ANOVA followed by Tukey's multiple comparison test or Two-way ANOVA followed by Bonferroni's multiple comparison test was used respectively. $P < 0.05$ were considered statistically significant. Rhythmicity of ATP, NAD^+, NADH, and mROS was assessed using a non-parametric algorithm previously described for determination of rhythmic transcripts (Hughes et al., 2010). The JTK-cycle algorithm was used as implemented in R by Kronauer as previously described (Dallmann et al., 2012). A window of 24 h was used for the determination of circadian periodicity and a P-value of < 0.05 was considered as statistically significant.

RESULTS

Aβ Disturbs Circadian Period Length *In vitro*

To address the question whether Aβ is able to disturb the circadian function, we first characterized the circadian period length of synchronized fibroblasts in the presence of different Aβ fragments (**Figures 1A–C**). For that purpose, we infected cells with a circadian reporter construct (Bmal1 promoter-driven expression of firefly luciferase-harboring lentivirus). First, the effect of $A\beta_{1-42}$, the major component of amyloid plaques in AD brains that is more aggregation prone and exhibits higher neurotoxicity than $A\beta_{1-40}$, was investigated. Notably, cells had a significantly longer period length in the presence of aggregated $A\beta_{1-42}$ at concentrations from 10 up to 500 nM compared to controls (**Figures 1A,B**), while 1 nM was not yet effective. At a concentration of 250 nM the maximum effect on prolongation of period length was already reached. However, amplitude (the difference between peak and nadir expression values) was unchanged (data not shown). Notably, up to a concentration of 500 nM, cell viability was not significantly impaired in these experimental settings (data not shown). Consistent with findings showing that the reverse control peptide $A\beta_{42-1}$ is inactive (Zhang et al., 2002), $A\beta_{42-1}$ did not disturb the cellular circadian properties. Similarly, $A\beta_{1-42}$ treatment also induced an increase in the period length in synchronized glioma A172

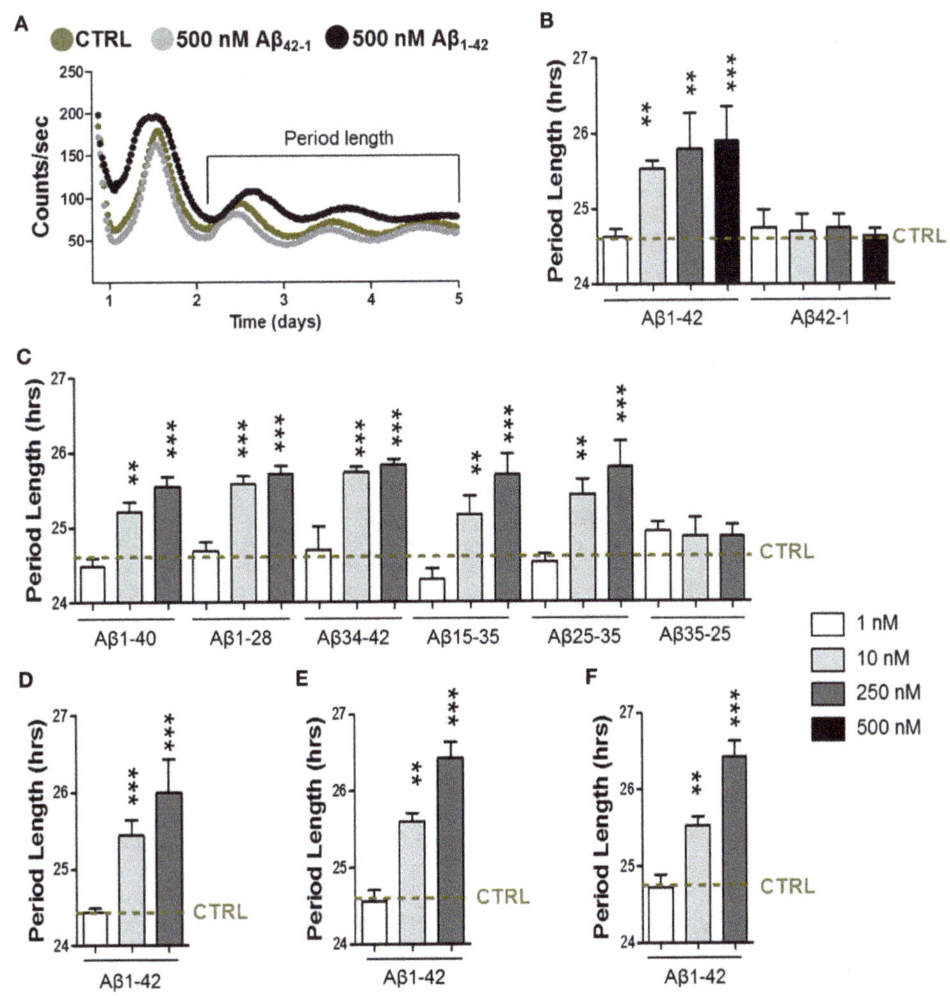

FIGURE 1 | Amyloid-β increases the circadian period length. (A) Representative luminescence records from human skin fibroblasts transfected with mice Bmal1::luciferase reporter in presence of amyloid-β 1–42 (500 nM) or of the reverse peptide amyloid-β 42-1 (500 nM) compared to the condition in the absence of Aβ species (CRTL). **(B, C)** Circadian period length determined in synchronized human skin fibroblasts transfected with mice Bmal1::luciferase reporter in presence of amyloid-β 1–42 and 42-1 **(B)**, 1–40, 1–24, 34–42, 25–35, 35-25, and 15–25 **(C)** compared to the condition in the absence of Aβ species (CRTL) (dashed line). **(D)** Circadian period length determined in synchronized human glioma A172 cells transfected with Bmal1::luciferase reporter in presence of amyloid-β 1–42 compared to control (CRTL) (dashed line). **(E)** Circadian period length determined in synchronized cortical primary mouse neurons transfected with Bmal1::luciferase reporter in presence of amyloid-β 1–42 compared to control (CRTL) (dashed line). **(F)** Circadian period length determined in synchronized hippocampal primary mouse neurons transfected with Bmal1::luciferase reporter in presence of amyloid-β 1–42 compared to control (CRTL) (dashed line). Bars represent the mean of at least three independent experiments ± SD. $^{**}P < 0.01$; $^{***}P < 0.001$ for Student's two-tailed *t*-test, compared to control.

cells as well as in cortical and hippocampal primary mouse neurons (**Figures 1D–F**). In order to identify the specific Aβ fragment/s responsible for the increase in the period length, we then treated the synchronized fibroblasts with different Aβ species ($A\beta_{1-40}$, the most abundant Aβ isoform in the brain, $A\beta_{1-28}$, $A\beta_{34-42}$, $A\beta_{15-25}$, and $A\beta_{25-35}$) within the same range of concentrations (**Figure 1C**). Surprisingly, all the fragments induced a significant alteration of the circadian function to a similar extent as $A\beta_{1-42}$ did itself. Together, these results suggest that the aggregated nature of the Aβ species seem to represent an important factor for the AD-related disruption of the circadian rhythm.

Aβ Induces a Decline in the Circadian Bioenergetic Homeostasis

Since mitochondria were found to be a target of Aβ (Schmitt et al., 2012), leading to mitochondrial dysfunction including a decline in OxPhos and ultimately in ATP content, we investigated the impact of Aβ on ATP content and on mitochondrial oxidative metabolism with regard to rhythmic changes due to the the tight relationship between the circadian clock and metabolism (Brown, 2016; Panda, 2016). As ATP is primarily generated via mitochondrial oxidative phosphorylation (OxPhos), we first monitored whole cell ATP content as readout of OxPhos in $A\beta_{1-42}$-treated (500 nM) compared with untreated synchronized human skin fibroblasts. Under normal conditions, total ATP levels displayed a circadian rhythmicity in control cells (with the peak at 16 h and the trough at 28 h), whereas ATP levels in the Aβ-treated cells did not oscillate and were, in addition, significantly reduced (**Figure 2A**).

We then monitored the real-time oxygen consumption rate (OCR), an indicator of mitochondrial respiration in Aβ-treated human skin fibroblasts compared to untreated cells at 16 h corresponding to the ATP peak and at 28 h related to the ATP trough using the Seahorse Bioscience XF24 Flux Analyzer (**Figure 2B**). In untreated control cells, the OCR was significantly decreased at the time point of the ATP trough (at 28 h) compared to that of the ATP peak (at 16 h) (**Figure 2B**). Thus, the circadian oscillations of OCR and ATP appear to be in the same phase and fit well together in the way that at the time point of high energy production, the oxidative phosphorylation system provides the maximum performance. In contrast, $A\beta_{1-42}$ treatment completely dampened the variation in the OCR and no differences were found at 16 and 28 h after synchronization (**Figure 2B**). Overall, these observations support the hypothesis that circadian control of the mitochondrial function is strongly disturbed by Aβ which may lead to a mitochondrial inability to respond to an increasing metabolic demand. In addition, we characterized the cellular bioenergetic profile of Aβ-treated human skin fibroblasts compared to untreated cells, by mapping OCR (basal respiration) vs. ATP for the indicated time points (**Figure 2C**). Remarkably, untreated cells switched between a metabolically active state corresponding to the high ATP (16 h) and a metabolically resting state corresponding to low ATP levels (28 h), while Aβ-treated cells remained in the metabolically inactive state at both time points.

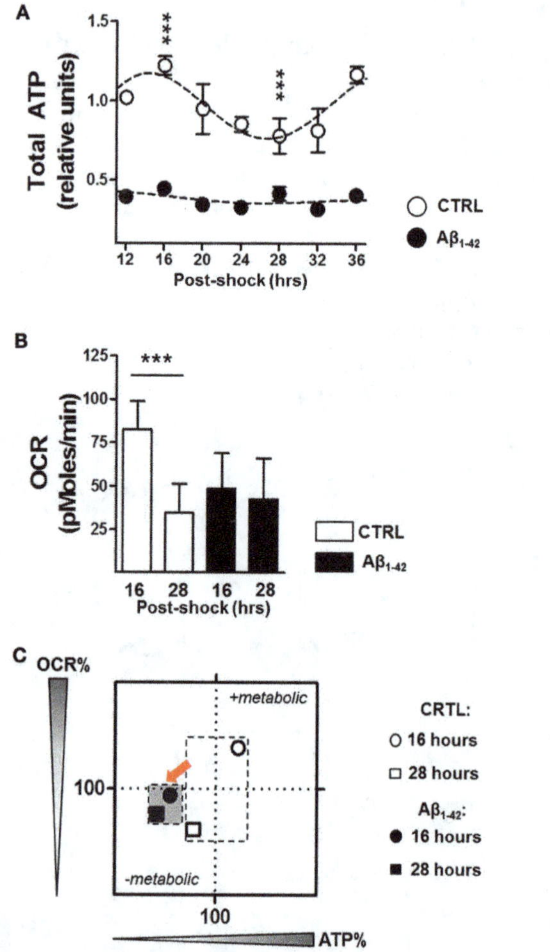

FIGURE 2 | Aβ induces a decline in circadian bioenergetic homeostasis. (A) Total ATP levels from synchronized human skin fibroblasts treated with Aβ 1–42 compared to non-treated cells (CTRL) measured at the indicated time points (6 time points, $n = 6$ for each) (Two-way ANOVA; Aβ effect: $Df = 1$, $F = 3890$, $P < 0.0001$; time effect: $Df = 6$, $F = 34.25$, $P < 0.0001$; *post hoc* Bonferroni, ctrl vs. Aβ: at 16 h, $t = 23.43$, $^{***}P < 0.0001$, at 28 h, $t = 11$, $^{***}P < 0.0001$). Rhythmicity of ATP was assessed using the JTK_Cycle algorithm as previously described (Dallmann et al., 2012): JTK_Cycle, $P_{CTRL} = 2.07 \times 10^{-15}$, $P_{A\beta} = 0.691$. **(B)** Oxygen Consumption Rate (OCR) was evaluated in Aβ-treated human skin fibroblasts compared to untreated control cells at 16 and 28 h after synchronization, respectively. ($n = 11$ replicates /group, three independent experiments) (Two-way ANOVA, Aβ effect: $Df = 1$, $F = 9.948$, $P = 0.0021$; time effect: $Df = 1$, $F = 44.08$, $P < 0.0001$; *post hoc* Bonferroni, ctrl vs. Aβ: at 16 h, $t = 5.886$, $^{***}P < 0.0001$, at 28 h, $t = 1.448$, $P > 0.05$). **(C)** OCR/ATP: The basal OCR corresponding to the ATP peak (at 16 h) and the ATP trough (at 28 h) are plotted against the respective ATP content in control (white symbols) and Aβ conditions (black symbols). Values represent the mean of each group (mean of the ATP levels in abscissa/mean of the OCR in ordinate); $n = 11–12$ replicates/group of three independent experiments. The red arrows highlight the Aβ-induced metabolic shift at 16 and 28 h after cell synchronization.

Alterations in Aβ-Related Mitochondrial Functions Lead to Oxidative Stress

To further investigate the Aβ-induced imbalance in mitochondrial homeostasis, we next evaluated the mitochondrial

ROS levels as well as the $NAD^+/NADH$ ratio as oxidative stress readout in synchronized human skin fibroblasts in the presence or absence of Aβ (**Figure 3**). Again under normal conditions, we found circadian oscillations for mitochondrial ROS (mROS) levels exhibiting a peak at 16 h and a trough at 28 h after synchronization consistent with our findings on ATP oscillations. Interestingly, $A\beta_{1-42}$ (500 nM) increased globally the mROS levels in the Aβ-treated cells, but it did not induce a dampening of the circadian rhythmicity compared to the untreated cells as found for bioenergetic readouts (**Figure 3A**). In contrast, the $NAD^+/NADH$ ratio did not exhibit a circadian pattern in control cells (**Figure 3B**). However, the ratio was significantly augmented by $A\beta_{1-42}$ treatment (about 10 times) compared to untreated cells (**Figure 3B**). Together, our findings suggest that Aβ triggers a decline of mitochondrial bioenergetics including an abolishment of variations in ATP levels coupled to a shift in the redox homeostasis toward a highly oxidized state.

DISCUSSION

In our study, we aimed to investigate, on the one hand, whether Aβ can directly play a role in the molecular circadian clock disturbances associated with AD and on the other hand, whether Aβ impacts the integrity of the circadian regulation of mitochondrial function, which could, in part, contribute to the AD pathogenesis. The major findings were that, (i) AD-related Aβ species are able to induce alterations in the molecular circadian rhythms; (ii) Aβ provoked a drastic dysregulation in the circadian control of the mitochondrial respiratory capacity including reduced energy levels along with increased ROS production.

Given that circadian rhythms become weaker and less synchronized in specific regions of the brain (i.e., SCN) with aging (Farajnia et al., 2012; Hastings and Goedert, 2013), the progressive desynchrony likely promotes Aβ aggregation contributing to the pathogenesis of AD. Comparable to human studies (Weldemichael and Grossberg, 2010), it was shown for several animal models of AD that they exhibit disturbances of behavioral and physiological circadian rhythms (Musiek, 2015). In mice, the circadian disturbances appear to correlate with the degree of amyloid plaque burden and it has been suggested that aggregated forms of Aβ might disrupt the circadian clock (Sterniczuk et al., 2010; Roh et al., 2012). One proposed explanation of circadian dysfunction in AD is the Aβ-related impairment of the SCN caused by the drastic loss of vasopressin- and vasoactive intestinal peptide-expressing neurons which are essential in the maintenance of the SCN circadian function (Swaab et al., 1985; Zhou et al., 1995; Farajnia et al., 2012).

Moreover, considerable evidence has emerged linking the sleep-wake cycle with Aβ regulation in the brains of mice and humans (Kang et al., 2009; Huang et al., 2012; Lim et al., 2014). The diurnal variation of Aβ levels suggests that neuronal activities related to the sleep/ wake cycle directly influence levels of Aβ in the brain (Nir et al., 2011). Synaptic activity has been shown to increase interstitial fluid Aβ release from neurons in both mice and men (Cirrito et al., 2005; Brody et al., 2008). Similarly, sleep deprivation increases plaque formation (Kang et al., 2009), whereas enhanced sleep reduces Aβ deposition (Tabuchi et al., 2015). The most active brain regions during quiet wakefulness are located in the default mode network (DMN) and have been reported as the first network affected by AD (Greicius et al., 2004) exhibiting the most Aβ deposition during the development of AD pathology (Mormino et al., 2011). Consistent with observations of an alteration of circadian behavior in MCI and AD patients, it can be speculated that the effects of Aβ protein on the circadian period length can be related to disturbances in the circadian rhythm and the sleep/wake cycle in MCI and early-stage AD patients where a functional disruption of the SCN is even observed in early disease stages. These age-associated changes in the SCN have been proposed to be responsible for the impairment of circadian clock synchronization throughout the

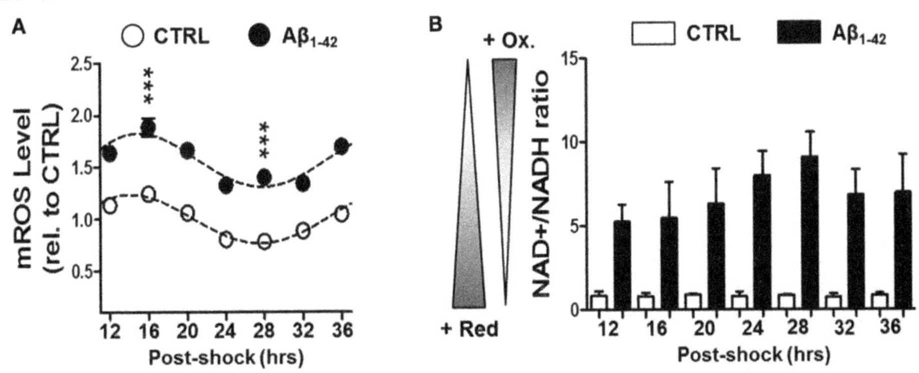

FIGURE 3 | Aβ induces a disruption in the cellular redox state. (A) Mitochondrial (mROS) reactive oxygen species levels were evaluated in synchronized human skin fibroblasts treated with Aβ 1–42 compared to non-treated cells (CTRL) measured at the indicated time points (6 time points, $n = 4$ for each) (Two-way ANOVA; Aβ effect: $Df = 1$, $F = 859$, $P < 0.0001$; time effect: $Df = 6$, $F = 33.16$, $P < 0.0001$; *post hoc* Bonferroni, ctrl vs. Aβ: at 16 h, $t = 9.757$, $^{***}P < 0.0001$, at 28 h, $t = 9.035$, $^{***}P < 0.0001$). Rhythmicity of mROS was assessed using the JTK_Cycle algorithm as previously described (Dallmann et al., 2012): JTK_Cycle, $P(CTRL)_{mROS} = 5.40 \times 10^{-21}$, $P(A\beta)_{mROS} = 3.9 \times 10^{-18}$. **(B)** The $NAD^+/NADH$ ratio evaluated in in synchronized Aβ-treated human skin fibroblasts compared to untreated control cells at the indicated time points. Values represent the mean ± SD; $n = 9–12$ replicates of three independents experiments (Two-way ANOVA; Aβ effect: $Df = 1$, $F = 408.7$, $P < 0.0001$; time effect: $Df = 6$, $F = 1.769$, $P = 0.1343$).

body causing circadian and sleep defects (Zhou et al., 1995; Stopa et al., 1999).

Indeed, physiologically relevant concentrations of $A\beta_{1-42}$, which were not yet cytotoxic, were able to alter circadian rhythms by increasing the period length in human fibroblasts, human A172 glioma cells as well as in mouse primary neurons. Unexpectedly, similar effects were detected with different synthetic Aβ peptides including peptides lacking the N- and C-terminus of the Aβ sequence ($A\beta_{1-28}$, $A\beta_{34-42}$, $A\beta_{25-35}$, and $A\beta_{15-25}$). The whole amino-acids sequence of $A\beta_{1-42}$ seems to be involved in the disruption of the circadian rhythm (Mariani et al., 2007), but already short Aβ fragments such as $A\beta_{25-35}$ which is processed *in vivo* by brain proteases (Clementi et al., 2005), retain the effect of the full-length peptide on the period length in our *in vitro* experiments, while Aβ fragments exhibiting the reverse amino acid sequence were devoid of any action ($A\beta_{42-1}$ and $A\beta_{35-25}$). Unlike the reverse Aβ peptides, several peptide fragments of Aβ, including our selection of Aβ species, form aggregates *in vitro* which have a similar fibrillary morphology in aqueous buffers (Serpell, 2000). Hence, the structure and the assembly of the Aβ protein might be crucial for its mode of action on circadian rhythmicity such as that of the period length.

Consistent with a growing body of evidence on the circadian regulation of the mitochondrial function (Manella and Asher, 2016), metabolic byproducts of mitochondrial metabolism including ATP and mROS exhibited circadian rhythmicity. Concurrent to the circadian rhythmicity in ATP levels, mitochondrial oxygen consumption analyses showed time-of-day-dependent variation in basal respiration (Isobe et al., 2011; Peek et al., 2013). When in resting state (low ATP), observed 28 h post-synchronization in cultured cells, the cells exhibited a low respiration as well. The reverse was seen at 16 h post-synchronization, when the cells showed high ATP levels and high respiration respectively. Thus, the circadian patterns of OCR, ATP and mROS seem likely to be in the same phase and fit well together in the way that at the time point of high energy production the oxidative phosphorylation system provides the maximum performance accordingly to the high energy demand, initiating at the same time a maximum in mROS production due to the high electron leakage from the electron transport chain. Surprisingly, we did not observe a circadian rhythmicity of the $NAD^+/NADH$ ratio, although it has been showed that this ratio exhibited distinct circadian rhythms in $ApoE^{-/-}$ and C57BL/6J SCN under the constant dark condition (Zhou et al., 2016). The difference with our *in vitro* observations might be possibly due to the fact that the SCN is a stronger clock than fibroblasts as peripheral oscillators (Welsh et al., 2004).

Since disturbances in mitochondrial bioenergetics are known as early and prominent features of AD-related neuronal toxicity induced by Aβ (Yao et al., 2009; Garcia-Escudero et al., 2013), we examined the potential impacts of Aβ on the integrity of the mitochondrial function. Concomitantly, defects in the mitochondrial function induced a decline in mitochondrial metabolism including decreased mitochondrial respiration, depletion in ATP content and increased oxidative stress through increased mitochondrial ROS levels and drastic changes in the $NAD^+/NADH$ ratio. Interestingly, only the rhythmicity of ATP and OCR was entirely dampened in the presence of Aβ. This Aβ-related loss of rhythmicity in basal respiration and energy production could be explained by altered expression patterns of the circadian clock genes caused by an Aβ-induced post-translational degradation of the circadian clock genes, Bmal1, and Per2 (Song et al., 2015), thereby probably impairing the expression of clock-controlled genes involved in the oxidative phosphorylation (Panda et al., 2002). This impairment may, in turn lead to alterations of the rhythmic assembly of mitochondrial supercomplexes to reach their maximum performance in OXPHOS. Moreover, in addition to the Aβ-related alterations in numerous enzymes essential for the mitochondrial functions (Gibson et al., 1998), it has been also recently proposed that the PERIOD proteins serve as a rheostat for mitochondrial nutrient utilization by regulating rate-limiting mitochondrial enzymes and therefore improving mitochondrial metabolism (Neufeld-Cohen et al., 2016). Overall, these observations suggest that Aβ likely induces alterations in the molecular clock gene expression, which lead, in turn, to changes in clock-controlled gene expressions and eventually to disturbances in mitochondrial respiration and in energy production.

Given the role of the circadian system in the regulation of ROS homeostasis (Kondratova and Kondratov, 2012; Lee et al., 2013), it is surprising that, while mROS levels increased drastically in the presence of Aβ, they retained their circadian rhythmicity despite the proposed Aβ-related alterations in the molecular clock. Indeed, it has been described that ROS levels oscillated in different mouse tissues and these rhythmic patterns were disrupted in mice bearing impaired circadian clocks (Kondratov et al., 2006). Our findings could be explained, at least in part, by the fact that fibroblasts are known to have stronger antioxidant defense mechanism than the brain (Cecchi et al., 2002). Other explanations might be that the expression of clock-controlled genes regulating the cellular antioxidant defense are less sensitive to Aβ-induced insults than those of the OXPHOS or that the antioxidant defense enzymes may act upstream of the electron transport chain which is disturbed in its function by Aβ in this way initiating and increasing oxidative stress. Further research is needed to elucidate the underlying molecular mechanisms of these cellular response systems. Our findings are in agreement with previous observations from both animal models and AD patients exhibiting mitochondrial failure as well as elevated oxidative stress in their brains (Cecchi et al., 2002; Shi and Gibson, 2007; Zhu et al., 2013).

In summary, we gained new insights into the Aβ-related molecular circadian impairments in AD. Based on the complexity of the multifactorial nature of AD, several vicious cycles are interconnected within a larger vicious cycle where mitochondria play a prominent role in the cascade of events leading to AD. All of them, once set in motion, amplify their own processes, thus accelerating the development of AD. One of these subordinate cycles may represent the impact of a disrupted circadian rhythm on mitochondrial function. Finally, the critical role of mitochondria in the early pathogenesis of AD may make them attractive as a preferential target for therapeutic strategies by sustaining mitochondrial metabolic function. Since the diurnal oscillations of Aβ levels in the brain appear to be closely related to the sleep-wake cycle and Aβ, in turn, impacts the circadian regulation of mitochondrial functions, the possibility exists that treating the aging-related sleep-wake impairments and upstream events of the circadian dysfunction early, even prior to the development of AD pathology, might prevent or slow down AD pathogenesis pathways.

AUTHOR CONTRIBUTIONS

KS and AG performed experiments. AE conceived the project, coordinated and supervised research. KS and AE wrote the manuscript.

ACKNOWLEDGMENTS

We thank Ginette Baysang and Fides Meier for technical assistance.

REFERENCES

Brody, D. L., Magnoni, S., Schwetye, K. E., Spinner, M. L., Esparza, T. J., Stocchetti, N., et al. (2008). Amyloid-β dynamics correlate with neurological status in the injured human brain. *Science* 321, 1221–1224. doi: 10.1126/science.1161591

Brown, S. A. (2016). Circadian metabolism: from mechanisms to metabolomics and medicine. *Trends Endocrinol. Metab.* 27, 415–426. doi: 10.1016/j.tem.2016.03.015

Brown, S. A., Fleury-Olela, F., Nagoshi, E., Hauser, C., Juge, C., Meier, C. A., et al. (2005). The period length of fibroblast circadian gene expression varies widely among human individuals. *PLoS Biol.* 3:E338. doi: 10.1371/journal.pbio.0030338

Cecchi, C., Fiorillo, C., Sorbi, S., Latorraca, S., Nacmias, B., Bagnoli, S., et al. (2002). Oxidative stress and reduced antioxidant defenses in peripheral cells from familial Alzheimer's patients. *Free Radic. Biol. Med.* 33, 1372–1379. doi: 10.1016/S0891-5849(02)01049-3

Cirrito, J. R., Yamada, K. A., Finn, M. B., Sloviter, R. S., Bales, K. R., May, P. C., et al. (2005). Synaptic activity regulates interstitial fluid Amyloid-β levels *in vivo*. *Neuron* 48, 913–922. doi: 10.1016/j.neuron.2005.10.028

Clementi, M. E., Marini, S., Coletta, M., Orsini, F., Giardina, B., and Misiti, F. (2005). Aβ(31-35) and Aβ(25-35) fragments of Amyloid β-protein induce cellular death through apoptotic signals: role of the redox state of methionine-35. *FEBS Lett.* 579, 2913–2918. doi: 10.1016/j.febslet.2005.04.041

Cooper, S. (2003). Rethinking synchronization of mammalian cells for cell cycle analysis. *Cell. Mol. Life Sci.* 60, 1099–1106. doi: 10.1007/s00018-003-2253-2

Dallmann, R., Viola, A. U., Tarokh, L., Cajochen, C., and Brown, S. A. (2012). The human circadian metabolome. *Proc. Natl. Acad. Sci. U.S.A.* 109, 2625–2629. doi: 10.1073/pnas.1114410109

Eckel-Mahan, K., and Sassone-Corsi, P. (2013). Metabolism and the circadian clock converge. *Physiol. Rev.* 93, 107–135. doi: 10.1152/physrev.00016.2012

Farajnia, S., Michel, S., Deboer, T., Vanderleest, H. T., Houben, T., Rohling, J. H., et al. (2012). Evidence for neuronal desynchrony in the aged suprachiasmatic nucleus clock. *J. Neurosci.* 32, 5891–5899. doi: 10.1523/JNEUROSCI.0469-12.2012

Froy, O. (2011). Circadian rhythms, aging, and life span in mammals. *Physiology* 26, 225–235. doi: 10.1152/physiol.00012.2011

Garcia-Escudero, V., Martin-Maestro, P., Perry, G., and Avila, J. (2013). Deconstructing mitochondrial dysfunction in Alzheimer disease. *Oxid. Med. Cell. Longev.* 2013:162152. doi: 10.1155/2013/162152

Gaspar, L., and Brown, S. A. (2015). Measuring circadian clock function in human cells. *Meth. Enzymol.* 552, 231–256. doi: 10.1016/bs.mie.2014.10.023

Gibson, G. E., Sheu, K. F., and Blass, J. P. (1998). Abnormalities of mitochondrial enzymes in Alzheimer disease. *J. Neural Transm. (Vienna)* 105, 855–870. doi: 10.1007/s007020050099

Greicius, M. D., Srivastava, G., Reiss, A. L., and Menon, V. (2004). Default-mode network activity distinguishes Alzheimer's disease from healthy aging: evidence from functional MRI. *Proc. Natl. Acad. Sci. U.S.A.* 101, 4637–4642. doi: 10.1073/pnas.0308627101

Hastings, M. H., and Goedert, M. (2013). Circadian clocks and neurodegenerative diseases: time to aggregate? *Curr. Opin. Neurobiol.* 23, 880–887. doi: 10.1016/j.conb.2013.05.004

Hastings, M., O'neill, J. S., and Maywood, E. S. (2007). Circadian clocks: regulators of endocrine and metabolic rhythms. *J. Endocrinol.* 195, 187–198. doi: 10.1677/JOE-07-0378

Hofman, M. A., and Swaab, D. F. (2006). Living by the clock: the circadian pacemaker in older people. *Ageing Res. Rev.* 5, 33–51. doi: 10.1016/j.arr.2005.07.001

Huang, Y., Potter, R., Sigurdson, W., Santacruz, A., Shih, S., Ju, Y. E., et al. (2012). Effects of age and amyloid deposition on Aβ dynamics in the human central nervous system. *Arch. Neurol.* 69, 51–58. doi: 10.1001/archneurol.2011.235

Hughes, M. E., Hogenesch, J. B., and Kornacker, K. (2010). JTK_CYCLE: an efficient nonparametric algorithm for detecting rhythmic components in genome-scale data sets. *J. Biol. Rhythms*, 25, 372–380. doi: 10.1177/0748730410379711

Invernizzi, F., D'Amato, I., Jensen, P. B., Ravaglia, S., Zeviani, M., and Tiranti, V. (2012). Microscale oxygraphy reveals OXPHOS impairment in MRC mutant cells. *Mitochondrion* 12, 328–335. doi: 10.1016/j.mito.2012.01.001

Isobe, Y., Hida, H., and Nishino, H. (2011). Circadian rhythm of enolase in suprachiasmatic nucleus depends on mitochondrial function. *J. Neurosci. Res.* 89, 936–944. doi: 10.1002/jnr.22610

Kang, J. E., Lim, M. M., Bateman, R. J., Lee, J. J., Smyth, L. P., Cirrito, J. R., et al. (2009). Amyloid-β dynamics are regulated by orexin and the sleep-wake cycle. *Science* 326, 1005–1007. doi: 10.1126/science.1180962

Kondratov, R. V., Kondratova, A. A., Gorbacheva, V. Y., Vykhovanets, O. V., and Antoch, M. P. (2006). Early aging and age-related pathologies in mice deficient in $BMAL_1$, the core componentof the circadian clock. *Genes Dev.* 20, 1868–1873. doi: 10.1101/gad.1432206

Kondratova, A. A., and Kondratov, R. V. (2012). The circadian clock and pathology of the ageing brain. *Nat. Rev. Neurosci.* 13, 325–335. doi: 10.1038/nrn3208

Lai, A. G., Doherty, C. J., Mueller-Roeber, B., Kay, S. A., Schippers, J. H., and Dijkwel, P. P. (2012). CIRCADIAN CLOCK-ASSOCIATED 1 regulates ROS homeostasis and oxidative stress responses. *Proc. Natl. Acad. Sci. U.S.A.* 109, 17129–17134. doi: 10.1073/pnas.1209148109

Lee, J., Moulik, M., Fang, Z., Saha, P., Zou, F., Xu, Y., et al. (2013). $Bmal_1$ and β-cell clock are required for adaptation to circadian disruption, and their loss of function leads to oxidative stress-induced β-cell failure in mice. *Mol. Cell. Biol.* 33, 2327–2338. doi: 10.1128/MCB.01421-12

Lim, M. M., Gerstner, J. R., and Holtzman, D. M. (2014). The sleep-wake cycle and Alzheimer's disease: what do we know? *Neurodegener. Dis. Manag.* 4, 351–362. doi: 10.2217/nmt.14.33

Manczak, M., Park, B. S., Jung, Y., and Reddy, P. H. (2004). Differential expression of oxidative phosphorylation genes in patients with Alzheimer's disease: implications for early mitochondrial dysfunction and oxidative damage. *Neuromolecular Med.* 5, 147–162. doi: 10.1385/NMM:5:2:147

Manella, G., and Asher, G. (2016). The circadian nature of mitochondrial biology. *Front. Endocrinol.* 7:162. doi: 10.3389/fendo.2016.00162

Mariani, E., Monastero, R., and Mecocci, P. (2007). Mild cognitive impairment: a systematic review. *J. Alzheimers Dis.* 12, 23–35.

Mormino, E. C., Smiljic, A., Hayenga, A. O., Onami, S. H., Greicius, M. D., Rabinovici, G. D., et al. (2011). Relationships between β-amyloid and functional connectivity in different components of the default mode network in aging. *Cereb. Cortex* 21, 2399–2407. doi: 10.1093/cercor/bhr025

Musiek, E. S. (2015). Circadian clock disruption in neurodegenerative diseases: cause and effect? *Front. Pharmacol.* 6:29. doi: 10.3389/fphar.2015.00029

Musiek, E. S., and Holtzman, D. M. (2016). Mechanisms linking circadian clocks, sleep, and neurodegeneration. *Science* 354, 1004–1008. doi: 10.1126/science.aah4968

Neufeld-Cohen, A., Robles, M. S., Aviram, R., Manella, G., Adamovich, Y., Ladeuix, B., et al. (2016). Circadian control of oscillations in mitochondrial rate-limiting enzymes and nutrient utilization by PERIOD proteins. *Proc. Natl. Acad. Sci. U.S.A.* 113, E1673–E1682. doi: 10.1073/pnas.1519650113

Nir, Y., Staba, R. J., Andrillon, T., Vyazovskiy, V. V., Cirelli, C., Fried, I., et al. (2011). Regional slow waves and spindles in human sleep. *Neuron* 70, 153–169. doi: 10.1016/j.neuron.2011.02.043

Pagani, L., Schmitt, K., Meier, F., Izakovic, J., Roemer, K., Viola, A., et al. (2011). Serum factors in older individuals change cellular clock properties. *Proc. Natl. Acad. Sci. U.S.A.* 108, 7218–7223. doi: 10.1073/pnas.1008882108

Panda, S. (2016). Circadian physiology of metabolism. *Science* 354, 1008–1015. doi: 10.1126/science.aah4967

Panda, S., Antoch, M. P., Miller, B. H., Su, A. I., Schook, A. B., Straume, M., et al. (2002). Coordinated transcription of key pathways in the mouse by the circadian clock. *Cell* 109, 307–320. doi: 10.1016/S0092-8674(02)00722-5

Peek, C. B., Affinati, A. H., Ramsey, K. M., Kuo, H. Y., Yu, W., Sena, L. A., et al. (2013). Circadian clock NAD+ cycle drives mitochondrial oxidative metabolism in mice. *Science* 342:1243417. doi: 10.1126/science.1243417

Roh, J. H., Huang, Y., Bero, A. W., Kasten, T., Stewart, F. R., Bateman, R. J., et al. (2012). Disruption of the sleep-wake cycle and diurnal fluctuation of β-amyloid in mice with Alzheimer's disease pathology. *Sci. Transl. Med.* 4:150ra122. doi: 10.1126/scitranslmed.3004291

Rosner, M., Schipany, K., and Hengstschlager, M. (2013). Merging high-quality biochemical fractionation with a refined flow cytometry approach to monitor nucleocytoplasmic protein expression throughout the unperturbed mammalian cell cycle. *Nat. Protoc.* 8, 602–626. doi: 10.1038/nprot.2013.011

Schmitt, K., Grimm, A., Kazmierczak, A., Strosznajder, J. B., Gotz, J., and Eckert, A. (2012). Insights into mitochondrial dysfunction: aging, Amyloid-β, and tau-A deleterious trio. *Antioxid. Redox Signal.* 16, 1456–1466. doi: 10.1089/ars.2011.4400

Serpell, L. C. (2000). Alzheimer's amyloid fibrils: structure and assembly. *Biochim. Biophys. Acta* 1502, 16–30. doi: 10.1016/S0925-4439(00)00029-6

Shi, Q., and Gibson, G. E. (2007). Oxidative stress and transcriptional regulation in Alzheimer disease. *Alzheimer Dis. Assoc. Disord.* 21, 276–291. doi: 10.1097/WAD.0b013e31815721c3

Song, H., Moon, M., Choe, H. K., Han, D. H., Jang, C., Kim, A., et al. (2015). Aβ-induced degradation of $BMAL_1$ and CBP leads to circadian rhythm disruption in Alzheimer's disease. *Mol. Neurodegener.* 10:13. doi: 10.1186/s13024-015-0007-x

Sterniczuk, R., Dyck, R. H., Laferla, F. M., and Antle, M. C. (2010). Characterization of the 3xTg-AD mouse model of Alzheimer's disease: Part 1. Circadian changes. *Brain Res.* 1348, 139–148. doi: 10.1016/j.brainres.2010.05.013

Stopa, E. G., Volicer, L., Kuo-Leblanc, V., Harper, D., Lathi, D., Tate, B., et al. (1999). Pathologic evaluation of the human suprachiasmatic nucleus in severe dementia. *J. Neuropathol. Exp. Neurol.* 58, 29–39. doi: 10.1097/00005072-199901000-00004

Swaab, D. F., Fliers, E., and Partiman, T. S. (1985). The suprachiasmatic nucleus of the human brain in relation to sex, age and senile dementia. *Brain Res.* 342, 37–44. doi: 10.1016/0006-8993(85)91350-2

Tabuchi, M., Lone, S. R., Liu, S., Liu, Q., Zhang, J., Spira, A. P., et al. (2015). Sleep interacts with Aβ to modulate intrinsic neuronal excitability. *Curr. Biol.* 25, 702–712. doi: 10.1016/j.cub.2015.01.016

Weldemichael, D. A., and Grossberg, G. T. (2010). Circadian rhythm disturbances in patients with Alzheimer's disease: a review. *Int. J. Alzheimers Dis.* 2010:716453. doi: 10.4061/2010/716453

Welsh, D. K., Yoo, S. H., Liu, A. C., Takahashi, J. S., and Kay, S. A. (2004). Bioluminescence imaging of individual fibroblasts reveals persistent, independently phased circadian rhythms of clock gene expression. *Curr. Biol.* 14, 2289–2295. doi: 10.1016/j.cub.2004.11.057

Wulff, K., Gatti, S., Wettstein, J. G., and Foster, R. G. (2010). Sleep and circadian rhythm disruption in psychiatric and neurodegenerative disease. *Nat. Rev. Neurosci.* 11, 589–599. doi: 10.1038/nrn2868

Yao, J., Irwin, R. W., Zhao, L., Nilsen, J., Hamilton, R. T., and Brinton, R. D. (2009). Mitochondrial bioenergetic deficit precedes alzheimer's pathology in female mouse model of Alzheimer's disease. *Proc. Natl. Acad. Sci. U.S.A.* 106, 14670–14675. doi: 10.1073/pnas.0903563106

Zhang, Y., Mclaughlin, R., Goodyer, C., and Leblanc, A. (2002). Selective cytotoxicity of intracellular amyloid β peptide1-42 through P53 and Bax in cultured primary human neurons. *J. Cell Biol.* 156, 519–529. doi: 10.1083/jcb.200110119

Zhou, J. N., Hofman, M. A., and Swaab, D. F. (1995). VIP neurons in the human SCN in relation to sex, age, and Alzheimer's disease. *Neurobiol. Aging* 16, 571–576. doi: 10.1016/0197-4580(95)00043-E

Zhou, L., Gao, Q., Nie, M., Gu, J. L., Hao, W., Wang, L., et al. (2016). Degeneration and energy shortage in the suprachiasmatic nucleus underlies the circadian rhythm disturbance in ApoE-/- mice: implications for Alzheimer's disease. *Sci. Rep.* 6:36335. doi: 10.1038/srep36335

Zhu, X., Perry, G., Smith, M. A., and Wang, X. (2013). Abnormal mitochondrial dynamics in the pathogenesis of Alzheimer's disease. *J. Alzheimers Dis.* 33(Suppl. 1), S253–S262. doi: 10.3233/JAD-2012-129005

11

Circadian Rhythms and Mood Disorders: Are the Phenomena and Mechanisms Causally Related?

*William Bechtel**

Department of Philosophy and Center for Circadian Biology, University of California San Diego, San Diego, CA, USA

Edited by:
DeoBruin,
VU University Amsterdam, Netherlands

Reviewed by:
Oksana Sorokina,
The University of Edinburgh, UK
Kyle B. Gustafson,
École Polytechnique Fédérale de Lausanne, Switzerland
Victor Gijsbers,
Universiteit Leiden, Netherlands

***Correspondence:**
William Bechtel,
Department of Philosophy, University of California San Diego, 9500 Gilman Drive, San Diego, CA 92093-0119, USA
bechtel@ucsd.edu

This paper reviews some of the compelling evidence of disrupted circadian rhythms in individuals with mood disorders (major depressive disorder, seasonal affective disorder, and bipolar disorder) and that treatments such as bright light, designed to alter circadian rhythms, are effective in treating these disorders. Neurotransmitters in brain regions implicated in mood regulation exhibit circadian rhythms. A mouse model originally employed to identify a circadian gene has proven a potent model for mania. While this evidence is suggestive of an etiological role for altered circadian rhythms in mood disorders, it is compatible with other explanations, including that disrupted circadian rhythms and mood disorders are effects of a common cause and that genes and proteins implicated in both simply have pleiotropic effects. In light of this, the paper advances a proposal as to what evidence would be needed to establish a direct causal link between disruption of circadian rhythms and mood disorders.

Keywords: mood disorders, circadian rhythms, mechanistic explanations, causal relations between mechanisms

Introduction

Much biological research over the past 200 years has proceeded by delineating individual phenomena and explaining each distinct phenomenon by characterizing the responsible mechanism (1). Discovering mechanisms involves localizing the phenomenon in a responsible system that is taken to be the mechanism and then decomposing that system structurally to discover its component parts and functionally to discover the operations those parts perform (2–4). To show that the parts and operations suffice for the phenomenon requires recomposing the mechanism by mentally rehearsing the operations or employing computational models. When the organization is non-sequential, and the operations, non-linear, computational modeling is often necessary to establish that the mechanism could generate the phenomenon (5). Overall, this has been a highly productive strategy. Much has been learnt about the mechanisms for various biological phenomena, but it has also succeeded in revealing the limitations of the approach. One important limitation is that the supposedly independent phenomena and mechanisms are not nearly as independent as initially thought.

Understanding the ways mechanisms are connected is turning out to be an important challenge in twenty-first century biology and medicine, in part because such connections afford useful ways of intervening on systems to control particular phenomena (e.g., to treat specific diseases). This paper explores the challenges in establishing that the mechanism advanced to explain the fact that one phenomenon is causally affected by that put forward to explain another. As in the project of advancing a philosophical analysis of mechanistic explanation, my aim is to ground an account of what is involved in establishing causal relations between mechanisms in the practice of scientific researchers. To do this, I focus on two biological phenomena in which important progress has been made in identifying mechanisms – circadian rhythms and moods – and engage in a detailed review of the research and the causal claims that have been advanced as to how the mechanisms relate to each other[1].

As much of the research on mood has focused not on the moods of healthy individuals, but mood disorders such as major depressive disorder (MDD) and bipolar disorder (BD), and these have been related to disruptions of normal circadian rhythms, I will generally treat the related phenomena as mood disorders and disruptions of circadian rhythms. While making for a somewhat complex discussion, this does not pose a substantive problem since disrupted phenomena often serve to guide development of the understanding of the mechanism underlying the normally occurring phenomenon (6).

Progress in characterizing and understanding circadian rhythms and moods has largely stemmed from treating the two independently. But research in the later decades of the twentieth century also revealed connections between the two phenomena by showing that mood disorders are accompanied by disruptions of circadian rhythms. During the last two decades research on both circadian rhythms and mood disorders has increasingly focused on the molecular components of the two mechanisms. This research has revealed that molecular components of the circadian clock mechanism also play a role in mood disorders. This has raised the possibility of causal links between the mechanisms so that either disruptions in the circadian mechanism might be viewed as a cause of mood disorders, or mood disorders might be the cause of altered circadian rhythms. Of course the causality could also go in both directions, but my focus is on another alternative – that despite involving shared components, the two mechanisms are really independent and that what researchers are observing are effects of a common cause or pleotropic effects of common components.

My goal in this paper is not to argue for a particular stance on whether circadian rhythm disorders cause mood disorders; rather I will show how research has raised and addressed the question of possible connections between the two phenomena in the Section "Establishing a Relation between Circadian Rhythms and Mood Disorders" and between the two mechanisms in the Section "Research Implicating Molecular Components of the Circadian Clock in Mood Disorders." I then explore whether a causal connection is supported by the evidence in the Section "How are the Mechanisms Related?" In particular, I am concerned with what it would take to establish a causal connection between these mechanisms. Focusing only on the relation between phenomena, the standard measure of independence is that each can be dissociated from the other. There is evidence that some features of mood disorders and circadian disruptions are independent, but the same is true of different features that are treated as aspects of just one phenomenon. The separateness or relatedness of the mechanisms is what ultimately will determine whether researchers judge the phenomena to be causally linked. Mechanisms comprise parts performing operations, which explains the focus on determining whether parts of the circadian mechanism are also implicated in mood phenomena. However, just knowing that two mechanisms employ the same type of part, even if it performs the same operation in each, does not causally link the two mechanisms. Two car engines may employ pistons, but that does not causally connect them. What is required is that the same individual part is a component of both mechanisms and that the parts of the first mechanism affect the second mechanism differently as the first mechanism is in different states. Only then can researchers relate activities in one mechanism to activities in another mechanism. In the case of circadian and mood mechanisms, one needs to show that a protein, for example, affects mood differently as a consequence of its role in different circadian states. This is a demanding standard that has not yet been realized. But before raising these skeptical worries about how circadian disruptions and mood disorders relate, I turn first to the evidence that has been invoked in relating them. As noted above, my objective is to show that the question of how to understand the relation between the generation of circadian rhythm disorders and mood disorders is a real concern for science, not purely an abstract philosophical concern. Subsequent sections, thus, provide a review of how claims about the relation between circadian rhythms and mood developed and the current state of attempts to evaluate whether a causal claim can be substantiated.

Establishing a Relation between Circadian Rhythms and Mood Disorders

Reports of daily cycles of leaf folding in plants stem from ancient times and were first shown experimentally not to be a response to light when De Mairan (7) placed plants in a dark cupboard and observed that they continued to fold. Other examples of daily rhythms followed, such as, Wunderlich's (8) demonstration that body temperature in humans oscillates by over 1°C/day. Although a variety of researchers tried to maintain that these were responses to external cues, by the time of the International Symposium on Biological Clocks in 1960, the recognition that these oscillations continue but with periods of only approximately 24 h (thus, *circa* + *dies*) when light, temperature, and other environmental cues are removed had established that these rhythms were generated endogenously. That fact, plus the ability of these oscillations to be entrained by light or other cues (referred to as *Zeitgebers*) and the determination that they were maintained with the same period at different temperatures, has come to characterize the phenomenon of circadian rhythmicity. Although many researchers sought clues as to the nature of the mechanism, little progress was made until the 1990s. Instead, during the period 1960–1990, much circadian research focused on developing more detailed accounts of circadian phenomena, such as, how the phase of circadian oscillations is affected by light pulses of different strengths and durations.

Whereas the focus on circadian rhythms was largely motivated by trying to understand the phenomenon as it is normally manifested (disruptions of circadian rhythms were largely used to

[1] The relation between circadian rhythms and mood disorders is just one example of relations between circadian and other phenomena/mechanisms that have been the focus of intense research in recent years. Two other major examples are the relations between circadian rhythms and basic metabolism and circadian rhythms and cognition. See Venkataraman et al. (47) for a review of recent research addressing all three of these linkages between circadian rhythms and other phenomena.

identify the responsible mechanism), mood, like other psychiatric phenomena, is typically characterized in terms of disorders. The identification of *melancholia* stems from ancient times, with the term *depression* acquiring general currency by the end of the nineteenth century. DSM-I, in 1952, included the category of *depressive reaction*, and DSM-II (1968) included *depressive neurosis*. Mania, and the shifting from manic to depressive states, was also recognized in the DSM-II as manic-depressive psychosis. The former was subsequently labeled *unipolar* and the later *bipolar*. The terms *major depressive disorder* (MDD) and *bipolar disorder* (BD) were introduced in the 1970s and incorporated into DSM-III in 1980.

Suggestions of a link between mood disorders and circadian rhythms developed about the same time as the endogenous nature of circadian rhythms was established. Many of these focused on sleep disruptions in patients with mood disorders, for which there were case reports but no systematic studies until Hinton (9) performed a detailed study of currently depressed and recovered patients. He showed less sleep during each hour of the night as well as greater motility in those currently depressed. Sleep, however, is only partially under circadian control and Hinton's, as well as a number of other studies in the 1960s and 1970s, such as, Taub and Berger's (10) examination of the effects of altered sleep patterns on mood in healthy individuals, faced the problem of how to differentiate the effects of disrupted sleep and disrupted circadian rhythms. By employing a forced desynchrony protocol using a light–dark period longer than the circadian system could adapt to, Boivin et al. (11) were able to establish that although subjective happiness declined over each daily awake period, it clearly also oscillated in accord with underlying circadian rhythms (as measured, for example, by core body temperature).

A number of researchers in the 1970s and 1980s demonstrated correlations between measures of mood and measures of circadian rhythms. For example, Kripke et al. (12) found altered circadian periods in the manic-depressive patients they studied and determined that only those with shortened rhythms responded to lithium treatment. In another example, Souetre et al. (13) measured body temperature, plasma cortisol, norepinephrine, thyrotropin, and melatonin concentrations in depressed, recovered, and controls with no diagnosis of depression and demonstrated that the phase remained normal but the amplitude was significantly diminished in depressed participants but returned to normal after recovery.

A different strategy for establishing the linkage between mood disorders and circadian rhythms focused on various therapies found to be effective for mood disorders. Perhaps the best known is light therapy for seasonal affective disorders (SADs). After establishing that sunlight and bright artificial light (2000 lux) can suppress melatonin levels in humans, Lewy et al. (14) employed bright light therapy during 3 h after awakening on a seasonally manic-depressive patient during winter when his depression was greatest. This considerably reduced his depressive symptoms. Based on studies with additional patients, Rosenthal et al. (15) introduced the category SAD and presented further evidence of temporary reduction in depression with bright light therapy (the effects usually ceased when light treatment was stopped). The researchers went beyond the correlation to propose the *phase shift hypothesis*, which holds that depression results from the delayed phase of circadian rhythms (or, in a few cases, from an advanced phase) and that the therapeutic effect of light on depression resulted from shifting the phase of circadian rhythms earlier (or later in phase advanced patients). They supported this with evidence of advance (or delay) in the phase of melatonin expression in treated patients [(16, 17); for a more recent review, see Ref. (18)].

The evidence reviewed in this section demonstrated a connection between the phenomena of mood disorders and circadian rhythms. Mood changes according to circadian time and correlates with a number of other measures of circadian rhythmicity. Therapies that treat mood disorders, such as bright light at dawn, serve to alter the phase of circadian rhythms. The success of light therapy alleviating depression suggested a causal account, whereby circadian rhythms when altered are a causal factor in depression. Light therapy, on this account, restores normal rhythmicity and relieves depression. This idea was picked up in other theoretical proposals, such as, the *social Zeitgeber theory* (19), which proposed that in individuals vulnerable to depression, social stress events can disrupt circadian rhythms and that this in turn leads to depression. But to show that there is a direct causal connection between the phenomena requires more than evidence that they are correlated or even that the same treatments affect both. Information about the mechanism is required. Otherwise, one cannot discount the possibility that neither phenomenon directly affects the other but both phenomena are the product of other factors that are correlated or causally related.

Research Implicating Molecular Components of the Circadian Clock in Mood Disorders

The initial clues to the mechanism responsible for circadian rhythms in animals were developed in the early 1970s when circadian researchers both linked the central clock mechanism in mammals to a structure in the hypothalamus known as the suprachiasmatic nucleus (SCN) (20, 21) and, in fruit flies, identified a gene, *Period* (*Per*)[2], in which mutations caused short or long period oscillations or rendered the organisms arrhythmic (22). However, little progress was made until it was possible to clone *Per* and measure concentrations of its mRNA and protein at different times of day. This revealed that both *Per* mRNA the PER protein oscillated, with the protein peaking several hours after the mRNA. Hardin et al. (23) proposed on this basis a delayed negative feedback mechanism in which the protein PER would feedback on its own gene, temporarily inhibiting its own synthesis until concentrations decayed, at which point the inhibition would cease and new PER could be synthesized (**Figure 1**).

In the 15 years after 1990, many more clock genes were identified, including many homologs between the genes found in fruit

[2]Conventions for naming genes differ between insects and mammals. For this paper, I will adopt the mammalian convention of italics and capitalizing the first letter in the case of genes and upper case Roman for proteins regardless of species.

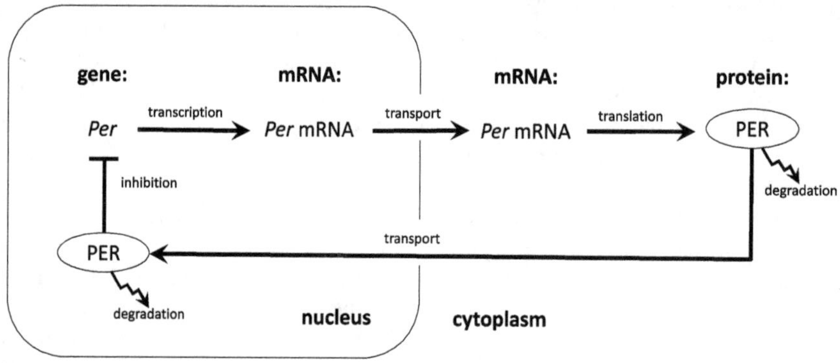

FIGURE 1 | The transcription–translation feedback loop proposed by Hardin et al. (23) to explain circadian rhythms. Transcription of the gene *Per* and translation into protein, PER is followed by the transport of PER back to the nucleus where it inhibits the transcription of its own gene.

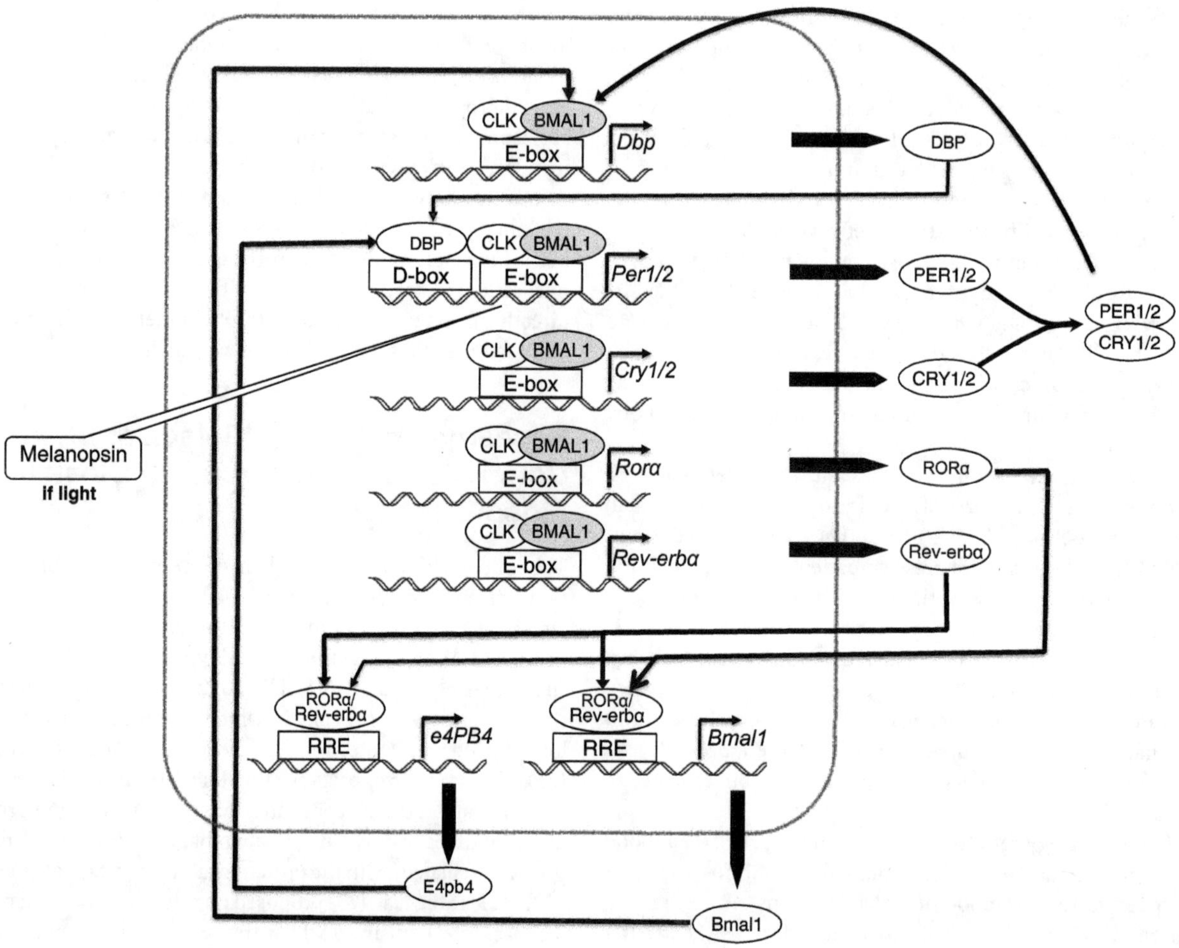

FIGURE 2 | The parts, operations, and organization of the mammalian circadian clock, as understood circa 2005.

flies and mice. Of particular, relevance for the relations between circadian rhythms and mood was the discovery of *Clock* in mice (24), which was shown to bind to the *Per* promoter and to be the target of inhibitory activity by PER. **Figure 2** shows the conception of the circadian mechanism in mammalian cells that had been generated by 2005. Two variant proteins, PER1 and PER2, were now recognized as forming dimers with CRY1 and CRY2, respectively. The inhibition is directed at a dimer between CLOCK (CLK) and BMAL1, which otherwise would bind to the promoter on *Per* and several other genes, activating their transcription. In addition, there is a negative feedback loop involving *E4pb4* and a positive feedback loop involving *Bmal1*.

Much of the research on the mechanisms underlying depression has focused on several monoamine neurotransmitters, especially serotonin, but also norepinephrine and dopamine. These were identified primarily through the fact that many antidepressant drugs increase levels of these monoamines (25). Caspi et al. (26) targeted serotonin as playing a mediating role between stressful life events and depression since individuals with short alleles of serotonin transporter were more prone to experience depression after such events. The different monoamines are associated with particular brain regions that figure centrally in research on depression. The dorsal raphe nuclei are the only source of serotonin in the brain. Dopamine, which is synthesized in decreased amounts in depression, functions in projections from the ventral tegmental area (VTA) to the nucleus accumbens. Norepinephrine is expressed in the locus coeruleus.

One clue to the linkage between circadian rhythms and these neurotransmitters that are altered in depression is that serotonin, norepinephrine, and dopamine all exhibit circadian oscillations in their concentrations (27). Moreover, the connection between the circadian mechanism and synthesis of these monoamines is quite direct: *monoamine oxidase A*, *Maoa*, is a transcriptional target of clock genes *Bmal1* and *Per2* and the protein MAOA serves to terminate dopamine signaling. On the other side, several clock genes have been linked to mood disorders. *Clock*, *Bmal1*, and *Per3* have been implicated in bipolar disease. SNPs of *Per2*, *Npas2*, and *Bmal1* are linked to increased risk for SAD, while there is suggestive evidence of a link between *Cry2* and depression (28). There is also evidence suggestive of a role of mood disorders in affecting circadian rhythms. The SCN has among the densest serotonergic innervation in the brain (all five 5-HT receptor types are employed) and the innervated region of the SCN significantly overlaps areas that receive retinal input and figure in entrainment. This suggests that mood may modulate the ability of the circadian clock to be entrained to local environments, a hypothesis supported by the fact that lesioning the raphe nucleus, thereby eliminating serotonergic innervation of the SCN, alters entrainment. Moreover, applying an agonist of 5-HT receptor generates phase advances (29).

Even stronger evidence indicative of a connection between parts of the circadian mechanism and mood is found in the affects of mutant forms of clock genes on mood. Vitaterna et al.'s discovery that *Clock* is a circadian gene resulted from the generation of a mutant (*Clock*Δ19) that exhibited a long period (27 h) and arrhythmia after several days in darkness. This same mutant has provided a mouse model for mania (30). Both the mutant mice and humans with mania exhibit (1) disrupted circadian rhythms, (2) hyperactivity, and (3) decreased sleep. In addition, the mice exhibit other traits closely resembling those of mania in humans: (4) humans describe feelings of extreme euphoria, while the mice exhibit hyperhedonia and less helplessness, (5) humans engage in increased risk taking, while the mice exhibit reduced anxiety, and (6) while humans exhibit a propensity to drug abuse, the mice show increased preference for cocaine. The mutant mice exhibit increased dopamine in the VTA, rendering neurons there more excitable. As in humans, lithium normalizes manic behavior, and since one effect of lithium is to increase dopamine levels in the VTA, the link appears to be causal.

McClung and her colleagues have investigated *Clock*Δ19 mice to acquire clues into the mechanism underlying human mania. They have found deficits involving the entrainment of low gamma (30–50 Hz) oscillations to delta (1–4 Hz) oscillations in the nucleus accumbens in these mutant mice. In wild-type mice, such entrainment is negatively correlated with amount of exploration in a novel environment. This entrainment is seriously impaired in ClockΔ19 mice, which also exhibit hyperactivity in response to novelty. When treated with lithium, the coupling is restored and the hyperactivity stops (31). Knockdown of *Clock* in the VTA alone results in a manic-like state of less anxiety and hyperactivity but also depressive behavior (32), which seems to fit the fact that manic patients typically also exhibit depressive episodes. Lithium has been shown to lengthen circadian period, likely by inhibiting GSK3β, which phosphorylates PER2 and REV–ERBα, and to produce phase delays as well as affecting the amplitude and period of circadian oscillations (33). It, thus, has the opposite effects on the clock as light treatment, appropriate since it affects mania, not depression.

In an extremely ambitious study, Li et al. (34) provided yet additional evidence pointing to a causal link between circadian genes and mood disorders. They examined gene expression in six brain areas in cadavers of 55 normal controls and 34 patients with MDD post-mortem, analyzing them by circadian time of death. By plotting concentrations of mRNA by the patient's circadian time of death, they generated pseudo-time series data for each gene across the subject pool. In the controls, they identified several hundred genes exhibiting cyclic expression in the dorsolateral prefrontal cortex, amygdala, cerebellum, nucleus accumbens, anterior cingulate cortex, and hippocampus. Many core clock genes were among the genes with the strongest cyclic patterns. These are labeled in yellow on the left in **Figure 3**, in which the *p*-values for those genes with the highest overall significance levels on a measure of oscillation are shown. Red indicates genes whose oscillation is significant ($p < 0.05$) in a given tissue. On the right are the comparable data for the patients with MDD. Comparing the two plots reveals that oscillation reaches statistical significance for many fewer genes in many fewer tissues among the patients. Especially noteworthy is the decrease of rhythmicity in ARNTL (BMAL1) and PER2, two central clock genes, in most brain tissues.

As a measure of the power of the post-mortem gene expression data, Li et al. used the data from 60 randomly selected subjects (both normal controls and patients) to construct an algorithm designed to predict time of death from the pattern of gene expression at death. **Figure 4** shows, for all subjects, the actual time of death in the outer circle and the predicted time of death in the inner circle. Lines connect the corresponding data points and it is clear that the predictions for normal controls align better than for those for patients with MDD. This indicates substantial disruption in the circadian pattern of gene expression in the depressed patients.

Another type of evidence suggestive of a causal connection between the circadian mechanism and that involved in mood disorders is that several of the interventions designed to affect either mood or circadian rhythms also affect the other. One of the most popular drugs used to treat depression, the serotonin reuptake inhibitor (SSRI) fluoxetine, also induces phase advance in the SCN in slices of rat brain in culture. Other SSRIs shorten

A

Symbol	DLPFC	AnCg	HC	AMY	NAcc	CB
ARNTL*	0.0005	0.0005	0.001	0.001	0.0005	0.0005
PER2*	0.001	0.0005	0.0005	0.005	0.008	0.0005
PER3*	0.0005	0.0005	0.0005	0.094	0.0005	0.001
NR1D1*	0.0005	0.0005	0.0005	0.102	0.0005	0.008
DBP*	0.0005	0.0005	0.003	0.066	0.002	0.001
SFPQ	0.0005	0.152	0.013	0.134	0.001	0.029
ITIH5	0.0005	0.021	0.009	0.577	0.007	0.027
LDLR	0.001	0.002	0.004	0.014	0.561	0.204
PER1*	0.0005	0.005	0.008	0.559	0.044	0.071
INSIG1	0.007	0.003	0.001	0.025	0.727	0.183
SLC39A14	0.007	0.0005	0.029	0.067	0.077	0.262
NFIL3*	0.011	0.0005	0.104	0.181	0.03	0.198
SNTB2	0.023	0.038	0.17	0.001	0.013	0.368
PDZRN3	0.002	0.001	0.037	0.333	0.207	0.195
BHLHE40*	0.0005	0.014	0.147	0.42	0.02	0.127
BHLHE41	0.005	0.003	0.997	0.751	0.051	0.003

Color scale: 1, 0.8, 0.6, 0.4, 0.2, 0

B **MDD:**

	DLPFC	ACG	HC	AMY	NACC	CB
ARNTL	0.121	0.072	0.732	0.084	0.005	0.141
PER2	0.015	0.083	0.213	0.342	0.075	0.582
PER3	0.42	0.652	0.432	0.999	0.29	0.531
NR1D1	0.04	0.029	0.285	0.097	0.003	0.111
DBP	0.102	0.236	0.025	0.79	0.121	0.118
SFPQ	0.135	0.124	0.165	0.265	0.047	0.089
ITIH5	0.936	0.47	0.117	0.603	0.15	0.832
LDLR	0.012	0.385	0.315	0.307	0.005	0.028
PER1	0.006	0.21	0.137	0.619	0.124	0.061
INSIG1	0.056	0.534	0.668	0.869	0.318	0.88
SLC39A14	0.641	0.21	0.301	0.393	0.157	0.354
NFIL3*	0.565	0.326	0.633	0.478	0.179	0.617
SNTB2	0.928	0.194	0.123	0.765	0.365	0.293
PDZRN3	0.13	0.003	0.503	0.229	0.075	0.139
BHLHE40	0.19	0.897	0.433	0.963	0.14	0.009
BHLHE41	0.497	0.781	0.754	0.433	0.875	0.246

Color scale: 1, 0.8, 0.6, 0.4, 0.2, 0

FIGURE 3 | (A) Top oscillating genes in six brain tissues in normal controls in a cadaver study in which time of death was known. Shown in yellow are genes known to figure in the circadian clock. The numbers indicate significance levels on a measure of oscillation and color coding, with color coding differentiating five groups. **(B)** Data for patients with major depressive disorder analyzed in the same manner, making it clear that these genes achieved much lower significance levels in almost all tissues. Reproduced from Li et al. (34), Figures 2 and 4A.

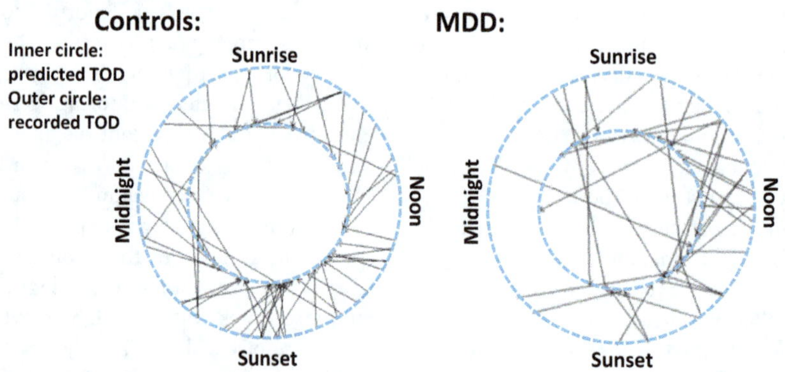

FIGURE 4 | In normal controls, as shown on the left, the pattern of gene expression at death, shown on the inner circle, was a good predictor of time of death, shown on the outer circle. Most of the lines connect nearby points on the two circles. In depressed patients (shown on the right), however, gene expression at death provided a must less reliable predictor of time of death. Reproduced from Li et al. (34), Figure 4C.

the circadian period. Agomelatine, a relatively recent drug that advances the phase in melatonin expression, has proven effective in treating depression (it also, though, functions as an agonist to serotonin 2C receptors so the effects might not just be through altering circadian phase).

In this section, I have discussed the development of mechanistic accounts of both circadian rhythms and mood disorders. What the research has revealed is a host of possible connections between these mechanisms and many have found these highly suggestive that circadian disruption might cause mood disorders, or vice versa. But is such evidence sufficient to establish that the mechanisms are causally linked? I turn to that question in the next section.

How are the Mechanisms Related?

The evidence discussed in the previous sections, claiming both phenomenal and mechanistic connections between circadian rhythms and mood, invites a causal interpretation: disrupted circadian rhythms cause mood disorders (or vice versa). In fact, though, there are four different possibilities to consider:

1. Circadian disruptions cause mood disorders.
2. Mood disorders cause circadian disorders.
3. Causation goes in both directions.
4. Both circadian disruptions and mood disorders are common effects of something else or pleiotropic effects of common components.

Most interpretations adopt the first possibility. Yet, if there is a connection in that direction, there is likely also to be feedback from mood disorders to circadian disorders. However, my concern in this section is with the fourth possibility, which rejects a direct causal connection between circadian rhythms and mood disorders. I will argue that the evidence to date does not allow one to reject possibility.

One way some researchers have tried to support a causal connection is to identify intervening pathways between the two mechanisms. McClung (35) identifies several pathways by which circadian rhythms might regulate mood, of which I discuss three.

There are no direct projections from locus of the central circadian clock, the SCN, to the main loci of mood mechanisms, the dorsal raphe nucleus, the VTA, or the locus coereleus. But McClung shows that there are indirect pathways through a number of hypothalamic nuclei (e.g., the SCN projects to the dorsomedial hypothalamus which then projects to all three areas). These pathways appear to enable circadian oscillations in the SCN to regulate monoamine synthesis in these tissues. These pathways would explain how monoamine levels are altered in mutant mice in which clock genes are mutated or knocked down. McClung identifies a second pathway through the immune system. Alternations to circadian rhythms have effects on the immune system, leading to increased levels of proinflammatory cytokines. Increased levels of proinflammatory cytokines have previously been implicated in depression (36) as well as reduced neurogenesis, neural plasticity, and long-term potentiation. Moreover, the reduction in neurogenesis as well as depressive behaviors can be blocked in environments otherwise inducing stress by applying an inhibitor of nuclear factor-κB (NF-κB). This points to the NF-κB pathway as figuring in generating depression in animals with altered circadian rhythms. The determination that CLOCK itself interacts with NF-κB to activate transcription at NF-κB responsive promoters (37) further supports this as a candidate pathway for linking circadian mechanisms and mood disorders. A third pathway McClung proposed involves glucocorticoids. Concentrations of glucocorticoids increase in stress situations, a condition correlated with mood disorders. A neuronal and hormonal excitatory pathway from the SCN through the paraventricular nucleus (PVN) and the pituitary to the adrenal gland results in the rhythmic synthesis and release of glucocorticoids that then feed back onto the PVN and adrenal glands to maintain stable levels. Two clock proteins figure in regulating glucocorticoid levels. CRY proteins repress glucocorticoid receptors on the PVN and adrenal glands, thereby generating oscillation in the response to glucocorticoids. The receptors are also acetylated by CLOCK, which also decreases their sensitivity to glucocorticoids in the morning and increases it in the evening when acetylation is reversed (38).

Together with the evidence that components of the circadian clock are involved in mood, the evidence of pathways through which the circadian clock could regulate moods makes the case that the circadian clock plays a role in regulating seem plausible. But such evidence alone does not address the question as to whether the mechanisms themselves are actually linked. They may share components, but the roles these components play in each mechanism may be impendent of the role they play in the other. If that were the case, then, even if there are pathways that could connect the two mechanisms, the two mechanisms are not affecting each other – the generation of circadian rhythms is not affecting moods. Each mechanism operates on its own. Establishing that the circadian mechanism is what is affecting moods requires demonstrating that when common components contribute to one phenomenon, they do so in a way that is responsive to their role in the mechanism responsible for the other phenomenon.

Invoking the phenomenon of pleiotropy – the same gene having multiple functions – Landgraf et al. (39) make the case that the mechanisms responsible for circadian rhythms and moods may operate independently while sharing components:

> it is important to point out that, although commonly called 'clock genes', the molecular components of the circadian clock have pleiotropic functions, including many functions that have nothing to do with the clock: manipulating clock genes affects more than just circadian rhythms.

Landgraf et al. marshal their argument by considering several of the kinds of evidence for a causal link from circadian phenomena or mechanisms to mood such as I have presented in previous sections. In response to each, they argue that the evidence is compatible with the circadian and mood mechanisms operating independently while using common components. In fact, given differences in the way the two mechanisms operate, Landgraf et al. suggest there is reason to distinguish, not integrate, the two mechanisms. I will briefly present four of their examples.

One phenomenal linkage between circadian rhythms and mood involves the use of sleep deprivation as a means of transiently ameliorating symptoms of depression in both MDD and BD patients (40, 41). Sleep deprivation has also been found to induce mania in mice (42), which could then be successfully treated with lithium or tamoxifen. Sleep deprivation has been shown as well to have effects on circadian rhythms in mice, hamsters, and humans. A possible explanation for the dual affects of sleep deprivation on both mood and circadian rhythms is that they are the product of one integrated mechanism. But Landgraf et al. note there are also important differences between the phenomena. For example, a brief nap the following day can result in a relapse of depression, but does not have any effect on the circadian system. Sleep is only partially a circadian phenomenon, and it is possible that the effects on depression depend on a non-circadian pathway, perhaps involving cytokines, cortisol, or brain-derived neurotrophic factor.

A second example involves one of the possible pathways that might link circadian disruptions and mood disorders I discussed above: the NF-κB signal transduction pathway. Monje et al. (43) have provided intriguing evidence that the immune system, specifically the NF-κB signal transduction pathway, may be a common cause of circadian disruption and mood disorders, not an intermediary. They appeal to the effects of constant darkness, a known strategy for inducing depression-like behavior in rats. It is known that total darkness results in apoptosis of noradrenergic neurons in the locus coeruleus, serotinergic neurons in the dorsal raphe, and dopaminergic neurons in the VTA. Citing evidence of the role of the immune system in depression, they show that constant darkness results in increased levels of proinflammatory cytokine IL-6 in the hippocampus, leading to increased ERK activation. Manipulation of NF-κB inhibitors indicates that NF-κB played a causal role in mood disorders. The authors also demonstrated a causal effect of NF-κB in decreasing PER2 and increasing BMAL1 levels in the hippocampus. Rather than the effect of constant darkness on mood being mediated by an effect on the circadian system, the two may be independent consequences mediated by a common immunological pathway.

I turn now to claim about two common components of the circadian and mood mechanisms: *Clock* and *Per2*. Without challenging that the appearance of manic symptoms in the *Clock*Δ19 mouse are a result of higher dopamine levels in the VTA, which are themselves the result of the *Clock* gene mutation, Landgraf et al. note that there is little evidence of endogenous circadian rhythms in the VTA (when projections from the SCN are cut, the VTA exhibits no sustained PER2:LUC rhythms). Rather, when rhythms are found in the VTA, they may be driven by the SCN. In the VTA, where *Clock* has an effect on mood, it may not be performing a circadian function at all. It might instead be an independent contribution of the same genes.

PER2 is one of the proteins most clearly oscillating in brain tissues of normal controls. As we saw in discussing Li et al.'s study, its oscillation is greatly reduced in patients with MDD. Mouse studies have shown that stress, which leads to depression-like behaviors, results in lower amplitude oscillations in PER2 (44). But the effects can be dissociated. PER2 rhythms are restored more rapidly than recovery from depression-like behaviors. The link between PER2 and mood is thought to involve MAOA, which, as discussed above, serves to terminate dopamine signaling. MAOA contains an E-box through which its transcription is made rhythmic by fluctuating PER2 and BMAL1 concentrations (45). However, one *Per2* mutant, $Per2^{Brdm1-/-}$, despite no longer generating rhythmic expression of *Maoa*, still exhibits oscillation in dopamine levels in the VTA and its overall dopamine levels are higher than in the wild type. It exhibits much less depression-like behavior in response to a stressful activity like forced swim. Landgraf et al. suggest that the behavioral changes may be due to decrease in constitutive expression of dopamine, not its oscillation.

These and other examples that Landgraf et al. present illustrate a variety of ways to discount the suggestive links between the phenomena of circadian disruption and mood disorders and between the mechanisms for each. The two phenomena may be independent effects of a common cause[3] and the responses to therapeutic intervention, while similar, may show differences to yet other manipulations. The two mechanisms may involve the same parts without the parts figuring in a common mechanism. The roles in the different mechanisms may be pleiotropic. Moreover, the mood mechanism may not be responsive to the oscillation in dopamine but to how much is expressed. Altogether these results raise doubts about whether the correlations discussed earlier between circadian disruptions and mood disorders are due to a causal linkage between the mechanisms responsible for the two phenomena.

Raising doubts about whether two phenomena or their respective mechanisms are causally connected is very different from showing that they are not. Given the variety of correlations between mood disorders and circadian disruptions, it seems highly plausible that they are causally connected. What the challenges by Landgraf et al. indicate is that different evidence is required to establish a causal link than has been provided by most of the research to date. What would seem to be required is a demonstration that perturbations that alter one phenomenon affect the other in virtue of the way they altered the first phenomenon. This might be most clearly shown in by focusing on common parts of the circadian mechanism and the mood mechanism and the way they function in each mechanism. If the effect the part has on mood depends on how it behaves in the circadian mechanism that would indicate a causal link between the mechanisms. Experimental perturbations would provide the most compelling evidence: if perturbing how a part functions within the circadian clock thereby perturbs how it behaves in the mood mechanism, then one would have strong evidence that the two mechanisms are causally integrated. Procuring such evidence will be experimentally challenging and the evidence available to date does not support such direct causal connections.

Conclusion

Research on both circadian rhythms and mood disorders has been pursued in the quest for mechanistic explanations of each. This requires delineating the respective phenomena, linking the phenomena with a particular mechanism, and decomposing that mechanism into its parts and operations. I have reviewed several major studies that provide evidence that the phenomena of altered circadian rhythms and mood disorders are correlated and of common components in that the respective mechanisms share components. This research strongly suggests that altered circadian rhythms are a causal factor in the generation of mood disorders. Drawing on arguments advanced by Landgraf et al., however, I have argued that the evidence advanced so far does not yet justify such a claim. The phenomena may be due to common causes and the components of the mechanisms may function independently in each one. My goal, however, is not simply to make the point that correlation does not establish causation but rather to point to what would provide stronger support for the claim that circadian disruptions cause mood disorders. What is required is to show that it is as a contributor to the circadian mechanism that a component affects moods. One way this can be done is to establish that as its state in the circadian mechanism changes, the contribution of the component to the generation of moods and mood disorders changes.

The general issue of how mechanisms hypothesized to explain different phenomena are connected to one another is becoming increasingly important in biology and medicine. The investigation of proteins or the genes that code for them has often revealed components that figure in two or more cellular functions, sometimes in the same tissue. The question, as I have tried to argue here, is then whether the common component actually provides a causal linkage between the mechanisms. One factor accelerating the need to address this question is that researchers are moving beyond classical techniques that typically only identify a handful of very important components to a mechanism, such as *Per*, *Cry*, *Clock*, and *Bmal1*, in the case of circadian rhythms. Newer techniques reveal a plethora of components. For example, using small interfering RNAs to screen the whole

[3] If one opens the investigation into common causes, one finds many possible candidates. In footnote 1, I alluded to the growing evidence of multiple points of connection between circadian mechanisms and metabolic processes. Metabolic processes are one for common causes between the circadian mechanisms and mood mechanisms.

genome, Zhang et al. (46) identified an additional 200 genes beyond those thought to constitute the core clock which have affects on the amplitude or period of circadian rhythms. Many of these genes were previously characterized in terms of their roles in other cellular functions and it becomes relevant to know whether they are operating within their role in these other cellular functions in affecting circadian rhythms. If they do, then manipulating these other phenomena may be a viable strategy for altering circadian rhythms, or vice versa.

My concern has been to present issues of this sort as arising within ongoing science. Accordingly, I have examined in detail how the issue has arisen in the case of circadian rhythm research and mood. But the issue is a general one. Finding relations between phenomena and common parts within the mechanisms proposed to explain them can be very suggestive of a causal relation. Yet, until one has shown that a component has its effect on one mechanism in virtue of its role in the other, one has not established a causal connection between the phenomena.

References

1. Bechtel W, Richardson RC. *Discovering Complexity: Decomposition and Localization as Strategies in Scientific Research.* 1993 ed. Cambridge, MA: MIT Press, Princeton University Press (1993/2010).
2. Bechtel W, Abrahamsen A. Explanation: a mechanist alternative. *Stud Hist Philos Biol Biomed Sci* (2005) **36**:421–41. doi:10.1016/j.shpsc.2005.03.010
3. Craver CF, Darden L. *In Search of Mechanisms: Discoveries Across the Life Sciences.* Chicago, IL: University of Chicago Press (2013).
4. Machamer P, Darden L, Craver CF. Thinking about mechanisms. *Philos Sci* (2000) **67**:1–25. doi:10.1086/392759
5. Bechtel W, Abrahamsen A. Dynamic mechanistic explanation: computational modeling of circadian rhythms as an exemplar for cognitive science. *Stud Hist Philos Sci* (2010) **41**:321–33. doi:10.1016/j.shpsa.2010.07.003
6. Simon HA. *The Sciences of the Artificial.* 2nd ed. Cambridge, MA: MIT Press (1980).
7. De Mairan J. Observation botanique. *Histoire de l'Académie royale des sciences* (1729). p. 35.
8. Wunderlich KRA. *Das Verhalten der Eigenwärme in Krankheiten.* Leipzig: Otto Wigard (1868).
9. Hinton JM. Patterns of insomnia in depressive states. *J Neurol Neurosurg Psychiatry* (1963) **26**:184–9. doi:10.1136/jnnp.26.2.184
10. Taub JM, Berger RJ. Performance and mood following variations in the length and timing of sleep. *Psychophysiology* (1973) **10**:559–70. doi:10.1111/j.1469-8986.1973.tb00805.x
11. Boivin DB, Czeisler CA, Dijk DJ, Duffy JF, Folkard S, Minors DS, et al. Complex interaction of the sleep-wake cycle and circadian phase modulates mood in healthy subjects. *Arch Gen Psychiatry* (1997) **54**:145–52. doi:10.1001/archpsyc.1997.01830140055010
12. Kripke DF, Mullaney DJ, Atkinson M, Wolf S. Circadian rhythm disorders in manic-depressives. *Biol Psychiatry* (1978) **13**:335–51.
13. Souetre E, Salvati E, Belugou JL, Pringuey D, Candito M, Krebs B, et al. Circadian rhythms in depression and recovery: evidence for blunted amplitude as the main chronobiological abnormality. *Psychiatry Res* (1989) **28**:263–78. doi:10.1016/0165-1781(89)90207-2
14. Lewy AJ, Kern HA, Rosenthal NE, Wehr TA. Bright artificial light treatment of a manic-depressive patient with a seasonal mood cycle. *Am J Psychiatry* (1982) **139**:1496–8. doi:10.1176/ajp.139.11.1496
15. Rosenthal NE, Sack DA, Gillin JC, Lewy AJ, Goodwin FK, Davenport Y, et al. Seasonal affective disorder. A description of the syndrome and preliminary findings with light therapy. *Arch Gen Psychiatry* (1984) **41**:72–80. doi:10.1001/archpsyc.1984.01790120076010
16. Lewy AJ, Sack RL, Singer CM, White DM. The phase shift hypothesis for bright light's therapeutic mechanism of action: theoretical considerations and experimental evidence. *Psychopharmacol Bull* (1987) **23**:349–53.
17. Lewy AJ, Sack RL, Singer CM, White DM, Hoban TM. Winter depression and the phase-shift hypothesis for bright light's therapeutic effects: history, theory, and experimental evidence. *J Biol Rhythms* (1988) **3**:121–34. doi:10.1177/074873048800300203
18. Lewy AJ, Emens JS, Songer JB, Sims N, Laurie AL, Fiala SC, et al. Winter depression: integrating mood, circadian rhythms, and the sleep/wake and light/dark cycles into a bio-psycho-social-environmental model. *Sleep Med Clin* (2009) **4**:285–99. doi:10.1016/j.jsmc.2009.02.003
19. Ehlers CL, Frank E, Kupfer DJ. Social zeitgebers and biological rhythms: a unified approach to understanding the etiology of depression. *Arch Gen Psychiatry* (1988) **45**:948–52. doi:10.1001/archpsyc.1988.01800340076012
20. Moore RY. Retinohypothalamic projection in mammals: a comparative study. *Brain Res* (1973) **49**:403–9. doi:10.1016/0006-8993(73)90431-9
21. Moore RY, Eichler VB. Loss of a circadian adrenal corticosterone rhythm following suprachiasmatic lesions in the rat. *Brain Res* (1972) **42**:201–6. doi:10.1016/0006-8993(72)90054-6
22. Konopka RJ, Benzer S. Clock mutants of *Drosophila melanogaster*. *Proc Natl Acad Sci U S A* (1971) **89**:2112–6. doi:10.1073/pnas.68.9.2112
23. Hardin PE, Hall JC, Rosbash M. Feedback of the *Drosophila period* gene product on circadian cycling of its messenger RNA levels. *Nature* (1990) **343**:536–40. doi:10.1038/343536a0
24. Vitaterna MH, King DP, Chang A-M, Kornhauser JM, Lowrey PL, McDonald JD, et al. Mutagenesis and mapping of a mouse gene, *Clock*, essential for circadian behavior. *Science* (1994) **264**:719–25. doi:10.1126/science.8171325
25. Nutt DJ. Relationship of neurotransmitters to the symptoms of major depressive disorder. *J Clin Psychiatry* (2008) **69**(Suppl E1):4–7.
26. Caspi A, Sugden K, Moffitt TE, Taylor A, Craig IW, Harrington H, et al. Influence of life stress on depression: moderation by a polymorphism in the 5-HTT gene. *Science* (2003) **301**:386–9. doi:10.1126/science.1083968
27. Hampp G, Ripperger JA, Houben T, Schmutz I, Blex C, Perreau-Lenz S, et al. Regulation of monoamine oxidase A by circadian-clock components implies clock influence on mood. *Curr Biol* (2008) **18**:678–83. doi:10.1016/j.cub.2008.04.012
28. Albrecht U. Circadian clocks and mood-related behaviors. In: Kramer A, Merrow M, editors. *Circadian Clocks.* (Vol. 217), Berlin: Springer (2013). p. 227–39.
29. Sollars PJ, Pickard GE, Sprouse JS. Serotonin and the regulation of mammalian circadian rhythms. In: Squire LR, editor. *Encyclopedia of Neuroscience.* Oxford: Academic Press (2009). p. 723–30.
30. Roybal K, Theobold D, Graham A, DiNieri JA, Russo SJ, Krishnan V, et al. Mania-like behavior induced by disruption of CLOCK. *Proc Natil Acad Sci U S A* (2007) **104**:6406–11. doi:10.1073/pnas.0609625104
31. McClung CA. Circadian rhythms and mood regulation: insights from pre-clinical models. *Eur Neuropsychopharmacol* (2011) **21**(Suppl 4):S683–93. doi:10.1016/j.euroneuro.2011.07.008
32. Mukherjee S, Coque L, Cao J-L, Kumar J, Chakravarty S, Asaithamby A, et al. Knockdown of *Clock* in the ventral tegmental area through RNA interference results in a mixed state of mania and depression-like behavior. *Biol Psychiatry* (2010) **68**:503–11. doi:10.1016/j.biopsych.2010.04.031
33. Li JZ, Lu WQ, Beesley S, Loudon AS, Meng QJ. Lithium impacts on the amplitude and period of the molecular circadian clockwork. *PLoS One* (2012) **7**:e33292. doi:10.1371/journal.pone.0033292
34. Li JZ, Bunney BG, Meng F, Hagenauer MH, Walsh DM, Vawter MP, et al. Circadian patterns of gene expression in the human brain and disruption in major depressive disorder. *Proc Natl Acad Sci U S A* (2013) **110**:9950–5. doi:10.1073/pnas.1305814110
35. McClung CA. How might circadian rhythms control mood? Let me count the ways. *Biol Psychiatry* (2013) **74**:242–9. doi:10.1016/j.biopsych.2013.02.019
36. Miller AH, Maletic V, Raison CL. Inflammation and its discontents: the role of cytokines in the pathophysiology of major depression. *Biol Psychiatry* (2009) **65**:732–41. doi:10.1016/j.biopsych.2008.11.029
37. Spengler ML, Kuropatwinski KK, Comas M, Gasparian AV, Fedtsova N, Gleiberman AS, et al. Core circadian protein CLOCK is a positive regulator of NF-κB-mediated transcription. *Proc Natil Acad Sci U S A* (2012) **109**:E2457–65. doi:10.1073/pnas.1206274109
38. Charmandari E, Chrousos GP, Lambrou GI, Pavlaki A, Koide H, Ng SSM, et al. Peripheral CLOCK regulates target-tissue glucocorticoid receptor transcriptional activity in a circadian fashion in man. *PLoS One* (2011) **6**:e25612. doi:10.1371/journal.pone.0025612

39. Landgraf D, McCarthy MJ, Welsh DK. The role of the circadian clock in animal models of mood disorders. *Behav Neurosci* (2014) **128**:344–59. doi:10.1037/a0036029
40. Giedke H, Schwarzler F. Therapeutic use of sleep deprivation in depression. *Sleep Med Rev* (2002) **6**:361–77. doi:10.1016/S1087-0792(02)90235-2
41. Selvi Y, Gulec M, Agargun MY, Besiroglu L. Mood changes after sleep deprivation in morningness-eveningness chronotypes in healthy individuals. *J Sleep Res* (2007) **16**:241–4. doi:10.1111/j.1365-2869.2007.00596.x
42. Armani F, Andersen ML, Andreatini R, Frussa R, Tufik S, Galduroz JCF. Successful combined therapy with tamoxifen and lithium in a paradoxical sleep deprivation-induced mania model. *CNS Neurosci Ther* (2012) **18**:119–25. doi:10.1111/j.1755-5949.2010.00224.x
43. Monje FJ, Cabatic M, Divisch I, Kim E-J, Herkner KR, Binder BR, et al. Constant darkness induces IL-6-dependent depression-like behavior through the NF-κB signaling pathway. *J Neurosci* (2011) **31**:9075–83. doi:10.1523/JNEUROSCI.1537-11.2011
44. Jiang WG, Li SX, Zhou SJ, Sun Y, Shi J, Lu L. Chronic unpredictable stress induces a reversible change of PER2 rhythm in the suprachiasmatic nucleus. *Brain Res* (2011) **1399**:25–32. doi:10.1016/j.brainres.2011.05.001
45. Hampp G, Albrecht U. The circadian clock and mood-related behavior. *Commun Integr Biol* (2008) **1**:1–3. doi:10.4161/cib.1.1.6286
46. Zhang EE, Liu AC, Hirota T, Miraglia LJ, Welch G, Pongsawakul PY, et al. A genome-wide RNAi screen for modifiers of the circadian clock in human cells. *Cell* (2009) **139**:199–210. doi:10.1016/j.cell.2009.08.031
47. Venkataraman A, Ballance H, Hogenesch JB. The role of the circadian system in homeostasis. In: Walhout AJM, Vidal M, Dekker J, editors. *Handbook of Systems Biology: Concepts and Insights*. Amsterdam: Elsevier (2013). p. 407–26.

12

Transcriptome Analysis of Hypothalamic Gene Expression during Daily Torpor in Djungarian Hamsters (*Phodopus sungorus*)

Ceyda Cubuk, Julia Kemmling, Andrej Fabrizius and Annika Herwig *

Zoologisches Institut, Universität Hamburg, Hamburg, Germany

Edited by:
Etienne Challet,
CNRS UPR3212, University of Strasbourg, France

Reviewed by:
Fabien Pifferi,
UMR 7179 Centre National de la Recherche Scientifique, Muséum National d'Histoire Naturelle, France
Dietmar Weinert,
Martin Luther University of Halle-Wittenberg, Germany

Correspondence:
Annika Herwig
annika.herwig@uni-hamburg.de

Animals living at high or temperate latitudes are challenged by extensive changes in environmental conditions over seasons. Djungarian hamsters (*Phodopus sungorus*) are able to cope with extremely cold ambient temperatures and food scarcity in winter by expressing spontaneous daily torpor. Daily torpor is a circadian controlled voluntary reduction of metabolism that can reduce energy expenditure by up to 65% when used frequently. In the past decades it has become more and more apparent, that the hypothalamus is likely to play a key role in regulating induction and maintenance of daily torpor, but the molecular signals, which lead to the initiation of daily torpor, are still unknown. Here we present the first transcriptomic study of hypothalamic gene expression patterns in Djungarian hamsters during torpor entrance. Based on Illumina sequencing we were able to identify a total number of 284 differentially expressed genes, whereby 181 genes were up- and 103 genes down regulated during torpor entrance. The 20 most up regulated group contained eight genes coding for structure proteins, including five collagen genes, *dnha2* and *myo15a*, as well as the procoagulation factor *vwf*. In a proximate approach we investigated these genes by quantitative real-time PCR (qPCR) analysis over the circadian cycle in torpid and normothermic animals at times of torpor entrance, mid torpor, arousal and post-torpor. These qPCR data confirmed up regulation of *dnah2, myo15a,* and *vwf* during torpor entrance, but a decreased mRNA level for all other investigated time points. This suggests that gene expression of structure genes as well as the procoagulation factor are specifically initiated during the early state of torpor and provides evidence for protective molecular adaptions in the hypothalamus of Djungarian hamsters including changes in structure, transport of biomolecules and coagulation.

Keywords: metabolic depression, seasonal adaptations, circadian, hypothalamus, Illumina, RNA-Seq

Abbreviations: *col17a1,* collagen, type XVII, alpha 1; *dnah2,* dynein, axonemal, heavy chain 2; *myo15a,* myosin XVA; NGS, next generation sequencing; qPCR, quantitative real-time PCR; T_a, ambient temperature; T_b, body temperature; *vwf,* von Willebrand factor; ZT, Zeitgebertime.

INTRODUCTION

Metabolic depression (torpor) is a commonly used strategy of mammals to survive winter. A reduction in energy expenditure as well as energy requirements is necessary to compensate for harsh environmental conditions during winter season when ambient temperature (T_a) drops and food availability is reduced (Jastroch et al., 2016).

The Djungarian hamster (also known as Siberian hamster, *P. sungorus*) has evolved a number of physiological and morphological adaptations (e.g., voluntary reduction of body weight, molt to dense white winter coat, gonadal regression, torpor) to seasonally reduce energy requirements (Figala et al., 1973; Scherbarth and Steinlechner, 2010). In Djungarian hamsters, winter adaptations are driven by photoperiod and can easily be induced by changes of the artificial light-dark cycle at moderate T_a in the laboratory (Steinlechner and Heldmaier, 1982; Vitale et al., 1985). The most effective adaptive trait is the expression of daily torpor that spontaneously occurs after 10–12 weeks in short days once all other physiological adaptations are completed and the corresponding hormonal systems are in winter state (reduced levels of prolactin, testosterone and leptin) (Cubuk et al., 2016). Daily torpor is initiated by an active depression of metabolic rate (25% below the level of resting metabolic rate), accompanied by reduced heart rate and ventilation as well as a decrease in body temperature (T_b) to > 15°C and reduced physical locomotor activity (Heldmaier and Ruf, 1992; Heldmaier et al., 2004). Torpor bouts are usually timed into the light phase of the light-dark cycle and have been shown to be under circadian control. The average duration of a torpor episode is 6 h and it is terminated by a spontaneous arousal prior to the hamsters' naturally active phase (Kirsch et al., 1991). The incidence of daily torpor is highly variable between individuals as well as in the same animal (1–7 torpor bouts per week) and can save up to 65% of total energy requirements, when torpor is used on a daily basis (Heldmaier, 1981; Kirsch et al., 1991; Ruf et al., 1991).

Spontaneous daily torpor is dependent on signaling of various hormonal systems changing with seasons and morphology, nutritional state as well as circadian timing mechanisms, hence, the hypothalamus is the brain area most likely involved in its regulation. Manipulations of prolactin levels lead to reduced torpor incidence and when testosterone, leptin or T3 are supplemented peripherally torpor is almost completely blocked (Ouarour et al., 1991; Ruby et al., 1993; Freeman et al., 2004; Bank et al., 2015). It has already been shown, that lesion of various hypothalamic nuclei (suprachiasmatic nuclei, arcuate nucleus, paraventricular nucleus) alters torpor behavior. Moreover, the pharmacological activation of NPY mechanisms in arcuate nucleus induces torpor like hypothermia and hypothalamic application of T3 is able to block the expression of torpor (Ruby and Zucker, 1992; Ruby, 1995; Paul et al., 2005; Pelz and Dark, 2007; Dark and Pelz, 2008; Pelz et al., 2008). However, although torpor physiology has been extensively studied in this species, the regulatory systems in the brain ultimately initiating entrance into torpor on some days but not on others are entirely unknown.

Here we carried out a next generation sequencing (NGS) study to impartially screen for potential candidate genes playing a role in molecular hypothalamic torpor induction mechanisms. NGS allows the investigation of all transcripts of a genome by counting the number of mRNA sequencing reads of a specific tissue. To date, only few transcriptomic studies are available investigating gene expression patterns in the 13-lined ground squirrel (*Ictidomys tridecemlieatus*) during hibernation in various tissues, like cerebral cortex, hypothalamus, heart, skeletal muscle, brown adipose tissue and white adipose tissue (Hampton et al., 2011, 2013; Schwartz et al., 2013, 2015; Grabek et al., 2015). Except for one study investigating brown adipose tissue during entrance into torpor (Grabek et al., 2015), these studies were focused on time points before animals enter hibernation season, while being in deep hibernation or during the interbout arousals. The Djungarian hamster is an excellent animal model to investigate gene expression patterns during torpor entrance, because torpor is precisely timed into the circadian cycle and allows precise sampling with timed controls that are winter adapted but do not show torpor on that particular day. Moreover, substantial knowledge exists about hypothalamic mechanisms regulating seasonal adaptations in body weight and reproduction in this species (Ebling and Barrett, 2008).

Here we present a summary of differentially expressed genes during torpor entrance in the hypothalamus of *P. sungorus*. Moreover, we provide information about circadian regulation of mRNA expression patterns for selected candidate genes by relative gene expression analysis in torpid and normothermic hamsters.

MATERIALS AND METHODS

Animals

All experiments and procedures were conducted in accordance with the German Animal Welfare Law and approved by the local animal welfare authorities (No. 114_14, Hamburg, Germany). All animals originated from our own breeding colony at the Institute of Zoology University of Hamburg. Djungarian hamsters (*P. sungorus*) were bred and raised under artificial long photoperiod (16:8-h light:dark cycle) at 21°C ± 1°C T_a. The animals were individually housed in plastic cages (Macrolon Type III). Before and during the experiments, hamsters were fed a hamster breeding diet (Altromin 7014, Germany) *ad libitum* and had free access to drinking water. For the experiments, 3–4 months old Djungarian hamsters were transferred to short day conditions (8:16-h light:dark cycle) at constant T_a of 18°C ± 1°C. After 12 weeks in short days they were implanted i.p. with DSI-transmitters (Model TA-F10, St. Paul, MN, USA) under 1.5–2% isoflurane anesthesia and carprofen (5 mg/kg) analgesia as previously described (Bank et al., 2015) to monitor T_b on line. T_b was recorded every 3 min.

Experiment 1: Transcriptomic Analysis of Hypothalamic Gene Expression at Torpor Entrance

Sampling

Between week 13 and week 16, three animals were euthanized by carbon dioxide during entrance into torpor (T_b 30.4°C ± 0.6°C) at Zeitgebertime 1 (ZT1; ZT0 = lights on) (**Figure 1**, group 1).

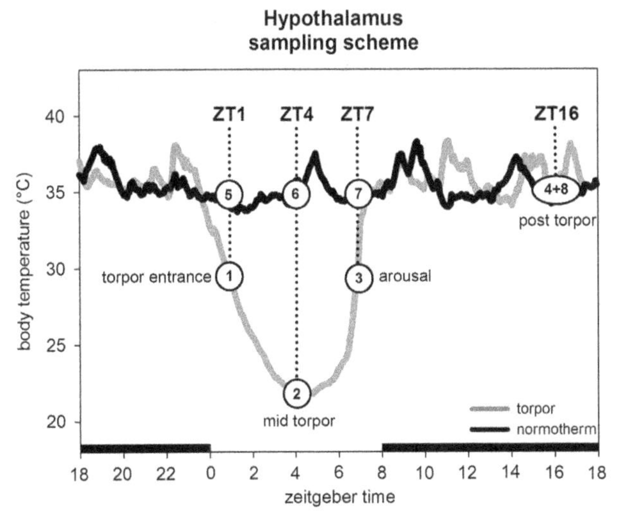

FIGURE 1 | Hypothalamus sampling scheme. For experiment 1 one hamster group ($n = 3$) was sampled during torpor entrance (1) and a corresponding normothermic group ($n = 3$) at same ZT (5). For experiment 2 four hamster groups ($n = 5$ for each group) were sampled in the torpid state during torpor entrance at ZT1 (1), mid torpor at ZT4 (2), arousal at ZT7 (3) and post-torpor at ZT16 (4). For each time point a corresponding normothermic group ($n = 5$ for each group) was sampled (5–8).

Additionally, three hamsters were culled in a normothermic state (T_b 36.1°C ± 0.7°C) at the same ZT as control group (**Figure 1**, group 5). The brain was dissected from each hamster, frozen on dry ice and stored at −80°C.

Isolation of Total RNA

Hypothalamic blocks were cut from frozen tissues between Bregma −0.20 and −2.70 mm, laterally at the hypothalamic sulci and dorsally 3–4 mm from the ventral surface. Tissue samples were homogenized in 500 µl TriFast using a micropestle. Total RNA was obtained using peqGOLD Trifast™ (Peqlab, Erlangen, Germany) according to the manufacturer's instructions. Total RNA was purified with the Crystal RNA MiniKit (Biolabproducts, Bebensee, Germany) including an on-column digestion with RNase-free DNase (Qiagen, Hilden, Germany). RNA integrity was proven by gel electrophoresis, total RNA was quantified spectrometrically and RNA purity was assessed by the 260/280 nm ratio on a NanoDrop 1000 spectrophotometer.

Illumina Sequencing

In total, 2 µg total RNA per sample were used for transcriptome analysis. Library preparation and Illumina sequencing were performed by *GENterprise* Genomics (Mainz, Germany). For library preparation the TruSeq RNA Library Preparation Kit (Illumina, San Diego, CA) was used. All RNA samples had a RIN ≥ 6.9. The samples were sequenced by Illumina NextSeq 500 with a calculated output of 50 million paired-end reads (2 × 150 bp) per sample. The raw Illumina data are available at the NCBI SRA database under the accession numbers biosample: SAMN062002211 to SAMN06200226 (Bioproject PRJNA360070). Since currently no annotated *Phodopus sungorus* genome is available, the reads were mapped against the genome of the Chinese hamster (*Cricetulus griseus*), that showed best compliance, using the CLC-Genomics Workbench 7.5.1 (Qiagen, Hilden, Germany). Only reads with intact pairs mapping with an 85% read identity and 85% read length were used for RPKM (reads per kilobase per million mapped reads) calculation (Mortazavi et al., 2008). Supplementary Table 1 shows the total number of reads and the number of reads mapped in pairs for each sample. Statistically significant expression changes between normothermic and torpid hamsters were calculated by an empirical analysis of digital gene expression (DGE) statistics, performing an "Exact Test" (Robinson and Smyth, 2008). This tool is implemented in CLC-Genomics Workbench 7.5.1. To correct for multiple testing, a false discovery rate (FDR) correction of p-values was applied (see Supplementary Table 2).

Transcripts with an RPKM-value ≥ 0.1 in one of the samples were chosen for further analysis. Transcripts with a fold change ≥ 1.2 and an FDR-corrected $p \leq 0.05$ were considered as differentially expressed. The identified differentially expressed transcripts were functionally classified using the PANTHER Classification System (Protein ANalysis THrough Evolutionary Relationships; www.pantherdb.org) version 10.0 (Mi et al., 2013). Differentially expressed transcripts were additionally analyzed using the PANTHER Overrepresentation Test (release 20160715) applying the PANTHER GO-slim terms as annotated, followed by Bonferroni correction for multiple testing. The PANTHER Overrepresentation Test was conducted for all 284 differentially expressed genes as well as the 181 up regulated genes and the 103 down regulated genes respectively. *Mus musculus* was selected as reference organism for the GO annotation and for the statistical calculation of overrepresented GO-terms. Overrepresented terms with a Bonferroni corrected $p \leq 0.05$ were considered as significant.

Experiment 2: Relative Quantification of Hypothalamic Gene Expression in Different Torpor Stages

Sampling

To validate our Illumina results, we selected eight genes for further investigations by qPCR analysis. A group of seven genes immediately attracted attention for their potential role in structural changes (five collagens, myosin and dynein). Additionally, the von Willebrand factor (*vwf*) was chosen for its role in blood clotting. To provide more detailed information about gene expression changes over a circadian cycle in torpid and normothermic state, 40 hamsters were used for gene expression analysis by real-time PCR (qPCR). A total of 20 animals were culled by carbon dioxide on a day with torpor expression at ZT1 (entrance into torpor: T_b 30.8°C ± 0.5°C, $n = 5$), ZT4 (mid torpor: T_b 22.5°C ± 1.5°C, $n = 5$), ZT7 (arousal: T_b 30.4°C ± 0.4°C, $n = 5$) and ZT16 (active phase after torpor bout: T_b 35.7°C ± 0.6°C, $n = 5$) (**Figure 1**, groups 1–4). Five normothermic animals were sampled for each time point as respective control group (ZT1: Tb 35.7°C ± 0.5°C; ZT4: T_b 35.7°C ± 0.4°C; ZT7: T_b 35.6°C ± 0.4°C;

ZT16: T_b 36.2°C ± 1.3°C) (**Figure 1**, groups 5–8). Brains were dissected, frozen on dry ice and stored at −80°C for qPCR analysis.

Isolation of RNA and cDNA Synthesis

Hypothalami were dissected from frozen brains and isolation of total RNA was performed as described for Experiment 1. For qPCR templates and generation of standard plasmids, cDNA was synthesized from every total RNA sample using RevertAid H Minus First Strand cDNA Synthesis Kit (Thermo Scientific, Waltham, MA, USA) and oligo-(dT)18 oligonucleotide primers following manufacturer's instructions. Reverse transcription was conducted using 1 μg total RNA per sample.

Cloning and Sequencing

For standard plasmids, coding sequence fragments (100–200 bp long) of collagen alpha-1(XXIV) chain-like (*LOC103164493*), collagen, type XX, alpha 1 (*col20a1*), collagen, type XVII, alpha 1 (*col17a1*), collagen, type XVIII, alpha 1 (*col18a1*), collagen, type V, alpha 3 (*col5a3*), dynein, axonemal, heavy chain 2 (*dnah2*), myosin XVA (*myo15a*), von Willebrand factor (*vwf*) and hypoxanthine phosphoribosyltransferase (*hprt*) were amplified by gene specific primers (**Table 1**). All primers were designed on the *P. sungorus* specific sequences generated by Illumina sequencing using the onlinetool OligoAnalyzer 3.1. The primers were designed with a melting temperature at 60°C ± 1.1°C. After cloning of the amplicons using the pGEM®-T Easy Vector System (Promega, Madison, USA) following the manufacturer's instructions, the cDNA fragments were Sanger-sequenced by GATC Biotech (Konstanz, Germany).

Real-Time qPCR and Analysis of Expression Data

qPCR was performed using Power SYBR® Green PCR Master Mix (Applied Biosystems, Darmstadt, Germany) on an ABI Prism 7300 Real Time PCR System (Applied Biosystems). Due to the large number of samples, qPCRs were performed on two 96-well plates for each target gene. For comparability, the normothermic ZT16 group was applied to all plates as inter-plate calibrator. *Hprt* was selected as reference gene, based on the stability of expression values across all samples. All samples were run in triplicates (for 5 biological replicates per group), using 1 μl cDNA as template in a reaction volume of 20 μl, and a series of six 10-fold dilutions of specific standard plasmids were used to generate the standard curve to calculate qPCR efficiencies. Additionally, a no-template control was included on each plate in duplicates for each target gene. Quantification was performed with the following cycling parameters for 40 cycles: 50°C 2 min; 95°C 10 min; 95°C 15 s; 60°C 15 s; 72°C 30 s. Amplification specificity was controlled by dissociation curve analysis referring to the qPCR run.

First evaluation of qPCR results was carried out using the 7300 System Software v1.4.0 (ABI Prism, Applied Biosystems) and subsequently exported to Microsoft Excel 2010 to identify differences in expression levels using the $\Delta\Delta$CT method. All statistical testings and figures were done with SigmaPlot 12.5 (Systat Software Inc.). All results were statistically analyzed by two-way ANOVA with time of day (Zeitgebertime) and metabolic state (torpid/normothermic) as factors, followed by Tukey's test for pairwise comparison of relative expression levels between torpid and normothermic hamsters and within the torpid and normothermic groups.

TABLE 1 | *P. sungorus* specific primer sequences.

Gene		5′3′sequence	Melting temperature (°C)	Amplicon length (bp)
LOC103164493	Forward	CATGCAGCAGTAACGCCAACC	59.4	136
	Reverse	GTGGCAATTGTGCTTCACCAACTC	59.2	
col20a1	Forward	GCTCCTACCTCCACGTCTGTCTC	60.5	174
	Reverse	CTGCCATAGGTGTCACCTGCAC	60.2	
col17a1	Forward	CATAACCTCCTCCTGGGCTGATG	59.2	126
	Reverse	GCTCTTCCTACAGTGCTCCCATG	59.4	
col18a1	Forward	CAGGACCAAAGGGTGACAAAGGAG	59.7	189
	Reverse	GGCCAGGTACACTTGAGCTGAAG	59.8	
col5a3	Forward	GAACAAGGAGACCTCAAGGCTGAG	59.2	166
	Reverse	CTGCAAGACAGTGGCATTTCGTTC	58.9	
dnah2	Forward	CTTCGTGCTCAATGATATGGGCCG	60.6	102
	Reverse	CTGCGATGGCTCTTGTCAATGCTG	60.1	
myo15a	Forward	CATGGCACCCAGGAGATGATCTTG	59.7	136
	Reverse	CACGCTTGGCATTGTAGGCATTG	59.4	
vwf	Forward	CCACAAGGTCATTTCTCCAGCCAC	60.1	109
	Reverse	GGTCCGACAGAGGTGAGCATAAG	59.1	
hprt	Forward	AGTCCCAGCGTCGTGATTAGTGATG	60.4	140
	Reverse	CGAGCAAGTCTTTCAGTCCTGTCCA	60.5	

RESULTS

Transcriptomic Expression Analysis in the Hypothalamus of *P. sungorus* during Torpor Entrance

We identified a total number of 27,830 transcripts with 284 transcripts being differentially expressed in hamsters during torpor entrance as compared to ZT matched normothermic hamsters (**Table 2**). A total of 181 transcripts were significantly upregulated whereas 103 transcripts were significantly downregulated. All transcripts identified had an RPKM-value $\geq$ 0.1 and a FDR $p \leq 0.05$.

Functional Classification of Differentially Expressed Genes

Differentially expressed transcripts during torpor entrance were classified according to gene ontology categories. It has to be noted, that some genes were included in more than one category.

Of the 181 up regulated genes 154 could be classified and assigned to 389 biological processes (**Figure 2A**). The majority of up regulated genes are involved in metabolic (18%) and cellular processes (18%), followed by localization (12%), biological regulation (9%), developmental processes (9%), cellular component organization or biogenesis (7%), multicellular organismal processes (7%), biological adhesion (6%), immune system processes (5%), response to stimulus (5%), apoptotic processes (2%), and reproduction (2%).

TABLE 2 | Overview of Illumina sequencing data and transcriptomic expression analysis.

		Up regulated	Down regulated
Identified genes	27,830		
Differentially expressed genes	284	⬆ 181	⬇ 103

A total number of 82 out of the 103 down regulated genes could be classified and assigned to 117 biological process hits (**Figure 2B**). The majority of down regulated genes was assigned to metabolic processes (33%), followed by cellular processes (20%), biological regulation (10%), developmental processes (9%), multicellular organismal processes (5%), localization (4%), immune system processes (4%), cellular component organization or biogenesis (3%), reproduction (3%), response to stimulus (3%), apoptotic processes (3%), and biological adhesion (3%).

The PANTHER overrepresentation test showed significant enrichments of the GO-slim terms only for the up regulated group of genes, comprising "transmembrane transporter activity" (9.64-fold, $p = 0.034$) in the domain molecular function and "extracellular matrix" (6.02-fold, $p = 0.000397$) in the domain cellular component.

Analysis of Most Affected Genes during Torpor Entrance

To determine the most affected genes during torpor entrance, we ranked the identified genes into the 20 most up- and 20 most down regulated genes, based on their fold changes.

Most up regulated genes (**Table 3**) showed fold changes in a range of 1.55–2.66. Within this group we found 8 genes coding for structure proteins (*LOC103164493, col20a1, myo15a, col17a1, micalcl, dnah2, col18a1, col5a3*), 4 involved in transporter function (*abca6, atp2a1, kcnh3, atp1a4*), 2 with signaling function (*OR2K2, LOC100773864*) and one gene each involved in stress defense (*klk8*), coagulation (*vwf*) and cell death (*steap3*). Three genes have so far unknown function (*LOC103160902_1, LOC100766933, catip*).

Fold changes of the most down regulated genes (**Table 4**) ranged between −1.5 and −4.0. This group contained 7 genes coding for transcription factors (*stk31, LOC100768314, LOC102638674, LOC100756005, LOC102632383, LOC102642077, smim11*), 4 with enzymatic activity (*top2a, clk1, coq3, LOC100772408_2*), 2 with transporter

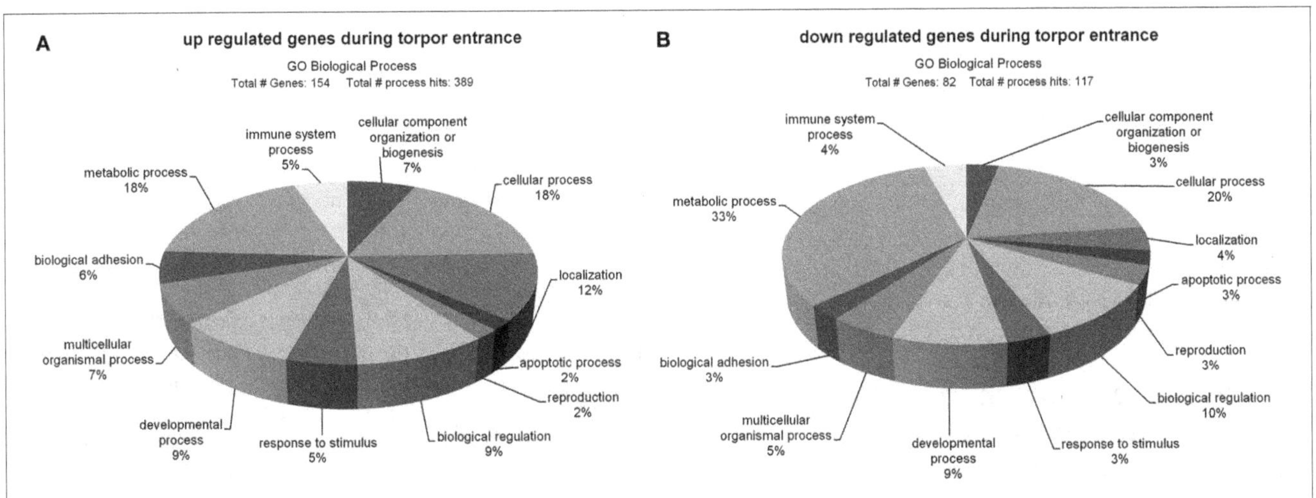

FIGURE 2 | Ontology of genes up- (A) and down regulated **(B)** during torpor entrance in the hypothalamus. Sequences were classified according to http://pantherdb.org and assigned into biological process hits. Some genes were assigned to more than one category.

TABLE 3 | Most up regulated genes in the hypothalamus during torpor entrance.

Function	Gene	Gene symbol	Fold change
Structure	Collagen alpha-1(XXIV) chain-like	*LOC103164493*	2.03
	Collagen, type XX, alpha 1	*col20a1*	1.97
	Myosin XVA	*myo15a*	1.93
	Collagen, type XVII, alpha 1	*col17a1*	1.77
	MICAL C-terminal like	*micalcl*	1.77
	Dynein, axonemal, heavy chain 2	*dnah2*	1.67
	Collagen, type XVIII, alpha 1	*col18a1*	1.62
	Collagen, type V, alpha 3	*col5a3*	1.55
Transporter	ATP-binding cassette, sub-family A (ABC1), member 6	*abca6*	2.07
	ATPase, Ca^{++} transporting, cardiac muscle, fast twitch 1	*atp2a1*	1.9
	Potassium voltage-gated channel, subfamily H, member 3	*kcnh3*	1.6
	ATPase, Na^{+}/K^{+} transporting, alpha 4 polypeptide	*atp1a4*	1.58
Signaling	Olfactory receptor, family 2, subfamily K, member 2	*OR2K2*	2.66
	Cyclin-dependent kinase 11B-like	*LOC100773864*	1.67
Stress defense	Kallikrein-related peptidase 8	*klk8*	1.87
Coagulation	von Willebrand factor	*vwf*	1.59
Cell death	STEAP family member 3, metalloreductase	*steap3*	1.69
Unknown	EF-hand calcium-binding domain-containing protein 8	*LOC103160902_1*	1.94
	Protein ARMCX6-like	*LOC100766933*	1.73
	Ciliogenesis associated TTC17 interacting protein	*catip*	1.63

functions (*slc47a1, nipsnap3b*), one gene each involved in cellular structure (*cornifin-A*), signaling (*psmc3ip*), rRNA maturation (*rrp15*) and ORF (*swt1*) and 3 genes with so far unknown function (*LOC100754037, LOC103159055, LOC100753290*).

Verification of Most up Regulated Gene Expression by qPCR

To verify the Illumina results, we calculated hypothalamic relative mRNA expression of *col17a1, dnah2, myo15a,* and *vwf* during torpor entrance by qPCR (**Figure 3**). Up regulation could be confirmed for *dnah2* (qPCR: 1.6-fold, $p = 0.016$; Illumina: 1.7-fold, $p < 0.001$), *myo15a* (qPCR: 2.5-fold, $p = 0.005$; Illumina: 1.9-fold, $p = 0.035$) and *vwf* (qPCR: 1.6-fold, $p < 0.001$; Illumina: 1.6-fold; $p = 0.046$). Up regulation of *col17a1* did not reach significance in the qPCR analysis (qPCR: 1.2-fold, $p = 0.462$; Illumina: 1.8-fold, $p = 0.027$). Also the other collagens identified by Illumina did not reach significance by qPCR (*col5a3*: 1.3-fold, $p = 0.550$; *col18a1*: 1.2-fold, $p = 0.450$; *col20a1*: 2.0-fold, $p = 0.361$; *LOC103164493*: 1.4-fold, $p = 0.563$) (data not shown).

Relative Gene Expression Patterns over the Circadian Cycle in Torpid and Normothermic Hamsters

To determine, whether differential candidate gene expression is restricted to torpor entrance and to assess circadian regulation, we investigated relative mRNA expression at ZT1, ZT4, ZT7, and ZT16 in animals undergoing torpor and animals remaining normothermic. Differences within each investigated time point are shown relative to normothermic control group at same ZT respectively (**Figures 4A,C,E,G**). Circadian variations for normothermic animals are shown relative to the normothermic ZT1 group. Circadian variations for torpid animals are presented relative to torpor ZT1 group (**Figures 4B,D,F,H**).

There was no effect of time of day on *col17a1* mRNA levels for normothermic animals, but there was an effect of time of day for torpid animals (two-way ANOVA: $p < 0.001$). *Col17a1* mRNA expression was reduced in the post-torpor group (ZT16) as compared to torpor entrance (ZT1, Tukey's test: $p = 0.004$) and to arousal (ZT7, Tukey's test: $p = 0.002$) (**Figure 4B**).

There were no significant changes in mRNA expression during torpor entrance (ZT1), mid torpor (ZT4) or arousal (ZT7) relative to normothermic control groups at the same ZTs. Post-torpor (ZT16), mRNA expression was 0.57-fold down regulated (Tukey's test: $p = 0.014$) (**Figure 4A**).

There was an effect of time of day on *dnah2* mRNA levels both, in normothermic and torpid animals (two-way ANOVA: $p < 0.001$). Normothermic animals showed lowest mRNA expression at ZT1 (Tukey's test: ZT1 vs. ZT4 $p = 0.006$, ZT1 vs. ZT7 $p < 0.001$, ZT1 vs. ZT16 $p = 0.004$) that increased at ZT4, peaked at ZT7 (Tukey's test: ZT7 vs. ZT4 $p = 0.011$) and decreased again at ZT16 (Tukey's test: ZT16 vs. ZT7 $p = 0.015$) (**Figure 4D**). Over the investigated torpor stages (ZT1, 4, 7) no significant changes were found, but post-torpor (ZT16) mRNA expression

TABLE 4 | Most down regulated genes in the hypothalamus during torpor entrance.

Function	Gene	Gene symbol	Fold change
Trancription factor	Serine/Threonine kinase 31	*stk31*	−2.69
	Zinc finger protein 93-like	*LOC100768314*	−1.69
	Zinc finger protein 26-like	*LOC102638674*	−1.62
	Zinc finger protein 420-like	*LOC100756005*	−1.61
	Zinc finger protein 431-like	*LOC102632383*	−1.56
	Zinc finger protein 431-like	*LOC102642077*	−1.55
	Small integral membrane protein 11	*smim11*	−1.47
Enzyme	Topoisomerase (DNA) II alpha 170kDa	*top2a*	−2.08
	CDC-like kinase 1	*clk1*	−1.93
	Coenzyme Q3 methyltransferase	*coq3*	−1.51
	2-hydroxyacylsphingosine 1-beta-galactosyltransferase	*LOC100772408_2*	
Transporter	Solute carrier family 47 (multidrug and toxin extrusion), member 1	*slc47a1*	−1.87
	Nipsnap homolog 3B	*nipsnap3b*	−1.48
Structure	SMALL PROLINE-RICH PROTEIN 1A	*cornifin-A*	−4.04
Signaling	PSMC3 interacting protein	*psmc3ip*	−1.71
rRNA maturation	Ribosomal RNA processing 15 homolog	*rrp15*	−1.61
ORF	SWT1 RNA endoribonuclease homolog	*swt1*	−1.56
Unknown	Chromosome unknown open reading frame, human C5orf46	*LOC100754037*	−2.99
	Uncharacterized LOC103159055	*LOC103159055*	−2.87
	Chromosome unknown open reading frame, human C5orf63	*LOC100753290*	−1.51

was 0.38-fold down regulated as compared to torpor entrance (ZT1, Tukey's test $p < 0.001$), mid torpor (ZT4, Tukey's test $p = 0.003$) and arousal (ZT7, Tukey's test $p < 0.001$) (**Figure 4D**).

Relative to their normothermic control groups, *dnah2* expression was 1.64-fold up regulated during torpor entrance (ZT1, Tukey's test $p = 0.016$), 0.56-fold down regulated during mid-torpor (ZT4, Tukey's test $p = 0.014$), 0.40-fold down regulated during arousal (ZT7, Tukey's test $p < 0.001$) and 0.26-fold down regulated post-torpor (ZT16, Tukey's test $p < 0.001$) (**Figure 4C**).

There was an effect of time of day on *myo15a* mRNA levels both, in normothermic and torpid animals (two-way ANOVA: $p < 0.001$). Normothermic animals showed low mRNA expression at ZT1 that increased at ZT4 (Tukey's test $p = 0.019$) and ZT7 (Tukey's test $p < 0.001$), before decreasing again at ZT16 (Tukey's test: ZT16 vs. ZT7 $p = 0.030$). Torpid animals showed highest mRNA expression during torpor entrance (ZT1) differing significantly from mid torpor (ZT4, Tukey's test $p = 0.010$) and post-torpor (ZT16, Tukey's test $p < 0.001$). mRNA expression at mid torpor (ZT4) was also down regulated as compared to arousal (ZT7, Tukey's test $p = 0.047$) and mRNA expression during arousal (ZT7) was up regulated relative to post-torpor (ZT16, Tukey's test $p < 0.001$) (**Figure 4F**).

Myo15a expression was 2.51-fold up regulated during torpor entrance (ZT1, Tukey's test $p = 0.005$), 0.32-fold down regulated at mid torpor (ZT4, Tukey's test $p = 0.002$), 0.40-fold down regulated during arousal (ZT7, Tukey's test $p = 0.006$) and 0.29-fold down regulated in post-torpor group (ZT16, Tukey's test $p < 0.001$) (**Figure 4E**) as compared to the normothermic control groups.

There was an effect of time of day on *vwf* mRNA levels both, in normothermic and torpid animals (two-way ANOVA: $p < 0.001$). Normothermic animals showed low mRNA expression at ZT1 that increased at ZT4 (Tukey's test $p = 0.038$) and further at ZT7 (Tukey's test: ZT1 vs. ZT7 $p < 0.001$, ZT4 vs. ZT7 $p = 0.017$), before decreasing at ZT16 (Tukey's test: ZT7 vs. ZT16 $p < 0.001$). The mRNA expression in torpid animals was significantly up regulated during torpor entrance (ZT1) as compared to mid torpor (ZT4, Tukey's test $p = 0.002$) and post-torpor (ZT16, Tukey's test $p < 0.001$) and during arousal (ZT7) compared to post-torpor (ZT16, Tukey's test $p = 0.002$) (**Figure 4H**).

Vwf expression was 1.61-fold up regulated during torpor entrance (ZT1, Tukey's test $p < 0.001$), 0.58-fold down regulated during mid-torpor (ZT4, Tukey's test $p = 0.004$), 0.51-fold down regulated during arousal (ZT7, Tukey's test $p < 0.001$) and 0.60-fold down regulated in post-torpor group (ZT16, Tukey's test $p = 0.003$) (**Figure 4G**) as compared to the normothermic control groups.

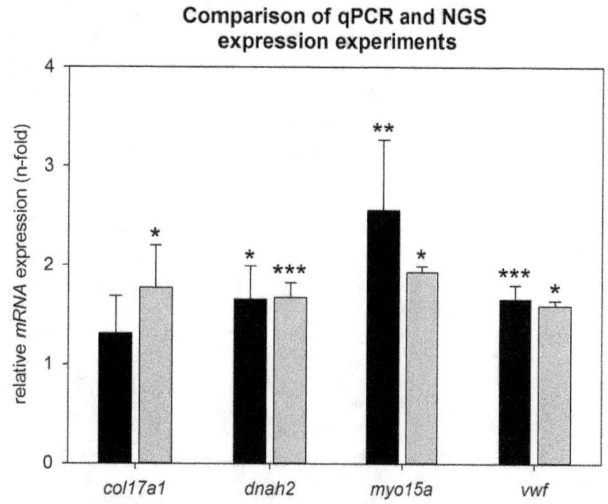

FIGURE 3 | Comparison of NGS- and qPCR data during torpor entrance. Expression changes were calculated by comparison of torpid animals at ZT1 to normothermic animals at ZT1 in both experiments. Gray bars represent torpid animals at ZT1(±SEM) analyzed by NGS and black bars represent torpid animals at ZT1(±SEM) analyzed by qPCR. Significant differences to their relative control groups are marked with $^*p < 0.05$, $^{**}p < 0.01$, $^{***}p < 0.001$.

DISCUSSION

Our data show 284 differentially expressed genes out of 27,830 identified genes in the hypothalamus of *P. sungorus* during entrance into the torpid state, implying that just a small set of genes is affected by the metabolic depression initiating torpor entrance. These results are in accordance with previous studies showing that transcript levels of most genes are unaffected during torpor (Storey and Storey, 2004). In accordance with the fact that daily torpor is a state of extreme metabolic adjustment, the majority of differentially regulated genes was found in cellular and metabolic processes for both, up and down regulated genes.

The majority of the top 20 down regulated genes were transcription factors, which could be responsible for a delay or suppression of mRNA transcription during the torpid state. It has been shown before, that transcriptional initiation as well as elongation rates are reduced during hibernation in golden-mantled ground squirrels (van Breukelen and Martin, 2002). Also in *P. sungorus* metabolic depression is associated with reduced transcriptional initiation (Berriel Diaz et al., 2004). This may contribute to the generally suppressed protein synthesis during torpor that has been demonstrated in various tissues from different species (Gulevsky et al., 1992; Frerichs et al., 1998; Hittel and Storey, 2002).

Within the top 20 up regulated group our data show a remarkable number of genes coding for structure proteins. Except for the up regulation in collagen genes we were able to verify these results by qPCR for *dnah2*, *myo15a* and the procoagulation factor *vwf*.

Collagens are extracellular matrix structural components, which are involved in neuronal development of the brain. Collagens play a role in axonal guidance, synaptogenesis and establishment of brain architecture (Chernousov et al., 2006; Fox, 2008; Hubert et al., 2009). A study of Schwartz et al. (2013) identified an up regulation of several collagen genes in the cerebral cortex, but not in the hypothalamus, of thirteen-lined ground squirrels during deep hibernation and interbout arousals, indicating synaptic plasticity during hibernation (Schwartz et al., 2013). Although we obtained a significant up regulation in mRNA expression of five collagen genes during torpor entrance by NGS and a significant enrichment of extracellular matrix components in up regulated gens, we were not able to verify these results by qPCR. There was only a trend of increased *col17a1* during torpor entrance as well as slightly lower mRNA levels during all other torpor stages and no diurnal changes could be detected in normothermic animals. Investigation of all other collagens identified in the 20 up regulated group showed a similar picture with a slight up regulation at torpor entrance and trend to lower mRNA levels during the other torpor stages that did not reach significance (data not shown). There was a high variability in the mRNA expression levels of qPCR samples, especially at torpor entrance, which might have caused the non-significant result. Different groups of animals were used for NGS and qPCR study and data might reflect inter-individual differences. A larger sample size might help to resolve expression patterns in collagen genes more precisely. Hence, whether collagens are involved in synaptic remodeling and plasticity during torpid states remains to be revealed.

Elevated expression of *dnah2*- and *myo15a* mRNA during torpor entrance could be identified by both, NGS and qPCR approach. Myosin and dynein are structural components of cytoskeleton and represent two out of three superfamilies of molecular motor proteins in neurons. They are able to transport biomolecules, such as vesicles, protein complexes and mRNAs in axons, dendrites and pre- and post-synaptic regions. Intracellular transport is necessary for neuronal morphogenesis, function and survival (Hirokawa et al., 1998, 2010; Vale, 2003). During deep hibernation, elevated mRNA levels of three different myosin types and one dynein have been detected in the cerebral cortex of *S. tridecemlineatus*, indicating dynamic structural changes (Schwartz et al., 2013).

In our study, hamsters showed elevated *dnah2* and *myo15a* expression only during torpor entrance (ZT1), whereas mRNA expression was reduced at all other investigated torpor states (mid torpor, arousal, post-torpor) compared to normothermic animals. The higher expression of *dnah2* and *myo15a* during torpor entrance could be important to ensure maintenance of synaptic transmission and neuron survival during torpor by an elevated transport of biomolecules. It might also be possible that higher mRNA amounts are produced at the beginning and stored during the torpid state to provide transcripts for a fast utilization of these molecular motors during arousal. However, we think this possibility is unlikely because mRNA levels are already declining during mid-torpor (ZT4).

In normothermic animals *dnah2* as well as *myo15a* show a diurnal regulation in its mRNA expression with a peak at ZT7 in normothermic animals. This might suggest a higher demand of these motor proteins during the hamster's naturally active phase.

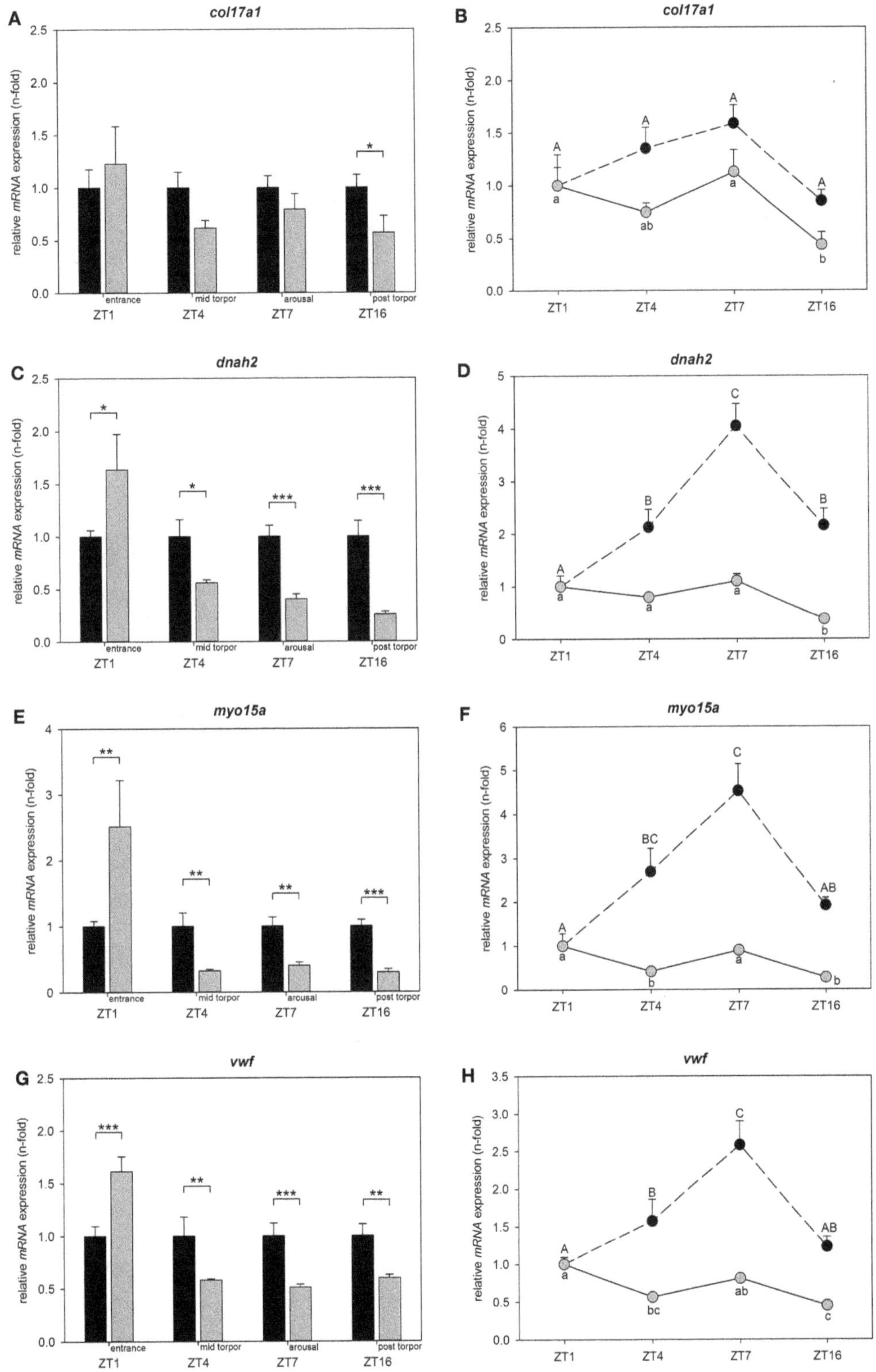

FIGURE 4 | Circadian regulation of *col17a1*, *dnah2*, *myo15a*, and *vwf* in torpid and normothermic Djungarian hamsters. Bar graphs on the left side show differences in *mRNA* expression of *col17a1* **(A)**, *dnah2* **(C)**, *myo15a* **(E)**, and *vwf* **(G)** in torpid animals (gray bars, ±SEM) relative to normothermic control group at same ZT (black bars, ±SEM). Significant differences are marked with $^{*}p < 0.05$, $^{**}p < 0.01$, and $^{***}p < 0.001$. Line graphs on the right side show relative differences in *mRNA* expression of *col17a1* **(B)**, *dnah2* **(D)**, *myo15a* **(F)**, and *vwf* **(H)** over the course of a day within normothermic animals relative to normothermic ZT1 group marked with upper case (black circles, ±SEM) and within torpid animals relative to torpid ZT1 group marked with lower case (gray circles, ±SEM). Data points with different characters are significantly different ($p < 0.05$).

Taken together changes in structural protein shows evidence for plasticity in the hypothalamus of torpid hamsters and thereby confirm studies in deep hibernation that have proposed plastic changes in the brain before.

In addition to structure gene expression changes, we chose to investigate *vwf* in more detail, because of its function in blood clotting. In torpid animals the reduced heart rate, ventilation and T_b results in a decreased blood flow that increases relatively fast to its euthermic flow rate during arousal. In contrast to all other mammalian species, torpor expressing mammals are able to survive these periods of low blood flow and consequent reperfusion without apparent formations of deep vein thrombi, stroke or pulmonary embolism (Lyman and O'Brien, 1961; Frerichs et al., 1994).

vWF is a major factor involved in platelet adhesion and thrombus formation (Denis and Wagner, 2007). Higher vWF levels increase the risk for thrombosis and embolism whereas deficiency in vWF activity leads to the human bleeding disorder von Willebrand's disease (Sadler, 1998, 2005). Moreover, Zhao et al. (2009) identified vWF as an important protein regulating the occurrence of cerebral ischemia and showed that a lack of vWF is able to reduce infarct volume (Zhao et al., 2009). Based on this knowledge, a reduced level of vWF would be expected during the torpid state to prevent blood clotting during periods of low blood flow. Indeed, in plasma samples of hibernating thirteen-lined ground squirrels vWF collagen binding is 10-fold decreased and in lung tissues *vwf* mRNA expression is 3-fold down regulated during torpor (Cooper et al., 2016). Unexpectedly, our NGS and qPCR data show an elevated level of *vwf* mRNA during torpor entrance in the hypothalamus. The elevated level of *vwf* mRNA might either not directly translate into protein variation or alternatively translate into protein without damaging effects, namely inactive vWF. vWF is a large multimeric glycoprotein which can be cleaved in smaller multimers by ADAMTS13, a zinc-containing metalloprotease enzyme. These smaller multimers of vWF have a strongly decreased activity resulting in a reduced platelet adhesion and aggregation (Chauhan et al., 2006; Zhao et al., 2009). In this case, no damage of brain structures would be expected even when higher *vwf* levels are present. Moreover, apart from the up regulation during torpor entrance, *vwf* expression was lower in torpid animals at all other investigated states, supporting the hypothesis of low *vwf* levels facilitating blood flow during the torpid state. Diurnal changes of *vwf* could be detected in either group. Normothermic animals displayed highest *vwf* level at ZT7, suggesting a higher demand of *vwf* at the beginning of the active time. In torpid animals *vwf* level is lowest at mid torpor (ZT4) and post-torpor (ZT16). Taken together, our data provide evidence for readjustment of blood clotting during different torpor stages as well as times of day.

In general, the diurnal mRNA expression of all investigated genes of this study is less pronounced in torpid animals, which is likely to be caused by the suppression of transcription and translation during torpor. The transcriptional depression during torpor has been shown to result from both, down regulated transcriptional initiation and suppressed elongation van Breukelen and Martin, 2002; Berriel Diaz et al., 2004). Low T_b during torpor affects biochemical process, leading to a decline in gene expression caused by the temperature sensitivity of transcriptional elongation (van Breukelen and Martin, 2002; Berriel Diaz et al., 2004).

The NGS technology allows a whole transcriptome survey of gene expression changes and our analysis provide an overview of gene expression changes during torpor initiation in *P. sungorus* for the first time.

Although we could not determine signaling pathways regulating torpor initiation with this approach, we identified molecular adaptions in the hypothalamus of *P. sungorus* initiated during the early state of torpor. Our data provide evidence for synaptic remodeling and plasticity, an elevated transport of biomolecules and readjustment of coagulation. Comparable gene expression changes have already been found in deep hibernators. This would support the hypothesis that daily torpor and hibernation are similar physiological states only differing in amplitude and duration. Interestingly, the molecular changes already occur within the short time span of daily torpor. These adaptations may, just like in deep hibernation, help the brain cells to better survive or reduce cell damages during the extreme physiological conditions in the torpid state. In the future, precise anatomical investigation of identified genes is necessary to eventually gain insights into their functions.

AUTHOR CONTRIBUTIONS

CC, AF, and AH designed experiments, CC and JK performed experiments. CC, JK, AF, and AH analyzed and interpreted the data. CC and AH drafted the manuscript which was critically revised by JK and AF.

REFERENCES

Bank, J. H., Kemmling, J., Rijntjes, E., Wirth, E. K., and Herwig, A. (2015). Thyroid hormone status affects expression of daily torpor and gene transcription in Djungarian hamsters (*Phodopus sungorus*). *Horm. Behav.* 75, 120–129. doi: 10.1016/j.yhbeh.2015.09.006

Berriel Diaz, M., Lange, M., Heldmaier, G., and Klingenspor, M. (2004). Depression of transcription and translation during daily torpor in the Djungarian hamster (*Phodopus sungorus*). *J. Comp. Physiol. B. Biochem. Syst. Environ. Physiol.* 174, 495–502. doi: 10.1007/s00360-004-0436-2

Chauhan, A. K., Motto, D. G., Lamb, C. B., Bergmeier, W., Dockal, M., Plaimauer, B., et al. (2006). Systemic antithrombotic effects of ADAMTS13. *J. Exp. Med.* 203, 767–776. doi: 10.1084/jem.20051732

Chernousov, M. A., Rothblum, K., Stahl, R. C., Evans, A., Prentiss, L., and Carey, D. J. (2006). Glypican-1 and alpha4(V) collagen are required for Schwann cell myelination. *J. Neurosci.* 26, 508–517. doi: 10.1523/JNEUROSCI.2544-05.2006

Cooper, S., Sell, S., Nelson, L., Hawes, J., Benrud, J. A., Kohlnhofer, B. M., et al. (2016). Von Willebrand factor is reversibly decreased during torpor in 13-lined ground squirrels. *J. Comp. Physiol. B Biochem. Syst. Environ. Physiol.* 186, 131–139. doi: 10.1007/s00360-015-0941-5

Cubuk, C., Bank, J. H., and Herwig, A. (2016). The chemistry of cold: mechanisms of torpor regulation in the siberian hamster. *Physiology* 31, 51–59. doi: 10.1152/physiol.00028.2015

Dark, J., and Pelz, K. M. (2008). NPY Y1 receptor antagonist prevents NPY-induced torpor-like hypothermia in cold-acclimated Siberian hamsters. *Am. J. Physiol. Regul. Integr. Comp. Physiol.* 294, R236–R245. doi: 10.1152/ajpregu.00587.2007

Denis, C. V., and Wagner, D. D. (2007). Platelet adhesion receptors and their ligands in mouse models of thrombosis. *Arterioscler. Thromb. Vasc. Biol.* 27, 728–739. doi: 10.1161/01.ATV.0000259359.52265.62

Ebling, F. J., and Barrett, P. (2008). The regulation of seasonal changes in food intake and body weight. *J. Neuroendocrinol.* 20, 827–833. doi: 10.1111/j.1365-2826.2008.01721.x

Figala, J., Hoffmann., K. and Goldau, G. (1973). Zur Jahresperiodik beim Dsungarischen Zwerghamster *Phodopus sungorus. Oecologia (Berl)* 13, 89–118. doi: 10.1007/BF00345511

Fox, M. A. (2008). Novel roles for collagens in wiring the vertebrate nervous system. *Curr. Opin. Cell Biol.* 20, 508–513. doi: 10.1016/j.ceb.2008.05.003

Freeman, D. A., Lewis, D. A., Kauffman, A. S., Blum, R. M., and Dark, J. (2004). Reduced leptin concentrations are permissive for display of torpor in Siberian hamsters. American journal of physiology. *Regul. Integr. Comp. Physiol.* 287, R97–R103. doi: 10.1152/ajpregu.00716.2003

Frerichs, K. U., Kennedy, C., Sokoloff, L., and Hallenbeck, J. M. (1994). Local cerebral blood flow during hibernation, a model of natural tolerance to "cerebral ischemia". *J. Cereb. Blood Flow Metab.* 14, 193–205. doi: 10.1038/jcbfm.1994.26

Frerichs, K. U., Smith, C. B., Brenner, M., DeGracia, D. J., Krause, G. S., Marrone, L., et al. (1998). Suppression of protein synthesis in brain during hibernation involves inhibition of protein initiation and elongation. *Proc. Natl. Acad. Sci. U.S.A.* 95, 14511–14516. doi: 10.1073/pnas.95.24.14511

Grabek, K. R., Diniz Behn, C., Barsh, G. S., Hesselberth, J. R., and Martin, S. L. (2015). Enhanced stability and polyadenylation of select mRNAs support rapid thermogenesis in the brown fat of a hibernator. *Elife* 4:e04517. doi: 10.7554/eLife.04517

Gulevsky, A. K., Grischenko, V. I., Zagnoiko, V. I., Shchenyavsky, I. I., and Ilyasova, E. N. (1992). Peculiarities of functioning of protein-synthesizing apparatus of the hibernator (*Citellus undulatus*). *Cryobiology* 29, 679–684. doi: 10.1016/0011-2240(92)90071-9

Hampton, M., Melvin, R. G., and Andrews, M. T. (2013). Transcriptomic analysis of brown adipose tissue across the physiological extremes of natural hibernation. *PLoS ONE* 8:e85157. doi: 10.1371/journal.pone.0085157

Hampton, M., Melvin, R. G., Kendall, A. H., Kirkpatrick, B. R., Peterson, N., and Andrews, M. T. (2011). Deep sequencing the transcriptome reveals seasonal adaptive mechanisms in a hibernating mammal. *PLoS ONE* 6:e27021. doi: 10.1371/journal.pone.0027021

Heldmaier, G., Ortmann, S., and Elvert, R. (2004). Natural hypometabolism during hibernation and daily torpor in mammals. *Respir. Physiol. Neurobiol.* 141, 317–329. doi: 10.1016/j.resp.2004.03.014

Heldmaier, G., and Ruf, T. (1992). Body temperature and metabolic rate during natural hypothermia in endotherms. *J. Comp. Physiol. B Biochem. Syst. Environ. Physiol.* 162, 696–706. doi: 10.1007/BF00301619

Heldmaier, G. S. (1981). Seasonal control of energy requirements for thermoregulation in the Djungarian hamster (*Phodopus sungorus*), living in natural photoperiod. *J. Comp. Physiol. B Biochem. Syst. Environ. Physiol.* 142, 429–437. doi: 10.1007/BF00688972

Hirokawa, N., Niwa, S., and Tanaka, Y. (2010). Molecular motors in neurons: transport mechanisms and roles in brain function, development, and disease. *Neuron* 68, 610–638. doi: 10.1016/j.neuron.2010.09.039

Hirokawa, N., Noda, Y., and Okada, Y. (1998). Kinesin and dynein superfamily proteins in organelle transport and cell division. *Curr. Opin. Cell Biol.* 10, 60–73. doi: 10.1016/S0955-0674(98)80087-2

Hittel, D., and Storey, K. B. (2002). The translation state of differentially expressed mRNAs in the hibernating 13-lined ground squirrel (Spermophilus tridecemlineatus). *Arch. Biochem. Biophys.* 401, 244–254. doi: 10.1016/S0003-9861(02)00048-6

Hubert, T., Grimal, S., Carroll, P., and Fichard-Carroll, A. (2009). Collagens in the developing and diseased nervous system. *Cell. Mol. Life Scie.* 66, 1223–1238. doi: 10.1007/s00018-008-8561-9

Jastroch, M., Giroud, S., Barrett, P., Geiser, F., Heldmaier, G., and Herwig, A. (2016). Seasonal control of mammalian energy balance: recent advances in the understanding of daily torpor and hibernation. *J. Neuroendocrinol.* 28. doi: 10.1111/jne.12437

Kirsch, R., Ouarour, A., and Pévet, P. (1991). Daily torpor in the Djungarian hamster (*Phodopus sungorus*): photoperiodic regulation, characteristics and circadian organization. *J. Comp. Physiol. A Sens. Neural Behav. Physiol.* 168, 121–128. doi: 10.1007/BF00217110

Lyman, C. P., and O'Brien, R. C. (1961). Circulatory changes in the 13-lined ground squirrel during the hibernating cycle. *Tech. Rep. Arct. Aeromed. Lab.* 60, 1–18.

Mi, H., Muruganujan, A., Casagrande, J. T., and Thomas, P. D. (2013). Large-scale gene function analysis with the PANTHER classification system. *Nat. Protoc.* 8, 1551–1566. doi: 10.1038/nprot.2013.092

Mortazavi, A., Williams, B. A., McCue, K., Schaeffer, L., and Wold, B. (2008). Mapping and quantifying mammalian transcriptomes by RNA-Seq. *Nat. Methods* 5, 621–628. doi: 10.1038/nmeth.1226

Ouarour, A., Kirsch, R., and Pevet, P. (1991). Effects of temperature, steroids and castration on daily torpor in the Djungarian hamster (*Phodopus sungorus*). *J. Comp. Physiol. A Sen. Neural Behav. Physiol.* 168, 477–481. doi: 10.1007/BF00199607

Paul, M. J., Freeman, D. A., Park, J. H., and Dark, J. (2005). Neuropeptide Y induces torpor-like hypothermia in Siberian hamsters. *Brain Res.* 1055, 83–92. doi: 10.1016/j.brainres.2005.06.090

Pelz, K. M., and Dark, J. (2007). ICV NPY Y1 receptor agonist but not Y5 agonist induces torpor-like hypothermia in cold-acclimated Siberian hamsters. *Am. J. Physiol. Regula. Integr. Comp. Physiol.* 292, R2299–R2311. doi: 10.1152/ajpregu.00790.2006

Pelz, K. M., Routman, D., Driscoll, J. R., Kriegsfeld, L. J., and Dark, J. (2008). Monosodium glutamate-induced arcuate nucleus damage affects both natural torpor and 2DG-induced torpor-like hypothermia in Siberian hamsters. *Am. J. Physiol. Regul. Integr. Comp. Physiol.* 294, R255–R265. doi: 10.1152/ajpregu.00387.2007

Robinson, M. D., and Smyth, G. K. (2008). Small-sample estimation of negative binomial dispersion, with applications to SAGE data. *Biostatistics* 9, 321–332. doi: 10.1093/biostatistics/kxm030

Ruby, N. F. (1995). Paraventricular nucleus ablation disrupts daily torpor in Siberian hamsters. *Brain Res. Bull.* 37, 193–198. doi: 10.1016/0361-9230(94)00279-A

Ruby, N. F., Nelson, R. J., Licht, P., and Zucker, I. (1993). Prolactin and testosterone inhibit torpor in Siberian hamsters. *Am. J. Physiol.* 264, R123–R128.

Ruby, N. F., and Zucker, I. (1992). Daily torpor in the absence of the suprachiasmatic nucleus in Siberian hamsters. *Am. J. Physiol.* 263, R353–R362.

Ruf, T., Klingenspor, M., Preis, H., and Heldmaier, G. (1991). Daily torpor in the Djungarian hamster (*Phodopus sungorus*): interactions with food intake, activity, and social begaviour. *J. Comp. Physiol. B Biochem. Syst. Environ. Physiol.* 160, 609–615.

Sadler, J. E. (1998). Biochemistry and genetics of von Willebrand factor. *Annu. Rev. Biochem.* 67, 395–424. doi: 10.1146/annurev.biochem.67.1.395

Sadler, J. E. (2005). New concepts in von Willebrand disease. *Annu. Rev. Med.* 56, 173–191. doi: 10.1146/annurev.med.56.082103.104713

Scherbarth, F., and Steinlechner, S. (2010). Endocrine mechanisms of seasonal adaptation in small mammals: from early results to present understanding. *J. Comp. Physiol. B Biochem. Syst. Environ. Physiol.* 180, 935–952. doi: 10.1007/s00360-010-0498-2

Schwartz, C., Hampton, M., and Andrews, M. T. (2013). Seasonal and regional differences in gene expression in the brain of a hibernating mammal. *PLoS ONE* 8:e58427. doi: 10.1371/journal.pone.0058427

Schwartz, C., Hampton, M., and Andrews, M. T. (2015). Hypothalamic gene expression underlying pre-hibernation satiety. *Genes Brain Behav.* 14, 310–318. doi: 10.1111/gbb.12199

Steinlechner, S., and Heldmaier, G. (1982). Role of photoperiod and melatonin in seasonal acclimatization of the Djungarian hamster, *Phodopus sungorus*. *Int. J. Biometeorol.* 26, 329–337. doi: 10.1007/BF02219503

Storey, K. B., and Storey, J. M. (2004). Metabolic rate depression in animals: transcriptional and translational controls. *Biol. Rev. Camb. Philos. Soc.* 79, 207–233. doi: 10.1017/S1464793103006195

Vale, R. D. (2003). The molecular motor toolbox for intracellular transport. *Cell* 112, 467–480. doi: 10.1016/S0092-8674(03)00111-9

van Breukelen, F., and Martin, S. L. (2002). Reversible depression of transcription during hibernation. *J. Comp. Physiol. B Biochem. Syst. Environ. Physiol.* 172, 355–361. doi: 10.1007/s00360-002-0256-1

Vitale, P. M., Darrow, J. M., Duncan, M. J., Shustak, C. A., and Goldman, B. D. (1985). Effects of photoperiod, pinealectomy and castration on body weight and daily torpor in Djungarian hamsters (*Phodopus sungorus*). *J. Endocrinol.* 106, 367–375. doi: 10.1677/joe.0.1060367

Zhao, B. Q., Chauhan, A. K., Canault, M., Patten, I. S., Yang, J. J., Dockal, M., et al. (2009). von Willebrand factor-cleaving protease ADAMTS13 reduces ischemic brain injury in experimental stroke. *Blood* 114, 3329–3334. doi: 10.1182/blood-2009-03-213264

13

Regulation of Mammalian Physiology by Interconnected Circadian and Feeding Rhythms

Florian Atger[1,2†], Daniel Mauvoisin[1,3], Benjamin Weger[1], Cédric Gobet[1,3] and Frédéric Gachon[1,4]*

[1] *Department of Diabetes and Circadian Rhythms, Nestlé Institute of Health Sciences, Lausanne, Switzerland,* [2] *Department of Pharmacology and Toxicology, University of Lausanne, Lausanne, Switzerland,* [3] *School of Life Sciences, Institute of Bioengineering, Ecole Polytechnique Fédérale de Lausanne, Lausanne, Switzerland,* [4] *School of Life Sciences, Ecole Polytechnique Fédérale de Lausanne, Lausanne, Switzerland*

Edited by:
Etienne Challet,
University of Strasbourg, France

Reviewed by:
Akhilesh Basi Reddy,
University of Cambridge, UK
Susanne E. la Fleur,
University of Amsterdam, Netherlands

***Correspondence:**
Frédéric Gachon
frederic.gachon@rd.nestle.com

Circadian clocks are endogenous timekeeping systems that adapt in an anticipatory fashion the physiology and behavior of most living organisms. In mammals, the master pacemaker resides in the suprachiasmatic nucleus and entrains peripheral clocks using a wide range of signals that differentially schedule physiology and gene expression in a tissue-specific manner. The peripheral clocks, such as those found in the liver, are particularly sensitive to rhythmic external cues like feeding behavior, which modulate the phase and amplitude of rhythmic gene expression. Consequently, the liver clock temporally tunes the expression of many genes involved in metabolism and physiology. However, the circadian modulation of cellular functions also relies on multiple layers of posttranscriptional and posttranslational regulation. Strikingly, these additional regulatory events may happen independently of any transcriptional oscillations, showing that complex regulatory networks ultimately drive circadian output functions. These rhythmic events also integrate feeding-related cues and adapt various metabolic processes to food availability schedules. The importance of such temporal regulation of metabolism is illustrated by metabolic dysfunctions and diseases resulting from circadian clock disruption or inappropriate feeding patterns. Therefore, the study of circadian clocks and rhythmic feeding behavior should be of interest to further advance our understanding of the prevention and therapy of metabolic diseases.

Keywords: circadian rhythm, liver, metabolism, feeding behavior, genomics, proteomics

Most living organisms are subjected to daily environmental changes imposed by the 24-h rotation of the Earth around its own axis. To anticipate these environmental variations, organisms developed a self-sustained timekeeping system, called the circadian clock (from the Latin *circa* and *diem* meaning "about a day"), which regulates behavior and physiology. The mammalian clock is organized in a hierarchical manner by a master pacemaker located in the suprachiasmatic nucleus (SCN) of the hypothalamus. This synchronizes subsidiary peripheral oscillators present in nearly every cell of the body (1). At the molecular level, circadian rhythms in gene expression are generated by interconnected transcriptional and translational feedback loops (TTFLs), in which multiple layers of control, including temporal transcriptional, posttranscriptional, and posttranslational regulation, play important roles (2, 3).

The discovery of the prominent role of the SCN for circadian rhythmicity originates from extensive lesion studies reporting a region in the anterior hypothalamus necessary for rhythmic locomotor activities (4). Moreover, circadian rhythms were partially restored by transplantation of fetal SCN tissue in SCN-lesioned animals and also in genetically engineered clock-deficient animal models. In addition, SCN-lesioned hosts displayed altered locomotor activities following SCN transplantation from arrhythmic mutant mice (5, 6). The SCN regulates the daily adaptation of the internal clock to environmental light–dark cycles. Mammals perceive light information through the retina, where photoreceptors [termed intrinsically photosensitive retinal ganglion cells (ipRGCs)] express melanopsin, a photopigment that transmits the information directly to the SCN through the retinohypothalamic tract (7, 8). In addition, ipRGCs receive non-visual cues from rod and cone photoreceptors and transmit these to the SCN, showing their central role in photic input processing (9, 10).

As a master clock, the SCN provides robustness and plasticity to the circadian system. Indeed, the SCN exhibits an adaptive response to photoperiod lengths, as shown by the opposite consequences of exposures to varying photoperiods upon SCN oscillations (11). This flexibility of daily resetting may reside in the intracellular coupling of greatly heterogeneous SCN neurons (12, 13). Indeed, the mammalian SCN is composed of ~20,000 neurons, which contain a circadian clock (14) but exhibit a broad range of phases and periods of neural firing when isolated *in vivo* or in cell culture experiments (15). Furthermore, SCN neuron explants and high density cultures of SCN neurons produced robust synchronized neuronal firing, even when the circadian clock had been genetically altered (12, 13). At the cellular level, photic cues entrain the circadian clock through several signaling pathways. Notably, light pulses triggered during the dark phase induce the expression of the circadian clock *Period* (*Per*) genes through the activation of the extracellular signal-regulated kinase (ERK) pathway (16, 17). Interestingly, this occurs exclusively when light is provided during the dark phase, suggesting that *Per* genes are involved in night–day transition.

THE MOLECULAR CIRCADIAN CLOCK

As mentioned, the molecular clock has been conserved throughout evolution and works through TTFL (18). The circadian clock is also targeted by multiple posttranslational modifications that increase the robustness of the oscillatory system by fine-tuning the localization and degradation of core oscillator proteins (2). Notably, proteasome-mediated degradation of core circadian proteins is necessary for the rhythmic expression of core clock genes (19).

In mammals, the Circadian Locomotor Output Cycles Kaput (CLOCK) and Brain and Muscle ARNT Like protein 1 (BMAL1) proteins, two transcription factors belonging to the family of bHLH-PAS (basic helix-loop-helix; Per-Arnt-Sim domain) proteins, enhance the positive limb of the TTFL. CLOCK and BMAL1 heterodimerize and initiate transcription by binding to specific DNA elements like E-box-related motifs (5′-CACGT[G/T]) in the promoters of target genes, including the *Per* and *Cryptochrome* (*Cry*) paralogs. Subsequently, PER and CRY accumulate and dimerize in the cytoplasm and then translocate into the nucleus to inhibit the transcriptional activity of the CLOCK:BMAL1 heterodimer, resulting in the downregulation of their own expression (3). Another primordial loop operates to stabilize the molecular core oscillator by connecting it to metabolic effectors (20). This loop is composed of other targets of the CLOCK:BMAL1 heterodimer such as the nuclear receptors retinoic acid-related orphan receptor α (RORα) and reverse erythroblastosis virus α (REV-ERBα or NR1D1), which respectively activate and repress *Bmal1* expression by binding response elements (RORE) present in the *Bmal1* promoter (21, 22) (**Figure 1**). An additional feedback loop involving the bHLH proteins DEC1 (or BHLHE40) and DEC2 (or BHLHE41) plays a role in rhythmic metabolism by regulating BMAL1 activity through competitive binding to its cognate sites (23, 24). In addition, the circadian clock controls the rhythmic expression of the PARbZip transcription factors DBP, HLF, and TEF and their repressive counterpart E4BP4 (or NFIL3). These factors are not directly involved in clock regulation but play an important role in the regulation of metabolism and physiology by the circadian clock (25).

SYNCHRONIZATION OF PERIPHERAL CLOCKS BY THE SCN AND ITS DOWNSTREAM FEEDING RHYTHMS

Principally, SCN output signals are mediated by circadian variation of neuronal firing and transmitter release at SCN axons (13). Neuronal connection appeared as a major effector of the SCN control since surgical isolation of the SCN (which did not compromise SCN rhythms) resulted in the abolition of circadian rhythms in other brain regions (26). Peripheral organs also contain endogenous sustain oscillators as shown by *ex vivo* cultures of liver, lung, and skeletal muscle tissues (27). These oscillations in peripheral organs progressively dampened and were desynchronized after SCN lesion, suggesting that the SCN coordinates peripheral clocks to "tick" properly (28). However, local clocks are also necessary for circadian functions. Notably, the specific inactivation of the local oscillator in adipocytes, pancreatic islets, and the liver resulted in an alteration of lipid, insulin, and glucose homeostasis, respectively (29–31). Conversely, mice with a conditionally active liver clock lost daily variation of most liver transcripts following REV-ERBα overexpression and suppression of clock oscillation (32). However, several transcripts like *Per2* still exhibited robust oscillations, suggesting that besides a functional hepatocyte clock, systemic cues can drive hepatic rhythms independently. Indeed, the SCN fashions peripheral clock rhythmicity through the modulation of systemic cues such as hormones, body temperature, and feeding behavior (33–36).

Interestingly, feeding behavior interacts with both temperature and humoral synchronization of peripheral clocks. In most mammals, feeding behavior exhibits a pronounced circadian rhythmicity characterized by major food consumption during the active phase. Nocturnal rodents consume 70%–80% of their total daily food intake during the active dark phase. Lesion of the SCN led rats to eat similar proportions of food during the light

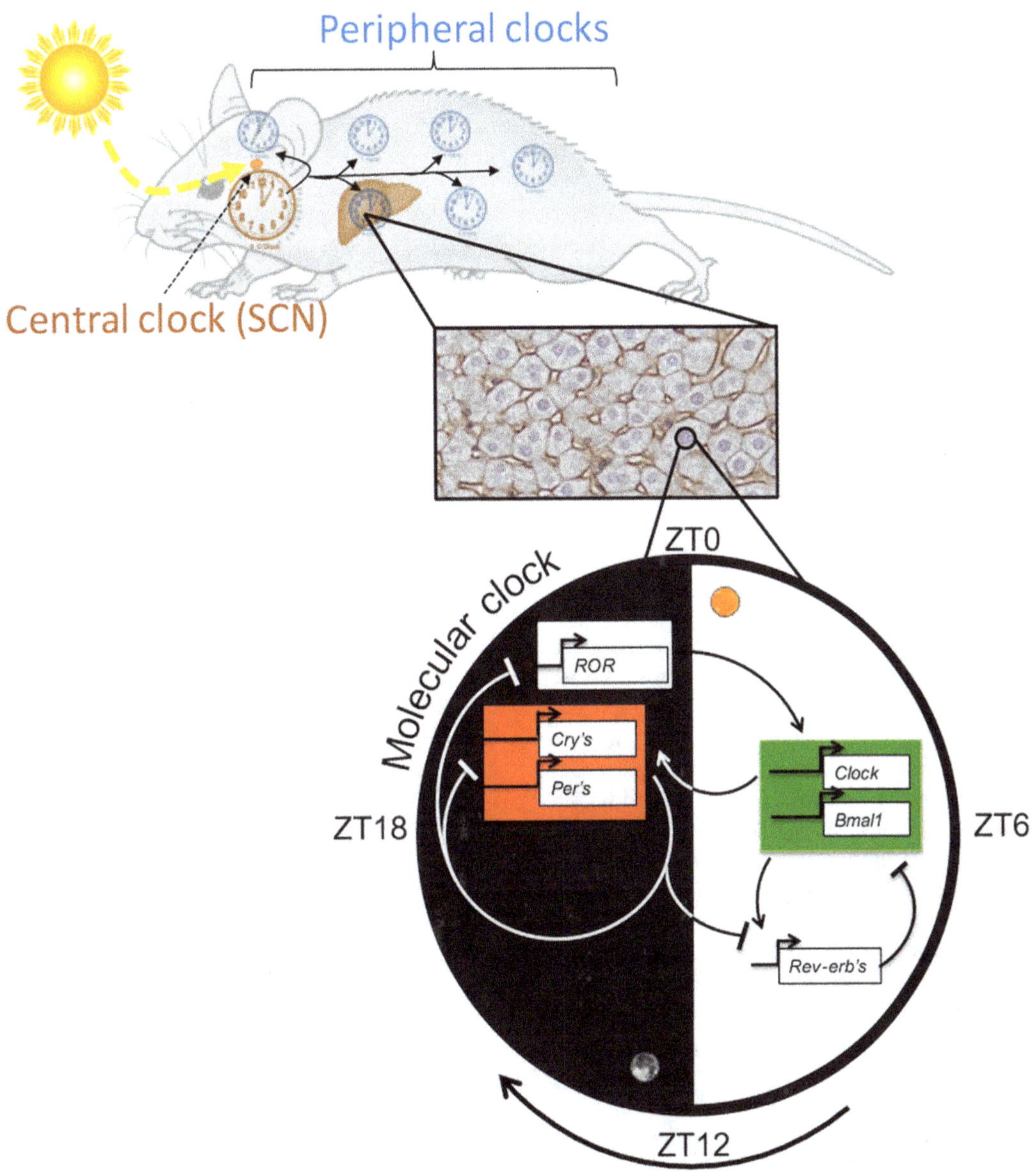

FIGURE 1 | Hierarchical organization of the circadian clock in mammals.

phase and the dark phase, showing that a functional master clock is necessary for proper feeding behavior (37). Conversely, genetic alteration of the molecular clock impaired the rhythmic food consumption in various whole-body circadian mutant models (31, 38, 39). Daily feeding–fasting cycles were shown to be primordial *Zeitgebers* (for time givers) for peripheral oscillators by shifting mealtimes to the resting period. This inverted feeding regimen rapidly inverted peripheral clocks in wild-type (WT) mouse liver, kidney, heart, and pancreas but had little to no effect on the central oscillator (36, 40). The food induction of phase shifting occurs in both light–dark and constant darkness conditions, indicating that entrainment of peripheral clocks under restricted feeding conditions may occur independently of the SCN. Indeed, the arrhythmic expression of *Per1* and *Per2* genes in the liver of SCN-lesioned mice was restored when food was restricted to a 4-h time window during the light phase (41). In addition, food restriction can partially restore rhythmicity of hepatic gene expression in mouse models with a defective circadian clock (39). However, food-induced shifting of peripheral clocks occurs progressively, and 12-h inversions of liver oscillations need slightly more than 1 week to be effective (36). Recently, the investigation of *in vivo Bmal1*-luciferase expression showed similar results (42). In addition, the authors revealed that entrainment of the liver clock by inverted feeding occurred rapidly in mice with ablated SCN. Therefore, the SCN may counteract peripheral clock uncoupling imposed by inverted food regimens, potentially through the rhythmic secretion of glucocorticoids (43).

Interestingly, the adrenal gland is connected by a polysynaptic pathway to the SCN, which controls the daily release of glucocorticoids (44). The SCN stimulates the daily release of corticosterone in a light-dependent manner, leading to a glucocorticoid surge during the light phase, which reaches maximum levels at the day–night transition, anticipating the active/feeding phase in nocturnal rodents (45). Glucocorticoids may be a way for the SCN to specify rhythms of peripheral clocks and to delay a phase shift under inverted feeding conditions. Indeed, adrenalectomized animals harbored fast food-induced resetting of peripheral clocks, similarly to SCN-ablated mice (43). Glucocorticoids act on peripheral clocks through the interaction with glucocorticoid receptors, which bind glucocorticoid response elements in the promoters of target genes. These regulatory elements have been found in the promoter of core clock genes such as *Bmal1, Cry1, Per1*, and *Per2* (46–48), showing the strong interconnection between the two systems (49). Conversely, glucocorticoids were shown to entrain peripheral clocks, as suggested by the ability of dexamethasone (a glucocorticoid analog) to trigger oscillations in rat fibroblasts (33).

In parallel, temperature modulation was proven to sustain and synchronize peripheral oscillators (34, 50, 51). Indeed, temperature fluctuations impact circadian periods in fibroblasts as shown in fibroblasts expressing *Bmal1*-luciferase reporters. Short periods were associated with higher temperatures, whereas an opposite effect was observed with lower temperatures (52). Interestingly, temperature compensation was dampened in *Per1* KO fibroblasts, which exhibited similar oscillations to control counterparts (52). In addition, the heat shock factor 1 is likely involved in temperature-mediated modulation of the liver clock (53). Conversely, in SCN-lesioned animals, food restriction induced both rhythmic locomotor activities and temperature rhythms (54, 55). Finally, temperature could also impact rhythmic gene expression through the regulation of mRNA splicing efficiency, as recently demonstrated for cold-inducible RNA-binding protein (56).

Restriction of feeding to a few hours during the resting phase enhances oscillation of metabolic factors including glucose, free fatty acids, and glucocorticoids (57). Similarly, this short supply of food during the day quickly alters daily behavioral rhythms such as locomotor activity to anticipate food availability (55, 58). This food-anticipatory activity (FAA) persists when mice are subsequently placed under food deprivation. Interestingly, most of the murine models with a defective circadian clock presented normal FAA (58–60). Entrainment to food can also occur in rodents with SCN lesions, indicating that the neuronal locations governing FAA are at least partially distinct from those who participate in light entrainment (54, 58).

Although the brain regions involved in FAA still need to be discovered, several studies suggest that peripheral organs participate in FAA through humoral routes. Notably, Ghrelin-secreting cells of the stomach were shown to constitute potential food-entrainable oscillators. Ghrelin stimulates food intake during feeding restriction, and Ghrelin receptor knockout animals show a reduction in FAA (61, 62). In addition, the gut-secreted oxyntomodulin is also involved in the synchronization of the circadian clock through feeding cues (63). In parallel, *Per2* has recently been shown to mediate hepatic action upon FAA. Although *Per2* mutation in the whole body is known to impair food anticipation in mice, the liver-specific *Per2* mutation (L-*Per2*) is sufficient to disrupt this circadian behavior (64, 65). Under inverted feeding conditions, PER2 modulates *Cpt1a* and *Hmgcs2* expression, two rate-limiting enzymes for β-hydroxybutyrate synthesis. Interestingly, β-hydroxybutyrate injection rescues FAA in L-*Per2* mice, which provides a way for the liver to participate in adaptation of feeding behavior. Another example is given by the adipocyte clock, which is involved in daily leptin secretion (30). Leptin reduces appetite, and its signaling is blunted in circadian clock-mutant animals and under chronic jetlag (66). Adipocyte-specific deletion of *Bmal1* resulted in the impairment of leptin levels in plasma, as well as defective feeding behavior. The regulation of feeding behavior appears to integrate multiple layers of control involving not only the central clock but also clock-independent food-entrainable oscillators employing central and peripheral organs.

TRANSCRIPTIONAL CONTROL OF CIRCADIAN OUTPUT GENES

Recently, the transcriptional landscape of circadian core clock transcriptional regulators has been revealed by time-resolved Chip-seq experiments (67). The DNA-binding preference for circadian activators (BMAL1, CLOCK, and NPAS2) and repressors (PER1, PER2, and CRY2) showed opposite phase specificity. DNA binding of circadian transcriptional regulators showed accompanying rhythms of histone modifications, indicating that rhythmic fluctuations of liver transcripts partially emerge as a result of transcriptional regulation (67, 68). Consequently, an important part of the liver transcriptome exhibits daily oscillations connected to genes encoding proteins involved in metabolic regulations (69–71). Conversely, several aspects of glucose and lipid metabolism are altered in circadian-deficient mice models (1).

As mentioned before, additional feedback loops connect the core loop to metabolic regulations. One connection is explained by the interaction of PER2 with nuclear receptors REV-ERBα, PPARα, and PPARγ involved in both glucose and lipid metabolism regulation (72, 73). These interactions likely specify oscillations of genes targeted by nuclear receptors. REV-ERBs have a dual role in stabilizing the core loop by binding RORE in their promoter and driving metabolic gene expression through their interaction with other transcription factors (74, 75). A secondary connection is the interaction of CRY proteins with glucocorticoid receptors, linking CRY to glucose metabolism (76). On the other hand, PPARα is activated by binding to fatty acids and regulates glucose and lipid metabolism. Importantly, PPARα activity is also indirectly controlled by the circadian effectors DBP, TEF, and HLF. Indeed, mice lacking these three PARbZip family members showed impaired hepatic fatty acid content, due to the loss of oscillations of rate-limiting enzymes involved in FA synthesis (77). Interestingly, PPARα activity could be rescued in PARbZip KO mice through the stimulation of *de novo* fatty acid synthesis induced by a fat-free diet. Another transcription factor, SREBP1, is controlled by the circadian clock and food inputs.

Indeed, SREBP1-mediated transcription is altered in *Bmal1* and *Rev-erbα* KO mice (78, 79). Conversely, day time food-induced resetting of the clock in WT mice led to a 12-h phase shift of SREBP1 activation (80) and rescued its rhythmic activity in *Cry1/Cry2* KO mice (39).

Contradicting these numerous examples of circadian clock-mediated transcriptional regulation, some studies suggested that a minor proportion of rhythmic transcripts were driven by transcriptional events (67, 81). In contrast, investigation of DNA-binding dynamics of the DNA polymerase II revealed a higher importance of transcriptional regulation in guiding mRNA oscillations (82). Similarly, we observed that most of the cyclic mRNA accumulation originated from rhythmic transcriptional events (83). These discrepancies may originate from differences in the analysis (84) or nature of the data. Indeed, experimental conditions such as light–dark schedule or constant darkness, as well as *ad libitum* or night-restricted feeding, play an important role in the quantitative rhythmic transcriptome. This is suggested by the consolidation of mRNA rhythms in mice subjected to night or day feeding restrictions (39, 85). Still these studies univocally demonstrate that posttranscriptional regulations are at least partially involved in circadian rhythmicity.

Indeed, transcriptional regulations are not necessarily reflected at the proteomic level. Early proteomic-based investigations showed that rhythmic variation of protein abundance is not fully explained by variation in mRNA levels (86). More recent studies with higher coverage of mouse liver and SCN also concluded that about half of the rhythmic proteins are encoded by non-rhythmic mRNA (87–89). Considering rhythmic protein contents in specific liver organelles such as nuclei and mitochondria, correlation between protein and mRNA levels is even worse, which suggests that rhythmicity likely results from cell trafficking (90, 91). Although protein secretion has been suggested as a possible explanation for rhythmic liver protein contents (89), other processes like mRNA translation could be also involved.

THE IMPACT OF CIRCADIAN AND FEEDING RHYTHMS ON mRNA TRANSLATION

The first evidence of a major role of mRNA translation in the generation of circadian rhythms came from the study of the rhythmic photosynthesis of the giant green algae *Acetabularia*. *Acetabularia* has a single nucleus located in the rhizoid, which allows the regeneration of the cell if its cap is completely removed. However, not only can the cell survive for several weeks without its nucleus, but the rhythmic photosynthesis of the plant continues under this condition (92). In addition, studies examining the reintroduction of an out-of-phase nucleus into the plant showed that the clock in the cytoplasm determines the phase of the rhythmic photosynthesis. The cytoplasmic clock entrains the nuclear clock, which suggests that the latter has a minimal effect on this rhythm (93, 94). Further experiments show that the rhythmic synthesis of a subset of proteins is dependent on the translation machinery, demonstrating for the first time the circadian translation of mRNA (95).

Secondary evidence came from the study of the luminescent unicellular dinoflagellate *Gonyaulax*, which presents circadian photosynthesis, motility, cell division, and luminescence (96). The nocturnal luminescence of *Gonyaulax* is produced by a complex of three proteins, whose synthesis is controlled by the circadian clock at a posttranscriptional level (97, 98). Further experiments show that this translational regulation is controlled by the UG-repeat sequence binding protein CCTR, which rhythmically binds the 3′-untranslated region (UTR) in the RNA of this luminescent protein and represses its expression during the day (99). In addition to these historical discoveries in unicellular organisms, recent evidence suggests that circadian clock-regulated translation also occurs in mammals.

The first observation suggesting a rhythmic translation in mammals is the description of a rhythmic polysome profile in rat liver, with around 25% more polysomes present during the dark phase than during the light phase (100). This observation was later confirmed by electron microscopy experiments, which showed that the polysomal volume density is four times higher at dusk than at dawn (101). In agreement with these observations, we have recently demonstrated that the circadian clock can coordinate the temporal translation of a subset of mRNAs involved in ribosome biogenesis by controlling the transcription of translation initiation factors, as well as the rhythmic activation of signaling pathways involved in their regulation (102). Later experiments using ribosome profiling allowed us to show that two main classes of mRNA are indeed subjected to rhythmic translation: the 5′-terminal oligopyrimidine tract (5′-TOP) mRNAs, translated in a TORC1-dependent manner and involved in ribosome biogenesis (103), and the translation initiator of short 5′ UTR (TISU) motif harboring mRNA coding mostly for mitochondrial proteins (104). Although both circadian clock and feeding rhythms appeared to be involved in the translational regulation of the latter class, only feeding rhythms seem to regulate the translation of 5′-TOP mRNA (83).

However, additional regulations of rRNA synthesis and maturation, as well as ribosome assembly, are subjected to rhythmic regulation potentially involving the circadian clock (91, 102). Because both size and organization of the nucleolus are directly related to ribosome production (105), it is notable that the size of the nucleolus in sympathetic neurons follows a diurnal pattern with a maximum in the middle of the dark period (106), in synchrony with the observed accumulation of ribosomal proteins in the liver.

Another level of circadian translational regulation has been described. While it has already been shown that the size of the poly(A) tail of some mRNA is subject to circadian variation (107), Kojima et al. showed that around 2% of the mRNAs expressed in mouse liver exhibit a rhythmic size of their poly(A) tail, even though their steady-state mRNA levels are not rhythmic (108). The size of the poly(A) tail is under the control of rhythmic cytoplasmic polyadenylation, regulated in part through the rhythmic expression of cytoplasmic polyadenylation element-binding proteins. Interestingly, they show that the rhythm of the length of the poly(A) tail of these mRNAs correlates with the rhythmic expression of the corresponding encoded proteins, with a several-hour delay between the time of longest poly(A) tail and the highest protein levels. Importantly, this study demonstrates that the rhythmic polyadenylation status of mRNAs can result in rhythmic protein expression independent of the steady-state levels of the mRNA. This rhythmic poly(A) length could likely be under the regulation of the clock-controlled NOCTURNIN (NOC) deadenylase (109). Remarkably, a search for NOC-regulated polyadenylated genes revealed that ribosome biogenesis and mitochondrial oxidative phosphorylation are the primary functions regulated by NOC, showing a convergent regulation of these pathways by the circadian clock (110). Therefore, it is not surprising that impaired mitochondrial activity is observed in several circadian clock-mutant mice (111–113).

CHARACTERIZATION OF THE CIRCADIAN PROTEOMES AND POSTTRANSLATIONAL REGULATIONS

During the previous decade and until recently, the literature in large-scale circadian expression studies relied on genomic approach technologies, and proteomics played a limited role due to technological limitations. Pioneer circadian proteomic studies relied on 2-dimensional gel electrophoresis (2D-GE) followed by mass spectrometry (MS). This approach allowed separation of complex protein mixtures and visualization of expression pattern changes in diverse conditions such as different times of the day. This technique was successfully applied to the study of circadian protein expression of organs such as the SCN (114), the rat pineal gland (115), and the mouse retina (116).

The first breakthrough came from the laboratory of M. Hastings where the liver circadian proteome was investigated. Their 2D-GE analyses detected 642 protein spots, of which 60 showed significant rhythmicity. MS identified 39 rhythmic proteins originating from 29 unique genes (86). Using the same experimental design, an exploration of the mouse SCN proteome was conducted in the same laboratory and 34 proteins exhibiting significant rhythmic patterns were identified. This rhythmic proteome was highly enriched with proteins implicated in vesicle trafficking and synaptic vesicle recycling. Moreover, both studies showed a small fraction of corresponding rhythmic mRNA, highlighting the importance of posttranscriptional regulation (86, 117). This work was published just after the study by Hatcher et al. (118) and before the study by Lee et al. (119), both of which characterized the circadian SCN peptides released by MS. Subsequently, an automated and integrated proteomics platform was designed to study the effect of light stimulation on the murine SCN proteome, and, from the 2,131 proteins identified, 387 were shown to be light regulated (120).

Recently, new quantitative proteomic techniques have been developed, from label-free (LF) proteomics to stable-isotope labeling by amino acids in cell culture (SILAC) (121). Accordingly, these tools were used to decipher the rhythmic circadian proteome in both SCN and liver. LF proteomics was used to quantify circadian-related peptides from the SCN (122), and more recently, SILAC was applied to quantify the rhythmic SCN proteome (87). We have used *in vivo* SILAC in mice (123) to characterize the diurnal oscillations of the liver proteome. We identified 5,827 proteins in total protein liver extract, of which 6% were rhythmic and accumulated mostly in the morning and during the night. Half of the rhythmic proteome did not display corresponding rhythmic mRNAs, and the rhythmicity of this group, in which secreted proteins were overrepresented, appeared to be clock independent. This indicates that feeding behavior might determine the rhythm of circulating proteins in the blood (89). This discovery was in accordance with previous data from the study by Martino et al. showing no association between the plasma proteome and the mouse liver transcriptome (124). A parallel study also using an *in vivo* SILAC approach but in constant darkness drew similar conclusions (88). This absence of rhythmicity at the mRNA level for nevertheless cyclic proteins suggests that the regulation of the rhythmic proteome results from posttranscriptional and even posttranslational modification events, since the circadian clock-regulated translation impacts only a limited subset of genes (83, 125, 126).

A caveat when working with total proteomes is their high level of complexity, which can result in difficulties detecting important proteins expressed at a low level such as the core clock proteins, transcription factors, or organelle-specific proteins. To bypass proteome complexity and enhance its resolution, initial organelle biochemical fractionations can be performed before applying quantitative proteomics. This strategy was applied to quantify the mitochondrial proteome using LF quantitative proteomics. Thirty-eight percent of the mitochondrial proteins were cycling, the majority peaking during the early light phase, with low corresponding rhythmic mRNA. These data highlighted the role of posttranscriptional regulation orchestrated by the clock and feeding rhythms in the regulation of mitochondrial function such as fatty acid oxidation. The rhythmic mitochondrial proteome was also correlated with the expression of the TIM/TOM complex, suggesting that protein entry in the mitochondria was temporally framed (90). Alternatively, mitochondrial fission fusion and autophagy, orchestrated by the circadian clock, might also influence the dynamics of the mitochondrial proteome (112).

By using *in vivo* SILAC, we recently produced unprecedented nuclear quantitative proteomic data. Indeed, among the 4,035 nuclear proteins quantified, more than 500 were highly rhythmic, including all the core clock components along with the clock-controlled transcription factors. These findings are in accordance with the absolute quantification of circadian clock proteins published in parallel (91, 127). The rhythmic nuclear proteins were mainly controlled at the posttranscriptional level and were members of complexes displaying robust diurnal nuclear accumulation. These complexes were involved in ribosome biogenesis and assembly (102), as well as DNA repair (128) and transcriptional regulation. In fact, we quantified the rhythmic temporal accumulation of around 100 transcription factors and transcriptional coregulators and provided new insights into the diurnal regulatory landscape in liver nuclei (91).

Reddy et al. already predicted that posttranslational modifications play a role in the regulation of the rhythmic proteome. They identified two different phosphorylated forms of peroxiredoxin 6 displaying antiphasic levels of phosphorylation and the other one being in phase with the transcript (86). This observation led to the discovery that peroxiredoxins undergo circadian redox cycles in association with oscillations in NADH and NADPH, independent of transcription (129, 130). This posttranslational clock is also conserved in all domains of life, probably as a sensor of rhythmic metabolism (131). NADPH, in eukaryotic cells, is provided by the pentose phosphate pathway, which was recently shown to regulate circadian redox oscillations and influence transcriptional oscillations (132). In response to daily changes in nutrient availability and physiological states, numerous posttranslational modifications of the circadian clock have been identified, and modifications such as phosphorylation, ubiquitination, acetylation, O-GlcNacylation, and SUMOylation were shown to have a direct role in fine-tuning the timing of the molecular circadian clock and related metabolic pathways [for reviews, see Ref. (2, 133)].

Phosphorylation has already been described as the base of the circadian clock system in cyanobacteria (134) and is by far the mostly studied posttranslational modification. Moreover, among signaling pathways rhythmically activated by phosphorylation in mouse liver, AMPK and ERK pathways are activated during the day, corresponding to the fasting period (102, 135), whereas AKT and TORC1 pathways are activated during the night, corresponding to the feeding period (102). These results were recently corroborated by total phosphoproteomics analysis, emphasizing the impact of the rhythmic activation of these pathways on the general regulation of metabolism and physiology (90). In parallel, nuclear phosphoproteomic analysis also underlined the alignment of the cell cycle and the circadian clock and its potential role in the regulation of hepatocyte ploidy (91). Both studies also identified rhythmic phosphorylation sites within the core clock proteins, such as the serine 446 and serine 440/441 of CLOCK implicated in regulating its transcriptional activity (136). We found that the serine 42 of BMAL1 is rhythmically phosphorylated in the nucleus (91). This phosphorylation event, under the control of the insulin-AKT-mTOR pathway, reduces the nuclear accumulation of BMAL1 and stabilizes the protein in the cytosol (136, 137). By finely tuning the clock, this mechanism could be one potential contributor to the beneficial effects of restricted feeding. Although the relative impact of feeding entrainable oscillators and circadian rhythms on these rhythmic pathway activations is still poorly described and understood, evidence suggested strong interactions between the circadian clock and metabolism might be key for rhythmic activation of the TORC1 pathway (138, 139).

Beyond phosphorylation, acetylation oscillations have also been shown to play an important role in the rhythmic regulation of liver physiology. In the nucleus, the SIRT1 deacetylase plays a critical role in the organization of the circadian clock in both SCN and peripheral tissues (140–142). In parallel, both SIRT6 and HDAC3 are more involved in the transcriptional regulation of rhythmic metabolism, in particular lipid metabolism (143, 144). SIRT7, another nuclear located deacetylase, was also linked *in vivo* to lipid metabolism, since its expression alleviates ER stress and prevents fatty liver development (145). Moreover, in mouse liver, it specifically locates the promoter of ribosomal proteins for transcriptional silencing and its activity is potentiated by ribosomal RNAs (145, 146). We showed that SIRT7 accumulation is rhythmic in the nucleus, in phase with rRNAs and in opposite phase with translation (91, 102). Hence, in mammals, SIRT7 may be certainly an important contributor to the rhythmic regulation of ribosomal biogenesis and result in rhythmic protein translation. In the cytoplasm, SIRT2 regulates the pentose phosphate pathway by deacetylating glucose-6-phosphate dehydrogenase, which might be important for the regulation of circadian redox oscillations (132, 147). In accordance with our nuclear proteomic data, SIRT2 transiently peaks in the nucleus during mitosis where it has several functions such as the regulation of nuclear envelope reassembly (91, 148).

To date, one large-scale proteomic study looked at the circadian acetylome, finding 306 acetylation sites within 179 proteins (highly enriched in mitochondrial proteins), of which a few sites showed disrupted rhythm in CLOCK-mutant animals (149). The circadian activity of Sirtuins is mainly the consequence of the circadian clock-dependent synthesis of its cofactor NAD^+ through the NAD^+ salvage pathway (150, 151). Therefore, this rhythmic NAD^+ synthesis controls SIRT3 activity in the mitochondria and is involved in the rhythmic mitochondrial activity controlled by the circadian clock (111). Our recent characterization of the rhythmic acetylome identified around 100 rhythmic acetylation sites in mouse liver, mostly originating from mitochondrial proteins. These rhythmic mitochondrial acetylations are correlated with a SIRT3-dependant deacetylation process (unpublished observation).

THE INTERACTION BETWEEN HOST CIRCADIAN RHYTHMS AND GUT MICROBIOTA

In addition to the regulation of transcription, translation and posttranslational modifications by the circadian clock, recent studies also point out the impact of circadian and feeding rhythms on host gut microbiota adding a new layer of complexity to this interplay. The gut microbiome is a complex assembly of more than a thousand microorganisms, mostly commensal bacteria. Gut microbiota play an important role in gut physiology and host metabolism (152). A decrease in microbiota diversity has been associated with metabolic diseases that include obesity and type 2 diabetes (153). Recent studies show that both the composition and the activity of the gut microbiome (154–157), as well as its adherence to the intestinal epithelium (158), are highly dynamic and exhibit a diurnal pattern. This rhythm appears to be dependent on a functional circadian clock in the host (154, 156). Indeed, the cyclic changes in composition and diversity of gut microbiota are absent in mouse models in which clock function is genetically compromised. However, these absent rhythms can be restored by a time-restricted feeding regimen, strongly suggesting that the main driver of daily fluctuation of gut microbiota composition is feeding rhythm (154, 155, 158, 159). Conversely, gut microbiota has been reported to feedback on host clock gene expression. Germ-free or antibiotic-treated mice that are devoid of gut microbiota were shown to have perturbation of the liver and the intestinal circadian clock. However, the reported effects on peripheral clock gene expression are highly variable, ranging from disruption of clock gene expression in the ileum and colon

(160), to rather mild changes in phases and amplitude (157, 161) and virtually no alteration in mouse liver (158). Future studies will evaluate the impact of gut microbiota on host circadian rhythms in more detail to improve our understanding of the mechanism underlying this interaction. Moreover, gut microbiota has also been described as an important modulator of brain function and behavior, including feeding behavior and appetite control (162). It will be interesting to understand how this layer of bacteria–host communication feeds into interaction between the host's circadian clock and gut microbiota.

CONCLUSION: IMPACT OF FEEDING RHYTHMS ON METABOLIC HEALTH

In this review, we summarized the impact of circadian and feeding rhythms not only on rhythmic transcriptional regulations but also on rhythmic posttranscriptional events orchestrated by these tightly interconnected rhythms (**Figure 2**). Interestingly, imposed feeding rhythms have the capacity to synchronize or increase oscillations in models characterized by decreased amplitude of metabolic and feeding rhythms. For example, imposed day feeding is able to restore liver rhythmic gene expression in clock-deficient mice (39). In addition, deleterious metabolic effect of high-fat diet has been successfully counteract by imposed restricted feeding during the night, the active phase of the animals (85, 163–166). Indeed, limiting access to a high-fat diet during the night increased the amplitude of metabolic rhythms and reduced the health consequences of a high-fat diet without changing the global quantity of ingested calories. This regimen also limits the deleterious impact of high-fat diet-induced obesity on gut microbiota (155, 159). Moreover, the same kind of observation is also true for humans (167) as imposed feeding patterns improved weight loss under calorie restriction (168). Therefore, these studies constitute the basis of chrononutrition, an approach that aims to improve metabolic health through the synchronization of the circadian clock with downstream feeding and sleeping cycles strongly impacted by living environment (169).

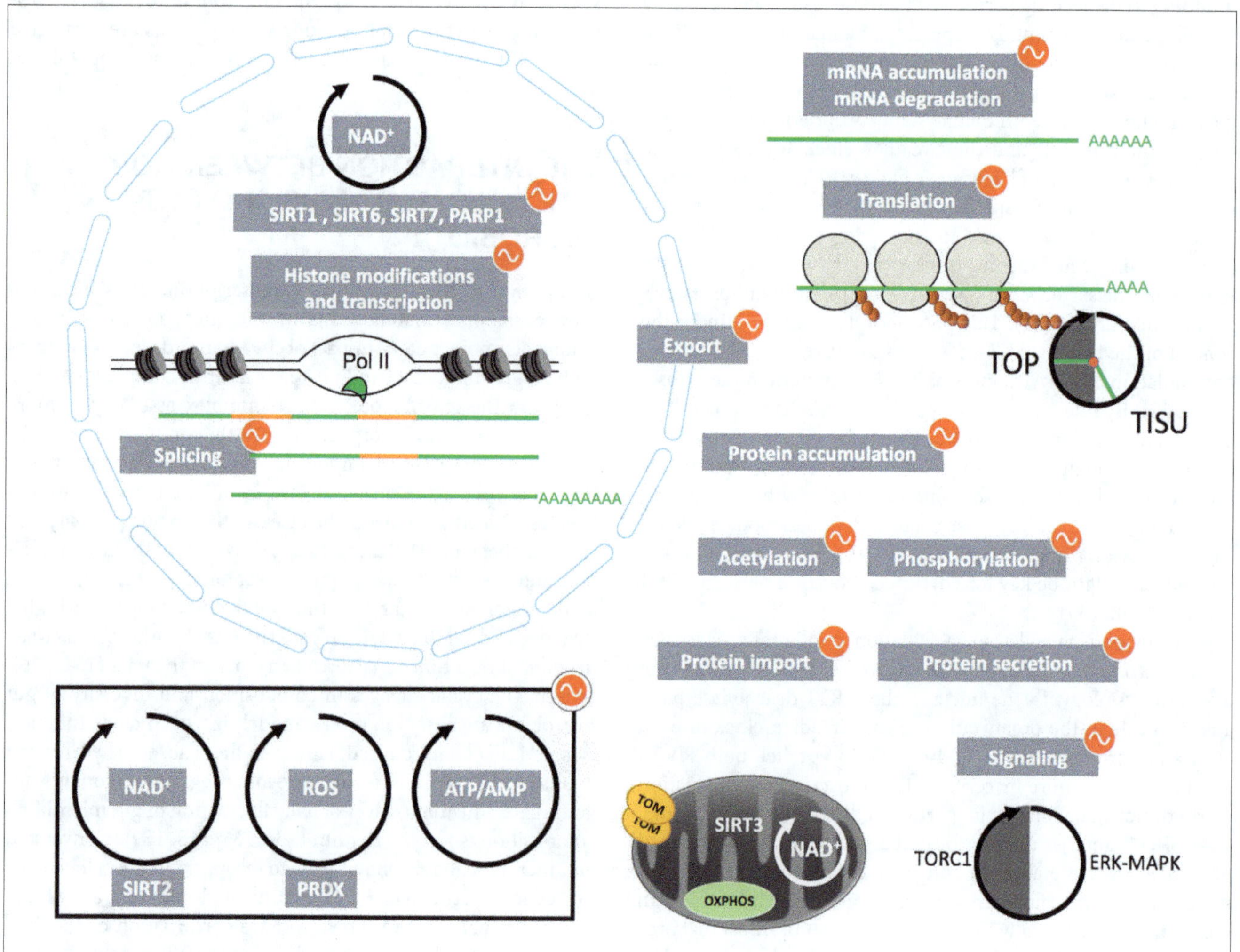

FIGURE 2 | The multisteps regulated by circadian and feeding rhythms involved in genes product expression: from mRNA transcription to posttranslational modifications and cell trafficking.

AUTHOR CONTRIBUTIONS

All authors listed have made substantial, direct, and intellectual contribution to the work and approved it for publication.

REFERENCES

1. Panda S. Circadian physiology of metabolism. *Science* (2016) 354:1008. doi:10.1126/science.aah4967
2. Hirano A, Fu YH, Ptacek LJ. The intricate dance of post-translational modifications in the rhythm of life. *Nat Struct Mol Biol* (2016) 23:1053–60. doi:10.1038/nsmb.3326
3. Papazyan R, Zhang Y, Lazar MA. Genetic and epigenomic mechanisms of mammalian circadian transcription. *Nat Struct Mol Biol* (2016) 23:1045–52. doi:10.1038/nsmb.3324
4. Stephan FK, Zucker I. Circadian rhythms in drinking behavior and locomotor activity of rats are eliminated by hypothalamic lesions. *Proc Natl Acad Sci U S A* (1972) 69:1583–6. doi:10.1073/pnas.69.6.1583
5. Ralph MR, Foster RG, Davis FC, Menaker M. Transplanted suprachiasmatic nucleus determines circadian period. *Science* (1990) 247:975–8. doi:10.1126/science.2305266
6. Sujino M, Masumoto KH, Yamaguchi S, van der Horst GTJ, Okamura H, Inouye ST. Suprachiasmatic nucleus grafts restore circadian behavioral rhythms of genetically arrhythmic mice. *Curr Biol* (2003) 13:664–8. doi:10.1016/S0960-9822(03)00222-7
7. Berson DM, Dunn FA, Takao M. Phototransduction by retinal ganglion cells that set the circadian clock. *Science* (2002) 295:1070–3. doi:10.1126/science.1067262
8. Hattar S, Liao HW, Takao M, Berson DM, Yau KW. Melanopsin-containing retinal ganglion cells: architecture, projections, and intrinsic photosensitivity. *Science* (2002) 295:1065–70. doi:10.1126/science.1069609
9. Chen SK, Badea TC, Hattar S. Photoentrainment and pupillary light reflex are mediated by distinct populations of ipRGCs. *Nature* (2011) 476:92–5. doi:10.1038/nature10206
10. Guler AD, Ecker JL, Lall GS, Haq S, Altimus CM, Liao HW, et al. Melanopsin cells are the principal conduits for rod-cone input to non-image-forming vision. *Nature* (2008) 453:102–5. doi:10.1038/nature06829
11. Inagaki N, Honma S, Ono D, Tanahashi Y, Honma KI. Separate oscillating cell groups in mouse suprachiasmatic nucleus couple photoperiodically to the onset and end of daily activity. *Proc Natl Acad Sci U S A* (2007) 104:7664–9. doi:10.1073/pnas.0607713104
12. Liu AC, Welsh DK, Ko CH, Tran HG, Zhang EE, Priest AA, et al. Intercellular coupling confers robustness against mutations in the SCN circadian clock network. *Cell* (2007) 129:605–16. doi:10.1016/j.cell.2007.02.047
13. Welsh DK, Takahashi JS, Kay SA. Suprachiasmatic nucleus: cell autonomy and network properties. *Annu Rev Physiol* (2010) 72:551–77. doi:10.1146/annurev-physiol-021909-135919
14. Herzog ED. Neurons and networks in daily rhythms. *Nat Rev Neurosci* (2007) 8:790–802. doi:10.1038/nrn2215
15. Welsh DK, Logothetis DE, Meister M, Reppert SM. Individual neurons dissociated from rat suprachiasmatic nucleus express independently phased circadian firing rhythms. *Neuron* (1995) 14:697–706. doi:10.1016/0896-6273(95)90214-7
16. Ginty DD, Kornhauser JM, Thompson MA, Bading H, Mayo KE, Takahashi JS, et al. Regulation of CREB phosphorylation in the suprachiasmatic nucleus by light and a circadian clock. *Science* (1993) 260:238–41. doi:10.1126/science.8097062
17. Shigeyoshi Y, Taguchi K, Yamamoto S, Takekida S, Yan L, Tei H, et al. Light-induced resetting of a mammalian circadian clock is associated with rapid induction of the mPer1 transcript. *Cell* (1997) 91:1043–53. doi:10.1016/S0092-8674(00)80494-8
18. Partch CL, Green CB, Takahashi JS. Molecular architecture of the mammalian circadian clock. *Trends Cell Biol* (2014) 24:90–9. doi:10.1016/j.tcb.2013.07.002
19. Stratmann M, Suter DM, Molina N, Naef F, Schibler U. Circadian Dbp transcription relies on highly dynamic BMAL1-CLOCK interaction with E boxes and requires the proteasome. *Mol Cell* (2012) 48:277–87. doi:10.1016/j.molcel.2012.08.012
20. Gerhart-Hines Z, Lazar MA. Rev-erbα and the circadian transcriptional regulation of metabolism. *Diabetes Obes Metab* (2015) 17:12–6. doi:10.1111/dom.12510
21. Preitner N, Damiola F, Lopez-Molina L, Zakany J, Duboule D, Albrecht U, et al. The orphan nuclear receptor REV-ERBα controls circadian transcription within the positive limb of the mammalian circadian oscillator. *Cell* (2002) 110:251–60. doi:10.1016/S0092-8674(02)00825-5
22. Sato TK, Panda S, Miraglia LJ, Reyes TM, Rudic RD, McNamara P, et al. A functional genomics strategy reveals Rora as a component of the mammalian circadian clock. *Neuron* (2004) 43:527–37. doi:10.1016/j.neuron.2004.07.018
23. Honma S, Kawamoto T, Takagi Y, Fujimoto K, Sato F, Noshiro M, et al. *Dec1* and *Dec2* are regulators of the mammalian molecular clock. *Nature* (2002) 419:841–4. doi:10.1038/nature01123
24. Kato Y, Kawamoto T, Fujimoto K, Noshiro M. DEC1/STRA13/SHARP2 and DEC2/SHARP1 coordinate physiological processes, including circadian rhythms in response to environmental stimuli. *Curr Top Dev Biol* (2014) 110:339–72. doi:10.1016/B978-0-12-405943-6.00010-5
25. Gachon F. Physiological function of PARbZip circadian clock-controlled transcription factors. *Ann Med* (2007) 39:562–71. doi:10.1080/07853890701491034
26. Inouye ST, Kawamura H. Persistence of circadian rhythmicity in a mammalian hypothalamic "island" containing the suprachiasmatic nucleus. *Proc Natl Acad Sci U S A* (1979) 76:5962–6. doi:10.1073/pnas.76.11.5962
27. Yamazaki S, Numano R, Abe M, Hida A, Takahashi R, Ueda M, et al. Resetting central and peripheral circadian oscillators in transgenic rats. *Science* (2000) 288:682–5. doi:10.1126/science.288.5466.682
28. Yoo SH, Yamazaki S, Lowrey PL, Shimomura K, Ko CH, Buhr ED, et al. PERIOD2::LUCIFERASE real-time reporting of circadian dynamics reveals persistent circadian oscillations in mouse peripheral tissues. *Proc Natl Acad Sci U S A* (2004) 101:5339–46. doi:10.1073/pnas.0308709101
29. Marcheva B, Ramsey KM, Buhr ED, Kobayashi Y, Su H, Ko CH, et al. Disruption of the clock components CLOCK and BMAL1 leads to hypoinsulinaemia and diabetes. *Nature* (2010) 466:627–31. doi:10.1038/nature09253
30. Paschos GK, Ibrahim S, Song WL, Kunieda T, Grant G, Reyes TM, et al. Obesity in mice with adipocyte-specific deletion of clock component *Arntl*. *Nat Med* (2012) 18:1768–77. doi:10.1038/nm.2979
31. Lamia KA, Storch KF, Weitz CJ. Physiological significance of a peripheral tissue circadian clock. *Proc Natl Acad Sci U S A* (2008) 105:15172–7. doi:10.1073/pnas.0806717105
32. Kornmann B, Schaad O, Bujard H, Takahashi JS, Schibler U. System-driven and oscillator-dependent circadian transcription in mice with a conditionally active liver clock. *PLoS Biol* (2007) 5:e34. doi:10.1371/journal.pbio.0050034
33. Balsalobre A, Brown SA, Marcacci L, Tronche F, Kellendonk C, Reichardt HM, et al. Resetting of circadian time in peripheral tissues by glucocorticoid signaling. *Science* (2000) 289:2344–7. doi:10.1126/science.289.5488.2344
34. Brown SA, Zumbrunn G, Fleury-Olela F, Preitner N, Schibler U. Rhythms of mammalian body temperature can sustain peripheral circadian clocks. *Curr Biol* (2002) 12:1574–83. doi:10.1016/S0960-9822(02)01145-4
35. Vujović N, Davidson AJ, Menaker M. Sympathetic input modulates, but does not determine, phase of peripheral circadian oscillators. *Am J Physiol Regul Integr Comp Physiol* (2008) 295:R355–60. doi:10.1152/ajpregu.00498.2007
36. Damiola F, Le Minh N, Preitner N, Kornmann B, Fleury-Olela F, Schibler U. Restricted feeding uncouples circadian oscillators in peripheral tissues from the central pacemaker in the suprachiasmatic nucleus. *Genes Dev* (2000) 14:2950–61. doi:10.1101/gad.183500

37. Nagai K, Nishio T, Nakagawa H, Nakamura S, Fukuda Y. Effect of bilateral lesions of the suprachiasmatic nuclei on the circadian rhythm of food-intake. *Brain Res* (1978) 142:384–9. doi:10.1016/0006-8993(78)90648-0
38. Turek FW, Joshu C, Kohsaka A, Lin E, Ivanova G, McDearmon E, et al. Obesity and metabolic syndrome in circadian clock mutant mice. *Science* (2005) 308:1043–5. doi:10.1126/science.1108750
39. Vollmers C, Gill S, DiTacchio L, Pulivarthy SR, Le HD, Panda S. Time of feeding and the intrinsic circadian clock drive rhythms in hepatic gene expression. *Proc Natl Acad Sci U S A* (2009) 106:21453–21458. doi:10.1073/pnas.0909591106
40. Stokkan KA, Yamazaki S, Tei H, Sakaki Y, Menaker M. Entrainment of the circadian clock in the liver by feeding. *Science* (2001) 291:490–3. doi:10.1126/science.291.5503.490
41. Hara R, Wan K, Wakamatsu H, Aida R, Moriya T, Akiyama M, et al. Restricted feeding entrains liver clock without participation of the suprachiasmatic nucleus. *Genes Cells* (2001) 6:269–78. doi:10.1046/j.1365-2443.2001.00419.x
42. Saini C, Liani A, Curie T, Gos P, Kreppel F, Emmenegger Y, et al. Real-time recording of circadian liver gene expression in freely moving mice reveals the phase-setting behavior of hepatocyte clocks. *Genes Dev* (2013) 27:1526–36. doi:10.1101/gad.221374.113
43. Le Minh N, Damiola F, Tronche F, Schutz G, Schibler U. Glucocorticoid hormones inhibit food-induced phase-shifting of peripheral circadian oscillators. *EMBO J* (2001) 20:7128–36. doi:10.1093/emboj/20.24.7128
44. Buijs RM, Wortel J, Van Heerikhuize JJ, Feenstra MGP, Ter Horst GJ, Romijn HJ, et al. Anatomical and functional demonstration of a multisynaptic suprachiasmatic nucleus adrenal (cortex) pathway. *Eur J Neurosci* (1999) 11:1535–44. doi:10.1046/j.1460-9568.1999.00575.x
45. Ishida A, Mutoh T, Ueyama T, Bando H, Masubuchi S, Nakahara D, et al. Light activates the adrenal gland: timing of gene expression and glucocorticoid release. *Cell Metab* (2005) 2:297–307. doi:10.1016/j.cmet.2005.09.009
46. Reddy AB, Maywood ES, Karp NA, King VM, Inoue Y, Gonzalez FJ, et al. Glucocorticoid signaling synchronizes the liver circadian transcriptome. *Hepatology* (2007) 45:1478–88. doi:10.1002/hep.21571
47. Yamamoto T, Nakahata Y, Tanaka M, Yoshida M, Soma H, Shinohara K, et al. Acute physical stress elevates mouse *period1* mRNA expression in mouse peripheral tissues via a glucocorticoid-responsive element. *J Biol Chem* (2005) 280:42036–42043. doi:10.1074/jbc.M509600200
48. So AYL, Bernal TU, Pillsbury ML, Yamamoto KR, Feldman BJ. Glucocorticoid regulation of the circadian clock modulates glucose homeostasis. *Proc Natl Acad Sci U S A* (2009) 106:17582–7. doi:10.1073/pnas.0909733106
49. Weger BD, Weger M, Görling B, Schink A, Gobet C, Keime C, et al. Extensive regulation of diurnal transcription and metabolism by glucocorticoids. *PLoS Genet* (2016) 12:e1006512. doi:10.1371/journal.pgen.1006512
50. Buhr ED, Yoo SH, Takahashi JS. Temperature as a universal resetting cue for mammalian circadian oscillators. *Science* (2010) 330:379–85. doi:10.1126/science.1195262
51. Saini C, Morf J, Stratmann M, Gos P, Schibler U. Simulated body temperature rhythms reveal the phase-shifting behavior and plasticity of mammalian circadian oscillators. *Genes Dev* (2012) 26:567–80. doi:10.1101/gad.183251.111
52. Dibner C, Sage D, Unser M, Bauer C, d'Eysmond T, Naef F, et al. Circadian gene expression is resilient to large fluctuations in overall transcription rates. *EMBO J* (2009) 28:123–34. doi:10.1038/emboj.2008.262
53. Reinke H, Saini C, Fleury Olela F, Dibner C, Benjamin IJ, Schibler U. Differential display of DNA-binding proteins reveals heat-shock factor 1 as a circadian transcription factor. *Genes Dev* (2008) 22:331–45. doi:10.1101/gad.453808
54. Krieger DT, Hauser H, Krey LC. Suprachiasmatic nuclear lesions do not abolish food-shifted circadian adrenal and temperature rhythmicity. *Science* (1977) 197:398. doi:10.1126/science.877566
55. Stephan FK, Swann JM, Sisk CL. Entrainment of circadian rhythms by feeding schedules in rats with suprachiasmatic lesions. *Behav Neural Biol* (1979) 25:545–54. doi:10.1016/S0163-1047(79)90415-1
56. Gotic I, Omidi S, Fleury-Olela F, Molina N, Naef F, Schibler U. Temperature regulates splicing efficiency of the cold-inducible RNA-binding protein gene *Cirbp*. *Genes Dev* (2016) 30:2005–17. doi:10.1101/gad.287094.116
57. Krieger DT. Food and water restriction shifts corticosterone, temperature, activity and brain amine periodicity. *Endocrinology* (1974) 95:1195–201. doi:10.1210/endo-95-5-1195
58. Stephan FK. The "other" circadian system: food as a Zeitgeber. *J Biol Rhythms* (2002) 17:284–92. doi:10.1177/074873002129002591
59. Pitts S, Perone E, Silver R. Food-entrained circadian rhythms are sustained in arrhythmic *Clk/Clk* mutant mice. *Am J Physiol Regul Integr Comp Physiol* (2003) 285:R57–67. doi:10.1152/ajpregu.00023.2003
60. Storch KF, Weitz CJ. Daily rhythms of food-anticipatory behavioral activity do not require the known circadian clock. *Proc Natl Acad Sci U S A* (2009) 106:6808–13. doi:10.1073/pnas.0902063106
61. Laermans J, Vancleef L, Tack J, Depoortere I. Role of the clock gene Bmal1 and the gastric ghrelin-secreting cell in the circadian regulation of the ghrelin-GOAT system. *Sci Rep* (2015) 5:16748. doi:10.1038/srep16748
62. LeSauter J, Hoque N, Weintraub M, Pfaff DW, Silver R. Stomach ghrelin-secreting cells as food-entrainable circadian clocks. *Proc Natl Acad Sci U S A* (2009) 106:13582–7. doi:10.1073/pnas.0906426106
63. Landgraf D, Tsang AH, Leliavski A, Koch CE, Barclay JL, Drucker DJ, et al. Oxyntomodulin regulates resetting of the liver circadian clock by food. *Elife* (2015) 4:e06253. doi:10.7554/eLife.06253
64. Chavan R, Feillet C, Costa SSF, Delorme JE, Okabe T, Ripperger JA, et al. Liver-derived ketone bodies are necessary for food anticipation. *Nat Commun* (2016) 7:10580. doi:10.1038/ncomms10580
65. Feillet CA, Ripperger JA, Magnone MC, Dulloo A, Albrecht U, Challet E. Lack of food anticipation in *Per2* mutant mice. *Curr Biol* (2006) 16:2016–22. doi:10.1016/j.cub.2006.08.053
66. Kettner NM, Mayo SA, Hua J, Lee C, Moore DD, Fu L. Circadian dysfunction induces leptin resistance in mice. *Cell Metab* (2015) 22:448–59. doi:10.1016/j.cmet.2015.06.005
67. Koike N, Yoo SH, Huang HC, Kumar V, Lee C, Kim TK, et al. Transcriptional architecture and chromatin landscape of the core circadian clock in mammals. *Science* (2012) 338:349–54. doi:10.1126/science.1226339
68. Ripperger JA, Schibler U. Rhythmic CLOCK-BMAL1 binding to multiple E-box motifs drives circadian *Dbp* transcription and chromatin transitions. *Nat Genet* (2006) 38:369–74. doi:10.1038/ng1738
69. Panda S, Antoch MP, Miller BH, Su AI, Schook AB, Straume M, et al. Coordinated transcription of key pathways in the mouse by the circadian clock. *Cell* (2002) 109:307–20. doi:10.1016/S0092-8674(02)00722-5
70. Storch KF, Lipan O, Leykin I, Viswanathan N, Davis FC, Wong WH, et al. Extensive and divergent circadian gene expression in liver and heart. *Nature* (2002) 417:78–83. doi:10.1038/nature744
71. Ueda HR, Chen W, Adachi A, Wakamatsu H, Hayashi S, Takasugi T, et al. A transcription factor response element for gene expression during circadian night. *Nature* (2002) 418:534–9. doi:10.1038/nature00906
72. Grimaldi B, Bellet MM, Katada S, Astarita G, Hirayama J, Amin RH, et al. PER2 controls lipid metabolism by direct regulation of PPARg. *Cell Metab* (2010) 12:509–20. doi:10.1016/j.cmet.2010.10.005
73. Schmutz I, Ripperger JA, Baeriswyl-Aebischer S, Albrecht U. The mammalian clock component PERIOD2 coordinates circadian output by interaction with nuclear receptors. *Genes Dev* (2010) 24:345–57. doi:10.1101/gad.564110
74. Cho H, Zhao X, Hatori M, Yu RT, Barish GD, Lam MT, et al. Regulation of circadian behaviour and metabolism by REV-ERB-α and REV-ERB-β. *Nature* (2012) 485:123–7. doi:10.1038/nature11048
75. Zhang Y, Fang B, Emmett MJ, Damle M, Sun Z, Feng D, et al. Discrete functions of nuclear receptor Rev-erbα couple metabolism to the clock. *Science* (2015) 348:1488–92. doi:10.1126/science.aab3021
76. Lamia KA, Papp SJ, Yu RT, Barish GD, Uhlenhaut NH, Jonker JW, et al. Cryptochromes mediate rhythmic repression of the glucocorticoid receptor. *Nature* (2011) 480:552–6. doi:10.1038/nature10700
77. Gachon F, Leuenberger N, Claudel T, Gos P, Jouffe C, Fleury Olela F, et al. Proline- and acidic amino acid-rich basic leucine zipper proteins modulate peroxisome proliferator-activated receptor α (PPARα) activity. *Proc Natl Acad Sci U S A* (2011) 108:4794–9. doi:10.1073/pnas.1002862108
78. Gilardi F, Migliavacca E, Naldi A, Baruchet M, Canella D, Le Martelot G, et al. Genome-wide analysis of SREBP1 activity around the clock reveals its combined dependency on nutrient and circadian signals. *PLoS Genet* (2014) 10:e1004155. doi:10.1371/journal.pgen.1004155

79. Le Martelot G, Claudel T, Gatfield D, Schaad O, Kornmann B, Sasso GL, et al. REV-ERBα participates in circadian SREBP signaling and bile acid homeostasis. *PLoS Biol* (2009) 7:e1000181. doi:10.1371/journal.pbio.1000181
80. Brewer M, Lange D, Baler R, Anzulovich A. SREBP-1 as a transcriptional integrator of circadian and nutritional cues in the liver. *J Biol Rhythms* (2005) 20:195–205. doi:10.1177/0748730405275952
81. Menet JS, Rodriguez J, Abruzzi KC, Rosbash M. Nascent-Seq reveals novel features of mouse circadian transcriptional regulation. *Elife* (2012) 1:e00011. doi:10.7554/eLife.00011
82. Le Martelot G, Canella D, Symul L, Migliavacca E, Gilardi F, Liechti R, et al. Genome-wide RNA polymerase II profiles and RNA accumulation reveal kinetics of transcription and associated epigenetic changes during diurnal cycles. *PLoS Biol* (2012) 10:e1001442. doi:10.1371/journal.pbio.1001442
83. Atger F, Gobet C, Marquis J, Martin E, Wang J, Weger B, et al. Circadian and feeding rhythms differentially affect rhythmic mRNA transcription and translation in mouse liver. *Proc Natl Acad Sci U S A* (2015) 112:E6579–88. doi:10.1073/pnas.1515308112
84. Lück S, Thurley K, Thaben PF, Westermark PO. Rhythmic degradation explains and unifies circadian transcriptome and proteome data. *Cell Rep* (2014) 9:741–51. doi:10.1016/j.celrep.2014.09.021
85. Hatori M, Vollmers C, Zarrinpar A, DiTacchio L, Bushong EA, Gill S, et al. Time-restricted feeding without reducing caloric intake prevents metabolic diseases in mice fed a high-fat diet. *Cell Metab* (2012) 15:848–60. doi:10.1016/j.cmet.2012.04.019
86. Reddy AB, Karp NA, Maywood ES, Sage EA, Deery M, O'Neill JS, et al. Circadian orchestration of the hepatic proteome. *Curr Biol* (2006) 16:1107–15. doi:10.1016/j.cub.2006.04.026
87. Chiang CK, Mehta N, Patel A, Zhang P, Ning Z, Mayne J, et al. The proteomic landscape of the suprachiasmatic nucleus clock reveals large-scale coordination of key biological processes. *PLoS Genet* (2014) 10:e1004695. doi:10.1371/journal.pgen.1004695
88. Robles MS, Cox J, Mann M. In-vivo quantitative proteomics reveals a key contribution of post-transcriptional mechanisms to the circadian regulation of liver metabolism. *PLoS Genet* (2014) 10:e1004047. doi:10.1371/journal.pgen.1004047
89. Mauvoisin D, Wang J, Jouffe C, Martin E, Atger F, Waridel P, et al. Circadian clock-dependent and -independent rhythmic proteomes implement distinct diurnal functions in mouse liver. *Proc Natl Acad Sci U S A* (2014) 111:167–72. doi:10.1073/pnas.1314066111
90. Neufeld-Cohen A, Robles MS, Aviram R, Manella G, Adamovich Y, Ladeuix B, et al. Circadian control of oscillations in mitochondrial rate-limiting enzymes and nutrient utilization by PERIOD proteins. *Proc Natl Acad Sci U S A* (2016) 113:E1673–82. doi:10.1073/pnas.1519650113
91. Wang J, Mauvoisin D, Martin E, Atger F, Galindo AN, Dayon L, et al. Nuclear proteomics uncovers diurnal regulatory landscapes in mouse liver. *Cell Metab* (2017) 25:102–17. doi:10.1016/j.cmet.2016.10.003
92. Sweeney BM, Haxo FT. Persistence of a photosynthetic rhythm in enucleated *Acetabularia*. *Science* (1961) 134:1361–3. doi:10.1126/science.134.3487.1361
93. Schweiger E, Wallraff HG, Schweiger HG. Endogenous circadian rhythm in cytoplasm of *Acetabularia*: influence of the nucleus. *Science* (1964) 146:658–9. doi:10.1126/science.146.3644.658
94. Woolum JC. A re-examination of the role of the nucleus in generating the circadian rhythm in *Acetabularia*. *J Biol Rhythms* (1991) 6:129–36. doi:10.1177/074873049100600203
95. Hartwig R, Schweiger M, Schweiger R, Schweiger HG. Identification of a high molecular weight polypeptide that may be part of the circadian clockwork in *Acetabularia*. *Proc Natl Acad Sci U S A* (1985) 82:6899–902. doi:10.1073/pnas.82.20.6899
96. Hastings JW. The *Gonyaulax* clock at 50: translational control of circadian expression. *Cold Spring Harb Symp Quant Biol* (2007) 72:141–4. doi:10.1101/sqb.2007.72.026
97. Johnson CH, Roeber JF, Hastings JW. Circadian changes in enzyme concentration account for rhythm of enzyme activity in *Gonyaulax*. *Science* (1984) 223:1428–30. doi:10.1126/science.223.4643.1428
98. Morse D, Milos PM, Roux E, Hastings JW. Circadian regulation of bioluminescence in *Gonyaulax* involves translational control. *Proc Natl Acad Sci U S A* (1989) 86:172–6. doi:10.1073/pnas.86.1.172
99. Mittag M, Lee DH, Hastings JW. Circadian expression of the luciferin-binding protein correlates with the binding of a protein to the 3' untranslated region of its mRNA. *Proc Natl Acad Sci U S A* (1994) 91:5257–61. doi:10.1073/pnas.91.12.5257
100. Fishman B, Wurtman RJ, Munro HN. Daily rhythms in hepatic polysome profiles and tyrosine transaminase activity: role of dietary protein. *Proc Natl Acad Sci U S A* (1969) 64:677–82. doi:10.1073/pnas.64.2.677
101. Uchiyama Y, Asari A. A morphometric study of the variations in subcellular structures of rat hepatocytes during 24 hours. *Cell Tissue Res* (1984) 236:305–15. doi:10.1007/BF00214231
102. Jouffe C, Cretenet G, Symul L, Martin E, Atger F, Naef F, et al. The circadian clock coordinates ribosome biogenesis. *PLoS Biol* (2013) 11:e1001455. doi:10.1371/journal.pbio.1001455
103. Meyuhas O, Kahan T. The race to decipher the top secrets of TOP mRNAs. *Biochim Biophys Acta* (2015) 1849:801–11. doi:10.1016/j.bbagrm.2014.08.015
104. Sinvani H, Haimov O, Svitkin Y, Sonenberg N, Tamarkin-Ben-Harush A, Viollet B, et al. Translational tolerance of mitochondrial genes to metabolic energy stress involves TISU and eIF1-eIF4GI cooperation in start codon selection. *Cell Metab* (2015) 21:479–92. doi:10.1016/j.cmet.2015.02.010
105. Hernandez-Verdun D. The nucleolus: a model for the organization of nuclear functions. *Histochem Cell Biol* (2006) 126:135–48. doi:10.1007/s00418-006-0212-3
106. Seïte R, Pébusque MJ. Chronobiological studies on the nucleolus. *Chronobiol Int* (1985) 2:69–91. doi:10.3109/07420528509055546
107. Robinson BG, Frim DM, Schwartz WJ, Majzoub JA. Vasopressin mRNA in the suprachiasmatic nuclei: daily regulation of polyadenylate tail length. *Science* (1988) 241:342–4. doi:10.1126/science.3388044
108. Kojima S, Sher-Chen EL, Green CB. Circadian control of mRNA polyadenylation dynamics regulates rhythmic protein expression. *Genes Dev* (2012) 26:2724–36. doi:10.1101/gad.208306.112
109. Stubblefield JJ, Terrien J, Green CB. Nocturnin: at the crossroads of clocks and metabolism. *Trends Endocrinol Metab* (2012) 23:326–33. doi:10.1016/j.tem.2012.03.007
110. Kojima S, Gendreau KL, Sher-Chen EL, Gao P, Green CB. Changes in poly(A) tail length dynamics from the loss of the circadian deadenylase Nocturnin. *Sci Rep* (2015) 5:17059. doi:10.1038/srep17059
111. Peek CB, Affinati AH, Ramsey KM, Kuo HY, Yu W, Sena LA, et al. Circadian clock NAD^+ cycle drives mitochondrial oxidative metabolism in mice. *Science* (2013) 342:1243417. doi:10.1126/science.1243417
112. Jacobi D, Liu S, Burkewitz K, Kory N, Knudsen NH, Alexander RK, et al. Hepatic Bmal1 regulates rhythmic mitochondrial dynamics and promotes metabolic fitness. *Cell Metab* (2015) 22:709–20. doi:10.1016/j.cmet.2015.08.006
113. Woldt E, Sebti Y, Solt LA, Duhem C, Lancel S, Eeckhoute J, et al. Rev-erb-α modulates skeletal muscle oxidative capacity by regulating mitochondrial biogenesis and autophagy. *Nat Med* (2013) 19:1039–46. doi:10.1038/nm.3213
114. Fahrenkrug J, Hannibal J, Honoré B, Vorum H. Altered calmodulin response to light in the suprachiasmatic nucleus of PAC1 receptor knockout mice revealed by proteomic analysis. *J Mol Neurosci* (2005) 25:251–8. doi:10.1385/JMN:25:3:251
115. Møller M, Sparre T, Bache N, Roepstorff P, Vorum H. Proteomic analysis of day-night variations in protein levels in the rat pineal gland. *Proteomics* (2007) 7:2009–18. doi:10.1002/pmic.200600963
116. Tsuji T, Hirota T, Takemori N, Komori N, Yoshitane H, Fukuda M, et al. Circadian proteomics of the mouse retina. *Proteomics* (2007) 7:3500–8. doi:10.1002/pmic.200700272
117. Deery MJ, Maywood ES, Chesham JE, Sládek M, Karp NA, Green EW, et al. Proteomic analysis reveals the role of synaptic vesicle cycling in sustaining the suprachiasmatic circadian clock. *Curr Biol* (2009) 19:2031–6. doi:10.1016/j.cub.2009.10.024
118. Hatcher NG, Atkins N, Annangudi SP, Forbes AJ, Kelleher NL, Gillette MU, et al. Mass spectrometry-based discovery of circadian peptides. *Proc Natl Acad Sci U S A* (2008) 105:12527–32. doi:10.1073/pnas.0804340105
119. Lee JE, Atkins N, Hatcher NG, Zamdborg L, Gillette MU, Sweedler JV, et al. Endogenous peptide discovery of the rat circadian clock: a focused study of the suprachiasmatic nucleus by ultrahigh performance tandem

mass spectrometry. *Mol Cell Proteomics* (2010) 9:285–97. doi:10.1074/mcp.M900362-MCP200
120. Tian R, Alvarez-Saavedra M, Cheng HYM, Figeys D. Uncovering the proteome response of the master circadian clock to light using an autoproteome system. *Mol Cell Proteomics* (2011) 10:M110.007252. doi:10.1074/mcp.M110.007252
121. Bantscheff M, Lemeer S, Savitski MM, Kuster B. Quantitative mass spectrometry in proteomics: critical review update from 2007 to the present. *Anal Bioanal Chem* (2012) 404:939–65. doi:10.1007/s00216-012-6203-4
122. Lee JE, Zamdborg L, Southey BR, Atkins N, Mitchell JW, Li M, et al. Quantitative peptidomics for discovery of circadian-related peptides from the rat suprachiasmatic nucleus. *J Proteome Res* (2013) 12:585–93. doi:10.1021/pr300605p
123. Krüger M, Moser M, Ussar S, Thievessen I, Luber CA, Forner F, et al. SILAC mouse for quantitative proteomics uncovers kindlin-3 as an essential factor for red blood cell function. *Cell* (2008) 134:353–64. doi:10.1016/j.cell.2008.05.033
124. Martino TA, Tata N, Bjarnason GA, Straume M, Sole MJ. Diurnal protein expression in blood revealed by high throughput mass spectrometry proteomics and implications for translational medicine and body time of day. *Am J Physiol Regul Integr Comp Physiol* (2007) 293:R1430–7. doi:10.1152/ajpregu.00183.2007
125. Jang C, Lahens NF, Hogenesch JB, Sehgal A. Ribosome profiling reveals an important role for translational control in circadian gene expression. *Genome Res* (2015) 25:1836–47. doi:10.1101/gr.191296.115
126. Janich P, Arpat AB, Castelo-Szekely V, Lopes M, Gatfield D. Ribosome profiling reveals the rhythmic liver translatome and circadian clock regulation by upstream open reading frames. *Genome Res* (2015) 25:1848–59. doi:10.1101/gr.195404.115
127. Narumi R, Shimizu Y, Ukai-Tadenuma M, Ode KL, Kanda GN, Shinohara Y, et al. Mass spectrometry-based absolute quantification reveals rhythmic variation of mouse circadian clock proteins. *Proc Natl Acad Sci U S A* (2016) 113:E3461–7. doi:10.1073/pnas.1603799113
128. Sancar A, Lindsey-Boltz LA, Kang TH, Reardon JT, Lee JH, Ozturk N. Circadian clock control of the cellular response to DNA damage. *FEBS Lett* (2010) 584:2618–25. doi:10.1016/j.febslet.2010.03.017
129. O'Neill JS, Reddy AB. Circadian clocks in human red blood cells. *Nature* (2011) 469:498–503. doi:10.1038/nature09702
130. O'Neill JS, van Ooijen G, Dixon LE, Troein C, Corellou F, Bouget FY, et al. Circadian rhythms persist without transcription in a eukaryote. *Nature* (2011) 469:554–8. doi:10.1038/nature09654
131. Edgar RS, Green EW, Zhao Y, van Ooijen G, Olmedo M, Qin X, et al. Peroxiredoxins are conserved markers of circadian rhythms. *Nature* (2012) 485:459–64. doi:10.1038/nature11088
132. Rey G, Valekunja UK, Feeney KA, Wulund L, Milev NB, Stangherlin A, et al. The pentose phosphate pathway regulates the circadian clock. *Cell Metab* (2016) 24:462–73. doi:10.1016/j.cmet.2016.07.024
133. Asher G, Sassone-Corsi P. Time for food: the intimate interplay between nutrition, metabolism, and the circadian clock. *Cell* (2015) 161:84–92. doi:10.1016/j.cell.2015.03.015
134. Johnson CH, Mori T, Xu Y. A cyanobacterial circadian clockwork. *Curr Biol* (2008) 18:R816–25. doi:10.1016/j.cub.2008.07.012
135. Lamia KA, Sachdeva UM, DiTacchio L, Williams EC, Alvarez JG, Egan DF, et al. AMPK regulates the circadian clock by cryptochrome phosphorylation and degradation. *Science* (2009) 326:437–40. doi:10.1126/science.1172156
136. Robles MS, Humphrey SJ, Mann M. Phosphorylation is a central mechanism for circadian control of metabolism and physiology. *Cell Metab* (2017) 25:118–27. doi:10.1016/j.cmet.2016.10.004
137. Dang F, Sun X, Ma X, Wu R, Zhang D, Chen Y, et al. Insulin post-transcriptionally modulates Bmal1 protein to affect the hepatic circadian clock. *Nat Commun* (2016) 7:12696. doi:10.1038/ncomms12696
138. Khapre RV, Kondratova AA, Patel S, Dubrovsky Y, Wrobel M, Antoch MP, et al. BMAL1-dependent regulation of the mTOR signaling pathway delays aging. *Aging (Albany NY)* (2014) 6:48–57. doi:10.18632/aging.100633
139. Khapre RV, Patel SA, Kondratova AA, Chaudhary A, Velingkaar N, Antoch MP, et al. Metabolic clock generates nutrient anticipation rhythms in mTOR signaling. *Aging (Albany NY)* (2014) 6:675–89. doi:10.18632/aging.100686
140. Asher G, Gatfield D, Stratmann M, Reinke H, Dibner C, Kreppel F, et al. SIRT1 regulates circadian clock gene expression through PER2 deacetylation. *Cell* (2008) 134:317–28. doi:10.1016/j.cell.2008.06.050
141. Nakahata Y, Kaluzova M, Grimaldi B, Sahar S, Hirayama J, Chen D, et al. The NAD^+-dependent deacetylase SIRT1 modulates CLOCK-mediated chromatin remodeling and circadian control. *Cell* (2008) 134:329–40. doi:10.1016/j.cell.2008.07.002
142. Chang HC, Guarente L. SIRT1 mediates central circadian control in the SCN by a mechanism that decays with aging. *Cell* (2013) 153:1448–60. doi:10.1016/j.cell.2013.05.027
143. Feng D, Liu T, Sun Z, Bugge A, Mullican SE, Alenghat T, et al. Orchestrated by histone deacetylase 3 controls hepatic lipid metabolism. *Science* (2011) 331:1315–9. doi:10.1126/science.1198125
144. Masri S, Rigor P, Cervantes M, Ceglia N, Sebastian C, Xiao C, et al. Partitioning circadian transcription by SIRT6 leads to segregated control of cellular metabolism. *Cell* (2014) 158:659–72. doi:10.1016/j.cell.2014.06.050
145. Shin J, He M, Liu Y, Paredes S, Villanova L, Brown K, et al. SIRT7 represses Myc activity to suppress ER stress and prevent fatty liver disease. *Cell Rep* (2013) 5:654–65. doi:10.1016/j.celrep.2013.10.007
146. Tong Z, Wang M, Wang Y, Kim DD, Grenier JK, Cao J, et al. SIRT7 is an RNA-activated protein lysine deacylase. *ACS Chem Biol* (2017) 12:300–10. doi:10.1021/acschembio.6b00954
147. Wang YP, Zhou LS, Zhao YZ, Wang SW, Chen LL, Liu LX, et al. Regulation of G6PD acetylation by SIRT2 and KAT9 modulates NADPH homeostasis and cell survival during oxidative stress. *EMBO J* (2014) 33:1304–20. doi:10.1002/embj.201387224
148. Kaufmann T, Kukolj E, Brachner A, Beltzung E, Bruno M, Kostrhon S, et al. SIRT2 regulates nuclear envelope reassembly through ANKLE2 deacetylation. *J Cell Sci* (2016) 129:4607–21. doi:10.1242/jcs.192633
149. Masri S, Patel VR, Eckel-Mahan KL, Peleg S, Forne I, Ladurner AG, et al. Circadian acetylome reveals regulation of mitochondrial metabolic pathways. *Proc Natl Acad Sci U S A* (2013) 110:3339–44. doi:10.1073/pnas.1217632110
150. Nakahata Y, Sahar S, Astarita G, Kaluzova M, Sassone-Corsi P. Circadian control of the NAD^+ salvage pathway by CLOCK-SIRT1. *Science* (2009) 324:654–7. doi:10.1126/science.1170803
151. Ramsey KM, Yoshino J, Brace CS, Abrassart D, Kobayashi Y, Marcheva B, et al. Circadian clock feedback cycle through NAMPT-mediated NAD^+ biosynthesis. *Science* (2009) 324:651–4. doi:10.1126/science.1171641
152. Tremaroli V, Backhed F. Functional interactions between the gut microbiota and host metabolism. *Nature* (2012) 489:242–9. doi:10.1038/nature11552
153. Nieuwdorp M, Gilijamse PW, Pai N, Kaplan LM. Role of the microbiome in energy regulation and metabolism. *Gastroenterology* (2014) 146:1525–33. doi:10.1053/j.gastro.2014.02.008
154. Thaiss CA, Zeevi D, Levy M, Zilberman-Schapira G, Suez J, Tengeler AC, et al. Transkingdom control of microbiota diurnal oscillations promotes metabolic homeostasis. *Cell* (2014) 159:514–29. doi:10.1016/j.cell.2014.09.048
155. Zarrinpar A, Chaix A, Yooseph S, Panda S. Diet and feeding pattern affect the diurnal dynamics of the gut microbiome. *Cell Metab* (2014) 20:1006–17. doi:10.1016/j.cmet.2014.11.008
156. Liang X, Bushman FD, FitzGerald GA. Rhythmicity of the intestinal microbiota is regulated by gender and the host circadian clock. *Proc Natl Acad Sci U S A* (2015) 112:10479–84. doi:10.1073/pnas.1501305112
157. Leone V, Gibbons SM, Martinez K, Hutchison AL, Huang EY, Cham CM, et al. Effects of diurnal variation of gut microbes and high-fat feeding on host circadian clock function and metabolism. *Cell Host Microbe* (2015) 17:681–9. doi:10.1016/j.chom.2015.03.006
158. Thaiss CA, Levy M, Korem T, Dohnalová L, Shapiro H, Jaitin DA, et al. Microbiota diurnal rhythmicity programs host transcriptome oscillations. *Cell* (2016) 167:1495.e–510.e. doi:10.1016/j.cell.2016.11.003
159. Voigt RM, Forsyth CB, Green SJ, Mutlu E, Engen P, Vitaterna MH, et al. Circadian disorganization alters intestinal microbiota. *PLoS One* (2014) 9:e97500. doi:10.1371/journal.pone.0097500
160. Mukherji A, Kobiita A, Ye T, Chambon P. Homeostasis in intestinal epithelium is orchestrated by the circadian clock and microbiota cues transduced by TLRs. *Cell* (2013) 153:812–27. doi:10.1016/j.cell.2013.04.020

161. Montagner A, Korecka A, Polizzi A, Lippi Y, Blum Y, Canlet C, et al. Hepatic circadian clock oscillators and nuclear receptors integrate microbiome-derived signals. *Sci Rep* (2016) 6:20127. doi:10.1038/srep20127
162. Fetissov SO. Role of the gut microbiota in host appetite control: bacterial growth to animal feeding behaviour. *Nat Rev Endocrinol* (2017) 13:11–25. doi:10.1038/nrendo.2016.150
163. Chaix A, Zarrinpar A, Miu P, Panda S. Time-restricted feeding is a preventative and therapeutic intervention against diverse nutritional challenges. *Cell Metab* (2014) 20:991–1005. doi:10.1016/j.cmet.2014.11.001
164. Sundaram S, Yan L. Time-restricted feeding reduces adiposity in mice fed a high-fat diet. *Nutr Res* (2016) 36:603–11. doi:10.1016/j.nutres.2016.02.005
165. Duncan MJ, Smith JT, Narbaiza J, Mueez F, Bustle LB, Qureshi S, et al. Restricting feeding to the active phase in middle-aged mice attenuates adverse metabolic effects of a high-fat diet. *Physiol Behav* (2016) 167:1–9. doi:10.1016/j.physbeh.2016.08.027
166. Sherman H, Genzer Y, Cohen R, Chapnik N, Madar Z, Froy O. Timed high-fat diet resets circadian metabolism and prevents obesity. *FASEB J* (2012) 26:3493–502. doi:10.1096/fj.12-208868
167. Gill S, Panda S. A smartphone app reveals erratic diurnal eating patterns in humans that can be modulated for health benefits. *Cell Metab* (2015) 22:789–98. doi:10.1016/j.cmet.2015.09.005
168. Jakubowicz D, Barnea M, Wainstein J, Froy O. High caloric intake at breakfast vs. dinner differentially influences weight loss of overweight and obese women. *Obesity (Silver Spring)* (2013) 21:2504–12. doi:10.1002/oby.20460
169. Oike H, Oishi K, Kobori M. Nutrients, clock genes, and chrononutrition. *Curr Nutr Rep* (2014) 3:204–12. doi:10.1007/s13668-014-0082-6

14

Abnormal Sleep, Circadian Rhythm Disruption, and Delirium in the ICU: Are they Related?

Marietou Daou [1,2], Irene Telias [1,2,3,4], Magdy Younes [5], Laurent Brochard [1,3,4] and M. Elizabeth Wilcox [1,2]*

[1] Interdepartment Division of Critical Care Medicine, University of Toronto, Toronto, ON, Canada, [2] Department of Medicine (Respirology), University Health Network, Toronto, ON, Canada, [3] Department of Medicine (Critical Care Medicine), St. Michael's Hospital, Toronto, ON, Canada, [4] Keenan Research Centre, Li Ka Shing Knowledge Institute, Toronto, ON, Canada, [5] Sleep Disorders Centre, Winnipeg, MB, Canada

Edited by:
Sairam Parthasarathy,
University of Arizona, United States

Reviewed by:
Gregory M. Brown,
University of Toronto, Canada
Mikhail G. Poluektov,
I. M. Sechenov First Moscow State Medical University, Russia

***Correspondence:**
M. Elizabeth Wilcox
elizabeth.wilcox@utoronto.ca

Delirium is a syndrome characterized by acute brain failure resulting in neurocognitive disturbances affecting attention, awareness, and cognition. It is highly prevalent among critically ill patients and is associated with increased morbidity and mortality. A core domain of delirium is represented by behavioral disturbances in sleep-wake cycle probably related to circadian rhythm disruption. The relationship between sleep, circadian rhythm and intensive care unit (ICU)-acquired delirium is complex and likely bidirectional. In this review, we explore the proposed pathophysiological mechanisms of sleep disruption and circadian dysrhythmia as possible contributing factors in transitioning to delirium in the ICU and highlight some of the most relevant caveats for understanding the relationship between these complex phenomena. Specifically, we will (1) review the physiological consequences of poor sleep quality and efficiency; (2) explore how the neural substrate underlying the circadian clock functions may be disrupted in delirium; (3) discuss the role of sedative drugs as contributors to delirium and chrono-disruption; and, (4) describe the association between abnormal sleep-pathological wakefulness, circadian dysrhythmia, delirium and critical illness. Opportunities to improve sleep and readjust circadian rhythmicity to realign the circadian clock may exist as therapeutic targets in both the prevention and treatment of delirium in the ICU. Further research is required to better define these conditions and understand the underlying physiologic relationship to develop effective prevention and therapeutic strategies.

Keywords: ICU acquired delirium, sleep, circadian rhythm, intervention, mechanisms

INTRODUCTION

Delirium is a syndrome characterized by acute brain failure typically arising over hours or few days that leads to a change in mental state (1–3). It primarily results in disturbances in attention (the ability of directing, focusing, sustaining, and shifting attention) and awareness of the environment (3). Prevalence can be as high as 80% in elderly patients receiving mechanical ventilation (4, 5). Delirium is associated with significant morbidity and mortality in the intensive care unit (ICU).

Risk factors for delirium include acute illness, coma, more severe illness, emergency surgery, polytrauma, and mechanical ventilation; patient characteristics that are related to a higher risk of developing delirium include age and chronic conditions (e.g., dementia, hypertension) (6, 7). Environmental characteristics specific to the ICU and related to sleep and circadian rhythm disruption (8) may worsen symptoms. Such factors include the lack of normal variability in light-dark cycle (9), noise (10), the use of mechanical ventilation (11, 12), and need for continuous infusions of sedative drugs (13). The available literature suggests that there may be a close relationship between delirium, sleep, circadian rhythm, and critical illness, however, no causal pathway has been yet clearly described or the directionality of the relationship understood.

ASSOCIATION BETWEEN SLEEP DISTURBANCES AND DELIRIUM

Sleep architecture changes throughout an individual's lifespan to support proper development and physiological function (14, 15). Normal sleep architecture varies among individuals but is made up of cycles of rapid eye movement (REM) and the 3 stages of non-REM (NREM) sleep; as an example, "normal" sleep in a healthy adult might be made up of 2–5% stage 1, 45–55% stage 2, 3–15% stage 3, or slow wave sleep and 20–25% REM (16). Transition from wake to sleep onset occurs within 10–20 min and the first period of REM typically occurs within 90–120 min. Poor sleep is associated with both neuropsychological and cognitive impairment (17). In a study by Zhou et al. (18) induced sleep deprivation in 13 young healthy men (mean age 23 yrs.) was associated with impairment in both attention and psychomotor vigilance. Further, in a study of 66 healthy adult volunteers chronic sleep deprivation was associated with increased reaction time to visual stimulus; experienced impairment was dose-dependent and variable time to recovery to baseline cognition was seen between individuals once normal sleep restored (19).

Poor sleep is common in the ICU (20, 21). Critically ill patients experience increases in stages 1 and 2 sleep with frequent arousals and awakenings. Further, they are less likely to transition into stage 3 or slow wave sleep or REM sleep (22–24). Poor sleep has been associated with delirium and other outcomes such as length of stay and long-term cognitive impairment (25–28). Additionally, there is a general believe among ICU clinicians that poor sleep is a risk factor for delirium as shown in a recent global survey, 97% of 1,223 ICU physicians and nurses (29). Moreover, the 2018 Clinical Practice Guidelines for Pain, Agitation, and Delirium (PAD), from the Society of Critical Care Medicine recommended using a sleep-promoting, multicomponent protocol in critically ill adults based on the pooled analysis of three observational before-after studies demonstrating an overall reduction in the prevalence of delirium when sleep promoting interventions were used (30, 31). Although a direct relationship between ICU delirium and sleep has yet to be shown, in long-term follow-up, total duration of ICU delirium was found by Altman et al. (32) to be significantly associated with increased sleep disturbance at long-term follow-up (mean 5 months after hospital discharge).

NEURAL NETWORKS INVOLVED IN CIRCADIAN DYSRHYTHMIA AND DELIRIUM

Two primary processes, the homeostatic process (Process S) interacts with the Process C, controlled by the circadian pacemaker to control the normal sleep-wake cycle, with time courses regulated from physiological and behavioral variables (33). The suprachiasmatic nucleus (SCN) acts as a central pacemaker coordinating daily physiological and behavioral cycles. The SCN is a neural network that entrains peripheral cellular clocks across the body achieving circadian control of behavior, neuroendocrine and autonomic signals in target tissues (34).

The circadian rhythm appears to be disrupted commonly in critically ill patients (35–40). It is hypothesized that chronodisruption may be associated with ICU-acquired delirium. Alterations in the structure and function of specific neural networks represent potential substrates for this relationship. Among patients with impaired consciousness during vegetative or comatose states resting state functional magnetic resonance imaging (MRI) showed a reduction in connectivity of posteromedial and anteromedial cortices as well as temporoparietal junctions with worsening impairment in consciousness (41). The posteromedial cortex, including the posterior cingulate cortex is responsible for maintenance of wakefulness and consciousness (42). In 22 medical inpatients with delirium, Choi et al. (43) found abnormalities in functional connectivity of the posterior cingulate cortex, intralaminar thalamic nuclei, and mesencephalic networks, including the nucleus basalis and the ventral tegmental area, part of the ascending reticular activating system (ARAS), during episodes of delirium. Interestingly, abnormal resting state connectivity of the SCN, as assessed by functional MRI, has been identified by Kyeong et al. (44) as a possible substrate for chronodisruption in 34 delirious patients admitted to various inpatient units for various medical conditions. In this study, abnormal resting state connectivity between the SCN, cortical nodes including the posteromedial/anteromedial cortices, and temporoparietal junctions, and subcortical regions was seen in delirious patients (44).

An important hallmark of delirium is decreased activity of the ARAS (5): a neuronal network located in the brainstem that controls wake, sleep and dreaming states through connections with the SCN and releasing acetylcholine during the individual's active phase (45). In delirium, due to transient hypoxic states, the depletion of acetylcholinergic projections and the dopaminergic overproduction from the ARAS result in alertness and attention disturbances (5, 46). Normal circadian distribution of sleep-wakefulness states has been attributed to the intimate relationship between the SCN and cholinergic neurons within the ARAS such as the locus coeruleus (47, 48). However, despite consistently described alterations in melatonin metabolism in critically ill

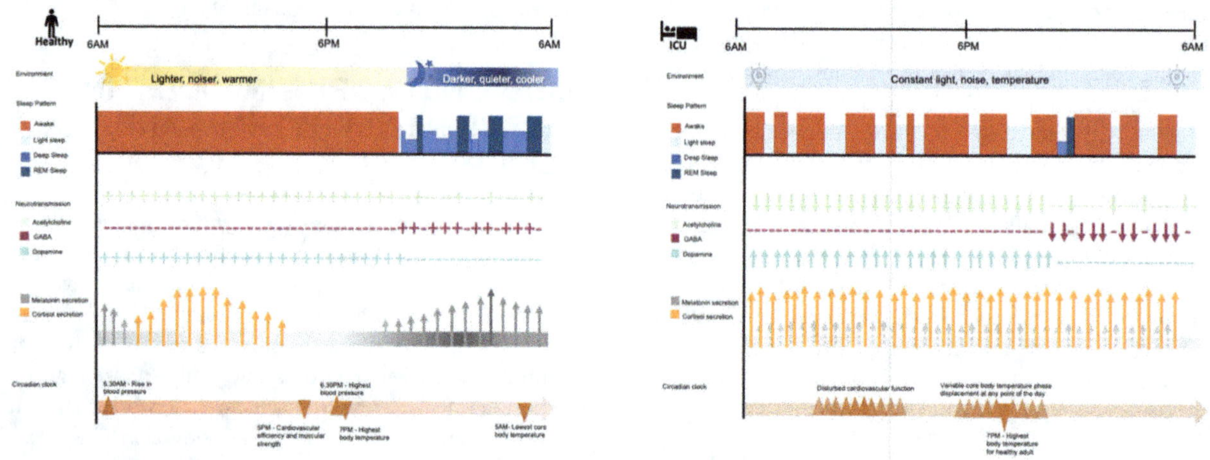

FIGURE 1 | Comparison of sleep and circadian rhythms in healthy adult and adult with critical illness in the ICU. In a healthy adult, the circadian clock is synced to the daily external cycle of changing light, sound, and temperature. The sleep stage of a healthy adult occurs during the night and is composed of 2–5% light sleep, 48–70% deep sleep, 20–25% rapid eye movement (REM) sleep. REM sleep reoccurs in cycles of 90–120 min. Acetylcholine is predominantly discharged during wakefulness and REM sleep; while GABAergic activity is predominant during deep sleep. Dopaminergic activity promotes alertness and reduces sleep. Melatonin secretion starts around 9.30 pm (dim light melatonin onset) and stops around 7.30 am, peaking around 3 am. Cortisol secretion starts in the early morning, peaks around 10 am in correspondence to the time of highest alertness, and keeps declining gradually throughout the day, and the night. Overall, these processes coordinate physiological functions including cardiovascular functions and temperature. In contrast, the intensive care unit (ICU) constant artificial environment disrupts the daily cycle of circadian functions. In the ICU critically ill patients, compared to healthy adults, present equal to normal sleep time in the course of 24 h but the majority of it consists of light sleep; 50% of sleep time is distributed during the day and disturbed by frequent arousals. For instance, benzodiazepine decrease sleep latency, slow wave sleep (SWS) and REM sleep duration and frequency; propofol suppresses SWS EEG bursts; opioids alter REM sleep; while, dexmedetomidine improve stage 2 and sleep efficiency by shifting 75% of sleep to nighttime. In ICU patients, the acute stress environment has been associated with decreased GABAergic and cholinergic transmission, and increased dopaminergic transmission, impaired melatonin secretion and increased cortisol production, along with displacement of physiological functions normally coordinated by the circadian clock. These disturbances have been associated with symptoms of delirium. ICU, intensive care unit; REM, rapid eye movement; GABA, gamma-aminobutyric acid.

patients (36, 40, 49, 50), abnormalities in circadian connectivity seen on neuroimaging studies were not associated with measured melatonin levels.

BIOCHEMICAL SUBSTRATE OF SLEEP DISTURBANCES, CIRCADIAN DYSRHYTHMIA, AND DELIRIUM IN CRITICAL ILLNESS

Abnormal sleep architecture (20), circadian dysrhythmia (8), and delirium (51–53) are all common in the ICU. Disturbance in sleep-wake cycle, alertness and altered sensorium often have multiple possible etiologies and likely share attributable pathophysiological mechanisms (See **Figure 1**).

Gamma-Aminobutyric Acid(GABA)-Ergic Mechanisms

The upregulation of GABA-A receptors, either through an increase in synthesis of endogenous GABA agonists or stimulation from exogenous GABA agonists, has been implicated in delirium (54, 55). GABA-ergic agents are thought to destabilize neurons preventing sleep transition (55), and upregulate inhibitory tone in the central nervous system contributing to neural connectivity and cognitive disintegration (56). Both benzodiazepines and propofol, commonly administered sedatives in the ICU, mediate their effect by modulating the effects of GABA. Zaal et al. (13) demonstrated that continuous infusion as compared to intermittent bolus dosing was associated with delirium; suggesting that higher doses or greater exposure is an important factor in transitioning to delirium. Although the interpretation of sleep in the ICU can be difficult in sedated patients, benzodiazepines typically increase total sleep time through prolonging stage 2 NREM, while suppressing both stage 3 NREM or slow wave sleep and REM (57). Propofol has been shown to worsen overall sleep architecture; specifically, suppressing REM sleep (58).

In contrast to the potentially deleterious effects of GABA agonists, the use of the alpha-2 agonist dexmedetomidine has been shown to be relatively effective in decreasing the daily prevalence of delirium in mechanically ventilated ICU patients (59). Dexmedetomidine is a highly selective alpha-2 agonist that facilitates both sedation and analgesia, without much respiratory depression. It appears to be particularly effective in lowering the daily prevalence and duration of delirium when compared with benzodiazepines, such as lorazepam, the comparator in the randomized, double-blind MENDS trial (60). The daily prevalence of delirium in dexmedetomidine-treated patients was also significantly lower when compared to a midazolam group in the randomized, double-blind SEDCOM trial (61).

Recently, the prophylactic use of nocturnal dexmedetomidine was shown to reduce the incidence of delirium in the SKY-DEX trial (62). In the DahLIA, placebo-controlled trial (63), 74 mechanically ventilated patients with agitation and delirium were randomized to dexmedetomidine or placebo; patients treated with dexmedetomidine had increased ventilator-free hours at 7 days (median, 145 vs. 128 h) and faster resolution of their delirium symptoms (median, 23 vs. 40 h). The effect of dexmedetomidine on delirium prevention may be mediated both through its reduction in glutamate release, as glutamate toxicity has been previously associated with the development of delirium (64), but also through its decreased GABA receptor modulation or cholinergic receptor activity when compared to other commonly used sedatives (65). Furthermore, dexmedetomidine through the stimulation of alpha-2 receptors and resultant inhibition of noradrenergic neurons in the locus coeruleus and disinhibition of GABA neurons in the ventrolateral preoptic nucleus it may promote more natural sleep in the ICU environment (66).

Melatonergic Mechanisms

Disturbed melatonergic activity is also implicated in delirium pathogenesis. Risk factors for delirium including pre-existing cognitive impairment, old age, and psychotropic medication use are all associated with impaired melatonergic function. Melatonin deficiency and abnormal secretion contribute to impairment of the sleep-wake cycle. Perras et al. (67) report that the normal response of melatonin secretion to changes in light and darkness is impaired in critically ill patients suggesting a dysregulation of the mechanism of melatonin secretion or a shift in the circadian clock phase in the SCN. Altered urinary levels of the melatonin metabolite 6-sulfatoxymelatonin (6-SMT) has been reported in delirious patients as compared to patients who were not delirious; levels were elevated in hypoactive patients and lower in hyperactive patients (68). Urinary 6-SMT exhibited loss of circadian rhythmicity with no daytime decline in septic patients (36), a frequently present in critical illness. Recently, Li et al. (69) measured plasma levels of melatonin, TNF-α, IL-6 and messenger RNA of the circadian genes Cry-1 and Per-2 for 24-h in septic and non-septic ICU patients ($n = 22$). Altered circadian rhythm of melatonin secretion, reduced expression of Cry-1 and Per-2, and elevated levels of TNF-α and IL-6 were again seen in patients with sepsis (69).

Hypothalamic-Pituitary-Adrenal-Stress Axis

Hypothalamic-pituitary-adrenal-stress axis (HPA) dysregulation might also be related to incident delirium and circadian dysrhythmia and is intimately related to the SCN and melatonergic functions. Elevated plasma cortisol levels are associated with increased delirium risk after both cardiac- (70) and non-cardiac surgery (71). Pearson et al. (72) found that in post-operative patients over the age of 60 years with acute hip fracture, cortisol CSF levels were elevated in those who developed delirium as compared to those who did not. It has been postulated that aberrant stress responses related to disrupted function in the limbic-HPA axis and its interaction with the inflammatory response may be responsible for the increased risk of delirium with age as well as pre-existing cognitive impairment (73). In a cohort of ICU patients with severe sepsis and septic shock ($n = 140$), plasma cortisol level between 6 and 12 h post hemodynamic stabilization (odds ratio [OR]: 2.3, 95% CI 2.0–3.2; $p = 0.02$) and the combination of older age and plasma cortisol level (OR: 1.0, 95% CI 1.0–1.9; $p = 0.04$) were associated with increase delirium risk (74).

STRATEGIES TO IMPROVE SLEEP AND REALIGN CIRCADIAN RHYTHM IN THE ICU

Numerous opportunities exist to improve sleep and re-entrain circadian rhythm in the ICU. Easily modifiable risk factors associated with disruption of sleep and circadian rhythm such as mechanical ventilation strategies paired with sedation stewardship and multicomponent sleep improvement strategies in the ICU may help to reduce delirium duration or severity and facilitate recovery from critical illness (75) (See **Table 1**).

Mechanical Ventilation

Relationship between mechanical ventilation, sleep disturbances and circadian dysrhythmia are not well-understood as they are complex and likely associated with variation in the administration of sedative agents and subsequent patient-ventilator asynchrony management (8). However, this relationship strongly influences the weaning process as sleep disturbances and delirium are associated with greater duration of mechanical ventilation and prolonged ICU length of stay (78–80). An opportunity must therefore exist for intervention with the aim of modifying ventilator settings and practices for improving sleep and circadian rhythmicity.

Sedation is commonly used to help patients tolerate mechanical ventilation. The 2018 PADIS Clinical Guidelines recommend the use of light levels of sedation (Richmond Agitation Sedation Score of −2 to +1) during invasive mechanical ventilation (30). This inevitably results in patients breathing spontaneously during assisted ventilation and resultant abnormal patient-ventilator interactions named asynchronies. The typical reaction of physicians to the presence of asynchronies involves the administration of additional sedation boluses or increasing the dose of sedative infusions which can significantly affect sleep architecture, circadian rhythmicity and delirium risk. However, not all asynchronies are "improved" (81) with sedation (82, 83). Therefore, an understanding of the mechanisms leading to the experienced asynchrony and personalized adjustment of ventilator settings (81) might spare a patient from further exposure to sedative agents, possibly mitigating further risk of sleep and circadian rhythm disruption. The titration of pressure support settings during non-invasive ventilation by adjusting the amount of support to meet the needs of the patient has previously been shown to decrease the number of asynchronies and improve sleep architecture in patients with chronic neuromuscular diseases (84).

TABLE 1 | Strategies to improve sleep and realign circadian rhythm in the ICU.

Intervention	Mechanism	Evidence
Increase light-dark contrast in the ICU	Loss of exposure to natural light is associated with circadian rhythm disruption that may impact incident delirium and outcomes in critically ill patients	Existing evidence does not support routine light therapy in isolation, the optimal dose, timing, and patient population require further investigation and it may be that light therapy is best deployed as part of a multicomponent strategy
Melatonin therapy	Potential role of melatonin to regulate the circadian distribution of sleep and prevent ICU-acquired delirium	General interest in the potential prophylactic use of melatonin but no current recommendations exist supporting the exogenous administration of melatonin to treat ICU-acquired delirium • Recent meta-analysis indicated that the peri-operative supplementation of melatonin agonists reduced the risk of transitioning into delirium to 37% compared to placebo or no treatment ($p = 0.006$) (76) • Investigators are currently evaluating the use of melatonin as a prophylactic agent for delirium prevention in the ICU (77)
Mechanical ventilation	Relationship between mechanical ventilation, sleep disturbances, and circadian dysrhythmia not well-understood and likely complex as relate to the use of sedative agents	Attention should be paid to reducing over-assistance with pressure support ventilation and, as available, clinicians should consider modes such as proportional assist-ventilation, and neurally adjust ventilatory assist

Caution however needs to be exercised as over-assistance during pressure support can alternately lead to central apneas with resultant poor sleep, characterized by frequently awakenings and arousals leading to greater sleep fragmentation (85, 86). Ventilatory support in excess to a patient's metabolic need results in hyperventilation where CO_2 levels decrease below the apnea threshold (87). To eliminate over-assistance, which can also lead to other adverse outcomes such as disuse diaphragmatic atrophy (88), the amount of ventilatory support needs to be decreased (89). Alternatively, assist-controlled modes with a back-up respiratory rate can also be used to prevent apnea events which has been shown to reduce sleep fragmentation (86). Using assist-controlled modes however does not eliminate the risk of disuse diaphragmatic atrophy and might create the false impression that patients are not ready for liberation, potentially delaying extubation. Proportional modes of ventilation [i.e., proportional assist-ventilation [PAV+] and neurally adjust ventilatory assist [NAVA]] can be used to deliver pressure proportional to the patient's instantaneous efforts in terms of amplitude and timing which avoids over- and under-assistance and improves synchrony. The use of these modes has systematically been shown to decrease asynchronies (82, 90, 91) and improve sleep quality in cross-over studies of small size (92, 93).

Multicomponent Strategies

Recently a review by Flannery investigated whether interventions targeted at improving sleep in the ICU were associated with reductions in ICU delirium (94). Six of the ten identified studies demonstrated a statistically significant reduction in the incidence of ICU delirium associated with sleep intervention. Unfortunately, although sleep interventions seem to be a promising approach for improving delirium and related outcomes (e.g., ICU length of stay) conclusions are limited by confounding, variable methodology and bias issues. Further study is therefore needed. Based on available data, potentially effective interventions might include a combination of dexmedetomidine (62), oral melatonin (95), and cognitive behavioral sleep therapy (96) using modified polysomnography to quantify sleep quality and quantity (25, 78) and understand to which extent sleep actually affects delirium occurrence.

CONCLUSIONS

Despite advances in our understanding of the sleep-wake cycle its association with the underlying mechanism of delirium, and how both influence ICU patient outcome, significant knowledge gaps exist in understanding the relationships between sleep, circadian rhythm and delirium. Hypotheses for mechanistic relationships between the sleep-wake cycle and delirium have largely been derived from studies of non-ICU patients. A better understanding of mechanisms would guide the development of new methods for prevention and treatment that consequently may improve short- and long-term outcomes of ICU survivors.

AUTHOR CONTRIBUTIONS

MW, MD, and IT wrote the first draft and revised the manuscript. All authors revised and approved the final manuscript.

REFERENCES

1. Blazer DG, van Nieuwenhuizen AO. Evidence for the diagnostic criteria of delirium: an update. *Curr Opin Psychiatry.* (2012) 25:239–43. doi: 10.1097/YCO.0b013e3283523ce8
2. European Delirium A, American Delirium S. The DSM-5 criteria, level of arousal and delirium diagnosis: inclusiveness is safer. *BMC Med.* (2014) 12:141. doi: 10.1186/s12916-014-0141-2
3. American Psychiatric Association. *Diagnostic and Statistical Manual of Mental Disorders.* 5th ed. Arlington, VA: American Psychiatric Association (2013).

4. Salluh JI, Wang H, Schneider EB, Nagaraja N, Yenokyan G, Damluji A, et al. Outcome of delirium in critically ill patients: systematic review and meta-analysis. *BMJ.* (2015) 350:h2538. doi: 10.1136/bmj.h2538
5. Thom RP, Levy-Carrick NC, Bui M, Silbersweig D. Delirium. *Am J Psychiatry.* (2019) 176:785–93. doi: 10.1176/appi.ajp.2018.18070893
6. van Rompaey B, Elseviers MM, Schuurmans MJ, Shortridge-Baggett LM, Truijen S, Bossaert L. Risk factors for delirium in intensive care patients: a prospective cohort study. *Crit Care.* (2009) 13:R77. doi: 10.1186/cc7892
7. Zaal IJ, Devlin JW, Peelen LM, Slooter AJ. A systematic review of risk factors for delirium in the ICU. *Crit Care Med.* (2015) 43:40–7. doi: 10.1097/CCM.0000000000000625
8. Telias I, Wilcox ME. Sleep and circadian rhythm in critical illness. *Crit Care.* (2019) 23:82. doi: 10.1186/s13054-019-2366-0
9. Smonig R, Magalhaes E, Bouadma L, Andremont O, de Montmollin E, Essardy F, et al. Impact of natural light exposure on delirium burden in adult patients receiving invasive mechanical ventilation in the ICU: a prospective study. *Ann Intensive Care.* (2019) 9:120. doi: 10.1186/s13613-019-0592-x
10. Simons KS, Verweij E, Lemmens PMC, Jelfs S, Park M, Spronk PE, et al. Noise in the intensive care unit and its influence on sleep quality: a multicenter observational study in Dutch intensive care units. *Crit Care.* (2018) 22:250. doi: 10.1186/s13054-018-2182-y
11. Bulic D, Bennett M, Rodgers H, Nourse M, Rubie P, Looi JC, et al. Delirium after mechanical ventilation in intensive care units: the Cognitive and Psychosocial Assessment (CAPA) study protocol. *JMIR Res Protoc.* (2017) 6:e31. doi: 10.2196/resprot.6660
12. Ely EW, Evans GW, Haponik EF. Mechanical ventilation in a cohort of elderly patients admitted to an intensive care unit. *Ann Intern Med.* (1999) 131:96–104. doi: 10.7326/0003-4819-131-2-199907200-00004
13. Zaal IJ, Devlin JW, Hazelbag M, Klein Klouwenberg PM, van der Kooi AW, Ong DS, et al. Benzodiazepine-associated delirium in critically ill adults. *Intensive Care Med.* (2015) 41:2130–7. doi: 10.1007/s00134-015-4063-z
14. Cooke JR, Ancoli-Israel S. Normal and abnormal sleep in the elderly. *Handb Clin Neurol.* (2011) 98:653–65. doi: 10.1016/B978-0-444-52006-7.00041-1
15. Banks G, Nolan PM, Peirson SN. Reciprocal interactions between circadian clocks and aging. *Mamm Genome.* (2016) 27:332–40. doi: 10.1007/s00335-016-9639-6
16. Dement W, Kleitman N. Cyclic variations in EEG during sleep and their relation to eye movements, body motility, and dreaming. *Electroencephalogr Clin Neurophysiol.* (1957) 9:673–90. doi: 10.1016/0013-4694(57)90088-3
17. Honn KA, Hinson JM, Whitney P, van Dongen HPA. Cognitive flexibility: a distinct element of performance impairment due to sleep deprivation. *Accid Anal Prev.* (2019) 126:191–7. doi: 10.1016/j.aap.2018.02.013
18. Zhou X, Ferguson SA, Matthews RW, Sargent C, Darwent D, Kennaway DJ, et al. Dynamics of neurobehavioral performance variability under forced desynchrony: evidence of state instability. *Sleep.* (2011) 34:57–63. doi: 10.1093/sleep/34.1.57
19. Belenky G, Wesensten NJ, Thorne DR, Thomas ML, Sing HC, Redmond DP, et al. Patterns of performance degradation and restoration during sleep restriction and subsequent recovery: a sleep dose-response study. *J Sleep Res.* (2003) 12:1–12. doi: 10.1046/j.1365-2869.2003.00337.x
20. Pisani MA, Friese RS, Gehlbach BK, Schwab RJ, Weinhouse GL, Jones SF. Sleep in the intensive care unit. *Am J Respir Crit Care Med.* (2015) 191:731–8. doi: 10.1164/rccm.201411-2099CI
21. Elliott R, McKinley S, Cistulli P, Fien M. Characterisation of sleep in intensive care using 24-hour polysomnography: an observational study. *Crit Care.* (2013) 17:R46. doi: 10.1186/cc12565
22. Cooper AB, Thornley KS, Young GB, Slutsky AS, Stewart TE, Hanly PJ. Sleep in critically ill patients requiring mechanical ventilation. *Chest.* (2000) 117:809–18. doi: 10.1378/chest.117.3.809
23. Freedman NS, Gazendam J, Levan L, Pack AI, Schwab RJ. Abnormal sleep/wake cycles and the effect of environmental noise on sleep disruption in the intensive care unit. *Am J Respir Crit Care Med.* (2001) 163:451–7. doi: 10.1164/ajrccm.163.2.9912128
24. Gabor JY, Cooper AB, Crombach SA, Lee B, Kadikar N, Bettger HE, et al. Contribution of the intensive care unit environment to sleep disruption in mechanically ventilated patients and healthy subjects. *Am J Respir Crit Care Med.* (2003) 167:708–15. doi: 10.1164/rccm.2201090
25. Drouot X, Roche-Campo F, Thille AW, Cabello B, Galia F, Margarit L, et al. A new classification for sleep analysis in critically ill patients. *Sleep Med.* (2012) 1:7–14. doi: 10.1016/j.sleep.2011.07.012
26. Barr J, Fraser GL, Puntillo K, Ely EW, Gelinas C, Dasta JF, et al. Clinical practice guidelines for the management of pain, agitation, and delirium in adult patients in the intensive care unit. *Crit Care Med.* (2013) 41:263–306. doi: 10.1097/CCM.0b013e3182783b72
27. Barr J, Fraser GL, Puntillo K, Ely EW, Gelinas C, Dasta JF, et al. Clinical practice guidelines for the management of pain, agitation, and delirium in adult patients in the Intensive Care Unit: executive summary. *Am J Health Syst Pharm.* (2013) 70:53–8. doi: 10.1093/ajhp/70.1.53
28. Wilcox ME, McAndrews MP, Van J, Jackson JC, Pinto R, Black SE, et al. Sleep fragmentation and cognitive trajectories after critical illness. *Chest.* (2020). doi: 10.1016/j.chest.2020.07.036. [Epub ahead of print].
29. Kamdar BB, Knauert MP, Jones SF, Parsons EC, Parthasarathy S, Pisani MA, et al. Perceptions and practices regarding sleep in the Intensive Care Unit. a survey of 1,223 critical care providers. *Ann Am Thorac Soc.* (2016) 13:1370–7. doi: 10.1513/AnnalsATS.201601-087OC
30. Devlin JW, Skrobik Y, Gelinas C, Needham DM, Slooter AJC, Pandharipande PP, et al. Clinical practice guidelines for the prevention and management of pain, agitation/sedation, delirium, immobility, and sleep disruption in adult patients in the ICU. *Crit Care Med.* (2018) 46:e825–73. doi: 10.1097/CCM.0000000000003299
31. Devlin JW, Skrobik Y, Gelinas C, Needham DM, Slooter AJC, Pandharipande PP, et al. Executive summary: clinical practice guidelines for the prevention and management of pain, agitation/sedation, delirium, immobility, and sleep disruption in adult patients in the ICU. *Crit Care Med.* (2018) 46:1532–48. doi: 10.1097/CCM.0000000000003259
32. Altman MT, Knauert MP, Murphy TE, Ahasic AM, Chauhan Z, Pisani MA. Association of intensive care unit delirium with sleep disturbance and functional disability after critical illness: an observational cohort study. *Ann Intensive Care.* (2018) 8:63. doi: 10.1186/s13613-018-0408-4
33. Borbely AA, Daan S, Wirz-Justice A, Deboer T. The two-process model of sleep regulation: a reappraisal. *J Sleep Res.* (2016) 25:131–43. doi: 10.1111/jsr.12371
34. Mohawk JA, Green CB, Takahashi JS. Central and peripheral circadian clocks in mammals. *Annu Rev Neurosci.* (2012) 35:445–62. doi: 10.1146/annurev-neuro-060909-153128
35. Guo X, Kuzumi E, Charman SC, Vuylsteke A. Perioperative melatonin secretion in patients undergoing coronary artery bypass grafting. *Anesth Analg.* (2002) 94:1085–91. doi: 10.1097/00000539-200205000-00006
36. Mundigler G, Delle-Karth G, Koreny M, Zehetgruber M, Steindl-Munda P, Marktl W, et al. Impaired circadian rhythm of melatonin secretion in sedated critically ill patients with severe sepsis. *Crit Care Med.* (2002) 30:536–40. doi: 10.1097/00003246-200203000-00007
37. Olofsson K, Alling C, Lundberg D, Malmros C. Abolished circadian rhythm of melatonin secretion in sedated and artificially ventilated intensive care patients. *Acta Anaesthesiol Scand.* (2004) 48:679–84. doi: 10.1111/j.0001-5172.2004.00401.x
38. Shilo L, Dagan Y, Smorjik Y, Weinberg U, Dolev S, Komptel B, et al. Patients in the intensive care unit suffer from severe lack of sleep associated with loss of normal melatonin secretion pattern. *Am J Med Sci.* (1999) 317:278–81. doi: 10.1016/S0002-9629(15)40528-2
39. Verceles AC, Silhan L, Terrin M, Netzer G, Shanholtz C, Scharf SM. Circadian rhythm disruption in severe sepsis: the effect of ambient light on urinary 6-sulfatoxymelatonin secretion. *Intensive Care Med.* (2012) 38:804–10. doi: 10.1007/s00134-012-2494-3
40. Madrid-Navarro CJ, Sanchez-Galvez R, Martinez-Nicolas A, Marina R, Garcia JA, Madrid JA, et al. Disruption of circadian rhythms and delirium, sleep impairment and sepsis in critically ill patients. Potential therapeutic implications for increased light-dark contrast and melatonin therapy in an ICU environment. *Curr Pharm Des.* (2015) 21:3453–68. doi: 10.2174/1381612821666150706105602
41. Vanhaudenhuyse A, Noirhomme Q, Tshibanda LJ, Bruno MA, Boveroux P, Schnakers C, et al. Default network connectivity reflects the level of consciousness in non-communicative brain-damaged patients. *Brain.* (2010) 133(Pt 1):161–71. doi: 10.1093/brain/awp313

42. Cavanna AE, Trimble MR. The precuneus: a review of its functional anatomy and behavioural correlates. *Brain.* (2006) 129(Pt 3):564–83. doi: 10.1093/brain/awl004
43. Choi SH, Lee H, Chung TS, Park KM, Jung YC, Kim SI, et al. Neural network functional connectivity during and after an episode of delirium. *Am J Psychiatry.* (2012) 169:498–507. doi: 10.1176/appi.ajp.2012.11060976
44. Kyeong S, Choi SH, Eun Shin J, Lee WS, Yang KH, Chung TS, et al. Functional connectivity of the circadian clock and neural substrates of sleep-wake disturbance in delirium. *Psychiatry Res.* (2017) 264:10–12. doi: 10.1016/j.pscychresns.2017.03.017
45. Hut RA, van der Zee EA. The cholinergic system, circadian rhythmicity, and time memory. *Behav Brain Res.* (2011) 221:466–80. doi: 10.1016/j.bbr.2010.11.039
46. Hughes CG, Pandharipande PP, Thompson JL, Chandrasekhar R, Ware LB, Ely EW, et al. Endothelial activation and blood-brain barrier injury as risk factors for delirium in critically Ill patients. *Crit Care Med.* (2016) 44:e809–17. doi: 10.1097/CCM.0000000000001739
47. Aston-Jones G, Chen S, Zhu Y, Oshinsky ML. A neural circuit for circadian regulation of arousal. *Nat Neurosci.* (2001) 4:732–8. doi: 10.1038/89522
48. Mistlberger RE. Circadian regulation of sleep in mammals: role of the suprachiasmatic nucleus. *Brain Res Brain Res Rev.* (2005) 49:429–54. doi: 10.1016/j.brainresrev.2005.01.005
49. Boyko Y, Holst R, Jennum P, Oerding H, Nikolic M, Toft P. Melatonin secretion pattern in critically Ill patients: a pilot descriptive study. *Crit Care Res Pract.* (2017) 2017:7010854. doi: 10.1155/2017/7010854
50. Maas MB, Lizza BD, Abbott SM, Liotta EM, Gendy M, Eed J, et al. Factors disrupting melatonin secretion rhythms during critical illness. *Crit Care Med.* (2020) 48:854–61. doi: 10.1097/CCM.0000000000004333
51. Arumugam S, El-Menyar A, Al-Hassani A, Strandvik G, Asim M, Mekkodithal A, et al. Delirium in the intensive care unit. *J Emerg Trauma Shock.* (2017) 10:37–46. doi: 10.4103/0974-2700.199520
52. Grover S, Ghosh A, Sarkar S, Desouza A, Yaddanapudi LN, Basu D. Delirium in intensive care unit: phenomenology, subtypes, and factor structure of symptoms. *Indian J.* (2018) 40:169–77. doi: 10.4103/IJPSYM.IJPSYM_274_17
53. Mori S, Takeda JR, Carrara FS, Cohrs CR, Zanei SS, Whitaker IY. Incidence and factors related to delirium in an intensive care unit. *Rev Esc Enferm USP.* (2016) 50:587–93. doi: 10.1590/S0080-623420160000500007
54. Maldonado JR. Neuropathogenesis of delirium: review of current etiologic theories and common pathways. *Am J Geriatr Psychiatry.* (2013) 21:1190–222. doi: 10.1016/j.jagp.2013.09.005
55. Maldonado JR. Delirium pathophysiology: an updated hypothesis of the etiology of acute brain failure. *Int J Geriatr Psychiatry.* (2018) 33:1428–57. doi: 10.1002/gps.4823
56. Sanders RD. Hypothesis for the pathophysiology of delirium: role of baseline brain network connectivity and changes in inhibitory tone. *Med Hypotheses.* (2011) 77:140–3. doi: 10.1016/j.mehy.2011.03.048
57. Weinhouse GL, Watson PL. Sedation and sleep disturbances in the ICU. *Anesthesiol Clin.* (2011) 29:675–85. doi: 10.1016/j.anclin.2011.09.007
58. Kondili E, Alexopoulou C, Xirouchaki N, Georgopoulos D. Effects of propofol on sleep quality in mechanically ventilated critically ill patients: a physiological study. *Intensive Care Med.* (2012) 38:1640–6. doi: 10.1007/s00134-012-2623-z
59. Reade MC, O'Sullivan K, Bates S, Goldsmith D, Ainslie WR, Bellomo R. Dexmedetomidine vs. haloperidol in delirious, agitated, intubated patients: a randomised open-label trial. *Crit Care.* (2009) 13:R75. doi: 10.1186/cc7890
60. Pandharipande PP, Pun BT, Herr DL, Maze M, Girard TD, Miller RR, et al. Effect of sedation with dexmedetomidine vs lorazepam on acute brain dysfunction in mechanically ventilated patients: the MENDS randomized controlled trial. *JAMA.* (2007) 298:2644–53. doi: 10.1001/jama.298.22.2644
61. Riker RR, Shehabi Y, Bokesch PM, Ceraso D, Wisemandle W, Koura F, et al. Dexmedetomidine vs midazolam for sedation of critically ill patients: a randomized trial. *JAMA.* (2009) 1:489–99. doi: 10.1001/jama.2009.56
62. Skrobik Y, Duprey MS, Hill NS, Devlin JW. Low-dose nocturnal dexmedetomidine prevents ICU delirium. A randomized, placebo-controlled trial. *Am J Respir Crit Care Med.* (2018) 197:1147–56. doi: 10.1164/rccm.201710-1995OC
63. Reade MC, Eastwood GM, Bellomo R, Bailey M, Bersten A, Cheung B, et al. Effect of dexmedetomidine added to standard care on ventilator-free time in patients with agitated delirium: a randomized clinical trial. *JAMA.* (2016) 315:1460–8. doi: 10.1001/jama.2016.2707
64. Pandharipande PP, Morandi A, Adams JR, Girard TD, Thompson JL, Shintani AK, et al. Plasma tryptophan and tyrosine levels are independent risk factors for delirium in critically ill patients. *Intensive Care Med.* (2009) 35:1886–92. doi: 10.1007/s00134-009-1573-6
65. Huang R, Hertz L. Receptor subtype and dose dependence of dexmedetomidine-induced accumulation of [14C]glutamine in astrocytes suggests glial involvement in its hypnotic-sedative and anesthetic-sparing effects. *Brain Res.* (2000) 873:297–301. doi: 10.1016/S0006-8993(00)02525-7
66. Hipp DM, Ely EW. Pharmacological and nonpharmacological management of delirium in critically ill patients. *Neurother.* (2012) 9:158–75. doi: 10.1007/s13311-011-0102-9
67. Perras B, Meier M, Dodt C. Light and darkness fail to regulate melatonin release in critically ill humans. *Intensive Care Med.* (2007) 33:1954–8. doi: 10.1007/s00134-007-0769-x
68. Balan S, Leibovitz A, Zila SO, Ruth M, Chana W, Yassica B, et al. The relation between the clinical subtypes of delirium and the urinary level of 6-SMT. *J Neuropsychiatry Clin Neurosci.* (2003) 15:363–6. doi: 10.1176/jnp.15.3.363
69. Li CX, Liang DD, Xie GH, Cheng BL, Chen QX, Wu SJ, et al. Altered melatonin secretion and circadian gene expression with increased proinflammatory cytokine expression in early-stage sepsis patients. *Mol Med Rep.* (2013) 7:1117–22. doi: 10.3892/mmr.2013.1331
70. Plaschke K, Fichtenkamm P, Schramm C, Hauth S, Martin E, Verch M, et al. Early postoperative delirium after open-heart cardiac surgery is associated with decreased bispectral EEG and increased cortisol and interleukin-6. *Intensive Care Med.* (2010) 36:2081–9. doi: 10.1007/s00134-010-2004-4
71. Shi CM, Wang DX, Chen KS, Gu XE. Incidence and risk factors of delirium in critically ill patients after non-cardiac surgery. *Chin Med J.* (2010) 123:993–9. doi: 10.3760/cma.j.issn.0366-6999.2010.08.004
72. Pearson A, de Vries A, Middleton SD, Gillies F, White TO, Armstrong IR, et al. Cerebrospinal fluid cortisol levels are higher in patients with delirium versus controls. *BMC Res Notes.* (2010) 3:33. doi: 10.1186/1756-0500-3-33
73. Maclullich AM, Ferguson KJ, Miller T, de Rooij SE, Cunningham C. Unravelling the pathophysiology of delirium: a focus on the role of aberrant stress responses. *J Psychosom Res.* (2008) 65:229–38. doi: 10.1016/j.jpsychores.2008.05.019
74. Nguyen DN, Huyghens L, Zhang H, Schiettecatte J, Smitz J, Vincent JL. Cortisol is an associated-risk factor of brain dysfunction in patients with severe sepsis and septic shock. *Biomed Res Int.* (2014) 2014:712742. doi: 10.1155/2014/712742
75. Kamdar BB, Needham DM, Collop NA. Sleep deprivation in critical illness: its role in physical and psychological recovery. *J Intensive Care Med.* (2012) 27:97–111. doi: 10.1177/0885066610394322
76. Campbell AM, Axon DR, Martin JR, Slack MK, Mollon L, Lee JK. Melatonin for the prevention of postoperative delirium in older adults: a systematic review and meta-analysis. *BMC Geriatr.* (2019) 19:272. doi: 10.1186/s12877-019-1297-6
77. Martinez FE, Anstey M, Ford A, Roberts B, Hardie M, Palmer R, et al. Prophylactic Melatonin for Delirium in Intensive Care (Pro-MEDIC): study protocol for a randomised controlled trial. *Trials.* (2017) 18:4. doi: 10.1186/s13063-016-1751-0
78. Dres M, Younes M, Rittayamai N, Kendzerska T, Telias I, Grieco DL, et al. Sleep and pathological wakefulness at the time of liberation from mechanical ventilation (SLEEWE). A prospective multicenter physiological study. *Am J Respir Crit Care Med.* (2019) 199:1106–15. doi: 10.1164/rccm.201811-2119OC
79. Rault C, Sangare A, Diaz V, Ragot S, Frat JP, Raux M, et al. Impact of sleep deprivation on respiratory motor output and endurance: a physiological study. *Am J Respir Crit Care Med.* (2020) 201:976–83. doi: 10.1164/rccm.201904-0819OC
80. Thille AW, Reynaud F, Marie D, Barrau S, Rousseau L, Rault C, et al. Impact of sleep alterations on weaning duration in mechanically ventilated patients: a prospective study. *Eur Respir J.* (2018) 51:1702465. doi: 10.1183/13993003.02465-2017
81. Pham T, Telias I, Piraino T, Yoshida T, Brochard LJ. Asynchrony consequences and management. *Crit Care Clin.* (2018) 34:325–41. doi: 10.1016/j.ccc.2018.03.008

82. Vaschetto R, Cammarota G, Colombo D, Longhini F, Grossi F, Giovanniello A, et al. Effects of propofol on patient-ventilator synchrony and interaction during pressure support ventilation and neurally adjusted ventilatory assist. *Crit Care Med.* (2014) 42:74–82. doi: 10.1097/CCM.0b013e31829e53dc
83. Chanques G, Kress JP, Pohlman A, Patel S, Poston J, Jaber S, et al. Impact of ventilator adjustment and sedation-analgesia practices on severe asynchrony in patients ventilated in assist-control mode. *Crit Care Med.* (2013) 41:2177–87. doi: 10.1097/CCM.0b013e31828c2d7a
84. Fanfulla F, Delmastro M, Berardinelli A, Lupo ND, Nava S. Effects of different ventilator settings on sleep and inspiratory effort in patients with neuromuscular disease. *Am J Respir Crit Care Med.* (2005) 172:619–24. doi: 10.1164/rccm.200406-694OC
85. Meza S, Mendez M, Ostrowski M, Younes M. Susceptibility to periodic breathing with assisted ventilation during sleep in normal subjects. *J Appl Physiol.* (1998) 85:1929–40. doi: 10.1152/jappl.1998.85.5.1929
86. Parthasarathy S, Tobin MJ. Effect of ventilator mode on sleep quality in critically ill patients. *Am J Respir Crit Care Med.* (2002) 166:1423–9. doi: 10.1164/rccm.200209-999OC
87. Vaporidi K, Akoumianaki E, Telias I, Goligher EC, Brochard L, Georgopoulos D. Respiratory drive in critically Ill patients. Pathophysiology and clinical implications. *Am J Respir Crit Care Med.* (2020) 201:20–32. doi: 10.1164/rccm.201903-0596SO
88. Goligher EC, Dres M, Fan E, Rubenfeld GD, Scales DC, Herridge MS, et al. Mechanical ventilation-induced diaphragm atrophy strongly impacts clinical outcomes. *Am J Respir Crit Care Med.* (2018) 197:204–13. doi: 10.1164/rccm.201703-0536OC
89. Thille AW, Cabello B, Galia F, Lyazidi A, Brochard L. Reduction of patient-ventilator asynchrony by reducing tidal volume during pressure-support ventilation. *Intensive Care Med.* (2008) 34:1477–86. doi: 10.1007/s00134-008-1121-9
90. Spahija J, de Marchie M, Albert M, Bellemare P, Delisle S, Beck J, et al. Patient-ventilator interaction during pressure support ventilation and neurally adjusted ventilatory assist. *Crit Care Med.* (2010) 38:518–26. doi: 10.1097/CCM.0b013e3181cb0d7b
91. Piquilloud L, Vignaux L, Bialais E, Roeseler J, Sottiaux T, Laterre PF, et al. Neurally adjusted ventilatory assist improves patient-ventilator interaction. *Intensive Care Med.* (2011) 37:263–71. doi: 10.1007/s00134-010-2052-9
92. Bosma K, Ferreyra G, Ambrogio C, Pasero D, Mirabella L, Braghiroli A, et al. Patient-ventilator interaction and sleep in mechanically ventilated patients: pressure support versus proportional assist ventilation. *Crit Care Med.* (2007) 35:1048–54. doi: 10.1097/01.CCM.0000260055.64235.7C
93. Delisle S, Ouellet P, Bellemare P, Tetrault JP, Arsenault P. Sleep quality in mechanically ventilated patients: comparison between NAVA and PSV modes. *Ann Intensive Care.* (2011) 1:42. doi: 10.1186/2110-5820-1-42
94. Flannery AH, Oyler DR, Weinhouse GL. The impact of interventions to improve sleep on delirium in the ICU. A systematic review and research framework. *Crit Care Med.* (2016) 44:2231–40. doi: 10.1097/CCM.0000000000001952
95. Burry L, Scales D, Williamson D, Foster J, Mehta S, Guenette M, et al. Feasibility of melatonin for prevention of delirium in critically ill patients: a protocol for a multicentre, randomised, placebo-controlled study. *BMJ Open.* (2017) 7:e015420. doi: 10.1136/bmjopen-2016-015420
96. Zhang Y, Su J, Wang J, Tang G, Hu W, Mao J, et al. Cognitive behavioral therapy for insomnia combined with eszopiclone for the treatment of sleep disorder patients transferred out of the intensive care unit: a single-centred retrospective observational study. *Medicine.* (2018) 97:e12383. doi: 10.1097/MD.0000000000012383

15

High-Resolution Recording of the Circadian Oscillator in Primary Mouse α- and β-Cell Culture

*Volodymyr Petrenko[1,2,3,4], Yvan Gosmain[4,5] and Charna Dibner[1,2,3,4]**

[1]Endocrinology, Diabetes, Hypertension and Nutrition Division, Department of Specialties of Medicine, University Hospital of Geneva, Geneva, Switzerland, [2]Faculty of Medicine, Department of Cell Physiology and Metabolism, University of Geneva, Geneva, Switzerland, [3]Institute of Genetics and Genomics in Geneva (iGE3), Geneva, Switzerland, [4]Diabetes Center of the Faculty of Medicine, University of Geneva, Geneva, Switzerland, [5]Molecular Diabetes Laboratory, Endocrinology, Diabetes, Hypertension and Nutrition Division, Faculty of Medicine, Department of Specialties of Medicine, University Hospital of Geneva, University of Geneva, Geneva, Switzerland

Edited by:
Andries Kalsbeek,
Academic Medical Center,
Netherlands

Reviewed by:
Aleksey V. Matveyenko,
Mayo Clinic Minnesota, USA
Elaine Vieira,
Researcher at Universidade
católica de Brasilia, Brazil

***Correspondence:**
Charna Dibner
charna.dibner@hcuge.ch

Circadian clocks have been developed in evolution as an anticipatory mechanism allowing for adaptation to the constantly changing light environment due to rotation of the Earth. This mechanism is functional in all light-sensitive organisms. There is a considerable body of evidence on the tight connection between the circadian clock and most aspects of physiology and metabolism. Clocks, operative in the pancreatic islets, have caught particular attention in the last years due to recent reports on their critical roles in regulation of insulin secretion and etiology of type 2 diabetes. While β-cell clocks have been extensively studied during the last years, α-cell clocks and their role in islet function and orchestration of glucose metabolism stayed unexplored, largely due to the difficulty to isolate α-cells, which represents a considerable technical challenge. Here, we provide a detailed description of an experimental approach for the isolation of separate mouse α- and β-cell population, culture of isolated primary α- and β-cells, and their subsequent long-term high-resolution circadian bioluminescence recording. For this purpose, a triple reporter *ProGlucagon-Venus*/RIP-*Cherry*/*Per2*:*Luciferase* mouse line was established, carrying specific fluorescent reporters for α- and β-cells, and luciferase reporter for monitoring the molecular clockwork. Flow cytometry fluorescence-activated cell sorting allowed separating pure α- and β-cell populations from isolated islets. Experimental conditions, developed by us for the culture of functional primary mouse α- and β-cells for at least 10 days, will be highlighted. Importantly, temporal analysis of freshly isolated α- and β-cells around-the-clock revealed preserved rhythmicity of core clock genes expression. Finally, we describe the setting to assess circadian rhythm in cultured α- and β-cells synchronized *in vitro*. The here-described methodology allows to analyze the functional properties of primary α- and β-cells under physiological or pathophysiological conditions and to assess the islet cellular clock properties.

Keywords: mouse pancreatic islet, α- and β-cells, primary culture, *in vitro* synchronization, circadian bioluminescence

INTRODUCTION

The circadian system represents a complex anticipatory mechanism developed during evolution in nearly all organisms, allowing to coordinate a plethora of physiological functions to the daily changes of geophysical time. Within this system, a master pacemaker in the hypothalamus orchestrates subsidiary oscillators situated in peripheral organs (1). In fact, myriads of these self-sustained and cell-autonomous oscillators are operative in most cells of the body (2, 3). The molecular composition of central and peripheral oscillators is identical, and it relies on primary and secondary feedback loops of transcription and translation of key core clock components (4). The primary loop comprises the positive limb transcription factors CLOCK and BMAL1, which induce expression of the negative limb elements PERIODS and CRYPTOCHROMES (5). Recent studies provide increasing evidence for a tight connection between the circadian system and metabolism, linking metabolic diseases to circadian misalignments associated with modern life-style, including frequent jetlag, shifted work schedules, and chronic social jetlag (4, 6–10). Studies in clock-deficient genetic rodent models suggest that a number of metabolic defects develop in mice that are deficient for one or two core clock components (11, 12). For instance, *Clock* mutant mice develop hyperphagia, obesity, hyperglycemia, and hypoinsulinemia (12).

There is an increasing evidence for the essential roles of the peripheral circadian clocks operative in endocrine tissues for their transcriptional and functional regulation (13–15). Indeed, most of the hormones, including myokines and adipokines, are secreted in a circadian manner and regulated by respective cell-autonomous oscillators (16, 17). Such cell-autonomous clocks have been recently characterized in pancreatic islets in mice (11, 18) and in humans (18–20). Loss of islet clock function in islet-specific *Bmal1* KO mouse models, either induced during development or in the adult age, resulted in the early onset of type 2 diabetes (T2D) in these mice (11, 18, 21). Moreover, siClock-mediated clock perturbation in adult human islet cells caused disruption in basal and glucose induced insulin secretion by these cells *in vitro* (20). Taken together, these data suggest that circadian oscillators operative in islet cells play an important role in regulating these cell function.

So far, most of the research works were conducted on whole islets, or on insulin secreting β-cells, representing about 80% of total islet cells in mice (22). Therefore, the circadian physiology of glucagon secreting α-cells stayed largely unexplored, due to the difficulty to identify these cells within the complex three dimensional islet structure and to isolate them due to their low abundance (less than 20% of the mouse islet cell population). In an attempt to fill this gap, we hereby report an experimental approach, which allows to (1) efficiently isolate nearly pure populations of mouse α- and β-cells; (2) establish and maintain mouse α- and β-cell primary cultures; (3) study endocrine function of separated α- and β-cells; and (4) assess the circadian properties of primary α- and β-cells, utilizing high-resolution circadian bioluminescence monitoring in living cells synchronized *in vitro*.

MATERIALS AND METHODS

Animal Care and Reporter Mouse Strain

For all experiments a triple reporter mouse strain *ProGlucagon-Venus*/RIP-*Cherry*/*Per2:Luciferase* (*ProGcg-Venus*/RIP-*Cherry*/*Per2:Luc*) was derived by crossing the *ProGlucagon-Venus* (*ProGcg-Venus*) reporter mouse (23) with Rat *Insulin2* promoter (RIP)-*Cherry* (RIP-*Cherry*) (24) and *Period2:Luciferase* (*Per2:Luc*) mice (25). *ProGcg-Venus* and *RIP-Cherry* reporters exhibit a high specificity for α- and β-cells, respectively, while the fusion protein PER2:Luciferase, encoded by *Per2:Luc*, is a circadian reporter functionally indistinguishable from the wild-type PER2 protein. The overview of the experimental procedures is illustrated in **Figure 1**. All experiments were conducted on male mice aged 7–16 weeks under standard animal housing conditions comprising *ad libitum* access to food and water and 12 h light/12 h dark cycles. Islet isolations were performed during morning hours (07:00 a.m.–12:00 a.m.). To study circadian rhythms in freshly isolated α- and β-cells *in vivo*, mice were subjected to night-restricted feeding 2 weeks prior to the experiment and during the entire period of sample collection as described previously (26), with half of the animals entrained with inversed light-dark and feeding cycles during the same period.

Pancreatic Islet Isolation and Separation of α- and β-Cells

Islets of Langerhans were isolated by a standard procedure based on collagenase (Type XI, Sigma) digestion of pancreas followed

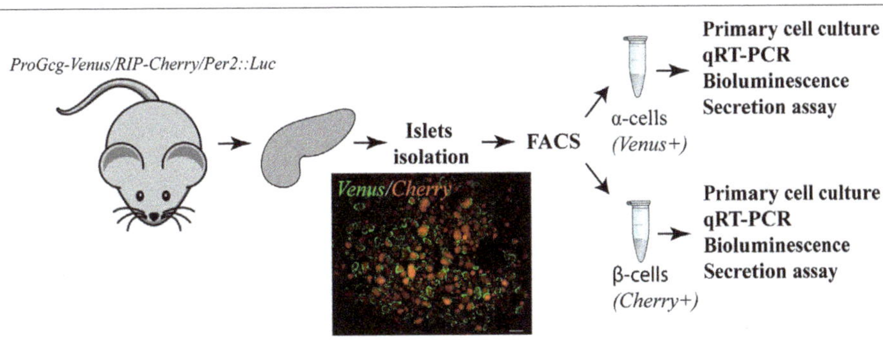

FIGURE 1 | Overview of the experimental procedures. Pancreatic islets were isolated from triple transgenic mice (ProGcg-Venus/RIP-Cherry/Per2:Luc). Representative fluorescent image demonstrates pancreatic islets comprising *Venus*-positive α-cells preferentially located on the periphery of islets and *Cherry*-positive β-cells in the core (labeled in green and red, respectively). Following fluorescence-activated cell sorting (FACS) separation, populations of α- and β-cells were subjected to further experimental procedures [primary cultures, quantitative RT-PCR (qRT-PCR) analysis, bioluminescence recording, and assessment of hormone secretion]. Scale bar = 200 μm.

by Ficoll purification (27). Briefly, 2 ml of a 2-mg/ml collagenase solution [diluted in Hanks Balanced Salt Solution (HBSS) (Gibco), 4.2 nM sodium bicarbonate, 1 M $CaCl_2$, and 1 M HEPES (Gibco)] was injected retrogradely through the ampulla of Vater into the exocrine part of the pancreas, which was dissected and digested in a water bath at 37°C (11–14 min, exact time needs to be calibrated for every new batch of enzyme). The digested mixture was then washed in HBSS, supplemented with 0.3% free fatty acid bovine serum albumin (BSA) (Sigma) with subsequent Ficoll gradient centrifugation (densities: 1.108, 1.096, and 1.069). Islets, collected from the gradient, were then washed in HBSS supplemented with 0.3% BSA. Islet cells were gently dissociated by trypsin (Gibco), re-suspended in KRB solution (pH 7.4, BSA, 1.4 mM glucose and 0.5 mM EDTA), and filtered through a 70-µm cell strainer (Falcon). α- and β-cell populations were separated by flow cytometry fluorescence-activated cell sorting [FACS; Astrios Sorter (Beckman Coulter)], based on fluorescence intensity and wavelength, single cell nature, size, and viability. Purity of the sorted cells was further assessed by a second, additional FACS analysis. The viability of treated cells was evaluated by FACS with DRAQ7™ (Abcam) or DAPI (ThermoFisher) dyes.

Immunohistochemistry

Sorted cells were plated on 35 mm dishes and fixed in 4% paraformaldehyde during 30 min. For immunohistochemistry, the fixed cells were incubated with mouse anti-Glucagon (1:500, Sigma) or guinea-pig anti-Insulin (1:500, ThermoFisher Scientific) primary antibodies. The signal was revealed by Alexa-Fluor anti-mouse 568 or Alexa-Fluor anti Guinea-pig 488 secondary antibodies, respectively (1:1,000, Molecular Probes). Bright-field and fluorescent images were obtained with EvosTL fluorescent microscope (ThermoFisher) using 4×, 10×, or 40× objectives.

In Vitro Islets/Islet Cell Culture

For the *in vitro* culture, intact islets or sorted cells were recovered in RPMI 1640 complete medium (11.2 mM glucose, 110 µg/ml sodium pyruvate) supplemented with 10% fetal calf serum, 110 U/mL penicillin, 110 µg/ml streptomycin, and 50 µg/ml gentamycin and attached to 35 mm dishes or multi-well plates (LifeSystemDesign) pre-coated with a laminin-5-rich extracellular matrix (28). For hormone secretion assays, approximately 15,000 cells were plated per dish, in three separated drops of 50 µl each. For bioluminescence recordings either 250 islets or approximately 50,000 separated cells were plated per well.

Quantitative RT-PCR (qRT-PCR)

Total RNA was prepared from homogenized islet cells using RNeasy® Plus Micro Kit (Qiagen). Ten nanograms of total RNA were reverse transcribed (PrimeScript RT reagent kit; Takara) and pre-amplified (TaqMan PreAmp Master Mix; Applied Biosystems) following the manufacturer's instructions. Specific target gene mRNA levels were analyzed by real-time quantitative PCR using the LightCycler technology (LC480; Roche Diagnostics). Mean values of gene expression were calculated from technical duplicates of each qRT-PCR analysis and normalized to the housekeeping gene *Hypoxanthine guanine phosphoribosyl transferase* (*Hprt*) exhibiting no significant variability of its expression level throughout each experiment, and therefore served as internal control. Primers used for this study are listed in **Table 1**.

Hormone Secretion Measurements

Insulin and glucagon basal secretion assays were performed on approximately 15,000 attached separated α- or β-cells at 3 days *in vitro*. For basal insulin secretion assessment, cells were washed in KRB solution (Krebs-Ringer bicarbonate, pH 7.4, supplemented with 0.3% BSA) containing 2.8 mM glucose for 1 h, with subsequent incubation in KRB solution, containing 2.8 mM glucose for 30 min at 37°C in a cell culture incubator. For glucagon assessment, cells were washed in KRB solution containing 7 mM glucose for 1 h, followed by additional 30 min incubation in the same solution at 37°C in a cell culture incubator. To assess the islet cell acute secretory response, FACS-separated α- (*Venus*-positive) and β- (*Cherry*-positive) cells were subjected to 2 h incubation in KRB solution containing 5.6 mM glucose, followed by additional 30 min incubation in KRB containing 5.6 mM glucose (basal condition), 30 min incubation in KRB containing 5.6 mM glucose supplemented with 10 mM arginine (stimulated secretion for *Venus*-positive cells) or in KRB containing 16.7 mM glucose (stimulated secretion for *Cherry*-positive cells), and additional 30 min incubation in KRB containing 5.6 mM glucose (re-basal condition). At the end of each experiment, cells were lysed in Acid/Ethanol mixture (1.5% HCl/75% Ethanol) for glucagon or insulin residual contents measurements. Insulin and glucagon concentrations were quantified in the supernatants and in lysed cells by the Mouse Insulin or Glucagon ELISA kits (Mercodia). For acute secretion assays, glucagon and insulin values were expressed as a percentage of appropriate released hormone to residual cell content.

Islet Cells Synchronization and Circadian Bioluminescence Monitoring

Adherent islets/islet cells were synchronized by a 1-h pulse of forskolin 10 µM (Sigma) prior to continuous bioluminescence recording in RPMI, supplemented with 100 µM luciferin (NanoLight Technology) (20). Photon counts of each well were

TABLE 1 | List of primers used for quantitative RT-PCR.

Target gene		Sequence primers, 5′-3′
Hprt	*Forward*	GCTCGAGATGTCATGAAGGAGAT
	Reverse	AAAGAACTTATAGCCCCCCTTGA
Clock	*Forward*	TTGCTCCACGGGAATCCTT
	Reverse	GGAGGGAAAGTGCTCTGTTGTAG
Per1	*Forward*	ACCAGCGTGTCATGATGACATAC
	Reverse	CTCTCCCGGTCTTGCTTCAG
Per2	*Forward*	GTAGCGCCGCTGCCG
	Reverse	GCGGTCACGTTTTCCACTATG
Ins1	*Forward*	TCTTCTACACACCCAAGT
	Reverse	TGCAGCACTGATCCACAA
Ins2	*Forward*	GCTCTCTACCTGGTGTGT
	Reverse	CTCCACCCAGCTCCAGTT
Gcg	*Forward*	GATCATTCCCAGCTTCCC
	Reverse	CTGGTAAAGGTCCCTTCA
MafA	*Forward*	CATTCTGGAGAGCGAGAA
	Reverse	TTTCTCCTTGTACAGGTC

integrated during 1 min, over 24 min intervals. For detrended time series, raw luminescence signals were smoothened by a moving average with a window of 24 h, allowing for a less biased comparison of bioluminescence values across experiments with regard to the measured circadian parameters (20).

RESULTS

Separating Primary Mouse α- and β-Cells

In order to simultaneously label α- and β-cells within the islets, a *ProGcg-Venus*/RIP-*Cherry*/*Per2:Luc* reporter mouse line was established (**Figure 1**), allowing for the highly specific separation of nearly pure endocrine cell populations. To this end, following islet isolation and gentle trypsinization, dispersed cells were sorted by FACS based on cellular fluorescence characteristics, cell size (based on the data of Forward Scatter detector, FSC), and granularity (based on the data of Side Scatter detector, SSC; see **Figures 2A,B**). Of note, *Cherry*-positive cells showed higher cell granularity than *Venus*-positive cells (compare two histograms in **Figure 2B**). In parallel, cell viability was assessed by utilizing DRAQ7™, a dye that binds to DNA when cell membrane permeability is altered after initiation of cell death. Overall viability across preparations was near 90% (**Figure 2C**), with almost a 10-fold higher percentage of cell death for *Cherry*-positive cells (up to 20%) than for *Venus*-positive cells (**Figures 2D,E**), suggesting a higher sensitivity of *Cherry*-positive cells to the islet isolation, trypsinization, and/or sorting processes. The average number of harvested viable *Cherry*-positive cells per mouse was 39,292 ± 6,887, which is more than threefold higher than for *Venus*-positive cells (12,521 ± 1,885) (**Figure 2F**), reflecting the physiological ratio between these two cell types within mouse islets (22). In addition, the purity of the obtained *Venus*- and *Cherry*-positive cell populations was assessed by a complementary round of FACS analysis (**Figures 3A–G**). According to this analysis, the α-cell population comprises more than 90% viable *Venus*-positive cells without detectable contamination with *Cherry*-positive cells (**Figures 3A–C,G**), while the β-cell population contained up to 96% viable *Cherry*-positive cells without visible *Venus*-positive contaminants (**Figures 3D,E,G**). Finally, the morphological examination of sorted cell populations with a fluorescent microscope confirmed their high purity (**Figure 3H**).

Primary Culture of Mouse α- and β-Cells

Insulin and glucagon transcript expression levels were assessed in separated *Venus*- and *Cherry*-positive cells by qRT-PCR analysis. As expected, *Gcg* transcription was the highest in the *Venus*-positive population, further confirming the α-cell identity, while both insulin transcripts *Ins1* and *Ins2* were abundant in *Cherry*-positive cells, indicating their β-cell identity (**Figure 4A**). Importantly, expression levels of the opposite cell hormone genes (*Ins1* and *Ins2* in *Venus*-positive cells, and *Gcg* in *Cherry*-positive cells) were more than 10-fold (for *Ins1* and *Ins2*) and 1,000-fold (for *Gcg*) lower, further confirming the satisfactory purity of the α- and β-cell populations. Furthermore, *Cherry*-positive cell population expressed β-cell-specific transcription factor *MafA* at the levels which were 1,000-fold higher compared to this transcript expression in *Venus*-positive counterparts (**Figure 4B**).

For cell culture, separated α- and β-cells were plated on plastic dishes covered with laminin-enriched matrix, which improves islet cell survival and function, and keeping them from de-diffentiation (28). Attached islet cells were maintained *in vitro* for at least 10 days. During the first 48 h of culture, attached β-cells formed monolayer cell aggregates resembling pseudo islets, while α- cells formed small domed structures composed by a few cells or stayed separated (**Figure 4C**). Immunofluorescence analysis demonstrated that *Venus*-positive cells in culture co-localized with glucagon-specific antibody, whereas *Cherry*-positive cells co-localized with insulin-specific antibody (**Figure 4D**), further validating these cell identity and high purity of α- and β-cell fractions.

Hormone secretion assays, performed after 3 days in culture, detected high basal levels of insulin in the supernatant of β-cells, and high basal levels of glucagon in α-cell supernatants, released during 30 min in the presence of constant glucose concentrations (2.8 mM for insulin and 7 mM for glucagon; **Figure 4E**). Noteworthy, secretion of the opposite hormones (glucagon by β-cells and insulin by α-cells) was below the detection level. Importantly, incubation of cultured α-cells with arginine induced about 2.5-fold increase in glucagon secretion, whereas incubation of cultured β-cells with high glucose stimulated secretion of insulin above two-fold (**Figure 4F**). Taken together, these data suggest that the here-described methodology ensures highly specific and efficient separation of the two main populations of islet cells, resulting in nearly pure populations of viable and functional α- and β-cells, which can be maintained in culture.

Assessment of Circadian Oscillator Properties in Separated α- and β-Cells

In view of the complexity of the separation procedure by FACS, we next explored if separated α- and β-cell populations maintain their circadian properties, as was previously reported to be the case in isolated intact islets (11, 18). To this end, mRNA levels for selected core clock transcripts have been assessed in sorted islet cells isolated every 4 h during 24 h. The qRT-PCR analysis revealed pronounced rhythmic patterns for *Per1* and *Per2* genes over 24 h, while the oscillation of *Clock* transcription was shallow, in agreement with previous reports (**Figure 5**) (11, 19).

Moreover, we explored cell-autonomous molecular clocks in separated α- and β-cell primary cultures synchronized *in vitro*. Similar to intact islets (**Figure 6A**), populations of pure α-cells (**Figure 6B**) and β-cells (**Figure 6C**) responded to a 1 h synchronizing pulse of forskolin by demonstrating high-amplitude self-sustained circadian oscillations of *Per2:Luc* reporter expression for at least 5 consecutive days following synchronization. Synchronizing effect of forskolin on cultured α- and β-cells was specific, since medium change alone had little synchronizing effect on the *Per2:Luc* expression in both cell types (**Figures 6B,C**). Collectively, these data suggest that circadian oscillations persist in pure populations of α- and β-cells following islet isolation, trypsinization, and FACS separation procedures.

DISCUSSION

The major obstacle for studying α- and β-cells is that they are organized in the tight three-dimensional structure within the

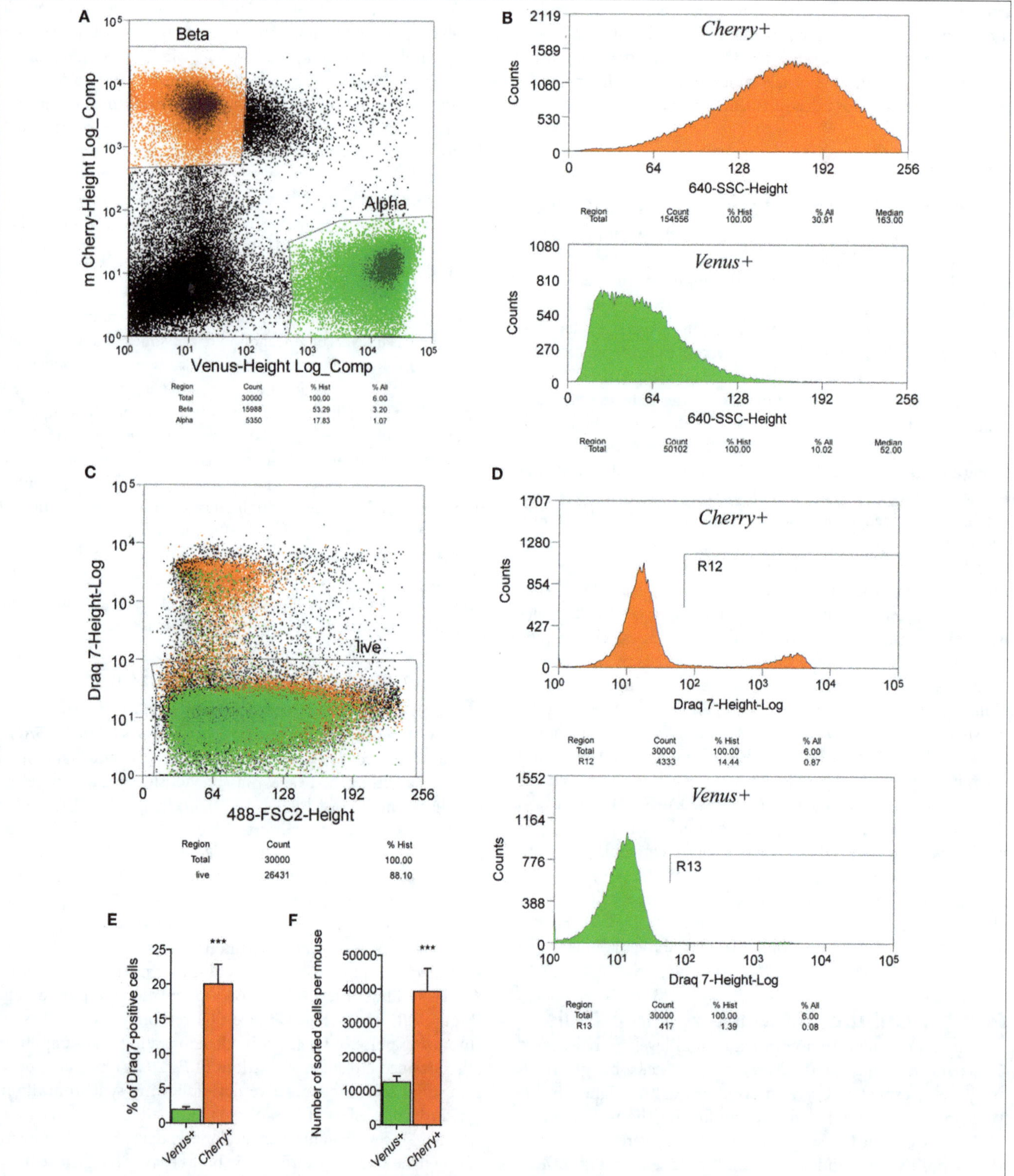

FIGURE 2 | Fluorescence-activated cell sorting of pancreatic islet cells from ProGcg-Venus/RIP-Cherry/Per2:Luc mice. (A) Dot plots indicating good separation of *Venus*- and *Cherry*-positive cells from gated cell population. **(B)** Histograms representing number of analyzed events versus cell complexity (granularity) of the sorted cells. Note that *Cherry*-positive β-cells have greater granularity when compared to *Venus*-positive α-cells. **(C)** Dot plots for DRAQ7-based assessment of sorted cell viability, indicating approximately 90% alive cells in the preparation. **(D)** Representative histograms showing number of dead α- and β-cells among analyzed events and **(E)** corresponding quantitative data from 12 independent experiments (three to six mice per experiment), suggesting higher cell death for β-cell population, as compared to α-cells (paired, two-tailed Student's *t*-test). **(F)** Histogram indicating average numbers of obtained α- and β-cells per mouse ($N = 12$ independent experiments with three to six mice per experiment), statistical difference illustrate more than three times greater content of β-cells within sorted population, as compared to α-cells (paired, two-tailed Student's *t*-test). Data expressed as mean ± SEM.

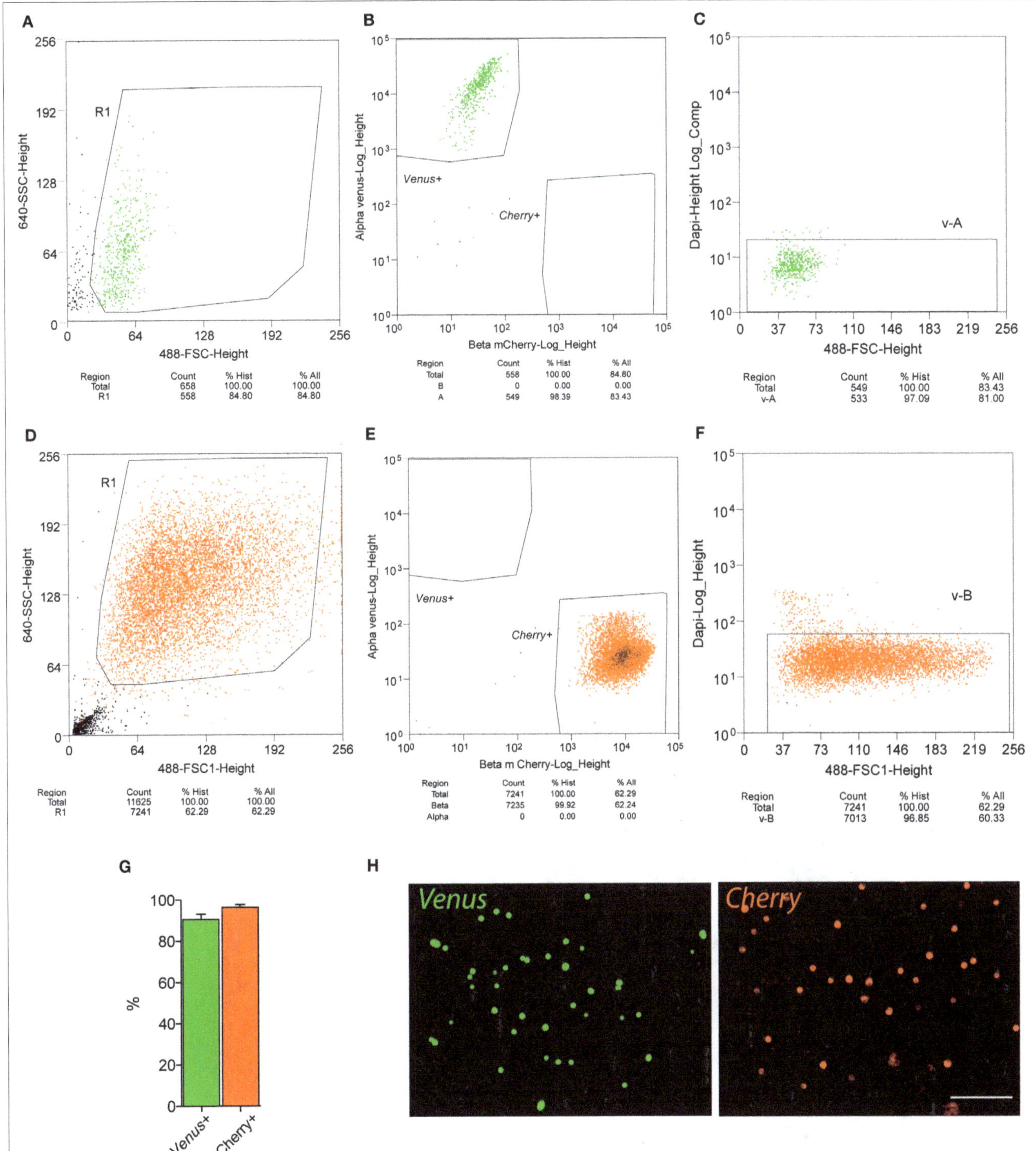

FIGURE 3 | Purity of α- and β-cell populations, separated by fluorescence-activated cell sorting (FACS) form ProGcg-Venus/RIP-Cherry/Per2:Luc mouse islets. Sorted samples of *Venus*- and *Cherry*-positive cells were subsequently analyzed by the second run of FACS. **(A–C)** FACS-assessed purity analysis of obtained α-cell population: **(A)** dot plot presenting distribution of cell size [forward scatter detector (FSC), *x*-axis] versus granularity [side scatter detector (SSC), *y*-axis] of *Venus*-positive cells within gated cell population; **(B)** dot plot showing sample enrichment for *Venus*-positive cells and complete absence of *Cherry*-positive cells; **(C)** DAPI-assessed analysis of α-cell viability after sorting, indicating 97% viable cells in the sample. **(D–F)** FACS-assessed purity analysis of obtained β-cell population: **(D)** dot plot presenting distribution of cell size (FSC, *x*-axis) versus granularity (SSC, *y*-axis) of *Cherry*-positive cells within gated cell population; **(E)** dot plot showing enrichment of sample for *Cherry*-positive cells and absence of *Venus*-positive contaminants; **(F)** DAPI-assessed analysis of β-cell viability after sorting, indicating approximately 97% viable cells in the sample. **(G)** Histogram representing average purity in analyzed samples (data are presented as mean ± SEM, $N = 6$ experiments for α-cells; and $N = 10$ for β-cells). **(H)** Representative fluorescent images illustrating sorted *Venus*- and *Cherry*-positive cell populations (α- and β-cells, respectively). Scale bar = 100 μm.

pancreatic islet. We successfully overcame this problem by utilizing transgenic mice, specifically expressing the *ProGcg-Venus* reporter in α-cells (23) and the RIP-*Cherry* reporter in β-cells (24) (**Figure 1**), allowing to separate these two cell populations by FACS with high viability and purity (**Figures 2** and **3**). The here-described methodology allows for extracting up to 40,000 β-cells and 12,500 α-cells per mouse (**Figure 2F**), and culturing thus separated primary α- and β-cells for at least 10 days. Importantly, the cell ratio after sorting reflects proportion between α- and β-cells in mouse pancreatic islets *in vivo* (60–80 versus 15–20%, respectively) (22, 29). The value obtained by FACS for this islet cell ratio following isolation and separation provides an estimation for the islet cell composition, which gives an advantage for studying the altered ratio between α- and β-cells upon different pathological conditions like obesity, T2D and others.

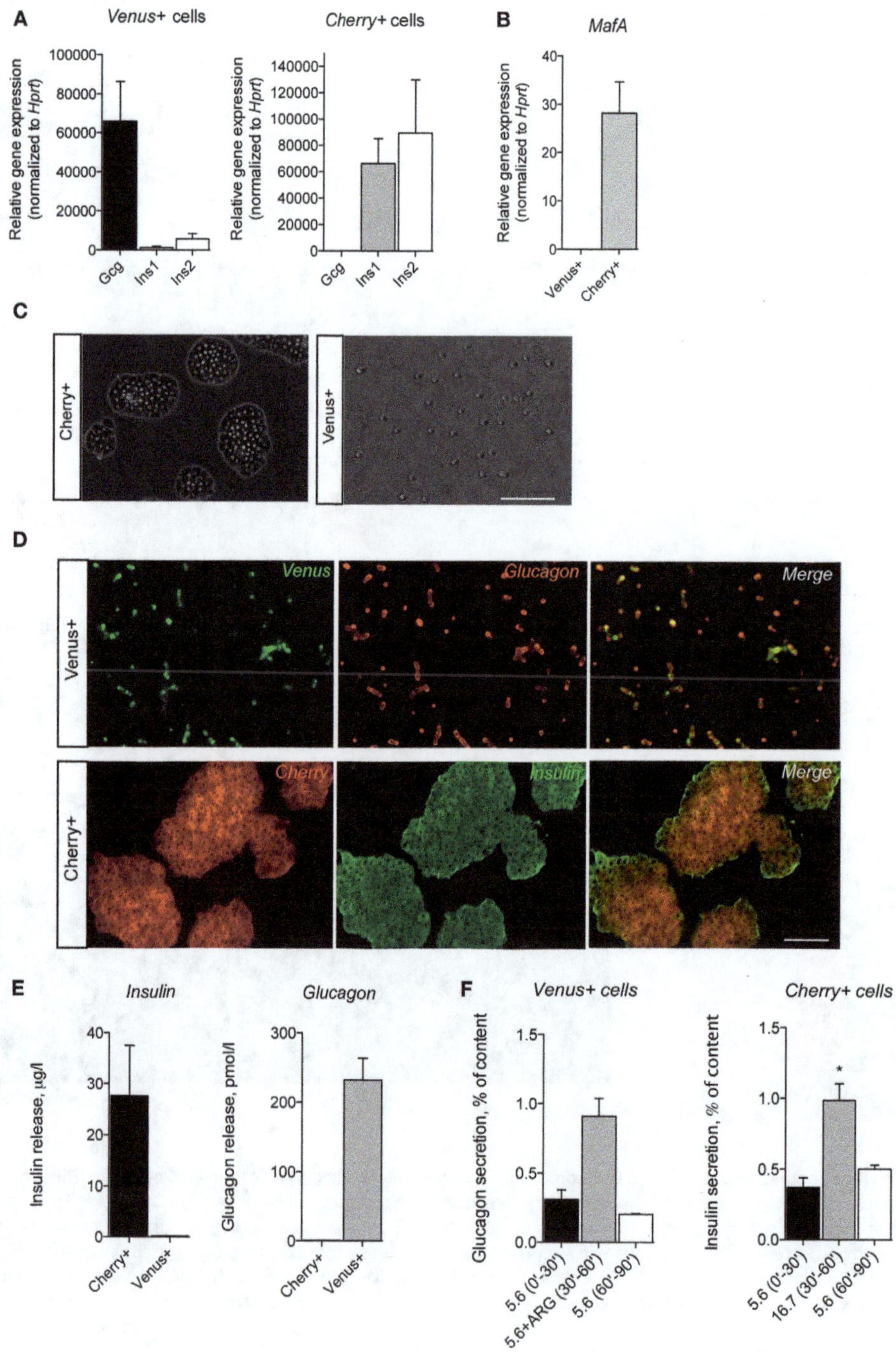

FIGURE 4 | Continued

FIGURE 4 | Continued
Endocrine identity of sorted *Venus*- and *Cherry*-positive cell populations, isolated from ProGcg-Venus/RIP-Cherry/Per2:Luc mouse islets by fluorescence-activated cell sorting (FACS). (A,B) Quantitative RT-PCR analysis of **(A)** insulin (*Ins1* and *Isn2*) and glucagon (*Gcg*) transcripts; or **(B)** V-Maf avian musculoaponeurotic fibrosarcoma oncogene homolog A (*MafA*) β-cell-specific transcript in freshly isolated *Venus*- and *Cherry*-positive cells. Data are presented as relative expression of the target gene normalized to the *Hprt* housekeeping gene (mean ± SEM, $N = 3$ independent experiments for **(A)** and $N = 4$ experiments for **(B)** with six mice each). **(C)** Representative bright-field images of cultured *Venus*- and *Cherry*-positive cells 48 h after plating. **(D)** Representative fluorescent images of ProGcg-Venus and Insulin-Cherry transgenic proteins (left panels) colocalizing with glucagon and insulin immunostaining, respectively (merge, right panels). Analysis of purified *Venus*- and *Cherry*-positive cell cultures prior the immunostaining showed no cross-contaminations. No *Venus*-positive cells appeared positive for insulin, and no *Cherry*-positive cells appeared positive for glucagon by immunostaining. Scale bars = 100 μm. **(E)** FACS-separated *Venus*- and *Cherry*-positive cells were plated in 35 mm dishes (approximately 15,000 cells per dish, as described in Section "Material and Methods"), and subjected to 30 min incubation with 2.8 mM glucose (for basal insulin assessment) or with 7 mM glucose (for basal glucagon assessment). Hormone levels were assessed in the incubation solution with Mouse Insulin and Glucagon ELISA kits (Mercodia). Data are expressed as absolute values (mean ± SD) for $N = 6$ mice used for two independent islet preparations. **(F)** Acute secretion assays performed on cultured *Venus*- and *Cherry*-positive cells 48 h after plating. Cell supernatants were collected for three successive 30-min periods (30 min basal condition, 30 min stimulated condition, and 30 min re-basal condition, as described in Section "Material and Methods") after 2 h of cell depletion in KRB solution. Hormone levels were assessed with Mouse Insulin and Glucagon ELISA kits and normalized to the residual hormone content in the end of the experiment. Data are expressed as percentage of glucagon or insulin from cell contents (mean ± SD; $N = 2$ experiments for *Venus*-positive cells and $N = 4$ experiments for *Cherry*-positive cells (two mice per experiment); * $p < 0.05$, two-tailed Student's *t*-test).

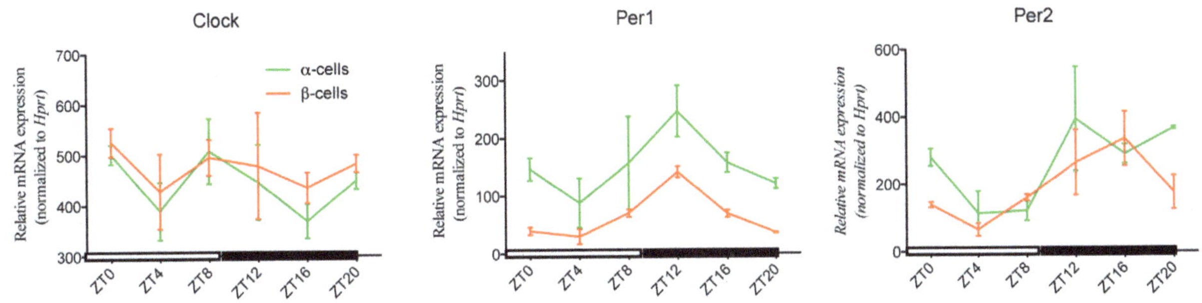

FIGURE 5 | Isolated around-the-clock α- and β-cells express *in vivo* circadian rhythm for selected core clock genes after fluorescence-activated cell sorting (FACS) separation. Triple transgenic mice (ProGcg-Venus/RIP-Cherry/Per2:Luc) were kept at standard 12 h/12 h light–dark cycles (ZT0 (Zeitgeber) corresponds to 07:00 a.m., and ZT12 corresponds to 07:00 p.m.), with constant access to the drinking water and night-restricted feeding regime for 2 weeks prior to islet collection. Pancreatic islets were isolated around-the-clock every 4 h and subjected to the FACS separation procedure. Temporal profiles of selected core clock transcripts (*Clock*, *Per1*, and *Per2*) were assessed in freshly extracted mRNA at each time point from α- and β-cell populations by quantitative RT-PCR analysis. Transcript levels were normalized to *Hprt* expression. Data expressed as mean ± SD ($N = 2$ biological replicates of 6 mice at each time point).

In an agreement with the previous studies, we demonstrate that a reporter-based separation of endocrine cells from pancreatic islets allows to obtain α- and β-cell populations bearing high expression levels of *glucagon*, and *insulin* and *MafA* transcripts, respectively (**Figures 4A,B**) (30, 31). Importantly, recently published by us circadian RNA sequencing analysis of thus separated α- and β-cell populations provides further extensive characterization of their differential transcriptional patterns (32). Indeed, *insulin*, *glucagon*, *MafA*, *Arx*, and additional cell-specific transcripts were expressed in a highly specific manner in the appropriate islet cell type (32). Additionally, separated primary α- and β-cells exhibited cell-specific glucagon and insulin positive immunostaining, respectively (**Figure 4D**), and inherent basal hormone release properties (**Figure 4E**). Moreover, cultured islet cells responded properly to the physiologically relevant secretagogues (high glucose for insulin, and arginine for glucagon), by inducing the respective hormone secretion about twofolds (**Figure 4F**). In line with these data, our recent work demonstrated that primary α-cells isolated from *ProGcg-Venus* mice responded to high glucose by a reduction in glucagon release (33), thus giving the opportunity to perform hormone secretion studies by these cells *in vitro*. This is particularly important for α-cells, since in mixed islet cell populations the glucagon secretion is altered by the amount of insulin secreted by adjacent β-cells, which represent the cell majority (34, 35). Furthermore, we have recently shown that both basal insulin secretion by synchronized β-cells and basal glucagon secretion by synchronized α-cells are circadian, further validating that thus isolated islet cells keep their cell-autonomous clocks and their functional properties (32).

Functional circadian oscillators have been previously characterized in mouse pancreatic islets (11, 18, 21, 36). However, circadian studies conducted in whole islets principally assess the more abundant β-cell population, and are unable to exclude complex functional interactions between different endocrine cell types (34, 35). At the same time, the circadian characteristics of α-cells remain largely unexplored and have only been assessed in a single study in primary cells to the best of our knowledge (37). The here presented efficient separation of islet cell populations paves the way for systematic analyses of circadian transcriptional outputs of the clock in pure populations of α- and β-cells *in vivo* (**Figure 5**), and *in vitro* following different synchronization stimuli upon selected conditions (as exemplified by forskolin synchronization in **Figure 6**). Our *in vivo* studies revealed circadian oscillations of *Per1* and *Per2* transcripts, exhibiting peak expression levels in the beginning of the dark phase in α- and β-cells, in accordance with a previous report for the intact islets (11). In contrast, the

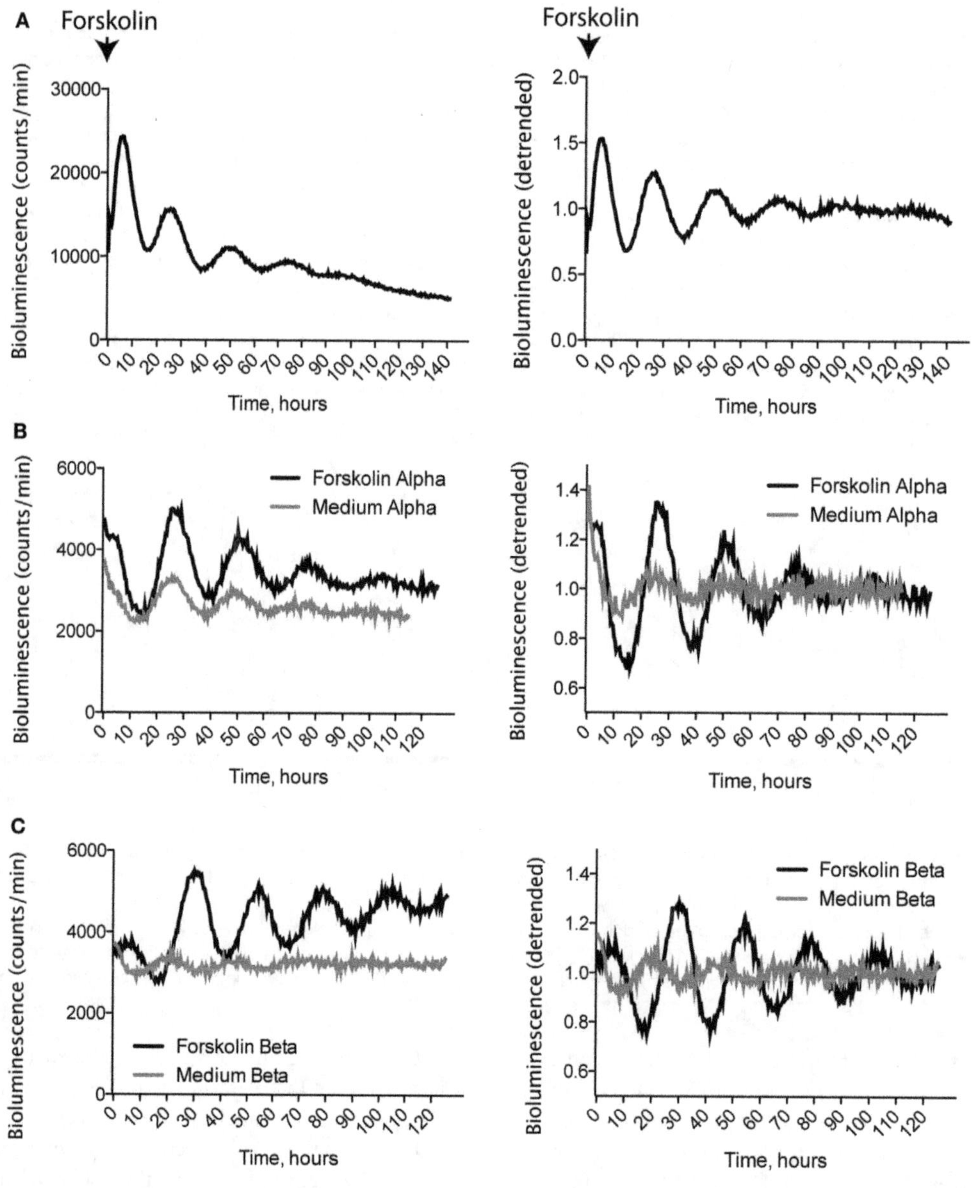

FIGURE 6 | *In vitro* monitoring of circadian rhythm in fluorescence-activated cell sorting-separated α- and β-cells. Representative Period2:Luciferase oscillation profiles of cultured whole islets **(A)**, α- cells **(B)**, and β-cells **(C)** isolated from ProGcg-Venus/RIP-Cherry/Per2:Luc mice, following 1-h synchronization with 10 μM forskolin or fresh medium **(A,B)**. Data are presented as absolute (left panels) or corresponding detrended (19) values (right panels).

temporal pattern of *Clock* expression was shallow, in agreement with earlier studies in mouse liver *in vivo* (26) and in synchronized human islets *in vitro* (19). These data strongly suggest that circadian oscillators persist in isolated α- and β-cells, following not only islet isolation procedure as previously demonstrated by Marcheva et al. (11), but also further trypsinization and FACS separation. Finally, in agreement with our previous observations in dispersed human islet cells compared to intact human islets (19, 20), our results further support that the three-dimensional islet structure is not essential for maintaining cell-autonomous molecular clocks in α- and β-cells (**Figure 6**). In agreement with previous publications (11, 18), demonstrating strong *in vitro* synchronizing properties of forskolin in pancreatic islets, we show high-amplitude, self-sustained circadian oscillations induced by a forskolin pulse in isolated islets, and in separated α- and β-cells (**Figure 6**). Moreover, our recent study suggests that α- and β-cell oscillators possess distinct circadian properties *in vivo* and *in vitro* (32). Importantly, this methodology allows to study the cell-autonomous impact of functional clocks on α- and β-cell hormone secretion *in vitro*, for instance by islet cell perifusion, as reported by us (38). The here-described strategy to study the circadian oscillator in separated primary mouse α- and β-cells will help to unravel the important functional roles of these cells in the regulation of glucose metabolism under physiological conditions, and upon metabolic diseases, including obesity and T2D.

AUTHOR CONTRIBUTIONS

VP contributed to data acquisition, analysis and interpretation, and drafted the manuscript. YG contributed to data acquisition and analysis. CD designed the study, contributed to the data acquisition and analysis, and drafted the manuscript. All authors took part in the revision of the manuscript and approved the final version.

ACKNOWLEDGMENTS

The authors thank Jacques Philippe for constructive discussions, and Ursula Loizides-Mangold for critical reading of the manuscript.

REFERENCES

1. Saini C, Brown SA, Dibner C. Human peripheral clocks: applications for studying circadian phenotypes in physiology and pathophysiology. *Front Neurol* (2015) 6:95. doi:10.3389/fneur.2015.00095
2. Balsalobre A, Damiola F, Schibler U. A serum shock induces circadian gene expression in mammalian tissue culture cells. *Cell* (1998) 93:929–37. doi:10.1016/S0092-8674(00)81199-X
3. Nagoshi E, Saini C, Bauer C, Laroche T, Naef F, Schibler U. Circadian gene expression in individual fibroblasts: cell-autonomous and self-sustained oscillators pass time to daughter cells. *Cell* (2004) 119:693–705. doi:10.1016/j.cell.2004.11.015
4. Dibner C, Schibler U. Circadian timing of metabolism in animal models and humans. *J Intern Med* (2015) 277:513–27. doi:10.1111/joim.12347
5. Partch CL, Green CB, Takahashi JS. Molecular architecture of the mammalian circadian clock. *Trends Cell Biol* (2014) 24:90–9. doi:10.1016/j.tcb.2013.07.002
6. Buxton OM, Cain SW, O'Connor SP, Porter JH, Duffy JF, Wang W, et al. Adverse metabolic consequences in humans of prolonged sleep restriction combined with circadian disruption. *Sci Transl Med* (2012) 4:129ra43. doi:10.1126/scitranslmed.3003200
7. Kalsbeek A, la Fleur S, Fliers E. Circadian control of glucose metabolism. *Mol Metab* (2014) 3:372–83. doi:10.1016/j.molmet.2014.03.002
8. Marcheva B, Ramsey KM, Peek CB, Affinati A, Maury E, Bass J. Circadian clocks and metabolism. *Handb Exp Pharmacol* (2013) 217:127–55. doi:10.1007/978-3-642-25950-0_6
9. Scheer FA, Hilton MF, Mantzoros CS, Shea SA. Adverse metabolic and cardiovascular consequences of circadian misalignment. *Proc Natl Acad Sci U S A* (2009) 106:4453–8. doi:10.1073/pnas.0808180106
10. Challet E. Circadian clocks, food intake, and metabolism. *Prog Mol Biol Transl Sci* (2013) 119:105–35. doi:10.1016/B978-0-12-396971-2.00005-1
11. Marcheva B, Ramsey KM, Buhr ED, Kobayashi Y, Su H, Ko CH, et al. Disruption of the clock components CLOCK and BMAL1 leads to hypoinsulinaemia and diabetes. *Nature* (2010) 466:627–31. doi:10.1038/nature09253
12. Turek FW, Joshu C, Kohsaka A, Lin E, Ivanova G, McDearmon E, et al. Obesity and metabolic syndrome in circadian clock mutant mice. *Science* (2005) 308:1043–5. doi:10.1126/science.1108750
13. Kalsbeek A, Fliers E. Daily regulation of hormone profiles. *Handb Exp Pharmacol* (2013) 217:185–226. doi:10.1007/978-3-642-25950-0_8
14. Philippe J, Dibner C. Thyroid circadian timing: roles in physiology and thyroid malignancies. *J Biol Rhythms* (2015) 30:76–83. doi:10.1177/0748730414557634
15. Tsang AH, Astiz M, Friedrichs M, Oster H. Endocrine regulation of circadian physiology. *J Endocrinol* (2016) 230:R1–11. doi:10.1530/JOE-16-0051
16. Perrin L, Loizides-Mangold U, Skarupelova S, Pulimeno P, Chanon S, Robert M, et al. Human skeletal myotubes display a cell-autonomous circadian clock implicated in basal myokine secretion. *Mol Metab* (2015) 4:834–45. doi:10.1016/j.molmet.2015.07.009
17. Shostak A, Husse J, Oster H. Circadian regulation of adipose function. *Adipocyte* (2013) 2:201–6. doi:10.4161/adip.26007
18. Perelis M, Marcheva B, Ramsey KM, Schipma MJ, Hutchison AL, Taguchi A, et al. Pancreatic beta cell enhancers regulate rhythmic transcription of genes controlling insulin secretion. *Science* (2015) 350:aac4250. doi:10.1126/science.aac4250
19. Pulimeno P, Mannic T, Sage D, Giovannoni L, Salmon P, Lemeille S, et al. Autonomous and self-sustained circadian oscillators displayed in human islet cells. *Diabetologia* (2013) 56:497–507. doi:10.1007/s00125-012-2779-7
20. Saini C, Petrenko V, Pulimeno P, Giovannoni L, Berney T, Hebrok M, et al. A functional circadian clock is required for proper insulin secretion by human pancreatic islet cells. *Diabetes Obes Metab* (2016) 18:355–65. doi:10.1111/dom.12616
21. Sadacca LA, Lamia KA, deLemos AS, Blum B, Weitz CJ. An intrinsic circadian clock of the pancreas is required for normal insulin release and glucose homeostasis in mice. *Diabetologia* (2011) 54:120–4. doi:10.1007/s00125-010-1920-8
22. Cabrera O, Berman DM, Kenyon NS, Ricordi C, Berggren PO, Caicedo A. The unique cytoarchitecture of human pancreatic islets has implications for islet cell function. *Proc Natl Acad Sci U S A* (2006) 103:2334–9. doi:10.1073/pnas.0510790103
23. Reimann F, Habib AM, Tolhurst G, Parker HE, Rogers GJ, Gribble FM. Glucose sensing in L cells: a primary cell study. *Cell Metab* (2008) 8:532–9. doi:10.1016/j.cmet.2008.11.002
24. Zhu X, Hu R, Brissova M, Stein RW, Powers AC, Gu G, et al. Microtubules negatively regulate insulin secretion in pancreatic beta cells. *Dev Cell* (2015) 34:656–68. doi:10.1016/j.devcel.2015.08.020
25. Yoo SH, Yamazaki S, Lowrey PL, Shimomura K, Ko CH, Buhr ED, et al. PERIOD2:LUCIFERASE real-time reporting of circadian dynamics reveals persistent circadian oscillations in mouse peripheral tissues. *Proc Natl Acad Sci U S A* (2004) 101:5339–46. doi:10.1073/pnas.0308709101
26. Atger F, Gobet C, Marquis J, Martin E, Wang J, Weger B, et al. Circadian and feeding rhythms differentially affect rhythmic mRNA transcription and translation in mouse liver. *Proc Natl Acad Sci U S A* (2015) 112:E6579–88. doi:10.1073/pnas.1515308112
27. Wojtusciszyn A, Andres A, Morel P, Charvier S, Armanet M, Toso C, et al. Immunomodulation by blockade of the TRANCE co-stimulatory pathway in murine allogeneic islet transplantation. *Transpl Int* (2009) 22:931–9. doi:10.1111/j.1432-2277.2009.00892.x
28. Parnaud G, Bosco D, Berney T, Pattou F, Kerr-Conte J, Donath MY, et al. Proliferation of sorted human and rat beta cells. *Diabetologia* (2008) 51:91–100. doi:10.1007/s00125-007-0855-1
29. Gomez Dumm CL, Console GM, Luna GC, Dardenne M, Goya RG. Quantitative immunohistochemical changes in the endocrine pancreas of nonobese diabetic (NOD) mice. *Pancreas* (1995) 11:396–401. doi:10.1097/00006676-199511000-00012
30. Adriaenssens AE, Svendsen B, Lam BY, Yeo GS, Holst JJ, Reimann F, et al. Transcriptomic profiling of pancreatic alpha, beta and delta cell populations identifies delta cells as a principal target for ghrelin in mouse islets. *Diabetologia* (2016) 59:2156–65. doi:10.1007/s00125-016-4033-1
31. Benner C, van der Meulen T, Caceres E, Tigyi K, Donaldson CJ, Huising MO. The transcriptional landscape of mouse beta cells compared to human beta cells reveals notable species differences in long non-coding RNA and protein-coding gene expression. *BMC Genomics* (2014) 15:620. doi:10.1186/1471-2164-15-620
32. Petrenko V, Saini C, Giovannoni L, Gobet C, Sage D, Unser M, et al. Pancreatic α- and β-cellular clocks have distinct molecular properties and impact on

islet hormone secretion and gene expression. *Genes Dev* (2017) 31:383–98. doi:10.1101/gad.290379

33. Dusaulcy R, Handgraaf S, Heddad-Masson M, Visentin F, Vesin C, Reimann F, et al. Alpha-cell dysfunctions and molecular alterations in male insulinopenic diabetic mice are not completely corrected by insulin. *Endocrinology* (2016) 157:536–47. doi:10.1210/en.2015-1725
34. Ishihara H, Maechler P, Gjinovci A, Herrera PL, Wollheim CB. Islet beta-cell secretion determines glucagon release from neighbouring alpha-cells. *Nat Cell Biol* (2003) 5:330–5. doi:10.1038/ncb951
35. Koh DS, Cho JH, Chen L. Paracrine interactions within islets of Langerhans. *J Mol Neurosci* (2012) 48:429–40. doi:10.1007/s12031-012-9752-2
36. Qian J, Block GD, Colwell CS, Matveyenko AV. Consequences of exposure to light at night on the pancreatic islet circadian clock and function in rats. *Diabetes* (2013) 62:3469–78. doi:10.2337/db12-1543
37. Vieira E, Marroqui L, Figueroa AL, Merino B, Fernandez-Ruiz R, Nadal A, et al. Involvement of the clock gene Rev-erb alpha in the regulation of glucagon secretion in pancreatic alpha-cells. *PLoS One* (2013) 8:e69939. doi:10.1371/journal.pone.0069939
38. Petrenko V, Saini C, Perrin L, Dibner C. Parallel measurement of circadian clock gene expression and hormone secretion in human primary cell cultures. *J Vis Exp* (2016) 117:e54673. doi:10.3791/54673

16

Sleep and Circadian Rhythms in Survivors of Acute Respiratory Failure

*Pei-Lin Yang[1], Teresa M. Ward[1], Robert L. Burr[1], Vishesh K. Kapur[2], Susan M. McCurry[1], Michael V. Vitiello[3], Catherine L. Hough[2] and Elizabeth C. Parsons[2,4]**

[1] School of Nursing, University of Washington, Seattle, WA, United States, [2] Division of Pulmonary, Critical Care and Sleep Medicine, University of Washington, Seattle, WA, United States, [3] Department of Psychiatry and Behavioral Sciences, University of Washington, Seattle, WA, United States, [4] VA Puget Sound Health Care System, Seattle, WA, United States

Edited by:
Xavier Drouot,
University of Poitiers, France

Reviewed by:
Axel Steiger,
Ludwig Maximilian University of Munich, Germany
Hiroshi Kadotani,
Shiga University of Medical Science, Japan

***Correspondence:**
Elizabeth C. Parsons
parsonse@uw.edu

Background: Little is known about sleep and circadian rhythms in survivors of acute respiratory failure (ARF) after hospital discharge.

Objectives: To examine sleep and rest-activity circadian rhythms in ARF survivors 3 months after hospital discharge, and to compare them with a community-dwelling population.

Methods: Sleep diary, actigraphy data, and insomnia symptoms were collected in a pilot study of 14 ARF survivors. Rest-activity circadian rhythms were assessed with wrist actigraphy and sleep diary for 9 days, and were analyzed by cosinor and non-parametric circadian rhythm analysis.

Results: All participants had remarkable actigraphic sleep fragmentation, 71.5% had subclinical or clinical insomnia symptoms. Compared to community-dwelling adults, this cohort had less stable rest-activity circadian rhythms ($p < 0.001$), and weaker circadian strength ($p < 0.001$).

Conclusion: Insomnia and circadian disruption were common in ARF survivors. Sleep improvement and circadian rhythm regularity may be a promising approach to improve quality of life and daytime function after ARF.

Keywords: acute respiratory distress syndrome, critical illness, sleep, circadian rhythm, actigraphy

INTRODUCTION

Survivors of Acute Respiratory Distress Syndrome (ARDS) experience impairments in physical, psychological, and cognitive functioning, as well as quality of life (1–4). Sleep disorders may play an important role in post-intensive care unit (ICU) syndrome, defined as a constellation of cognitive, psychological and physical impairment lasting months to years after discharge (5). A systematic literature review found that sleep disturbances affected an estimated 67% of ARDS survivors at 1-month post-hospitalization and 39% beyond 1-month post-hospitalization (6). The majority of these studies use self-report measures that focus on sleepiness or insomnia (6, 7). Few studies have incorporated objective sleep measures that could identify circadian rhythm (also known as sleep-wake) disorders for which ARDS survivors are at risk (7).

Many biobehavioral processes in humans, including sleep-wake behavior, follow a diurnal pattern, often called a circadian rhythm. Circadian rhythms are endogenous rhythmic patterns in multiple physiological and behavioral processes such as sleep-wake patterns, rest-activity patterns, mood, cognitive function, body temperature, heart rate, and hormone secretions that are entrained to a 24-h day to enable individuals to anticipate and adapt to periodic environmental changes (8–10). Optimal circadian entrainment, exhibiting a 24-h period with an appropriate amplitude (strength) and phase (timing), is essential for the optimization of physical, psychological, and behavioral functions and overall human health (9, 10). Abnormalities in the circadian rhythm have been identified in the acute ICU period, including a dampened circadian amplitude, and/or a delayed phase of physiological circadian biomarkers (i.e., melatonin, cortisol, cytokines) (11–13). Left untreated, circadian disruption may contribute to persistent sleep complaints including insomnia (9, 10) and/or influence mood and cognition (14, 15). However, to date, it is not known whether circadian rhythms are disrupted after hospital discharge among ARDS survivors.

Wrist actigraphy is a non-invasive, objective measure of sleep-wake patterns and circadian rest-activity rhythms recordable for extended periods of time in a natural environment. Estimates of sleep parameters (i.e., sleep onset and offset, total sleep time, sleep efficiency) and rest-activity circadian rhythms with actigraphy in conjunction with sleep diaries have been validated by polysomnography (PSG) and other circadian biomarkers such as melatonin and core body temperature (16–20). Wrist actigraphy has been accepted as a reliable surrogate measure of sleep and entrained endogenous circadian rhythms in both clinical and research settings (16–18, 21). To our knowledge, there are no published studies using actigraphy in conjunction with sleep diary to identify circadian disruption among ARDS survivors.

The purpose of this pilot study was to: (1) examine sleep duration, sleep quality, and rest-activity circadian rhythms as measured by sleep diary and actigraphy in ARDS survivors 3 months after hospital discharge; and (2) compare sleep and circadian rest-activity rhythms of ARDS survivors to community dwelling adults in the U.S. A better understanding of sleep and circadian rest-activity rhythms in ARDS survivors after hospital discharge may provide new knowledge for the development of interventions to improve sleep and daytime function on the ARDS population.

MATERIALS AND METHODS

Participants and Procedures

This study is a subset analysis from a prospective observational cohort pilot study named **S**leep **a**nd **R**ecovery after **A**cute Respiratory Failure (**SARA study**). SARA recruited 21 patients with acute respiratory failure admitted to an urban medical center in the Pacific Northwest, a tertiary care hospital from December 2012 to August 2013. Patients in the medical and surgical ICU were screened consecutively for eligibility in this prospective observational cohort study. Eligible patients (or their healthcare proxies) were approached before or shortly after hospital discharge (within 1 week of discharge) and invited to participate in the study. Enrolled patients included both medical and surgical ICU patients with a variety of primary diagnoses and varying lengths of stay. Inclusion criteria included (1) >18 years, (2) admitted to the ICU, and (3) required ≥ 48 h of mechanical ventilation. Participants were excluded if they had (1) chronic mechanical ventilation, (2) primary neurological injury or diagnosis, or pregnancy, or (3) inability to obtain patient or surrogate consent. The SARA study was reviewed and and approved by the University Human Subjects Institutional Review Board (No. 43516). Informed consent was obtained from all participants prior to data collection. Patients enrolled in the study were evaluated prospectively using sleep questionnaires, actigraphy and sleep diary. At 3 months post-discharge, study evaluation included a survey of sleep and quality of life symptoms, and 9 days of actigraphy and sleep diary. Of 21 patients enrolled in the SARA study, this subset analysis included the 14 patients with sleep diary and actigraphy data (the participant rate: 66.7%, two patients were lost to follow-up, 1 withdrew from the study, 4 refused actigraphy).

Measures

Sleep Characteristics

Sleep characteristics were evaluated objectively by actigraphy and subjectively by sleep diary for 9 consecutive days at home.

Objective sleep estimates

Participants were asked to wear a wrist actigraphy (Actiwatch2, Phillips-Respironics) on the non-dominant wrist to record raw activity counts in 1 min epochs. Actigraphy data were scored as sleep or wake with medium (40 activity count threshold) wake sensitivity settings under Actiware software (Mini-Mitter Philips Respironics, Inc.) (6, 19, 20, 22). The onset and offset of the rest intervals were determined by the sleep diaries and was based on the American Academy of Sleep Medicine (AASM) scoring actigraphy standard criteria (19, 20, 23). Five actigraphy sleep parameters were included in this study: (1) sleep onset, defined as the time of the first period of 10 or more consecutive minutes of immobility; (2) sleep offset, defined as the time of the last period of 10 or more consecutive minutes of immobility; (3) total sleep time (TST_A), defined as the total amount of nocturnal sleep duration in hours during the nighttime rest period scored as sleep; (4) actigraphy sleep efficiency (SE_A), defined as the ratio of TST to the nighttime rest period (multiplied by 100 to yield a percentage); and (5) amount of wake, defined as the wake time after sleep onset (WASO) in minutes.

Subjective sleep estimates

Three sleep parameters derived from sleep diary included (1) total sleep time (TST_D), defined as the time participants reported in the item as "the total amount of time they slept at night;" (2) diary-derived SE (SE_D), defined as the ratio of TST_D to total time in bed (multiplied by 100 to yield a percentage); and (3) self-reported sleep quality, assessed by how participant rated the item "when I woke up for the day, I felt" on the level of refreshed, somewhat refreshed, or fatigued.

Insomnia symptoms

Participants were administered the Insomnia Severity Index (ISI) to measure their perception of insomnia symptoms over the past 2 weeks. The ISI is a self-reported seven-item questionnaire designed to assess the severity of sleep problems (e.g., sleep-onset, difficulties in maintenance), satisfaction with current sleep patterns, interference with daily functioning, the impairment of quality of life and distress about sleep problems (24). Each item is rated with a five-point Likert scale ("not at all" to "extremely") and total score ranges from 0 to 28 with higher scores indicating greater severity of insomnia symptom. An ISI value between 8 and 14 was used to identify subclinical insomnia; a cut-off value of ≥15 was used to identify clinically significant insomnia (24). The ISI has established reliability and validity for survivors of critical illness (25, 26).

Rest-Activity Circadian Rhythm

Rest-activity circadian rhythms derived from actigraphy recordings in this study were analyzed by two different methods to account for both normal and non-normal distributions of data, using traditional parametric cosinor analysis and non-parametric circadian rhythm analysis (NPCRA) (16, 27, 28). Analysis of circadian rhythms requires specialized statistical analyses to account for the periodicity of the data, the distribution of the data, and temporal changes over time. Cosinor analysis is a traditional approach to characterize rest-activity circadian rhythms, in which a cosinor curve with a period of 24 h is fit to a multiple-day time series of measurements of raw activity counts by using least-squares methods (27–31). Three cosinor parameters were included in this study: (1) mesor, defined as mean activity count of the fitted 24-h circadian rhythm pattern; (2) magnitude, defined as mesor-to-peak difference, indicating half estimated extent of the variation within the cycle; and (3) acrophase, defined as highest activity timing in the cycle expressed in decimal hours [**Figure 1**; (28, 29)]. These three parameters were used to characterize the circadian phase (timing) and circadian strength. Clinically, acrophase is the measure of circadian phase; mesor and magnitude reflect the robustness of rest-activity circadian rhythms.

As the assumed temporal distribution of cosinor analysis may not always fit the real-world rest-activity patterns well, we also performed a non-parametric analysis (NPCRA) to make our data analysis more robust (32). Six NPCRA variables were included in this study: (1) interdaily stability (IS) provides an estimate of stability of rest-activity rhythms across days, ranging from 0 to 1, and a higher IS value indicates a better synchronization to 24-h environmental cues; (2) intradaily variability (IV) provides the estimate of fragmentation of the 24-h rest-activity rhythms, ranging from 0 to 2, and a higher IV value is found in individuals who have worse sleep efficiency or greater fragmented circadian rhythm patterns; (3) M10 midpoint is determined by the midpoint of the 10 most active consecutive hours, indicating the time of highest activity; (4) L5 midpoint is determined by the midpoint of the 5 least active consecutive hours, indicating the time of lowest activity; (5) amplitude is determined by difference between M10 and L5 levels, indicating the difference in activity level of highest and lowest activity periods; and (6) relative amplitude (RA) is determined by the amplitude divided by the sum of L5 and M10 levels, ranging from 0 to 1, and a higher RA indicates stronger circadian rhythm strength (27, 29, 33).

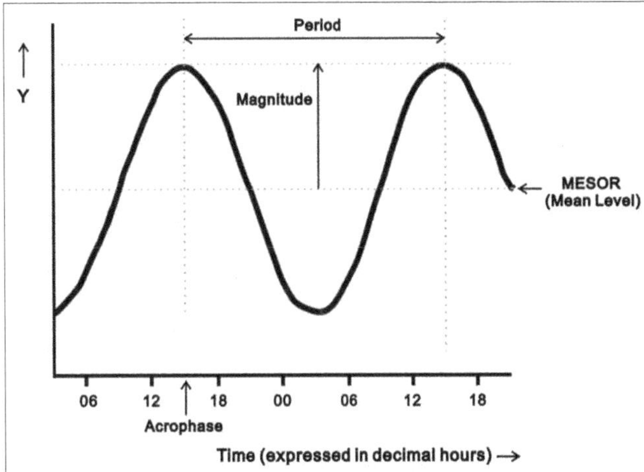

FIGURE 1 | Diagram illustrating four parameters of the oscillation from cosinor analysis: mesor (the estimated mean activity count of the fitted 24-h pattern), period (the duration of a full cycle), magnitude (mesor-to-peak difference, indicating robustness/strength of rhythm), and acrophase (the time of peak activity). Adapted from Cornelissen (28).

Demographic and Clinical Characteristics

Trained research personnel extracted demographic (i.e., age and gender) and clinical characteristics including pre-existing comorbidities (heart disease, sleep apnea, hypertension, diabetes, and depression), body mass index (BMI), diagnosis at ICU admission (trauma or medical), length of hospital stay and ICU stay, duration of medical ventilation, PaO_2/FiO_2 ratio, and illness severity at ICU admission based on Acute Physiology and Chronic Health Evaluation II classification system (APACHE II) (34) from electronic medical record. Participants were asked about living situation and employment status as well as if they needed any assistance with any of eight instrumental activities of daily living (IADLs) including using the telephone, walking, shopping for groceries, preparing meals, doing housework or handyman work, doing laundry, taking medication, and managing money (35) on a scale of 0 (unable to do at all), 1 (need some help), and 2 (need no help). The summed individual IADL scores were used to create a global IADL score, indicative of patient functional status; global IADL scores could range from 0 (low function, dependent) to 16 (high function, independent).

Statistical Analysis

Descriptive statistics were used to describe the demographic and clinical characteristics of the participants. As only actigraphy sleep data with matching sleep diary data were included in the analyses, participants had between 6 and 9 days of concurrent actigraphy sleep data (median = 9 days, five participants had <9 days of concurrent data). Actigraphy-measured sleep onset and offset, TST_A, SE_A, and WASO plus self-reported TST_D and SE_D from the sleep diary were averaged over consecutive study days for each participant. The sleep characteristics were skewed; consequently, medians and interquartile ranges (IQR) were reported for the actigraphy and self-report sleep measures.

Actigraphy circadian outcomes were analyzed by cosinor analysis and NPCRA analysis to quantify 24-h rest-activity circadian rhythms for each participant. Actigraphy raw activity data were transformed using natural log (ln) function followed by fitting a 24-h cosine curve through regression analysis. Given the activity count data were highly skewed, natural log transformation was able to make the activity count data at each time point more uniform and balanced over a 24-h period, especially important for the low-activity nighttime period (36). Circadian outcomes were presented as means ± standard deviation (SD) to depict rest-activity circadian rhythms.

Given the nature of this pilot study with the lack of comparison group, each of the mean actigraphy circadian parameters, TST_A, and SE_A used Hedges' G effect sizes to compare with those from a sample of 578 community-dwelling U.S. adults, which have been described in detail elsewhere (37). Data analyses were performed using SPSS (v 25).

RESULTS

Participant Demographic and Clinical Characteristics

Table 1 shows the demographic and clinical characteristics of the study sample. The mean age of the sample was 49.1 ± 15.9 years; 71% were male and lived independently. Fifty-seven percent were trauma patients and 79% met the criteria for moderate and severe ARDS (PaO2/FiO2 ratio ≤200) (38). The mean premorbid IADL score was 12.8 ± 2.5, indicating mild functional limitations, yet only 14% ($n = 2$) were full-time employed.

TABLE 1 | Demographic and clinical characteristics of ARDS survivors ($n = 14$).

Variables[a]	Total sample
Demographics	
Age, years	49.1 ± 15.9
Male, *n* (%)	10 (71)
Body mass index, kg/m^2	27.4 ± 3.5
Living situation	
House/apartment (independent)	10 (71)
Rehabilitation facility	2 (14)
Others	2 (14)
IADL scores (0-16)	12.8 ± 2.5
Full time employment, *n* (%)	2 (14)
Pre-existing comorbidities, *n* (%)	
Heart disease	5 (36)
Sleep apnea	2 (14)
Hypertension	5 (36)
Diabetes	4 (29)
Depression	1 (7)
ICU characteristics	
Diagnosis at ICU admission, *n* (%)	
Trauma	8 (57)
Medical	6 (43)
Disease severity, APACHE II score	24.5 ± 4.9
PaO_2/FiO_2 ratio	163.8 ± 90.0
PaO_2/FiO_2 ratio ≤ 200, *n* (%)	11(79)
Length of hospital stay, days	21 ± 17.5
Length of ICU stay, days	11 ± 8.8
Duration of mechanical ventilation, hours	175.8 ± 135.0

ARDS, acute respiratory distress syndrome; IADL, instrumental activities of daily living; ICU, intensive care unit; APACHE II, acute physiology and chronic health evaluation II (APACHE II) classification system.

[a]Reported as mean ± standard deviation unless specified.

Sleep Characteristics in ARDS Survivors

Table 2 summarizes the actigraphy and sleep diary data and insomnia symptom scores. The median TST_A was 7.8 h (IQR: 6.2–8.3 h), the median WASO was 59.8 min (IQR: 45.0–92.8 min) and the median SE_A was 81.9% (IQR: 78.9–86.0%). Based on sleep diary data, the median TST_D was 6.6 h (IQR: 5.3–6.9 h), with a median SE_D of 70.0% (IQR: 62.2–80.6%). The median ISS score was 12.0 (IQR: 6.8–15.0). 42.9% of participants had subclinical insomnia (8≤ ISS score ≤14), and 28.6% had clinically significant insomnia (ISI score ≥15).

Rest-Activity Circadian Rhythm

Table 3 summarizes circadian rest-activity measures, as well as TST_A and SE_A and compares them with a community-dwelling sample of US adults (37). Additionally, comparisons of age and BMI between the two samples were performed to examine the potential effects of age and BMI on rest-activity circadian rhythms (37, 39). No significant differences in age and BMI between two samples were found, indicating the sample of community-dwelling US adults was comparable to our sample on these important rest-activity measures.

24-h Rhythm Stability/Variability

ARDS survivors had a mean IS of 0.32 (±0.10) compared to a typical value of 0.6 in healthy adults (27), suggesting ARDS survivors had a less stable rest-activity rhythm across the days. ARDS survivors had a mean IV of 0.55 (±0.18) which was congruent to the typical value of <1 for healthy adults (27). This suggests that ARDS survivors have a fairly regular rest-activity rhythm within a single day. ARDS survivors had significantly less stable rest-activity circadian rhythms across days [Hedges' G effect size, $E.S._{(G)}$ for IS $= -1.42$, $p < 0.001$], and less fragmented rest-activity circadian rhythms within a single day [$E.S._{(G)}$ for IV $= -1.30$, $p < 0.001$] compared with the sample of community-dwelling US adults. Less stability of rest-activity circadian rhythms across days in ARDS survivors could represent the suboptimal entrainment of endogenous circadian rhythms to environmental and social cues (37).

24-h Rhythm Phase

ARDS survivors exhibited later timing for peak activity [$E.S._{(G)}$ for acrophase = 0.61, $E.S._{(G)}$ for M10 midpoint = 0.65] and rest periods [$E.S._{(G)}$ for L5 midpoint = 0.55], and it might indicate a delayed circadian phase (also known as circadian phenotype) in ARDS survivors (40); however, the mean acrophase, L5, and M10 midpoint values were not significantly different in the two samples. ARDS survivors exhibited greater variances in peak activity (SD for acrophase = 2.05 vs. 1.3, SD for M10 midpoint

TABLE 2 | Sleep characteristics measured by actigraphy, sleep diary, and symptom survey ($n = 14$).

Variables	Median (IQR)
Actigraphy	
Sleep onset[a]	23:29 (22:11–00:30)
Sleep offset[a]	7:24 (6:11–09:19)
TST_A, hours	7.8 (6.2–8.3)
TST_A <7 h, *n* (%)	5 (35)
SE_A, %	81.9 (78.9–86.0)
SE_A <85%, *n* (%)	9 (64.3)
WASO, minutes	59.8 (45.0–92.8)
WASO >30 min, *n* (%)	14 (100)
Sleep diary	
TST_D, hours	6.6 (5.3–6.9)
TST_D <7 h, *n* (%)	11 (79)
SE_D, %	70.0 (62.2–80.6)
SE_D <85%, *n* (%)	11 (79)
Self-reported sleep quality[b]	
Refreshing sleep >3 nights, *n* (%)	2 (14.3)
Somewhat refreshing night >3 nights, *n* (%)	9 (64.3)
Fatigued sleep >3 nights, *n* (%)	4 (28.6)
Insomnia symptoms, ISI score	12.0 (6.8–15.0)
Clinical insomnia (ISI ≥15), *n* (%)	4 (28.6)
Subthreshold (8≤ ISI ≤14), *n* (%)	6 (42.9)
No clinically significant insomnia (ISS<8), *n* (%)	4 (28.6)

IQR, interquartile range; TST_A, total sleep time estimated by actigraphy; SE_A, sleep efficiency estimated by actigraphy; WASO, wake after sleep onset; TST_D, total sleep time estimated by sleep diary; SE_D, sleep efficiency estimated by sleep diary; ISS, insomnia severity index.

[a]Sleep onset, sleep offset times are presented in 24-h clock format.

[b]Due to missing data (18 number of days), 96 number of days were included to examine self-reported sleep quality.

= 2.64 vs. 1.6, respectively) and rest periods (SD for L5 midpoint = 2.49 vs. 1.3, respectively) compared with the sample of community-dwelling US adults, indicating higher heterogeneity of circadian phase in ARDS survivors.

Activity Strength and 24-h Rhythm Strength

A large effect size in mesor [$E.S._{(G)} = -2.01$, $p < 0.001$], magnitude [$E.S._{(G)} = -1.61$, $p < 0.001$], amplitude [$E.S._{(G)} = -12.03$, $p < 0.001$], and RA [$E.S._{(G)} = -1.18$, $p < 0.001$] were found in ARDS survivors of the sample compared with the sample of community-dwelling US adults. These results indicate that ARDS survivors were less active and had weaker rest-activity circadian rhythms compared to community-dwelling adults.

Sleep Quantity and Efficiency

Both TST_A [$E.S._{(G)} = 0.51$, $p = 0.15$] and SE_A [$E.S._{(G)} = -0.55$, $p = 0.01$] produced moderate effect sizes, but only SE_A was statistically *significant*, indicating that ARDS survivors had a longer objective total nighttime sleep time but lower sleep efficiency at 3 months after hospital discharge relative to the comparison sample.

TABLE 3 | Comparisons of the results from actigraphy rest-activity circadian rhythm and sleep data with those from a sample of community-dwelling US adults[a].

Parameters	ARDS survivors ($n = 14$)	Community-dwelling US adults ($n = 578$)	$E.S._{(G)}$	*p*
Age, years	49.1 (15.9)	51.9 (14.9)	−0.19	0.489
Body mass index, kg/m²	27.4 (3.5)	27.5 (6.0)	−0.02	0.951
24-h rhythm stability /variability				
NPCRA IS	0.32 (0.10)	0.49 (0.12)	−1.42	**<0.001**
NPCRA IV	0.55 (0.18)	0.86 (0.24)	−1.30	**<0.001**
Activity strength				
Cosinor Mesor, ln counts	2.9 (0.43)	3.9 (0.5)	−2.01	**<0.001**
24-h rhythm strength				
Cosinor Magnitude, ln counts	1.8 (0.39)	2.6 (0.5)	−1.61	**<0.001**
NPCRA Amplitude, ln counts	3.23 (0.68)	7.0 (0.3)	−12.03	**<0.001**
NPCRA Relative Amplitude (RA)	0.64 (0.11)	0.77 (0.11)	−1.18	**<0.001**
24-h rhythm phase				
Cosinor Acrophase, decimal hours	15.40 (2.05)	14.6 (1.3)	0.61	0.261
NPCRA L5 midpoint, decimal hours	3.44 (2.49)	2.7 (1.3)	0.55	0.288
NPCRA M10 midpoint, decimal hours	15.26 (2.64)	14.2 (1.6)	0.65	0.158
Actigraphy sleep parameters				
Total sleep time, hours	7.4 (1.2)	6.90 (0.97)	0.51	0.146
Sleep efficiency, %	81.7 (4.8)	85.6 (7.10)	−0.55	**0.010**

ARDS, acute respiratory distress syndrome; NPCRA, non-parametric circadian rhythm analysis; Ln, natural log; IS, interdaily stability; IV, intradaily variability; $E.S._{(G)}$, Hedges' G effect sizes. Bold values denote the significance at the $p < 0.05$ level.

[a]Data reported by Cespedes et al. (37).

DISCUSSION

This study provides preliminary data regarding rest-activity circadian rhythms and sleep quality after discharge among acute respiratory failure survivors. At 3 months post-discharge, our cohort of ARDS survivors exhibited subclinical and clinical insomnia symptoms, supported by findings from actigraphy (sleep fragmentation) and sleep diaries (reduced sleep time and quality). Survivors' rest-activity circadian rhythms displayed less stability and lower amplitude compared to that of a published community-dwelling population. To the best of our knowledge, this is the first study to identify persistent circadian rhythm disruption in ARDS survivors after hospital discharge.

Sleep Disruption in ARDS Survivors

Resolving the literature on sleep disruption after critical illness can be challenging due to the heterogeneity of ICU populations across studies. ICU survivors are a heterogenous group of patients with a variety of diagnoses, pre-existing comorbidities, severity of illness, and long-term outcomes. ARDS survivors are a useful population to examine the link between sleep and/or disruption and functional impairment, because this population shares a common pathophysiology (respiratory failure) and has a high prevalence of long-term functional impairment (4). Our goal in this study was to identify sleep and/or circadian disruptions that could reasonably contribute to the functional impairment of post-ICU syndrome.

Our cohort of ARDS survivors reported moderately impaired sleep time and sleep efficiency on their sleep diaries, but these findings were less notable in the actigraphy data. Subjective sleep disturbance was pronounced, similar to prior questionnaire studies in ICU survivors (7). The prevalence of ISI-defined clinical insomnia at 3-months post-discharge was 28.6%, similar to the prevalence at 12-months post-discharge in our previous work of ICU survivors (26). Objective total sleep time is slightly better in our cohort compared than found among 1-month ICU survivors by Solverson et al. (TST_A: 7.8 vs. 6.2 h, respectively); sleep efficiency estimates are quite similar (SE_A: 81.9 vs. 78%, respectively) (41). The improved sleep time in our cohort compared to Solverson's may reflect methodological differences and/or the population studied (6, 7). We performed an average of 9 nights of actigraphy (Solverson et al. performed 3 nights). Given the potential for night-to-night variability, particularly among ICU survivors with insomnia (7, 42), a longer assessment period would be expected to generate more reliable sleep estimates. Factors that might explain slightly worse sleep in Solverson's cohort include the earlier assessment period (1 month post-ICU vs. 3 months after hospital discharge) and longer duration of mechanical ventilation (240 vs. 175 h, respectively). Solverson's study also included mostly medical ICU patients, who tend to be older and exhibit more pre-existing comorbidities than trauma ICU patients (57% of our cohort). Interestingly, our ARDS cohort exhibited higher severity of illness (APACHE II score: 24.5 vs. 20, respectively) and longer hospital length of stay (21 vs.15 days, respectively) than those in Solverson's cohort. The relative importance of pre-existing comorbidity and ICU factors in predicting post-ICU sleep disruption is a question that bears further investigation.

Most survivors in our cohort reported insomnia symptoms and subjective deficits in sleep quantity and quality, while standard actigraphy measures of sleep (total sleep time and sleep efficiency) were fairly normal. There are several possible reasons for these findings. First, sleep diary may align better with subjective sleep impairment than standard actigraphy measures, and sleep diary tends to underestimate sleep time and efficiency compared to actigraphy (22, 43, 44). Second, identifying circadian abnormalities requires specialized analyses that take into account the timing of the sleep period, which is not reflected in standard actigraphy parameters. Untreated circadian disruption may contribute to insomnia (45), and effective treatment must take account both sleep and circadian components. While limited in size and scope, this pilot study provides an intriguing potential insight into a circadian contribution to the subjective sleep complaints commonly described among survivors of critical illness (6, 42, 46).

Rest-Activity Circadian Disruption in ARDS Survivors

Our cohort exhibited multiple circadian abnormalities including a less stable rest-activity circadian rhythm, later timings for their peak activity and rest periods, a greater variance in circadian phase, and less active and weaker rest-activity circadian strength compared to the community-dwelling US adult sample with similar age and BMI distribution. To our knowledge, the present study is the first using actigraphy to examine rest-activity circadian rhythms after critical illness.

Possible contributors to circadian disruption after hospitalization among ARDS survivors include inflammation, delirium, side effects of ICU treatments (i.e., sedative medications, mechanical ventilation), and post-ICU depression, anxiety, and post-traumatic stress disorder (3, 11–13, 47–49). Our cohort represented weaker rest-activity circadian rhythms compared to community-dwelling adults supported the lower values of cosinor magnitude as well as NPCRA amplitude and RA. A recent population-based study showed that lower relative amplitude of rest-activity rhythms was related to depressed mood, mood instability, and poor subjective wellbeing (i.e., happiness, health satisfaction) (50). A lack of regular daily routine may be another possible explanation for post-ICU circadian disruption, supported by findings in our cohort including the low IS value, large variance in sleep offset times, and high percentage of unemployed participants. Regular daytime routines (i.e., work or social schedules; exposure to light, exercise, and food cues) are essential to strengthen the regularity of the circadian system (9, 10, 51, 52). Further work is needed to identify post-ICU mental health and behavioral factors that may be associated with circadian disruption and serve as appropriate targets for intervention.

Left untreated, rest-activity circadian disruption may exacerbate cognitive and psychological comorbidities in ARDS survivors. Participants in our study were able to live independently and had mild functional limitations in activities of daily living, but IADLs only reflect some domains of cognitive function. ARDS survivors often experience persistent impairments in physical activity and social functioning (3, 4, 53), both of which have been found to be associated with low activity and weak circadian strength (54, 55). Impairments in memory, executive functioning, attention, visual-spatial construction, and language have been described in ARDS survivors but were not measured in this study (56, 57). In other populations rather than ICU survivors, cognitive impairment has been associated with disrupted rest-activity circadian rhythms (i.e., less stability, more fragmentation or lower rest-activity amplitude) (39, 55, 58–60). A prospective study with 1,282 healthy older community-dwelling women reported that a less stable, lower rest-activity amplitude, and delayed peak activity timing of rest-activity circadian rhythms predicted the development of either mild cognitive impairment or dementia 4.9 years later, independently of SE and TST (58). Future studies are needed to identify if rest-activity circadian disruption may be a contributor to long-term cognitive deficits among ARDS survivors.

Circadian re-entrainment may be a valuable treatment for sleep and quality of life improvement after critical illness (13, 36, 47). Re-entrainment generally includes a combination of chronotherapy (light and/or melatonin exposure) and behavioral interventions (e.g., set wake time). The timing of these therapies differs by the patient's underlying circadian phenotype. Delayed circadian phase ("night owl" phenotype) is treated with morning light and evening melatonin, while advanced circadian phase ("morning lark" phenotype) is treated with evening light. In our cohort, we discovered large variances in circadian phase markers of acrophase, M10, and L5 midpoints. Some subjects displayed delayed circadian phase ("night owl" phenotype) while others displayed advanced circadian phase ("morning lark" phenotype) (61). In the ICU, morning light and/or evening melatonin have been prescribed to improve nighttime sleep, circadian rhythms, and decrease delirium (13, 47). This timing of therapy is likely beneficial in patients with delayed circadian phase (e.g., "night owl" phenotype). However, it could worsen advanced circadian phase (e.g., "morning lark" phenotype) and may yield minimal benefit among those with normal circadian phase. Larger studies are needed, but our findings suggest that sleep interventions in ICU survivors may need to account for multiple circadian phenotypes.

Limitations

Limitations of the current study include our small sample size and restriction of the sample to ARDS survivors. Our findings need replication in larger and more diverse samples of ICU survivors. Data analysis only included data from the ARDS survivors who completed actigraphy and sleep diary for 9 consecutive days. Participant bias may potentially limit our results to generalize a general population of ARDS survivors. Data on sleep prior to critical illness were not available, and therefore we cannot identify a causal role for critical illness in the circadian abnormalities found in our cohort. Our study suggests that actigraphy is a feasible method to identify circadian disruption in ARDS survivors. While actigraphy is a widely accepted method for estimating sleep and entrained circadian rhythms in other populations, its use has not formally been validated against PSG (the gold standard) in ARDS survivors. Additional study is warranted to examine the validity of actigraphy concurrently with PSG. Larger studies are needed to capture a more comprehensive picture of circadian rhythms after ARDS, potentially incorporating biological markers (i.e., melatonin) and measures of behavioral and environmental contributors (i.e., light exposure) that perpetuate circadian disruption.

CONCLUSIONS

Findings from this pilot study show that sleep and rest-activity circadian disruption is common among survivors of acute respiratory failure 3 months after hospital discharge. Sleep and circadian disruption are potentially treatable through chronotherapy (i.e., light, melatonin) as well as behavioral strategies. Sleep improvement and circadian rhythm regularity may be a promising approach to improve quality of life and daytime function in ARDS survivors. Future research is warranted in larger samples to validate these findings, their association with quality of life, and to target specific chronotypes with effective circadian interventions.

AUTHOR CONTRIBUTIONS

EP contributed to design, patient enrollment, data collection, management, analysis, and interpretation. VK, SM, MV, and CH contributed to the design and implementation of the research. P-LY, TW, and RB performed data analysis and interpretation. P-LY, TW, RB, and EP took the lead in writing manuscript. All authors provided critical feedback to this manuscript and approved the final manuscript for publication.

FUNDING

This project was supported by National Institutes of Health/National Institute of Nursing Research, Center for Research on the Management of Sleep Disturbances (P30 NR 011400-01); Center for Innovation in Sleep Self-Management (P30 NR 016585); and pre-doctoral scholarship from National Defense Medical Bureau, the Republic of China (Taiwan).

ACKNOWLEDGMENTS

The authors thank Ellen Caldwell for assistance with data management, and Dr. Horacio de la Iglesia (University of Washington) for consulting about circadian rhythms.

REFERENCES

1. Dodoo-Schittko F, Brandstetter S, Blecha S, Thomann-Hackner K, Brandl M, Knüttel H, et al. Determinants of quality of life and return to work following acute respiratory distress syndrome: a systematic review. *Dtsch Arztebl Int.* (2017) 114:103–9. doi: 10.3238/arztebl.2017.0103
2. Rubenfeld GD, Herridge MS. Epidemiology and outcomes of acute lung injury. *Chest.* (2007) 131:554–62. doi: 10.1378/chest.06-1976

3. Herridge MS, Moss M, Hough CL, Hopkins RO, Rice TW, Bienvenu OJ, et al. Recovery and outcomes after the acute respiratory distress syndrome (ARDS) in patients and their family caregivers. *Intensive Care Med.* (2016) 42:725–38. doi: 10.1007/s00134-016-4321-8
4. Bein T, Weber-Carstens S, Apfelbacher C. Long-term outcome after the acute respiratory distress syndrome: different from general critical illness? *Curr Opin Crit Care.* (2018) 24:35–40. doi: 10.1097/MCC.0000000000000476
5. Rawal G, Yadav S, Kumar R. Post-intensive care syndrome: an overview. *J Transl Int Med.* (2017) 5:90–2. doi: 10.1515/jtim-2016-0016
6. Dhooria S, Sehgal I, Agrawal A, Agarwal R, Aggarwal A, Behera D. Sleep after critical illness: study of survivors of acute respiratory distress syndrome and systematic review of literature. *Indian J Crit Care Med.* (2016) 20:323–31. doi: 10.4103/0972-5229.183908
7. Altman MT, Knauert MP, Pisani MA. Sleep disturbance after hospitalization and critical illness: a systematic review. *Ann Am Thorac Soc.* (2017) 14:1457–68. doi: 10.1513/AnnalsATS.201702-148SR
8. Foster RG, Kreitzman L. The rhythms of life: what your body clock means to you! *Exp Physiol.* (2014) 99:599–606. doi: 10.1113/expphysiol.2012.071118
9. Roenneberg T, Merrow M. The circadian clock and human health. *Curr Biol.* (2016) 26:R432–43. doi: 10.1016/j.cub.2016.04.011
10. Baron KG, Reid KJ. Circadian misalignment and health. *Int Rev Psychiatry.* (2014) 26:139–54. doi: 10.3109/09540261.2014.911149
11. Knauert MP, Haspel JA, Pisani MA. Sleep loss and circadian rhythm disruption in the intensive care unit. *Clin Chest Med.* (2015) 36:419–29. doi: 10.1016/j.ccm.2015.05.008
12. Telias I, Wilcox ME. Sleep and circadian rhythm in critical illness. *Crit Care.* (2019) 23:82 doi: 10.1186/s13054-019-2366-0
13. Oldham MA, Lee HB, Desan PH. Circadian rhythm disruption in the critically ill: an opportunity for improving outcomes. *Crit Care Med.* (2016) 44:207–17. doi: 10.1097/CCM.0000000000001282
14. Vadnie CA, McClung CA. Circadian rhythm disturbances in mood disorders: insights into the role of the suprachiasmatic nucleus. *Neural Plast.* (2017) 2017:1504507. doi: 10.1155/2017/1504507
15. Videnovic A, Lazar AS, Barker RA, Overeem S. 'The clocks that time us'–circadian rhythms in neurodegenerative disorders. *Nat Rev Neurol.* (2014) 10:683–93. doi: 10.1038/nrneurol.2014.206
16. Ancoli-Israel S, Cole R, Alessi C, Chambers M, Moorcroft W, Pollak CP. The role of actigraphy in the study of sleep and circadian rhythms. *Sleep.* (2003) 26:342–92. doi: 10.1093/sleep/26.3.342
17. Wirz-Justice A. How to measure circadian rhythms in humans. *Medicographia.* (2007) 29:84–90. doi: 10.13078/jksrs09013
18. Hofstra WA, de Weerd AW. How to assess circadian rhythm in humans: a review of literature. *Epilepsy Behav.* (2008) 13:438–44. doi: 10.1016/j.yebeh.2008.06.002
19. Taibi DM, Landis CA, Vitiello MV. Concordance of polysomnographic and actigraphic measurement of sleep and wake in older women with insomnia. *J Clin Sleep Med.* (2013) 9:217–25. doi: 10.5664/jcsm.2482
20. Ward TM, Lentz M, Kieckhefer GM, Landis CA. Polysomnography and actigraphy concordance in juvenile idiopathic arthritis, asthma and healthy children. *J Sleep Res.* (2012) 21:113–21. doi: 10.1111/j.1365-2869.2011.00923.x
21. Morgenthaler T, Alessi C, Friedman L, Owens J, Kapur V, Boehlecke B, et al. Practice parameters for the use of actigraphy in the assessment of sleep and sleep disorders: an update for 2007. *Sleep.* (2007) 30:519–29. doi: 10.1093/sleep/30.4.519
22. Schwab KE, Ronish B, Needham DM, To AQ, Martin JL, Kamdar BB. Actigraphy to evaluate sleep in the intensive care unit. A systematic review. *Ann Am Thorac Soc.* (2018) 15:1075–82. doi: 10.1513/AnnalsATS.201801-004OC
23. Iber C, American Academy of Sleep M. *The AASM Manual for the Scoring of Sleep and Associated Events: Rules, Terminology and Technical Specifications.* Westchester, IL: American Academy of Sleep Medicine (2007).
24. Bastien CH, Vallières A, Morin CM. Validation of the Insomnia Severity Index as an outcome measure for insomnia research. *Sleep Med.* (2001) 2:297–307. doi: 10.1016/S1389-9457(00)00065-4
25. McKinley S, Fien M, Elliott R, Elliott D. Sleep and psychological health during early recovery from critical illness: an observational study. *J Psychosom Res.* (2013) 75:539–45. doi: 10.1016/j.jpsychores.2013.09.007
26. Parsons EC, Hough CL, Vitiello MV, Zatzick D, Davydow DS. Insomnia is associated with quality of life impairment in medical-surgical intensive care unit survivors. *Heart Lung.* (2015) 44:89–94. doi: 10.1016/j.hrtlng.2014.11.002
27. Calogiuri G, Weydahl A, Carandente F. Methodological issues for studying the rest–activity cycle and sleep disturbances:a chronobiological approach using actigraphy data. *Biol Res Nurs.* (2013) 15:5–12. doi: 10.1177/1099800411416224
28. Cornelissen G. Cosinor-based rhythmometry. *Theor Biol Med Model.* (2014) 11:16. doi: 10.1186/1742-4682-11-16
29. Thomas KA, Burr RL, Spieker S. Maternal and infant activity: analytic approaches for the study of circadian rhythm. *Infant Behav Dev.* (2015) 41:80–7. doi: 10.1016/j.infbeh.2015.08.002
30. Lentz MJ. Time-series analysis–cosinor analysis: a special case. *West J Nurs Res.* (1990) 12:408–12. doi: 10.1177/019394599001200313
31. Refinetti R, Lissen GC, Halberg F. Procedures for numerical analysis of circadian rhythms. *Biol Rhythm Res.* (2007) 38:275–325. doi: 10.1080/09291010600903692
32. Swaab DF, Colenda CC, Cohen W, McCall WV, Rosenquist PB. Bright light therapy: improved sensitivity to its effects on rest-activity rhythms in Alzheimer patients by application of nonparametric methods. *Chronobiol Int.* (1999) 16:505–18. doi: 10.3109/07420529908998724
33. Thomas KA, Burr RL, Spieker S, Lee J, Chen J. Mother–infant circadian rhythm: Development of individual patterns and dyadic synchrony. *Early Hum Dev.* (2014) 90:885–90. doi: 10.1016/j.earlhumdev.2014.09.005
34. Knaus WAM, Draper EAM, Wagner DPP, Zimmerman JEM. APACHE II: a severity of disease classification system. *Crit Care Med.* (1985) 13:818–29. doi: 10.1097/00003246-198510000-00009
35. Hopkins RO, Suchyta MR, Kamdar BB, Darowski E, Jackson JC, Needham DM. Instrumental activities of daily living after critical illness: a systematic review. *Ann Am Thorac Soc.* (2017) 14:1332–43. doi: 10.1513/AnnalsATS.201701-059SR
36. Dowling GA, Burr RL, Van Someren EJ, Hubbard EM, Luxenberg JS, Mastick J, et al. Melatonin and bright-light treatment for rest-activity disruption in institutionalized patients with Alzheimer's disease. *J Am Geriatr Soc.* (2008) 56:239–46. doi: 10.1111/j.1532-5415.2007.01543.x
37. Cespedes Feliciano EM, Quante M, Weng J, Mitchell JA, James P, Marinac CR, et al. Actigraphy-derived daily rest-activity patterns and body mass index in community-dwelling adults. *Sleep.* (2017) 40:zsx168. doi: 10.1093/sleep/zsx168
38. Umbrello M, Formenti P, Bolgiaghi L, Chiumello D. Current concepts of ARDS: a narrative review. *Int J Mol Sci.* (2016) 18:64. doi: 10.3390/ijms18010064
39. Luik AI, Zuurbier LA, Hofman A, Van Someren EJW, Tiemeier H. Stability and fragmentation of the activity rhythm across the sleep-wake cycle: the importance of age, lifestyle, and mental health. *Chronobiol Int.* (2013) 30:1223–30. doi: 10.3109/07420528.2013.813528
40. Roveda E, Vitale J, Montaruli A, Galasso L, Carandente F, Caumo A. Predicting the actigraphy-based acrophase using the Morningness-Eveningness Questionnaire (MEQ) in college students of North Italy. *Chronobiol Int.* (2017) 34:551–62. doi: 10.1080/07420528.2016.1276928
41. Solverson KJ, Easton PA, Doig CJ. Assessment of sleep quality post-hospital discharge in survivors of critical illness. *Respir Med.* (2016) 114:97–102. doi: 10.1016/j.rmed.2016.03.009
42. Lee CM, Herridge MS, Gabor JY, Tansey CM, Matte A, Hanly PJ. Chronic sleep disorders in survivors of the acute respiratory distress syndrome. *Intensive Care Med.* (2009) 35:314–20. doi: 10.1007/s00134-008-1277-3
43. Harvey AG, Tang NK. (Mis)perception of sleep in insomnia: a puzzle and a resolution. *Psychol Bull.* (2012) 138:77–101. doi: 10.1037/a0025730
44. Hartmann JA, Carney CE, Lachowski A, Edinger JD. Exploring the construct of subjective sleep quality in patients with insomnia. *J Clin Psychiatry.* (2015) 76:e768–73. doi: 10.4088/JCP.14m09066
45. Borbely AA, Daan S, Wirz-Justice A, Deboer T. The two-process model of sleep regulation: a reappraisal. *J Sleep Res.* (2016) 25:131–43. doi: 10.1111/jsr.12371
46. Parsons EC, Kross EK, Caldwell ES, Kapur VK, McCurry SM, Vitiello MV, et al. Post-discharge insomnia symptoms are associated with quality of life impairment among survivors of acute lung injury. *Sleep Med.* (2012) 13:1106–9. doi: 10.1016/j.sleep.2012.05.010

47. McKenna HT, Reiss IK, Martin DS. The significance of circadian rhythms and dysrhythmias in critical illness. *J Intensive Care Soc.* (2017) 18:121–9. doi: 10.1177/1751143717692603
48. Huang M, Parker AM, Bienvenu OJ, Dinglas VD, Colantuoni E, Hopkins RO, et al. Psychiatric symptoms in acute respiratory distress syndrome survivors: a 1-year national multicenter study. *Crit Care Med.* (2016) 44:954–65. doi: 10.1097/CCM.0000000000001621
49. Hopkins RO, Weaver LK, Collingridge D, Parkinson RB, Chan KJ, Orme JF, Jr. Two-year cognitive, emotional, and quality-of-life outcomes in acute respiratory distress syndrome. *Am J Respir Crit Care Med.* (2005) 171:340–7. doi: 10.1164/rccm.200406-763OC
50. Lyall LM, Wyse CA, Graham N, Ferguson A, Lyall DM, Cullen B, et al. Association of disrupted circadian rhythmicity with mood disorders, subjective wellbeing, and cognitive function: a cross-sectional study of 91 105 participants from the UK Biobank. *Lancet Psychiatry.* (2018) 5:507–14. doi: 10.1016/S2215-0366(18)30139-1
51. Oosterman JE, Kalsbeek A, la Fleur SE, Belsham DD. Impact of nutrients on circadian rhythmicity. *Am J Physiol Regul Integr Comp Physiol.* (2015) 308:R337–50. doi: 10.1152/ajpregu.00322.2014
52. Honma S. The mammalian circadian system: a hierarchical multi-oscillator structure for generating circadian rhythm. *J Physiol Sci.* (2018) 68:207–19. doi: 10.1007/s12576-018-0597-5
53. Herridge MS, Tansey CM, Matte A, Tomlinson G, Diaz-Granados N, Cooper A, et al. Functional disability 5 years after acute respiratory distress syndrome. *N Engl J Med.* (2011) 364:1293–304. doi: 10.1056/NEJMoa1011802
54. Innominato PF, Komarzynski S, Palesh OG, Dallmann R, Bjarnason GA, Giacchetti S, et al. Circadian rest-activity rhythm as an objective biomarker of patient-reported outcomes in patients with advanced cancer. *Cancer Med.* (2018) 7:4396–405. doi: 10.1002/cam4.1711
55. Carvalho-Bos SS, Riemersma-van der Lek RF, Waterhouse J, Reilly T, Van Someren EJ. Strong association of the rest-activity rhythm with well-being in demented elderly women. *Am J Geriatr Psychiatry.* (2007) 15:92–100. doi: 10.1097/01.JGP.0000236584.03432.dc
56. Hopkins RO, Weaver LK, Chan KJ, Orme JF, Jr. Quality of life, emotional, and cognitive function following acute respiratory distress syndrome. *J Int Neuropsychol Soc.* (2004) 10:1005–17. doi: 10.1017/S135561770410711X
57. Jackson JC, Mitchell N, Hopkins RO. Cognitive functioning, mental health, and quality of life in ICU survivors: an overview. *Crit Care Clin.* (2009) 25:615–28, x. doi: 10.1016/j.ccc.2009.04.005
58. Tranah GJ, Blackwell T, Stone KL, Ancoli-Israel S, Paudel ML, Ensrud KE, et al. Circadian activity rhythms and risk of incident dementia and mild cognitive impairment in older women. *Ann Neurol.* (2011) 70:722–32. doi: 10.1002/ana.22468
59. Wu JQ, Li P, Stavitsky Gilbert K, Hu K, Cronin-Golomb A. Circadian rest-activity rhythms predict cognitive function in early parkinson's disease independently of sleep. *Mov Disord Clin Pract.* (2018) 5:614–9. doi: 10.1002/mdc3.12692
60. Cochrane A, Robertson IH, Coogan AN. Association between circadian rhythms, sleep and cognitive impairment in healthy older adults: an actigraphic study. *J Neural Transm.* (2012) 119:1233–9. doi: 10.1007/s00702-012-0802-2
61. Khalsa SBS, Jewett ME, Cajochen C, Czeisler CA. A phase response curve to single bright light pulses in human subjects. *J Physiol.* (2003) 549:945–52. doi: 10.1113/jphysiol.2003.040477

17

The Circadian Nature of Mitochondrial Biology

*Gal Manella and Gad Asher**

Department of Biomolecular Sciences, Weizmann Institute of Science, Rehovot, Israel

Edited by:
Etienne Challet,
CNRS and University of Strasbourg, France

Reviewed by:
Urs Albrecht,
University of Fribourg, Switzerland
Hai-Bin Ruan,
University of Minnesota, USA

Correspondence:
Gad Asher
gad.asher@weizmann.ac.il

Circadian clocks orchestrate the daily changes in physiology and behavior of light-sensitive organisms. These clocks measure about 24 h and tick in a self-sustained and cell-autonomous manner. Mounting evidence points toward a tight intertwining between circadian clocks and metabolism. Although various aspects of circadian control of metabolic functions have been extensively studied, our knowledge regarding circadian mitochondrial function is rudimentary. In this review, we will survey the current literature related to the circadian nature of mitochondrial biology: from mitochondrial omics studies (e.g., proteome, acetylome, and lipidome), through dissection of mitochondrial morphology, to analyses of mitochondrial processes such as nutrient utilization and respiration. We will describe potential mechanisms that are implicated in circadian regulation of mitochondrial functions in mammals and discuss the possibility of a mitochondrial-autonomous oscillator.

Keywords: circadian rhythms, clocks, mitochondria, mitochondrial respiration, reactive oxygen species, oxygen, mitochondrial dynamics

INTRODUCTION

Light-sensitive organisms harbor molecular oscillators that measure time with periodicity of about a day known as circadian clocks. These clocks enable organisms to optimize a wide range of biological functions with the geophysical time (1–3). In mammals, these activities include rest/activity cycles, feeding/fasting, and various other physiological processes. The mammalian circadian timing system consists of a central pacemaker in the suprachiasmatic nucleus (SCN) of the brain that synchronizes subsidiary oscillators in the rest of the body. While the brain's "master clock" is entrained by daily light–dark cycles, the dominant timing cue for clocks in peripheral organs appears to be feeding time. Circadian clocks are believed to function based on negative transcription–translation feedback loops generated through the action of several core clock genes. These include the transcriptional activators *Clock* and *Bmal1*, the repressors *Per1/2/3* and *Cry1/2*, and the nuclear receptors' family members *Rev-Erb* and *Ror*. These clocks tick in virtually every cell of the body and function in a self-sustained and cell-autonomous manner.

Growing evidence support the presence of an intricate interplay between circadian clocks and metabolism. Circadian clocks play a prominent role in the regulation of various metabolic pathways. In turn, several metabolites and metabolic processes are implicated in the clock's function. Several comprehensive reviews have covered in detail the molecular architecture of the core clock machinery (4–7) and their interplay with metabolism (2, 8–11). Among the large number of studies on circadian control of metabolism, only a handful of studies investigated in-depth circadian facets of mitochondrial function. Mitochondria constitute major metabolic hubs in eukaryotic cells involved in many vital processes including energy production via aerobic respiration, lipid biosynthesis, and calcium homeostasis. It is, therefore, conceivable that some of these functions might be under circadian clock control.

We review herein the current literature related to the circadian nature of mitochondrial biology in mammals. We elaborate on potential mechanisms underlying circadian control of mitochondrial functions and discuss the possibility of a mitochondrial-autonomous oscillator.

CIRCADIAN RHYTHMS IN MITOCHONDRIAL COMPOSITION

Rhythmic changes in the proteome, acetylome, and lipidome of mitochondria were uncovered lately as detailed below. These changes are expected to support rhythms in mitochondrial functions.

The Mitochondrial Proteome

The mitochondrial proteome consists of several hundred different proteins (12). While the majority of the mitochondrial proteome is encoded by the nuclear genome (13) and transported into mitochondria via protein import machinery, only 13 protein-coding genes are transcribed and synthesized locally. Substantial daily changes in the mitochondrial protein composition were uncovered by whole liver proteomics (14, 15) and more recently by proteomic analyses of isolated mitochondria (16). In fact, over a third of the mitochondrial proteins accumulated in mitochondria in a daily manner (16). Notably, the vast majority of rhythmic proteins reached their zenith levels about the same time, during the early light phase. Further functional annotation of the rhythmic mitochondrial proteome evinced that key catabolic and oxidative functions of mitochondria exhibit diurnal oscillation (16). Of note, several components of the pyruvate dehydrogenase complex (PDC) that catalyzes the rate-limiting step in mitochondrial carbohydrate metabolism accumulate early in the light phase. While carnitine palmitoyl-transferase 1 (CPT1), the rate-limiting enzyme in the entry of fatty acids into the mitochondrial matrix, oscillates with zenith levels between the late dark and early light phase.

Both transcriptional and posttranscriptional events can potentially account for the above-described changes in the mitochondrial proteome. Indeed, the transcript levels of several nuclear-encoded mitochondrial proteins are altered in clock genes mutant mice (17, 18). Moreover, BMAL1 was shown to bind their promoters by ChIP (19, 20). However, global analysis evinced poor correlation between the phase of the mitochondrial proteome and its respective transcriptome (16). It is therefore likely that the observed daily changes in the mitochondrial proteome arise from posttranscriptional mechanisms such as rhythmic translation, protein import, and/or degradation. Future studies are expected to shed light on the contribution of these different mechanisms.

The Mitochondrial Acetylome

Posttranslational modifications, such as phosphorylation, acetylation, and ubiquitinilation, control protein stability and activity. Global acetylome analysis of mouse liver identified daily changes in the acetylation status of many mitochondrial proteins (21). Remarkably, CLOCK-dependent acetylation sites were enriched for mitochondrial proteins including participants of the Krebs cycle and glutathione metabolism. Likewise, Peek and colleagues found that the acetylation status of many mitochondrial proteins differs between wild-type and BMAL1-deficient mice (22). For example, acetylation of fatty acid metabolism enzymes correlates with their activity and are BMAL1 dependant. In addition, the respiratory complex I is rhythmically acetylated, in accordance with changes in mitochondrial respiration (23). Overall, these results suggest that circadian clocks play a regulatory role in mitochondrial protein acetylation. It will be interesting to determine whether other posttranslational modifications of mitochondrial proteins, such as phosphorylation, are rhythmic as well, and further dissect their functional relevance.

The Mitochondrial Lipidome

Lipids are the principal building blocks of biological membranes and among others define the physical qualities of mitochondrial membranes, as well as their protein content (24). In addition, lipids serve as a major energy source for mitochondrial respiration and some lipids are even synthesized in mitochondria. We recently applied high-throughput lipidomic analyses on isolated mitochondria from mouse liver to investigate the daily mitochondrial lipidome (25). We found that about one third of the lipids in mitochondria exhibit daily rhythms. Both the composition and phase of the rhythmic lipids depend on feeding regimen (nighttime restricted vs. *ad libitum* feeding) and circadian clock (PER1/2 null vs. wild type mice). In *ad libitum* fed mice, the majority of mitochondrial lipids reach their peak levels at the transition between the light and the dark phase, while an opposite phase is observed in mice fed exclusively during the dark phase. By contrast, in the absence of the core clock proteins PER1 and PER2, the oscillating lipids exhibit a wide range of peak times without an overt phase, supporting a role for circadian clocks in coordination of mitochondrial lipid accumulation (25). Likewise, mitochondrial fatty acid composition as well as their metabolism was reported to depend on BMAL1 (22). Future studies on these rhythmic lipids are expected to further clarify their relevance to the daily changes in mitochondrial morphology and function as detailed below.

CIRCADIAN RHYTHMS IN MITOCHONDRIAL MORPHOLOGY

Mitochondrial dynamics, namely, changes in shape and size due to fission, fusion, and mitophagy, strongly affect mitochondrial function. In general, respiration is more efficient in fused mitochondria compared to fragmented mitochondria, primarily due to changes in nutrient availability (26).

Early electron microscopy works showed that the shape and volume of mitochondria change between the light and dark phase in rat hepatocytes (27). A recent study identified daily rhythms in mitochondrial dynamics in mouse liver and revealed that many genes participating in mitochondrial dynamics are expressed in a daily manner and are dependent on BMAL1 (20). Consequently, mitochondria isolated from *Bmal1* liver-specific knockout mice are bigger, more rounded, and do not exhibit morphological changes throughout the day. Additionally, in the absence of *Bmal1*, mitochondria are more susceptible to oxidative stress-related damage.

Dependency of mitochondrial morphology on clock genes was also reported in mouse skeletal muscle (28) and heart (17) and is linked to impaired mitochondrial function in these organs. Mitochondria in macrophages exhibit daily morphological changes *in vitro* as well (29). By contrast, the overall number of mitochondria, assessed by mitochondrial genome copy number, appears to be constant throughout the day and is independent of clock genes (16, 17, 20, 30). Collectively, these studies point to circadian regulation of mitochondrial dynamics, such as changes in mitochondrial mass and morphology, with major implications on mitochondrial function.

CIRCADIAN RHYTHMS IN MITOCHONDRIAL NUTRIENT UTILIZATION AND RESPIRATION

A central function of mitochondria is energy production through nutrient oxidation, a process known as oxidative phosphorylation. Pyruvate and fatty acids are catabolized into acetyl CoA in the mitochondrial matrix through the action of the PDC and fatty acid oxidation (FAO), respectively. The acetyl groups are then fed into the Krebs cycle, and the process culminates with the transfer of acetyl-derived high-energy electrons along the respiratory chain. This process is coupled to production of ATP by the ATP synthase complex upon flux of protons through the inner mitochondrial membrane. In recent years, several studies tested the circadian control of mitochondrial nutrient utilization and respiration, using assays that measure oxygen consumption rate (OCR) in cultured cells and isolated mitochondria as detailed below. OCR measurements of synchronized C2C12 muscle cells in culture are rhythmic with ~24 h period (22). Similar results were obtained with HepG2 cells, albeit with a significantly shorter period (~15 h) (23). Analysis of isolated hepatocytes from wild-type mice harvested in different times of the day revealed higher respiration levels during the dark phase compared to the light phase in the presence of pyruvate. These daily differences were diminished in hepatocytes derived from liver-specific BMAL1-deficient mice (20).

Additional analyses of mitochondrial respiration were conducted with isolated mitochondria from mouse liver, muscle, and rat brain (16, 22, 28, 31). Mitochondria isolated from livers of wild-type mice exhibit higher OCR than those of *Bmal1* knockout mice (22), *Bmal1* liver-specific knockout mice (20), and *Per1/2* double knockout mice (16). Likewise, measurements of FAO by [^{14}C]-labeled fatty acid supplementation evinced that this property is also reduced in *Bmal1* knockout mice (22). Experiments performed with mitochondria isolated from mice around the clock shed light on daily aspects of mitochondrial nutrient utilization. In the presence of succinate, the respiration of mitochondria is constant throughout the day (20) (Asher lab, unpublished data). By contrast, supplementation of FAO substrates such as palmitoyl-carnitine and palmitoyl-CoA + carnitine results in rhythmic respiration with zenith level early in the light phase, in accordance with CPT1 protein levels. Carbohydrates (i.e., pyruvate and malate) utilization is rhythmic as well, but peaks later during the light phase (16). The differences in peak time of mitochondrial respiration in experiments conducted with isolated mitochondria (16) vs. hepatocytes (20) might reflect the role of mitochondrial extrinsic cellular mechanism in controlling mitochondrial respiration. Remarkably, these daily rhythms in mitochondrial respiration are strongly influenced not only by the molecular circadian clock but also by nutrition type (e.g., high fat diet) and eating pattern (i.e., nighttime restricted feeding). Each of these factors differentially affects the overall level, rhythm, and phase of oscillation for several mitochondrial enzymes and the processing of their respective substrates (16).

Taken together, these studies suggest that mitochondrial respiration exhibits daily rhythms that are dependent on the molecular clock, nutrients, feeding pattern, and diet composition.

OXYGEN AND MITOCHONDRIAL RHYTHMICITY

Reactive oxygen species (ROS) are byproducts of mitochondrial oxidative activity. The ROS hydrogen peroxide (H_2O_2) is scavenged by the peroxiredoxins (Prx's) protein family members, which are reversibly oxidized to generate Prx-SOH. Upon high peroxide concentration, a hyperoxidized form of Prx, namely, Prx-SO_2, accumulate and can then be reduced by sulfiredoxin (Srx). Prx3, the mitochondrial isoform of Prx, exhibits daily oscillations in its oxidation state. These oscillations are dependent on Srx levels in mitochondria, which are rhythmic as well and are regulated through its mitochondrial import and degradation (32). The regulation on Srx is ROS dependent and therefore generates a metabolic feedback loop between ROS levels Prx3 and Srx. Of note, the oscillations in Prx3-SO_2 levels were shown to play an important role in rhythmic production of corticosterone from cholesterol in the adrenal gland mitochondria (33).

Oxygen is obligatory for mitochondrial aerobic respiration, and recent studies identified a reciprocal interplay between oxygen and the circadian clock (34–36). Rhythmic oxygen levels reset circadian clocks through HIF1α (34). Concomitantly, clock genes in concert with HIF1α regulate mitochondrial respiration upon changes in oxygen levels (35). Thus, both hands, namely, ROS and hypoxia, appear to intertwine with circadian control of mitochondrial function.

THE SCN CLOCK AND MITOCHONDRIAL FUNCTION

Several studies examined mitochondrial activity of SCN neuron in the context of circadian clock function. Notably, SCN cells exhibit daily rhythms in cytochrome *c* oxidase activity and mitochondrial membrane potential (37). Moreover, studies with SCN astrocytes identified circadian oscillation in calcium release from mitochondria (38, 39). These rhythms have been linked to oscillations in extracellular ATP concentration, which appear to play a role in coupling of SCN neurons (38, 39). Furthermore, treatment of mice with the mitochondrial toxin 3-nitropropionic acid results in disruption of SCN clock outputs, as monitored by behavioral rhythms and *ex vivo* reporter measurements (40).

AUTONOMOUS MITOCHONDRIAL RHYTHMS

Mitochondria are considered as successors of ancient aerobic bacteria, consumed by an early eukaryotic predator cell over 1.5 billion years ago (41). This theory, known as endosymbiotic theory, proposes that mitochondria were once independent free-living organisms and possessed the full machinery for survival and reproduction. However, throughout evolution, some of their capabilities have been lost or transferred to the host cell. It is possible that the mitochondrial ancestor has possessed some kind of an oscillator to temporally coordinate contradictory metabolic processes. As such, even the simplest mitochondria-possessing cells, i.e., the budding yeast, present oscillations in mitochondrial oxidative activity (42). The "yeast metabolic cycle" shares some conserved characteristics with the circadian clock (42, 43), although its period is only of few hours. Given the high conservation of mitochondrial rhythms from yeast to mammals, and the observed rhythms in ROS-related mitochondrial enzymes, it is tempting to speculate that mitochondria harbor their own autonomous clocks. Along this line, a self-sustained transcription-independent mitochondrial oscillator has been suggested in the form of Prx3-SO_2 (32), yet so far, its independency from the transcription–translation-based clock has not been established.

SUMMARY AND OPEN QUESTIONS

In this review, we discussed daily rhythmicity in mitochondrial composition, morphology, and function alongside their underlying regulatory mechanisms (**Figure 1**). As shown, experiments performed with different clock mutant models support the potential role of circadian clocks in control of mitochondrial rhythmicity. However, it cannot be excluded that some of these effects are attributed to specific clock genes irrespective of their function within the core clock oscillator. In this respect, CRY proteins were reported to localize also in mitochondria; however, their specific mitochondrial function is unknown (44).

Another question is whether mitochondrial rhythmicity is achieved through systemic cues (such as feeding–fasting or rest–activity cycles) or via cell-autonomous mechanisms. It is likely that both scenarios co-regulate mitochondrial homeostasis throughout the day. In this conjuncture, experiments addressing mitochondrial function in cultured cells support a cell-autonomous effect on mitochondrial function. Whereas experiments with mice show that feeding rhythms are sufficient to restore some mitochondrial functions even in the absence of a functional clock. Remarkably, the ability of mitochondria to preserve functional differences when isolated in different hours

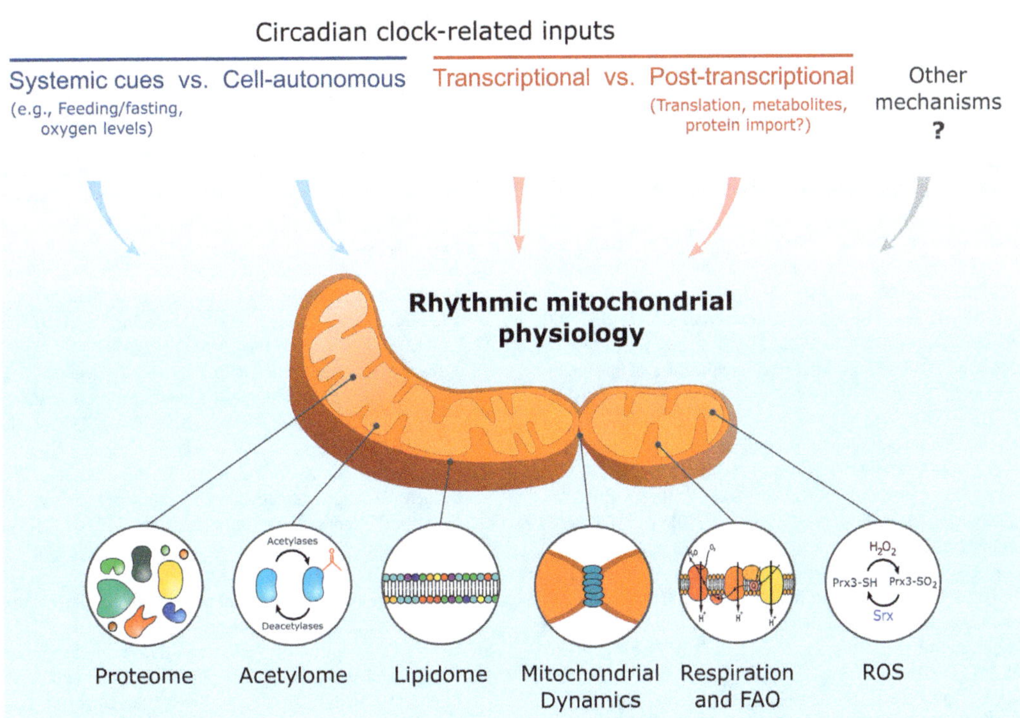

FIGURE 1 | Schematic depiction of key input mechanisms that participate in regulation of various circadian mitochondrial outputs. ROS, reactive oxygen species; FAO, fatty acid oxidation.

of the day indicates that these alterations are not simply because of daily changes in substrate availability, but rather due to an inherent change in mitochondrial composition.

The lack of phase correlation between the mitochondrial proteome and its respective transcriptome (16) is another puzzling point. This finding highlights the importance of post-transcriptional mechanisms in control of mitochondrial protein homeostasis throughout the day. Recently, translation efficiency was reported to exhibit daily rhythms, specifically with respect to genes implicated in mitochondrial function (45, 46). An additional potential mechanism involves rhythmic regulation of protein import into mitochondria. Mitochondrial import machinery consists of several membrane protein complexes, such as the translocase of the outer (TOM) and translocase of the inner (TIM) mitochondrial membranes. Many subunits of TOM and TIM complexes are rhythmic in mitochondria (16). Moreover, the assembly of these complexes is regulated by several kinases, including casein kinase (CK) 1 and 2 (47, 48), which are widely recognized as regulators of circadian rhythmicity (49). Interestingly, cardiolipin lipids that are known to stabilize the import protein complexes (24) are also rhythmic in mitochondria isolated from mouse liver (25, 50). Given that the majority of mitochondrial proteins accumulate early in the light phase (16), it is presumable that the import machinery is gated to this time of the day and therefore dictate the daily changes in the mitochondrial proteome and function.

Bass and colleagues (22) proposed another model wherein circadian clocks generate oscillations in NAD^+ levels, a cofactor for Sirtuin, a family of NAD^+-dependent deacetylases, among them the mitochondrial SIRT3. Thus, NAD^+ serves as a metabolic link between circadian clocks and mitochondrial function through NAD^+ and SIRT3-dependent deactylation. In support of this model, they reported that reduction in mitochondrial activity in the absence of BMAL1 could be rescued by restoring NAD^+ levels.

Future studies are expected to shed light on many of these and other open questions that are related to the circadian nature of mitochondrial biology.

AUTHOR CONTRIBUTIONS

GM and GA wrote the manuscript together.

ACKNOWLEDGMENTS

We apologize to all colleagues whose work could not be cited due to space limitations. We are grateful to R. Aviram for her valuable comments on the manuscript. GA is supported by the Israel Science Foundation (ISF 138/12), the European Research Council (ERC-2011 METACYCLES 310320). GA is recipient of the EMBO young investigator award and incumbent of the Pauline Recanati career development chair.

REFERENCES

1. Asher G, Schibler U. Crosstalk between components of circadian and metabolic cycles in mammals. *Cell Metab* (2011) 13(2):125–37. doi:10.1016/j.cmet.2011.01.006
2. Bass J. Circadian topology of metabolism. *Nature* (2012) 491(7424):348–56. doi:10.1038/nature11704
3. Mohawk JA, Green CB, Takahashi JS. Central and peripheral circadian clocks in mammals. *Annu Rev Neurosci* (2012) 35:445–62. doi:10.1146/annurev-neuro-060909-153128
4. Dardente H, Cermakian N. Molecular circadian rhythms in central and peripheral clocks in mammals. *Chronobiol Int* (2007) 24(2):195–213. doi:10.1080/07420520701283693
5. Feng D, Lazar MA. Clocks, metabolism, and the epigenome. *Mol Cell* (2012) 47(2):158–67. doi:10.1016/j.molcel.2012.06.026
6. Partch CL, Green CB, Takahashi JS. Molecular architecture of the mammalian circadian clock. *Trends Cell Biol* (2014) 24(2):90–9. doi:10.1016/j.tcb.2013.07.002
7. Dibner C, Schibler U. Circadian timing of metabolism in animal models and humans. *J Intern Med* (2015) 277:513–27. doi:10.1111/joim.12347
8. Marcheva B, Ramsey KM, Peek CB, Affinati A, Maury E, Bass J. Circadian clocks and metabolism. *Handb Exp Pharmacol* (2013) 217:127–55. doi:10.1007/978-3-642-25950-0_6
9. Bailey SM, Udoh US, Young ME. Circadian regulation of metabolism. *J Endocrinol* (2014) 222(2):R75–96. doi:10.1530/JOE-14-0200
10. Asher G, Sassone-Corsi P. Time for food: the intimate interplay between nutrition, metabolism, and the circadian clock. *Cell* (2015) 161(1):84–92. doi:10.1016/j.cell.2015.03.015
11. Reinke H, Asher G. Circadian clock control of liver metabolic functions. *Gastroenterology* (2016) 150(3):574–80. doi:10.1053/j.gastro.2015.11.043
12. Cotter D, Guda P, Fahy E, Subramaniam S. MitoProteome: mitochondrial protein sequence database and annotation system. *Nucleic Acids Res* (2004) 32(Database issue):D463–7. doi:10.1093/nar/gkh048
13. Taanman J-W. The mitochondrial genome: structure, transcription, translation and replication. *Biochim Biophys Acta* (1999) 1410(2):103–23. doi:10.1016/S0005-2728(98)00161-3
14. Mauvoisin D, Wang J, Jouffe C, Martin E, Atger F, Waridel P, et al. Circadian clock-dependent and -independent rhythmic proteomes implement distinct diurnal functions in mouse liver. *Proc Natl Acad Sci U S A* (2014) 111(1):167–72. doi:10.1073/pnas.1314066111
15. Robles MS, Cox J, Mann M. In-vivo quantitative proteomics reveals a key contribution of post-transcriptional mechanisms to the circadian regulation of liver metabolism. *PLoS Genet* (2014) 10(1):e1004047. doi:10.1371/journal.pgen.1004047
16. Neufeld-Cohen A, Robles MS, Aviram R, Manella G, Adamovich Y, Ladeuix B, et al. Circadian control of oscillations in mitochondrial rate-limiting enzymes and nutrient utilization by PERIOD proteins. *Proc Natl Acad Sci U S A* (2016) 113(12):E1673–82. doi:10.1073/pnas.1519650113
17. Kohsaka A, Das P, Hashimoto I, Nakao T, Deguchi Y, Gouraud SS, et al. The circadian clock maintains cardiac function by regulating mitochondrial metabolism in mice. *PLoS One* (2014) 9(11):e112811. doi:10.1371/journal.pone.0112811
18. Gong C, Li C, Qi X, Song Z, Wu J, Hughes ME, et al. The daily rhythms of mitochondrial gene expression and oxidative stress regulation are altered by aging in the mouse liver. *Chronobiol Int* (2015) 32(9):1254–63. doi:10.3109/07420528.2015.1085388
19. Koike N, Yoo SH, Huang HC, Kumar V, Lee C, Kim TK, et al. Transcriptional architecture and chromatin landscape of the core circadian clock in mammals. *Science* (2012) 338(6105):349–54. doi:10.1126/science.1226339
20. Jacobi D, Liu S, Burkewitz K, Kory N, Knudsen NH, Alexander RK, et al. Hepatic Bmal1 regulates rhythmic mitochondrial dynamics and promotes metabolic fitness. *Cell Metab* (2015) 22(4):709–20. doi:10.1016/j.cmet.2015.08.006
21. Masri S, Patel VR, Eckel-Mahan KL, Peleg S, Forne I, Ladurner AG, et al. Circadian acetylome reveals regulation of mitochondrial metabolic pathways. *Proc Natl Acad Sci U S A* (2013) 110(9):3339–44. doi:10.1073/pnas.1217632110

22. Peek CB, Affinati AH, Ramsey KM, Kuo HY, Yu W, Sena LA, et al. Circadian clock NAD+ cycle drives mitochondrial oxidative metabolism in mice. *Science* (2013) 342(6158):1243417. doi:10.1126/science.1243417
23. Cela O, Scrima R, Pazienza V, Merla G, Benegiamo G, Augello B, et al. Clock genes-dependent acetylation of complex I sets rhythmic activity of mitochondrial OxPhos. *Biochim Biophys Acta* (2016) 1863(4):596–606. doi:10.1016/j.bbamcr.2015.12.018
24. Osman C, Voelker DR, Langer T. Making heads or tails of phospholipids in mitochondria. *J Cell Biol* (2011) 192(1):7–16. doi:10.1083/jcb.201006159
25. Aviram R, Manella G, Kopelman N, Neufeld-Cohen A, Zwighaft Z, Elimelech M, et al. Lipidomics analyses reveal temporal and spatial lipid organization and uncover daily oscillations in intracellular organelles. *Mol Cell* (2016) 62(4):636–48. doi:10.1016/j.molcel.2016.04.002
26. Wai T, Langer T. Mitochondrial dynamics and metabolic regulation. *Trends Endocrinol Metab* (2016) 27(2):105–17. doi:10.1016/j.tem.2015.12.001
27. Uchiyama Y. Circadian alterations in tubular structures on the outer mitochondrial membrane of rat hepatocytes. *Cell Tissue Res* (1981) 214(3):519–27. doi:10.1007/BF00233492
28. Andrews JL, Zhang X, McCarthy JJ, McDearmon EL, Hornberger TA, Russell B, et al. CLOCK and BMAL1 regulate MyoD and are necessary for maintenance of skeletal muscle phenotype and function. *Proc Natl Acad Sci U S A* (2010) 107(44):19090–5. doi:10.1073/pnas.1014523107
29. Oliva-Ramirez J, Moreno-Altamirano MM, Pineda-Olvera B, Cauich-Sanchez P, Sanchez-Garcia FJ. Crosstalk between circadian rhythmicity, mitochondrial dynamics and macrophage bactericidal activity. *Immunology* (2014) 143(3):490–7. doi:10.1111/imm.12329
30. Magnone MC, Langmesser S, Bezdek AC, Tallone T, Rusconi S, Albrecht U. The mammalian circadian clock gene Per2 modulates cell death in response to oxidative stress. *Front Neurol* (2014) 5:289. doi:10.3389/fneur.2014.00289
31. Simon N, Papa K, Vidal J, Boulamery A, Bruguerolle B. Circadian rhythms of oxidative phosphorylation: effects of rotenone and melatonin on isolated rat brain mitochondria. *Chronobiol Int* (2003) 20(3):451–61. doi:10.1081/CBI-120021385
32. Kil IS, Ryu KW, Lee SK, Kim JY, Chu SY, Kim JH, et al. Circadian oscillation of sulfiredoxin in the mitochondria. *Mol Cell* (2015) 59(4):651–63. doi:10.1016/j.molcel.2015.06.031
33. Kil IS, Lee SK, Ryu KW, Woo HA, Hu MC, Bae SH, et al. Feedback control of adrenal steroidogenesis via H2O2-dependent, reversible inactivation of peroxiredoxin III in mitochondria. *Mol Cell* (2012) 46(5):584–94. doi:10.1016/j.molcel.2012.05.030
34. Adamovich Y, Ladeuix B, Golik M, Koeners MP, Asher G. Rhythmic oxygen levels reset circadian clocks through HIF1α. *Cell Metab* (2016). doi:10.1016/j.cmet.2016.09.014
35. Peek CB, Levine DC, Cedernaes J, Taguchi A, Kobayashi Y, Tsai SJ, et al. Circadian clock interaction with HIF1α mediates oxygenic metabolism and anaerobic glycolysis in skeletal muscle. *Cell Metab* (2016). doi:10.1016/j.cmet.2016.09.010
36. Wu Y, Tang D, Liu N, Xiong W, Huang H, Li Y, et al. Reciprocal regulation between the circadian clock and hypoxia signaling at the genome level in mammals. *Cell Metab* (2016). doi:10.1016/j.cmet.2016.09.009
37. Isobe Y, Hida H, Nishino H. Circadian rhythm of metabolic oscillation in suprachiasmatic nucleus depends on the mitochondrial oxidation state, reflected by cytochrome c oxidase and lactate dehydrogenase. *J Neurosci Res* (2011) 89(6):929–35. doi:10.1002/jnr.22609
38. Burkeen JF, Womac AD, Earnest DJ, Zoran MJ. Mitochondrial calcium signaling mediates rhythmic extracellular ATP accumulation in suprachiasmatic nucleus astrocytes. *J Neurosci* (2011) 31(23):8432–40. doi:10.1523/JNEUROSCI.6576-10.2011
39. Marpegan L, Swanstrom AE, Chung K, Simon T, Haydon PG, Khan SK, et al. Circadian regulation of ATP release in astrocytes. *J Neurosci* (2011) 31(23):8342–50. doi:10.1523/JNEUROSCI.6537-10.2011
40. Kudo T, Loh DH, Tahara Y, Truong D, Hernandez-Echeagaray E, Colwell CS. Circadian dysfunction in response to in vivo treatment with the mitochondrial toxin 3-nitropropionic acid. *ASN Neuro* (2014) 6(1):e00133. doi:10.1042/AN20130042
41. Dyall SD, Brown MT, Johnson PJ. Ancient invasions: from endosymbionts to organelles. *Science* (2004) 304(5668):253. doi:10.1126/science.1094884
42. Tu BP, Kudlicki A, Rowicka M, McKnight SL. Logic of the yeast metabolic cycle: temporal compartmentalization of cellular processes. *Science* (2005) 310(5751):1152–8. doi:10.1126/science.1120499
43. Causton HC, Feeney KA, Ziegler CA, O'Neill JS. Metabolic cycles in yeast share features conserved among circadian rhythms. *Curr Biol* (2015) 25(8):1056–62. doi:10.1016/j.cub.2015.02.035
44. Kobayashi K, Kanno S, Smit B, van der Horst GT, Takao M, Yasui A. Characterization of photolyase/blue-light receptor homologs in mouse and human cells. *Nucleic Acids Res* (1998) 26(22):5086–92. doi:10.1093/nar/26.22.5086
45. Atger F, Gobet C, Marquis J, Martin E, Wang J, Weger B, et al. Circadian and feeding rhythms differentially affect rhythmic mRNA transcription and translation in mouse liver. *Proc Natl Acad Sci U S A* (2015) 112(47):E6579–88. doi:10.1073/pnas.1515308112
46. Janich P, Arpat AB, Castelo-Szekely V, Lopes M, Gatfield D. Ribosome profiling reveals the rhythmic liver translatome and circadian clock regulation by upstream open reading frames. *Genome Res* (2015) 25(12):1848–59. doi:10.1101/gr.195404.115
47. Gallego M, Virshup DM. Post-translational modifications regulate the ticking of the circadian clock. *Nat Rev Mol Cell Biol* (2007) 8(2):139–48. doi:10.1038/nrm2106
48. Harbauer AB, Zahedi RP, Sickmann A, Pfanner N, Meisinger C. The protein import machinery of mitochondria - a regulatory hub in metabolism, stress, and disease. *Cell Metab* (2014) 19(3):357–72. doi:10.1016/j.cmet.2014.01.010
49. Reischl S, Kramer A. Kinases and phosphatases in the mammalian circadian clock. *FEBS Lett* (2011) 585(10):1393–9. doi:10.1016/j.febslet.2011.02.038
50. Adamovich Y, Rousso-Noori L, Zwighaft Z, Neufeld-Cohen A, Golik M, Kraut-Cohen J, et al. Circadian clocks and feeding time regulate the oscillations and levels of hepatic triglycerides. *Cell Metab* (2014) 19(2):319–30. doi:10.1016/j.cmet.2013.12.016

18

Synchronization by Daytime Restricted Food Access Modulates the Presence and Subcellular Distribution of β-Catenin and its Phosphorylated Forms in the Rat Liver

*Dalia Luz De Ita-Pérez and Mauricio Díaz-Muñoz**

Departamento de Neurobiología Celular y Molecular, Instituto de Neurobiología, Universidad Nacional Autónoma de México, Querétaro, Querétaro, México

Edited by:
Etienne Challet,
University of Strasbourg, France

Reviewed by:
Shigenobu Shibata,
Waseda University, Japan
Sabine Colnot,
INSERM, France

Correspondence:
Mauricio Díaz-Muñoz
mdiaz@comunidad.unam.mx

β-catenin, the principal effector of the Wnt pathway, is also one of the cadherin cell adhesion molecules; therefore, it fulfills signaling and structural roles in most of the tissues and organs. It has been reported that β-catenin in the liver regulates metabolic responses such as gluconeogenesis and histological changes in response to obesity-promoting diets. The function and cellular location of β-catenin is finely modulated by coordinated sequences of phosphorylation–dephosphorylation events. In this article, we evaluated the levels and cellular localization of liver β-catenin variants, more specifically β-catenin phosphorylated in serine 33 (this phosphorylation provides recognizing sites for β-TrCP, which results in ubiquitination and posterior proteasomal degradation of β-catenin) and β-catenin phosphorylated in serine 675 (phosphorylation that enhances signaling and transcriptional activity of β-catenin through recruitment of different transcriptional coactivators). β-catenin phosphorylated in serine 33 in the nucleus shows day–night fluctuations in their expression level in the *Ad Libitum* group. In addition, we used a daytime restricted feeding (DRF) protocol to show that the above effects are sensitive to food access-dependent circadian synchronization. We found through western blot and immunohistochemical analyses that DRF protocol promoted (1) higher total β-catenins levels mainly associated with the plasma membrane, (2) reduced the presence of cytoplasmic β-catenin phosphorylated in serine 33, (3) an increase in nuclear β-catenin phosphorylated in serine 675, (4) differential co-localization of total β-catenins/β-catenin phosphorylated in serine 33 and total β-catenins/β-catenin phosphorylated in serine 675 at different temporal points along day and in fasting and refeeding conditions, and (5) differential liver zonation of β-catenin variants studied along hepatic acinus. In conclusion, the present data comprehensively characterize the effect food synchronization has on the presence, subcellular distribution, and liver zonation of β-catenin variants. These results are relevant to understand the set of metabolic and structural liver adaptations that are associated with the expression of the food entrained oscillator (FEO).

Keywords: food entrained oscillator, β-catenin variants, liver, microscopy, phosphorylation

INTRODUCTION

Daytime restricted feeding (DRF) is an accepted protocol to study the dynamic relationship between the circadian timing system and metabolic networks (1, 2). It usually involves limited access to food (a few hours each day) during a period of 2–3 weeks. A daily increase in locomotor activity before food presentation becomes an evident adaptive response after a few days of DRF conditions; this behavioral display observed is known as food-anticipatory activity (FAA) (3). DRF (2-h food access per day) involves two underlying aspects of daily physiological adjustments: (1) a circadian synchronization that shifts the phases of clock genes and (2) a hypocaloric food intake. Both aspects influence the adaptive response that allows an optimal metabolic handling of nutrients when food availability is restricted to a particular time of day (4, 5). Furthermore, a consequence of DRF is the adoption of a new coordination between the master circadian pacemaker, the hypothalamic suprachiasmatic nucleus (SCN), and peripheral oscillators such as liver, lung, adipose tissue, and heart (6, 7). Key experiments show that a variety of 24-h rhythmic responses under the DRF protocol, including the onset and maintenance of FAA, are elicited even when SCN functions are disrupted [references within Ref. (8)], which support the existence of an SCN-independent circadian timing system known as the food entrained oscillator (FEO) (9). Defining the FEO's anatomical substrate has been elusive, in part because the existence of several FEOs in different organs and tissues (10) and the emergence of an alternative timing system that complements the SCN's pacemaker activity (11, 12).

The liver is one of the organs that show a faster change in 24-h rhythmicity and metabolic responses under the DRF protocol (13). In this context, it has been shown that a 2-h food access during the daytime modifies (1) the circadian phase of BMAL1 and PER1 clock proteins (14, 15), (2) metabolic liver regulation (16), (3) hepatic mitochondrial activity (17), (4) ureagenesis (15), and (5) gluconeogenesis (GNG) (18). In addition to these biochemical adaptations, DRF promotes histological and ultrastructural changes in hepatocytes (19).

Conversely, β-catenin is a polyfunctional protein; it acts as a subunit of the cadherin protein complex, and hence, it regulates cell–cell adhesion properties (20). Also, it functions as a transcriptional factor acting as an effector of the Wnt signaling pathway (21), and it is a metabolic regulator that facilitates gluconeogenic activity in the liver (22). The complex role played by β-catenin is accomplished by the selective actions of phosphorylated β-catenin forms (23). Indeed, two of the best characterized phosphorylated β-catenins are as follows: (1) β-catenin phosphorylated at serine 33 (pSer33 β-catenin). This phosphorylation is carried by the serine/threonine kinase glycogen synthase kinase 3β (GSK3β) (24) after initial phosphorylation by another serine/threonine kinase, casein kinase 1 α (CK1α), at residue serine 45. Subsequent phosphorylation by GSK3β at residues T41, S37, and S33 in the *N*-terminal promotes that β-catenin be recognized by the β-TrCP E3-ligase complex, ubiquitylated, and quickly degraded by the 26 S proteasome (25). Therefore, GSK3β, CK1α, and scaffold proteins such as adenomatous polyposis coli (APC) and axin are part of the multiprotein complex called the "destruction complex" of β-catenin, whose function is to regulate cytosolic β-catenin levels. (2) β-catenin phosphorylated at serine 675 (pSer675 β-catenin). This phosphorylation is performed either by protein kinase A (PKA), a cAMP-dependent protein kinase (26), or by p21-activated kinase, a serine/threonine protein kinase (27). Phosphorylation at serine 675 enhances β-catenin transcriptional activity by facilitating the interaction between the *C*-terminal tail of β-catenin with several transcriptional coactivators, including the CREB-binding protein (28). β-catenin is linked to physiology in the metabolic zonation and metabolism of the liver due to its participation in different metabolic pathways. The importance of this functional duality consists in the preservation of liver homeostasis. It has been reported that any disruption of homeostatic balance, like the one produced by a high-fat dietary manipulation in a biological system where β-catenin is absent (a hepatocyte-specific β-catenin transgenic or β-catenin knockout mice), fosters deleterious effects on hepatocyte function and morphology (29). These effects suggest that Wnt signaling in hepatocytes is essential for the development of diet-induced fatty liver and obesity.

Evidences of relationship between β-catenin and clock proteins have come from cancer experimental models both *in vitro* and *in vivo*, where the downregulation of PER1 or PER2 proteins increased β-catenin (30) and some of its target genes such as cyclin D and C-myc. It has been proposed that previous effect is because β-catenin promotes PER1 and PER2 degradation (31). Contrary, the downregulation of β-catenin by siRNA increases the PER2 protein level in human colon cancer cells (31) and in small intestine mucosa of mice with APC mutations ($APC^{Min/+}$). It was also observed that PER2 rhythm was lost concomitant to a reduced protein expression (31). In contrast, BMAL1, a positive regulator of the circadian clock, was demonstrated to be a transcriptional factor of the β-catenin protein and other components of the Wnt pathway (32). As a consequence, β-catenin levels in a BMAL1 null mice ($BMAL1^{-/-}$) were decreased in comparison to wild-type mice (32). In addition, molecular mechanisms of circadian rhythmicity reside on posttranslational modifications (PTMs) of clock proteins (33), mainly phosphorylation. Most known kinases in the circadian machinery are CK1α/ε and GSK3β, which are part of the Wnt/β-catenin pathway as well. In the context of circadian mechanism, these kinases can determinate clock proteins subcellular localization, stabilization, heterodimerization, and degradation, whereas in the β-catenin context, they are involved mostly in the degradation process. Taken together, all these antecedents strongly suggest that β-catenin could be influenced by the core of the circadian molecular clock. Therefore, the purpose of this study was to explore whether DRF and the associated FEO expression could influence the 24-h rhythmicity and subcellular distribution of β-catenin variants in the rat liver.

The daily profile data in our research showed that DRF promoted (1) an enhanced presence of total β-catenins mainly in the areas adjacent to the plasma membrane, (2) a reduction in pSer33 β-catenin levels, and (3) an increase in the nuclear presence of pSer675 β-catenin. Our research also demonstrated a dynamic rearrangement in the subcellular localization of β-catenins at different times of the day. Overall, our results indicate that the β-catenin system could be part of the functional and structural adaptations that take place in the liver during the FEO expression.

MATERIALS AND METHODS

Animals and Housing

Adult male Wistar rats weighing 200 ± 20 g at the beginning of the experiment were kept in groups in transparent acrylic cages (40 cm × 50 cm × 20 cm) and acclimated to laboratory conditions: 12:12 h light–dark cycle (lights on 08:00 hours), controlled temperature (22 ± 1°C), and free access to food (5001 rodent diet; LabDiet, St. Louis MO, USA) and water for a few days before starting the experimental procedures. Our study and the experimental protocols were approved by the Universidad Nacional Autónoma de México Institutional Animal Care and Use Committee, and all experiments were conducted in accordance to the recommendations of the Universidad Nacional Autónoma de México Institutional Animal Care and Use Committee. In addition, we took into account the International Ethical Standards reported by Portaluppi et al. (34).

Experimental Groups

For 3 weeks, rats were randomly assigned to one of the following feeding conditions, which are similar to those reported by Davidson and Stephan (35) and Ángeles-Castellanos et al. (36):

(1) *Ad libitum* group (AL), with free access to food and water throughout the 24-h period.
(2) Daytime restricted feeding (DRF) group, which had access to food for only 2 h per day, from 12:00 to 14:00 hours.At the end of feeding conditions 1 and 2, animals were processed at 3-h intervals over a 24-h period starting at 08:00 hours.To discard the possibility that observed effects were due to the daily fasting (22 h)–refeeding (2 h) cycle in the DRF group, two additional feeding control groups were included as follows:
(3) An acute 22-h fasting group (Fa), where rats were given free access to food for 3 weeks. On the last day of the experiment, food was removed at 14:00 hours, and animals were food deprived for the next 21 h. At the end of this acute fasting (at 11:00 hours), animals were sacrificed.
(4) An acute 2-h refeeding group (Rf), where rats were left for 22 h in fasting and then refed for 2 h (from 12:00 to 14:00 hours). They were sacrificed at 14:00 hours.

Previous reports of our work group have proved the effectiveness of the DRF protocol by testing different metabolic and physiological adaptations in the rat liver such as phase shift in the daily variations of clock proteins PER1 (37, 38) and BMAL1 (14) and serum corticosterone levels (37, 38). Besides, the appearance of FAA is always associated to DRF protocol.

Liver Sampling and Subcellular Fractionation

Animals were killed by a guillotine-like device. Livers were dissected, and a 5 g sample was processed immediately at 4°C in homogenization buffer (225 mM sucrose, 0.3 mM EGTA, 10 mM Tris-HCl, pH 7.4; 1:10 w/v), using a Potter-Elvehjem Teflon-glass homogenizer (40 rpm for 20 s). Total liver homogenate was centrifuged at 1,500 g for 15 min (Sorvall SS34 centrifuge), and the resulting pellet was isolated using the citric acid method, as reported by Reiners and Busch (39) to collect the nuclear fraction, while the resultant supernatant was decanted and centrifuged again at 10,000 g for 20 min to precipitate the mitochondrial fraction (which was discarded). The resultant supernatant was ultracentrifuged (Beckman 70Ti rotor) at 100,000 g for 70 min to obtain the microsomal fraction (which was removed) from the pellet and the cytosolic fraction from the supernatant (40). All fractions were collected, aliquoted, and stored at −70°C until further use.

Western Blot Analyses

The total homogenate and the cytosolic and nuclear fractions were used to measure the presence of total β-catenins, pSer33 β-catenin, and pSer675 β-catenin. Total protein was quantified using the Bradford method (41). Equal amounts of protein were mixed with 2× Laemmli sample buffer (Bio-Rad Laboratories, Hercules, CA, USA) and incubated at 80°C for 10 min. The proteins were separated with 10% SDS-PAGE under reducing conditions. Subsequently, gels were transferred to nitrocellulose membranes and blocked for 1 h with 5% non-fat milk. After three washouts with 20 mM Tris-Buffered Saline and Tween 20 (TBST) (pH 7.5), membranes were incubated overnight at 4°C with the following primary antibodies (all of them diluted in TBST): rabbit anti β-catenin antibody (ab 32572) 1:5,000 dilution, rabbit anti β-catenin (phospho S33) antibody (ab 73153) (Abcam, Cambridge, MA, USA) 1:30,000 dilution, and rabbit anti β-catenin (Ser675) antibody (D2F1, Cell Signaling Technology Inc., Danvers, MA, USA) 1:1,000 dilution. The following day, all membranes were washed three times with TBST and then incubated for 2 h with the alkaline phosphatase-conjugated secondary donkey anti-rabbit antibody (sc2083, Santa Cruz Biotechnology, Dallas, TX, USA), 1:5,000 dilution. Bands were revealed using the alkaline phosphatase conjugate substrate kit (Bio-Rad Laboratories, Hercules, CA, USA). β-tubulin antibody (ab 56676) at 1:1,000 dilution was used as a loading control for homogenate and cytosolic fractions, while lamin B1 antibody (ab184115) (Abcam, Cambridge, MA, USA) at 1:10,000 dilution was used as a marker for the nuclear fraction. Quantification was done by densitometric analysis using Image J Software (42) [National Institutes of Health (NIH), USA].

Immunofluorescence

Liver tissue was fixed in 10% formalin at 4°C for 1 week with changes every 2 days. Subsequently, the tissue was embedded in paraffin and sectioned into 7-μm slices. Liver slices were deparaffinized for 2 h at 60°C in a dry heat oven and then rehydrated in 100% xylol (10 min), 100% ethanol (5 min), 96% ethanol (5 min), 80% ethanol (5 min), and deionized water (10 min). Afterward, slices were bathed in permeabilization buffer (3.9 mM sodium citrate, 0.1% Tween 20) for 8 min and then boiled in EDTA buffer (1 mM EDTA, 0.05% Tween 20, pH 8.0) at 96°C for 1 h. Slices were blocked with 1% non-fat milk for 1 h, washed three times with TBST buffer, and incubated overnight at 4°C with the following antibodies (all diluted in TBST): rabbit anti β-catenin antibody (ab 32572) at 1:100 dilution, rabbit anti β-catenin (phospho S33) antibody (ab 73153) (Abcam, Cambridge, MA, USA) at 1:100 dilution, and rabbit anti β-catenin (Ser675) antibody (D2F1, Cell Signaling Technology Inc., Danvers, MA, USA) at 1:100 dilution.

The next day, slices were washed three times with TBST buffer and then incubated for 2 h with the secondary antibody Alexa Fluor 594 donkey anti-rabbit IgG (Invitrogen Molecular Probes Inc., Eugene, OR, USA) at 1:500 dilution. Subsequently, slices were blocked again with 1% non-fat milk for 1 h, washed three more times with TBST, and incubated overnight at 4°C with the second primary antibody, mouse anti-glutamine synthetase (GS) antibody (MAB302, Millipore Corporation, Billerica, MA, USA) at 1:300 dilution. Finally, slices were incubated for 2 h with the second secondary antibody Alexa Fluor 488 donkey anti-mouse IgG (A21202) or donkey anti-rabbit IgG (A21206) (Invitrogen, Molecular Probes Inc., Eugene, OR, USA) at 1:300 dilution. Fluorescence was visualized with both epi-fluorescence (Nikon Eclipse E600, Minato, Japan) and confocal microscopy (Zeiss Axiovert 200 LSM 510 Meta-Multiphotonic, Oberkochen, Germany), and it was quantified with Image J software (42) (NIH, USA).

Data Analysis

The data were grouped according to experimental conditions and times (at least four rats per temporal point) and expressed as the mean ± SEM. Results were compared using the one-way and two-way ANOVA test to determine time and treatment effects, respectively. Significant differences were detected with Tukey or Sidak *post hoc* tests ($p < 0.05$). A chronobiological analysis was also carried out using the ChronosFit program (43) with the following parameters: acrophase, mesor, and percentage of rhythmicity. Finally, a Student's t-test was used for the feeding condition control groups to identify significant differences between the following groups: acute fasted and refed; DRF and acute fasted (at 11:00 hours); DRF and acute refed (at 14:00 hours). All graphs and statistical analyses were performed using GraphPad Prism version 6.0 (GraphPad Software, San Diego, CA, USA).

RESULTS

The presence of free β-catenin in the cell cytoplasm is usually regulated across its degradation, unless β-catenin avoids the destruction complex. In this case, β-catenin increases in cytoplasm and can translocate into the nucleus. This function can be regulated by phosphorylation of a variety of kinases in the *N*-terminus or *C*-terminus of protein. First, in our experimental protocol, we evaluated β-catenin that is targeted to degradation (pSer33 β-catenin) and a β-catenin with an enhanced transcriptional activity (pSer675 β-catenin).

DRF Protocol Decreased the Level of pSer33 β-Catenin

The daily patterns of pSer33 β-catenin at different subcellular compartments of the liver are represented in **Figure 1**. The AL and DRF groups showed a constant presence of protein in the total homogenate and in the cytosolic fraction (**Figures 1A,B**) during the 24-h period. In the cytosolic fraction, the AL group at 08:00 hours presented a significant difference, two-way ANOVA hours of day: $F(1,48) = 23.85, p < 0.0001$, in comparison to DRF at same temporal point. Nevertheless, the DRF group showed a 16% decrease in the total homogenate and a 42% decrease in the cytosolic fraction. In the nuclear fraction, both groups displayed a gradual decrease of pSer33 β-catenin from the beginning of the light phase (08:00 hours) to the middle of dark phase (02:00 hours) (**Figure 1C**). In both groups, the one-way ANOVA showed significant difference. In the AL group: $F(7,32) = 2.74$, $p = 0.02$, and in the DRF group: $F(7,32) = 2.74, p = 0.02$. However, they did not present any rhythmicity when they were evaluated by the chronobiological analysis. The Fa group exhibited a similar expression of pSer33 β-catenin to DRF at 11:00 hours in all fractions tested, whereas the Rf group revealed a similar pattern in the total homogenate and in the nuclear fraction, but not in the cytosolic fraction; it showed a 61% reduction in pSer33 β-catenin compared to the DRF group (14:00 hours). The Fa group decreased its pSer33 β-catenin expression in the total homogenate by 23% with respect to the Rf group. In contrast, the Rf group decreased its pSer33 β-catenin expression in the cytosolic fraction by 51% with respect to the Fa group (**Figures 1A–C**).

DRF Increased the Nuclear Presence of pSer675 β-Catenin

The daily patterns of pSer675 β-catenin were quantified at different subcellular compartments of the liver in both AL and DRF groups (**Figure 2**). In total homogenate, AL rats showed a gradual decrease in pSer675 β-catenin expression throughout the light phase (from 08:00 to 20:00 hours) and a gradual increase in the dark phase (from 20:00 to 08:00 hours) until it reached a peak at 05:00 hours, one-way ANOVA hours of day $F(7,32) = 5.08$, $p = 0.0006$ (**Figure 2A**). This increment favors a 24-h rhythmic pattern that presented acrophase at 4.5 h (**Table 1**).

In the cytosolic fraction, the presence of pSer675 β-catenin was higher in the AL group during the dark phase (**Figure 2B**). In the nuclear fraction, a constant expression of pSer675 β-catenin was observed throughout the 24-h period. Regarding the DRF group, a uniform presence of pSer675 β-catenin was identified in all fractions tested in the 24-h cycle. It is relevant to mention that, compared to the DRF group, the AL group showed a 21% increase in the expression of pSer675 β-catenin in the cytosolic fraction throughout the 24-h period. This daily pattern is proportionately reversed in favor of the DRF group in the nuclear fraction (**Figure 2C**). The Fa and Rf groups showed a similar presence of protein in the total homogenate and in the nuclear fraction when compared to the DRF group (at 11:00 and 14:00 hours). The increase of pSer675 β-catenin in the cytosolic fraction of Fa group was greater than the observed in the DRF group at 11:00 hours (52%) and in the Rf group at 14:00 hours (50%).

To discriminate among the multiple forms of β-catenin in our protocol (phosphorylated and non-phosphorylated), we also evaluated the total liver β-catenins.

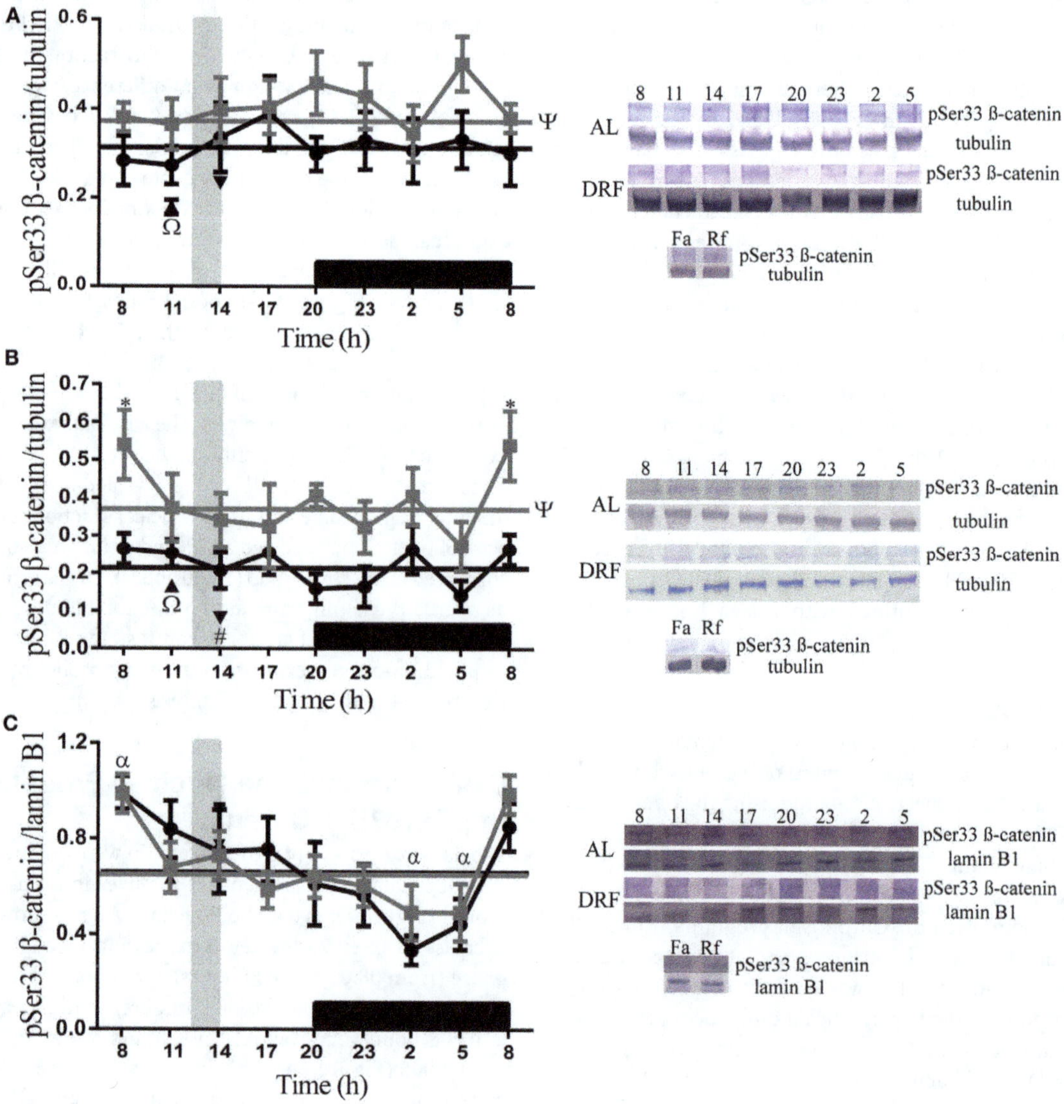

FIGURE 1 | Daily profile of pSer33 β-catenin in the rat liver under the daytime restricted feeding (DRF) protocol. Semiquantitative western blot analysis of pSer33 β-catenin at total homogenate **(A)**, cytosolic fraction **(B)**, and nuclear fraction **(C)**. Each value was normalized using the housekeeping proteins tubulin [for **(A,B)**] and lamin B1 [for **(C)**]. A representative western blot for each condition is shown. Gray squares, AL group; black circles, DRF group; triangles, Fa group; inverse triangles, Rf group. Data are represented as the mean ± SEM (n = 4–5 different animals per temporal point). Horizontal lines represent the 24-h cycle average. The vertical gray bar indicates food access (12:00–14:00 hours), and the horizontal black rectangle in the x-axis corresponds to the dark phase. ΨSignificant difference between AL and DRF groups in the 24-h average (Student's t-test, $p < 0.05$). *Significant difference between AL and DRF groups at the same temporal point (two-way ANOVA followed by Sidak *post hoc* test, $p < 0.0001$). αSignificant difference between points of the same group (one-way ANOVA followed by Tukey *post hoc* test, $p < 0.05$). ΩSignificant difference between Fa and Rf groups (Student's t-test, $p < 0.05$). #Significant difference between DRF (11:00 or 14:00 hours) versus Fa and Rf (Student's t-test, $p < 0.05$).

DRF Protocol Increased the Presence of Total β-Catenins

Figure 3 shows daily patterns of total β-catenins at different subcellular compartments of rat hepatocytes under AL and DRF conditions. The AL group showed a constant 24-h expression in all fractions tested. DRF rats did not show a 24-h rhythmic pattern. However, DRF protocol promoted significant increases in the 24-h cycle average as follows: 113% of total β-catenins in comparison to the liver homogenate in the AL group (**Figure 3A**), 39% in the cytosolic fraction (**Figure 3B**), and 75% in the nuclear fraction (**Figure 3C**). All three increases were greater in the light phase, when DRF animals had access to food. DRF only displayed temporal differences with the AL group, in the total homogenate at 14:00, 20:00, 02:00, and 05:00 hours; two-way ANOVA hours of day: $F(1,88) = 69.56$, $p < 0.0001$. The Fa and Rf groups showed similar total β-catenin levels to the AL group at 11:00 and 14:00 hours in the total homogenate and in the cytosolic fraction (**Figures 3A,B**). Nevertheless, total β-catenins

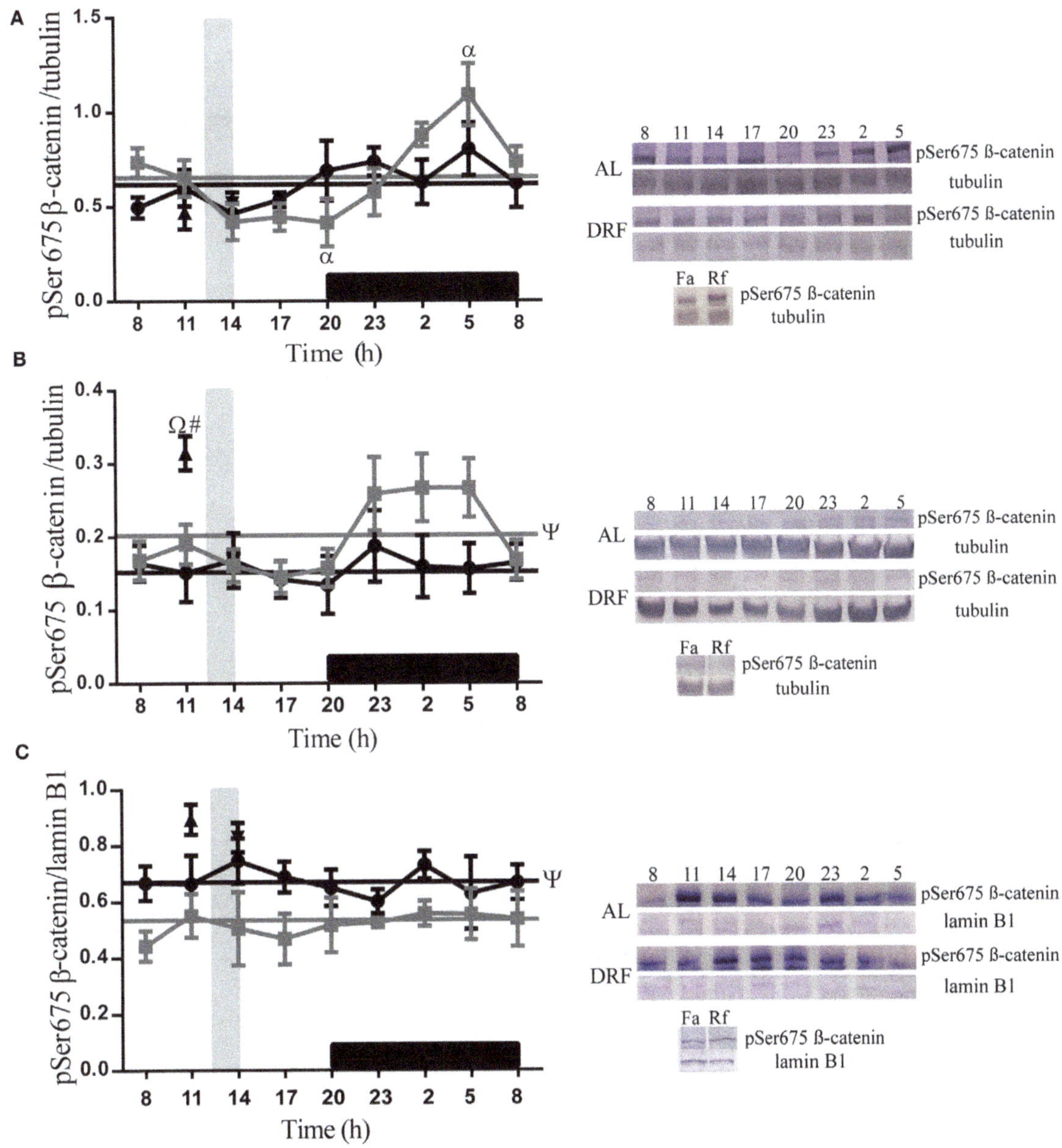

FIGURE 2 | Daily profile of pSer675 β-catenin in the rat liver under the daytime restricted feeding (DRF) protocol. Semiquantitative western blot analysis of pSer675 β-catenin at total homogenate **(A)**, cytosolic fraction **(B)**, and nuclear fraction **(C)**. Each value was normalized using the housekeeping proteins tubulin [for **(A,B)**] and lamin B1 [for **(C)**]. A representative western blot for each condition is shown. Gray squares, AL group; black circles, DRF group; triangles, Fa group; inverse triangles, Rf group. Data are represented as the mean ± SEM (n = 4–5 animals per temporal point). Horizontal lines represent the 24-h cycle average. The vertical gray bar indicates food access (12:00–14:00 hours), and the horizontal black rectangle in the x-axis corresponds to the dark phase. $^{\Psi}$Significant difference between AL and DRF groups in the 24-h average (Student's t-test, $p < 0.05$). $^{\alpha}$Significant difference between points of the same group (one-way ANOVA followed by Tukey *post hoc* test, $p < 0.05$). $^{\Omega}$Significant difference between Fa and Rf groups (Student's t-test, $p < 0.05$). $^{\#}$Significant difference between DRF (11:00 or 14:00 hours) versus Fa and Rf (Student's t-test, $p < 0.05$).

levels in the nuclear fraction were similar to those in the DRF group (**Figure 3C**).

Due to the structural function of β-catenin at adherens junctions (AJ), we evaluated the presence of the β-catenin variants in the plasma membrane through immunohistochemistry at 11:00 hours (before food access for DRF rats), 14:00 hours (after food access for DRF rats), and 02:00 hours (in the middle of the dark phase) and under Fa and Rf conditions.

Immunohistochemical observations were used to determine how the time of day and feeding conditions influence the subcellular distribution of phosphorylated and total forms of β-catenin within hepatocytes, as well as the correlations between them.

TABLE 1 | Chronobiological analysis of pSer675 β-catenin in total homogenate of *Ad libitum* group.

	MESOR	Amplitude	Acrophase (hours:minutes)	Rhythmicity (%)
pSer675 β-catenin	0.65 ± 0.24	0.30	04.55	87.43

CHRONOS-FIT analysis was performed to evaluate the daily rhythmicity. Amplitude represents the difference between the peak (or trough) and the mean value of a wave (Mesor). Acrophase represents the time at which the peak of a rhythm occurs. The existence of a rhythmic pattern was defined by one-way ANOVA.

DRF Protocol Augmented Total β-Catenins Placed in the Plasma Membrane

The AL group showed the presence of similar total β-catenins in all temporal points mentioned above, whereas the DRF group showed an enhanced expression of total β-catenins at 11:00 and 14:00 hours (**Figures 4A,B**). In contrast, the Fa and Rf groups showed the lowest expression of total β-catenins in the plasma membrane. To discover whether the expression of total β-catenins in the plasma membrane could be correlated

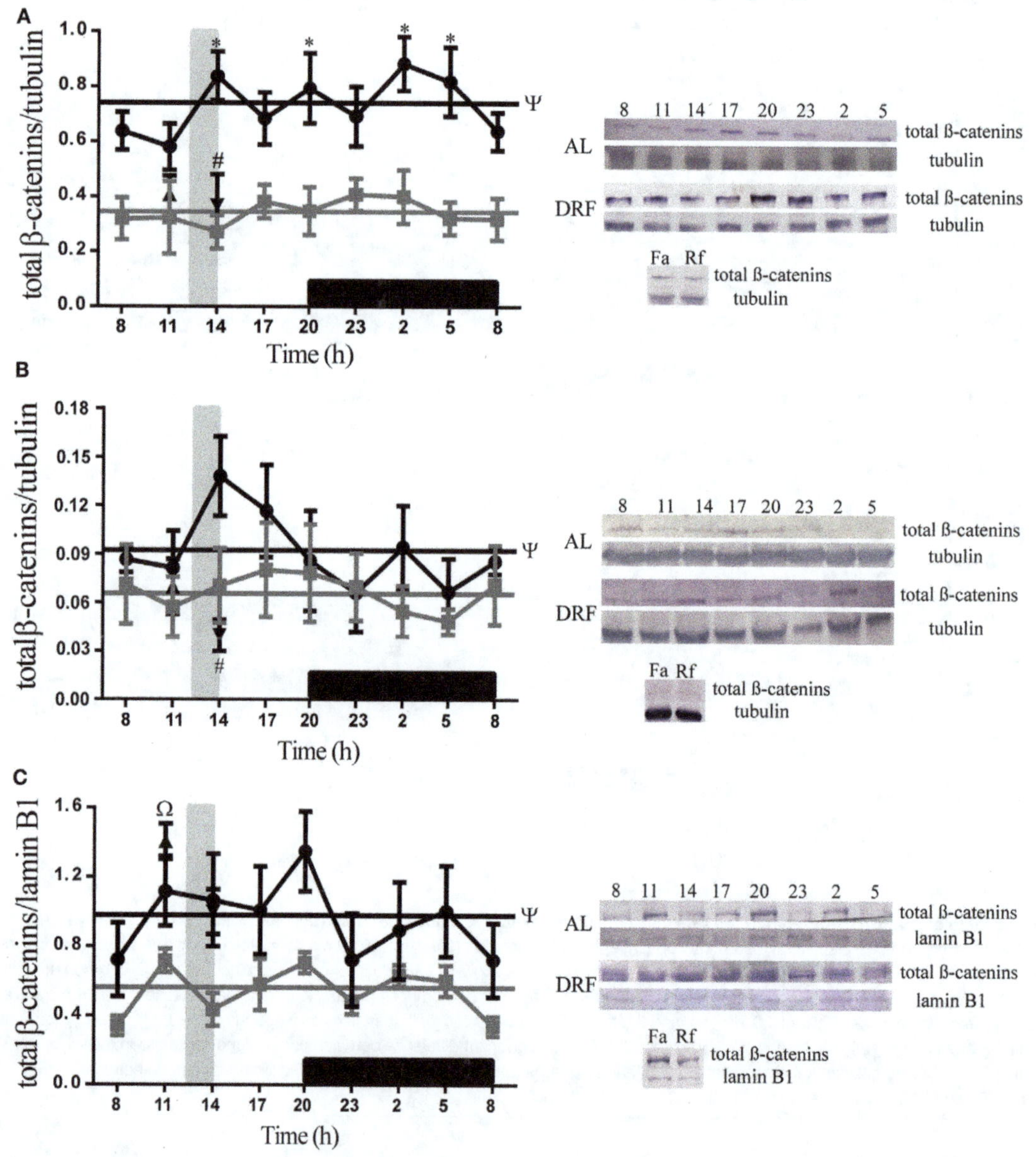

FIGURE 3 | Daily profile of total β-catenins presence in the rat liver under the daytime restricted feeding (DRF) protocol. Semiquantitative western blot analysis of total β-catenins at total homogenate **(A)**, cytosolic fraction **(B)**, and nuclear fraction **(C)**. Each value was normalized using the housekeeping proteins tubulin [for **(A,B)**] and lamin B1 [for **(C)**]. A representative western blot for each condition is shown. Gray squares, AL group; black circles, DRF group; triangles, Fa group; inverse triangles, Rf group. Data are represented as the mean ± SEM (n = 5–7 animals per temporal point). Horizontal lines represent the 24-h cycle average. The vertical gray bar indicates food access (12:00–14:00 hours), and the horizontal black rectangle in the x-axis corresponds to the dark phase. ΨSignificant difference between AL and DRF groups in the 24-h average (Student's t-test, $p < 0.05$). *Significant difference between AL and DRF groups at the same temporal point (two-way ANOVA followed by Sidak *post hoc* test, $p < 0.0001$). ΩSignificant difference between Fa and Rf groups (Student's t-test, $p < 0.05$). #Significant difference between DRF (11:00 or 14:00 hours) versus Fa and Rf (Student's t-test, $p < 0.05$).

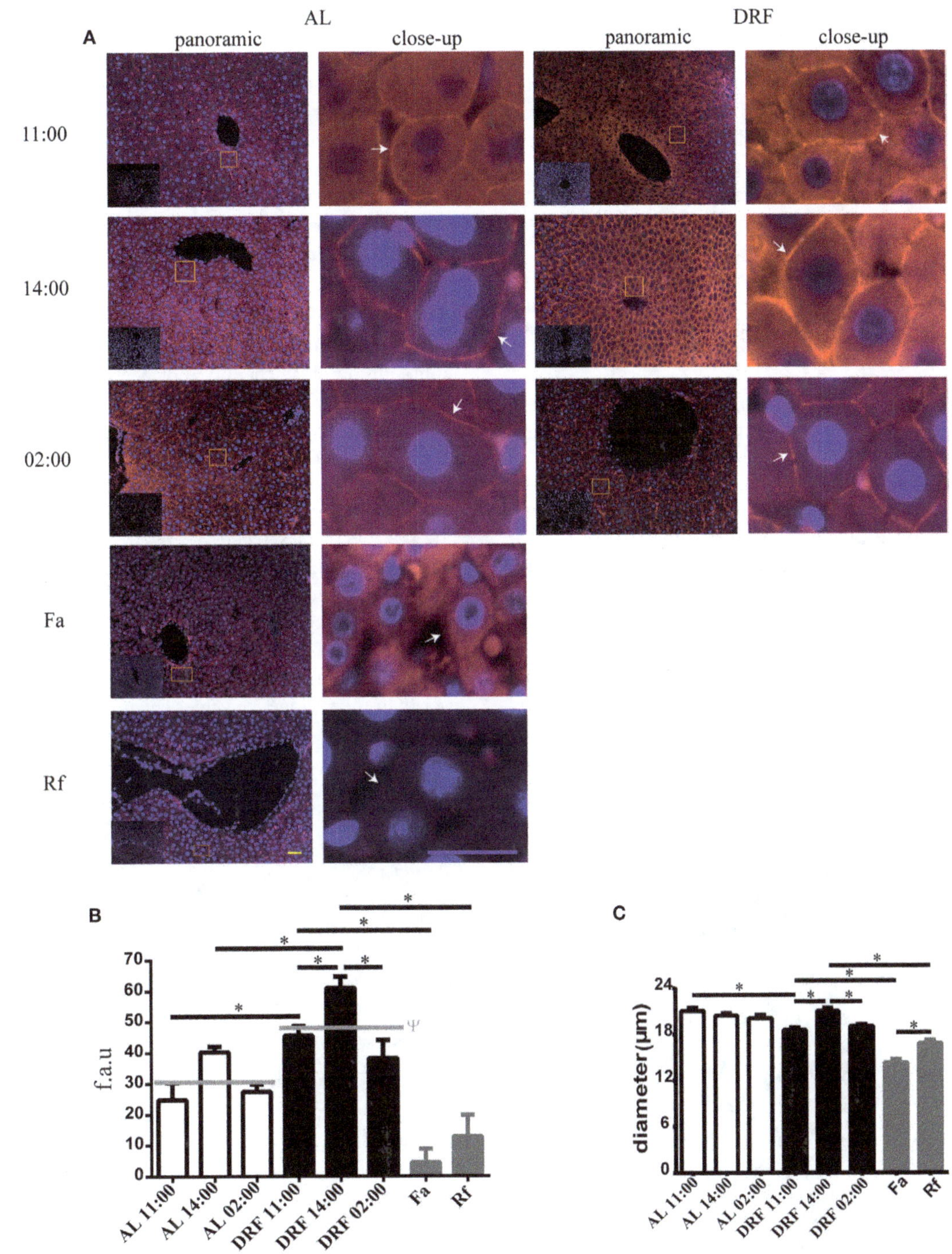

FIGURE 4 | Expression of the total β-catenins in the hepatocyte plasma membrane under the daytime restricted feeding (DRF) protocol. (A) Immunofluorescence signal for total β-catenins in three different temporal points: before food-anticipatory activity (FAA) (11:00 hours), after FAA (14:00 hours), and in the middle of the dark phase (02:00 hours), as well as under Fa and Rf conditions. Both a panoramic (yellow calibration bar = 50 µm) and a close-up view (blue calibration bar = 25 µm) indicated by an orange square are shown. A negative control (primary antibody omitted) is displayed in the insert of the panoramic panels. Histograms show quantification of **(B)** total β-catenins presence in hepatocyte plasma membrane (n = 3 animals) and **(C)** hepatocyte diameter at same temporal points described above under AL (white bars), DRF (black bars), and Fa and Rf (gray bars) conditions (n = 200). Data are represented as the mean ± SEM. The horizontal gray line represents the schedules average of each condition. $^{\Psi}$Significant difference between AL and DRF groups average (Student's t-test, $p < 0.05$). *Significant difference between AL and DRF groups at the same temporal point (Student's t-test, $p < 0.05$). f.a.u, fluorescence arbitrary units.

with hepatocyte size, we measured hepatocyte diameter under the conditions described in the Section "Materials and Methods" (only hepatocytes with an evident nucleus were considered for the morphometric study). According to the results, hepatocytes had a constant diameter under AL conditions (~20.5 μm) (**Figure 4C**). DRF treatment promoted fluctuations in hepatocyte diameter: 12% decrease at 11:00 hours, a subsequent increase at 14:00 hours similar to the diameters found in the AL group, and finally a 5% decrease at 02:00 hours (**Figure 4C**). In addition, the Fa group showed a 23% reduction in comparison to the DRF group at 11:00 hours, whereas the Rf group presented only a 12% reduction compared to the DRF group at 14:00 hours (**Figure 4C**). Hepatocyte diameters in the Fa and Rf groups differed significantly.

The Light to Dark Transition Changed pSer33 β-Catenin from the Cytosol to the Plasma Membrane

At two temporal points of the light phase (11:00 and 14:00 hours), both the AL and the DRF groups showed co-localization of total β-catenins and pSer33 β-catenin mainly in the cytosolic compartment of the hepatocytes (Figure S1A in Supplementary Material; **Figure 5**). Strikingly, the intracellular distribution of both forms of β-catenin changed in the dark phase (02:00 hours) since total β-catenins and pSer33 β-catenin were observed presumably next to the plasma membrane (Figure S1A Supplementary Material; **Figure 5**). Both total β-catenins and pSer33 β-catenin were still co-localized.

The Acute Fa–Rf Cycle Promoted pSer33 β-Catenin Location at the Hepatocyte Plasma Membrane

Unlike the AL and DRF groups, pSer33 β-catenin in Fa and Rf groups co-localized slightly with total β-catenins in the hepatocyte cytoplasm (**Figure 5**). Nevertheless, acute fasting and refeeding favored the location of pSer33 β-catenin next to the plasma membrane (**Figure 5**).

DRF Reduced pSer675 β-Catenin Located in the Plasma Membrane

Double immunohistochemistry of pSer675 β-catenin and total β-catenins proteins was performed to learn about pSer675 β-catenin's subcellular distribution, response to feeding protocols (DRF and Fa–Rf), and co-localization with total β-catenins. Results revealed plasma membrane distribution under AL (Figure S2 in Supplementary Material) and DRF conditions (**Figure 6**) at 11:00, 14:00, and 02:00 hours. Co-localization with total β-catenins were observed at these 3 h. However, after DRF rats had access to food (at 14:00 hours), they also exhibited pSer675 β-catenin with cytosolic distribution around the vasculature. Although AL and DRF groups exhibited pSer675 β-catenin in the plasma membrane (**Figure 6**), the average DRF values were 43% lower than the average AL values (Figure S2B in Supplementary

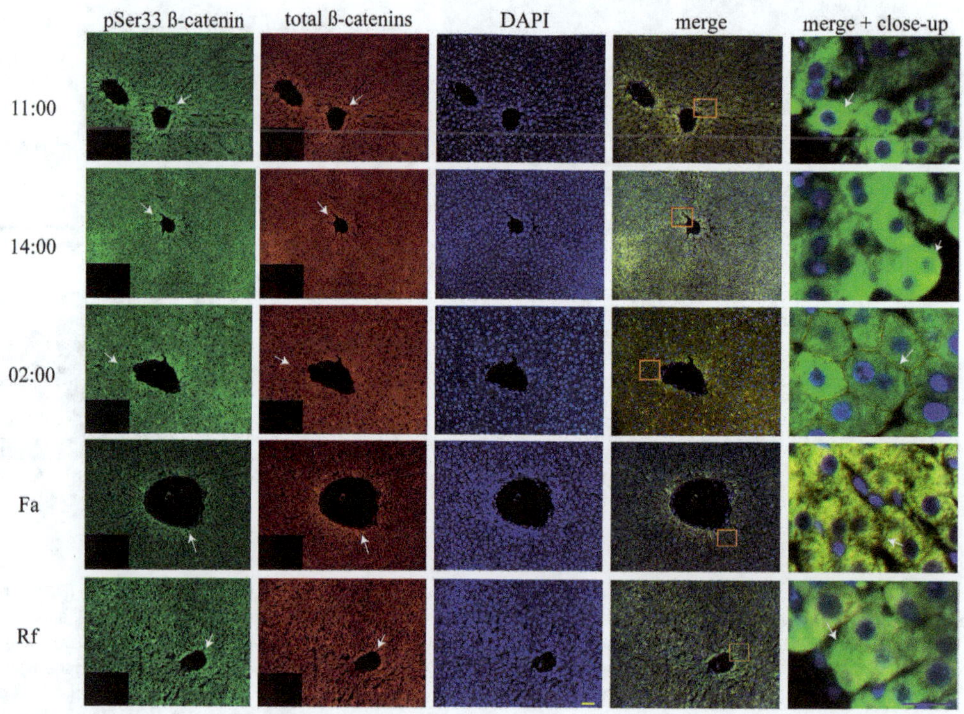

FIGURE 5 | Cytosolic co-localization of pSer33 β-catenin and total β-catenins in histological liver samples of rats under daytime restricted feeding (DRF) protocol. Immunofluorescence signal for the pSer33 β-catenin (green), the total β-catenins (red), and the DAPI (blue) in DRF conditions at three different temporal points: 11:00, 14:00, and 02:00 hours (see **Figure 4** for explanation), as well as Fa and Rf conditions. Both a panoramic (yellow calibration bar = 50 μm) and a close-up view (blue calibration bar = 25 μm) indicated by an orange square are shown. Negative controls (primary antibody omitted) are displayed in the insert of the panoramic panels. Histological liver samples from three different animals.

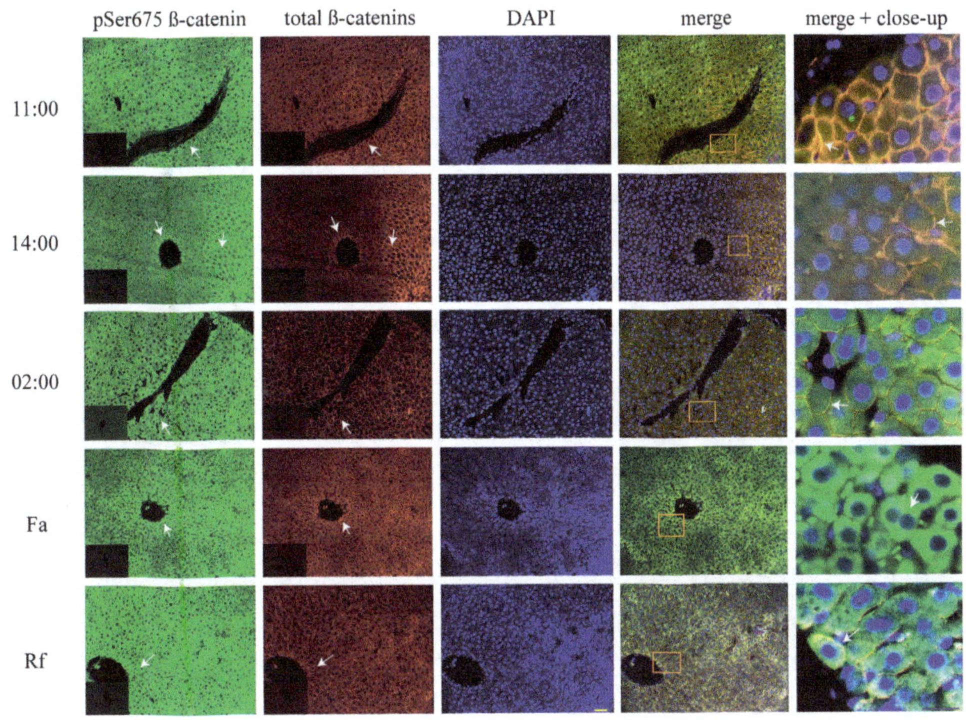

FIGURE 6 | Plasma membrane co-localization of total β-catenins and pSer675 β-catenin in histological liver samples of rats under daytime restricted feeding (DRF) protocol. Immunofluorescence signal for pSer675 β-catenin (green), total β-catenins (red), and DAPI (blue) under DRF conditions at three different temporal points: 11:00, 14:00, and 02:00 hours (see **Figure 4**, for explanation), as well as under Fa and Rf conditions. Both a panoramic (yellow calibration bar = 50 μm) and a close-up view (blue calibration bar = 25 μm) indicated by an orange square are shown. Negative controls (primary antibody omitted) are displayed in the insert of the panoramic panels. Histological liver samples from three different animals.

Material). Conversely, while the Fa group showed a presence of pSer675 β-catenin in cytosol, a relocation of this phosphorylated form of β-catenin was observed close to the plasma membrane in the Rf group. Both feeding condition groups expressed co-localization with total β-catenins (**Figure 6**).

Liver Zonation of β-Catenin Variants

The three forms of β-catenin (total β-catenin, pSer33 β-catenin, and pSer675 β-catenin) displayed distinctive subcellular expressions influenced by the time in the 24-h cycle and the feeding condition. Previous reports have shown that the expression of different forms of β-catenin vary in the pericentral (PC) and periportal (PP) hepatocytes in the hepatic lobule (44, 45). Therefore, to explore a putative enrichment in the presence of β-catenin forms in the PP and PC hepatocyte population, a double immunohistochemistry was performed on all β-catenin proteins, and the GS enzyme, the canonical marker of the PC zone of the hepatic acinus. Results exhibited that total β-catenins and the pSer675 β-catenin in all schedules and conditions (11:00, 14:00, and 02:00 hours and Fa and Rf) were located mostly in the cytosol of PC hepatocytes, while from the intermediate to the PP zone of acinus, they were located in the plasma membrane (**Figures 7** and **8**, respectively). On the other hand, the presence of both cytosolic and cell membrane pSer33 β-catenin was observed in PC hepatocytes (**Figure 9**); this presence disappears between the intermediate and PP zones. That was observed in all schedules and conditions proven (11:00, 14:00, and 02:00 hours and Fa and Rf).

DISCUSSION

Cell Biology and β-Catenin Signaling

Wnt/β-catenin is a conserved signaling pathway (46) that fulfills important metabolic roles in the adult liver. β-catenin plays a pivotal role that involves cell adhesion (a stable β-catenin pool associated with the cell membrane) and transcriptional activity (a soluble β-catenin cytoplasmic pool) (47). These roles are coordinated by PTMs, mainly phosphorylation (48).

Our results indicated a significant decrease of pSer33 β-catenin in the total homogenate and in the cytosol under DRF, which could indicate a lower rate for protein degradation and an opportunity for β-catenin to be translocated into the nucleus to promote transcription of its target genes.

Although the GSK3β phosphorylates β-catenin in the serine 33, this form of β-catenin did not show a rhythmic patron (**Figures 1A,B**). Presumably, this is because multiple and consecutive phosphorylation events are required. First, it is necessary that CK1α and GSK3β hyperphosphorylate the scaffold proteins of the destruction complex (APC and axin), which increase their affinity for β-catenin. Once the axin–APC–β-catenin complex is

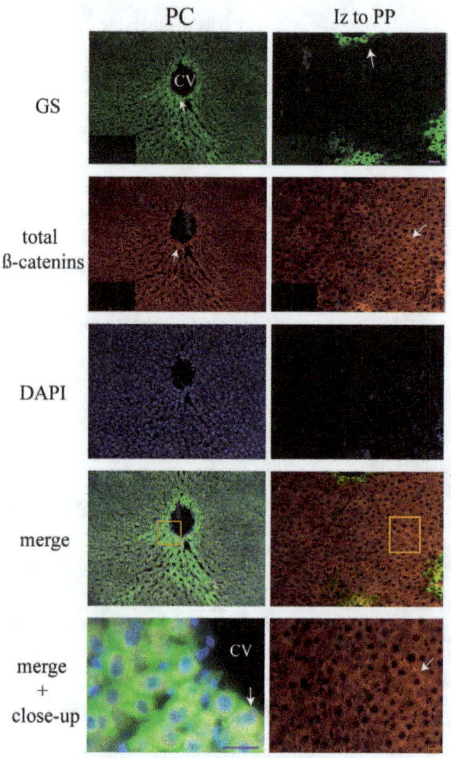

FIGURE 7 | Zonal distribution of total β-catenins in the hepatic acinus. Immunofluorescence signal for glutamine synthetase (green), total β-catenins (red), and DAPI (blue). Both a panoramic (purple calibration bar = 50 μm) and a close-up view (blue calibration bar = 25 μm and yellow calibration bar = 20 μm) indicated by an orange square are shown. Negative controls (primary antibody omitted) are displayed in the insert of the panoramic panels. Histological liver samples from three different animals. PC, pericentral zone; Iz, intermediate zone; PP, periportal zone; CV, central vein.

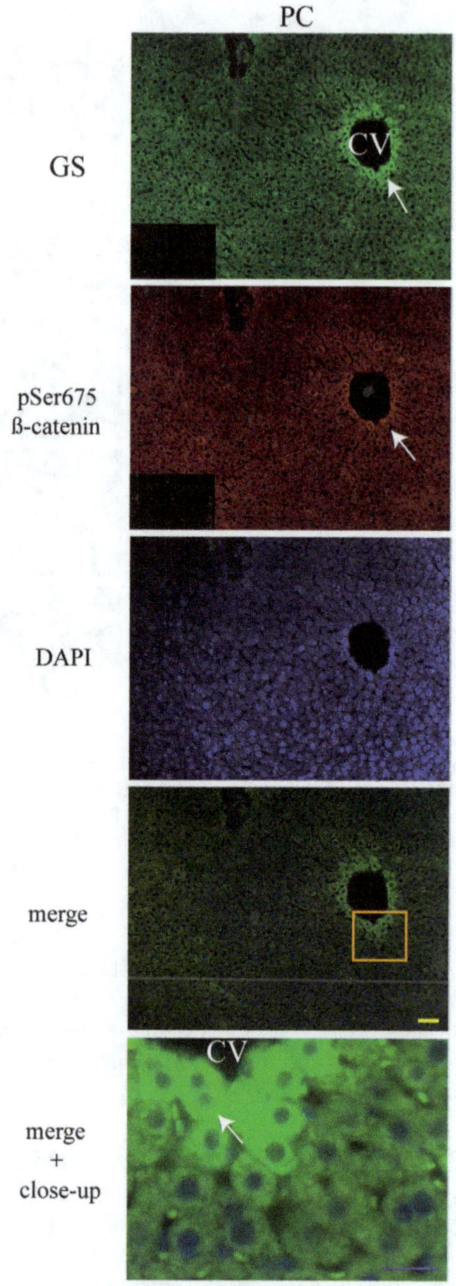

FIGURE 8 | Zonal distribution of pSer675 β-catenin in the hepatic acinus. Immunofluorescence signal for glutamine synthetase (green), pSer675 β-catenin (red), and DAPI (blue). Both a panoramic (yellow calibration bar = 50 μm) and a close-up view (blue calibration bar = 25 μm) indicated by an orange square are shown. Negative controls (primary antibody omitted) are displayed in the insert of the panoramic panels. Histological liver samples from three different animals. CV = central vein.

formed, CK1 phosphorylates the β-catenin in the serine 45; IkB kinase-α (49) and cyclin D1/Cdk6 (50) can also phosphorylate this site. This priming phosphorylation subsequently promotes that GSK3β phosphorylates threonine 41 and serines 37, and 33 (51), and these residues can be also phosphorylated by PKC (52). In this context, the protein phosphatase 1 acts on axin (53), and in consequence, GSK3β function is impeded. Also, in epithelial cells, β-catenin is constitutive synthesized to form AJ with the E-cadherin (54). Cytosolic presence of newly synthesized β-catenin and release of β-catenin from AJ are regulated by the destruction complex. Thus, we hypothesize that multifactorial equilibrium between phosphorylation and dephosphorylation events by a variety of cellular inputs maintains constant pSer33 β-catenin expression levels.

Differences among pSer33 β-catenin temporal points in the nucleus (**Figure 1C**) could be explained by the fact that pSer33 β-catenin is not transcriptionally active; consequently, it could be periodically exported from the cell nucleus.

Concerning the pSer675 β-catenin expression, AL group presented substantial changes in the night, where normally animals eat, and metabolic parameters such as glycemia and insulin are increased (18), a pattern expected for species with nocturnal feeding habits. In the case of DRF animals, pSer675 β-catenin expression was constant in all fractions, but it increased in nucleus (**Figure 2C**). It is known that DRF animals are hypoglycemic and they present high levels of corticosterone and glucagon as well as low levels of insulin (18), three positive regulators of GNG.

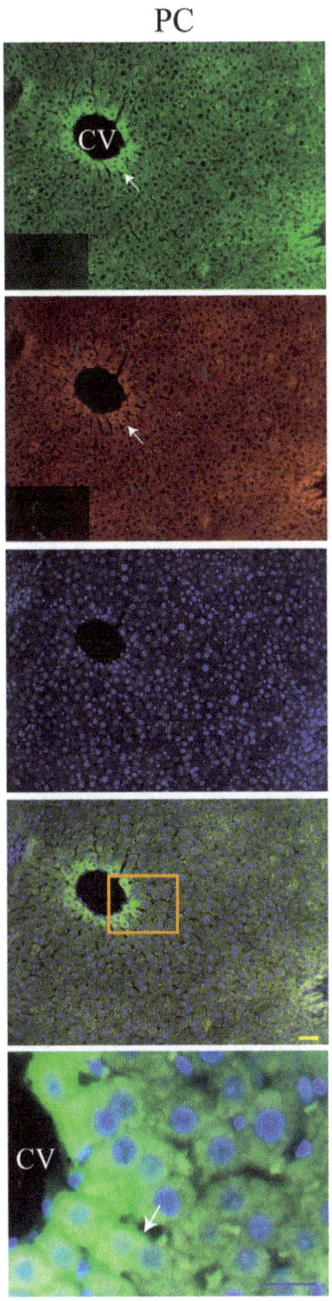

FIGURE 9 | Zonal distribution of pSer33 β-catenin in the hepatic acinus. Immunofluorescence signal for glutamine synthase (green), pSer33 β-catenin (red), and DAPI (blue). Both a panoramic (yellow calibration bar = 50 μm) and a close-up view (blue calibration bar = 25 μm) indicated by an orange square are shown. Negative controls (primary antibody omitted) are displayed in the insert of the panoramic panels. Histological liver samples from 3 different animals. PC = pericentral zone; CV = central vein.

Protein kinase A, which phosphorylates β-catenin at serine 675 (26), is stimulated by glucagon. This condition could be related to the pSer675 β-catenin transcriptional activity associated with repeated fasting and the consequent GNG activation. GNG is a physiological adaptation to starvation (short and medium fasting), stressful conditions, and short-term glycogen-replenishment activity in the liver after food intake (18). It has been confirmed that in the liver of starved animals, β-catenin regulates hepatic glucose metabolism through transcriptional regulation of cyclin D1, which controls the gluconeogenic response in addition to its role in the cell cycle (55, 56). Furthermore, β-catenin regulates the transcription of two of the rate-limiting enzymes in hepatic GNG: glucose-6-phosphatase (G6Pase) and phosphoenolpyruvate carboxykinase (PEPCK) by interacting with the FoxO1 transcription factor (22).

Indeed, GNG also increases under Fa and Rf conditions. However, when compared to DRF, Fa rats showed a higher presence of pSer675 in the cytosolic fraction (**Figure 2B**), which could be related to a synergic regulation by other signaling pathway elements such as Akt (57), glucagon-like peptide 1 (57), glucagon-like peptide 2 (58), p21 (27), or insulin growth factor 1 (59).

Substantial differences between DRF protocol and an acute 22 h fasting (Fa) are presented in a diversity of metabolic parameters (15, 17–19, 38, 60, 61), supporting the notion that the metabolic state of rats under DRF protocol is unique and distinct from fed and fasted animals. It is proposed under DRF protocol that hepatic physiology acquires a rheostatic state (12, 17) as a result of biochemical and physiological adaptations for a better handling of nutrients.

It has been also reported that the amount of nuclear active dephosphorylated form of β-catenin increases after an overnight fast (22), which could be probably related to the significant incremented expression of total β-catenins in the cytosol and in the cell nucleus under DRF, Fa, and Rf conditions as a response to both acute and repeated fasting (**Figure 3**). DRF shifted the peaks of PEPCK and G6Pase around the time of food access (18), which coincides with the increase of total β-catenins mainly in the light phase (**Figure 3**). DRF also enhanced hepatic PEPCK activity and increased the amount of hepatic G6Pase (18). Therefore, we propose that elevated levels of total β-catenins within the nucleus could exert transcriptional activity, and the increased expression of total β-catenins in the plasma membrane (**Figures 4A,B**) under DRF could be related to cell adhesion properties. β-catenin can bind to type I cadherins, and it plays an essential role in the structural organization of tissues forming the cadherin–catenin complex, which is the base of AJ, to establish and maintain epithelial polarity (62). In hepatocytes, the polarization arrangement is unique and contributes to form the bile canaliculus, the smallest branch of the bile duct that forms a complex interconnected network that spreads along the liver parenchyma, in which tight junctions (TJ) are essential (63). By using a microarray technique, our group detected that, under DRF conditions, both cadherin (AJ) and claudin (TJ) increased by 13.3- and 6.4-folds, respectively, (data not published) after food intake at 14:00 hours; this temporal point is coincident with the maximal expression of total β-catenins in the plasma membrane (**Figure 4B**). At 14:00 hours, hepatocytes showed a larger diameter in comparison to the other schedules and conditions. This fact exhibits a correlation between total β-catenins presence and proteins related to hepatocyte morphology. Díaz-Muñoz et al. (19) demonstrated that DRF can modify the cross-sectional area of hepatocytes during FAA because at 11:00 hours hepatocytes were about 53% larger than under DRF before (08:00 hours) and after FAA (14:00 hours). In addition, Steinberg and Takeichi (64) postulated that the expression level of adhesion molecules, such as cadherins, influences the strength of adhesion, which provides active adhesion gradients in both vertebrate and insect developing systems. These gradients can determine both morphogenetic movements and specific anatomical configurations (65). Considering that liver weight decreases (~15%) under DRF treatment mainly during the light phase (14), it is possible that the β-catenin–cadherin complex could act as a flexible cell border involved in daily cell size changes: a decrease in hepatocyte diameter after 22 h of fasting (11:00 hours) and an increase in hepatocyte diameter upon replenishing their glycogen after 2 h of food access (14:00 hours) (18) (**Figure 4C**). Indeed, this dynamic cycle of decrease/increase in cell proportion is more noticeable under Fa and Rf conditions (**Figure 4C**).

Regarding the cellular localization of the three different forms of β-catenin, Benhamouche et al. (44) demonstrated both a robust β-catenin expression in the hepatocyte membrane (related to cell adhesion) and a slight cytosolic accumulation of β-catenin in the PC zone of hepatic lobule, while in PP hepatocytes staining in hepatocyte membrane decreased. When they probed the unphosphorylated form of β-catenin (an active form of protein), localization was cytosolic in the both proximal and distal part of PC compartment, whereas its negative regulator APC was expressed in the PP zone. This complementary distribution of β-catenin and APC suggests opposite effects of β-catenin pathway along hepatic acinus.

We observed that pSer33 β-catenin is present in the cytosol mainly at 11:00 and 14:00 hours and in the plasma membrane at 02:00 hours, both under DRF (**Figure 5**) and AL (Figure S1 in Supplementary Material) conditions; probably to a daily target for β-catenin degradation that is more evident during the light phase. According to western blot results, β-catenin marked for degradation in the Fa and Rf groups is not as noticeable as the other two groups (**Figure 1B**). Presumably, pSer33 β-catenin localization in the plasma membrane is due to a dynamic equilibrium between phosphorylation and dephosphorylation. Unexpectedly, we found pSer675 β-catenin close to the plasma membrane (**Figure 6**; Figure S2A in Supplementary Material). Semiquantification of pSer675 at the hepatocyte periphery under AL and DRF conditions demonstrated a decreased average in the DRF group in comparison to the AL group (Figure S2B in Supplementary Material). Apparently, the above result indicate that pSer675 β-catenin under DRF could be acting as a reservoir for β-catenin to eventually be translocated to the nucleus. In the Fa group, pSer675 β-catenin cytosolic expression (**Figure 6**) correlates with western blot results (**Figure 2B**), probably due to further phosphorylation associated with other signaling pathways.

With respect to the localization of β-catenin pools in the hepatic acinus, these showed cytosolic distribution in the PC zone, whereas detection in the plasma membrane was evident from the intermediate to the PP zones (**Figures 6–8**). Benhamouche et al.'s report in 2006 established a key role of Wnt/β-catenin pathway in liver zonation, which entails a functional and structural cellular heterogeneity. This hepatic zonation suggests an anatomical specialization in β-catenin functions, where in the PC zone, β-catenin that is committed to cell signaling could be accumulated in the cytosol waiting to be shuttled into the nucleus or to be degraded, whereas in the PP zone, β-catenin that plays a structural/reservoir role could be accumulated in the plasma membrane. Recently, the molecular mechanism that controls metabolic liver zonation was determined (66), showing complexity of this phenomena, where the APC protein and the RSPO-LGR4/5-ZNRF3/RNF43 module play essential and complementary roles.

Our results indicate that β-catenin is sensitive to feeding conditions and that both its structural and transcriptional functions are differentially modulated by the DRF protocol. These findings are significant because it would establish β-catenin as an element of the liver metabolic network that is closely related to the circadian molecular clock. To integrate our western blot and immunohistochemical results of the three forms of β-catenin, we elaborated a dynamic model to depict the liver response and adaptation to 2 h of DRF protocol at different times of the day (11:00, 14:00, and 02:00 hours) and feeding conditions (Fa and Rf) (**Figure 10**). In this model, we represented the gradient in the expression of the three different pools of β-catenin studied (total β-catenins, pSer33 β-catenin, and pSer675 β-catenin), along the hepatic acinus [metabolic zonation from the central vein (CV) to the portal triad (T)] (**Figure 10A**). The intracellular location of each β-catenin within the hepatocyte, besides the hepatocyte morphometry (**Figure 10B**), is shown. The cytoplasmic location of the three β-catenins in the PC hepatocytes can be seen, whereas the presence of total β-catenins and pSer675 in the PP hepatocytes is mostly in the plasma membrane region.

The β-Catenin Protein and FEO Expression

The core of liver circadian clock is based on a molecular mechanism that includes transcriptional/translational loops (67). In this mechanism, we found positive regulators such as the BMAL1 protein and negative regulators such as the PER protein. Both BMAL1 and PER1 show circadian rhythmicity in the liver (68), whose acrophases are modified by the DRF protocol (14). In this sense, experiments with cell cultures of NIH-3T3 cells have shown that overexpressions of BMAL1 increase β-catenin mRNA levels, indicating a direct relationship between them (69). In addition, downregulation of PER2 increases β-catenin in human colon cancer cells (70) and in the breast cancer cell line (MTCL) (30). These data suggest that clock genes in peripheral tissues regulate β-catenin expression. In the liver and other organs, DRF protocol promotes metabolic adaptations and changes in the daily rhythmicity of a various proteins and enzymes from different metabolic pathways (18), hormones (14, 16), receptors (15), calcium dynamics (38), and nuclear receptors (71). Liu et al. (22) demonstrated that β-catenin in the liver acts as a regulator of circulating glucose, GNG and as a modulator of insulin signaling. Moreover, it plays a role in mitochondrial homeostasis and, consequently, in energy balance (72). Many of these metabolic functions show a daily rhythmicity that is affected by the DRF protocol.

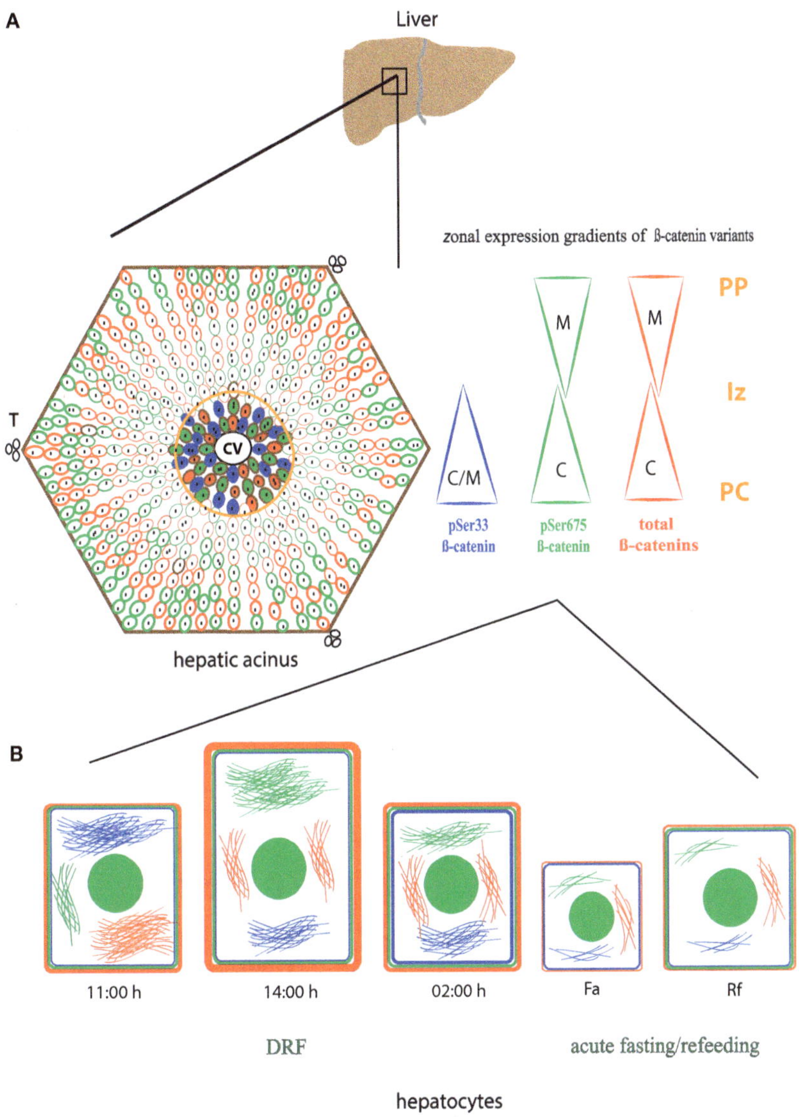

FIGURE 10 | Schematic model of the main changes and adaptations showed by total β-catenins and its phosphorylated forms: pSer33 and p675 in the hepatic acinus under daytime restricted feeding protocol. (A) Zonal localization of the three different pools of β-catenin studied, total β-catenins (red), pSer33 β-catenin (blue), and p675 β-catenin (green) within the functional unit of liver, the hepatic acinus. This localization is represented in the form of gradients (triangles) according to the distinct zones of the acinus. PC was signaled and delimited by an orange circle. **(B)** Intracellular and plasma membrane localization of the β-catenin pools mentioned in **(A)** in hepatocytes at 11:00, 14:00, and 02:00 hours, as well as under Fa and Rf conditions. Hepatocytes size varies according to the time of the day and the feeding condition. Color filaments represent cytosolic localization of distinct β-catenins, and the green circle inside hepatocytes represent cell nucleus. CV, central vein; T, portal triad; PC, pericentral zone; Iz, intermediate zone; PP, periportal zone; C, cytosolic expression; M, plasma membrane expression.

In mammals, the suprachiasmatic nuclei (SCN) of the hypothalamus is the main circadian pacemaker (68, 73), which is synchronized by light–dark cycle and organizes the timing of peripheral organs through neural and hormonal pathways (74). The core of circadian system is based on a transcriptional–translational feedback loops of genes and proteins whose oscillating period is near 24 h. Besides light cues, other environmental factors as periodic feeding can entrain circadian rhythms in peripheral oscillators as the liver. In this sense, when food availability is restricted 2–3 h per day (DRF), a new configuration of circadian system called FEO emerges. The most evident behavior associated to DRF in rodents is the FAA, which persists even when the SCN has been completed ablated (75) and for instance is considered the result of a circadian oscillator different to SCN.

DRF protocol implies both timed restricted feeding and calorie restriction to foster a generalized anticipatory state that optimizes searching, assimilation, and processing of nutrients. In peripheral oscillators, adaptations to restricted feeding paradigm includes a shift in the acrophase of clock genes, hormones, and many proteins (76–78) involved in metabolic pathways near the time of food accessibility. Under a DRF protocol, we found many interaction points between the molecular circadian clock and the metabolism that are under chronostatic regulation (12). Although the anatomical substrate of the FEO is unknown yet, the liver acts in a coordinated manner with other peripheral oscillators to induce an anticipatory behavior to prepare the animal to search for food.

Due to only a couple hours of food access in the DRF protocol, experimental animals consume lesser quantity of food (~36%) and reduce their body weight (~28%) (data not shown) and nutritional conditions change to be hypocaloric (79) compared to AL group. Calorie restriction involves a reduction in caloric intake (24–60%) from the macronutrients respect to AL animals (80). Animal below hypocaloric conditions did not present malnutrition (81), which had been corroborated in our laboratory by parameters such as albumin, hemoglobin concentration, and mean corpuscular hemoglobin (data not shown). Importance of calorie restriction combined or not with a DRF protocol resides in the resetting of the SCN (82), promoting interaction between the master circadian clock and metabolism. Moreover, the cross-talk between the circadian clock and Wnt signaling relies on two kinases: CK1 and GSK3β. These kinases phosphorylate clock proteins contributing to the fine-tuning regulation of the circadian clock (83), and they downregulate β-catenin activity in the Wnt/β-catenin pathway (84). The interactions between clock proteins, β-catenin, and different kinases could be a robust switch that coordinates metabolic changes in the liver under the DRF protocol. Further experiments are needed to elucidate if β-catenin, as a structural or as a signaling element, could be acting as an output factor of the hepatic circadian molecular clock.

Implications of β-Catenin in Liver Disease

β-catenin is a transcription factor for cell cycle regulators such as cyclin D1 (55) and c-myc (85). Moreover, β-catenin is essential in liver physiology (86). Aberrant β-catenin pathway activation has been associated with various liver pathologies such as defective bile acid metabolism, hepatosteatosis and cholestasis (87), chronic liver disease, hepatic fibrosis, and hepatocellular cancer (HCC) (88). In this sense, it has been reported that HCC cells from animal models and human patients show a constitutive activation of Wnt/β-catenin signaling (89). In addition, PER and BMAL1 could influence cell proliferation through Wnt pathway activation (69). It has also been proposed that cancer may be a circadian-related disorder (90) and that DRF decreases tumor size in HCC induced by dimethylnitrosamine (data not shown). All these data strengthen the idea that β-catenin could be considered a key factor in future therapeutic strategies for various liver pathologies.

In conclusion, our results suggest that β-catenin is an essential element in the metabolism and circadian context of liver physiology. Interestingly, β-catenin functions in the liver are zonated, which provides versatility for a good adaptation to metabolic challenges. Further studies are needed to define the mechanistic relationship between these findings and the FEO expression.

AUTHOR CONTRIBUTIONS

DI-P and MD-M designed the project and wrote the manuscript. DI-P was responsible for the acquisition, analysis of data, and the interpretation of experimental work. Both authors approved the final manuscript for publication and agreed to be accountable for all aspects of the work presented therein.

ACKNOWLEDGMENTS

We thank Ing. Elsa Nydia Hernández Ríos, Dr. Olivia Vázquez-Martínez, and Nut. Fernando López Barrera for their technical assistance. We also thank Lic. Jessica González Norris for her careful revision of the English version of this manuscript and MSc Leonor Casanova Rico for her academic support. Dalia Luz De Ita Pérez is a doctoral student from *Programa de Doctorado en Ciencias Biomédicas*, Universidad Nacional Autónoma de México (UNAM), and she received fellowship number 339099 from CONACYT.

SUPPLEMENTARY MATERIAL

FIGURE S1 | Cytosolic co-localization of pSer33 β-catenin and total β-catenins in histological liver samples of AL rats. Immunofluorescence signal for pSer33 β-catenin (green), total β-catenins (red), and DAPI (blue) under AL conditions at three different temporal points: 11:00, 14:00, and 02:00 hours (see **Figure 4**, for explanation). Both a panoramic (yellow calibration bar = 50 μm) and a close-up view (blue calibration bar = 25 μm) indicated by an orange square are shown. Negative controls (primary antibody omitted) are displayed in the insert of the panoramic panels. Histological liver samples from three different animals.

FIGURE S2 | Plasma membrane co-localization of total β-catenins and pSer675 β-catenin in histological liver samples of AL rats. (A) Immunofluorescence signal for pSer675 β-catenin (green), total β-catenins (red), and DAPI (blue) under AL conditions at three different temporal points: 11:00, 14:00, and 02:00 hours (see **Figure 4**, for explanation). Both a panoramic (yellow calibration bar = 50 μm) and a close-up view (blue calibration bar = 25 μm) indicated by an orange square are shown. Negative controls (primary antibody omitted) are displayed in the insert of the panoramic panels. Histological liver samples from three different animals. Histogram showing quantification of **(B)** plasma membrane presence of pSer675 β-catenin in hepatocytes ($n = 3$ animals) at same temporal points described above under AL (white bars), DRF (black bars), and Fa and Rf (gray bars). Data are represented as the mean ± SEM. The horizontal gray lines represent the schedules average of each condition. ΨSignificant difference between AL and DRF groups average (Student's *t*-test, $p < 0.05$). *Significant difference between AL and DRF groups at the same temporal point (Student's *t*-test, $p < 0.05$). f.a.u, fluorescence arbitrary units; nd, not detected.

REFERENCES

1. Challet E, Caldelas I, Graff C, Pévet P. Synchronization of the molecular clockwork by light- and food-related cues in mammals. *Biol Chem* (2003) 384(5):711–9. doi:10.1515/BC.2003.079
2. Mendoza J. Circadian clocks: setting time by food. *J Neuroendocrinol* (2007) 19(2):127–37. doi:10.1111/j.1365-2826.2006.01510.x
3. Mistlberger RE. Food-anticipatory circadian rhythms: concepts and methods. *Eur J Neurosci* (2009) 30(9):1718–29. doi:10.1111/j.1460-9568.2009.06965.x
4. Challet E, Solberg LC, Turek FW. Entrainment in calorie-restricted mice: conflicting zeitgebers and free-running conditions. *Am J Physiol* (1998) 274(6 Pt 2):R1751–61.
5. de Vasconcelos AP, Bartol-Munier I, Feillet CA, Gourmelen S, Pevet P, Challet E. Modifications of local cerebral glucose utilization during circadian food-anticipatory activity. *Neuroscience* (2006) 139(2):741–8. doi:10.1016/j.neuroscience.2005.12.045
6. Pezuk P, Mohawk JA, Yoshikawa T, Sellix MT, Menaker M. Circadian organization is governed by extra-SCN pacemakers. *J Biol Rhythms* (2010) 25(6):432–41. doi:10.1177/0748730410385204
7. Oosterman JE, Kalsbeek A, la Fleur SE, Belsham DD. Impact of nutrients on circadian rhythmicity. *Am J Physiol Regul Integr Comp Physiol* (2015) 308(5):R337–50. doi:10.1152/ajpregu.00322.2014
8. Hiroshige T, Honma K, Honma S. SCN-independent circadian oscillators in the rat. *Brain Res Bull* (1991) 27(3–4):441–5. doi:10.1016/0361-9230(91)90139-B
9. Stephan FK. The 'other' circadian system: food as a zeitgeber. *J Biol Rhythms* (2002) 17(4):284–92. doi:10.1177/074873040201700402
10. LeSauter J, Hoque N, Weintraub M, Pfaff DW, Silver R. Stomach ghrelin-secreting cells as food-entrainable circadian clocks. *Proc Natl Acad Sci U S A* (2009) 106(32):13582–7. doi:10.1073/pnas.0906426106
11. Carneiro BT, Araujo JF. The food-entrainable oscillator: a network of interconnected brain structures entrained by humoral signals? *Chronobiol Int* (2009) 26(7):1273–89. doi:10.3109/07420520903404480
12. Aguilar-Roblero R, Díaz-Muñoz M. Chronostatic adaptations in the liver to restricted feeding: the FEO as an emergent oscillator. *Sleep and Biol Rhythms* (2010) 8(1):9–17. doi:10.1111/j.1479-8425.2009.00415.x
13. Schibler U, Ripperger J, Brown SA. Peripheral circadian oscillators in mammals: time and food. *J Biol Rhythms* (2003) 18(3):250–60. doi:10.1177/0748730403253381
14. Arellanes-Licea Edel C, Báez-Ruiz A, Carranza ME, Arámburo C, Luna M, Díaz-Muñoz M. Daily patterns and adaptation of the ghrelin, growth hormone and insulin-like growth factor-1 system under daytime food synchronisation in rats. *J Neuroendocrinol* (2014) 26(5):282–95. doi:10.1111/jne.12145
15. Luna-Moreno D, García-Ayala B, Díaz-Muñoz M. Daytime restricted feeding modifies 24 h rhythmicity and subcellular distribution of liver glucocorticoid receptor and the urea cycle in rat liver. *Br J Nutr* (2012) 108(11):2002–13. doi:10.1017/S0007114512000268
16. Díaz-Muñoz M, Vázquez-Martínez O, Aguilar-Roblero R, Escobar C. Anticipatory changes in liver metabolism and entrainment of insulin, glucagon, and corticosterone in food-restricted rats. *Am J Physiol Regul Integr Comp Physiol* (2000) 279(6):R2048–56.
17. Báez-Ruiz A, Escobar C, Aguilar-Roblero R, Vázquez-Martínez O, Díaz-Muñoz M. Metabolic adaptations of liver mitochondria during restricted feeding schedules. *Am J Physiol Gastrointest Liver Physiol* (2005) 289(6):G1015–23. doi:10.1152/ajpgi.00488.2004
18. Pérez-Mendoza M, Rivera-Zavala JB, Díaz-Muñoz M. Daytime restricted feeding modifies the daily variations of liver gluconeogenesis: adaptations in biochemical and endocrine regulators. *Chronobiol Int* (2014) 31(7):815–28. doi:10.3109/07420528.2014.908898
19. Díaz-Muñoz M, Vázquez-Martínez O, Báez-Ruiz A, Martínez-Cabrera G, Soto-Abraham MV, Avila-Casado MC, et al. Daytime food restriction alters liver glycogen, triacylglycerols, and cell size. A histochemical, morphometric, and ultrastructural study. *Comp Hepatol* (2010) 9:5. doi:10.1186/1476-5926-9-5
20. Amin N, Vincan E. The Wnt signaling pathways and cell adhesion. *Front Biosci (Landmark Ed)* (2012) 17:784–804. doi:10.2741/3957
21. Peifer M, Berg S, Reynolds AB. A repeating amino acid motif shared by proteins with diverse cellular roles. *Cell* (1994) 76(5):789–91. doi:10.1016/0092-8674(94)90353-0
22. Liu H, Fergusson MM, Wu JJ, Rovira II, Liu J, Lu T, et al. Metabolism Wnt signaling regulates hepatic metabolism. *Sci Signal* (2011) 4(158):1–22. doi:10.1126/scisignal.2001249
23. Niehrs C. The complex world of WNT receptor signalling. *Nat Rev Mol Cell Biol* (2012) 13(12):767–79. doi:10.1038/nrm3470
24. Dajani R, Fraser E, Roe SM, Yeo M, Good VM, Thompson V, et al. Structural basis for recruitment of glycogen synthase kinase 3beta to the axin-APC scaffold complex. *EMBO J* (2003) 22(3):494–501. doi:10.1093/emboj/cdg068
25. Hart M, Concordet JP, Lassot I, Albert I, del los Santos R, Durand H, et al. The F-box protein B-TrC associates with phosphorylated B-catenin and regulates its activity in the cell. *Curr Biol* (1999) 9:207–10. doi:10.1016/S0960-9822(99)80091-8
26. van Veelen W, Le NH, Helvensteijn W, Blonden L, Theeuwes M, Bakker ER, et al. B-catenin tyrosine 654 phosphorylation increases Wnt signalling and intestinal tumorigenesis. *Gut* (2011) 60(9):1204–12. doi:10.1136/gut.2010.233460
27. Zhu G, Wang Y, Huang B, Liang J, Ding Y, Xu A, et al. A Rac1/PAK1 cascade controls β-catenin activation in colon cancer cells. *Oncogene* (2012) 31(8):1001–12. doi:10.1038/onc.2011.294
28. Taurin S, Sandbo N, Qin Y, Browning D, Dulin NO. Phosphorylation of B-catenin by cyclic AMP-dependent protein kinase. *J Biol Chem* (2006) 281(15):9971–6. doi:10.1074/jbc.M508778200
29. Behari J, Li H, Liu S, Stefanovic-Racic M, Alonso L, O'Donnell CP, et al. B-catenin links hepatic metabolic zonation with lipid metabolism and diet-induced obesity in mice. *Am J Pathol* (2014) 184(12):3284–98. doi:10.1016/j.ajpath.2014.08.022
30. Wood PA, Yang X, Hrushesky WJ. Clock genes and cancer. *Integr Cancer Ther* (2009) 8(4):303–8. doi:10.1177/1534735409355292
31. Yang X, Wood PA, Ansell CM, Ohmori M, Oh EY, Xiong Y, et al. B-catenin induces B-TrCP-mediated PER2 degradation altering circadian clock gene expression in intestinal mucosa of ApcMin/+ Mice. *J Biochem* (2009) 145(3):289–97. doi:10.1093/jb/mvn167
32. Guo B, Chatterjee S, Li L, Kim JM, Lee J, Yechoor VK, et al. The clock gene, brain and muscle Arnt-like 1, regulates adipogenesis via Wnt signaling pathway. *FASEB J* (2012) 26(8):3453–63. doi:10.1096/fj.12-205781
33. Mehra A, Baker CL, Loros JJ, Dunlap JC. Post-translational modifications in circadian rhythms. *Trends Biochem Sci* (2009) 34(10):483–90. doi:10.1016/j.tibs.2009.06.006
34. Portaluppi F, Smolensky MH, Touitou Y. Ethics and methods for biological rhythm research on animals and human beings. *Chronobiol Int* (2010) 27:1911–29. doi:10.3109/07420528.2010.516381
35. Davidson AJ, Stephan FK. Plasma glucagon, glucose, insulin, and motilin in rats anticipating daily meals. *Physiol Behav* (1999) 66(2):309–15. doi:10.1016/S0031-9384(98)00308-4
36. Ángeles-Castellanos M, Mendoza J, Diaz-Munoz M, Escobar C. Food entrainment modifies the c-Fos expression pattern in brain stem nuclei of rats. *Am J Physiol Regul Integr Comp Physiol* (2005) 288(3):R678–84. doi:10.1152/ajpregu.00590.2004
37. Luna-Moreno D, Aguilar-Roblero R, Díaz-Muñoz M. Restricted feeding entrains rhythms of inflammation-related factors without promoting an acute-phase response. *Chronobiol Int* (2009) 26(7):1409–29. doi:10.3109/07420520903417003
38. Báez-Ruiz A, Cázares-Gómez K, Vázquez-Martínez O, Aguilar-Roblero R, Díaz-Muñoz M. Diurnal and nutritional adjustments of intracellular Ca2+ release channels and Ca2+ ATPases associated with restricted feeding schedules in the rat liver. *J Circadian Rhythms* (2013) 11(1):8. doi:10.1186/1740-3391-11-8
39. Reiners JJ, Busch H. Transcriptional and posttranscriptional modulation of cytoplasmic ribonucleic acids in regenerating liver and Novikoff hepatoma. *Biochemistry* (1980) 19:833–41. doi:10.1021/bi00546a002
40. Aguilar-Delfín I, López-Barrera R, Hernández-Muñoz F. Selective enhancement of lipid peroxidation in plasma membrane in two experimental models of liver regeneration : partial hepatectomy and acute CCl 4 administration. *Hepatology* (1996) 24(3):657–62. doi:10.1002/hep.510240331

41. Bradford M. A rapid and sensitive method for the quantitation of microgram quantities of protein utilizing the principle of protein–dye binding. *Anal Biochem* (1976) 72:248–54. doi:10.1016/0003-2697(76)90527-3
42. Abràmoff MD, Magalhaes PJ, Ram SJ. Image processing with Image J. *Biophotonics Int* (2004) 11(7):36–42.
43. Zuther P, Gorbery S, Lemmer B. Chronos-Fit. (2009). Available from: http://www.ma.uni-heidelberg.de/inst/phar/lehre/chrono.html
44. Benhamouche S, Decaens T, Godard C, Chambrey R, Rickman DS, Moinard C, et al. Apc tumor suppressor gene is the 'zonation-keeper' of mouse liver. *Dev Cell* (2006) 10(6):759–70. doi:10.1016/j.devcel.2006.03.015
45. Monga SP. Role and regulation of Β-catenin signaling during physiological liver growth. *Gene Expr* (2014) 16(2):51–62. doi:10.3727/105221614X13919976902138
46. Cadigan KM, Nusse R. Wnt signaling: a common theme in animal development. *Genes Dev* (1997) 11(24):3286–305. doi:10.1101/gad.11.24.3286
47. Bienz M. β-Catenin: a pivot between cell adhesion and Wnt signalling. *Curr Biol* (2005) 15(2):R64–7. doi:10.1016/j.cub.2004.12.058
48. Daugherty RL, Gottardi CJ. Phospho-regulation of beta-catenin adhesion and signaling functions. *Physiology (Bethesda)* (2007) 22(14):303–9. doi:10.1152/physiol.00020.2007
49. Provost E, Yamamoto Y, Lizardi I, Stern J, D'Aquila TG, Gaynor RB, et al. Functional correlates of mutations in Β-catenin exon 3 phosphorylation sites. *J Biol Chem* (2003) 278(34):31781–9. doi:10.1074/jbc.M304953200
50. Park CS, Lee MS, Oh HJ, Choi KY, Yeo MG, Chun JS, et al. Modulation of β-catenin by cyclin-dependent kinase 6 in Wnt-stimulated cells. *Eur J Cell Biol* (2007) 86(2):111–23. doi:10.1016/j.ejcb.2006.10.004
51. Liu C, Li Y, Semenov M, Han C, Baeg GH, Tan Y, et al. Control of Β-catenin phosphorylation/degradation by a dual-kinase mechanism. *Cell* (2002) 108(6):837–47. doi:10.1016/S0092-8674(02)00685-2
52. Gwak J, Cho M, Gong SJ, Won J, Kim DE, Kim EY, et al. Protein-kinase-C-mediated beta-catenin phosphorylation negatively regulates the Wnt/ beta-catenin pathway. *J Cell Sci* (2006) 119(22):4702–9. doi:10.1242/jcs.03256
53. Luo W, Peterson A, Garcia BA, Coombs G, Kofahl B, Heinrich R, et al. Protein phosphatase 1 regulates assembly and function of the Β-catenin degradation complex. *EMBO J* (2007) 26(6):1511–21. doi:10.1038/sj.emboj.7601607
54. Yap AS, Brieher WM, Gumbiner BM. Molecular and functional analysis of cadherin-based adherens junctions. *Annu Rev Cell Dev Biol* (1997) 13:119–46. doi:10.1146/annurev.cellbio.13.1.119
55. Shtutman M, Zhurinsky J, Simcha I, Albanese C, D'Amico M, Pestell R, et al. The cyclin D1 gene is a target of the beta-catenin/LEF-1 pathway. *Proc Natl Acad Sci U S A* (1999) 96(10):5522–7. doi:10.1073/pnas.96.10.5522
56. Bhalla K, Liu WJ, Thompson K, Anders L, Devarakonda S, Dewi R, et al. Cyclin D1 represses gluconeogenesis via inhibition of the transcriptional coactivator PGC1α. *Diabetes* (2014) 63(10):3266–78. doi:10.2337/db13-1283
57. Ying Y, Zhu H, Liang Z, Ma X, Li S. GLP1 protects cardiomyocytes from palmitate-induced apoptosis via Akt/GSK3b/b-catenin pathway. *J Mol Endocrinol* (2015) 55(3):245–62. doi:10.1530/JME-15-0155
58. Dubé PE, Rowland KJ, Brubaker PL. Glucagon-like peptide-2 activates β-catenin signaling in the mouse intestinal crypt: role of insulin-like growth factor-I. *Endocrinology* (2008) 149(1):291–301. doi:10.1210/en.2007-0561
59. Desbois-Mouthon C, Cadoret A, Blivet-Van Eggelpoel MJ, Cherqui G, Perret C, Capeau J. Insulin and IGF-1 stimulate the Β-catenin pathway through two signalling cascades involving GSK-3 Β inhibition and Ras activation. *Oncogene* (2001) 20(2):252–9. doi:10.1038/sj.onc.1204064
60. Aceves C, Escobar C, Rojas-Huidobro R, Vázquez-Martínez O, Martínez-Merlos T, Aguilar-Roblero R, et al. Liver 5'-deiodinase activity is modified in rats under restricted feeding schedules: evidence for post-translational regulation. *J Endocrinol* (2003) 179(1):91–6. doi:10.1677/joe.0.1790091
61. Luna-Moreno D, Vázquez-Martínez O, Báez-Ruiz A, Ramírez J, Díaz-Muñoz M. Food restricted schedules promote differential lipoperoxidative activity in rat hepatic subcellular fractions. *Comp Biochem Physiol A Mol Integr Physiol* (2007) 146(4):632–43. doi:10.1016/j.cbpa.2006.02.039
62. Gumbiner BM. Regulation of cadherin adhesive activity. *J Cell Biol* (2000) 148(3):399–404. doi:10.1083/jcb.148.3.399
63. Slim CL, Lázaro-Diéguez F, Bijlard M, Toussaint MJ, de Bruin A, Du Q, et al. Par1b induces asymmetric inheritance of plasma membrane domains via LGN-dependent mitotic spindle orientation in proliferating hepatocytes. *PLoS Biol* (2013) 11(12):e1001739. doi:10.1371/journal.pbio.1001739
64. Steinberg MS, Takeichi M. Experimental specification of cell sorting, tissue spreading, and specific spatial patterning by quantitative differences in cadherin expression. *Proc Natl Acad Sci U S A* (1994) 91(1):206–9. doi:10.1073/pnas.91.1.206
65. Nardi JB, Kafatos FC. Polarity and gradients in lepidopteran wing epidermis. *J Embryol Exp Morphol* (1976) 36(3):469–87.
66. Planas-Paz L, Orsini V, Boulter L, Calabrese D, Pikiolek M, Nigsch F, et al. The RSPO–LGR4/5–ZNRF3/RNF43 module controls liver zonation and size. *Nat Cell Biol* (2016) 18(5):467–79. doi:10.1038/ncb3337
67. Lowrey PL, Takahashi JS. Genetics of circadian rhythms in mammalian model organisms. *Adv Genet* (2011) 74:175–230. doi:10.1016/B978-0-12-387690-4.00006-4
68. Reppert SM, Weaver DR. Coordination of circadian timing in mammals. *Nature* (2002) 418(6901):935–41. doi:10.1038/nature00965
69. Lin F, Chen Y, Li X, Zhao Q, Tan Z. Over-expression of circadian clock gene Bmal1 affects proliferation and the canonical Wnt pathway in NIH-3T3 cells. *Cell Biochem Funct* (2013) 31(2):166–72. doi:10.1002/cbf.2871
70. Wood PA, Yang X, Taber A, Oh EY, Ansell C, Ayers SE, et al. Period 2 mutation accelerates ApcMin/+ tumorigenesis. *Mol Cancer Res* (2008) 6(11):1786–93. doi:10.1158/1541-7786.MCR-08-0196
71. Rivera-Zavala JB, Báez-Ruiz A, Díaz-Muoz M. Changes in the 24h rhythmicity of liver PPARs and peroxisomal markers when feeding is restricted to two daytime hours. *PPAR Res* (2011) 2011:261584. doi:10.1155/2011/261584
72. Lehwald N, Tao G, Jang KY, Papandreou I, Liu B, Liu B, et al. β-catenin regulates hepatic mitochondrial function and energy balance in mice. *Gastroenterology* (2012) 143(3):754–64. doi:10.1053/j.gastro.2012.05.048
73. Moore RY, Eichler VB. Loss of a circadian adrenal corticosterone rhythm following suprachiasmatic lesions in the rat. *Brain Res* (1972) 42(1):201–6. doi:10.1016/0006-8993(72)90054-6
74. Albrecht U. Timing to perfection: the biology of central and peripheral circadian clocks. *Neuron* (2012) 74(2):246–60. doi:10.1016/j.neuron.2012.04.006
75. Phillips JL, Mikulka PJ. The effects of restricted food access upon locomotor activity in rats with suprachiasmatic nucleus lesions. *Physiol Behav* (1979) 23(2):257–62. doi:10.1016/0031-9384(79)90364-0
76. Damiola F, Le Minh N, Preitner N, Kornmann B, Fleury-Olela F, Schibler U. Restricted feeding uncouples circadian oscillators in peripheral tissues from the central pacemaker in the suprachiasmatic nucleus. *Genes Dev* (2000) 14(23):2950–61. doi:10.1101/gad.183500
77. Wakamatsu H, Yoshinobu Y, Aida R, Moriya T, Akiyama M, Shibata S. Restricted-feeding-induced anticipatory activity rhythm is associated with a phase-shift of the expression of mPer1 and mPer2 mRNA in the cerebral cortex and hippocampus but not in the suprachiasmatic nucleus of mice. *Eur J Neurosci* (2001) 13(6):1190–6. doi:10.1046/j.0953-816X.2001.01483.x
78. Hara R, Wan K, Wakamatsu H, Aida R, Moriya T, Akiyama M, et al. Restricted feeding entrains liver clock without participation of the suprachiasmatic nucleus. *Genes Cells* (2001) 6(3):269–78. doi:10.1046/j.1365-2443.2001.00419.x
79. Challet E. Interactions between light, mealtime and calorie restriction to control daily timing in mammals. *J Comp Physiol B* (2010) 180(5):631–44. doi:10.1007/s00360-010-0451-4
80. Masoro EJ, Shimokawa I, Higami Y, McMahan CA, Yu BP. Temporal pattern of food intake not a factor in the retardation of aging processes by dietary restriction. *J Gerontol A Biol Sci Med Sci* (1995) 50A(1):B48–53. doi:10.1093/gerona/50A.1.B48
81. Froy O. The relationship between nutrition and circadian rhythms in mammals. *Front Neuroendocrinol* (2007) 28(2–3):61–71. doi:10.1016/j.yfrne.2007.03.001
82. Mendoza J, Drevet K, Pévet P, Challet E. Daily meal timing is not necessary for resetting the main circadian clock by calorie restriction. *J Neuroendocrinol* (2008) 20(2):251–60. doi:10.1111/j.1365-2826.2007.01636.x
83. Gallego M, Virshup DM. Post-translational modifications regulate the ticking of the circadian clock. *Nat Rev Mol Cell Biol* (2007) 8(2):139–48. doi:10.1038/nrm2106
84. Stamos JL, Weis WI. The Β-catenin destruction complex. *Cold Spring Harb Perspect Biol* (2013) 5(1):1–16. doi:10.1101/cshperspect.a007898
85. He TC, Sparks AB, Rago C, Hermeking H, Zawel L, da Costa LT, et al. Identification of c-MYC as a target of the APC pathway. *Science* (1998) 281(5382):1509–12. doi:10.1126/science.281.5382.1509

86. Thompson MD, Monga SP. WNT/B-catenin signaling in liver health and disease. *Hepatology* (2007) 45(5):1298–305. doi:10.1002/hep.21651
87. Behari J, Yeh TH, Krauland L, Otruba W, Cieply B, Hauth B, et al. Liver-specific B-catenin knockout mice exhibit defective bile acid and cholesterol homeostasis and increased susceptibility to diet-induced steatohepatitis. *Am J Pathol* (2010) 176(2):744–53. doi:10.2353/ajpath.2010.090667
88. Boyault S, Rickman DS, De Reyniès A, Balabaud C, Rebouissou S, Jeannot E, et al. Transcriptome classification of HCC is related to gene alterations and to new therapeutic targets. *Hepatology* (2007) 45(1):42–52. doi:10.1002/hep.21467
89. Okabe H, Kinoshita H, Imai K, Nakagawa S, Higashi T, Arima K, et al. Diverse basis of B-catenin activation in human hepatocellular carcinoma: implications in biology and prognosis. *PLoS One* (2016) 11(4):e0152695. doi:10.1371/journal.pone.0152695
90. Rana S, Mahmood S. Circadian rhythm and its role in malignancy. *J Circadian Rhythms* (2010) 8(1):1–13. doi:10.1186/1740-3391-8-3

19

Circadian Metabolomics in Time and Space

Kenneth A. Dyar[1] *and Kristin L. Eckel-Mahan*[2]*

[1] *Molecular Endocrinology, Institute for Diabetes and Obesity, Helmholtz Diabetes Center (HMGU) and German Center for Diabetes Research (DZD), Munich, Germany,* [2] *Brown Foundation of Molecular Medicine for the Prevention of Human Diseases of McGovern Medical School, University of Texas Health Science Center at Houston, Houston, TX, United States*

Edited by:
Etienne Challet,
UPR3212 Institut des Neurosciences Cellulaires et Intégratives (INCI), France

Reviewed by:
Frédéric Gachon,
Nestlé Institute of Health Sciences, Switzerland
Gad Asher,
Weizmann Institute of Science, Israel

***Correspondence:**
Kristin L. Eckel-Mahan
kristin.l.mahan@uth.tmc.edu

Circadian rhythms are widely known to govern human health and disease, but specific pathogenic mechanisms linking circadian disruption to metabolic diseases are just beginning to come to light. This is thanks in part to the development and application of various "omics"-based tools in biology and medicine. Current high-throughput technologies allow for the simultaneous monitoring of multiple dynamic cellular events over time, ranging from gene expression to metabolite abundance and sub-cellular localization. These fundamental temporal and spatial perspectives have allowed for a more comprehensive understanding of how various dynamic cellular events and biochemical processes are related in health and disease. With advances in technology, metabolomics has become a more routine "omics" approach for studying metabolism, and "circadian metabolomics" (i.e., studying the 24-h metabolome) has recently been undertaken by several groups. To date, circadian metabolomes have been reported for human serum, saliva, breath, and urine, as well as tissues from several species under specific disease or mutagenesis conditions. Importantly, these studies have consistently revealed that 24-h rhythms are prevalent in almost every tissue and metabolic pathway. Furthermore, these circadian rhythms in tissue metabolism are ultimately linked to and directed by internal 24-h biological clocks. In this review, we will attempt to put these data-rich circadian metabolomics experiments into perspective to find out what they can tell us about metabolic health and disease, and what additional biomarker potential they may reveal.

Keywords: circadian, metabolism, metabolomics, metabolites, chronotherapy

INTRODUCTION

The word "circadian" is derived from Latin, and literally means "around a day". Thus, circadian rhythms oscillate with ~24-h periodicity. "Circadian metabolism" refers to 24-h oscillating biochemical changes in a given biological context (tissue, cell, sub-cellular compartment), and are readily apparent throughout human physiology. These include several systemic and tissue-specific metabolic pathways associated with activity/rest cycles, feeding/fasting rhythms, reproductive cycles, body temperature, and related rhythms of circulating hormones and metabolites. As such, time of day is a fundamental determinant of metabolic flux and pathway activity, and thus cannot be ignored. Metabolomics studies performed at a single time point provide only a static glimpse of metabolism relevant to that particular time point, and depending on the time selected and experimental condition, may easily miss the bigger picture. The same can be said for the particular tissue selected. High-resolution sampling of steady-state metabolite abundance over time and in space, i.e., combining multiple time points and different tissues throughout the circadian cycle, more faithfully captures the dynamic nature of metabolic pathways and inter-organ metabolite dynamics. This allows one to reconstruct a moving picture of circadian metabolism within or among tissues, and even postulate how related changes in metabolite concentrations reflect the actual metabolic pathway activity and dynamics within a tissue or compartment throughout the 24-h cycle. Subcellular resolution within metabolomics experiments likewise allows for a more complete picture, including a better inference of flux, since the transport of substrates into cells and across intracellular compartments are often rate-limiting steps regulating metabolic flux.

RHYTHMICITY ACROSS TISSUES AND ORGANS

One major reason that rhythmic metabolites are important is that they provide key mechanisms by which clocks across the body communicate- whether in alignment or misalignment. Clocks in different cells and tissues respond to different synchronizing *zeitgebers* ("time-givers"), and proper communication between them is important for maintaining circadian homeostasis (Bass and Takahashi, 2010). Accordingly, cells isolated from organisms (i.e., mouse embryonic fibroblasts in culture) quickly become desynchronized in the absence of rhythmic synchronizing cues.

Often referred to as the "central pacemaker," the suprachiasmatic nucleus of the brain is a light-responsive region of the anterior hypothalamus that allows for entrainment to the environment, and assists in the synchronization of tissues within the organism (Eastman et al., 1984; Akhtar et al., 2002; Welsh et al., 2004; Yoo et al., 2004; Reddy et al., 2007; Mendoza and Challet, 2009). The SCN maintains its light-responsiveness via melanopsin-containing neurons of the retinohypothalamic tract, which transmit light information from the retina to the SCN (Hattar et al., 2002; Ruby et al., 2002; Gooley et al., 2003). Circadian timing information regarding the light/dark cycle is then transmitted from the SCN to the periphery via sympathetic and parasympathetic neural circuits. Accordingly, lesion studies of the SCN in rodents reveal arrhythmic physiology.

One major SCN target is the pineal gland (Klein and Moore, 1979), and SCN-dependent neural activity results in the rhythmic release of melatonin, which is induced upon darkness in both nocturnal and diurnal species. Melatonin functions as a *zeitgeber*, binding to receptors located throughout the body, promoting oscillations in blood pressure, and buffering the body's immune response (Slominski et al., 2012; Carrillo-Vico et al., 2013). Other pathways of the sympathetic and parasympathetic nervous system also contribute to time-keeping in peripheral tissues. For example, hepatic rhythms in glucose output are a result of sympathetic innervation from the SCN to the liver via the paraventricular nucleus (PVN; Kalsbeek et al., 2004; Cailotto et al., 2005). The adrenal gland, which contributes to humoral regulation of peripheral clocks via the secretion of glucocorticoids, is also a key SCN-driven source of circadian communication to the peripheral organs. Glucocorticoids and their analogs can alter the phase of peripheral rhythms and even restore hepatic rhythmicity in the absence of a functioning SCN (Balsalobre et al., 2000; Reddy et al., 2007).

Indeed, several peripheral tissue circadian clocks seem to respond more robustly to non-neuronal *zeitgebers*, including circulating nutrients and hormones associated with feeding (Damiola et al., 2000; Stokkan et al., 2001; Vollmers et al., 2009). Specific examples of the robust response of peripheral clocks to nutrients include the restoration of hepatic rhythmicity in *Cry1/2* double knockout mice under time-restricted feeding (Vollmers et al., 2009), or the rescue of kidney and liver rhythmicity in forebrain/SCN-specific *Bmal1* knockout mice under constant darkness, again, by restricted feeding (Izumo et al., 2014). While the latter study suggests that not all peripheral tissues are entrained by feeding, there is clear evidence that circadian clocks in the liver, adipose, muscle, and kidney are all highly responsive to nutrients and/or the downstream signaling pathways that arise from acute changes in energy supply (i.e., high glucose). For example, liver expression of *Per2*, part of the negative feedback loop of the core circadian clock, is robustly driven by food intake (Zani et al., 2013), and liver *Per2* retains normal circadian oscillation even in the midst of hepatic circadian clock disruption (Kornmann et al., 2007; Lamia et al., 2008). Thus, relevant information regarding current energy substrate supply can be rapidly integrated into the circadian transcriptional program as it becomes available, serving to synchronize individual cells within a tissue and coordinating their functional response. One can easily imagine this would be particularly important for the major energy storing and energy consuming tissues.

Activation of various metabolic pathways within a cell is largely dependent on the cycling availability, sensitivity and transport of specific substrates. Thus, metabolic flux (the rate of flow/conversion of metabolites through a given metabolic pathway) is another rhythmic feature that groups individual cells within a given tissue into a functionally coherent unit, and reflects tissue-specific synchronization. Specific examples of metabolites that cycle, and that have also been revealed to be important for specific clock functions are discussed in subsequent sections (also see **Figure 1** for examples).

MAINTENANCE OF CELLULAR CIRCADIAN CLOCKS

While there remains much to uncover, genomics studies have already revealed a wealth of information about the cellular determinants of circadian rhythmicity. Circadian rhythms of gene expression and metabolism are driven in part by circadian clock transcription factors (CLOCK and BMAL1 in mammals) that heterodimerize and activate target gene expression. Among these gene targets are their own negative regulators, the *Period* and *Cryptochrome* genes. Multiple peripheral loops of kinases, other transcription factors, phosphatases, and ubiquitin ligases, have been identified which keep the CLOCK:BMAL1 protein heterodimer and PER/CRY activity operating in a 24-h fashion

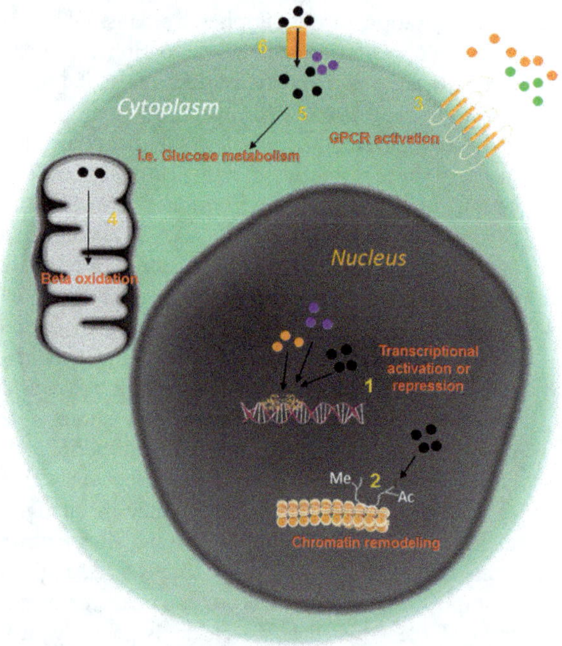

Process	Example Metabolite Ligands/Activators	Example Targets
1, gene regulation by transcription factors	Fatty acids, heme, NAD+, polyamines	PPARα, PPARγ, CLOCK, BMAL1, REV-ERBα, REV-ERBβ, SIRT1, SIRT6, SIRT3, NPAS2
2, gene regulation by chromatin modification	SAM/SAH, NAD^+/NADH, FAD/FADH2, AMP/ATP	SIRT1, SIRT6, MLL1
3, G protein coupled receptor (GPCR) activation	Fatty acids, vasopressin	Vipr2, Gpr176
4, mitochondrial function, oxidative metabolism	NAD^+	SIRT3
5, metabolic pathway enzyme activation	Glucose, NAD^+, FAD^+, AMP/ATP	AMPK, FMO
6, channel activation	Calcium, polyamines	BK, Kir, and glutamate channels
7, translation, post-translational modifications	Magnesium, O-GlcNAc	mTOR, BMAL1, PER2

- Fatty acids
- Energy metabolites (NAD^+, FAD^+, SAM, glucose, heme, etc.)
- Hormones
- Polyamines (spermine, spermidine, putrescine)

FIGURE 1 | Circadian metabolites have pleiotropic mechanisms by which to maintain cellular rhythmicity. Metabolites are an essential part of the cellular circadian clock, and function intracellularly in a variety of ways, from direct metabolic pathway activation to mitochondrial and nuclear events.

(Partch et al., 2014). While these are largely outside the scope of this article, it is important to mention that disruption of these proteins and some of their ancillary regulators disrupts rhythmic metabolism in tissue-specific ways.

Much of the rhythmic activity of the core clock transcriptional feedback loop depends on interactions with other transcriptional regulators, as well as a large group of chromatin modifying enzymes (Aguilar-Arnal and Sassone-Corsi, 2015). For example, histone acetyl transferases, such as p300 and CREB-binding protein (CBP), can interact with the CLOCK:BMAL1 transcriptional complex (Etchegaray et al., 2003; Lee et al., 2015). Similarly, methyltransferases, such as the EZH2, WDR5 and the Mixed-Lineage Leukemia proteins have been shown to interact with the core clock proteins (Brown et al., 2005; Etchegaray et al., 2006; Katada and Sassone-Corsi, 2010). In short, rhythmic chromatin dynamics, much of which center on interactions with the clock proteins, are essential for driving rhythmic transcription and, ultimately, rhythms in metabolism (Koike et al., 2012; Menet et al., 2014). However, the transcriptional feedback loop supported by the CLOCK:BMAL1/PER:CRY system is not only maintained by ancillary proteins but also by small metabolites themselves, which activate specific components of this transcriptional feedback system as well as some of their associating factors.

Several small metabolites have been demonstrated to be important for 24-h rhythmicity in the cell across multiple organisms. In fact, to date, there are few cellular processes which have not been shown to be impinged upon by the circadian abundance or activity of small metabolites. Some of the many circadian processes directly regulated by metabolites are displayed in **Figure 1**. Many metabolites function by affecting rhythmic gene expression, either by activating proteins that directly bind to the core clock machinery or by acting at one or more of the many chromatin modifying enzymes involved in rhythmic gene expression. One well studied example is the metabolite nicotinamide adenine dinucleotide (NAD^+), which as an activator of several NAD^+-dependent sirtuin proteins, and controls the rhythmic circadian output at the level of gene expression of the CLOCK:BMAL1 transcriptional complex itself (Asher et al., 2008; Nakahata et al., 2008, 2009; Ramsey et al., 2009). In addition to nuclear activation of the sirtuins, rhythmic activation of SIRT3 by NAD^+ in the mitochondria promotes oscillations in acetylation and activity of downstream enzymes important for mitochondrial oxidative function (Peek et al., 2013). Heme is another energy metabolite that controls circadian timekeeping at the cellular level. Heme is thought to bind directly to the circadian transcriptional repressors REV-ERBα and REV-ERBβ and thus influence their transcriptional activity (Raghuram et al., 2007; Yin et al., 2007). Heme is also considered to affect other clock components, including the NPAS2-BMAL1 heterodimer (Dioum et al., 2002; Ben-Shlomo et al., 2005). Nuclear receptors, including the REV-ERB proteins, are highly rhythmic in a tissue-specific way (Yang et al., 2006). This allows the cell to integrate and decode a diverse array of circadian changes in metabolite/ligand abundance directly into gene expression in a temporally and spatially precise manner. Many nuclear receptor ligands (some of which are diet-derived) are highly oscillatory (Sladek, 2011;

Solt et al., 2011). Other oscillatory metabolites with specific effects on circadian metabolism include acetyl-CoA, which, via rhythmic sirtuin-dependent acetylation of the enzyme acetyl-CoA synthetase 1 (AceCS1), induces rhythmicity in fatty acid elongation (Sahar et al., 2014). DNA methylation, which depends on availability of S-adenosylmethionine (SAM) and S-adenosylhomocysteine (SAH), has also been reported to undergo circadian oscillations throughout the circadian cycle (Xia et al., 2015). While these serve as some of the better-characterized examples of metabolites that directly control the circadian clock, additional metabolites have been studied in this context. For example, polyamines (compounds with more than one primary amino [-NH2] group) have recently been shown to oscillate and provide feedback into the clock system (Zwighaft et al., 2015). Polyamines, which decrease with age, play important roles in the cell (**Figure 1**), binding to both DNA and proteins, and regulating processes as disparate as gene expression and ion channel function (Pegg, 2009). Rhythmicity in polyamine abundance is both clock- and feeding-dependent, with the rate-limiting enzyme in polyamine synthesis, ornithine decarboxylase (ODC), oscillating throughout the circadian cycle in response to BMAL1:CLOCK transactivation. Interestingly, polyamine depletion in cells and mice results in a longer circadian period due to impaired PER2:CRY1 protein interaction, whereas increasing polyamine content shortens circadian period (Zwighaft et al., 2015).

HOW CAN HIGH-THROUGHPUT METABOLOMICS HELP US UNDERSTAND CIRCADIAN METABOLISM?

Just as genomics and transcriptomics studies have shed light on mechanisms regulating gene expression, global metabolomics experiments (if of sufficient temporal and spatial resolution) can help us understand circadian metabolism by revealing whole pathways of related metabolites that are changing in concert throughout the circadian cycle. Many good reviews already cover various technological aspects of metabolomics experiments (Zamboni et al., 2015).

While most of the studies reviewed here rely on datasets acquired by liquid chromatography/mass spectrometry (LC-MS), metabolite quantification has traditionally been performed using nuclear magnetic resonance spectroscopy (NMR) and MS. While considerably less sensitive than MS, NMR analysis can be performed with limited sample preparation, making it a preferable method in some situations. However, since sensitivity is lower than MS, higher initial sample volume is generally required.

Mass spectrometry, usually coupled with gas or liquid chromatography (GC-MS or LC-MS), can be performed in a high-throughput manner, and usually results in increased sensitivity. However, the more elaborate sample preparation may result in some metabolite losses. Also, the type of tissue under investigation may negatively impact ionization, and some poorly ionizing metabolites and metabolite classes may be underrepresented or missed altogether.

Overall, these should only be considered as very minor limitations, as ever more powerful MS-based metabolomics platforms have continued to evolve, and currently thousands of signals are normally collected and assigned a metabolite identity. However, many metabolites still cannot be assigned, as the specific metabolite identity may not have yet been described. Further complicating matters, mapping of many known metabolites to specific metabolic pathways (i.e., KEGG) is still incomplete, as the relatively slow pace of biological knowledge has not kept up with the accelerated pace of detection. While these "orphan" metabolites currently lack biological meaning, the breadth of information provided by circadian metabolomics studies can provide a unique context from which to predict their metabolic pathways, based on how they behave in relation to known metabolites. Thus, the size of the "known" metabolome in any given biological sample is likely to continue to rise substantially as more metabolite identities and their metabolic pathways are confirmed over time. Typically, assignment of LC-MS data to a particular metabolite is made based on the mass-to-charge value, retention time, fragmentation data, and isotopic detail. Various programs have been developed to assist with metabolite identification based on this information and have been described elsewhere (Zamboni et al., 2015).

While the specific number of metabolites identified in a typical metabolomics experiment is still currently some orders of magnitude smaller than analogous proteomics and transcriptomics experiments, coverage across various metabolite classes and metabolic pathways is usually sufficient to gain important biological insight. For example, comparative statistics and bioinformatics analyses, including metabolic pathway enrichment analysis, time-series (ANOVA), circadian analysis (e.g., JTK_Cycle) provide valuable starting points for investigation.

Spatial resolution is currently a major limitation for many circadian metabolomics studies. Metabolites can serve very different physiological roles depending on their intracellular localization. They can move across various intracellular compartments, either by diffusion or active transport, or even remain in different intracellular pools. While most circadian metabolomics studies published to date have largely ignored relevant information regarding subcellular localization of metabolites (i.e., mitochondrial vs. cytosolic pools), recent technological improvements are certain to change this trend. Subcellular fractionation and organelle purification prior to performing metabolomics is already used to help obtain a slightly clearer picture of intracellular metabolite distribution, but the time-consuming steps involved likely introduce additional confounders. On the other hand, matrix-assisted laser desorption/ionization coupled to Imaging Mass Spectrometry (MALDI-IMS) is already proving to be a very promising technology for mapping distribution of metabolites and proteins within tissue sections *in situ* (Norris and Caprioli, 2013; Ly et al., 2016).

We previously mentioned that relative changes in pathway activity and circadian dynamics may be inferred based on the relative changes in tissue steady-state metabolite levels. However, it is important to stress that these types of analyses can serve only as imperfect surrogates, and not as substitutes for actual metabolic flux analysis. Targeted pulse-chase biochemical and functional assays are still necessary for proper validation of these circadian dynamics. However, this may all soon change, as the increasing development and availability of specific fluorescent probes for monitoring 24-h metabolic flux *in vivo* are poised to provide additional essential tools in the near future.

WHAT HAVE WE LEARNED SO FAR FROM CIRCADIAN METABOLOMICS STUDIES?

To date, several circadian metabolomes from a variety of organisms and tissues have been published. For obvious practical reasons related to collecting sufficient numbers of samples under tightly controlled genetic or environmental conditions, most circadian metabolome studies have been performed on rodent tissues. However, several high-resolution human circadian metabolomes have also been reported, which biologists and clinicians can already utilize for hypothesis generation/validation and biomarker discovery. For example, several human serum metabolomes have provided high-resolution snapshots of robustly changing metabolic pathways across the circadian cycle (Minami et al., 2009; Dallmann et al., 2012; Kasukawa et al., 2012; Davies et al., 2014; Giskeodegard et al., 2015). Importantly, these studies have yielded interesting information that must be interpreted in the context of the experimental paradigm. Specifically, Dallman et al. (Zamboni et al., 2015) provided the first global circadian metabolome from humans, in which approximately 15% of the metabolome in plasma or saliva was shown to oscillate throughout the circadian cycle under constant conditions of sleep deprivation and isocaloric hourly feeding. As feeding is a strong driver of peripheral circadian rhythms, it may be expected that a much higher percentage of metabolites would be found to oscillate throughout a more typical 24-h day, with normal eating and sleeping rhythms. Indeed, subsequent studies have revealed that a majority of detected metabolites show circadian rhythmicity when the sleep/wake cycle and energy intake patterns are rhythmic (Davies et al., 2014). Specifically, human plasma samples collected every 2 h for 48 h revealed that a majority of metabolites oscillate under controlled laboratory conditions (environmental light, sleep, meals, and posture) during a complete 24-h wake/sleep cycle. Furthermore, acute sleep deprivation over the following 24 h alters only a small percentage of oscillating metabolites (under 20%). Interestingly, metabolites elevated by sleep deprivation, including serotonin, tryptophan and taurine, may explain why acute sleep deprivation has been shown to have an antidepressive effect (Voderholzer, 2003). Similar studies involving chronic sleep deprivation have not yet been performed. Thus, for humans, most circulating metabolites display rhythmic diurnal oscillation under normal physiological conditions. This rhythmicity likely helps to coherently communicate time of day to tissues throughout the body, maintains tissue-specific synchronization of circadian clocks, and promotes efficient temporal gating of circadian metabolic pathways.

In a similar study comparing the effects of sleep deprivation on a smaller group of metabolites obtained from human urine, 22% of metabolites were observed to be rhythmic, either under normal or sleep-deprived conditions (Giskeodegard et al., 2015). Approximately half of the metabolites were altered by acute 24-h sleep deprivation, with similar numbers being increased or decreased as a result of sleep deprivation. Similar to results obtained from human plasma, metabolites related to tryptophan metabolism and taurine were also increased in urine as a result of sleep deprivation. Consistent with human 40-h sleep deprivation results (Dallmann et al., 2012), the tryptophan metabolite 3-indoxyl sulfate (which is produced from tryptophan by gut bacteria and hepatic cytochrome P450 enzymes) was also significantly elevated after acute sleep deprivation.

Circadian metabolomics studies performed on rodent tissues have also revealed a high degree of circadian oscillation among metabolites, largely reflecting diurnal rhythms of local tissue metabolism. For example, numerous amino acids oscillate in the liver throughout the circadian cycle (Eckel-Mahan et al., 2012), with pathways involved in lysine and glutamate metabolism particularly rhythmic. In addition, nicotinamide-related metabolites, including nicotinamide adenine dinucleotide (NAD^+), oscillate robustly in mouse liver (Eckel-Mahan et al., 2012, 2013; Masri et al., 2014). As previously mentioned, NAD^+ has substantial influence over cell rhythmicity as an activator of NAD^+-dependent sirtuins and their interactions with the clock transcriptional machinery (Asher et al., 2008; Nakahata et al., 2008, 2009; Ramsey et al., 2009; Masri et al., 2014). Some lipid species are also highly rhythmic in livers, and even persist in livers of clock-disrupted *Per1/2* null mice, likely due to the maintenance of diurnal expression of *Pparα*, a master regulator of lipid metabolism (Adamovich et al., 2014). In this study, feeding time again emerged as a particularly strong driver for some oscillating liver metabolites. *Per1/2* null mice showed arrhythmic feeding patterns and a drastically shifted diurnal cycle of triglyceride accumulation. However, restricting food access to exclusively the dark phase was sufficient to consolidate peak diurnal triglyceride accumulation in *Per1/2* null mice to around ZT12, as occurred in wildtype mice (Adamovich et al., 2014), suggesting that rhythmic liver triglyceride accumulation is driven by systemic feeding/fasting cycles independently of a functional hepatocyte circadian clock.

Uncovering the molecular mechanisms that drive circadian metabolite oscillations in tissues, and understanding the extent to which they are linked to tissue-specific circadian clocks remains an important and active area of research. A few studies have examined how the core circadian clock regulates circadian oscillations of specific metabolites (Eckel-Mahan et al., 2013; Dyar et al., 2014; Aviram et al., 2016). For example, while muscle-specific *Bmal1* knockout mice (mKO) display reduced muscle insulin sensitivity and impaired muscle glucose oxidation compared to wildtype littermates, robust circadian cycles of most glycolytic intermediates are apparently normal (Dyar et al., 2014). However, mKO muscles show a large general accumulation of sugar metabolites from several pathways directly linked to glycolysis, including the pentose phosphate, polyol, and glucuronic acid pathways. This suggests that muscle clock disruption uncouples glycolysis from glucose oxidation, and diverts glycolytic intermediates toward alternative metabolic fates. Interestingly, many of these metabolites were found to be increased predominantly around the transition from the fasting+rest phase to the feeding+activity phase, when glycolytic flux is increased, and glucose becomes the predominant fuel source for skeletal muscle. In conditional and inducible muscle-specific *Bmal1* knockout mouse models, the authors noted impaired circadian oscillation of PDP1 mRNA and protein, the main activator of the pyruvate dehydrogenase complex (PDH), as well as persistent circadian oscillation of PDK4 mRNA and protein, the main inhibitor of PDH. Likewise, diurnal PDH activity was found to be impaired, especially around the transition from the fasting+rest phase to the feeding+activity phase. Thus, BMAL1-driven rhythms are important for muscle insulin sensitivity and for maintaining metabolic flexibility by promoting glucose oxidation during the fasting to feeding transition. Similar to the loss of BMAL1, lack of its heterodimer, CLOCK, results in profound disruption of the hepatic circadian clock (Eckel-Mahan et al., 2012). *Clock*-deficient livers show impaired circadian pyrimidine metabolism due to loss of CLOCK-dependent transcriptional activation of specific enzymes, such as uridine phosphorylase. In addition, circadian carbohydrate metabolism is considerably flattened, while many feeding-related metabolites peak prior to the onset of the dark phase, consistent with an advanced onset of food intake. The circadian metabolomes of these and other circadian models can be found at the website for CircadiOmics (http://circadiomics.igb.uci.edu/). (For data integration and analysis with the corresponding transcriptomes also see Patel et al., 2012, 2015).

Another open issue based on these results is the extent to which rhythmicity in cell metabolism is cell autonomous. To help answer this question, metabolite profiling was recently performed on mouse liver as well as a cell autonomous system [human U2 OS (bone osteosarcoma) cells] with a 1–2 h resolution over the course of 48-h (Krishnaiah et al., 2017). Similar to prior studies, approximately half of the detected metabolites from liver were determined as rhythmic following circadian synchronization. Enrichment was observed for metabolites associated with nucleotide and amino acid metabolism, but methylation pathway-associated metabolites were also observed to by highly rhythmic. Interestingly, in both hepatocytes and autonomous osteosarcoma cells, metabolite oscillations, in terms of percent of detected metabolites, exceeded the percent of transcript oscillations, suggesting an increase in oscillatory function in the cell from transcription to metabolism. Cell-autonomous osteosarcoma cells showed less rhythmicity at the level of individual metabolites than liver (which could also be due to their transformed state); however, metabolites that were observed to be rhythmic in both cell types included several involved in epigenetic regulation. Loss of the circadian proteins BMAL1 generally decreased the amplitude of metabolite rhythms, while CRY1-depletion actually induced 8-h oscillation patterns for a number of metabolites. Thus, rhythmicity of many metabolites is a clock-driven and cell autonomous process (Krishnaiah et al., 2017).

In addition to global and tissue-specific genetic perturbation of clock genes, and restricting access to food, high fat diet (HFD) is another common experimental model used to elicit circadian clock disruption. Circadian metabolomics studies performed under different diets (i.e., chow vs. HFD) suggest that the serum circadian metabolome may be more susceptible to disruption by nutrient challenge than other tissues (Abbondante et al., 2016). Serum metabolites are profoundly affected by HFD, with over half of metabolites changing significantly at some circadian time point following prolonged high fat diet feeding. Similar to studies looking at oscillating metabolites in humans during relatively normal sleeping and feeding behaviors (Davies et al., 2014), mice engaged in *ad libitum* (rhythmic) feeding on a typical chow diet reveal metabolite oscillations in approximately half of the serum metabolome. However, unlike the liver, where many metabolite and transcript oscillations persist under HFD feeding (Eckel-Mahan et al., 2013), oscillating serum metabolites are highly prone to disruption by nutrient challenge, with the majority of oscillating metabolites eliminated after HFD in spite of rhythmic eating patterns (Eckel-Mahan et al., 2013; Abbondante et al., 2016). A profound contributor to this loss of oscillation is the ablation of rhythmic lipid metabolites. Similar to the circadian imbalance of some circadian lipid metabolites under conditions of *Bmal1* deficiency in adipose tissue (Paschos et al., 2012), it is worth speculating that hypothalamic sensing of fatty acids under conditions of HFD feeding is temporally impaired. This loss of circadian oscillations in the circulation under HFD reveals that not only is there unlikely to be temporal coherence across tissues that release metabolites into the blood, but also that the circulation is unable to provide rhythmic information from one tissue to another under conditions of nutrient challenge. This has tremendous implications as to the extent to which diet may misalign circadian clocks in the body, a process which is thought to be disadvantageous in terms of energy balance (Froy, 2010; Roenneberg et al., 2012; Asher and Sassone-Corsi, 2015; Ribas-Latre and Eckel-Mahan, 2016). Further circadian analyses of additional tissue metabolomes under conditions of nutrient challenge is likely to reveal the extent to which such misalignment across tissues might occur.

Recent studies suggest that many metabolites oscillate according to the organelle in which they reside. For example, a recent study looking at circadian lipidomics in the mitochondria and nucleus revealed that while many lipids oscillated in both compartments, some lipid species oscillate distinctly based on their location (Aviram et al., 2016). Nuclear lipid species tend to peak early in the light phase (ZT2-4) while most of the oscillating lipid species within the mitochondria peaked between ZT10-14, in line with the onset of the dark period. Feeding is again an important modulator of oscillating lipids in both compartments, with dark phase restricted feeding inducing more nuclear lipid oscillations, while decreasing the number of oscillating lipid species in the mitochondria. While the direct functional relevance of these differentially oscillating species has not been fully explored, it is likely that they reflect the unique demands associated with each compartment during different times of the day.

While numerous metabolites and hormones oscillate in a circadian manner *in vivo*, **Figure 2** represents only a few of the many disparate rhythmic metabolites or hormones that orchestrate circadian responses within target tissues. For example, the phosphatidylcholine metabolites PC 18:0/18:1 have been shown to circulate in the serum as a result of rhythmic hepatic PPARδ activity, and in a manner which drives fatty acid use in the muscle (Liu et al., 2013). Interestingly, HFD reduces the circadian oscillation of this metabolite in the circulation. The dark-induced hormone melatonin is released by the pineal gland in a circadian fashion and targets many tissues via its rhythmic circulation and widespread expression of its receptors (Slominski et al., 2012). Interestingly, non-diabetic obese individuals have a significantly higher amplitude of melatonin oscillation compared to weight matched obese patients with type II diabetes, and lean non-diabetic individuals (Mantele et al., 2012). The antidiuretic hormone vasopressin is released in a circadian manner and has target effects on the liver (gluconeogenesis and glycogenolysis) and kidney, where it exerts its primary antidiuretic effects. Genetic variance in the vasopressin receptor AVPR1B have recently been linked to weight regulation, and copeptin, a C-terminal fragment of the arginine vasopressin pro-hormone is predictive of diabetes mellitus and abdominal obesity (Enhorning et al., 2009, 2013). Adrenocorticotrophic hormone (ACTH) is released rhythmically by the pineal gland, yet antiphase to melatonin. Subsequent stimulation of the adrenal cortex results in rhythmic cortisol release in humans as well as rhythmicity in aldosterone production and release. Cushing's disease, characterized by an overproduction of ACTH by the pituitary, severely diminishes the amplitude of oscillating cortisol in human patients (Boyar et al., 1979). Glucose and insulin, both elevated in the context of metabolic disease, are also present in the circulation in a rhythmic fashion, and directly depend on the circadian clock (Marcheva et al., 2011; Kalsbeek et al., 2014).

CONCLUSIONS AND FUTURE DIRECTIONS

Circadian metabolomics is just beginning to shed light on some of the mechanisms underlying our circadian behavior and physiology, and much more remains to be gained by such experiments. The opportunity to discover new biomarkers, to better predict physiological time, and to develop novel insights for personalized medicine are key areas for which circadian metabolomics experiments are likely to be extremely valuable in the near future.

New Biomarkers

As the number of published circadian metabolomics experiments continues to increase, one hope is that these uniquely robust and rich datasets will help serve to uncover novel biomarkers or complex metabolic signatures of various diseases. For example, jet-lag paradigms in mice have recently been shown to induce hepatocellular carcinoma (HCC), a phenomenon that appears to depend at least in part on impaired circadian metabolism in the liver (Kettner et al., 2016). Interestingly, jet-lag and mouse models of circadian disruption share this predisposition for HCC, as well as the altered circadian profile of numerous serum and hepatic carnitines, lipids and prostaglandins, TCA metabolites, and acetyl-CoA metabolites. Other studies looking at lung tumor-bearing mice also reveal altered circadian metabolite signatures

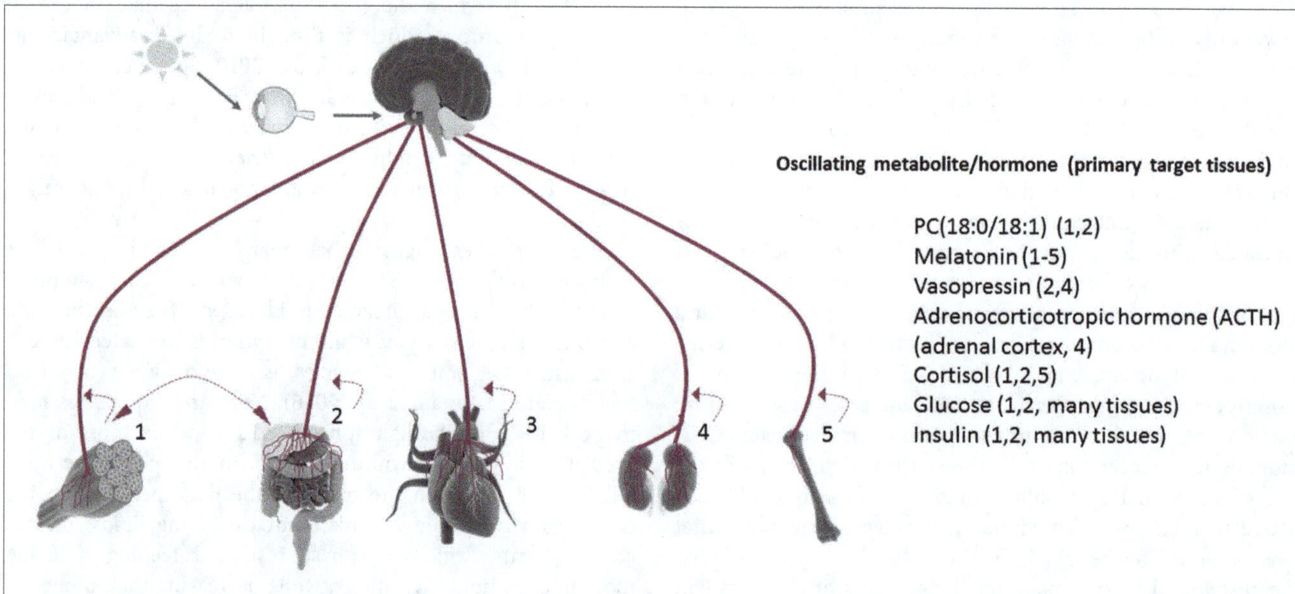

FIGURE 2 | Tissue rhythmicity is in part driven by oscillating metabolites in the circulation. Some examples of rhythmic circulating metabolites (many of which are controlled by the central clock) which are linked to metabolic disruption when aberrantly released. Under nutrient challenge conditions, the majority of circadian metabolite oscillations in the serum are abolished. Most tissues release metabolites back into the circulation in a manner which reflects their circadian biological activities [examples: (1) activity/exercise, (2) nutrient metabolism, (3) myocardial contraction, (4) fluid filtration, (5) bone resorption]. Many tissue-derived circadian metabolites released in the circulation have been shown to directly influence the rhythmic energy use in another tissue (example: hepatic-derived PC18:0/18:1).

(Masri et al., 2016). If circadian neuroendocrine and metabolic markers could collectively or in isolation be an indication of predisposition to tumorigenesis, or alternatively as evidence of existing tumorigenesis, this would greatly assist in cancer prevention and treatment.

Time Prediction

One hope already envisioned by several groups is that a clear temporal mapping of gene and metabolite oscillations and interactions will help us to better predict internal time. For example, can we predict drug efficacy or toxicity based on metabolite-based chronotype determinations? Can we determine the time of death? Blood metabolomics in mice has been studied for the purpose of predicting internal time (Minami et al., 2009) and metabolomics performed by breath analysis, where "breathprinting" is accomplished over hourly intervals, has revealed the potential for circadian rhythms in a large number of metabolites (Martinez-Lozano Sinues et al., 2014). Such an approach could greatly assist with chronotype determination. As the metabolomes of more subjects are studied with greater resolution, and better categorized into specific health and disease states, time prediction is likely to be a powerful end point of circadian metabolomics data for a variety of research areas.

A potentially fruitful outcome for circadian metabolomics as it relates to time prediction is its use in chronotherapy. Pharmacometabolomics is used to understand drug pharmacokinetics and pharmacodynamics. However, a better understanding of circadian fluctuations throughout the day and under specific environmental conditions could facilitate determination of optimal drug administration times, considering the toxicity and efficacy achieved in the body by the drug. Some drugs have already been shown to be more effective and/or less toxic when taken at a specific time of the day. One example is 5-fluorouracil (5-FU), which targets the oscillating thymidylate synthase, and which is already exploited for its effectiveness when administered at specific circadian times (Levi et al., 1992), when its toxicity is lowest at the level of bone marrow and gut, while concomitantly having the most antitumor effects (Wood et al., 2006). A recent high-throughput analysis importantly stressed that many more widely used drugs remain to be studied in this context (Zhang et al., 2014). Accordingly, personalized chronotherapy will undoubtedly emerge as a critical component of personalized medicine's future, as it holds great promise for disease treatment (Ballesta et al., 2017). It is hoped that additional knowledge gained from existing and future circadian metabolomics studies will facilitate and expedite our progression into this future.

AUTHOR CONTRIBUTIONS

All authors listed, have made substantial, direct and intellectual contribution to the work, and approved it for publication.

REFERENCES

Abbondante, S., Eckel-Mahan, K. L., Ceglia, N. J., Baldi, P., and Sassone-Corsi, P. (2016). Comparative circadian metabolomics reveal differential effects of nutritional challenge in the serum and liver. *J. Biol. Chem.* 291, 2812–2828. doi: 10.1074/jbc.M115.681130

Adamovich, Y., Rousso-Noori, L., Zwighaft, Z., Neufeld-Cohen, A., Golik, M., Kraut-Cohen, J., et al. (2014). Circadian clocks and feeding time regulate the oscillations and levels of hepatic triglycerides. *Cell Metab.* 19, 319–330. doi: 10.1016/j.cmet.2013.12.016

Aguilar-Arnal, L., and Sassone-Corsi, P. (2015). Chromatin dynamics of circadian transcription. *Curr. Mol. Biol. Rep.* 1, 1–9. doi: 10.1007/s40610-015-0001-7

Akhtar, R. A., Reddy, A. B., Maywood, E. S., Clayton, J. D., King, V. M., Smith, A. G., et al. (2002). Circadian cycling of the mouse liver transcriptome, as revealed by cDNA microarray, is driven by the suprachiasmatic nucleus. *Curr. Biol.* 12, 540–550. doi: 10.1016/S0960-9822(02)00759-5

Asher, G., Gatfield, D., Stratmann, M., Reinke, H., Dibner, C., Kreppel, F., et al. (2008). SIRT1 regulates circadian clock gene expression through PER2 deacetylation. *Cell* 134, 317–328. doi: 10.1016/j.cell.2008.06.050

Asher, G., and Sassone-Corsi, P. (2015). Time for food: the intimate interplay between nutrition, metabolism, and the circadian clock. *Cell* 161, 84–92. doi: 10.1016/j.cell.2015.03.015

Aviram, R., Manella, G., Kopelman, N., Neufeld-Cohen, A., Zwighaft, Z., Elimelech, M., et al. (2016). Lipidomics analyses reveal temporal and spatial lipid organization and uncover daily oscillations in intracellular organelles. *Mol. Cell* 62, 636–648. doi: 10.1016/j.molcel.2016.04.002

Ballesta, A., Innominato, P. F., Dallmann, R., Rand, D. A., and Levi, F. A. (2017). Systems chronotherapeutics. *Pharmacol. Rev.* 69, 161–199. doi: 10.1124/pr.116.013441

Balsalobre, A., Brown, S. A., Marcacci, L., Tronche, F., Kellendonk, C., Reichardt, H. M., et al. (2000). Resetting of circadian time in peripheral tissues by glucocorticoid signaling. *Science* 289, 2344–2347. doi: 10.1126/science.289.5488.2344

Bass, J., and Takahashi, J. S. (2010). Circadian integration of metabolism and energetics. *Science* 330, 1349–1354. doi: 10.1126/science.1195027

Ben-Shlomo, R., Akhtar, R. A., Collins, B. H., Judah, D. J., Davies, R., and Kyriacou, C. P. (2005). Light pulse-induced heme and iron-associated transcripts in mouse brain: a microarray analysis. *Chronobiol. Int.* 22, 455–471. doi: 10.1081/CBI-200062353

Boyar, R. M., Witkin, M., Carruth, A., and Ramsey, J. (1979). Circadian cortisol secretory rhythms in Cushing's disease. *J. Clin. Endocrinol. Metab.* 48, 760–765. doi: 10.1210/jcem-48-5-760

Brown, S. A., Ripperger, J., Kadener, S., Fleury-Olela, F., Vilbois, F., Rosbash, M., et al. (2005). PERIOD1-associated proteins modulate the negative limb of the mammalian circadian oscillator. *Science* 308, 693–696. doi: 10.1126/science.1107373

Cailotto, C., La Fleur, S. E., Van Heijningen, C., Wortel, J., Kalsbeek, A., Feenstra, M., et al. (2005). The suprachiasmatic nucleus controls the daily variation of plasma glucose via the autonomic output to the liver: are the clock genes involved? *Eur. J. Neurosci.* 22, 2531–2540. doi: 10.1111/j.1460-9568.2005.04439.x

Carrillo-Vico, A., Lardone, P. J., Alvarez-Sanchez, N., Rodriguez-Rodriguez, A., and Guerrero, J. M. (2013). Melatonin: buffering the immune system. *Int. J. Mol. Sci.* 14, 8638–8683. doi: 10.3390/ijms14048638

Dallmann, R., Viola, A. U., Tarokh, L., Cajochen, C., and Brown, S. A. (2012). The human circadian metabolome. *Proc. Natl. Acad. Sci. U.S.A.* 109, 2625–2629. doi: 10.1073/pnas.1114410109

Damiola, F., Le Minh, N., Preitner, N., Kornmann, B., Fleury-Olela, F., and Schibler, U. (2000). Restricted feeding uncouples circadian oscillators in peripheral tissues from the central pacemaker in the suprachiasmatic nucleus. *Genes Dev.* 14, 2950–2961. doi: 10.1101/gad.183500

Davies, S. K., Ang, J. E., Revell, V. L., Holmes, B., Mann, A., Robertson, F. P., et al. (2014). Effect of sleep deprivation on the human metabolome. *Proc. Natl. Acad. Sci. U.S.A.* 111, 10761–10766. doi: 10.1073/pnas.1402663111

Dioum, E. M., Rutter, J., Tuckerman, J. R., Gonzalez, G., Gilles-Gonzalez, M. A., and McKnight, S. L. (2002). NPAS2: a gas-responsive transcription factor. *Science* 298, 2385–2387. doi: 10.1126/science.1078456

Dyar, K. A., Ciciliot, S., Wright, L. E., Bienso, R. S., Tagliazucchi, G. M., Patel, V. R., et al. (2014). Muscle insulin sensitivity and glucose metabolism are controlled by the intrinsic muscle clock. *Mol. Metab.* 3, 29–41. doi: 10.1016/j.molmet.2013.10.005

Eastman, C. I., Mistlberger, R. E., and Rechtschaffen, A. (1984). Suprachiasmatic nuclei lesions eliminate circadian temperature and sleep rhythms in the rat. *Physiol. Behav.* 32, 357–368. doi: 10.1016/0031-9384(84)90248-8

Eckel-Mahan, K. L., Patel, V. R., de Mateo, S., Orozco-Solis, R., Ceglia, N. J., Sahar, S., et al. (2013). Reprogramming of the circadian clock by nutritional challenge. *Cell* 155, 1464–1478. doi: 10.1016/j.cell.2013.11.034

Eckel-Mahan, K. L., Patel, V. R., Mohney, R. P., Vignola, K. S., Baldi, P., and Sassone-Corsi, P. (2012). Coordination of the transcriptome and metabolome by the circadian clock. *Proc. Natl. Acad. Sci. U.S.A.* 109, 5541–5546. doi: 10.1073/pnas.1118726109

Enhorning, S., Bankir, L., Bouby, N., Struck, J., Hedblad, B., Persson, M., et al. (2013). Copeptin, a marker of vasopressin, in abdominal obesity, diabetes and microalbuminuria: the prospective Malmo Diet and Cancer Study cardiovascular cohort. *Int. J. Obes.* 37, 598–603. doi: 10.1038/ijo.2012.88

Enhorning, S., Leosdottir, M., Wallstrom, P., Gullberg, B., Berglund, G., Wirfalt, E., et al. (2009). Relation between human vasopressin 1a gene variance, fat intake, and diabetes. *Am. J. Clin. Nutr.* 89, 400–406. doi: 10.3945/ajcn.2008.26382

Etchegaray, J. P., Lee, C., Wade, P. A., and Reppert, S. M. (2003). Rhythmic histone acetylation underlies transcription in the mammalian circadian clock. *Nature* 421, 177–182. doi: 10.1038/nature01314

Etchegaray, J. P., Yang, X., DeBruyne, J. P., Peters, A. H., Weaver, D. R., Jenuwein, T., et al. (2006). The polycomb group protein EZH2 is required for mammalian circadian clock function. *J. Biol. Chem.* 281, 21209–21215. doi: 10.1074/jbc.M603722200

Froy, O. (2010). Metabolism and circadian rhythms–implications for obesity. *Endocr. Rev.* 31, 1–24. doi: 10.1210/er.2009-0014

Giskeodegard, G. F., Davies, S. K., Revell, V. L., Keun, H., and Skene, D. J. (2015). Diurnal rhythms in the human urine metabolome during sleep and total sleep deprivation. *Sci. Rep.* 5:14843. doi: 10.1038/srep14843

Gooley, J. J., Lu, J., Fischer, D., and Saper, C. B. (2003). A broad role for melanopsin in nonvisual photoreception. *J. Neurosci.* 23, 7093–7106.

Hattar, S., Liao, H. W., Takao, M., Berson, D. M., and Yau, K. W. (2002). Melanopsin-containing retinal ganglion cells: architecture, projections, and intrinsic photosensitivity. *Science* 295, 1065–1070. doi: 10.1126/science.1069609

Izumo, M., Pejchal, M., Schook, A. C., Lange, R. P., Walisser, J. A., Sato, T. R., et al. (2014). Differential effects of light and feeding on circadian organization of peripheral clocks in a forebrain *Bmal1* mutant. *eLife* 3:e04617. doi: 10.7554/eLife.04617

Kalsbeek, A., la Fleur, S., and Fliers, E. (2014). Circadian control of glucose metabolism. *Mol. Metab.* 3, 372–383. doi: 10.1016/j.molmet.2014.03.002

Kalsbeek, A., La Fleur, S., Van Heijningen, C., and Buijs, R. M. (2004). Suprachiasmatic GABAergic inputs to the paraventricular nucleus control plasma glucose concentrations in the rat via sympathetic innervation of the liver. *J. Neurosci.* 24, 7604–7613. doi: 10.1523/JNEUROSCI.5328-03.2004

Kasukawa, T., Sugimoto, M., Hida, A., Minami, Y., Mori, M., Honma, S., et al. (2012). Human blood metabolite timetable indicates internal body time. *Proc. Natl. Acad. Sci. U.S.A.* 109, 15036–15041. doi: 10.1073/pnas.1207768109

Katada, S., and Sassone-Corsi, P. (2010). The histone methyltransferase MLL1 permits the oscillation of circadian gene expression. *Nat. Struct. Mol. Biol.* 17, 1414–1421. doi: 10.1038/nsmb.1961

Kettner, N. M., Voicu, H., Finegold, M. J., Coarfa, C., Sreekumar, A., Putluri, N., et al. (2016). Circadian homeostasis of liver metabolism suppresses hepatocarcinogenesis. *Cancer Cell* 30, 909–924. doi: 10.1016/j.ccell.2016.10.007

Klein, D. C., and Moore, R. Y. (1979). Pineal N-acetyltransferase and hydroxyindole-O-methyltransferase: control by the retinohypothalamic tract and the suprachiasmatic nucleus. *Brain Res.* 174, 245–262. doi: 10.1016/0006-8993(79)90848-5

Koike, N., Yoo, S. H., Huang, H. C., Kumar, V., Lee, C., Kim, T. K., et al. (2012). Transcriptional architecture and chromatin landscape of the core circadian clock in mammals. *Science* 338, 349–354. doi: 10.1126/science.1226339

Kornmann, B., Schaad, O., Bujard, H., Takahashi, J. S., and Schibler, U. (2007). System-driven and oscillator-dependent circadian transcription in mice with a conditionally active liver clock. *PLoS Biol.* 5:e34. doi: 10.1371/journal.pbio.0050034

Krishnaiah, S. Y., Wu, G., Altman, B. J., Growe, J., Rhoades, S. D., Coldren, F., et al. (2017). Clock regulation of metabolites reveals coupling between transcription and metabolism. *Cell Metab.* 25, 961–974 e964. doi: 10.1016/j.cmet.2017.04.023

Lamia, K. A., Storch, K. F., and Weitz, C. J. (2008). Physiological significance of a peripheral tissue circadian clock. *Proc. Natl. Acad. Sci. U.S.A.* 105, 15172–15177. doi: 10.1073/pnas.0806717105

Lee, Y., Chun, S. K., and Kim, K. (2015). Sumoylation controls CLOCK-BMAL1-mediated clock resetting via CBP recruitment in nuclear transcriptional foci. *Biochim. Biophys. Acta* 1853, 2697–2708. doi: 10.1016/j.bbamcr.2015.07.005

Levi, F., Misset, J. L., Brienza, S., Adam, R., Metzger, G., Itzakhi, M., et al. (1992). A chronopharmacologic phase II clinical trial with 5-fluorouracil, folinic acid, and oxaliplatin using an ambulatory multichannel programmable pump. High antitumor effectiveness against metastatic colorectal cancer. *Cancer* 69, 893–900. doi: 10.1002/1097-0142(19920215)69:4<893::AID-CNCR2820690410>3.0.CO;2-X

Liu, S., Brown, J. D., Stanya, K. J., Homan, E., Leidl, M., Inouye, K., et al. (2013). A diurnal serum lipid integrates hepatic lipogenesis and peripheral fatty acid use. *Nature* 502, 550–554. doi: 10.1038/nature12710

Ly, A., Buck, A., Balluff, B., Sun, N., Gorzolka, K., Feuchtinger, A., et al. (2016). High-mass-resolution MALDI mass spectrometry imaging of metabolites from formalin-fixed paraffin-embedded tissue. *Nat. Protoc.* 11, 1428–1443. doi: 10.1038/nprot.2016.081

Mantele, S., Otway, D. T., Middleton, B., Bretschneider, S., Wright, J., Robertson, M. D., et al. (2012). Daily rhythms of plasma melatonin, but not plasma leptin or leptin mRNA, vary between lean, obese and type 2 diabetic men. *PLoS ONE* 7:e37123. doi: 10.1371/journal.pone.0037123

Marcheva, B., Ramsey, K. M., and Bass, J. (2011). Circadian genes and insulin exocytosis. *Cell. Logist.* 1, 32–36. doi: 10.4161/cl.1.1.14426

Martinez-Lozano Sinues, P., Tarokh, L., Li, X., Kohler, M., Brown, S. A., Zenobi, R., et al. (2014). Circadian variation of the human metabolome captured by real-time breath analysis. *PLoS ONE* 9:e114422. doi: 10.1371/journal.pone.0114422

Masri, S., Papagiannakopoulos, T., Kinouchi, K., Liu, Y., Cervantes, M., Baldi, P., et al. (2016). Lung adenocarcinoma distally rewires hepatic circadian homeostasis. *Cell* 165, 896–909. doi: 10.1016/j.cell.2016.04.039

Masri, S., Rigor, P., Cervantes, M., Ceglia, N., Sebastian, C., Xiao, C., et al. (2014). Partitioning circadian transcription by SIRT6 leads to segregated control of cellular metabolism. *Cell* 158, 659–672. doi: 10.1016/j.cell.2014.06.050

Mendoza, J., and Challet, E. (2009). Brain clocks: from the suprachiasmatic nuclei to a cerebral network. *Neuroscientist* 15, 477–488. doi: 10.1177/1073858408327808

Menet, J. S., Pescatore, S., and Rosbash, M. (2014). CLOCK:BMAL1 is a pioneer-like transcription factor. *Genes Dev.* 28, 8–13. doi: 10.1101/gad.228536.113

Minami, Y., Kasukawa, T., Kakazu, Y., Iigo, M., Sugimoto, M., Ikeda, S., et al. (2009). Measurement of internal body time by blood metabolomics. *Proc. Natl. Acad. Sci. U.S.A.* 106, 9890–9895. doi: 10.1073/pnas.0900617106

Nakahata, Y., Kaluzova, M., Grimaldi, B., Sahar, S., Hirayama, J., Chen, D., et al. (2008). The NAD+-dependent deacetylase SIRT1 modulates CLOCK-mediated chromatin remodeling and circadian control. *Cell* 134, 329–340. doi: 10.1016/j.cell.2008.07.002

Nakahata, Y., Sahar, S., Astarita, G., Kaluzova, M., and Sassone-Corsi, P. (2009). Circadian control of the NAD+ salvage pathway by CLOCK-SIRT1. *Science* 324, 654–657. doi: 10.1126/science.1170803

Norris, J. L., and Caprioli, R. M. (2013). Analysis of tissue specimens by matrix-assisted laser desorption/ionization imaging mass spectrometry in biological and clinical research. *Chem. Rev.* 113, 2309–2342. doi: 10.1021/cr3004295

Partch, C. L., Green, C. B., and Takahashi, J. S. (2014). Molecular architecture of the mammalian circadian clock. *Trends Cell Biol.* 24, 90–99. doi: 10.1016/j.tcb.2013.07.002

Paschos, G. K., Ibrahim, S., Song, W. L., Kunieda, T., Grant, G., Reyes, T. M., et al. (2012). Obesity in mice with adipocyte-specific deletion of clock component Arntl. *Nat. Med.* 18, 1768–1777. doi: 10.1038/nm.2979

Patel, V. R., Ceglia, N., Zeller, M., Eckel-Mahan, K., Sassone-Corsi, P., and Baldi, P. (2015). The pervasiveness and plasticity of circadian oscillations: the coupled circadian-oscillators framework. *Bioinformatics* 31, 3181–3188. doi: 10.1093/bioinformatics/btv353

Patel, V. R., Eckel-Mahan, K., Sassone-Corsi, P., and Baldi, P. (2012). CircadiOmics: integrating circadian genomics, transcriptomics, proteomics and metabolomics. *Nat. Methods* 9, 772–773. doi: 10.1038/nmeth.2111

Peek, C. B., Affinati, A. H., Ramsey, K. M., Kuo, H. Y., Yu, W., Sena, L. A., et al. (2013). Circadian clock NAD+ cycle drives mitochondrial oxidative metabolism in mice. *Science* 342:1243417. doi: 10.1126/science.1243417

Pegg, A. E. (2009). Mammalian polyamine metabolism and function. *IUBMB Life* 61, 880–894. doi: 10.1002/iub.230

Raghuram, S., Stayrook, K. R., Huang, P., Rogers, P. M., Nosie, A. K., McClure, D. B., et al. (2007). Identification of heme as the ligand for the orphan nuclear receptors REV-ERBalpha and REV-ERBbeta. *Nat. Struct. Mol. Biol.* 14, 1207–1213. doi: 10.1038/nsmb1344

Ramsey, K. M., Yoshino, J., Brace, C. S., Abrassart, D., Kobayashi, Y., Marcheva, B., et al. (2009). Circadian clock feedback cycle through NAMPT-mediated NAD+ biosynthesis. *Science* 324, 651–654. doi: 10.1126/science.1171641

Reddy, A. B., Maywood, E. S., Karp, N. A., King, V. M., Inoue, Y., Gonzalez, F. J., et al. (2007). Glucocorticoid signaling synchronizes the liver circadian transcriptome. *Hepatology* 45, 1478–1488. doi: 10.1002/hep.21571

Ribas-Latre, A., and Eckel-Mahan, K. (2016). Interdependence of nutrient metabolism and the circadian clock system: importance for metabolic health. *Mol. Metab.* 5, 133–152. doi: 10.1016/j.molmet.2015.12.006

Roenneberg, T., Allebrandt, K. V., Merrow, M., and Vetter, C. (2012). Social jetlag and obesity. *Curr. Biol.* 22, 939–943. doi: 10.1016/j.cub.2012.03.038

Ruby, N. F., Brennan, T. J., Xie, X., Cao, V., Franken, P., Heller, H. C., et al. (2002). Role of melanopsin in circadian responses to light. *Science* 298, 2211–2213. doi: 10.1126/science.1076701

Sahar, S., Masubuchi, S., Eckel-Mahan, K., Vollmer, S., Galla, L., Ceglia, N., et al. (2014). Circadian control of fatty acid elongation by SIRT1-mediated Deacetylation of Acetyl-CoA Synthetase 1. *J. Biol. Chem.* 289, 6091–6097. doi: 10.1074/jbc.M113.537191

Sladek, F. M. (2011). What are nuclear receptor ligands? *Mol. Cell. Endocrinol.* 334, 3–13. doi: 10.1016/j.mce.2010.06.018

Slominski, R. M., Reiter, R. J., Schlabritz-Loutsevitch, N., Ostrom, R. S., and Slominski, A. T. (2012). Melatonin membrane receptors in peripheral tissues: distribution and functions. *Mol. Cell. Endocrinol.* 351, 152–166. doi: 10.1016/j.mce.2012.01.004

Solt, L. A., Kojetin, D. J., and Burris, T. P. (2011). The REV-ERBs and RORs: molecular links between circadian rhythms and lipid homeostasis. *Future Med. Chem.* 3, 623–638. doi: 10.4155/fmc.11.9

Stokkan, K. A., Yamazaki, S., Tei, H., Sakaki, Y., and Menaker, M. (2001). Entrainment of the circadian clock in the liver by feeding. *Science* 291, 490–493. doi: 10.1126/science.291.5503.490

Voderholzer, U. (2003). Sleep deprivation and antidepressant treatment. *Dialogues Clin. Neurosci.* 5, 366–369.

Vollmers, C., Gill, S., DiTacchio, L., Pulivarthy, S. R., Le, H. D., and Panda, S. (2009). Time of feeding and the intrinsic circadian clock drive rhythms in hepatic gene expression. *Proc. Natl. Acad. Sci. U.S.A.* 106, 21453–21458. doi: 10.1073/pnas.0909591106

Welsh, D. K., Yoo, S. H., Liu, A. C., Takahashi, J. S., and Kay, S. A. (2004). Bioluminescence imaging of individual fibroblasts reveals persistent, independently phased circadian rhythms of clock gene expression. *Curr. Biol.* 14, 2289–2295. doi: 10.1016/j.cub.2004.11.057

Wood, P. A., Du-Quiton, J., You, S., and Hrushesky, W. J. (2006). Circadian clock coordinates cancer cell cycle progression, thymidylate synthase, and 5-fluorouracil therapeutic index. *Mol. Cancer Ther.* 5, 2023–2033. doi: 10.1158/1535-7163.MCT-06-0177

Xia, L., Ma, S., Zhang, Y., Wang, T., Zhou, M., Wang, Z., et al. (2015). Daily variation in global and local DNA methylation in mouse livers. *PLoS ONE* 10:e0118101. doi: 10.1371/journal.pone.0118101

Yang, X., Downes, M., Yu, R. T., Bookout, A. L., He, W., Straume, M., et al. (2006). Nuclear receptor expression links the circadian clock to metabolism. *Cell* 126, 801–810. doi: 10.1016/j.cell.2006.06.050

Yin, L., Wu, N., Curtin, J. C., Qatanani, M., Szwergold, N. R., Reid, R. A., et al. (2007). Rev-erbalpha, a heme sensor that coordinates metabolic and circadian pathways. *Science* 318, 1786–1789. doi: 10.1126/science.1150179

Yoo, S. H., Yamazaki, S., Lowrey, P. L., Shimomura, K., Ko, C. H., Buhr, E. D., et al. (2004). PERIOD2::LUCIFERASE real-time reporting of circadian dynamics reveals persistent circadian oscillations in mouse peripheral tissues. *Proc. Natl. Acad. Sci. U.S.A.* 101, 5339–5346. doi: 10.1073/pnas.0308709101

Zamboni, N., Saghatelian, A., and Patti, G. J. (2015). Defining the metabolome: size, flux, and regulation. *Mol. Cell* 58, 699–706. doi: 10.1016/j.molcel.2015.04.021

Zani, F., Breasson, L., Becattini, B., Vukolic, A., Montani, J. P., Albrecht, U., et al. (2013). PER2 promotes glucose storage to liver glycogen during feeding and acute fasting by inducing Gys2 PTG and G L expression. *Mol. Metab.* 2, 292–305. doi: 10.1016/j.molmet.2013.06.006

Zhang, R., Lahens, N. F., Ballance, H. I., Hughes, M. E., and Hogenesch, J. B. (2014). A circadian gene expression atlas in mammals: implications for biology and medicine. *Proc. Natl. Acad. Sci. U.S.A.* 11, 16219–16224. doi: 10.1073/pnas.1408886111

Zwighaft, Z., Aviram, R., Shalev, M., Rousso-Noori, L., Kraut-Cohen, J., Golik, M., et al. (2015). Circadian clock control by polyamine levels through a mechanism that declines with age. *Cell Metab.* 22, 874–885. doi: 10.1016/j.cmet.2015.09.011

20

High-Fat Feeding does Not Disrupt Daily Rhythms in Female Mice because of Protection by Ovarian Hormones

*Brian T. Palmisano[1], John M. Stafford[1,2,3] and Julie S. Pendergast[3,4]**

[1] Department of Molecular Physiology and Biophysics, Vanderbilt University School of Medicine, Nashville, TN, USA, [2] VA Tennessee Valley Healthcare System, Nashville, TN, USA, [3] Division of Diabetes, Endocrinology, and Metabolism, Department of Medicine, Vanderbilt University School of Medicine, Nashville, TN, USA, [4] Department of Biology, University of Kentucky, Lexington, KY, USA

Edited by:
Andries Kalsbeek,
Academic Medical Center, Netherlands

Reviewed by:
Valerie Simonneaux,
Centre national de la recherche scientifique (CNRS), France
Shin Jae Lee,
ETH Zurich, Switzerland

****Correspondence:***
Julie S. Pendergast
julie.pendergast@uky.edu

Obesity in women is increased by the loss of circulating estrogen after menopause. Shift work, which disrupts circadian rhythms, also increases the risk for obesity. It is not known whether ovarian hormones interact with the circadian system to protect females from obesity. During high-fat feeding, male C57BL/6J mice develop profound obesity and disruption of daily rhythms. Since C57BL/6J female mice did not develop diet-induced obesity (during 8 weeks of high-fat feeding), we first determined if daily rhythms in female mice were resistant to disruption from high-fat diet. We fed female PERIOD2:LUCIFERASE mice 45% high-fat diet for 1 week and measured daily rhythms. Female mice retained robust rhythms of eating behavior and locomotor activity during high-fat feeding that were similar to chow-fed females. In addition, the phase of the liver molecular timekeeping (PER2:LUC) rhythm was not altered by high-fat feeding in females. To determine if ovarian hormones protected daily rhythms in female mice from high-fat feeding, we analyzed rhythms in ovariectomized mice. During high-fat feeding, the amplitudes of the eating behavior and locomotor activity rhythms were reduced in ovariectomized females. Liver PER2:LUC rhythms were also advanced by ~4 h by high-fat feeding, but not chow, in ovariectomized females. Together these data show circulating ovarian hormones protect the integrity of daily rhythms in female mice during high-fat feeding.

Keywords: circadian, C57BL/6J, female, bioluminescence, liver, eating rhythm, high-fat diet, obesity

INTRODUCTION

Disruption of circadian rhythms contributes to obesity and its comorbidities. Circadian rhythms are approximately 24-h fluctuations in physiology and behavior that are synchronized to the environment. In mammals, the circadian system is composed of a network of clocks that are located in nearly every tissue in the body. The master circadian clock in the suprachiasmatic nucleus (SCN) in the brain receives information about the timing of the environmental light–dark cycle and in turn coordinates the timing (or phases) of the other clocks located throughout the body (1, 2). Numerous epidemiological studies of shift workers as well as laboratory studies of healthy people showed that disruption of the circadian system increases the risk for obesity and metabolic dysfunction (3–10).

Animal studies have probed the mechanisms underlying the reciprocal interactions between the circadian system and metabolism. Disabling the molecular timekeeping mechanism of circadian clocks in rodents altered glucose regulation and caused obesity (11–14). And, conversely, diet-induced obesity disrupted the circadian system (15–19). We and others found the daily rhythm of eating behavior was altered during high-fat feeding such that mice ate across the day instead of eating mostly at night, which is the normal feeding time for rodents (15, 16). This disrupted eating rhythm was a determinant of obesity since restricting high-fat diet feeding only to the nighttime inhibited obesity (20, 21). We also previously showed that high-fat feeding disrupted the temporal coordination between the timing of body clocks by altering the phase of the liver circadian clock (16).

The drawback of these previous animal studies, including our own, was they were performed exclusively in male animals. This is problematic because obesity and its related complications develop differently in men and women. Pre-menopausal women are protected from the negative consequences of obesity such as the metabolic syndrome (22). However, the loss of estrogen after menopause increases the risk of life-threatening, obesity-related complications such as cardiovascular disease and stroke (22–24). To our knowledge, no study has investigated the integrity of metabolic circadian rhythms in females or the role of ovarian hormones in regulating high-fat diet-induced disruption of daily rhythms. In this study, we addressed these questions by investigating daily rhythms in intact and ovariectomized female mice during high-fat feeding.

MATERIALS AND METHODS

Animals

Heterozygous C57BL/6J PERIOD2:LUCIFERASE (PER2:LUC) (2) and wild-type littermate (N23 to 25 generations of back-crossing with C57BL/6J mice, Jackson Laboratory, Bar Harbor, ME, USA) mice were born and raised in 12-h light/12-h dark (12L:12D; light intensity ~350 lux) at Vanderbilt University. At weaning (21 days old), mice were group housed (2–4 mice/cage). Genotype was determined by measuring bioluminescence from tail snips from 21-day-old mice. All mice (breeders and pups) were fed chow (13.5% kcal from fat, LabDiet 5L0D) *ad libitum* until they underwent experimental diet manipulations. All procedures were conducted in accordance with the guidelines of the National Institutes of Health Guide for the Care and Use of Laboratory Animals and were approved by the Institutional Animal Care and Use Committee at Vanderbilt University (protocol number M/13/081).

Experimental Protocols

Experiment I. Effect of Chronic High-Fat Diet Consumption on Body Weight in Female Mice

Heterozygous PER2:LUC C57BL/6J and wild-type female mice were single housed in cages (33 cm × 17 cm × 14 cm) with locked running wheels (wheels could not rotate) in light-tight boxes in 12L:12D (light intensity 200–300 lux; temperature inside light-tight boxes: 25.5 ± 1.5°C) at 7 weeks old and maintained on chow *ad libitum*. Beginning at 8 weeks old, mice were fed either chow or 45% high-fat diet (Research Diets D01060502) for 8 weeks. Body weight was measured weekly (always within 3 h before lights off).

Experiment II. Effects of Acute High-Fat Diet Consumption on Circadian Organization and the Eating Behavior and Locomotor Activity Rhythms in Female Mice

Heterozygous PER2:LUC C57BL/6J female mice were single housed in cages with locked running wheels at 7 weeks old in light-tight boxes in 12L:12D and fed chow. Body weight and food intake were measured weekly (always within 3 h before lights off). Locomotor activity and eating behavior were continuously measured. Beginning at 8 weeks old, mice were fed either chow or 45% high-fat diet for 1 week. At 9 weeks old, tissues were explanted and cultured to measure bioluminescence rhythms.

Experiment III. Effect of Ovariectomy in Mediating High-Fat Diet Effects on Daily Rhythms

Heterozygous PER2:LUC C57BL/6J female mice were ovariectomized at 6 weeks old and single housed following the surgery in light-tight boxes in 12L:12D. Body weight and food intake were measured weekly (always within 3 h before lights off). Locomotor activity and eating behavior were continuously measured. Mice were fed chow *ad libitum* for 2 weeks. Beginning at 8 weeks old, mice were fed either chow or 45% high-fat diet for 1 week. At 9 weeks old, livers were explanted, cultured, and bioluminescence rhythms were measured.

Bioluminescence Recording and Analysis

Within 1.5 h before lights out, tissue explants were prepared as previously described (25). In the first experiment (Figure S1 in Supplementary Material), SCN, arcuate complex, pituitary, liver, lung, aorta, spleen, and white adipose tissue were collected from each mouse and cultured as previously described (16). In the subsequent experiments in intact and ovariectomized mice, only liver explants were cultured from female mice. Bioluminescence was measured with the LumiCycle in 10-min intervals (Actimetrics Inc., Evanston, IL, USA). The data were detrended (by subtracting the 24 h moving average) and smoothed (0.5 h adjacent average) using LumiCycle software. Then ClockLab analysis software was used to determine the phase (peak of bioluminescence occurring between 12 h and 36 h in culture) of PER2:LUC expression.

Behavior Recording and Analysis

General locomotor activity data were collected every minute using passive infrared sensors (sensors record a maximum of one count every 6 s; model 007.1, Visonic LTD). Double-plotted actograms of locomotor activity were created with Clocklab (6-min bins; scaled setting). Cosinor analysis was performed for each mouse on activity profiles of 5 days of chow feeding or 5 days of high-fat feeding with Clocklab software. Cosinor analysis fits a cosine curve to the time series data and determines the amplitude (half of the peak-to-trough value), mesor (midline or rhythm-adjusted mean), and acrophase (the timing of the peak of the rhythm) of the rhythm (period was 24 h) (27). Mean activity profiles were generated by averaging daily locomotor activity in 6-min bins during either chow or high-fat feeding for all mice.

Eating behavior was continuously recorded using an infrared video camera (PYLE PLCM22IR Flush Mount Rear View Camera with 0.5 lux Night Vision, Pyle Audio Inc., Brooklyn, NY, USA) interfaced to a computer with VideoSecu4 (16). Eating behavior was analyzed in 1-min bins (coded as 1 for eating behavior and 0 for no eating behavior) as previously described (16). Eating behavior data were plotted in circular histograms and analyzed with circular statistics (Oriana 4.0; Kovach Computing Services, Wales, UK). Circular histograms show the distribution of eating events across the day (lights on 0–12). Circular statistics were used to determine the vector of the rhythm. Grand mean vectors describe the phase (direction) and amplitude (length) of the mean rhythms of female mice ($n = 5$) during chow (day 7) or high-fat diet (days 9 and 14) feeding.

Ovariectomy Surgery

At 6 weeks of age, female mice were ovariectomized as described previously (28). Briefly, animals were anesthetized under inhaled isoflurane and administered analgesic pre-operatively. After midline dorsal skin incision, two lateral incisions of the dorsal peritoneal wall were made and ovaries were removed. Peritoneal incisions were closed with single simple interrupted stiches and the skin incision was closed with autoclips. Mice were housed individually following surgery and allowed to recover for 7 days prior to study.

Statistical Analyses

Two-way Repeated Measures ANOVA (with *post hoc* Fisher LSD test) was used to determine if body weight was affected by high-fat diet compared to chow consumption over time and to determine the effects of sex, diet, and ovariectomy on eating behavior rhythms (OriginPro 2016, Northhampton, MA, USA). Independent *t*-tests (two-tailed) were used to compare the phases of liver PER2:LUC rhythms in intact or ovariectomized mice (OriginPro 2016). Paired *t*-tests (two-tailed) were used to compare the amplitudes, phases, and mesors of the locomotor activity rhythms. Circular data were plotted and analyzed using Oriana 4.0. The mean vector of each day of behavior data (for individual mice) was determined by Rayleigh's uniformity test to indicate the angle (μ) and degree of clustering (length; r). Grand mean vectors (to analyze groups of mice) were analyzed using Hotelling's one sample test. The length of the vector describes the uniformity of the distribution of activity such that short vectors indicate that activity is more evenly distributed across the cycle. Significance was ascribed at $p < 0.05$.

RESULTS

Female C57BL/6J Mice Are Resistant to Diet-Induced Obesity

Male C57BL/6J mice become obese when they consume high-fat diet (29, 30). We first tested whether female C57BL/6J mice fed 45% high-fat diet developed diet-induced obesity. We fed female mice chow or high-fat diet for 8 weeks and measured body weight weekly (**Figure 1**). Although all mice gained weight over the 8-week experiment (time: $F = 40.83$, $p < 0.001$), there was no significant interaction between diet and time ($F = 2.6$, $p = 0.11$). Therefore, female mice were resistant to diet-induced weight gain.

High-Fat Feeding Does Not Alter Molecular Timekeeping Rhythms in Tissues in Female Mice

We previously found that consumption of high-fat diet disrupted the temporal relationship between tissue molecular rhythms in male mice by advancing the phase of the liver circadian clock rhythm (16). Thus, we next determined the effects of high-fat diet consumption on circadian rhythms in central and peripheral tissues in female mice. PERIOD2 is a component of the molecular timekeeping mechanism of the circadian clock and is a target gene of the Clock/Bmal1 transcription factor network (31, 32). In PER2:LUC mice, the luciferase gene is knocked in to the 3′ end of the *Period2* locus resulting in the expression of the PER2:LUC fusion protein (2). We assessed the molecular circadian clock rhythm by measuring bioluminescence from tissues explanted from PER2:LUC reporter mice (2).

We fed female mice either chow or high-fat diet for 1 week and measured rhythms of PER2:LUC bioluminescence in explanted tissues (Figure S1 in Supplementary Material). Similar to our previous study in males, we found that the phases of the PER2:LUC rhythms in the SCN, pituitary, lung, aorta, spleen, arcuate nucleus, and white adipose tissue were not affected by high-fat diet consumption. We also found that the phase of the liver PER2:LUC rhythm was not affected by high-fat feeding in female mice (Figure S1 in Supplementary Material). This surprisingly

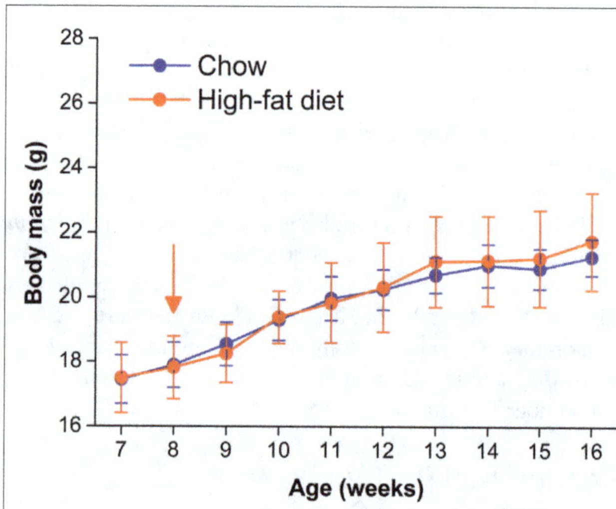

FIGURE 1 | Female C57BL/6J mice are resistant to diet-induced obesity. Body masses (mean grams ± SD) of female C57BL/6J mice fed either chow (blue circles, $n = 8$) or 45% high-fat diet (red circles, $n = 9$) for 8 weeks. High-fat feeding began at 8 weeks old (at red arrow).

contrasted with our previous finding that the phase of the liver PER2:LUC rhythm was advanced by ~5 h in male mice consuming high-fat diet (16). We therefore repeated the experiment in female mice, cultured only livers, and confirmed the phase of the liver PER2:LUC rhythm was not altered by 1 week of high-fat diet consumption (**Figure 2**: $p = 0.60$).

The Eating Behavior Rhythm Is Not Affected by High-Fat Feeding in Female Mice

Several studies, including our own, have shown that the amplitude of the daily rhythm of eating behavior was markedly reduced or eliminated during high-fat diet consumption in male C57BL/6J mice (15, 16, 26, 33). We examined the eating behavior rhythm in females using an infrared video camera (**Figure 3**; Figure S2 in Supplementary Material; data from all mice shown in Figure S3 in Supplementary Material). During chow feeding, females had a robust, high-amplitude eating behavior rhythm characterized by a few snacks during the day and the majority of eating during the night [a pattern indistinguishable from chow-fed males (16)] (**Figure 3A**: days 5–7; **Figures 3B,E**). During the first 24 h of high-fat diet feeding, females exhibited continuous eating behavior, resulting in a low-amplitude eating behavior rhythm, which is also similar to males on high-fat diet (16, 26, 33) (**Figure 3A**: day 9; **Figures 3C,F**). However, by 1 week of high-fat feeding, females had high-amplitude robust daily rhythms of eating behavior (**Figure 3A**: days 11–14; **Figures 3D,G**). Thus, females displayed the novelty response to palatable high-fat diet, but this response extinguished and their chow-like eating behavior rhythm returned. These data demonstrate that high-fat diet was not aversive to females. In fact, caloric intake increased 15% during 1 week of high-fat feeding, but the females did not gain more weight than chow-fed controls (Figure S2 in Supplementary Material; caloric intake did not increase during chow feeding). Moreover, females had fewer eating events (Figure S4A in Supplementary Material: intact) and ate fewer grams of food (Figure S4B in Supplementary Material: intact) during high-fat feeding compared to chow. These data suggest that the females had the appropriate homeostatic response to the calorie-dense high-fat diet by reducing the mass of food eaten in an attempt to scale down caloric intake to constrain their body weight gain.

We next compared the amplitudes and phases of the eating behavior rhythms between males [data from our previous study using an identical protocol (26)] and females during chow and high-fat feeding (**Figures 3H,I**). There was a significant interaction of sex and diet ($F = 12.3$, $p = 0.02$) on the amplitudes of the eating behavior rhythms (**Figure 3H**). Compared to chow, 1 week of high-fat feeding significantly reduced the amplitude of the eating behavior rhythm in males ($p = 0.04$), but not females ($p = 0.99$). There were no significant effects of sex and/or diet on the phase of the eating behavior rhythms (**Figure 3I**). Thus, although female mice initially responded to high-fat diet with disrupted low-amplitude eating behavior, within 1 week female mice, unlike males, reverted to the high-amplitude eating rhythm of chow-fed mice.

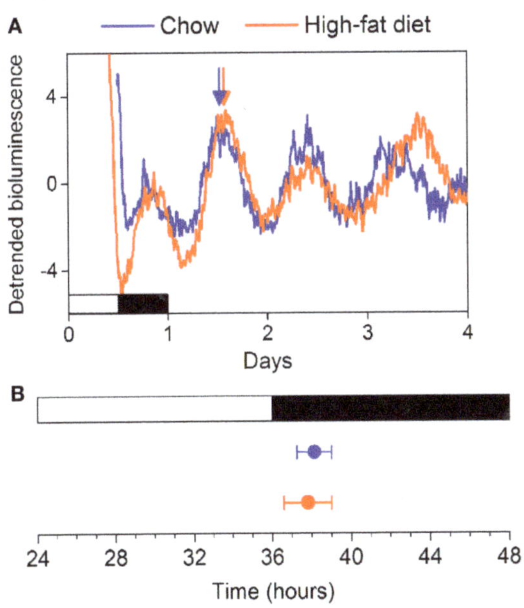

FIGURE 2 | High-fat diet does not alter the phase of the liver circadian clock in female mice. (A) Female C57BL/6J PER2:LUC mice were fed chow (blue circles) or high-fat diet (red circles) for 1 week and liver explants were cultured. **(B)** The mean phases (±SD) of the peaks of the bioluminescence rhythms were plotted relative to last lights on (12L:12D cycle indicated by white and black bars, respectively). Number of livers/total number cultured: Chow 7/7; High-fat diet: 5/7 ($p = 0.60$).

The Amplitude of the Locomotor Activity Rhythm Is Not Affected by High-Fat Feeding in Female Mice

The amplitude of the locomotor activity rhythm is reduced in male C57BL/6J mice (15, 18, 33). Thus, we next measured the locomotor activity rhythm with infrared motion sensors in female mice fed chow for 1 week and then high-fat diet for 1 week (**Figure 4**, actograms from all mice shown in Figure S5 in Supplementary Material; $n = 5$). In contrast to male mice, we found the amplitude and phase of the locomotor activity rhythm were not affected by high-fat feeding (**Figure 4**; **Table 1**). The mesor, or mean level of activity, was reduced slightly during high-fat feeding compared to chow feeding (**Table 1**).

Ovariectomy Abolishes Protection of Daily Rhythms from High-Fat Diet Feeding

We and others have previously shown that female mice are susceptible to diet-induced obesity after ovariectomy (34–37). Thus, we next determined if ovarian hormones were required to confer protection of daily rhythms from high-fat feeding in females. We ovariectomized female mice and then fed them chow or high-fat diet for 1 week (Figure S6 in Supplementary Material). In contrast to intact females, the phase of the liver PER2:LUC rhythm was advanced ~4 h in ovariectomized mice fed high-fat diet compared to those fed chow (**Figure 5**).

We next measured daily rhythm of eating behavior (**Figure 6**) in ovariectomized females fed chow or high-fat diet.

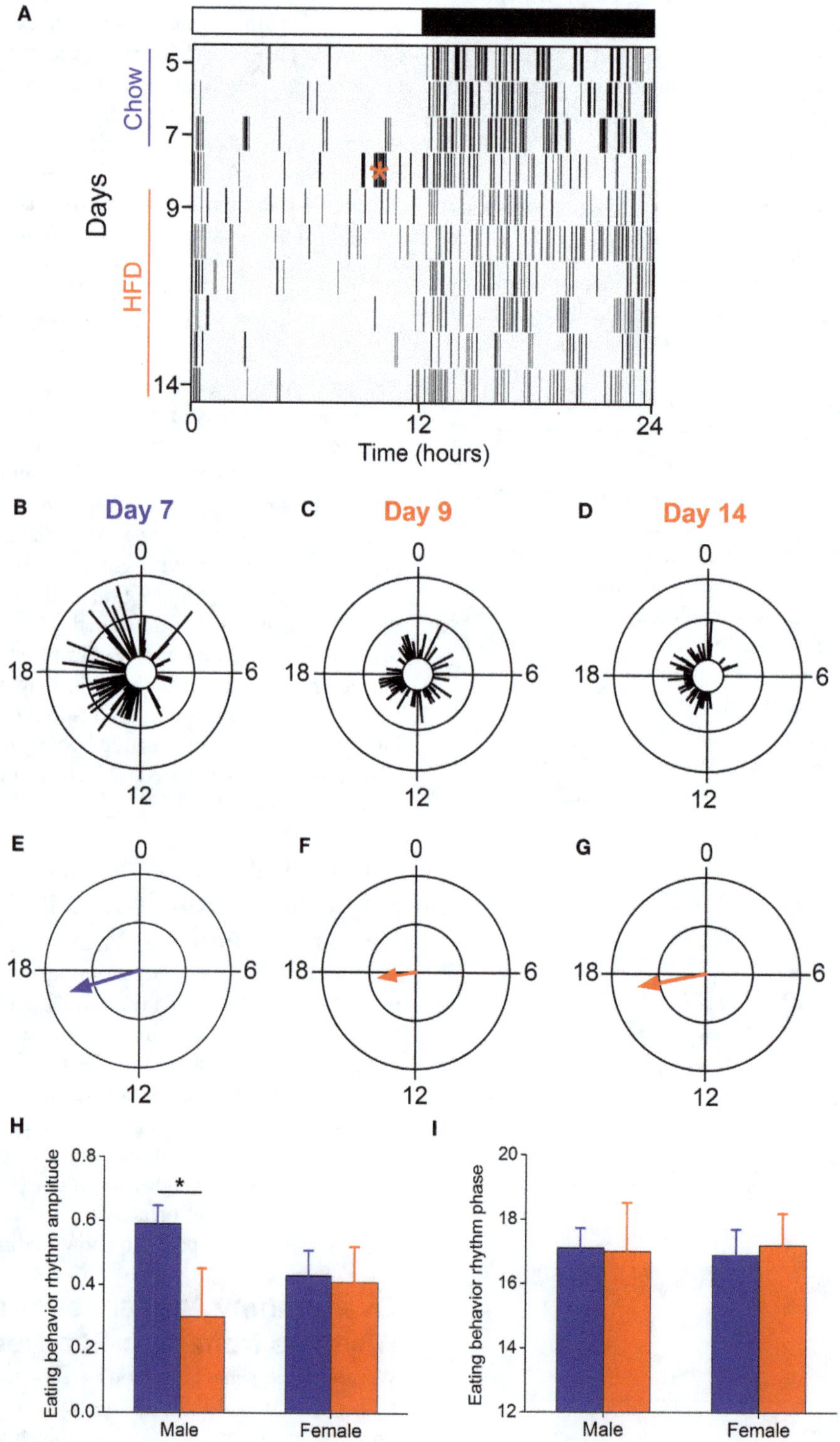

FIGURE 3 | The eating behavior rhythm is robust in females fed high-fat diet. Eating behavior was measured with infrared video cameras. **(A)** Representative actogram of eating behavior (1-min bins) of a female mouse fed chow (days 1–7, blue) and then switched to 45% high-fat diet (days 9–14, red, HFD added at red asterisk on day 8). Each vertical line is an eating event (1-min bins). Representative circular histograms show the distribution of eating behavior across the day (10-min bins) in an individual mouse during one day of chow [**(B)**: day 7], during the first day of HFD [**(C)**: day 9], and during the sixth day of HFD feeding [**(D)**: day 14]. Scale: inner circle, 0; middle circle, 5; outer circle, 10. Grand mean vectors of eating behavior show the average eating behavior of female mice ($n = 5$) during chow [**(E)**: day 7] and HFD [**(F)**: day 9; **(G)**: day 14] feeding. Scale: inner circle, 0; middle circle, 0.3; outer circle, 0.6. Lights were on from 0 to 12. Circular statistics are shown in Table S1 in Supplementary Material. Mean (±SD) amplitudes [**(H)**, *y*-axis: length of grand mean vector] and phases [**(I)**, *y*-axis: phase in ZT of grand mean vector] of male ($n = 5$) and female ($n = 5$) mice. Male data were taken from our previous study (26).

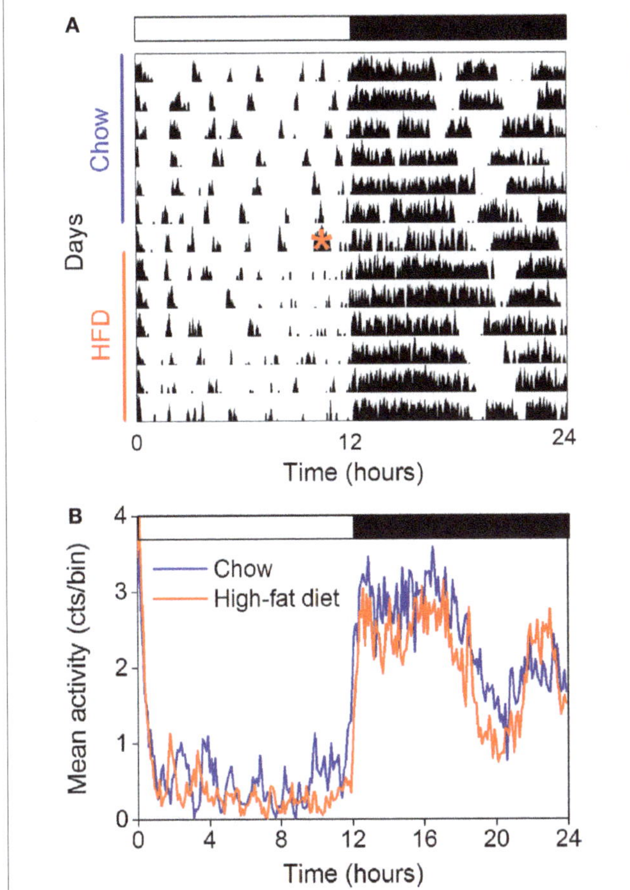

FIGURE 4 | The amplitude of the locomotor activity rhythm in females is not affected by high-fat feeding. Locomotor activity was measured with passive infrared sensors. **(A)** Representative actogram of locomotor activity (6-min bins; scale: 5) of a female mouse fed chow (days 1–7) and then switched to 45% high-fat diet (days 9–14, high-fat diet added at red asterisk on day 8). **(B)** Group average activity profiles (*y*-axis: counts/6 min bin) of females fed chow (blue) for 1 week and then high-fat diet (red) for 1 week ($n = 5$ mice).

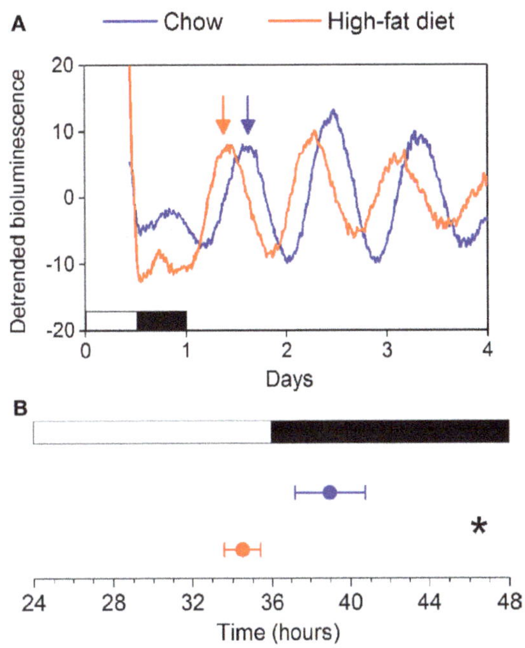

FIGURE 5 | High-fat diet feeding advances the phase of the liver clock in ovariectomized females. (A) Representative traces of PER2:LUC bioluminescence recorded from ovariectomized mice fed chow (blue) or 45% high-fat diet (red) for 1 week (*y*-axis: counts per second). Phases were determined from the peaks of bioluminescence occurring between 12 and 36 h in culture (indicated by arrows). **(B)** Mean phases (±SD) of liver PER2:LUC rhythms from chow ($n = 6$)- and high-fat diet ($n = 6$)-fed ovariectomized mice ($p < 0.001$).

TABLE 1 | Cosinor analysis of locomotor activity rhythms in intact female mice.

	Amplitude	Phase	Mesor
Chow	2.5 ± 1.1	17.2 ± 0.4	1.5 ± 0.6
High-fat diet	2.2 ± 1.1	18.0 ± 0.6	1.3 ± 0.6
p	0.19	0.06	0.03

Ovariectomized females fed chow had robust, high-amplitude eating behavior rhythms (**Figure 6A**: days 5–7; **Figures 6B,E**; all mice shown in Figure S7 in Supplementary Material). The amplitude of the eating behavior rhythm was reduced by high-fat feeding in ovariectomized females such that eating events were spread across the day and night (**Figure 6A**: days 9–14; **Figures 6C,D,F,G**; all mice shown in Figure S7 in Supplementary Material). The low-amplitude eating rhythm persisted 7 days after high-fat diet was introduced (**Figures 6D,G**). When we compared the amplitudes of the eating behavior rhythms between intact and ovariectomized females, there was a significant interaction of ovariectomy and diet ($F = 9.2$, $p = 0.04$) on the amplitudes of the eating behavior rhythms (**Figure 6H**). Compared to chow, 1 week of high-fat feeding significantly reduced the amplitude of the eating behavior rhythm in ovariectomized females ($p = 0.04$), but not intact females ($p = 0.74$). There were no significant effects of ovariectomy and diet on the phase of the eating behavior rhythm ($p = 0.06$). Ovariectomized females ate more calories during high-fat feeding compared to chow feeding (Figure S6 in Supplementary Material). Similar to intact females, ovariectomized mice had fewer eating events (Figure S4A in Supplementary Material: OVX) and ate fewer grams of food (Figure S4B in Supplementary Material: OVX) during high-fat feeding compared to chow.

We also measured the locomotor activity rhythm in ovariectomized females fed chow and high-fat diet (**Figure 7**). Immediately upon addition of high-fat diet, consolidated bouts of locomotor activity dissipated into shorter activity bouts (**Figure 7A**). This effect of high-fat diet persisted for the entire week of high-fat feeding. The amplitude and mesor (mean) of the locomotor activity rhythm were also reduced during high-fat feeding in ovariectomized females (**Figure 7B**; **Table 2**). There were no significant effects of ovariectomy and/or diet on the phase of the locomotor activity rhythm.

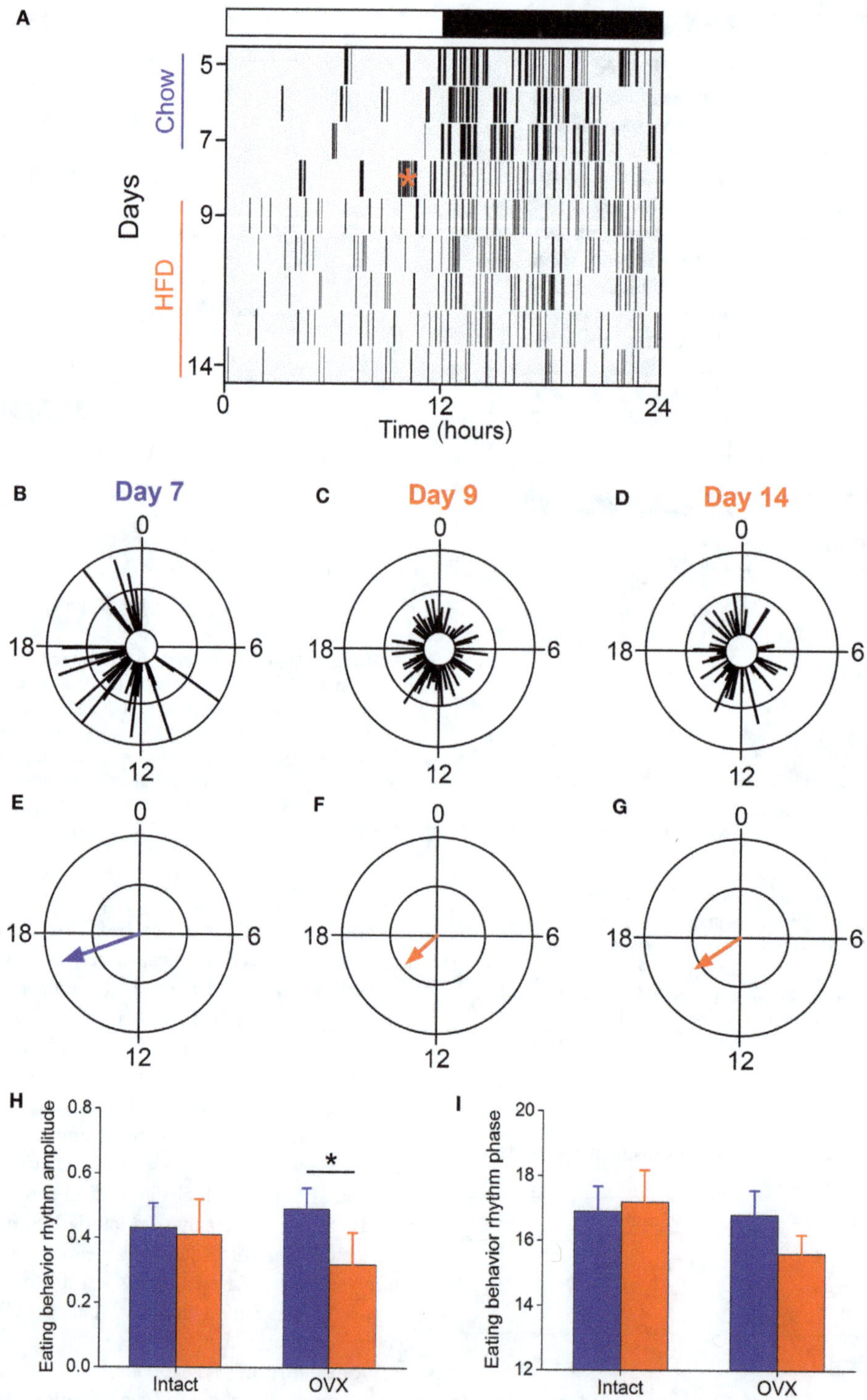

FIGURE 6 | The eating behavior rhythm is compromised in ovariectomized females fed high-fat diet. Eating behavior was measured with infrared video cameras. **(A)** Representative actogram of eating behavior (1-min bins) of an ovariectomized female mouse fed chow (days 1–7, blue) and then switched to 45% high-fat diet (days 9–14, red, high-fat diet added at red asterisk on day 8). Each vertical line is an eating event. Representative circular histograms show the distribution of eating behavior across the day (10-min bins) in an individual ovariectomized female mouse during 1 day of chow [**(B)**: day 7], during the first day of HFD [**(C)**: day 9], and during the sixth day of HFD feeding [**(D)**: day 14]. Scale: inner circle, 0; middle circle, 5; outer circle, 10. Grand mean vectors of eating behavior show the average eating behavior of ovariectomized female mice (n = 5) during chow [**(E)**: day 7] and HFD [**(F)**: day 9; **(G)**: day 14] feeding. Scale: inner circle, 0; middle circle, 0.3; outer circle, 0.6. Lights were on from 0 to 12. Circular statistics are shown in Table S1 in Supplementary Material. Mean (±SD) amplitudes [**(H)**, y-axis: length of grand mean vector] and phases [**(I)**, y-axis: phase in ZT of grand mean vector] of intact (n = 5; data from **Figure 3**) and ovariectomized (n = 5) female mice.

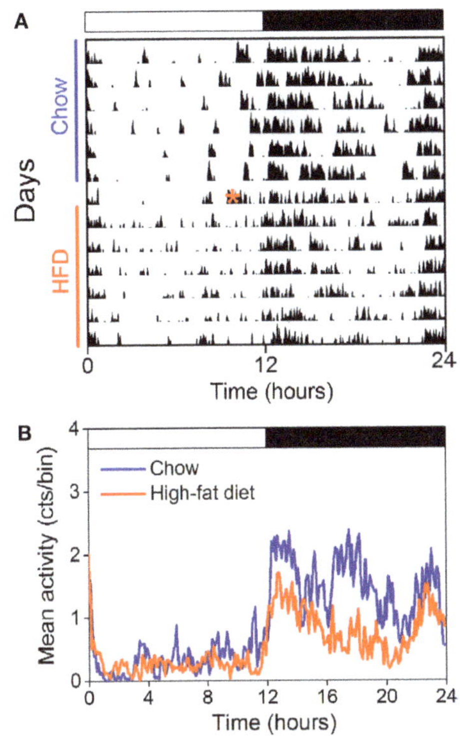

FIGURE 7 | The locomotor activity rhythm is reduced by high-fat feeding in ovariectomized female mice. Locomotor activity was measured with passive infrared sensors. **(A)** Representative actogram of locomotor activity (6-min bins; scale: 5) of an ovariectomized female mouse fed chow (days 1–7) and then switched to 45% high-fat diet (days 9–14, high-fat diet added at red asterisk on day 8). **(B)** Group average activity profiles (*y*-axis: counts/6-min bin) of ovariectomized females fed chow (blue) for 1 week and then high-fat diet (red) for 1 week (*n* = 5 mice).

TABLE 2 | Cosinor analysis of locomotor activity rhythms in ovariectomized female mice.

	Amplitude	Phase	Mesor
Chow	1.6 ± 0.6	17.0 ± 0.7	0.9 ± 0.4
High-fat diet	0.6 ± 0.1	17.1 ± 0.8	0.6 ± 0.2
p	0.02	0.77	0.06

DISCUSSION

Obesity and metabolic dysfunction are linked to disruption of circadian rhythms in human and animal studies. Studies in male mice have shown that high-fat feeding alters tissue, hormone, and behavior (eating and locomotor activity) rhythms (15–18). The disruption of daily rhythms in male mice is accompanied by development of profound obesity. However, the effects of high-fat feeding on daily metabolic rhythms in females have not been investigated. In this study, we showed that, in contrast to male mice, daily rhythms in females are protected from disruption by high-fat feeding.

Molecular rhythms of circadian gene expression and metabolites are altered in the livers of male mice fed high-fat diet acutely and chronically (15, 16, 19, 26, 33). We have postulated that temporal misalignment of the liver circadian clock and its rhythmic outputs are determinants of obesity. The current study further supports this hypothesis. We found the phase of the liver circadian clock is not affected by high-fat feeding in female mice, which are also resistant to diet-induced obesity. After ovariectomy, female mice are susceptible to diet-induced obesity (34, 35, 37), and the phases of their liver molecular clocks are markedly altered (liver phase is advanced 4 h). It is possible that circulating estrogen, or lack thereof, directly alters the circadian clock in the liver. Indeed, estradiol has been shown to alter the PER2:LUC rhythms in cultures of explanted uteruses and kisspeptin neurons(38, 39). Moreover, estrogen receptor signaling in the liver is incredibly responsive to estrogen *in vivo* (40). In future studies, we will investigate the mechanism whereby estrogen or other ovarian hormones regulate the phase of the liver circadian clock.

Disruption of the eating behavior rhythm contributes to the development of diet-induced obesity in males (20). When given high-fat diet, the amplitude of the eating rhythm is markedly reduced such that male mice eat throughout the 24-h day (light and dark phases) (15, 16). Restricting high-fat feeding to only the nighttime, which is when mice consume most of their calories, protects males from diet-induced obesity (20). In contrast to males, we found that females were resistant to the effects of high-fat diet on daily rhythms. Thus, in females, the daily rhythm of eating behavior in female mice is robust during high-fat feeding such that eating is consolidated during the nighttime. This robust eating behavior rhythm during high-fat feeding is lost after ovariectomy. Thus, ovarian hormones play a critical role in maintaining circadian feeding behavior rhythms despite high-fat diet feeding in female mice.

Our study also suggests that ovarian hormones differentially regulate the effects of high-fat feeding on the daily eating rhythm and homeostatic regulation of caloric intake. Ovariectomy abolished protection of the eating rhythm from high-fat feeding. In contrast, both intact and ovariectomized females had reduced eating events and food intake (measured in grams of food consumed) during high-fat feeding compared to chow. Thus, in ovariectomized mice, the homeostatic reduction in food intake is intact, since the mice eat significantly less of the calorie-dense high-fat diet compared to chow (Figure S4 in Supplementary Material), while the daily eating rhythm is markedly altered.

The role of ovarian hormones in maintaining circadian rhythms may be critical in protecting females from diet-induced obesity. It is likely that estrogen plays a major role in regulating circadian eating behavior during high-fat feeding. Previous studies have shown that estrogen acutely reduces feeding and the daily rhythm of food intake varies across the estrous cycle in rats (41, 42). In this study, we did not control for the estrous cycle in the intact females. It will be interesting to determine in future studies if the amplitude of the eating behavior rhythm during high-fat feeding fluctuates with the stage of the estrous cycle. In future studies, we will treat ovariectomized females with estrogen to determine if this restores protection of daily rhythms during high-fat feeding.

Studies in rodents and humans have demonstrated the roles of estrogen in controlling energy homeostasis and glucose metabolism [for review, see Ref (43)]. While the prevalence of obesity is equivalent in males and pre-menopausal women, obesity prevalence increases sharply in post-menopausal women (42%) (44). Estrogen deficiency after menopause predisposes women to obesity, the metabolic syndrome, and type 2 diabetes (22). Likewise, ovariectomy increases adiposity in rodents, and this increase in adiposity is prevented by estrogen replacement (41, 45). Thus, estrogens play an important role in energy homeostasis in both humans and rodents. We hypothesize that estrogen may play a role in protecting daily rhythms from the effects of high-fat feeding in female mice since ovariectomy abolished this protection. Alternatively, other ovarian hormones, such as progesterone, may confer protection of rhythms from high-fat feeding. Future studies will determine whether estrogen or other ovarian hormones are responsible for this protection.

The SCN controls the daily rhythm of food intake (46). It is possible that estrogen acts directly on SCN neurons to control the eating behavior rhythm. However, we speculate instead that estrogen acts downstream of the SCN to protect the daily rhythm of eating behavior from high-fat feeding. The reasons are twofold. First, the circadian rhythm in the SCN and its outputs are only moderately, at best, altered by high-fat feeding (15, 16, 18). This is in contrast to our observation that the eating behavior rhythm is all but eliminated during high-fat feeding in male mice and ovariectomized female mice (16). Second, the circadian rhythm in the SCN and its outputs are only moderately affected by manipulations of estrogen signaling (47). Moreover, estrogen receptors are expressed in few cells in the SCN (48). Taken together, we propose that estrogen acts outside of the SCN, perhaps in other feeding-related hypothalamic nuclei, to modulate the eating behavior rhythm during high-fat feeding.

High-fat feeding reduces the amplitude of the locomotor activity rhythm in male C57BL/6J mice (15, 18, 33). In contrast to males, the amplitude of the locomotor activity rhythm in female mice was not altered by high-fat feeding. Consistent with a previous study, the amplitude of the activity rhythm was reduced by ovariectomy in chow-fed mice (49). Additionally, in the absence of ovarian hormones, the amplitude of locomotor activity was reduced by half during high-fat feeding relative to chow feeding. Thus, ovarian hormones were also required to protect the daily activity rhythm. Similar to previous studies in males (15, 18), high-fat diet feeding reduced the mean activity level in both intact and ovariectomized females. Estrogen could act directly on SCN neurons or outside of the SCN to regulate the amplitude of the locomotor activity rhythm. It is difficult, if not impossible, to address this question because there is currently no way to eliminate the function of estrogen receptors exclusively in SCN cells (e.g., there is no Cre driver that is exclusively expressed in SCN cells).

Diet-induced obesity studies in rodents have provided promising avenues for "repairing" circadian disruption and improving metabolism. For example, restricting eating to specific times of day, called time-restricted feeding, is gaining traction as a plausible behavioral strategy to reduce obesity (50). However, while proof-of-concept for this therapy is strong in studies of male mice (20), our study suggests this therapy may not be effective in females. This study highlights the necessity of studying female models of diet-induced obesity when developing and testing novel therapeutics.

The current study elucidates protection of daily rhythms as a putative mechanism whereby females are resistant to diet-induced obesity. Notably, daily rhythms in females, compared to males, respond oppositely to high-fat feeding. Understanding the circadian mechanisms conferring obesity and designing therapeutics will employ distinct approaches in males and females.

AUTHOR CONTRIBUTIONS

BP performed experiments and participated in the discussion and writing of the manuscript. JS contributed to the design of the experiments and participated in discussion and writing of the manuscript. JP designed and performed experiments, analyzed data, and wrote the manuscript.

REFERENCES

1. Yamazaki S, Numano R, Abe M, Hida A, Takahashi R, Ueda M, et al. Resetting central and peripheral circadian oscillators in transgenic rats. *Science* (2000) 288:682–5. doi:10.1126/science.288.5466.682
2. Yoo SH, Yamazaki S, Lowrey PL, Shimomura K, Ko CH, Buhr ED, et al. PERIOD2:LUCIFERASE real-time reporting of circadian dynamics reveals persistent circadian oscillations in mouse peripheral tissues. *Proc Natl Acad Sci U S A* (2004) 101:5339–46. doi:10.1073/pnas.0308709101
3. Peplonska B, Bukowska A, Sobala W. Association of rotating night shift work with BMI and abdominal obesity among nurses and midwives. *PLoS One* (2015) 10:e0133761. doi:10.1371/journal.pone.0133761
4. Sookoian S, Gemma C, Fernandez Gianotti T, Burgueno A, Alvarez A, Gonzalez CD, et al. Effects of rotating shift work on biomarkers of metabolic syndrome and inflammation. *J Intern Med* (2007) 261:285–92. doi:10.1111/j.1365-2796.2007.01766.x
5. Tada Y, Kawano Y, Maeda I, Yoshizaki T, Sunami A, Yokoyama Y, et al. Association of body mass index with lifestyle and rotating shift work in Japanese female nurses. *Obesity (Silver Spring)* (2014) 22:2489–93. doi:10.1002/oby.20908
6. Pan A, Schernhammer ES, Sun Q, Hu FB. Rotating night shift work and risk of type 2 diabetes: two prospective cohort studies in women. *PLoS Med* (2011) 8:e1001141. doi:10.1371/journal.pmed.1001141
7. Di Lorenzo L, De Pergola G, Zocchetti C, L'Abbate N, Basso A, Pannacciulli N, et al. Effect of shift work on body mass index: results of a study performed in 319 glucose-tolerant men working in a Southern Italian industry. *Int J Obes Relat Metab Disord* (2003) 27:1353–8. doi:10.1038/sj.ijo.0802419

8. Suwazono Y, Dochi M, Oishi M, Tanaka K, Kobayashi E, Sakata K. Shiftwork and impaired glucose metabolism: a 14-year cohort study on 7104 male workers. *Chronobiol Int* (2009) 26:926–41. doi:10.1080/07420520903044422
9. Scheer FA, Hilton MF, Mantzoros CS, Shea SA. Adverse metabolic and cardiovascular consequences of circadian misalignment. *Proc Natl Acad Sci U S A* (2009) 106:4453–8. doi:10.1073/pnas.0808180106
10. Morris CJ, Purvis TE, Hu K, Scheer FA. Circadian misalignment increases cardiovascular disease risk factors in humans. *Proc Natl Acad Sci U S A* (2016) 113:E1402–11. doi:10.1073/pnas.1516953113
11. Lamia KA, Storch KF, Weitz CJ. Physiological significance of a peripheral tissue circadian clock. *Proc Natl Acad Sci U S A* (2008) 105:15172–7. doi:10.1073/pnas.0806717105
12. Turek FW, Joshu C, Kohsaka A, Lin E, Ivanova G, McDearmon E, et al. Obesity and metabolic syndrome in circadian Clock mutant mice. *Science* (2005) 308:1043–5. doi:10.1126/science.1108750
13. Rudic RD, McNamara P, Curtis AM, Boston RC, Panda S, Hogenesch JB, et al. BMAL1 and CLOCK, two essential components of the circadian clock, are involved in glucose homeostasis. *PLoS Biol* (2004) 2:e377. doi:10.1371/journal.pbio.0020377
14. Marcheva B, Ramsey KM, Buhr ED, Kobayashi Y, Su H, Ko CH, et al. Disruption of the clock components CLOCK and BMAL1 leads to hypoinsulinaemia and diabetes. *Nature* (2010) 466:627–31. doi:10.1038/nature09253
15. Kohsaka A, Laposky AD, Ramsey KM, Estrada C, Joshu C, Kobayashi Y, et al. High-fat diet disrupts behavioral and molecular circadian rhythms in mice. *Cell Metab* (2007) 6:414–21. doi:10.1016/j.cmet.2007.09.006
16. Pendergast JS, Branecky KL, Yang W, Ellacott KL, Niswender KD, Yamazaki S. High-fat diet acutely affects circadian organisation and eating behavior. *Eur J Neurosci* (2013) 37:1350–6. doi:10.1111/ejn.12133
17. Cano P, Jimenez-Ortega V, Larrad A, Reyes Toso CF, Cardinali DP, Esquifino AI. Effect of a high-fat diet on 24-h pattern of circulating levels of prolactin, luteinizing hormone, testosterone, corticosterone, thyroid-stimulating hormone and glucose, and pineal melatonin content, in rats. *Endocrine* (2008) 33:118–25. doi:10.1007/s12020-008-9066-x
18. Mendoza J, Pevet P, Challet E. High-fat feeding alters the clock synchronization to light. *J Physiol* (2008) 586:5901–10. doi:10.1113/jphysiol.2008.159566
19. Eckel-Mahan KL, Patel VR, de Mateo S, Orozco-Solis R, Ceglia NJ, Sahar S, et al. Reprogramming of the circadian clock by nutritional challenge. *Cell* (2013) 155:1464–78. doi:10.1016/j.cell.2013.11.034
20. Hatori M, Vollmers C, Zarrinpar A, DiTacchio L, Bushong EA, Gill S, et al. Time-restricted feeding without reducing caloric intake prevents metabolic diseases in mice fed a high-fat diet. *Cell Metab* (2012) 15:848–60. doi:10.1016/j.cmet.2012.04.019
21. Arble DM, Bass J, Laposky AD, Vitaterna MH, Turek FW. Circadian timing of food intake contributes to weight gain. *Obesity (Silver Spring)* (2009) 17:2100–2. doi:10.1038/oby.2009.264
22. Carr MC. The emergence of the metabolic syndrome with menopause. *J Clin Endocrinol Metab* (2003) 88:2404–11. doi:10.1210/jc.2003-030242
23. Matthews KA, Kuller LH, Sutton-Tyrrell K, Chang YF. Changes in cardiovascular risk factors during the perimenopause and postmenopause and carotid artery atherosclerosis in healthy women. *Stroke* (2001) 32:1104–11. doi:10.1161/01.STR.32.5.1104
24. Sugiyama MG, Agellon LB. Sex differences in lipid metabolism and metabolic disease risk. *Biochem Cell Biol* (2012) 90:124–41. doi:10.1139/o11-067
25. Yamazaki S, Takahashi JS. Real-time luminescence reporting of circadian gene expression in mammals. *Methods Enzymol* (2005) 393:288–301. doi:10.1016/S0076-6879(05)93012-7
26. Branecky KL, Niswender KD, Pendergast JS. Disruption of daily rhythms by high-fat diet is reversible. *PLoS One* (2015) 10:e0137970. doi:10.1371/journal.pone.0137970
27. Cornelissen G. Cosinor-based rhythmometry. *Theor Biol Med Model* (2014) 11:16. doi:10.1186/1742-4682-11-16
28. Palmisano BT, Le TD, Zhu L, Lee YK, Stafford JM. Cholesteryl ester transfer protein alters liver and plasma triglyceride metabolism through two liver networks in female mice. *J Lipid Res* (2016) 57:1541–51. doi:10.1194/jlr.M069013
29. Surwit RS, Kuhn CM, Cochrane C, McCubbin JA, Feinglos MN. Diet-induced type II diabetes in C57BL/6J mice. *Diabetes* (1988) 37:1163–7. doi:10.2337/diab.37.9.1163
30. Krawczewski Carhuatanta KA, Demuro G, Tschop MH, Pfluger PT, Benoit SC, Obici S. Voluntary exercise improves high-fat diet-induced leptin resistance independent of adiposity. *Endocrinology* (2011) 152:2655–64. doi:10.1210/en.2010-1340
31. Bae K, Jin X, Maywood ES, Hastings MH, Reppert SM, Weaver DR. Differential functions of mPer1, mPer2, and mPer3 in the SCN circadian clock. *Neuron* (2001) 30:525–36. doi:10.1016/S0896-6273(01)00302-6
32. Zheng B, Albrecht U, Kaasik K, Sage M, Lu W, Vaishnav S, et al. Nonredundant roles of the mPer1 and mPer2 genes in the mammalian circadian clock. *Cell* (2001) 105:683–94. doi:10.1016/S0092-8674(01)00380-4
33. Pendergast JS, Branecky KL, Huang R, Niswender KD, Yamazaki S. Wheel-running activity modulates circadian organization and the daily rhythm of eating behavior. *Front Psychol* (2014) 5:177. doi:10.3389/fpsyg.2014.00177
34. Grove KL, Fried SK, Greenberg AS, Xiao XQ, Clegg DJ. A microarray analysis of sexual dimorphism of adipose tissues in high-fat-diet-induced obese mice. *Int J Obes (Lond)* (2010) 34:989–1000. doi:10.1038/ijo.2010.12
35. Hong J, Stubbins RE, Smith RR, Harvey AE, Nunez NP. Differential susceptibility to obesity between male, female and ovariectomized female mice. *Nutr J* (2009) 8:11. doi:10.1186/1475-2891-8-11
36. Cao JJ, Gregoire BR. A high-fat diet increases body weight and circulating estradiol concentrations but does not improve bone structural properties in ovariectomized mice. *Nutr Res* (2016) 36:320–7. doi:10.1016/j.nutres.2015.12.008
37. Zhu L, Brown WC, Cai Q, Krust A, Chambon P, McGuinness OP, et al. Estrogen treatment after ovariectomy protects against fatty liver and may improve pathway-selective insulin resistance. *Diabetes* (2013) 62:424–34. doi:10.2337/db11-1718
38. Nakamura TJ, Sellix MT, Menaker M, Block GD. Estrogen directly modulates circadian rhythms of PER2 expression in the uterus. *Am J Physiol Endocrinol Metab* (2008) 295:E1025–31. doi:10.1152/ajpendo.90392.2008
39. Chassard D, Bur I, Poirel VJ, Mendoza J, Simonneaux V. Evidence for a putative circadian kiss-clock in the hypothalamic AVPV in female mice. *Endocrinology* (2015) 156:2999–3011. doi:10.1210/en.2014-1769
40. Ciana P, Raviscioni M, Mussi P, Vegeto E, Que I, Parker MG, et al. In vivo imaging of transcriptionally active estrogen receptors. *Nat Med* (2003) 9:82–6. doi:10.1038/nm809
41. Blaustein JD, Wade GN. Ovarian influences on the meal patterns of female rats. *Physiol Behav* (1976) 17:201–8. doi:10.1016/0031-9384(76)90064-0
42. ter Haar MB. Circadian and estrual rhythms in food intake in the rat. *Horm Behav* (1972) 3:213–9. doi:10.1016/0018-506X(72)90034-7
43. Mauvais-Jarvis F, Clegg DJ, Hevener AL. The role of estrogens in control of energy balance and glucose homeostasis. *Endocr Rev* (2013) 34:309–38. doi:10.1210/er.2012-1055
44. Ogden CL, Carroll MD, Kit BK, Flegal KM. Prevalence of obesity in the United States, 2009-2010. *NCHS Data Brief* (2012) 82:1–8.
45. Geary N, Asarian L, Korach KS, Pfaff DW, Ogawa S. Deficits in E2-dependent control of feeding, weight gain, and cholecystokinin satiation in ER-alpha null mice. *Endocrinology* (2001) 142:4751–7. doi:10.1210/en.142.11.4751
46. Nagai K, Nishio T, Nakagawa H, Nakamura S, Fukuda Y. Effect of bilateral lesions of the suprachiasmatic nuclei on the circadian rhythm of food-intake. *Brain Res* (1978) 142:384–9. doi:10.1016/0006-8993(78)90648-0

47. Blattner MS, Mahoney MM. Estrogen receptor 1 modulates circadian rhythms in adult female mice. *Chronobiol Int* (2014) 31:637–44. doi:10.3109/07420528.2014.885528
48. Vida B, Hrabovszky E, Kalamatianos T, Coen CW, Liposits Z, Kallo I. Oestrogen receptor alpha and beta immunoreactive cells in the suprachiasmatic nucleus of mice: distribution, sex differences and regulation by gonadal hormones. *J Neuroendocrinol* (2008) 20:1270–7. doi:10.1111/j.1365-2826.2008.01787.x
49. Royston SE, Yasui N, Kondilis AG, Lord SV, Katzenellenbogen JA, Mahoney MM. ESR1 and ESR2 differentially regulate daily and circadian activity rhythms in female mice. *Endocrinology* (2014) 155:2613–23. doi:10.1210/en.2014-1101
50. Arble DM, Bass J, Behn CD, Butler MP, Challet E, Czeisler C, et al. Impact of sleep and circadian disruption on energy balance and diabetes: a summary of workshop discussions. *Sleep* (2015) 38:1849–60. doi:10.5665/sleep.5226

21

A Life without Hunger: The Ups (and Downs) to Modulating Melanocortin-3 Receptor Signaling

Andrew A. Butler[1*]*, Clemence Girardet*[1†]*, Maria Mavrikaki*[1†]*, James L. Trevaskis*[2]*, Heather Macarthur*[1]*, Daniel L. Marks*[3] *and Susan A. Farr*[4,5]

[1] Department of Pharmacology and Physiology, Saint Louis University School of Medicine, St. Louis, MO, USA, [2] In vivo Pharmacology, Cardiovascular and Metabolic Disease, Medimmune, Gaithersburg, MD, USA, [3] Papé Family Pediatric Research Institute, Oregon Health and Science University, Portland, OR, USA, [4] Department of Internal Medicine, Division of Geriatrics, Saint Louis University School of Medicine, St. Louis, MO, USA, [5] VA Medical Center, St. Louis, MO, USA

Edited by:
Andries Kalsbeek, Academic Medical Center, Netherlands

Reviewed by:
Ruud Buijs, National Autonomous University of Mexico, Mexico
Miguel Lopez, Universidade de Santiago de Compostela, Spain

***Correspondence:**
Andrew A. Butler
butleraa@slu.edu

Melanocortin neurons conserve body mass in hyper- or hypo-caloric conditions by conveying signals from nutrient sensors into areas of the brain governing appetite and metabolism. In mice, melanocortin-3 receptor (MC3R) deletion alters nutrient partitioning independently of hyperphagia, promoting accumulation of fat over muscle mass. Enhanced rhythms in insulin and insulin-responsive metabolic genes during hypocaloric feeding suggest partial insulin resistance and enhanced lipogenesis. However, exactly where and how MC3Rs affect metabolic control to alter nutrient partitioning is not known. The behavioral phenotypes exhibited by MC3R-deficient mice suggest a contextual role in appetite control. The impact of MC3R-deficiency on feeding behavior when food is freely available is minor. However, homeostatic responses to hypocaloric conditioning involving increased expression of appetite-stimulating (orexigenic) neuropeptides, binge-feeding, food anticipatory activity (FAA), entrainment to nutrient availability and enhanced feeding-related motivational responses are compromised with MC3R-deficiency. Rescuing *Mc3r* transcription in hypothalamic and limbic neurons improves appetitive responses during hypocaloric conditioning while having minor effects on nutrient partitioning, suggesting orexigenic functions. Rescuing hypothalamic MC3Rs also restores responses of fasting-responsive hypothalamic orexigenic neurons in hypocaloric conditions, suggesting actions that sensitize fasting-responsive neurons to signals from nutrient sensors. MC3R signaling in ventromedial hypothalamic SF1(+ve) neurons improves metabolic control, but does not restore appetitive responses or nutrient partitioning. In summary, desensitization of fasting-responsive orexigenic neurons may underlie attenuated appetitive responses of MC3R-deficient mice in hypocaloric situations. Further studies are needed to identify the specific location(s) of MC3Rs controlling appetitive responses and partitioning of nutrients between fat and lean tissues.

Keywords: obesity, diabetes, appetite, neuropeptide, hypothalamus, limbic system, homeostasis, metabolism

Obesity is often attributed to a combination of genetic susceptibility and imbalances between energy intake and expenditure (Hill et al., 2012; Speakman and O'Rahilly, 2012). The problem facing modern societies is that obesity is now common: two-thirds of the population in the United States are overweight or obese (Lewis et al., 2009). Obesity increases risk of cardiometabolic disease and some cancers, reducing quality and duration of life (Lewis et al., 2009). Determining why some become obese and some do not is fundamental to solving and perhaps reversing current obesity trends. MC3Rs are a component of a canonical hypothalamic neural network regulating body mass and substrate partitioning between adipose and lean tissues (Girardet and Butler, 2014). While not widely considered a target for obesity treatment, here we discuss recent studies suggesting the importance of MC3Rs in appetite and metabolic control.

AN OVERVIEW OF THE CENTRAL NERVOUS MELANOCORTIN SYSTEM

At the core of central nervous melanocortin system are two neuronal populations sending projections throughout the brain from soma in the hypothalamic arcuate nucleus (ARC). These neurons integrate humoral cues of metabolic condition (insulin, acyl-ghrelin, leptin, glucagon-like peptide-1, glucocorticoids, interleukins and estrogen) (Mauvais-Jarvis et al., 2013; Gautron et al., 2015), metabolites such as glucose (Ibrahim et al., 2003; Parton et al., 2007), and inputs from neurons releasing serotonin (Burke and Heisler, 2015), glutamate (Krashes et al., 2014), orexin (van den Top et al., 2004; Morello et al., 2016), and cannabinoids (Koch et al., 2015; Morello et al., 2016).

GABA-ergic neurons co-expressing orexigenic neuropeptides agouti-related peptide (AgRP) and neuropeptide Y (NPY) are activated upon fasting (Hahn et al., 1998; Betley et al., 2015). Activation of NPY/AgRP/GABA (NAG) neurons rapidly induces feeding and learned instrumental actions to obtain food (Aponte et al., 2011; Krashes et al., 2011). In contrast, ablation causes anorexia and impairs adaptation to hypocaloric conditioning (Bewick et al., 2005; Luquet et al., 2005; Tan et al., 2014). Another population of ARC neurons express proopiomelanocortin (POMC), a propeptide converted to β-endorphin (an endogenous opioid) and melanocortins (α–, β- and γ–MSH and ACTH) (**Figure 1A**; Cone, 2006). Activation of ARC POMC neurons in mice inhibits feeding behavior, albeit over longer time frames compared to NAG neurons (Zhan et al., 2013). In contrast, ablating POMC neurons or suppressing ARC *Pomc* expression causes hyperphagic obesity syndromes (Smart et al., 2006; Bumaschny et al., 2012; Zhan et al., 2013). Activation of small population of POMC neurons in the nucleus of the solitary tract of the hindbrain rapidly inhibits feeding, however their ablation does not produce obesity (Zhan et al., 2013).

Cloning of the Melanocortin Receptors

Physiological responses to melanocortin ligands are mediated by five receptors (MC1R-MC5R) (Cortés et al., 2014). Melanocortin receptor pharmacology is complex, with two antagonists/inverse agonists (AgRP and agouti signaling peptide) and MSH ligands that exhibit varying degrees of receptor specificity (**Figure 1B**; Cone et al., 1996). Other ligands and cell-surface proteins have been identified that regulate melanocortin signaling (e.g., melanocortin receptor accessory proteins 1 and 2, mahogany, mahoganoid, attractin-like protein, syndecans, ion channels and defensins) (Kaelin et al., 2008; Nix et al., 2013, 2015; Anderson et al., 2016).

Melanocortin regulation of energy balance is mediated by two receptors expressed in the central nervous system. *Mc3r* and *Mc4r* mRNA are expressed in overlapping and distinct brain regions linked to appetite and metabolic control (Roselli-Rehfuss et al., 1993; Mountjoy et al., 1994; Kishi et al., 2003; Liu et al., 2003; Lippert et al., 2014; Mavrikaki et al., 2016). *Mc3r* expression is concentrated in hypothalamic and limbic structures, with dense expression in the ARC, ventromedial hypothalamus (VMH), ventral tegmental area (VTA), and medial habenula (MHb) (Roselli-Rehfuss et al., 1993; Cone, 2005; Lippert et al., 2014; Mavrikaki et al., 2016). Initial observations of expression of both receptors in areas of the rodent brain linked to appetite control (Roselli-Rehfuss et al., 1993; Mountjoy et al., 1994), and stimulation of feeding by melanocortin antagonists administered centrally (Fan et al., 1997), were crucial early steps in revealing the physiological significance of the central nervous melanocortin system. Chronic intracerebroventricular infusion of AgRP, an MC3R/MC4R antagonist/inverse agonist (Ollmann et al., 1997; Shutter et al., 1997), causes a hyperphagic obesity syndrome (Small et al., 2001). The central nervous melanocortin system is thus viewed as a promising target for developing obesity therapies. The first trials of melanocortin agonists for treating obesity failed due to cardiovascular responses (Greenfield, 2011). However, a recent trial investigating RM-493, a small peptide MC3R/MC4R agonist shown to have MC4R-dependent effects on food intake and body weight (Kumar et al., 2009), produced promising outcomes. In humans, RM-493 increased resting energy expenditure and reduced the respiratory quotient (RQ), suggesting enhanced fat oxidation (Chen et al., 2015). In obese non-human primates, administration of RM-493 resulted in weight loss with a transient suppression of food intake, increased total energy expenditure and improvements in insulin resistance and cardiovascular function (Kievit et al., 2013). Importantly, adverse cardiovascular responses that led to the discontinuation of earlier compounds were not evident.

In the absence of selective melanocortin receptor ligands, targeted deletion of the melanocortin receptors provided important information concerning the functional specificity of neural melanocortin receptors. MC3Rs are not required for suppression of food intake in response to MSH analogs (Marsh et al., 1999; Chen et al., 2000a,b; Kumar et al., 2009), and for appetite control during exposure to palatable high-fat/high sucrose diets (Butler et al., 2000, 2001; Albarado et al., 2004; Sutton et al., 2006; Srisai et al., 2011). Unlike MC4Rs, MC3Rs are not required for appetitive and metabolic responses to serotoninergic compounds (Heisler et al., 2002, 2006; Zhou et al., 2007). Deletion of the gene encoding either MC3R or MC4R causes obesity in mice, with both affecting partitioning of nutrients between adipose and non-adipose tissues (Huszar et al., 1997; Butler et al., 2000; Chen et al., 2000a). The two receptors were originally considered to function independently, as *Mc3r;Mc4r* double knockouts exhibit an additive obese phenotype (Chen et al., 2000a). As discussed later in this review, our data suggest MC3Rs may regulate MC4R activity by altering

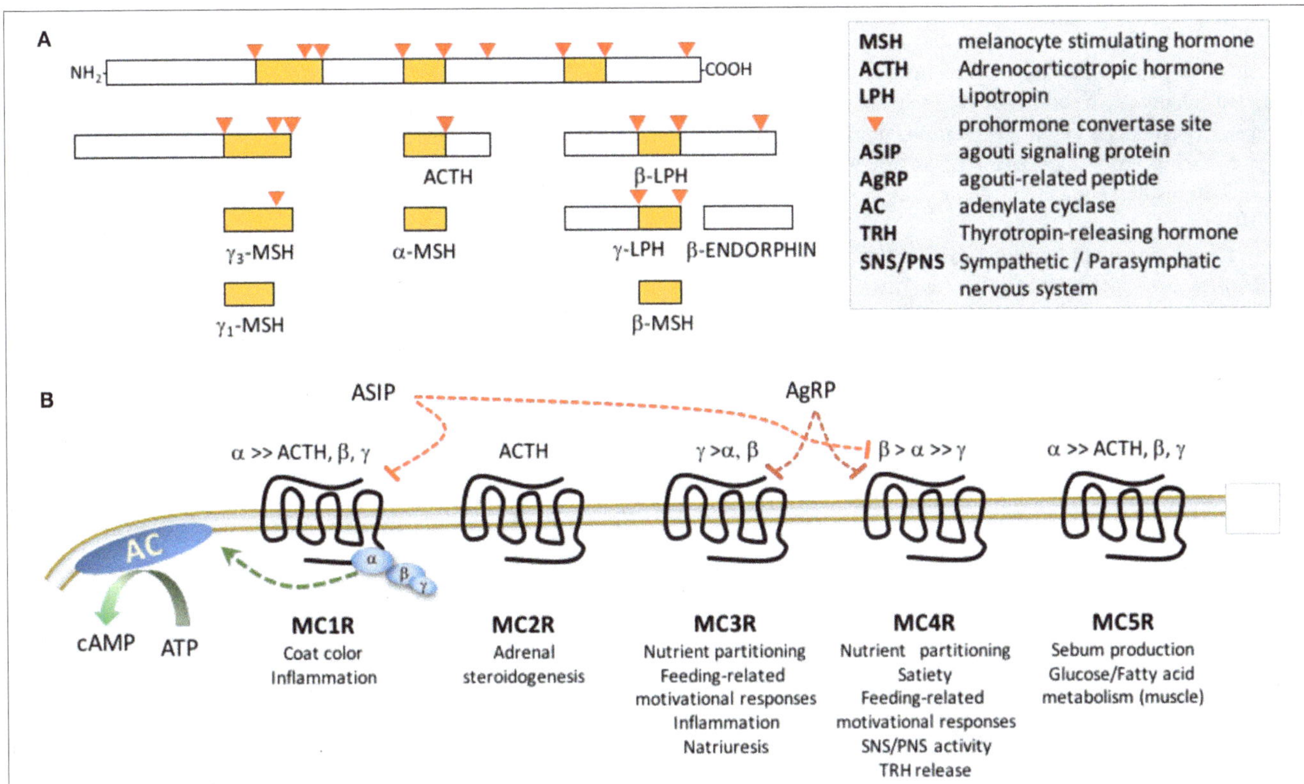

FIGURE 1 | Post-translational processing of POMC (A) and melanocortin receptor pharmacology **(B)**. **(A)** The propeptide proopiomelanocortin (POMC) is post-translationally modified by serine proteases propeptide (also known as prohormone) convertases 1/3 and 2. **(B)** MSH peptides and ACTH peptides activated following release from POMC differ in affinity for the 5 members of the melanocortin receptor family: γ-MSH exhibits preferential affinity for MC3Rs; ACTH is the only agonist for MC2Rs; ASIP exhibits high affinity for MC1R and MC4R, while AgRP is a selective antagonist for MC3R and MC4R. Note that this is a simplified schematic, and does not show the melanocortin receptor accessory proteins (MRAP1, MRAP2) that associate with the melanocortin receptors to modify receptor activity or coupling to β–arrestins which mediates receptor internalization and activation of intracellular signaling cascades. Receptor binding of the MSH results in activation of the stimulatory subunit of trimeric G protein receptor complex (α,β,γ) for all members of the family, resulting in increased adenylate cyclase (AC) activity and accumulation of cAMP. Agouti signaling peptide (ASIP) and agouti-related peptide (AgRP) were initially described as antagonists, however they may have biased agonist properties, activating receptor coupling to other G protein complexes. Lists of physiological processes are shown below each receptor.

the response of "1st order" neurons releasing the endogenous ligands to signals of metabolic state.

Genetic screens of obese populations confirmed the importance of normal melanocortin receptor function in the defense of body weight from early childhood. Missense mutations in the *POMC* and *MC4R* genes are associated with severe hyperphagic obesity syndromes that manifests within the first 1–2 years of life (Farooqi and O'Rahilly, 2008). The central nervous melanocortin system responds to environmental cues through epigenetic modifications that have long-lasting effects on expression of genes promoting lean phenotypes (Benite-Ribeiro et al., 2016; Kühnen et al., 2016). Methylation in a variably methylated region (VMR) of the *POMC* gene allele is associated with altered body mass in humans (Kühnen et al., 2016). Methylation of this region is sensitive to metabolic conditions *in utero*, and to paternal methylation patterns. Altered *POMC* expression as a consequence of developmental conditions could therefore contribute to obesity later in life. While the evidence for direct causality is less clear, *MC3R* haploinsufficiency is linked to increased risk of childhood obesity (Feng et al., 2005; Tao, 2010; Lee, 2012; Lee et al., 2016).

IS THERE A ROLE FOR MC3Rs IN APPETITE REGULATION?

Expression of MC3Rs in limbic and hypothalamic structures suggests functions related to controlling complex behaviors, including appetite (Roselli-Rehfuss et al., 1993; Lippert et al., 2014; Mavrikaki et al., 2016). However, as discussed above characterization of feeding behavior in *Mc3r* knockout (−/−) mice on mixed or congenic (C57BL/6J) backgrounds has been inconclusive (Butler et al., 2000; Chen et al., 2000a; Butler, 2006; Sutton et al., 2006; Ellacott et al., 2007; Begriche et al., 2011a).

Recent results from a recent experiment in mice with "humanized" MC3Rs may suggest a role in appetite control (Lee et al., 2016). Risk of childhood obesity is increased in homozygous carriers of two *MC3R* sequence variants (C17A+G241A) that reduce receptor binding and maximal cAMP accumulation in cell-based assays (Feng et al., 2005). Mice homozygous for the mutant *hMC3R* containing the double mutation ($MC3R^{hDM/hDM}$) exhibit reduced musculoskeletal mass and increased adiposity when compared to mice inheriting "wild type" hMC3Rs ($MC3R^{hWT/hWT}$) (Lee et al., 2016). $MC3R^{hDM/hDM}$ mice are also hyperphagic; while the difference is small (1–2 kcal/mouse/day), over time this could produce significant changes in adiposity (Butler and Kozak, 2010). However, hyperphagia does not explain the nutrient-partitioning defect reducing musculoskeletal growth, which has been postulated to result from a mild Cushingoid phenotype (Renquist et al., 2012).

How the feeding phenotype of $MC3R^{hDM/hDM}$ mice compares to outcomes from other studies using *Mc3r*-deficient mice is unclear. While classical gene targeting techniques result in complete loss of MC3R signaling, some signaling is presumably retained in $MC3R^{hDM/hDM}$ mice. Information on the impact of the (C17A+G241A) mutation on second messenger signaling thus far has been limited to measuring cAMP accumulation in the presence of the synthetic analog [Nle^4, D-Phe^7]-α-MSH. Information on how the mutation alter other signaling mechanisms and responses to other ligands such as AgRP are not available, but could be relevant given that physiological responses to centrally administered melanocortin agonists involve distinct G protein signaling mechanisms (Li et al., 2016).

MC3R Role in Appetite Regulation Is Context-Dependent and Exposed in Hypocaloric Conditions

Overall, the lack of conclusive evidence supporting a role for MC3Rs in appetite control in *ad libitum* fed situations, combined with comparatively modest changes in body mass (Butler et al., 2000, 2001; Chen et al., 2000a), explains why many laboratories overlooked neural MC3Rs. Evaluating behavioral and/or metabolic responses of mice to environmental challenges can be informative when investigating the functions of genes involved in behavior and metabolism. For example, cold stress is often used to assess mobilization of energy reserves and futile cycles to maintain body temperature (Kozak and Anunciado-Koza, 2008). Another example is transitioning between chows and obesogenic diets to assess behavioral and metabolic control (Collins et al., 2004). *Mc3r*-deficient mice tolerate cold and control appetite when challenged with palatable diets (Butler et al., 2000, 2001; Chen et al., 2000a; Sutton et al., 2006; Ellacott et al., 2007). However, a behavioral phenotype is observed in *Mc3r−/−* mice subjected to hypocaloric restricted feeding protocols to assess motivational responses anticipating food presentation (Sutton et al., 2008; Begriche et al., 2011a,b, 2012; Girardet et al., 2014a, 2017). These outcomes suggest that MC3Rs play a role in mediating appetite responses to situations of nutrient scarcity.

Mice provided unrestricted access to a running wheel exhibit food anticipatory activity (FAA) when subjected to a hypocaloric diet (70–75% of habitual intake) presented at 24 h intervals (Mistlberger, 2011). FAA involves a progressive rise in activity preceding food access, and has been suggested to involve a circadian oscillator ("food-entrainable oscillator," or FEO) that is independent of the light-entrained master clock. FAA is attenuated in *Mc3r−/−* mice housed in a 12 h light:dark setting (Sutton et al., 2008); the same study reported that *Mc3r−/−* mice failed to increase wakefulness in anticipation of food presentation. Entrainment to food presentation is also attenuated, but not completely inhibited, when FAA is assessed in constant dark (Begriche et al., 2011b). Based on the weakened anticipatory responses observed during restricted feeding, MC3Rs may act as a modulator of the inputs (or outputs) of FEOs (Mistlberger, 2011). Entrainment to food availability is thought to involve coordinated responses of FEO distributed throught the body (Mohawk et al., 2012). However, it is no clear how MC3Rs exert regulatory control over rhythms in FEO activity.

A recent paper from Roger Cone's laboratory suggested another interpretation of the FAA phenotype associated with loss of MC3R. Renquist et al. reported that the fasting responses of NAG neurons are not observed in *Mc3r−/−* mice (Renquist et al., 2012). We subsequently reported increased hypothalamic *AgRP* and *Npy* expression in the hypocaloric conditions used to induce FAA is also not observed in *Mc3r*-deficient mice (Girardet et al., 2014a, 2017). Collectively, these results suggest activation of NAG neurons by signals of negative energy balance contributes to the expression of FAA. Adult mice lacking NAG neurons adapt poorly to a hypocaloric feeding protocol used to induce FAA (Tan et al., 2014). FAA involves increased food seeking and motivational responses to seek food (Aponte et al., 2011; Krashes et al., 2011). Similar responses occur upon activation of NAG neurons (Aponte et al., 2011; Krashes et al., 2011), although another interpretation is that activation of NAG neurons delivers a "negative valence" signal (Betley et al., 2015) causing avoidance of situations associated with a painful experience (hunger).

Mc3r-deficient mice also exhibit attenuated appetitive responses to hypocaloric conditioning. Wild-type mice subjected to hypocaloric feeding protocols exhibit binge-feeding behavior, reducing meal frequency and increasing meal size to consume most of the food within 1 h of presentation (Bruss et al., 2010; Begriche et al., 2012; Girardet et al., 2017). This behavioral adaptation is attenuated in *Mc3r−/−* mice: food intake in the 1 h following presentation is markedly reduced with no compensation later in the feeding cycle and changes in meal structure (fewer, larger meals) are also attenuated (Begriche et al., 2012; Girardet et al., 2017). Motivation to self-administer food-rewards during hypocaloric conditions is also attenuated in *Mc3r*-deficient mice (Mavrikaki et al., 2016). However, self-administration is normal in *Mc3r*-deficient mice in *ad libitum* feeding conditions and increased motivation to self-administer more palatable sucrose diets is retained (Mavrikaki et al., 2016). The behavioral phenotype associated with MC3R-deficiency is therefore contextual and dependent on energy balance. *Mc3r*-deficient mice may not experience the "pain" of hunger, and are not be motivated to avoid unpleasant experiences associated with nutrient insufficiency.

These observations also suggest a new and perhaps simpler interpretation of the phenomenon observed in *Mc3r−/−* mice during restricted feeding. In the absence of MC3Rs, NAG neurons are desensitized to internal cues of metabolic state provided by hormones and metabolites, the release of which follows patterns that are sensitive to food consumption (Tschop et al., 2006). This model also explains why the release of other neuropeptides and neurotransmitters from NAG neurons does not compensate for the absence of MC3Rs. The rapid stimulation of feeding behavior following activation of NAG neurons requires the release of GABA or NPY from NAG neurons, while release of AgRP elicits a delayed yet prolonged increase in feeding behavior that is dependent on MC4Rs (Krashes et al., 2013).

MC3Rs in Hypothalamic and Limbic Structures Promote Appetitive Responses to Hypocaloric Conditions

We developed the LoxTB*Mc3r* mouse, allowing us to reactivate of *Mc3r* transcription using Cre transgenics, inserting a "lox-stop-lox" sequence in the 5′UTR (Begriche et al., 2011a). The response of NAG neurons to hypocaloric conditioning is restored in LoxTB*Mc3r* mice in which hypothalamic expression was rescued using Nkx2.1-Cre (Girardet et al., 2017). This study also observed that restoring FAA in LoxTB*Mc3r* mice is independent of improvements in adiposity. These results suggest that actions involving NKX2.1(+ve);MC3R(+ve) neurons in the hypothalamus are sufficient to restore "normal" activity of NAG neurons. This could indicate a developmental role in which NAG neurons fail to develop normal responses to altered signals of metabolic state in the absence of MC3Rs. Alternatively, MC3Rs in the mature hypothalamus may exert an active "gating" function; determining whether rescuing MC3Rs in the adult mouse restores responses of NAG neurons to metabolic cues could address this question.

MC3Rs expressed in the limbic system may regulate feeding-related motivational responses. MC3Rs are expressed in dopamine transporter (DAT) (+ve) and (−ve) neurons in the VTA, with female *Mc3r*-deficient mice exhibiting lower dopamine and altered sucrose consumption and taste preferences (Lippert et al., 2014). Operant conditioning experiments suggest increased food-related motivational responses associated with hypocaloric diets are attenuated in *Mc3r*-deficient mice. Rescuing *Mc3r* transcription in DAT(+ve) neurons in the VTA improved motivational responses (Mavrikaki et al., 2016) without restoring binge-feeding observed following the prolonged inter-meal interval. Compulsive behavioral responses to consume large meals in situations of negative energy balance may thus require MC3R activation in additional brain areas, and not only in the limbic system. A caveat to interpreting these studies is that they only used male mice; sex differences in the functions of MC3Rs in regulating feeding-related reward pathways exist (Lippert et al., 2014). Further studies using LoxTB*MC3R* mice to investigate the role of MC3Rs expressed in the VTA of females in regulate sucrose consumption and taste preferences are clearly needed.

MELANOCORTIN-3 RECEPTORS: ROLE IN METABOLIC CONTROL

Early experiments examining hypophyseal and autonomic outputs from the CNS controlling metabolism by melanocortins suggested no requirement for MC3R signaling. Acute stimulation of sympathetic activity by melanotan-II (MTII), an α–MSH analog, requires functional MC4Rs (Haynes et al., 1999). The regulation of energy expenditure by melanocortins is mediated by MC4Rs expressed by cholinergic sympathetic preganglionic neurons; glucose control involves MC4Rs expressed on both sympathetic and parasympathetic cholinergic preganglionic neurons (Rossi et al., 2011; Sohn et al., 2013; Berglund et al., 2014).

Similar to appetite control, the role of MC3Rs in metabolic homeostasis may also be contextual. We have reported two studies suggesting that MC3R signaling has a role in maintaining metabolic homeostasis and insulin sensitivity. The first study examined metabolic responses of *Mc3r−/−* mice subjected to the hypocaloric conditioning protocol used to induce FAA (Sutton et al., 2010; Begriche et al., 2011b; Girardet et al., 2014b). *Mc3r−/−* mice fed a single low-fat/high carbohydrate meal at 24 h intervals exhibited rhythms in hyperinsulinemia and insulin-regulated genes involved in lipid synthesis in the liver that peaked around meal presentation. This outcome suggests partial insulin resistance, with hepatic insulin sensitivity retained while other tissues (presumably skeletal muscle) are insulin resistant. While rhythms in insulin and glucose *ad libitum* fed *Mc3r−/−* mice were normal, this result might be misleading. Fasting insulin, fasting glucose and glucose tolerance are normal in muscle-specific insulin receptor knockout mice (MIRKO) (Bruning et al., 1998). Moreover, muscle insulin resistance redistributes nutrients to adipose tissue, increasing adiposity (Kim et al., 2000). It is therefore possible that *Mc3r−/−* mice are insulin resistant in skeletal muscle; showing this is the case requires more sensitive methodologies for measuring glucose metabolism. It might also be informative to examine entrainment of metabolic control to hypocaloric conditioning in MIRKO.

The second study involved rescuing *Mc3r* expression in steroidogenic factor-1 (SF1, also known as NR5A1) expressing neurons in the VMH (Begriche et al., 2011a). Early studies using in situ hybridization revealed the VMH as a site of dense *Mc3r* expression (Roselli-Rehfuss et al., 1993). Mice expressing Cre in VMH SF1(+ve) neurons (SF1-Cre) have been used to manipulate the expression of genes expressing hormone and growth factor receptors (leptin, insulin, estrogen, BDNF), second messenger signaling pathways and transcription factors involved in metabolic control (Kim et al., 2011; Klöckener et al., 2011; Orozco-Solis et al., 2015, 2016; Berger et al., 2016). VMH SF1(+ve) regulate glucose metabolism, regulate glucose production (Tong et al., 2007; Garfield et al., 2014; Meek et al., 2016). SF1(+ve) neurons are thus involved in the defense of body weight and metabolic control.

We crossed SF1-Cre and LoxTB*Mc3r* mice, rescuing Mc3r expression in the VMH (VMH-MC3R). Analysis of body composition (fat mass, fat-free mass) using a regression approach (Packard and Boardman, 1988; Allison et al., 1995) indicates that the nutrient partitioning phenotype is not rescued (**Figures 2A–C**). The expression of FAA was also not rescued (Begriche et al., 2011a). However, significant improvements in fasting insulin were observed in the absence of changes in fasting glucose (**Figures 2D,E**). In addition, changes in hepatic gene expression suggesting increased fatty acid flux were also partially reversed (Begriche et al., 2011a). The dissociation of the effects of MC3R on obesity from altered metabolic control suggests that MC3Rs expressed by SF1(+ve) neurons in the VMH are involved in metabolic control.

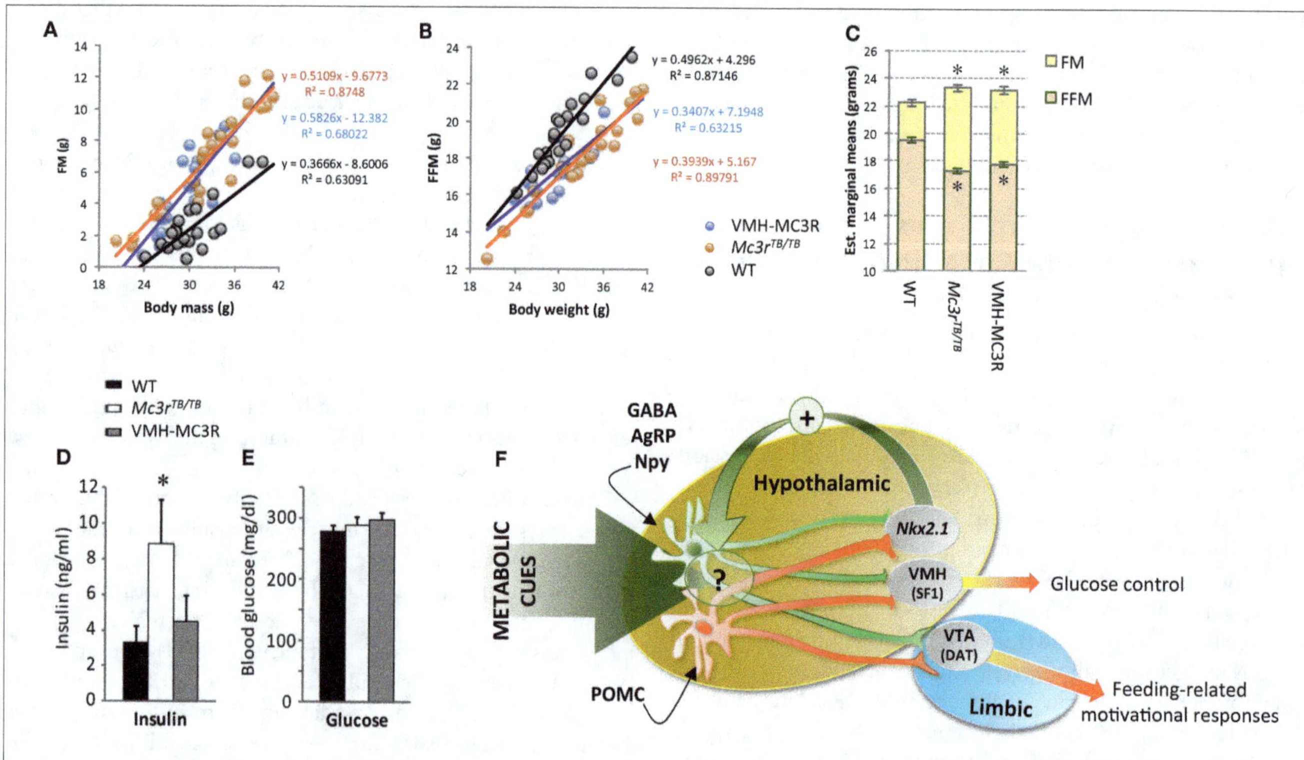

FIGURE 2 | Improved insulin sensitivity in VMH-MC3R mice is independent of reduced adiposity (A–E) and model describing the physiological roles of MC3Rs in the brain **(F)**. A regression approach plotting fat mass (FM, **A**) and fat-free mass (FFM, **B**) determined using NMR demonstrates the nutrient partitioning phenotype. As body mass increases, gains in FM are proportionately increased while gains in FFM are proportionately reduced in homozygous carriers of the "lox-stop-stop" suppressed *Mc3r* gene (*Mc3r*$^{TB/TB}$). Analysis of body composition using analysis of covariance (ANCOVA) using total body mass as a covariate indicates the predicted reduction of FFM and increased FM in *Mc3r*$^{TB/TB}$ mice. In *Mc3r*$^{TB/TB}$ mice where transcription in the ventromedial hypothalamus has been rescued (VMH-MC3R), the slope of association between FM and FFM as a function of body mass is similar to *Mc3r*$^{TB/TB}$ mice **(A,B)**; estimated marginal means derived from ANCOVA are also similar in VMH-MC3R and *Mc3r*$^{TB/TB}$ mice **(C)**. Fasting insulins are significantly increased in *Mc3r*$^{TB/TB}$ mice compared to controls and VMH-MC3R mice (**D**, $^{*}p < 0.05$), with no difference in blood glucose **(E)**. Model describing functional distribution of MC3Rs in the CNS suggested by studies using Cre transgenes to restore transcription in the VMH (SF1-Cre), VTA (DAT-Cre) and hypothalamus (Nkx2.1-Cre). MC3Rs expressed on SF1(+ve) neurons in the VMH are sufficient to improve metabolic control, while MC3Rs expressed in dopamine transporter (DAT) (+ve) neurons in the VTA restore feeding-related motivational responses during situations of caloric insufficiency. MC3Rs expressed in Nkx2.1-Cre(+ve) neurons are sufficient to restore normal responses of NAG (GABA/AgRP/Npy) neurons to signals of negative energy state, and for expression of food anticipatory activity and binge-feeding responses during situations of negative balance. While some Nkx2.1(+ve);MC3R(+ve) neurons reside in the hypothalamus, their specific location and identity remain unknown. In addition, while the actions of Nkx2.1(+ve);MC3R(+ve) neurons appears to be critical for the normal regulation of NAG neurons in response to metabolic cues, the underlying mechanism remains unknown.

Regulation of peripheral metabolism by MC3Rs may not be "acute," in that stimulation of MC3Rs in the absence of MC4Rs does not produce rapid changes. However, reduced fasting insulin in *Mc4r−/−* mice treated with an MSH analog for 14d suggests MC4R-independent effects on insulin sensitivity (Kumar et al., 2009). Whether this response involved MC3Rs expressed in the VMH or elsewhere has not been determined.

SUMMARY AND FUTURE PERSPECTIVES

The functions of neural MC3Rs received little attention after the publication of the phenotypes of *Mc3r−/−* mice in 2000. However, MC3Rs in the CNS regulate feeding-related motivational behaviors and glucose homeostasis. Both phenotypes appear to be context-dependent, increasing in prevalence with negative energy balance. Hypothalamic MC3R signaling maintains sensitivity of the nutrient-sensing networks in the hypothalamus to signals of metabolic condition (**Figure 2E**). In humans, *MC3R* polymorphisms have been associated with reduced interest in food (Lee et al., 2007; Obregon et al., 2010; Aris et al., 2015). Given the contextual nature of the feeding phenotype in mice, studies examining feeding behavior in humans with *MC3R* polymorphisms should consider energy balance in their experimental design. Finally, while making progress in identifying MC3Rs involved in appetite control, the location(s) of MC3Rs affecting nutrient partitioning remains unclear.

AUTHOR CONTRIBUTIONS

AB prepared the first manuscript draft. CG, MM, JT, HM, DM, and SF reviewed and edited the manuscript.

Biomedical Research Foundation, Clinical Nutrition Center Grant P30 DK072476 ("Nutritional Programming: Environmental and Molecular Interactions"), The Scripps Florida Fund and financial support from Saint Louis University.

REFERENCES

Albarado, D. C., McClaine, J., Stephens, J. M., Mynatt, R. L., Ye, J., Bannon, A. W., et al. (2004). Impaired coordination of nutrient intake and substrate oxidation in melanocortin-4 receptor knockout mice. *Endocrinology* 145, 243–252. doi: 10.1210/en.2003-0452

Allison, D. B., Paultre, F., Goran, M. I., Poehlman, E. T., and Heymsfield, S. B. (1995). Statistical considerations regarding the use of ratios to adjust data. *Int. J. Obes. Relat. Metab. Disord.* 19, 644–652.

Anderson, E. J., Çakir, I., Carrington, S. J., Cone, R. D., Ghamari-Langroudi, M., Gillyard, T., et al. (2016). 60 YEARS OF POMC: regulation of feeding and energy homeostasis by α-MSH. *J. Mol. Endocrinol.* 56, T157–T174. doi: 10.1530/JME-16-0014

Aponte, Y., Atasoy, D., and Sternson, S. M. (2011). AGRP neurons are sufficient to orchestrate feeding behavior rapidly and without training. *Nat. Neurosci.* 14, 351–355. doi: 10.1038/nn.2739

Aris, I. M., Tint, M. T., Teh, A. L., Holbrook, J. D., Quah, P. L., Chong, M. F., et al. (2015). MC3R gene polymorphisms are associated with early childhood adiposity gain and infant appetite in an Asian population. *Pediatr. Obes.* 11, 450–458. doi: 10.1111/ijpo.12086

Begriche, K., Levasseur, P. R., Zhang, J., Rossi, J., Skorupa, D., Solt, L. A., et al. (2011a). Genetic dissection of the functions of the melanocortin-3 receptor, a seven-transmembrane G-protein-coupled receptor, suggests roles for central and peripheral receptors in energy homeostasis. *J. Biol. Chem.* 286, 40771–40781. doi: 10.1074/jbc.M111.278374

Begriche, K., Marston, O. J., Rossi, J., Burke, L. K., McDonald, P., Heisler, L. K., et al. (2012). Melanocortin-3 receptors are involved in adaptation to restricted feeding. *Genes Brain Behav.* 11, 291–302. doi: 10.1111/j.1601-183X.2012.00766.x

Begriche, K., Sutton, G. M., and Butler, A. A. (2011b). Homeostastic and non-homeostatic functions of melanocortin-3 receptors in the control of energy balance and metabolism. *Physiol. Behav.* 104, 546–554. doi: 10.1016/j.physbeh.2011.04.007

Benite-Ribeiro, S. A., Putt, D. A., Soares-Filho, M. C., and Santos, J. M. (2016). The link between hypothalamic epigenetic modifications and long-term feeding control. *Appetite* 107, 445–453. doi: 10.1016/j.appet.2016.08.111

Berger, A., Kablan, A., Yao, C., Ho, T., Podyma, B., Weinstein, L. S., et al. (2016). Gsalpha deficiency in the ventromedial hypothalamus enhances leptin sensitivity and improves glucose homeostasis in mice on a high-fat diet. *Endocrinology* 157, 600–610. doi: 10.1210/en.2015-1700

Berglund, E. D., Liu, T., Kong, X., Sohn, J. W., Vong, L., Deng, Z., et al. (2014). Melanocortin 4 receptors in autonomic neurons regulate thermogenesis and glycemia. *Nat. Neurosci.* 17, 911–913. doi: 10.1038/nn.3737

Betley, J. N., Xu, S., Cao, Z. F., Gong, R., Magnus, C. J., Yu, Y., et al. (2015). Neurons for hunger and thirst transmit a negative-valence teaching signal. *Nature* 521, 180–185. doi: 10.1038/nature14416

Bewick, G. A., Gardiner, J. V., Dhillo, W. S., Kent, A. S., White, N. E., Webster, Z., et al. (2005). Post-embryonic ablation of AgRP neurons in mice leads to a lean, hypophagic phenotype. *FASEB J.* 19, 1680–1682. doi: 10.1096/fj.04-3434fje

Brüning, J. C., Michael, M. D., Winnay, J. N., Hayashi, T., Hörsch, D., Accili, D., et al. (1998). A muscle-specific insulin receptor knockout exhibits features of the metabolic syndrome of NIDDM without altering glucose tolerance. *Mol. Cell* 2, 559–569. doi: 10.1016/S1097-2765(00)80155-0

Bruss, M. D., Khambatta, C. F., Ruby, M. A., Aggarwal, I., and Hellerstein, M. K. (2010). Calorie restriction increases fatty acid synthesis and whole body fat oxidation rates. *Am. J. Physiol. Endocrinol. Metab.* 298, E108–E116. doi: 10.1152/ajpendo.00524.2009

Bumaschny, V. F., Yamashita, M., Casas-Cordero, R., Otero-Corchón, V., de Souza, F. S., Rubinstein, M., et al. (2012). Obesity-programmed mice are rescued by early genetic intervention. *J. Clin. Invest.* 122, 4203–4212. doi: 10.1172/JCI62543

Burke, L. K., and Heisler, L. K. (2015). 5-hydroxytryptamine medications for the treatment of obesity. *J. Neuroendocrinol.* 27, 389–398. doi: 10.1111/jne.12287

Butler, A. A. (2006). The melanocortin system and energy balance. *Peptides* 27, 281–290. doi: 10.1016/j.peptides.2005.02.029

Butler, A. A., Kesterson, R. A., Khong, K., Cullen, M. J., Pelleymounter, M. A., Dekoning, J., et al. (2000). A unique metabolic syndrome causes obesity in the melanocortin-3 receptor-deficient mouse. *Endocrinology* 141, 3518–3521. doi: 10.1210/endo.141.9.7791

Butler, A. A., and Kozak, L. P. (2010). A recurring problem with the analysis of energy expenditure in genetic models expressing lean and obese phenotypes. *Diabetes* 59, 323–329. doi: 10.2337/db09-1471

Butler, A. A., Marks, D. L., Fan, W., Kuhn, C. M., Bartolome, M., and Cone, R. D. (2001). Melanocortin-4 receptor is required for acute homeostatic responses to increased dietary fat. *Nat. Neurosci.* 4, 605–611. doi: 10.1038/88423

Chen, A. S., Marsh, D. J., Trumbauer, M. E., Frazier, E. G., Guan, X. M., Yu, H., et al. (2000a). Inactivation of the mouse melanocortin-3 receptor results in increased fat mass and reduced lean body mass. *Nat. Genet.* 26, 97–102. doi: 10.1038/79254

Chen, A. S., Metzger, J. M., Trumbauer, M. E., Guan, X. M., Yu, H., Frazier, E. G., et al. (2000b). Role of the melanocortin-4 receptor in metabolic rate and food intake in mice. *Transgenic Res.* 9, 145–154. doi: 10.1023/A:1008983615045

Chen, K. Y., Muniyappa, R., Abel, B. S., Mullins, K. P., Staker, P., Brychta, R. J., et al. (2015). RM-493, a melanocortin-4 receptor (MC4R) agonist, increases resting energy expenditure in obese individuals. *J. Clin. Endocrinol. Metab.* 100, 1639–1645. doi: 10.1210/jc.2014-4024

Collins, S., Martin, T. L., Surwit, R. S., and Robidoux, J. (2004). Genetic vulnerability to diet-induced obesity in the C57BL/6J mouse: physiological and molecular characteristics. *Physiol. Behav.* 81, 243–248. doi: 10.1016/j.physbeh.2004.02.006

Cone, R. D. (2005). Anatomy and regulation of the central melanocortin system. *Nat. Neurosci.* 8, 571–578. doi: 10.1038/nn1455

Cone, R. D. (2006). Studies on the physiological functions of the melanocortin system. *Endocr. Rev.* 27, 736–749. doi: 10.1210/er.2006-0034

Cone, R. D., Lu, D., Koppula, S., Vage, D. I., Klungland, H., Boston, B., et al. (1996). The melanocortin receptors: agonists, antagonists, and the hormonal control of pigmentation. *Recent Prog. Horm. Res.* 51, 287–317. discussion: 318.

Cortés, R., Navarro, S., Agulleiro, M. J., Guillot, R., García-Herranz, V., Sánchez, E., et al. (2014). Evolution of the melanocortin system. *Gen. Comp. Endocrinol.* 209C, 3–10. doi: 10.1016/j.ygcen.2014.04.005

Ellacott, K. L., Murphy, J. G., Marks, D. L., and Cone, R. D. (2007). Obesity-induced inflammation in white adipose tissue is attenuated by loss of melanocortin-3 receptor signaling. *Endocrinology* 148, 6186–6194. doi: 10.1210/en.2007-0699

Fan, W., Boston, B. A., Kesterson, R. A., Hruby, V. J., and Cone, R. D. (1997). Role of melanocortinergic neurons in feeding and the agouti obesity syndrome. *Nature* 385, 165–168. doi: 10.1038/385165a0

Farooqi, I. S., and O'Rahilly, S. (2008). Mutations in ligands and receptors of the leptin-melanocortin pathway that lead to obesity. *Nat. Clin. Pract. Endocrinol. Metab.* 4, 569–577. doi: 10.1038/ncpendmet0966

Feng, N., Young, S. F., Aguilera, G., Puricelli, E., Adler-Wailes, D. C., Sebring, N. G., et al. (2005). Co-occurrence of two partially inactivating polymorphisms of MC3R is associated with pediatric-onset obesity. *Diabetes* 54, 2663–2667. doi: 10.2337/diabetes.54.9.2663

Garfield, A. S., Shah, B. P., Madara, J. C., Burke, L. K., Patterson, C. M., Flak, J., et al. (2014). A parabrachial-hypothalamic cholecystokinin neurocircuit controls counterregulatory responses to hypoglycemia. *Cell Metab.* 20, 1030–1037. doi: 10.1016/j.cmet.2014.11.006

Gautron, L., Elmquist, J. K., and Williams, K. W. (2015). Neural control of energy balance: translating circuits to therapies. *Cell* 161, 133–145. doi: 10.1016/j.cell.2015.02.023

Girardet, C., Begriche, K., Ptitsyn, A., Koza, R. A., and Butler, A. A. (2014b). Unravelling the mysterious roles of melanocortin-3 receptors in metabolic homeostasis and obesity using mouse genetics. *Int. J. Obes. Suppl.* 4, S37–S44. doi: 10.1038/ijosup.2014.10

Girardet, C., and Butler, A. A. (2014). Neural melanocortin receptors in obesity and related metabolic disorders. *Biochim. Biophys. Acta* 1842, 482–494. doi: 10.1016/j.bbadis.2013.05.004

Girardet, C., Mavrikaki, M., Southern, M. R., Smith, R. G., and Butler, A. A. (2014a). Assessing interactions between Ghsr and Mc3r reveals a role for AgRP in the expression of food anticipatory activity in male mice. *Endocrinology* 155, 4843–4855. doi: 10.1210/en.2014-1497

Girardet, C., Mavrikaki, M., Stevens, J. R., Marks, D. L., Miller, C. A., and Butler, A. A. (2017). Melanocortin-3 receptors expressed in Nkx2.1(+ ve) neurons are sufficient for controlling appetitive responses to hypocaloric conditioning. *Sci. Rep.* 7:44444. doi: 10.1038/srep44444

Greenfield, J. R. (2011). Melanocortin signalling and the regulation of blood pressure in human obesity. *J. Neuroendocrinol.* 23, 186–193. doi: 10.1111/j.1365-2826.2010.02088.x

Hahn, T. M., Breininger, J. F., Baskin, D. G., and Schwartz, M. W. (1998). Coexpression of Agrp and NPY in fasting-activated hypothalamic neurons. *Nat. Neurosci.* 1, 271–272. doi: 10.1038/1082

Haynes, W. G., Morgan, D. A., Djalali, A., Sivitz, W. I., and Mark, A. L. (1999). Interactions between the melanocortin system and leptin in control of sympathetic nerve traffic. *Hypertension* 33, 542–547. doi: 10.1161/01.HYP.33.1.542

Heisler, L. K., Cowley, M. A., Tecott, L. H., Fan, W., Low, M. J., Smart, J. L., et al. (2002). Activation of central melanocortin pathways by fenfluramine. *Science* 297, 609–611. doi: 10.1126/science.1072327

Heisler, L. K., Jobst, E. E., Sutton, G. M., Zhou, L., Borok, E., Thornton-Jones, Z., et al. (2006). Serotonin reciprocally regulates melanocortin neurons to modulate food intake. *Neuron* 51, 239–249. doi: 10.1016/j.neuron.2006.06.004

Hill, J. O., Wyatt, H. R., and Peters, J. C. (2012). Energy balance and obesity. *Circulation* 126, 126–132. doi: 10.1161/CIRCULATIONAHA.111.087213

Huszar, D., Lynch, C. A., Fairchild-Huntress, V., Dunmore, J. H., Fang, Q., Berkemeier, L. R., et al. (1997). Targeted disruption of the melanocortin-4 receptor results in obesity in mice. *Cell* 88, 131–141. doi: 10.1016/S0092-8674(00)81865-6

Ibrahim, N., Bosch, M. A., Smart, J. L., Qiu, J., Rubinstein, M., RØnnekleiv, O. K., et al. (2003). Hypothalamic proopiomelanocortin neurons are glucose responsive and express K(ATP) channels. *Endocrinology* 144, 1331–1340. doi: 10.1210/en.2002-221033

Kaelin, C. B., Candille, S. I., Yu, B., Jackson, P., Thompson, D. A., Nix, M. A., et al. (2008). New ligands for melanocortin receptors. *Int. J. Obes.* 32(Suppl. 7), S19–S27. doi: 10.1038/ijo.2008.234

Kievit, P., Halem, H., Marks, D. L., Dong, J. Z., Glavas, M. M., Sinnayah, P., et al. (2013). Chronic treatment with a melanocortin-4 receptor agonist causes weight loss, reduces insulin resistance, and improves cardiovascular function in diet-induced obese rhesus macaques. *Diabetes* 62, 490–497. doi: 10.2337/db12-0598

Kim, J. K., Michael, M. D., Previs, S. F., Peroni, O. D., Mauvais-Jarvis, F., Neschen, S., et al. (2000). Redistribution of substrates to adipose tissue promotes obesity in mice with selective insulin resistance in muscle. *J. Clin. Invest.* 105, 1791–1797. doi: 10.1172/JCI8305

Kim, K. W., Sohn, J. W., Kohno, D., Xu, Y., Williams, K., and Elmquist, J. K. (2011). SF-1 in the ventral medial hypothalamic nucleus: a key regulator of homeostasis. *Mol. Cell. Endocrinol.* 336, 219–223. doi: 10.1016/j.mce.2010.11.019

Kishi, T., Aschkenasi, C. J., Lee, C. E., Mountjoy, K. G., Saper, C. B., and Elmquist, J. K. (2003). Expression of melanocortin 4 receptor mRNA in the central nervous system of the rat. *J. Comp. Neurol.* 457, 213–235. doi: 10.1002/cne.10454

Klöckener, T., Hess, S., Belgardt, B. F., Paeger, L., Verhagen, L. A., Husch, A., et al. (2011). High-fat feeding promotes obesity via insulin receptor/PI3K-dependent inhibition of SF-1 VMH neurons. *Nat. Neurosci.* 14, 911–918. doi: 10.1038/nn.2847

Koch, M., Varela, L., Kim, J. G., Kim, J. D., Hernández-Nuño, F., Simonds, S. E., et al. (2015). Hypothalamic POMC neurons promote cannabinoid-induced feeding. *Nature* 519, 45–50. doi: 10.1038/nature14260

Kozak, L. P., and Anunciado-Koza, R. (2008). UCP1: its involvement and utility in obesity. *Int. J. Obes.* 32(Suppl. 7), S32–S38. doi: 10.1038/ijo.2008.236

Krashes, M. J., Koda, S., Ye, C., Rogan, S. C., Adams, A. C., Cusher, D. S., et al. (2011). Rapid, reversible activation of AgRP neurons drives feeding behavior in mice. *J. Clin. Invest.* 121, 1424–1428. doi: 10.1172/JCI46229

Krashes, M. J., Shah, B. P., Koda, S., and Lowell, B. B. (2013). Rapid versus delayed stimulation of feeding by the endogenously released AgRP neuron mediators GABA, NPY, and AgRP. *Cell Metab.* 18, 588–595. doi: 10.1016/j.cmet.2013.09.009

Krashes, M. J., Shah, B. P., Madara, J. C., Olson, D. P., Strochlic, D. E., Garfield, A. S., et al. (2014). An excitatory paraventricular nucleus to AgRP neuron circuit that drives hunger. *Nature* 507, 238–242. doi: 10.1038/nature12956

Kühnen, P., Handke, D., Waterland, R. A., Hennig, B. J., Silver, M., Fulford, A. J., et al. (2016). Interindividual variation in DNA methylation at a putative POMC metastable epiallele is associated with obesity. *Cell Metab.* 24, 502–509. doi: 10.1016/j.cmet.2016.08.001

Kumar, K. G., Sutton, G. M., Dong, J. Z., Roubert, P., Plas, P., Halem, H. A., et al. (2009). Analysis of the therapeutic functions of novel melanocortin receptor agonists in MC3R- and MC4R-deficient C57BL/6J mice. *Peptides* 30, 1892–1900. doi: 10.1016/j.peptides.2009.07.012

Lee, B., Koo, J., Yun Jun, J., Gavrilova, O., Lee, Y., Seo, A. Y., et al. (2016). A mouse model for a partially inactive obesity-associated human MC3R variant. *Nat. Commun.* 7:10522. doi: 10.1038/ncomms10522

Lee, Y. S. (2012). Melanocortin 3 receptor gene and melanocortin 4 receptor gene mutations: the Asian Perspective. *Diabetes Metab. Res. Rev.* 28(Suppl. 2), 26–31. doi: 10.1002/dmrr.2351

Lee, Y. S., Poh, L. K., Kek, B. L., and Loke, K. Y. (2007). The role of melanocortin 3 receptor gene in childhood obesity. *Diabetes* 56, 2622–2630. doi: 10.2337/db07-0225

Lewis, C. E., McTigue, K. M., Burke, L. E., Poirier, P., Eckel, R. H., Howard, B. V., et al. (2009). Mortality, health outcomes, and body mass index in the overweight range: a science advisory from the American Heart Association. *Circulation* 119, 3263–3271. doi: 10.1161/CIRCULATIONAHA.109.192574

Li, Y. Q., Shrestha, Y., Pandey, M., Chen, M., Kablan, A., Gavrilova, O., et al. (2016). G(q/11)alpha and G(s)alpha mediate distinct physiological responses to central melanocortins. *J. Clin. Invest.* 126, 40–49. doi: 10.1172/JCI76348

Lippert, R. N., Ellacott, K. L., and Cone, R. D. (2014). Gender-specific roles for the melanocortin-3 receptor in the regulation of the mesolimbic dopamine system in mice. *Endocrinology* 155, 1718–1727. doi: 10.1210/en.2013-2049

Liu, H., Kishi, T., Roseberry, A. G., Cai, X., Lee, C. E., Montez, J. M., et al. (2003). Transgenic mice expressing green fluorescent protein under the control of the melanocortin-4 receptor promoter. *J. Neurosci.* 23, 7143–7154.

Luquet, S., Perez, F. A., Hnasko, T. S., and Palmiter, R. D. (2005). NPY/AgRP neurons are essential for feeding in adult mice but can be ablated in neonates. *Science* 310, 683–685. doi: 10.1126/science.1115524

Marsh, D. J., Hollopeter, G., Huszar, D., Laufer, R., Yagaloff, K. A., Fisher, S. L., et al. (1999). Response of melanocortin-4 receptor-deficient mice to anorectic and orexigenic peptides. *Nat. Genet.* 21, 119–122. doi: 10.1038/5070

Mauvais-Jarvis, F., Clegg, D. J., and Hevener, A. L. (2013). The role of estrogens in control of energy balance and glucose homeostasis. *Endocr. Rev.* 34, 309–338. doi: 10.1210/er.2012-1055

Mavrikaki, M., Girardet, C., Kern, A., Faruzzi Brantley, A., Miller, C. A., Macarthur, H., et al. (2016). Melanocortin-3 receptors in the limbic system mediate feeding-related motivational responses during weight loss. *Mol. Metab.* 5, 566–579. doi: 10.1016/j.molmet.2016.05.002

Meek, T. H., Nelson, J. T., Matsen, M. E., Dorfman, M. D., Guyenet, S. J., Damian, V., et al. (2016). Functional identification of a neurocircuit regulating blood glucose. *Proc. Natl. Acad. Sci. U.S.A.* 113, E2073–E2082. doi: 10.1073/pnas.1521160113

Mistlberger, R. E. (2011). Neurobiology of food anticipatory circadian rhythms. *Physiol. Behav.* 104, 535–545. doi: 10.1016/j.physbeh.2011.04.015

Mohawk, J. A., Green, C. B., and Takahashi, J. S. (2012). Central and peripheral circadian clocks in mammals. *Annu. Rev. Neurosci.* 35, 445–462. doi: 10.1146/annurev-neuro-060909-153128

Morello, G., Imperatore, R., Palomba, L., Finelli, C., Labruna, G., Pasanisi, F., et al. (2016). Orexin-A represses satiety-inducing POMC neurons and contributes to obesity via stimulation of endocannabinoid signaling. *Proc. Natl. Acad. Sci. U.S.A.* 113, 4759–4764. doi: 10.1073/pnas.1521304113

Mountjoy, K. G., Mortrud, M. T., Low, M. J., Simerly, R. B., and Cone, R. D. (1994). Localization of the melanocortin-4 receptor (MC4-R) in neuroendocrine and autonomic control circuits in the brain. *Mol. Endocrinol.* 8, 1298–1308.

Nix, M. A., Kaelin, C. B., Palomino, R., Miller, J. L., Barsh, G. S., and Millhauser, G. L. (2015). Electrostatic similarity analysis of human β-defensin binding in the melanocortin system. *Biophys. J.* 109, 1946–1958. doi: 10.1016/j.bpj.2015.09.005

Nix, M. A., Kaelin, C. B., Ta, T., Weis, A., Morton, G. J., Barsh, G. S., et al. (2013). Molecular and functional analysis of human beta-defensin 3 action at melanocortin receptors. *Chem. Biol.* 20, 784–795. doi: 10.1016/j.chembiol.2013.04.015

Obregon, A. M., Amador, P., Valladares, M., Weisstaub, G., Burrows, R., and Santos, J. L. (2010). Melanocortin-3 receptor gene variants: association with childhood obesity and eating behavior in Chilean families. *Nutrition* 26, 760–765. doi: 10.1016/j.nut.2009.07.005

Ollmann, M. M., Wilson, B. D., Yang, Y. K., Kerns, J. A., Chen, Y., Gantz, I., et al. (1997). Antagonism of central melanocortin receptors *in vitro* and *in vivo* by agouti-related protein. *Science* 278, 135–138. doi: 10.1126/science.278.5335.135

Orozco-Solis, R., Aguilar-Arnal, L., Murakami, M., Peruquetti, R., Ramadori, G., Coppari, R., et al. (2016). The circadian clock in the ventromedial hypothalamus controls cyclic energy expenditure. *Cell Metab.* 23, 467–478. doi: 10.1016/j.cmet.2016.02.003

Orozco-Solis, R., Ramadori, G., Coppari, R., and Sassone-Corsi, P. (2015). SIRT1 relays nutritional inputs to the circadian clock through the Sf1 neurons of the ventromedial hypothalamus. *Endocrinology* 156, 2174–2184. doi: 10.1210/en.2014-1805

Packard, G. C., and Boardman, T. J. (1988). The misuse of ratios, indices, and percentages in ecophysiological research. *Physiol. Zool.* 61, 1–9. doi: 10.1086/physzool.61.1.30163730

Parton, L. E., Ye, C. P., Coppari, R., Enriori, P. J., Choi, B., Zhang, C. Y., et al. (2007). Glucose sensing by POMC neurons regulates glucose homeostasis and is impaired in obesity. *Nature* 449, 228–232. doi: 10.1038/nature06098

Renquist, B. J., Murphy, J. G., Larson, E. A., Olsen, D., Klein, R. F., Ellacott, K. L., et al. (2012). Melanocortin-3 receptor regulates the normal fasting response. *Proc. Natl. Acad. Sci. U.S.A.* 109, E1489–E1498. doi: 10.1073/pnas.1201994109

Roselli-Rehfuss, L., Mountjoy, K. G., Robbins, L. S., Mortrud, M. T., Low, M. J., Tatro, J. B., et al. (1993). Identification of a receptor for gamma melanotropin and other proopiomelanocortin peptides in the hypothalamus and limbic system. *Proc. Natl. Acad. Sci. U.S.A.* 90, 8856–8860. doi: 10.1073/pnas.90.19.8856

Rossi, J., Balthasar, N., Olson, D., Scott, M., Berglund, E., Lee, C. E., et al. (2011). Melanocortin-4 receptors expressed by cholinergic neurons regulate energy balance and glucose homeostasis. *Cell Metab.* 13, 195–204. doi: 10.1016/j.cmet.2011.01.010

Shutter, J. R., Graham, M., Kinsey, A. C., Scully, S., Luthy, R., and Stark, K. L. (1997). Hypothalamic expression of ART, a novel gene related to agouti, is up-regulated in obese and diabetic mutant mice. *Genes Dev.* 11, 593–602. doi: 10.1101/gad.11.5.593

Small, C. J., Kim, M. S., Stanley, S. A., Mitchell, J. R., Murphy, K., Morgan, D. G., et al. (2001). Effects of chronic central nervous system administration of agouti-related protein in pair-fed animals. *Diabetes* 50, 248–254. doi: 10.2337/diabetes.50.2.248

Smart, J. L., Tolle, V., and Low, M. J. (2006). Glucocorticoids exacerbate obesity and insulin resistance in neuron-specific proopiomelanocortin-deficient mice. *J. Clin. Invest.* 116, 495–505. doi: 10.1172/JCI25243

Sohn, J. W., Harris, L. E., Berglund, E. D., Liu, T., Vong, L., Lowell, B. B., et al. (2013). Melanocortin 4 receptors reciprocally regulate sympathetic and parasympathetic preganglionic neurons. *Cell* 152, 612–619. doi: 10.1016/j.cell.2012.12.022

Speakman, J. R., and O'Rahilly, S. (2012). Fat: an evolving issue. *Dis. Model. Mech.* 5, 569–573. doi: 10.1242/dmm.010553

Srisai, D., Gillum, M. P., Panaro, B. L., Zhang, X. M., Kotchabhakdi, N., Shulman, G. I., et al. (2011). Characterization of the hyperphagic response to dietary fat in the MC4R knockout mouse. *Endocrinology* 152, 890–902. doi: 10.1210/en.2010-0716

Sutton, G. M., Begriche, K., Kumar, K. G., Gimble, J. M., Perez-Tilve, D., Nogueiras, R., et al. (2010). Central nervous system melanocortin-3 receptors are required for synchronizing metabolism during entrainment to restricted feeding during the light cycle. *FASEB J.* 24, 862–872. doi: 10.1096/fj.09-142000

Sutton, G. M., Perez-Tilve, D., Nogueiras, R., Fang, J., Kim, J. K., Cone, R. D., et al. (2008). The melanocortin-3 receptor is required for entrainment to meal intake. *J. Neurosci.* 28, 12946–12955. doi: 10.1523/JNEUROSCI.3615-08.2008

Sutton, G. M., Trevaskis, J. L., Hulver, M. W., McMillan, R. P., Markward, N. J., Babin, M. J., et al. (2006). Diet-genotype interactions in the development of the obese, insulin-resistant phenotype of C57BL/6J mice lacking melanocortin-3 or -4 receptors. *Endocrinology* 147, 2183–2196. doi: 10.1210/en.2005-1209

Tan, K., Knight, Z. A., and Friedman, J. M. (2014). Ablation of AgRP neurons impairs adaption to restricted feeding. *Mol. Metab.* 3, 694–704. doi: 10.1016/j.molmet.2014.07.002

Tao, Y. X. (2010). Mutations in the melanocortin-3 receptor (MC3R) gene: impact on human obesity or adiposity. *Curr. Opin. Investig. Drugs* 11, 1092–1096.

Tong, Q., Ye, C., McCrimmon, R. J., Dhillon, H., Choi, B., Kramer, M. D., et al. (2007). Synaptic glutamate release by ventromedial hypothalamic neurons is part of the neurocircuitry that prevents hypoglycemia. *Cell Metab.* 5, 383–393. doi: 10.1016/j.cmet.2007.04.001

Tschop, M. H., Castaneda, T. R., and Woods, S. C. (2006). The brain is getting ready for dinner. *Cell Metab.* 4, 257–258. doi: 10.1016/j.cmet.2006.09.001

van den Top, M., Lee, K., Whyment, A. D., Blanks, A. M., and Spanswick, D. (2004). Orexigen-sensitive NPY/AgRP pacemaker neurons in the hypothalamic arcuate nucleus. *Nat. Neurosci.* 7, 493–494. doi: 10.1038/nn1226

Zhan, C., Zhou, J., Feng, Q., Zhang, J. E., Lin, S., Bao, J., et al. (2013). Acute and long-term suppression of feeding behavior by POMC neurons in the brainstem and hypothalamus, respectively. *J. Neurosci.* 33, 3624–3632. doi: 10.1523/JNEUROSCI.2742-12.2013

Zhou, L., Sutton, G. M., Rochford, J. J., Semple, R. K., Lam, D. D., Oksanen, L. J., et al. (2007). Serotonin 2C receptor agonists improve type 2 diabetes via melanocortin-4 receptor signaling pathways. *Cell Metab.* 6, 398–405. doi: 10.1016/j.cmet.2007.10.008

22

Retinoid X Receptors Intersect the Molecular Clockwork in the Regulation of Liver Metabolism

*Salvatore De Cosmo and Gianluigi Mazzoccoli**

Department of Medical Sciences, Division of Internal Medicine and Chronobiology Unit, IRCCS "Ospedale Casa Sollievo della Sofferenza", San Giovanni Rotondo, Italy

Edited by:
Andries Kalsbeek,
Academic Medical Center, Netherlands

Reviewed by:
Alena Sumova,
Czech Academy of Sciences, Czechia
Weizhen Zhang,
University of Michigan, USA

****Correspondence:***
Gianluigi Mazzoccoli
g.mazzoccoli@operapadrepio.it

Liver metabolic pathways are driven by the biological clock, and appropriate timing of 24-h patterns of metabolic gene expression as well as anabolic/catabolic processes with wake-related activity/feeding and sleep-related resting/fasting cycles preserves hepatic healthiness. The interplay among the liver metabolic pathways and the molecular clockwork is geared by the nuclear receptors, and ligand-dependent transcription factors that gauge the cellular nutritional status and redox balance, bind hormones and metabolites, and modulate the transcription of thousands target genes through their DNA-binding domain. Several nuclear receptors in the liver oscillate with circadian rhythmicity, and among these, the retinoid X receptors play a key role in metabolism regulation, intersecting with the cogs of the molecular clockwork.

Keywords: RXR, circadian, rhythm, clock, liver, metabolism

INTRODUCTION

The regulation of lipid and glucose metabolism in the liver requires cell sensors capable of monitoring the concentration of nutrients and coordinating the enzyme cascades that regulate the synthesis and oxidation of metabolites. In this regard, the nuclear receptors are transcription factors that act as intracellular sensors, which are able to regulate lipid and glucose metabolism. Unlike extracellular receptors, which bind to protein ligands (e.g., growth factors and insulin) at the plasma membrane and activate cytoplasmic cascades, nuclear receptors interact directly with lipophilic ligands and regulate the expression of target genes (1). Members of the nuclear receptor superfamily function as ligand-dependent transcription factors that bind to promoters of specific DNA sequences. The nuclear receptors bind hormones, such as cortisol, melatonin, and 3,5,3′-triiodothyronine, and metabolites, such as lipids, oxysterols, heme, and bile acids, and sense redox balance and nutrient levels in the cell. The nuclear receptors have in common similar domain organizations, especially the DNA-binding domain (DBD) and the ligand-binding domain (LBD) that are crucial in amplifying hormone and metabolite signaling by specifically targeted genes. Binding of specific ligands to the precise receptor prompts ligand-induced conformational variations in the receptor, receptor translocation to the nucleus, receptor dimerization, interaction with target gene promoter elements, release/recruitment of coactivators or corepressors, chromatin remodeling, and finally interplay with the polymerase II complex to start transcription (2).

THE RETINOID X RECEPTORS (RXRs)

The RXR subtypes or isotypes α–γ (NR2B1–3) are encoded by RXRα–γ genes located on chromosomes 9 (band q34.3), 6 (band 21.3), and 1 (band q22–q23), respectively, and are members of the orphan nuclear receptor family since natural ligands were unidentified at the time of their discovery (3). The first candidate natural ligand was 9-*cis*-retinoic acid (9-*cis*-RA), but many researchers were not capable to identify endogenous 9-*cis*-RA in cells either in culture or *in vivo* without existence or addition of its isomer all-trans retinoic acid (ATRA) (3). Other RXR ligands are polyunsaturated fatty acids, such as docosahexaenoic acid (22:6), arachidonic acid (20:4), and oleic acid (18:1), and a saturated metabolite of chlorophyll, phytanic acid. In the nucleus, RXR works as a transcription factor and binds as a homodimer or heterodimer (bound to a different nuclear receptor) to definite 6 bp sequences of DNA in the promoter regions of specific genes (3). The promoter site [response element (RE)] composed of two 6 bp sequences (half-sites) separated by a discrete number of bases to which the RXR–nuclear receptor heterodimer binds [5′-PuG(G/T)TCA-(X)*n*-PuG(G/T)TCA-3′] is determined through binding by the ligand of the nuclear receptor partner. The sequences may be reiterated directly (DR), inverted (IR), everted (ER), palindromic (pal), or disordered in relation to the dimer bound (3).

CIRCADIAN RHYTHMICITY AND NUCLEAR RECEPTORS

The nuclear receptor superfamily encompasses 49 members, which manage lipid and carbohydrate metabolism and harmonize various features of organ physiology, as well as tissue development and organism reproduction (4). The nuclear receptors are expressed differently in the various tissues (5) and particularly in metabolically active tissues (liver, muscle, and white and brown adipose tissues), some of which show tissue-specific rhythmic fluctuations of expression characterized by 24-h periodicity (circadian) (6). Intermediate metabolism is hallmarked by time-related changes consistent with the daily light/darkness alternation, and periodic circadian variations in the levels of nuclear receptors may prompt rhythmic oscillations of the metabolic pathways (7). The interplay between rhythmic changes of nutrient levels and ligand binding by the nuclear receptors drives periodic variations in downstream transcriptional events steering different metabolism facets. The array of rhythms is driven by the biological clock and in turn the nuclear receptors feedback to the molecular clockwork connecting circadian and metabolic pathways (7).

THE BIOLOGICAL CLOCK

The organization of about 24-h rhythmicity in organism and cellular physiology is handled in mammals by the circadian timing system, a multilevel hierarchical network comprising central oscillators in the suprachiasmatic nuclei (SCN) of the hypothalamus and self-sustaining oscillators in peripheral tissues. The SCN biological clocks respond to several entraining factors: external, such as the photic inputs perceived by the retinal ganglion cells and conveyed by the retinohypothalamic tracts, and internal, such as temperature, hormones, and metabolites. The SCN neurons drive the peripheral oscillators by way of output pathways represented by hormones (cortisol, melatonin) and autonomic nervous fibers (8). At the molecular level, the biological clock is hardwired by transcription–translation feedback loops (TTFL) revolving one cycle in approximately 24 h and operated by circadian genes and proteins. The positive limb of the loop is worked by the transcription factors Clock and Arntl, which heterodimerize and bind to E-box enhancer elements in the promoters of *Period* (*Per1-3*) and *Cryptochrome* (*Cry1-2*) genes. These genes in turn prompt the negative limb of the loop encoding Per1–3 and Cry1–2 proteins, which interact to form a repression complex that along with casein kinase Iϵ (CKIϵ) translocates back into the nucleus, where it hinders Clock:Arntl transcriptional activity (9, 10). In addition, Clock:Arntl heterodimer induces the circadian expression of *Rev-erbα* and *Rora* genes, which encode the nuclear receptors Rev-Erbα alpha and RORα respectively. In turn, Rev-Erbα negatively controls the rhythmic transcription of *Arntl* gene, competing with RORα at the specific REs (11). The circadian proteins undergo posttranslational modifications, in particular phosphorylation/dephosphorylation and acetylation/deacetylation cycles. Per1–3 and Cry1–2 proteins are substrates for at least three different enzymes operating phosphorylation: CKIδ and CKIϵ, AMPK, and glycogen synthase kinase (GSK) 3β. In particular, phosphorylation by CKIδ/ϵ targets Per1–3/Cry1–2 proteins for degradation and regulates their nuclear translocation, AMPK targets Cry1–2 proteins, and GSK3β targets Arntl (12–15). Acetylation is operated by Clock, which has protein and histone acetyltransferase activity (16), and deacetylation by SIRT1, an NAD^+-dependent protein, and histone deacetylase assuring high-magnitude circadian transcription of several core clock genes, including *Arntl*, *Per2*, and *Cry1*. SIRT1 offsets the acetyltransferase activity of Clock, binds Clock–Arntl heterodimer in a circadian manner and promotes the deacetylation and degradation of Per2 (17–19).

RXRs AND THE NUCLEAR RECEPTOR SUPERFAMILY

The molecular clockwork controls the expression of numerous clock-controlled genes and tissue-specific output genes, so that about 15–20% of the transcriptome oscillates with circadian rhythmicity and manage the rhythmic changes of cell processes (metabolism, redox and oxphos balance, autophagy, cell cycle, DNA damage response) and tissue functions (liver and renal physiology, heart function, endocrine gland secretion) (20).

Among the clock-controlled genes, some encode nuclear receptors oscillating with circadian pattern in metabolically active tissues and specifically in the liver, such as RXRs, constitutive androstane receptor (CAR), estrogen-related receptor α, β, and γ, farnesoid receptor (FXR) α and β, glucocorticoid receptor, Nur-related protein 1 (NURR1), peroxisome proliferator-activated receptor (PPAR) α, δ/β, and γ, retinoic acid receptor (RAR) α, β, and γ, small heterodimeric partner, and thyroid hormone receptor (TR) α (6). Among these, a particularly intriguing role is played by RXRs, forming heterodimers with numerous members of the nuclear receptor superfamily including PPARs, RARs, FXRs, LXRs, TRs, CAR, NURR1, and vitamin D3 receptors (VDRs) (3, 21–23). Indeed, RXRs unrestrainedly heterodimerize with these members of the nuclear receptor superfamily, and by means of these interaction, RXR ligands, also called rexinoids, either transcriptionally stimulate *per se* the permissive subclass of heterodimers (PPAR/RXR, LXR/RXR, FXR/RXR, and CAR/RXR) or synergize with partner ligands in the non-permissive subclass of heterodimers (RAR/RXR, VDR/RXR, and TR/RXR) (24–26). The permissive heterodimers become transcriptionally active in the presence of either an RXR-selective ligand (rexinoid) or a nuclear receptor partner ligand, and the simultaneous presence of both RXR and partner receptor ligands results in a cooperative, synergistic response (1). By contrast, non-permissive heterodimers are unresponsive to rexinoids alone, but these agonists superactivate transcription by synergizing with partner agonists (27).

The TR/RXR heterodimer is generally defined as non-permissive, so that RXR is supposed to act as a silent partner not capable to bind specific ligands and full activity of the TR/RXR heterodimer is achieved only upon 3,3′,5-triiodo-L-thyronine (T3) binding and not by the RXR agonist. Anyway, studies performed with a sensitive derepression assay system showed that the RXR component can bind its ligand *in vivo* in a TR/RXR heterodimer without straight activation of the TR/RXR heterodimer, but with the TR dissociating from inhibitor(s)/corepressor(s), as a minimum in a temporary or dynamic manner, leading to TR-mediated repression in the absence of a ligand and/or TR-mediated activation upon ligand binding (28). Besides, 9-*cis*-RA was proved to induce conformational changes within the TR/RXR complex and to act as an allosteric repressor of transactivation (29).

Retinoid X receptor heterodimers with PPAR, RAR, VDR, and TR consist of two directly repeated (DR) half-sites separated by one, two or five, three, and four bases (*n*), respectively, typically with RXR in the 5′-position. When the RXR heterodimer with RAR is bound to a DR-1 RE, RXR can lodge either to the 5′- or 3′-position. The RXR homodimer favorably binds two 5′-(A/G)GGTCA-3′ half-sites disjointed by one base (DR-1).

Kinases modulate the function of RXRs homo- and heterodimers. In particular, AMPK activators hinder FXRRE-bound RXR/FXR heterodimers exclusively acting on FXR hindering FXR coactivator recruitment to promoters of FXR-regulated genes and FXR transcriptional activity, whereas RXRs are not impacted (30). On the other hand, studies performed in cancer cells showed that RXRs are targeted by the CK1 family, and precisely RXR is bound and phosphorylated by CK1α in an agonist-dependent manner (31), as well as by GSK3β, with modulation of cell predisposition to RXR agonist-induced growth arrest and apoptosis and support of cell survival (32).

RXRs AND THE BIOLOGICAL CLOCK

A tight interplay has been evidenced between RXRs and the cogs of the molecular clockwork. RXRs are capable to join with members of the positive limb of TTFL with an interaction influenced by circulating factors, and RA was found able to hinder clock genes transcription both in cultured muscle cells and in cardiovascular organs from intact animals (33) (**Figure 1**). Precisely, RXRα interacted in a ligand-dependent manner with the basic helix-loop-helix proteins Npas2 and Clock (the interaction strength boosted up to 15-fold upon specific ligand binding), but not with Bmal1, hindering, as a minimum *in vitro*, transcriptional activity of Clock/Npas2–Bmal1 heterodimers at the promoters of clock genes, and RA injection prompted small phase shifts of peripheral clocks in the heart and aorta (33). Besides, ATRA, 9-*cis*-RA, and 13-*cis*-RA were found capable to entrain circadian rhythmicity in cultured fibroblasts expressing Per2-luciferase (34), and retinoic acid signaling elicited central clock resetting upon light sensing (35, 36). Moreover, RXRα–cofactor proteins interaction as well as RXR nuclear receptors heterodimerization and ligand-dependent transactivation by RXR was found to be modified and inhibited, respectively, by the basic helix-loop-helix proteins differentiated embryo chondrocyte (Dec) 1 and Dec2 (37). The expression of Dec1–2 is driven by the biological clock, oscillates with circadian pattern in the mouse SCN and liver peaking in the subjective day, and takes part in the molecular clockwork, thereby blocking Clock/Arntl-induced transactivation of the mouse *Per1* promoter through direct protein–protein interactions with Arntl and/or competition for E-box elements (38, 39). Interestingly, experiments performed in the rat showed that insulin prompts the transcription of the *Dec1* gene *via* a phosphoinositide 3-kinase pathway, further supporting a direct link between intermediary metabolism and the molecular clockwork (40).

Besides, the interplay between RXRs and the biological clock showed up remarkably in an animal model of liver regeneration, represented by partial hepatectomy in RXRα-null compared to wild-type mouse. Hepatocyte proliferation showed approximately 20-h delay after partial hepatectomy in liver RXRα-deficient mice and numerous pathways were dwindled, in particular circadian cell cycle regulation. Furthermore, in accordance with the evidence that PPARα regulates the transcription of both Arntl and Rev-erbα *via* PPAR-response and *cis*-regulatory elements in their promoters (41), the PPARα/Arntl/Rev-erbα/P21 pathway was disrupted, and Cry1/Cry2 and Wee1/Per1 expression as well as the expression and regulation of cyclin D1/cyclin-dependent kinase (Cdk) 4, cyclin E1/Cdk2, cyclin A2/Cdk2, and cyclin B1/Cdk1 were deranged in regenerating RXRα-null livers (42).

Accordingly, studies performed on the hippocampus specimens of Holtzman rats harvested at 4-h intervals for 24 h showed clock-responsive canonical and non-canonical E-box elements and RORE sites in the regulatory regions of genes encoding RARs and RXRβ, as well as retinoic acid response elements (RAREs) and RXREs in *Bmal1* and *Per1* promoters (43).

Furthermore, an interplay between the PPARs/RXRα-regulated system and the molecular clockwork was shown. PPARα/RXRα modulated Period and Cryptochrome genes transcription driven by Clock/Bmal1 heterodimers (44). In turn, Clock/Bmal1 heterodimers binding to consensus E-box elements modulated PPARs/RXRα-dependent transcription through peroxisome proliferator response element of target genes, comprising those encoding acyl-CoA oxidase (AOX), lipoprotein lipase, acyl-CoA synthase, cellular retinol-binding protein II, and 3-hydroxy-3-methylglutaryl coenzyme A (HMG-CoA) synthase (44).

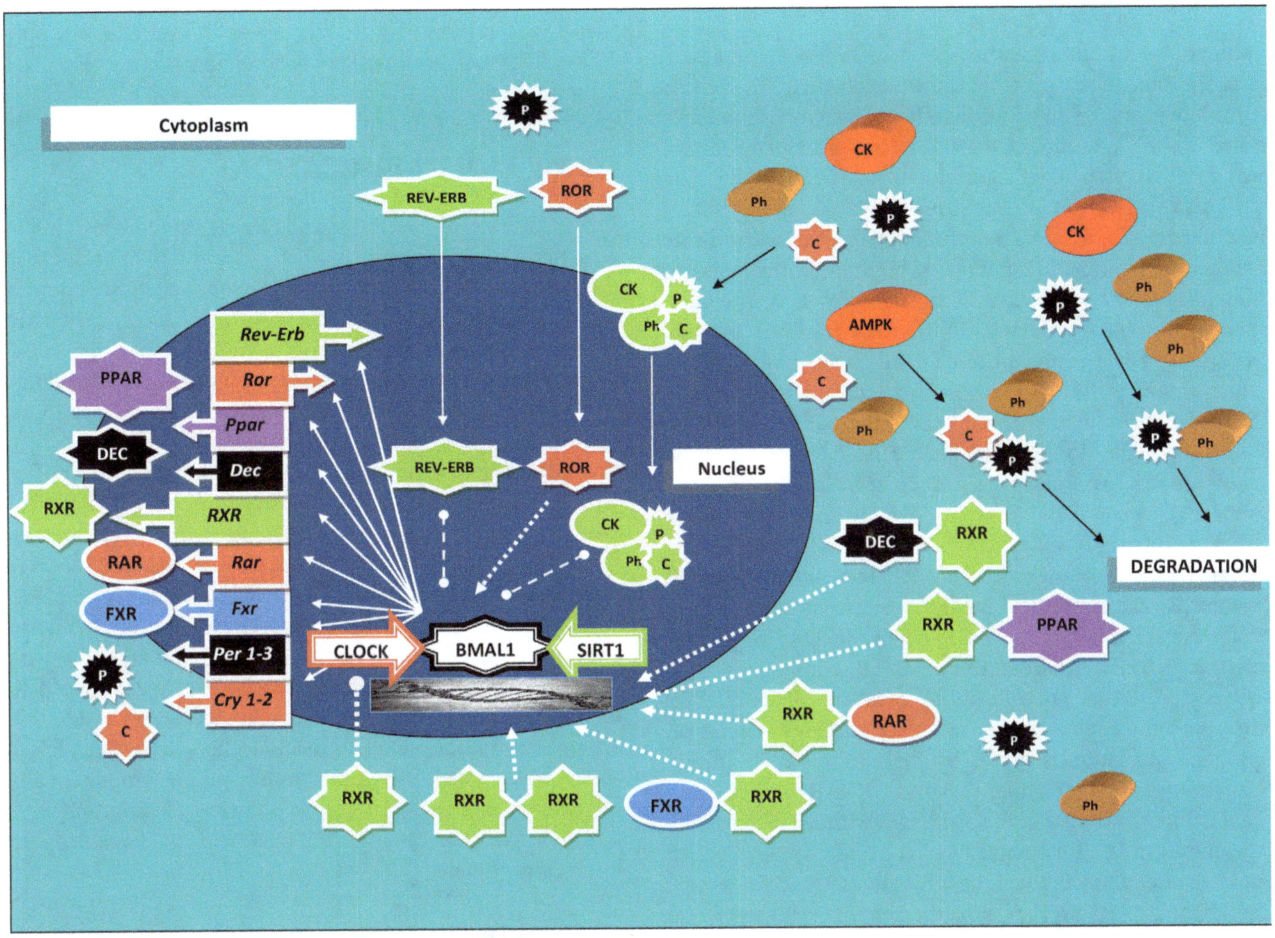

FIGURE 1 | Scheme rendering the interaction between the molecular clockwork, the retinoid X receptors, and other nuclear receptors oscillating with circadian rhythmicity; see text for acronyms explanation. Ball-ended dashed lines indicate inhibition; arrow-ended dashed lines indicate activation; arrow-ended continuous lines indicate translocation; black lines indicate modification.

RXRs AND TRANSCRIPTIONAL ACTIVITY

Retinoid X receptors as homodimers or heterodimerizing with RARs manage the signaling pathways and genetic transcriptional programs dependent on retinoids, crucial for vertebrates development and homeostasis (1, 3, 45). Non-steroid nuclear receptors bind to a core recognition element represented by the consensus sequence 5-AGGTCA-3, but RXRs and RARs minimally bind to this consensus site as monomers (45). Heterodimerization boosts their cooperative affinity and selectivity for RAREs, which are set up as coupled binding sites, so that RXR/RAR heterodimer binding to RAREs is more proficient respect to the homodimeric forms of RXR or RAR (1, 45). The nuclear receptor superfamily DBD maintains a highly conserved core sequence comprised of two zinc-nucleated modules and two α-helices folding into a single globular domain, with approximately 40% amino acid identity over a 67-residue region. In spite of the use of a highly conserved receptor DBD and a single major core binding sequence, complex DNA sites can be exploited with better selectivity by means of RXR forming combinatorial receptor heterodimers so that eventually two different ligands can co-regulate transcription from the same gene-regulatory element (45). The nuclear receptors DBDs can produce the same pattern of DNA selectivity and dimerization as the full-length receptors (3, 45), whereas the LBDs dimerization function of some receptors can additionally stabilize some dimeric assemblies but has no selective role for RE recognition (3, 45). The nuclear receptor superfamily members exploit the same consensus AGGTCA sequence, and transcriptional control selectivity is furthermore warranted by multiple arrangements of AGGTCA sites in the REs. RXR/RAR heterodimers preferentially bind to two AGGTCA sites set up in a direct repeat (DR) configuration hallmarked by inter-half-site spacings of 1–5 bp acknowledged as DR1–DR5, respectively (3, 45). The spacer size differentiates more respect to the sequence, with the maximum affinity binding sites for each RXR heterodimer and the discriminating binding of DRs based on inter-half-site spacings rated on a scale of 1–5. Other members of the nuclear superfamily link powerfully to inverted and everted repeats of core hexamer so that the usage of direct repeat geometry is less crucial (3, 45).

RXR HETERODIMERS

Combinatorial nuclear receptors are characterized by an amazing recognition mechanism that permits them to decipher a binding site geometry in addition to its sequence, with polarity adopted by the subunits of the bound receptor heterodimer representing an associated feature of any asymmetric RE. The RXR/RAR complex can assume diverse polarities when bound to its different REs, with different functions on the heterodimer dependent on ligand and corepressor binding. In this context, although the two hexameric binding sites may have the same sequence, the non-symmetric RXR/RAR complexes permits the position of every receptor to be distinguished as upstream or downstream (3, 45). A preceding structural analysis of the RXR/TR DBD complex linked to a DR4 thyroid RE permitted the direct configuration of the polarity related to that complex. The asymmetric assembly was recognized through the collaboration between DBD subunits, which arises exclusively with a 4-bp inter-half-site spacing length and RXR positioning upstream of TR (3, 45). The RXR/RAR heterodimer, whose RE repertoire is relatively small, mediates transcriptional control with low selectivity through DR1, DR2, and DR5 sequences located in REREs, whereas the RXR/TR complex is only restricted to DR4. A great flexibility measure of their DBDs in forming valid interaction surfaces with different effects on target gene regulation is hinted by the multiple high-affinity DNA-binding targets (3, 45). *In vivo*, RXR/RAR heterodimers on DR1 inhibit transcription with or without occurrence of specific ligands. The complex structure allows the DR1 to identify the polar assembly of the RXR and RAR DBDs as well as the aptitude of a DNA regulatory element to work as a typical allosteric ligand, triggering new conformations and/or interactions eventually augmenting its own binding.

RXRs AND DNA REs

DNA REs induce two different types of allosteric changes on nuclear receptors: (i) conformational changes ensuing within a DBD, such as the T-box α-helix deformation, prompting increased RXR binding DNA; (ii) DNA structures reshaping to facilitate protein–protein contacts. Effective RXR:RAR interactions induce a considerable improvement in their DNA affinity. The REs effectively impinge on the interactions of full-length nuclear receptors with their ligands, corepressors, coactivators, AP-1, and other players that can impact gene expression (3, 45). Other factors are represented by protein flexibility and DNA surfaces exactly changing on a DNA site. The retinoid REs inter-halfsite spacing identifies a fixed geometry for a pair of nuclear receptors to intermingle on, with one nucleotide change in the spacer inducing RXR and its partners to rotate ~35° around the double helix and be dislocated from each other by 3.4 Å. Consequently, RXR DBD must retain several fixed and different surfaces to put up its many combinatorial interactions, or utilize a small number of adaptable protein elements that can adjust to the rotations, displacements, and polarity of these binding sites with one or more receptor partners. Besides, the numerous RXR combinatorial complexes must be prearranged only when needed at particular control sites, to avoid wasting, considering the numerous pairwise interactions that RXR can form with its partners and the crucial role played by the DNA in the definition of the protein structures entailed for dimerization (3, 45).

RXRs' MULTIMERIZATION

In the absence of specific ligands RXRs expressly assemble as tetramers, which disengage when a ligand is bound, causing dimerization surface changes and development of RXR homodimers or heterodimers if adequate partners are present. In particular, ligand binding triggers conformational changes that modify receptor multimerization capability and changes RXRs' homo-/heterodimerization as well as cofactor-binding surface (mostly related to helices 10/11 and 12 reshuffle) inducing a ligand prompted shift to act as an activator and not as a repressor of gene transcription (46). Other than as receptor dimers, RXRs can also bind to DNA as larger protein complexes (trimers, tetramers, and pentamers) assembling supportively on REs containing appropriately repeated half-sites and crucially guaranteeing unambiguous DNA recognition. In particular, RXR tetramers display important functional plasticity and gather on REs hallmarked by varied half-site alignments and arrangements. The capability of RXRs to create tetramers and correlated oligomers seems to add to the synergistic transcriptional activation observed when multiple, spatially separated REs locate into a single promoter. RXRs oligomer formation contributes to isoform-specific promoter utilization and allows recognition of DNA sequences not recognized by receptor dimers (47).

RXRs AND THE BIOLOGICAL CLOCK IN LIVER METABOLISM

The hepatic metabolic pathways managing glycolysis/gluconeogenesis, lipogenesis/fatty acid oxidation, and protein biosynthesis are essential for glucose, lipid, and amino acid homeostasis. These divergent metabolic processes require temporal separation warranted by the biological clock, which drives rhythmic fluctuations of liver transcripts encoding rate-limiting enzymes and regulators of major metabolic processes, so that metabolic diseases ensue when the ordered sequence of activation of the numerous metabolic pathways is deranged (48, 49). A huge number of hepatic metabolites changes with 24-h periodicity and, for example, the circadian regulation of hepatic function sets up the alternation of glycolysis and gluconeogenesis, with the highest levels of the former in the morning and the lowest levels of the latter in the evening in nocturnal respect to diurnal species. Among the factors which RXRs are capable to interact with, Clock plays a key role in the molecular clockwork and liver metabolism as well, as evidenced by metabolic phenotyping studies performed on mice bearing a dominant negative mutation in the Clock gene (ClockΔ19 mice), which show hyperlipidemia, hyperglycemia, and hepatic steatosis (50). Other important RXRs heterodimerization partners involved in liver metabolism are the PPAR family members, which show 24-h oscillations in mouse liver (6). PPARα, the prevailing hepatic isoform, stimulates fatty acid catabolism by peroxisomal β-oxidation and mitochrondrial β- and O-oxidation in liver (3) and peaks in the early evening, oscillating in phase with the PGC-1α (51) and lipin 1, which magnifies the PPARα/PGC-1α module effects, upholding fatty acids utilization in early nocturnal feeding phase of rodents and anticipating hepatocyte capability to increase energy support for physical activity needs (52). Besides, PPARγ plays an important role in regulating glucose metabolism and fatty acid homeostasis: its functional activity depends on the establishment of RXR/PPARγ heterodimers, which can be activated not only by PPARγ agonists, such as anti-hyperglycemic and anti-diabetic thiazolidinediones, but also by RXR modulators, in particular partial agonists and even antagonists more than full agonists, which cause severe side effects (53).

Other important RXR partners are two nuclear receptors managing the transcription of genes enriching signaling pathways that regulate intestinal and hepatic lipid homeostasis: the LXRs, which control whole-body cholesterol, fatty acid, and glucose homeostasis, and the FXRs, which bind bile acids and are entailed in feedback inhibition of bile acid synthesis and cholesterol catabolism (54). RXR/LXR heterodimers manage cholesterol homeostasis controlling cholesterol transport and catabolism and triacyl glycerol synthesis gene regulation triggering ATP-binding cassette transporters (such as ABCA1) for cholesterol and phospholipids efflux from intracellular receptor stores to extracellular acceptors, sterol responsive element binding protein 1c, a transcription factor controlling fatty acid synthesis, apolipoproteins ApoD and ApoE, lipoprotein-modifying enzymes such as cholesterol ester (CETP), and phospholipid transfer proteins (3). Rexinoid agonists binding to RXR/FXR heterodimers act as antagonists to reduce DNA binding and coactivator recruitment (3). In its side, NURR1 prompts fatty acid-binding protein 5 *via* its promoter NBRE independent of RXR, whereas CAR is involved in response to endobiotic or xenobiotic challenge with induction of P450 enzymes (3).

RXRs AND THERAPEUTIC POTENTIAL

The reciprocal modulation deriving from the interplay between the ticking of biological clocks and the circadian fluctuations of nutrients and metabolites in the extracellular as well as intracellular milieu highlighted at present by animal experiments suggests a critical role played by nutrient sensors and RXRs as well as other rhythmically oscillating nuclear receptors in body physiology as well as in pathophysiological mechanisms of disease (55). In particular, RXR agonists (e.g., bexarotene) impact target genes of numerous permissive partners hinting that these molecules may pharmacologically influence numerous metabolically important pathways *in vivo* (56). Accordingly, RXR liver-specific deletion in mice provokes changes in all metabolic pathways regulated by RXR heterodimers, suggesting RXRs are essential and pleiotropic actors (57). Anyway, even if RXR agonists' multipotentiality hints therapeutic significance on several important signaling pathways and provides boosted effectiveness by permissive heterodimers panactivation, poor selectivity represents an important drawback. Furthermore, considering that RXR agonists trigger hypertriglyceridemia and hypothyroidism in animals and humans, more appropriate therapeutically valuable targets could be represented by RXRs' heterodimeric partners (58).

CONCLUSION

Various ligands ranging from cholesterol to fatty acids and fat-soluble vitamins bind to RXR heterodimers and the cell and context-dependent interaction of the ligand–receptor complexes with co-regulators induces modulation of gene networks, which impact transcriptional and posttranscriptional regulatory factors managing intermediary metabolism and involved in metabolic disorders pathophysiology when deranged. RXR modulators function as agonists, partial agonists, and inverse agonists or antagonists depending on the structure of the ligand–receptor complex, and heterodimer-selective rexinoids could represent future valuable therapeutic tools for metabolic diseases. Accordingly, RXR heterodimers and their interplay with the biological clock are crucial in the time-related regulation of metabolic pathways and represent future druggable targets.

AUTHOR CONTRIBUTIONS

All the authors listed have made substantial, direct, and intellectual contribution to the work and approved it for publication.

REFERENCES

1. Evans RM, Mangelsdorf DJ. Nuclear receptors, RXR, and the Big Bang. *Cell* (2014) 157:255–66. doi:10.1016/j.cell.2014.03.012
2. Mazzoccoli G, Vinciguerra M, Oben J, Tarquini R, De Cosmo S. Non-alcoholic fatty liver disease: the role of nuclear receptors and circadian rhythmicity. *Liver Int* (2014) 34:1133–52. doi:10.1111/liv.12534
3. Dawson MI, Xia Z. The retinoid X receptors and their ligands. *Biochim Biophys Acta* (2012) 1821:21–56. doi:10.1016/j.bbalip.2011.09.014
4. Chawla A, Repa JJ, Evans RM, Mangelsdorf DJ. Nuclear receptors and lipid physiology: opening the X-files. *Science* (2001) 294:1866–70. doi:10.1126/science.294.5548.1866
5. Bookout AL, Jeong Y, Downes M, Yu RT, Evans RM, Mangelsdorf DJ. Anatomical profiling of nuclear receptor expression reveals a hierarchical transcriptional network. *Cell* (2006) 126:789–99. doi:10.1016/j.cell.2006.06.049
6. Yang X, Downes M, Yu RT, Bookout AL, He W, Straume M, et al. Nuclear receptor expression links the circadian clock to metabolism. *Cell* (2006) 126:801–10. doi:10.1016/j.cell.2006.06.050

7. Yang X, Lamia KA, Evans RM. Nuclear receptors, metabolism, and the circadian clock. *Cold Spring Harb Symp Quant Biol* (2007) 72:387–94. doi:10.1101/sqb.2007.72.058
8. Lowrey PL, Takahashi JS. Genetics of circadian rhythms in mammalian model organisms. *Adv Genet* (2011) 74:175–230. doi:10.1016/B978-0-12-387690-4.00006-4
9. Hastings MH, Reddy AB, Maywood ES. A clockwork web: circadian timing in brain and periphery, in health and disease. *Nat Rev Neurosci* (2003) 4:649–61. doi:10.1038/nrn1177
10. Bass J, Takahashi JS. Circadian integration of metabolism and energetics. *Science* (2010) 330:1349–54. doi:10.1126/science.1195027
11. Yin L, Wu N, Lazar MA. Nuclear receptor Rev-erbalpha: a heme receptor that coordinates circadian rhythm and metabolism. *Nucl Recept Signal* (2010) 8:e001. doi:10.1621/nrs.08001
12. Eide EJ, Vielhaber EL, Hinz WA, Virshup DM. The circadian regulatory proteins BMAL1 and cryptochromes are substrates of casein kinase Iε. *J Biol Chem* (2002) 277:17248–54. doi:10.1074/jbc.M111466200
13. Agostino PV, Harrington ME, Ralph MR, Golombek DA. Casein kinase-1-epsilon (CK1epsilon) and circadian photic responses in hamsters. *Chronobiol Int* (2009) 26:126–33. doi:10.1080/07420520802675177
14. Lamia KA, Sachdeva UM, Ditacchio L, Williams EC, Alvarez JG, Egan DF, et al. AMPK regulates the circadian clock by cryptochrome phosphorylation and degradation. *Science* (2009) 326:437–40. doi:10.1126/science.1172156
15. Sahar S, Zocchi L, Kinoshita C, Borrelli E, Sassone-Corsi P. Regulation of BMAL1 protein stability and circadian function by GSK3beta-mediated phosphorylation. *PLoS One* (2010) 5:e8561. doi:10.1371/journal.pone.0008561
16. Hirayama J, Sahar S, Grimaldi B, Tamaru T, Takamatsu K, Nakahata Y, et al. CLOCK-mediated acetylation of BMAL1 controls circadian function. *Nature* (2007) 450:1086–90. doi:10.1038/nature06394
17. Nakahata Y, Kaluzova M, Grimaldi B, Sahar S, Hirayama J, Chen D, et al. The NAD+-dependent deacetylase SIRT1 modulates CLOCK-mediated chromatin remodeling and circadian control. *Cell* (2008) 134:329–40. doi:10.1016/j.cell.2008.07.002
18. Nakahata Y, Sahar S, Astarita G, Kaluzova M, Sassone-Corsi P. Circadian control of the NAD+ salvage pathway by CLOCK-SIRT1. *Science* (2009) 324:654–7. doi:10.1126/science.1170803
19. Asher G, Gatfield D, Stratmann M, Reinke H, Dibner C, Kreppel F, et al. SIRT1 regulates circadian clock gene expression through PER2 deacetylation. *Cell* (2008) 134:317–28. doi:10.1016/j.cell.2008.06.050
20. Mazzoccoli G, Pazienza V, Vinciguerra M. Clock genes and clock-controlled genes in the regulation of metabolic rhythms. *Chronobiol Int* (2012) 29:227–51. doi:10.3109/07420528.2012.658127
21. Leblanc BP, Stunnenberg HG. 9-cis retinoic acid signaling: changing partners causes some excitement. *Genes Dev* (1995) 9:1811–6. doi:10.1101/gad.9.15.1811
22. Mangelsdorf DJ, Evans RM. The RXR heterodimers and orphan receptors. *Cell* (1995) 83:841–50. doi:10.1016/0092-8674(95)90200-7
23. Mangelsdorf DJ, Thummel C, Beato M, Herrlich P, Schütz G, Umesono K, et al. The nuclear receptor superfamily: the second decade. *Cell* (1995) 83:835–9. doi:10.1016/0092-8674(95)90199-X
24. Gilardi F, Desvergne B. RXRs: collegial partners. *Subcell Biochem* (2014) 70:75–102. doi:10.1007/978-94-017-9050-5_5
25. Kojetin DJ, Matta-Camacho E, Hughes TS, Srinivasan S, Nwachukwu JC, Cavett V, et al. Structural mechanism for signal transduction in RXR nuclear receptor heterodimers. *Nat Commun* (2015) 6:8013. doi:10.1038/ncomms9013
26. Domínguez M, Alvarez S, de Lera AR. Natural and structure-based RXR ligand scaffolds and their functions. *Curr Top Med Chem* (2017) 17(6):631–62. doi:10.2174/1568026616666160617072521
27. Pérez E, Bourguet W, Gronemeyer H, de Lera AR. Modulation of RXR function through ligand design. *Biochim Biophys Acta* (2012) 1821:57–69. doi:10.1016/j.bbalip.2011.04.003
28. Li D, Li T, Wang F, Tian H, Samuels HH. Functional evidence for retinoid X receptor (RXR) as a nonsilent partner in the thyroid hormone receptor/RXR heterodimer. *Mol Cell Biol* (2002) 22:5782–92. doi:10.1128/MCB.22.16.5782-5792.2002
29. Putcha BD, Wright E, Brunzelle JS, Fernandez EJ. Structural basis for negative cooperativity within agonist-bound TR:RXR heterodimers. *Proc Natl Acad Sci U S A* (2012) 109:6084–7. doi:10.1073/pnas.1119852109
30. Lien F, Berthier A, Bouchaert E, Gheeraert C, Alexandre J, Porez G, et al. Metformin interferes with bile acid homeostasis through AMPK-FXR crosstalk. *J Clin Invest* (2014) 124:1037–51. doi:10.1172/JCI68815
31. Zhao Y, Qin S, Atangan LI, Molina Y, Okawa Y, Arpawong HT, et al. Casein kinase 1alpha interacts with retinoid X receptor and interferes with agonist-induced apoptosis. *J Biol Chem* (2004) 279:30844–9. doi:10.1074/jbc.M404651200
32. Gao W, Liu J, Hu M, Huang M, Cai S, Zeng Z, et al. Regulation of proteolytic cleavage of retinoid X receptor-α by GSK-3β. *Carcinogenesis* (2013) 34:1208–15. doi:10.1093/carcin/bgt043
33. McNamara P, Seo SB, Rudic RD, Sehgal A, Chakravarti D, FitzGerald GA. Regulation of CLOCK and MOP4 by nuclear hormone receptors in the vasculature: a humoral mechanism to reset a peripheral clock. *Cell* (2001) 105:877–89. doi:10.1016/S0092-8674(01)00401-9
34. Nakahata Y, Akashi M, Trcka D, Yasuda A, Takumi T. The in vitro real-time oscillation monitoring system identifies potential entrainment factors for circadian clocks. *BMC Mol Biol* (2006) 7:5. doi:10.1186/1471-2199-7-5
35. Thompson CL, Selby CP, Van Gelder RN, Blaner WS, Lee J, Quadro L, et al. Effect of vitamin A depletion on nonvisual phototransduction pathways in cryptochromeless mice. *J Biol Rhythms* (2004) 19(6):504–17. doi:10.1177/0748730404270519
36. Fu Y, Zhong H, Wang MH, Luo DG, Liao HW, Maeda H, et al. Intrinsically photosensitive retinal ganglion cells detect light with a vitamin A-based photopigment, melanopsin. *Proc Natl Acad Sci U S A* (2005) 102:10339–44. doi:10.1073/pnas.0501866102
37. Cho Y, Noshiro M, Choi M, Morita K, Kawamoto T, Fujimoto K, et al. The basic helix-loop-helix proteins differentiated embryo chondrocyte (DEC) 1 and DEC2 function as corepressors of retinoid X receptors. *Mol Pharmacol* (2009) 76:1360–9. doi:10.1124/mol.109.057000
38. Hamaguchi H, Fujimoto K, Kawamoto T, Noshiro M, Maemura K, Takeda N, et al. Expression of the gene for Dec2, a basic helix-loop-helix transcription factor, is regulated by a molecular clock system. *Biochem J* (2004) 382(Pt 1):43–50. doi:10.1042/BJ20031760
39. Honma S, Kawamoto T, Takagi Y, Fujimoto K, Sato F, Noshiro M, et al. Dec1 and Dec2 are regulators of the mammalian molecular clock. *Nature* (2002) 419:841–4. doi:10.1038/nature01123
40. Yamada K, Kawata H, Shou Z, Mizutani T, Noguchi T, Miyamoto K. Insulin induces the expression of the SHARP-2/Stra13/DEC1 gene via a phosphoinositide 3-kinase pathway. *J Biol Chem* (2003) 278:30719–24. doi:10.1074/jbc.M301597200
41. Canaple L, Rambaud J, Dkhissi-Benyahya O, Rayet B, Tan NS, Michalik L, et al. Reciprocal regulation of brain and muscle Arnt-like protein 1 and peroxisome proliferator-activated receptor alpha defines a novel positive feedback loop in the rodent liver circadian clock. *Mol Endocrinol* (2006) 20:1715–27. doi:10.1210/me.2006-0052
42. Yang X, Guo M, Wan YJ. Deregulation of growth factor, circadian clock, and cell cycle signaling in regenerating hepatocyte RXRalpha-deficient mouse livers. *Am J Pathol* (2010) 176:733–43. doi:10.2353/ajpath.2010.090524
43. Navigatore-Fonzo LS, Golini RL, Ponce IT, Delgado SM, Plateo-Pignatari MG, Gimenez MS, et al. Retinoic acid receptors move in time with the clock in the hippocampus. Effect of a vitamin-A-deficient diet. *J Nutr Biochem* (2013) 24:859–67. doi:10.1016/j.jnutbio.2012.05.006
44. Nakamura K, Inoue I, Takahashi S, Komoda T, Katayama S. Cryptochrome and period proteins are regulated by the CLOCK/BMAL1 gene: crosstalk between the PPARs/RXRalpha-regulated and CLOCK/BMAL1-regulated systems. *PPAR Res* (2008) 2008:348610. doi:10.1155/2008/348610
45. Rastinejad F, Wagner T, Zhao Q, Khorasanizadeh S. Structure of the RXR-RAR DNA-binding complex on the retinoic acid response element DR1. *EMBO J* (2000) 19:1045–54. doi:10.1093/emboj/19.5.1045
46. Szanto A, Narkar V, Shen Q, Uray IP, Davies PJ, Nagy L. Retinoid X receptors: X-ploring their (patho)physiological functions. *Cell Death Differ* (2004) 11(Suppl 2):S126–43. doi:10.1038/sj.cdd.4401533
47. Lin BC, Wong CW, Chen HW, Privalsky ML. Plasticity of tetramer formation by retinoid X receptors. An alternative paradigm for DNA recognition. *J Biol Chem* (1997) 272:9860–7. doi:10.1074/jbc.272.15.9860
48. Maury E, Ramsey KM, Bass J. Circadian rhythms and metabolic syndrome: from experimental genetics to human disease. *Circ Res* (2010) 106:447–62. doi:10.1161/CIRCRESAHA.109.208355

49. Asher G, Schibler U. Crosstalk between components of circadian and metabolic cycles in mammals. *Cell Metab* (2011) 13:125–37. doi:10.1016/j.cmet.2011.01.006
50. Turek FW, Joshu C, Kohsaka A, Lin E, Ivanova G, McDearmon E, et al. Obesity and metabolic syndrome in circadian clock mutant mice. *Science* (2005) 308:1043–5. doi:10.1126/science.1108750
51. Liu C, Li S, Liu T, Borjigin J, Lin JD. Transcriptional coactivator PGC-1alpha integrates the mammalian clock and energy metabolism. *Nature* (2007) 447:477–81. doi:10.1038/nature05767
52. Finck BN, Gropler MC, Chen Z, Leone TC, Croce MA, Harris TE, et al. Lipin 1 is an inducible amplifier of the hepatic PGC-1alpha/PPARalpha regulatory pathway. *Cell Metab* (2006) 4:199–210. doi:10.1016/j.cmet.2006.08.005
53. Morishita KI, Kakuta H. Retinoid X receptor ligands with anti-type 2 diabetic activity. *Curr Top Med Chem* (2017) 17(6):696–707. doi:10.2174/15680266 16666160617085545
54. Moschetta A. Nuclear receptors and cholesterol metabolism in the intestine. *Atheroscler Suppl* (2015) 17:9–11. doi:10.1016/S1567-5688(15)50003-2
55. Ribas-Latre A, Eckel-Mahan K. Interdependence of nutrient metabolism and the circadian clock system: importance for metabolic health. *Mol Metab* (2016) 5:133–52. doi:10.1016/j.molmet.2015.12.006
56. Repa JJ, Turley SD, Lobaccaro JA, Medina J, Li L, Lustig K, et al. Regulation of absorption and ABC1-mediated efflux of cholesterol by RXR heterodimers. *Science* (2000) 289:1524–9. doi:10.1126/science.289.5484.1524
57. Wan YJ, An D, Cai Y, Repa JJ, Hung-Po Chen T, Flores M, et al. Hepatocyte-specific mutation establishes retinoid X receptor alpha as a heterodimeric integrator of multiple physiological processes in the liver. *Mol Cell Biol* (2000) 20:4436–44. doi:10.1128/MCB.20.12.4436-4444.2000
58. Shulman AI, Mangelsdorf DJ. Retinoid X receptor heterodimers in the metabolic syndrome. *N Engl J Med* (2005) 353:604–15. doi:10.1056/NEJMra043590

23

The Role of Circadian Rhythms in Muscular and Osseous Physiology and their Regulation by Nutrition and Exercise

Shinya Aoyama[1,2] *and Shigenobu Shibata*[2*]

[1] *Organization for University Research Initiatives, Waseda University, Tokyo, Japan,* [2] *Laboratory of Physiology and Pharmacology, School of Advanced Science and Engineering, Waseda University, Tokyo, Japan*

Edited by:
Etienne Challet,
CNRS and University of Strasbourg, France

Reviewed by:
Stefano Schiaffino,
Venetian Institute of Molecular Medicine, Italy
Ke Ma,
Baylor College of Medicine, USA

****Correspondence:***
Shigenobu Shibata
shibatas@waseda.jp

The mammalian circadian clock regulates the day and night cycles of various physiological functions. The circadian clock system consists of a central clock in the suprachiasmatic nucleus (SCN) of the hypothalamus and peripheral clocks in peripheral tissues. According to the results of circadian transcriptomic studies in several tissues, the majority of rhythmic genes are expressed in a tissue-specific manner and are influenced by tissue-specific circadian rhythms. Here we review the diurnal variations of musculoskeletal functions and discuss the impact of the circadian clock on homeostasis in skeletal muscle and bone. Peripheral clocks are controlled by not only photic stimulation from the central clock in the SCN but also by external cues, such as feeding and exercise. In this review, we discuss the effects of feeding and exercise on the circadian clock and diurnal variation of musculoskeletal functions. We also discuss the therapeutic potential of chrono-nutrition and chrono-exercise on circadian disturbances and the failure of homeostasis in skeletal muscle and bone.

Keywords: circadian rhythm, clock gene, skeletal muscle, bone, chrono-exercise, chrono-nutrition

INTRODUCTION

Various physiological functions, including the sleep wake cycle, body temperature, hormone secretion, and locomotor activity, exhibit circadian rhythms. This time-dependent regulation is driven by an internal circadian clock. In mammals, the circadian clock is divided into two parts, the master clock in the suprachiasmatic nucleus (SCN) of the hypothalamus and peripheral clocks in the peripheral tissues, such as the liver, skeletal muscle and so on, as well as brain areas other than the SCN. The master clock in the SCN acts as a time keeper in the whole body; thus, it integrates and entrains the peripheral circadian clocks by regulating neural and endocrine pathways, such as the sympathetic nervous system and glucocorticoid signaling (Schibler et al., 2003; Shibata, 2004). Light is the major entraining factor for the SCN. On the other hand, the peripheral clocks are entrained by not only the light-dependent regulation of the SCN but also scheduled feeding and scheduled exercise in an SCN-independent manner (Tahara and Shibata, 2013). The molecular mechanisms of circadian clock systems in mammals have been investigated since *Clock* (*Circadian locomotor output cycles kaput*) was discovered in 1997 (King et al., 1997). Circadian rhythm is produced by the transcriptional and translational regulation feedback loop of core clock genes, which include *Bmal1* (*Bain and muscle ARNT-like 1*), *Clock*, *Per1* (*Period1*), *Per2*, *Cry1* (*cryptochrome1*), and *Cry2*. CLOCK and BMAL1 are transcriptional factors that have a basic helix-loop-helix PAS domain, and the heterodimer of CLOCK and BMAL1 proteins binds to an E-box binding element in the promoter regions of *Per* and *Cry*, and its binding activates the transcription of these genes (Gekakis et al., 1998). After transcription and translation, PER1/2 proteins localize to the cytoplasm and are phosphorylated by CKIε (Casein kinase Iε) (Lowrey et al., 2000). The phosphorylated PER1/2 proteins are not stable and are degraded by ubiquitination systems. CRY1/2 proteins in the cytoplasm are also degraded by ubiquitination systems via FBXL3 (F-box and leucine rich repeat protein 3) (Busino et al., 2007). The localization of CRY1/2 and PER1/2 to the cytoplasm promotes the formation of the PERs/CRYs/CKIε complex. This complex accumulates in the nucleus and suppresses the transcription of *Pers* and *Crys* by CLOCK and BMAL1. In addition, *Rev-erbs* (*nuclear receptor subfamily 1, group D*) and *Rors* (*RAR-related orphan receptor*) genes are the target genes of the complex of BMAL1 and CLOCK (Preitner et al., 2002; Sato et al., 2004). REV-ERBs and RORs act as the repressor and activator of *Bmal1* and *Clock* transcription, respectively, via binding to an ROR-responsive element (Preitner et al., 2002; Sato et al., 2004). Recent circadian transcriptomic studies revealed that clock genes are expressed in several tissues, and that the expression of rhythmic genes in each tissue occurs in a tissue-specific manner (Miller et al., 2007; Zhang et al., 2014), suggesting that peripheral clocks in each tissue generate the biological rhythm of tissue-specific functions.

Clock genes are also expressed in skeletal muscle and bones of the skeleton, and it is thought that the clock genes regulate muscular- or osseous-specific biological functions (Dudek and Meng, 2014; Mayeuf-Louchart et al., 2015; Chatterjee and Ma, 2016; Yang and Meng, 2016). Skeletal muscle and bone have roles in not only the regulation of locomotion and postural support but also the control of nutritional homeostasis, such as maintaining glucose and calcium levels. Feeding and exercise stimulate these tissues and change their functions, including the maintenance of tissue mass and metabolism. Here, we review and discuss mainly two topics as follows: (1) the role of circadian rhythms in the biological functions of muscles and bone, and (2) the entrainment or regulation of the circadian clock or biological rhythm in skeletal muscle and bone by feeding and exercise.

CIRCADIAN RHYTHM IN SKELETAL MUSCLES

Most mammalian cells express molecular clock genes and have a circadian clock system. Skeletal muscle cells also express molecular clock genes and show a circadian rhythm expression pattern. Using DNA microarray and RNA-seq methods Zhang et al. reported on the circadian transcriptome of 12 mouse organs and found that most rhythmic genes show an organ-specific pattern (Zhang et al., 2014). The circadian transcriptome of adult mouse skeletal muscle has also been identified by Miller et al., McCarthy et al., and Dyar et al. (McCarthy et al., 2007; Miller et al., 2007; Dyar et al., 2015). A small number, 3.4%, of the expressed genes in skeletal muscle show a circadian rhythm expression pattern (Miller et al., 2007). In addition, it has been reported that the number of rhythmic genes in skeletal muscle depends on the muscle fiber type; 684 rhythmic genes were found in the fast-twitch tibialis anterior muscle, while 1359 were identified in the slow-twitch soleus muscle (Dyar et al., 2015). The phase of expression of many rhythmic genes in skeletal muscle occurs at the mid-point of the subjective active phase (McCarthy et al., 2007; Miller et al., 2007). In liver, the phase expression of many rhythmic genes is different from that in skeletal muscle, the large cluster of phase expression occurs at the mid-point of subjective day and subjective night, respectively. One of the reasons for this may be that scheduled exercise can entrain the circadian clocks in skeletal muscles (Wolff and Esser, 2012), i.e., the phase of rhythmic gene expression in skeletal muscle may be regulated by the rhythm of locomotor activity. These results from circadian transcriptomic studies in skeletal muscle suggest circadian regulation of several muscle functions. For example, *Myod1* (*myogenic differentiation 1*), *Ucp3* (*uncoupling protein 3*), *Atrogin1* (*F-box protein 32*), *Myh1* (*myosin heavy chain 1*) are muscle-specific genes that play roles in myogenesis, muscle lipid utilization, protein metabolism and the organization of myofilaments, respectively. They have shown the circadian rhythms of gene expression, some of which have been shown to be directly regulated by clock genes (Andrews et al., 2010; Zhang et al., 2012). On the other hand, since the rhythmic expressions of *Myod1* and *Atrogin1* in *ad libitum feeding* mice are not observed in fasting mice (Shavlakadze et al., 2013), feeding and fasting patterns may be important factors for the rhythmic expression of muscle specific genes.

THE ROLE OF THE CIRCADIAN CLOCK IN MUSCLE MASS, MUSCLE STRENGTH, AND MYOFIBER TYPE

The roles of molecular circadian clocks in skeletal muscle mass, strength, and myofiber type are demonstrated with the use of molecular clock gene-deficient or mutant mice (**Table 1**). Kondratov et al. were the first to report on the effect of the molecular clock on muscle phenotype (Kondratov et al., 2006). Whole body *Bmal1* knockout in mice causes sarcopenia, i.e., age-dependent reduction of muscle mass, thus muscle loss is not observed in young *Bmal1* knockout mice (Kondratov et al., 2006). In recent years, the muscular phenotypes of some *Bmal1* knockout mice have been reported, with time-dependent knockout or tissue-specific knockout (Dyar et al., 2014; Schroder et al., 2015; Harfmann et al., 2016; Schiaffino et al., 2016; Yang et al., 2016). Yang et al. reported that body weight loss and early aging were not observed in tamoxifen-inducible *Bmal1* knockout mice under the treatment of tamoxifen after muscle development (>3 months) (Yang et al., 2016). In addition, Dyar et al. showed that reductions in muscle weight and strength were not observed in inducible muscle-specific *Bmal1* knockout mice once *Bmal1* knockout was induced after development (Dyar et al., 2014). These reports suggest that *Bmal1* expression during development is important for the maintenance of weight gain and muscular strength. In addition to the timing of *Bmal1* expression, the role of intrinsic muscular *Bmal1* in

TABLE 1 | Summary of the muscular and osseous phenotypes in clock gene mutant mice.

Genotype	Muscular or osseous phenotypes
Bmal1 knockout	Muscle
	Age-related muscle loss (sarcopenia) (Kondratov et al., 2006)
	Reduction in muscle fiber size (Kondratov et al., 2006; Chatterjee et al., 2013)
	Fiber-type shift (Dyar et al., 2014; Schroder et al., 2015)
	Disruption of myofiber architecture (Andrews et al., 2010)
	Reduction of mitochondrial volume (Andrews et al., 2010)
	Impaired muscle regeneration (Chatterjee et al., 2015)
	Bone
	High bone mass at young age (Fu et al., 2005)
	Age-related bone loss (Samsa et al., 2016)
	Abnormal bone calcification and arthropathy (McDearmon et al., 2006)
Inducible *Bmal1* knockout mice after development (> 3 months)	Bone
	Normal bone and joint (Yang et al., 2016)
Muscle-specific *Bmal1* knockout	Muscle
	Insulin resistance and glucose intolerance (Dyar et al., 2014; Harfmann et al., 2016)
	Impaired insulin stimulated glucose uptake (Dyar et al., 2014; Harfmann et al., 2016)
	Increased muscle mass and size (Dyar et al., 2014)
	Decreased muscle strength (Dyar et al., 2014)
	Slight shift in fiber type (Dyar et al., 2014)
	Bone
	Thick bone (Schroder et al., 2015)
Muscle-specific inducible *Bmal1* knockout after development (> 3 months)	Muscle
	Normal muscle weight and normal size (Dyar et al., 2014)
	No significant change (Dyar et al., 2014) or a slight decrease in muscle strength (Schroder et al., 2015)
	No significant change (Dyar et al., 2014) or a slight shift in fiber type (Schroder et al., 2015)
Osteoclast-specific *Bmal1* knockout	Bone
	High bone mass (Xu et al., 2016)
Clock mutant	Muscle
	The disruption of myofiber architecture (Andrews et al., 2010)
	Reduction in muscle strength (Andrews et al., 2010)
	Reduction in mitochondria (Andrews et al., 2010)
Per1 knockout	Muscle
	No significant change in muscle mass (Bae et al., 2006)
	Bone
	No significant change in bone mass (Fu et al., 2005)
Per2 knockout or *Per2* mutant	Muscle
	No change in muscle mass and lower exercise tolerance (Bae et al., 2006)
	Bone
	High bone mass at 3 months of age (Maronde et al., 2010)
	No significant change in bone mass (Fu et al., 2005)
Per1/2 knockout or *Per1/2* mutant mice	Bone
	High bone mass (Fu et al., 2005)
Per1$^{-/-}$/Osteoblast-specific-*Per2* mutant mice	Bone
	High bone mass (Fu et al., 2005)

(Continued)

TABLE 1 | Continued

Genotype	Muscular or osseous phenotypes
Cry1 knockout	Bone
	No significant change in bone mass (Fu et al., 2005)
Cry2 knockout	Bone
	High bone mass at 3 months of age (Maronde et al., 2010)
	No significant change in bone mass (Fu et al., 2005)
	Bone
	High bone mass (Fu et al., 2005)
Per2 mutant / *Cry2* knockout	Bone
	No significant change in bone mass (Maronde et al., 2010)
Rev-erbaα knockout	Muscle
	Disruption of myofiber architecture (Woldt et al., 2013)
	Reduction of mitochondrial volume (Woldt et al., 2013)
	Lower exercise capacity (Woldt et al., 2013)
	Slight fiber-type shift (Pircher et al., 2005)

the muscle weight and strength has also been reported (Dyar et al., 2014; Schroder et al., 2015). Muscle-specific *Bmal1* knockout mice showed an increase in muscle weight and a decrease in muscle strength, although the whole body *Bmal1* knockout mice exhibited muscle loss. These reports indicate that while a circadian clock during development regulates muscle mass, an intrinsic skeletal muscular clock may not directly regulate it. Lack of muscle use and the lowering of daily locomotor activity levels reduce muscle mass (Powers et al., 2005). Disruption of *Bmal1* in the whole body, and not in only skeletal muscle, induces the disappearance of an activity rhythm and a reduction in daily locomotor activity levels (Kondratov et al., 2006). In another report, muscle-specific over expression of *Bmal1* partially restores the *Bmal1* knockout-induced reduction of activity levels and body weight loss without improving arrhythmic behavior (McDearmon et al., 2006). In addition, the locomotor activity of muscle-specific *Bmal1* knockout mice, which show an increase in muscle mass, have a normal circadian rhythm, and is increased activity during the active phase (Dyar et al., 2014). These reports suggest that circadian clock-regulated activity levels may have an important role in the growth of skeletal muscle. Taken together, the results suggests that early aging and muscle weight loss in whole body *Bmal1* knockout mice are controlled in non-myofiber cells by *Bmal1* during development. Although the role of *Bmal1* for the developing fetus has not been described, it is possible that the rhythmic expression-independent functions of *Bmal1* in skeletal muscle growth are observed because *Bmal1*, just as other core clock genes, does not show rhythmic expression in the embryo (Dolatshad et al., 2010). Indeed, Lipton et al. found that the phosphorylation of BMAL1 by S6K1 (ribosomal S6 protein kinase 1) regulates translation, independently of its regulatory role in transcription (Lipton et al., 2015), suggesting that the phosphorylation of BMAL1 may affect the synthesis of muscle proteins, which is an important process for muscle growth. Further investigation is required of the role of molecular clocks in skeletal muscle growth.

Bmal1 knockout mice and *Clock* mutant mice have disrupted myofilament architecture in their skeletal muscle and decreased muscle strength at a single-fiber level (Andrews et al., 2010). The disruption of the myofilament architecture is observed in *Myod* knockout mice as well as *Bmal1* knockout mice (Andrews et al., 2010). There is a binding site for the heterodimer of CLOCK and BMAL1 in the promoter region of *Myod1* and this heterodimer directly regulates the rhythmic expression of *Myod1*, which is not seen in *Bmal1* knockout mice or *Clock* mutant mice (Andrews et al., 2010; Zhang et al., 2012). MyoD plays a role in myogenesis, which includes the formation of myofibers from satellite cells and myoblast cells. Cahtterjee et al. demonstrated that BMAL1 is one of the key players of myogenesis (Chatterjee et al., 2013). Deficiency of *Bmal1* in myoblast cells suppresses myogenesis related-gene expression, including *Myod*, *Myf5* (*myogenic factor* 5), and *Myogenin* expression, and impairs the differentiation of myoblasts to myofibers (Chatterjee et al., 2013). Moreover, they have shown a role for the Wnt (wingless-type MMTV integration site family) pathway in *Bmal1*-induced myoblast differentiation, since the circadian regulation of Wnt pathway-related genes is regulated by *Bmal1* (Chatterjee et al., 2013). In addition, they have demonstrated that *Bmal1* in skeletal muscle also promotes skeletal muscle regeneration via satellite cell proliferation using *in vivo* muscle injury models (Chatterjee et al., 2015). However, Schiaffino et al. reported that *Myod1* expression in the skeletal muscle of muscle-specific *Bmal1* knockout mice showed rhythmicity and was increased during the active phase (Schiaffino et al., 2016), while a previous study showed that whole body $Clock^{\Delta 19}$ mice did not show rhythmicity (Andrews et al., 2010). As one of the reasons, the up regulation of *Myod1* in muscle-specific *Bmal1* knockout mice may be due to the increase in locomotor activity during the active phase (Dyar et al., 2014); this hypothesis is supported by the finding that mechanical stimulation, such as during exercise, increases *Myod* expression (Legerlotz and Smith, 2008). Indeed, a stimulation such as fasting, which might cause hypolocomotion, down regulated the rhythmic expression of *Myod1* under conditions when the rhythmic expression of *Bmal1* is maintained (Shavlakadze et al., 2013). As another reason, the rhythmic expression of *Myod1* in muscle-specific *Bmal1* knockout mice may be because of the tissue-specific promoter driving genetic ablation. *Myosin light chain 1f* (*Mlc1f*) promoter was used to drive the ablation of muscle-specific *Bmal1* (Dyar et al., 2014). *Mlc1f* promoter is active in mature myocytes, but not in muscle precursor cells, such as satellite cells (Lee et al., 2012), suggesting that deficiency of *Bmal1* occurs only in mature myocytes. *Myod* is expressed not only in muscle precursor cells, such as activated satellite cells and myoblasts, but also in the mature muscle myocytes, albeit at low levels (Voytik et al., 1993; Hughes et al., 1997). The transcriptional regulation of *Myod* occurs through two elements, the "core enhancer" and a bipartite element containing the "distal regulatory region" and the "proximal regulatory region" (Charge et al., 2008). *Myod* expression in myoblasts is activated through the core enhancer, and its expression in mature myocytes is up regulated through the bipartite element (Charge et al., 2008). In addition, BMAL1 and CLOCK bind to the core enhancer, but not the bipartite element (Andrews et al., 2010). The rhythmic expression of *Myod1* in muscle-specific *Bmal1* knockout mice may reflect its rhythmic expression in activated satellite cells and myoblasts, which are included in adult skeletal muscles. Therefore, these reports indicate that clocks in myoblasts and satellite cells and locomotor activity rhythms regulate skeletal muscle functions, including the formation and growth of skeletal muscle, via skeletal muscle specific regulators such as MyoD.

Skeletal muscle fiber is divided into the two types, slow-twitch fiber and fast-twitch fiber, according to the myosin heavy chain isoform composition (Schiaffino and Reggiani, 1996). The slow-twitch fiber is mainly composed of myosin heavy chain isoforms I and IIa. It has high oxidative capacity and mitochondrial volume. On the other hand, the fast-twitch fiber is mainly composed of myosin heavy chain isoforms IIx and IIb. Some circadian clock genes regulate fiber type composition in skeletal muscle. Muscle-specific *Bmal1* knockout mice show a shift in their fiber type from slow- to fast-twitch compared with wild type mice (Dyar et al., 2014; Schroder et al., 2015). Deficiency of *Rev-erbα*, a repressor of *Bmal1* transcription, induces a shift in fiber type from fast- to slow-twitch in the slow-twitch soleus muscle, however, its effects are small (Pircher et al., 2005). On the other hand, Woldt et al. showed that fiber type did not shift significantly in the wild type and *Rev-erbα* mice, although the genetic expression of slow-twitch fiber markers was lower in muscle from *Rev-erbα* mice than in wild type mice (Woldt et al., 2013). The reason for this discrepancy may be in the independent line of the global genetic targeting of the *Rev-erbα* allele. While there are few reports regarding the relationship between molecular clocks and muscle fiber types, *Bmal1* has the potential to shift fiber types from fast- to slow-twitch. In contrast, *Rev-erbα*, the repressor of *Bmal1*, has opposing effects on fiber types.

THE ROLE OF THE CIRCADIAN CLOCK ON LIPID AND CARBOHYDRATE METABOLISM IN SKELETAL MUSCLE

As mentioned previously, there is a lot of evidence regarding the regulatory effects of circadian rhythm on lipid and carbohydrate metabolism in the liver (Tahara and Shibata, 2016). In skeletal muscle, circadian rhythm-regulated lipid and carbohydrate metabolism may be due to intrinsic molecular clocks or could be a response to a behavior such as feeding/fasting or neural and hormonal cues. Hodge et al. have reported that *Bmal1* in skeletal muscle-regulated genes is involved in the utilization and storage of energy substrates, independent of circadian activity (Hodge et al., 2015). For example, the peak time of lipogenic and lipolytic gene expression occurs at the end of the active phase and at the middle of the inactive phase, respectively. Carbohydrate catabolism and storage peak at the beginning of the active phase and in the middle of the active phase, respectively. These substrate-dependent peak times for metabolic genes in skeletal muscle are partially controlled by an intrinsic skeletal muscle molecular clock (Hodge et al., 2015). Other reports have demonstrated that insulin-stimulated glucose uptake, its metabolism, and its related factors are down-regulated in skeletal muscle-specific *Bmal1* knockout mice (Dyar et al., 2014; Harfmann et al., 2016). Glucose transporter 4 (GLUT4) is a key molecule for glucose transport in skeletal muscle. Insulin translocates GLUT4 from the cytoplasm to the plasma membrane via the activation of the insulin signaling pathway, which includes TBC1 domain family, member 1 (TBC1D1). Quantities of GLUT4 and TBC1D1 show a diurnal change, with increased levels during the active phase and decreased levels during the inactive phase (Dyar et al., 2014). These diurnal changes are not observed in muscle-specific *Bmal1* knockout mice (Dyar et al., 2014) and a deficiency in *Bmal1* reduces levels of these molecules throughout the day (Dyar et al., 2014; Harfmann et al., 2016). On the other hand, the deficiency of muscular *Bmal1* did not affect insulin signaling, including the phosphorylation of Akt (Dyar et al., 2014). In addition to affecting the transport of glucose, a deficiency in *Bmal1* causes dysregulation of glycolysis and glucose oxidation via the inactivity of metabolic enzymes, such as Hexokinase 2 (HK2) and Pyruvate dehydrogenase (PDH), suggesting abnormal glucose metabolism (Dyar et al., 2014; Harfmann et al., 2016). Owing to the dysregulation of the glycolytic pathway, a deficiency of *Bmal1* in skeletal muscle increases levels of the metabolites related to the pentose phosphate pathway, the polyol pathway, and glucuronic acid pathway (Dyar et al., 2014). These results, which relate not only to the transcriptome, but also to protein levels and metabolite levels, strongly support the notion that a major physiological role of the muscle clock is to prepare for the transition from the rest/fasting phase to the active/feeding phase, when glucose becomes the predominant fuel for skeletal muscle. Another investigation, using C2C12 myotubes, showed the role of muscle clocks in insulin sensitivity through Sirtuin 1 (*Sirt1*) (Liu et al., 2016). In this report, the knockdown of *Clock* and *Bmal1* caused insulin resistance via *Sirt1* (Liu et al., 2016). The muscular clock-regulated *Rev-erbα* also shows high expression levels in slow-twitch fiber type muscle, such as soleus muscle, and regulates lipid uptake and oxidative capacity in skeletal muscle by controlling mitochondrial biogenesis and autophagy (Woldt et al., 2013). A deficiency in *Rev-erbα* reduces oxidative capacity, which causes exercise intolerance (Woldt et al., 2013). RORα is highly expressed in skeletal muscles (Becker-Andre et al., 1993). A deficiency in *Rorα* inhibits the expression of genes involved in lipid homeostasis in skeletal muscle cells (Lau et al., 2004). In particular, RORα directly regulates the transcription of *Carnitine palmitoyltransferase-1* (*Cpt-1*) and *Caveolin-3* (Cav3) (Lau et al., 2004). These data suggest that the molecular clock generates the circadian rhythm of metabolism in skeletal muscle and that the disruption of circadian rhythm occurs owing to metabolic dysfunction in skeletal muscle.

THE PHASE-SHIFTED EFFECTS OF EXERCISE AND FEEDING TIME ON MUSCULAR CIRCADIAN CLOCKS

The hierarchy of tissue-specific clocks exists in the mammalian circadian clock system. The clock in the SCN is termed the master clock while clocks in other brain areas, such as the cerebral cortex and hippocampus, and peripheral tissues, such as the liver and skeletal muscle, are termed brain clocks and peripheral clocks, respectively. Brain and peripheral clocks are under the control of the master clock. Classically, the master clock is entrained by a photic cue, such as the light-dark cycle, and it is thought that peripheral clocks are also regulated by the central clock in the SCN. On the other hand, peripheral clocks are controlled in a central-clock-independent manner under certain conditions, such as scheduled exercise and restricted feeding (Damiola et al., 2000; Stokkan et al., 2001). Exercise is one of the non-photic phase-shifting cues (**Figure 1**). Several studies have shown scheduled exercise during the daytime or subjective daytime advancing of the phase of circadian rhythms in rodents (Reebs and Mrosovsky, 1989; Marchant and Mistlberger, 1996). Wolff et al. have shown the phase advanced effects of scheduled exercise in *ex-vivo* experiments (Wolff and Esser, 2012). After scheduled voluntary or involuntary (treadmill running) exercise during the daytime for 4 weeks, the phase expression of *Per2::Luc* advances in skeletal muscle and lung but not in the SCN (Wolff and Esser, 2012). Scheduled exercise also accelerates re-entrainment in mouse skeletal muscle and lung but not liver or the SCN to a new light-dark cycle (Yamanaka et al., 2008). In addition, Yamanaka et al. have shown that exercise-induced re-entrainment depends on the timing of exercise and on the peripheral tissues (Yamanaka et al., 2016). In the phase advanced light/dark cycle condition, wheel running at the beginning of the active phase (onset) accelerates the re-entrainment of the skeletal muscle clock but not the SCN. On the other hand, in the phase delayed light/dark cycle condition, wheel running at the end of the active-phase (offset) interferes with the re-entrainment of the skeletal muscle clock. These reports have indicated the potential of exercise to induce a phase shifting effect in skeletal muscle with the use of *ex vivo* experiments. In recent years, we have reported that exercise advances the phase of circadian rhythm in peripheral clocks, such as liver and gastrocnemius muscle, in *in vivo* experiments (Sasaki et al., 2016). In this report, the exercise-induced phase advance of the liver clock was stronger following forced exercise rather than voluntary exercise, although the difference between the two kinds of exercise to cause entrainment was not observed in the skeletal muscle clock. While the mechanism of exercise-induced phase shifting has not been fully elucidated, the role of some factors has been proposed to date. Adrenocortical hormone (Balsalobre et al., 2000; Hayasaka et al., 2007; Sujino et al., 2012; Tahara et al., 2015) and the sympathetic nervous system (Terazono et al., 2003; Tahara et al., 2015) play roles as entraining factors of peripheral clocks, and they are released and activated by exercise (Fediuc et al., 1985; Chennaoui et al., 2002; Stranahan et al., 2008; Zouhal et al., 2008; Hansen et al., 2012). In fact, we have shown that forced treadmill running increases serum corticosterone and tissue norepinephrine levels and their elevations play an important role in the forced exercise-induced phase shifting of peripheral clocks (Sasaki et al., 2016). The effects of inactivity on peripheral clocks have also been reported (Dyar et al., 2015; Nakao et al., 2015). Nakao et al. showed that the expression of *Bmal1*, *Per1*, *Per2*, *Rora*, *Nr1d1*, and *Dbp* were decreased, and the expression of *Clock* was increased, in inactive muscles by denervation of the sciatic nerve (Nakao et al., 2015). In denervated muscles, *Bmal1* and *Dbp* showed phase advance, compared with the contralateral muscle. The denervation-induced phase advance of muscular clocks has also reported by Dyar et al. (2015). Although the loss of muscle activity did not completely abolish the rhythms of muscular clocks, the rhythmic expressions of many cyclic genes were altered by denervation (Dyar et al., 2015; Nakao et al., 2015). These data suggest that physical activity affects muscular clocks. Further investigation is needed into the role of neuronal signals and physical activity in the direct and indirect regulation of muscular clocks; physical activity causes several physiological changes, such as to body temperature and hormonal status, which are known to affect the peripheral clocks (Tahara et al., 2017). The phase shifting effects of exercise have been observed in human studies (Van Reeth et al., 1994; Buxton et al., 1997, 2003; Miyazaki et al., 2001; Barger et al., 2004). For example, Yamanaka et al. reported that the sleep-wake cycle but not melatonin rhythm is accelerated by exercise under dim light conditions and a phase-advanced sleep schedule (Yamanaka et al., 2010). Zambon et al. reported that resistant exercise changed the gene expression of the circadian clock in the skeletal muscle of humans (Zambon et al., 2003). These reports indicate that exercise acts as a potential entrainer of skeletal muscle clocks in humans as well as rodents.

As mentioned before, the peripheral clock is regulated by restricted feeding (Damiola et al., 2000; Stokkan et al., 2001). To date, restricted feeding shifts and entrains the liver clock in an SCN-independent manner (Hara et al., 2001; Tahara and Shibata, 2014). It is thought that insulin is the hormone responsible for the feeding-induced phase advance of the peripheral clock (Kuriyama et al., 2004; Tahara et al., 2011; Dang et al., 2016). Skeletal muscle is one of the major insulin sensitive organs and it controls whole body blood glucose levels via insulin-stimulated glucose uptake (DeFronzo, 1988). This evidence

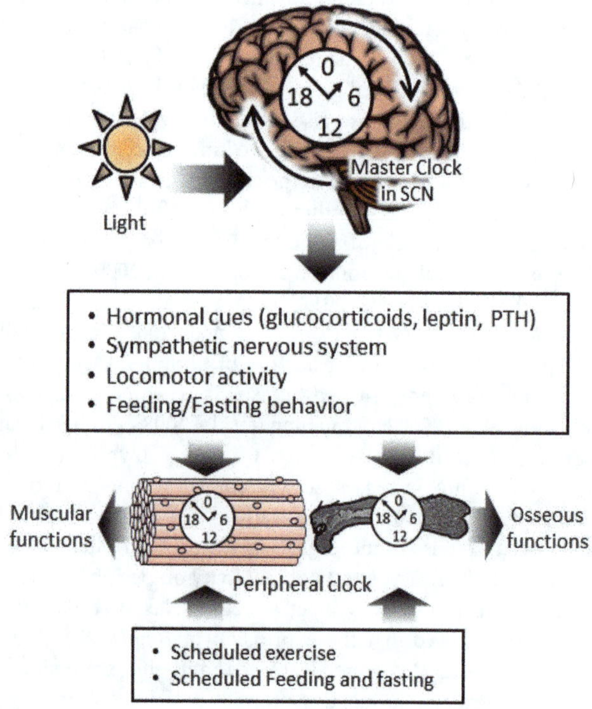

FIGURE 1 | The diurnal regulation of skeletal muscle and osseous functions by circadian clock systems and chrono-exercise and –nutrition. The master clock in the suprachiasmatic nucleus (SCN) is reset by a photic cue and it regulates the peripheral circadian clock and homeostasis in skeletal muscle and bone via hormonal cues, the nervous system, locomotor activity and feeding behavior. Muscular clocks are regulated by scheduled exercise in an SCN-independent manner. Circadian variation of osseous markers are regulated by scheduled feeding.

gives the expectation that clocks in insulin-sensitive organs are regulated by restricted feeding, in other words restricted feeding regulates the peripheral clock not only in the liver but also in skeletal muscle. However, Guo et al. reported tissue-dependent regulation of the peripheral clock by hormonal cues in SCN-lesioned mice (Guo et al., 2005). When circulating factors in SCN-lesioned mice and intact mice are shared by parabiosis, the arrhythmic clock gene expression in the liver of SCN-lesioned mice is restored. On the other hand, the disturbance of the skeletal muscle clock is not restored by parabiosis, indicating that circulating factors, such as hormones, are not important for the regulation of the skeletal muscle clock. In fact, some reports have shown that the expression of core clock genes, such as *Bmal1* and *Per2,* is synchronized by day time feeding in the liver but not skeletal muscle (Reznick et al., 2013; Yasumoto et al., 2016). On the other hand, some rhythmic genes, such as *Pdk4* (*pyruvate dehydrogenase kinase 4*) and *Ucp3*, in skeletal muscles show arrhythmic or dampened expression patterns owing to day time feeding. These data suggest that restricted feeding does not have a major effect on the skeletal muscle clock. However, further evidence is needed because reports about the effect of restricted feeding on circadian rhythm in skeletal muscle have been limited.

CIRCADIAN RHYTHM OF BONE FUNCTIONS

Bone is one of the organs to play a major role in the storage of calcium and phosphorus. Three kinds of cells exist in bone, namely osteocytes, osteoblasts, and osteoclasts, (Prideaux et al., 2016). More than 90% of cells in bone are osteocytes, and these cells play a role in the storage of bone matrix (Prideaux et al., 2016), whereas osteoblasts and osteoclasts regulate bone remodeling. Bone homeostasis is regulated by the balance between the production of bone matrix by osteoblasts, called bone formation, and the breakdown of bone matrix by osteoclasts, called bone resorption (Rodan and Martin, 2000). Not only the process of bone remodeling but also serum concentrations of some hormones regulating bone metabolism show diurnal variation (Dudek and Meng, 2014). For example, it has been reported that serum concentrations of calcitonin, calcium, osteocalcin, parathyroid hormone C-telopeptide, skeletal alkaline phosphatase, and tartate-resistant acid phosphatase show diurnal variation (Greenspan et al., 1997; Srivastava et al., 2001; Shao et al., 2003; Yang and Meng, 2016). In addition, Zvonic et al. reported on the circadian transcriptome in calvarial bone (Zvonic et al., 2007). In this report, more than 26% of genes expressed in calvarial bone show a rhythmic expression (Zvonic et al., 2007). Interestingly, among the rhythmic genes in calvarial bone 64% of genes do not exhibit rhythmic expression in liver, brown adipose tissue or white adipose tissue. In other words, a lot of rhythmic gene expression is controlled in a tissue-specific manner. For example, calcium channels, ADAMs (a disintegrin and metalloproteinases), FGFs (fibroblast growth factors), and Runxs (runt related transcription factors), which have critical roles in bone formation, bone remodeling, bone metabolism regulated cytokines and bone-specific transcriptional factors, show diurnal gene expression patterns (Zvonic et al., 2007). The transcriptomic results from calvarial bone suggest that the process of metabolism in several bones is regulated by circadian rhythm.

Indeed, it has been reported that some molecular clocks regulate and maintain bone homeostasis (**Table 1**). Fu et al. demonstrated that both *Per1* deficient and *Per2* PAS domain mutant mice have high bone mass (Fu et al., 2005). This phenotype is also exhibited by other clock gene modified mice, i.e., *Per1* and *2* double knockout mice, *Cry1* and *2* double knockout mice, *Bmal1* knockout mice, *Per2* mutant mice and *Cry2* knockout mice (Fu et al., 2005; Maronde et al., 2010). These reports have suggested that the molecular clock is a negative regulator of bone mass. The high bone mass induced by molecular clock-deficiency is controlled by osteoblast differentiation via leptin-Adrβ2 (adrenoceptor beta 2)-Creb1 cascades (Fu et al., 2005). Indeed, leptin levels are elevated in mice with both genotypes, $Per1^{-/-}$ and $Per2^{-/-}$ *mutant* mice, and the elevation of leptin levels may be involved in osteoblast differentiation via Adrβ2 activation. In fact, it has been reported that both leptin deficient mice and *Adrb2* deficient mice display a low bone mass phenotype (Ducy et al., 2000; Takeda et al., 2002). Therefore, clock deficiency-induced high bone mass is involved in leptin-dependent sympathetic activation via the Adrβ2. In contrast, Samsa et al. reported that deficiency of *Bmal1* in mice results in age-related bone loss (Samsa et al., 2016), which is in contrast to the results of a previous report (Fu et al., 2005). The different bone phenotypes in these reports may be due to the age differences of the mice. *Pers, Crys,* or *Bmal1* deficiency-induced high bone mass is observed during young and adolescent ages (Fu et al., 2005; Maronde et al., 2010). On the other hand, *Bmal1* deficiency-induced low bone mass is observed at geriatric age (Samsa et al., 2016). *Bmal1* knockout mice also show age-associated phenotypes such as body weight loss and sarcopenia (Kondratov et al., 2006). In addition, abnormal bone calcification and arthropathy in *Bmal1* knockout mice did not replicate in tamoxifen-inducible *Bmal1* knockout mice after development (Yang et al., 2016). While the reason for the opposing effects of *Bmal1* on bone mass have not been well elucidated, the age-dependent effects of *Bmal1* on bone mass may be one explanation.

The effects of circadian clock genes on bone resorption have been examined using osteoclast-specific *Bmal1* knockout mice (Xu et al., 2016). The osteoclast-specific *Bmal1* knockout mice have a high bone mass. The upregulation of *Nfatc1* via the direct regulation of the heterodimer of BMAL1 and CLOCK induces osteoclast differentiation and then reduces bone mass (Xu et al., 2016). This report suggests that the osteoclast clock genes reduce bone mass via the activation of osteoclast differentiation.

Interestingly, in recent years it has been reported that skeletal muscle clocks are linked to the maintenance of bone homeostasis. Schroder et al. reported that muscle specific-*Bmal1* knockout mice show thickening of the distal tibia (Schroder et al., 2015). Muscle and bone may communicate with each other via endocrine factors and mechanical loading (Karsenty and Olson, 2016). For example, myostatin, one of the hormones secreted from skeletal muscle, regulates osteoclast differentiation (Dankbar et al., 2015). While the mechanism of interaction of these tissues has not been fully elucidated yet, the skeletal muscle clock is closely linked to the maintenance of bone homeostasis.

REGULATION OF THE OSSEOUS CIRCADIAN RHYTHM BY INTERNAL AND EXTERNAL CUES

The circadian rhythms of bone functions are controlled by internal or external cues to maintain a balance between bone formation and bone resorption. The master clock in the SCN controls the peripheral circadian clocks via output signals such as hormonal and sympathetic nervous system signaling. Leptin is known to be one of the entraining factors of the circadian clock in osteoblasts (Fu et al., 2005) (**Figure 1**). Leptin activates the sympathetic nervous system via the Adrβ2, of which Creb1 is a downstream factor (Fu et al., 2005). These reports indicate that the osteoblast clock is regulated by sympathetic nervous system signals. In addition, in human osteoblasts, treatment with a β-adrenergic receptor agonist, isoprenaline, or synthetic glucocorticoids, dexamethasone, induces the circadian expression of clock genes (Komoto et al., 2012), suggesting that both sympathetic nervous system and glucocorticoid signals are involved in the circadian rhythm in osteoblasts and act as mediators from the SCN to osteoblasts. On the other hand, in osteoclasts, glucocorticoid signals rather than sympathetic signals have the ability to regulate rhythmic gene expression. Fujihara et al. demonstrated that the rhythmic expression of clock genes is changed by stimulation with dexamethasone but not isoprenaline (Fujihara et al., 2014). Osteoclast-specific genes, *Nfatc1 (nuclear factor of activated T cells 1)* and *Ctsk (cathepsin K)*, show rhythmic expressions (Fujihara et al., 2014). The rhythmic expression of *Nfatc1* participates in *Bmal1*-regulated bone resorption, as described above (Xu et al., 2016). These rhythmic expressions are dampened in cancellous bone from adrenalectomized mice, and glucocorticoid injection restores the rhythmic expression of these genes (Fujihara et al., 2014). This evidence indicates that glucocorticoid signaling acts as a mediator between the SCN and osteoclasts for the synchronization of circadian rhythms in osteoclasts.

Feeding and fasting regulate the diurnal variation of the bone resorption marker serum C-telopeptide fragments of collagen type 1 degradation (s-CTx) (Gertz et al., 1998) (**Figure 1**). The levels of s-CTx in humans are higher during early morning, from 05:00 to 08:00, and lower in the late afternoon, from 12:00 to 16:00. The levels of s-CTx show diurnal variation under normal feeding conditions, such as the consumption of breakfast, lunch and dinner, while fasting dampens the diurnal variation of s-CTx (Bjarnason et al., 2002; Qvist et al., 2002). In addition, the feeding-induced generation of this diurnal variation is also observed in the intake of glucose, protein, and fat (Bjarnason et al., 2002). The diurnal variation of levels of s-CTx under normal feeding conditions only occurs during breakfast but not lunch or dinner (Bjarnason et al., 2002). A reason for this may be that fasting plays a role in the feeding-induced generation of the s-CTx rhythm, since the fasting period from breakfast to lunch and from lunch to dinner is shorter than that from dinner to breakfast. These reports suggest that the feeding and fasting rhythm is an important factor in regulating and maintaining the circadian rhythm of bone resorption, although the mechanism for the preventative effects of food intake on bone resorption has not been well investigated.

Mechanical loading, such as exercise, protects against age-related bone loss, whereas unloading, such as bed rest, induces bone loss (Qi et al., 2016). Some reports have shown the effects of unloading on circadian rhythms of bone resorption markers (Halloran et al., 1988; Pedersen et al., 1995; Kim et al., 2000). Pedersen et al. showed that 5 days of bed rest in healthy women did not change the circadian rhythm of s-CTx or other serum bone resorption markers, such as alkaline phosphatase and osteocalcin (Pedersen et al., 1995). No effects of unloading on diurnal variation of bone resorption markers have been shown by other reports (Halloran et al., 1988; Kim et al., 2000). These reports suggest that a common physical activity rhythm, which also includes low intensity exercise, does not have the potential to regulate the circadian rhythm of bone resorption. However, moderate or high intensity scheduled exercise may affect the circadian variation of bone metabolism, since mechanical loading influences bone resorption and bone formation, as well as circulating factors such as glucocorticoids and parathyroid hormone (Fragala et al., 2011; Gardinier et al., 2015; Qi et al., 2016; Sasaki et al., 2016).

PERSPECTIVES

Based on recent findings, circadian rhythms in skeletal muscle and bone maintain their homeostasis. The disruption of muscle clocks occurs owing to dysregulation of whole body glucose metabolism (Harfmann et al., 2016) and bone clocks could be negative regulators of bone mass through the inhibition of bone formation and the activation of bone resorption (Fu et al., 2005; Xu et al., 2016). These finding suggest that disturbances of circadian rhythms by social or environmental factors, such as shift work, may result in dysfunctions of skeletal muscle and bone. In epidemiological studies, the prevalence of metabolic syndrome, osteoporosis and bone fractures is increased in shift workers (Feskanich et al., 2009; Pietroiusti et al., 2010; Quevedo and Zuniga, 2010). In addition, it has been reported that long term constant light exposure reduces muscle strength and bone mass in mice (Lucassen et al., 2016). These findings indicate that the regulation of circadian rhythms in skeletal muscle and bone by external cues, such as feeding and exercise, are important for the maintenance of homeostasis in these tissues, since circadian rhythm in these tissues can be entrained or regulated by the feeding/fasting rhythm and the physical activity rhythm, including scheduled exercise. We report that disturbances of circadian rhythms in peripheral clocks under constant light conditions are partially improved by scheduled feeding and scheduled exercise, although the circadian clocks in skeletal muscle and bone have not been measured (Hamaguchi et al., 2015). In addition, the reductions in both mitochondrial content and exercise tolerance in the skeletal muscle of *Clock* mutant mice are restored by endurance exercise training (Pastore and Hood, 2013), suggesting that exercise can prevent circadian disturbance-induced muscular dysfunctions. In addition, some reports have shown the importance of the circadian timing of exercise for the prevention of diseases. Schroeder et al. have reported that rhythmic deficits observed in vasointestinal polypeptide-deficient mice are improved by wheel running exercise (Schroeder et al., 2012). Interestingly, greater preventative effects are observed when wheel running occurs at the end of the active phase but not at the beginning of the active phase (Schroeder et al., 2012). We have also reported that wheel running exercise at the end of the active phase has more preventative effects on high fat diet-induced obesity than that occurring at the beginning of the active phase (Sasaki et al., 2014). In addition, exercise in the morning but not in the afternoon or evening increases fat oxidation over 24 h in healthy humans (Iwayama et al., 2015). These reports suggest the importance of scheduled feeding or exercise for skeletal muscle and bone health. However, the importance of the circadian timing of exercise and nutritional intake for muscular and osseous health has not been well elucidated. Further advanced evidence is required and it is expected to lead to a better understanding of the mutual interaction between the circadian clock and muscle/bone.

AUTHOR CONTRIBUTIONS

SA and SS were involved in conceptualizing and writing the manuscript.

REFERENCES

Andrews, J. L., Zhang, X., McCarthy, J. J., McDearmon, E. L., Hornberger, T. A., Russell, B., et al. (2010). CLOCK and BMAL1 regulate MyoD and are necessary for maintenance of skeletal muscle phenotype and function. *Proc. Natl. Acad. Sci. U.S.A.* 107, 19090–19095. doi: 10.1073/pnas.1014523107

Bae, K., Lee, K., Seo, Y., Lee, H., Kim, D., and Choi, I. (2006). Differential effects of two period genes on the physiology and proteomic profiles of mouse anterior tibialis muscles. *Mol. Cells* 22, 275–284.

Balsalobre, A., Brown, S. A., Marcacci, L., Tronche, F., Kellendonk, C., Reichardt, H. M., et al. (2000). Resetting of circadian time in peripheral tissues by glucocorticoid signaling. *Science* 289, 2344–2347. doi: 10.1126/science.289.5488.2344

Barger, L. K., Wright, K. P. Jr., Hughes, R. J., and Czeisler, C. A. (2004). Daily exercise facilitates phase delays of circadian melatonin rhythm in very dim light. *Am. J. Physiol. Regul. Integr. Comp. Physiol.* 286, R1077–R1084. doi: 10.1152/ajpregu.00397.2003

Becker-Andre, M., Andre, E., and DeLamarter, J. F. (1993). Identification of nuclear receptor mRNAs by RT-PCR amplification of conserved zinc-finger motif sequences. *Biochem. Biophys. Res. Commun.* 194, 1371–1379.

Bjarnason, N. H., Henriksen, E. E., Alexandersen, P., Christgau, S., Henriksen, D. B., and Christiansen, C. (2002). Mechanism of circadian variation in bone resorption. *Bone* 30, 307–313. doi: 10.1016/S8756-3282(01)00662-7

Busino, L., Bassermann, F., Maiolica, A., Lee, C., Nolan, P. M., Godinho, S. I., et al. (2007). SCFFbxl3 controls the oscillation of the circadian clock by directing the degradation of cryptochrome proteins. *Science* 316, 900–904. doi: 10.1126/science.1141194

Buxton, O. M., Frank, S. A., L'Hermite-Baleriaux, M., Leproult, R., Turek, F. W., and Van Cauter, E. (1997). Roles of intensity and duration of nocturnal exercise in causing phase delays of human circadian rhythms. *Am. J. Physiol.* 273, E536–E542.

Buxton, O. M., Lee, C. W., L'Hermite-Baleriaux, M., Turek, F. W., and Van Cauter, E. (2003). Exercise elicits phase shifts and acute alterations of melatonin that vary with circadian phase. *Am. J. Physiol. Regul. Integr. Comp. Physiol.* 284, R714–R724. doi: 10.1152/ajpregu.00355.2002

Charge, S. B., Brack, A. S., Bayol, S. A., and Hughes, S. M. (2008). MyoD- and nerve-dependent maintenance of MyoD expression in mature muscle fibres acts through the DRR/PRR element. *BMC Dev. Biol.* 8:5. doi: 10.1186/1471-213X-8-5

Chatterjee, S., and Ma, K. (2016). Circadian clock regulation of skeletal muscle growth and repair. *F1000Research* 5:1549. doi: 10.12688/f1000research.9076.1

Chatterjee, S., Nam, D., Guo, B., Kim, J. M., Winnier, G. E., Lee, J., et al. (2013). Brain and muscle Arnt-like 1 is a key regulator of myogenesis. *J. Cell Sci.* 126, 2213–2224. doi: 10.1242/jcs.120519

Chatterjee, S., Yin, H., Nam, D., Li, Y., and Ma, K. (2015). Brain and muscle Arnt-like 1 promotes skeletal muscle regeneration through satellite cell expansion. *Exp. Cell Res.* 331, 200–210. doi: 10.1016/j.yexcr.2014.08.041

Chennaoui, M., Gomez Merino, D., Lesage, J., Drogou, C., and Guezennec, C. Y. (2002). Effects of moderate and intensive training on the hypothalamo-pituitary-adrenal axis in rats. *Acta Physiol. Scand.* 175, 113–21. doi: 10.1046/j.1365-201x.2002.00971.x

Damiola, F., Le Minh, N., Preitner, N., Kornmann, B., Fleury-Olela, F., and Schibler, U. (2000). Restricted feeding uncouples circadian oscillators in peripheral tissues from the central pacemaker in the suprachiasmatic nucleus. *Genes Dev.* 14, 2950–2961. doi: 10.1101/gad.183500

Dang, F., Sun, X., Ma, X., Wu, R., Zhang, D., Chen, Y., et al. (2016). Insulin post-transcriptionally modulates Bmal1 protein to affect the hepatic circadian clock. *Nat. Commun.* 7:12696. doi: 10.1038/ncomms12696

Dankbar, B., Fennen, M., Brunert, D., Hayer, S., Frank, S., Wehmeyer, C., et al. (2015). Myostatin is a direct regulator of osteoclast differentiation and its inhibition reduces inflammatory joint destruction in mice. *Nat. Med.* 21, 1085–1090. doi: 10.1038/nm.3917

DeFronzo, R. A. (1988). Lilly lecture 1987. The triumvirate:β-cell, muscle, liver. A collusion responsible for NIDDM. *Diabetes* 37, 667–687.

Dolatshad, H., Cary, A. J., and Davis, F. C. (2010). Differential expression of the circadian clock in maternal and embryonic tissues of mice. *PLoS ONE* 5:e9855. doi: 10.1371/journal.pone.0009855

Ducy, P., Amling, M., Takeda, S., Priemel, M., Schilling, A. F., Beil, F. T., et al. (2000). Leptin inhibits bone formation through a hypothalamic relay: a central control of bone mass. *Cell* 100, 197–207. doi: 10.1016/s0092-8674(00)81558-5

Dudek, M., and Meng, Q. J. (2014). Running on time: the role of circadian clocks in the musculoskeletal system. *Biochem. J.* 463, 1–8. doi: 10.1042/BJ20140700

Dyar, K. A., Ciciliot, S., Tagliazucchi, G. M., Pallafacchina, G., Tothova, J., Argentini, C., et al. (2015). The calcineurin-NFAT pathway controls activity-dependent circadian gene expression in slow skeletal muscle. *Mol. Metab.* 4, 823–833. doi: 10.1016/j.molmet.2015.09.004

Dyar, K. A., Ciciliot, S., Wright, L. E., Bienso, R. S., Tagliazucchi, G. M., Patel, V. R., et al. (2014). Muscle insulin sensitivity and glucose metabolism are controlled by the intrinsic muscle clock. *Mol. Metab.* 3, 29–41. doi: 10.1016/j.molmet.2013.10.005

Fediuc, S., Campbell, J. E., and Riddell, M. C. (1985). Effect of voluntary wheel running on circadian corticosterone release and on HPA axis responsiveness to restraint stress in Sprague-Dawley rats. *J. Appl. Physiol.* 100, 1867–1875.

Feskanich, D., Hankinson, S. E., and Schernhammer, E. S. (2009). Nightshift work and fracture risk: the Nurses' Health Study. *Osteoporos. Int.* 20, 537–542. doi: 10.1007/s00198-008-0729-5

Fragala, M. S., Kraemer, W. J., Denegar, C. R., Maresh, C. M., Mastro, A. M., and Volek, J. S. (2011). Neuroendocrine-immune interactions and responses to exercise. *Sports Med.* 41, 621–639. doi: 10.2165/11590430-000000000-00000

Fu, L., Patel, M. S., Bradley, A., Wagner, E. F., and Karsenty, G. (2005). The molecular clock mediates leptin-regulated bone formation. *Cell* 122, 803–815. doi: 10.1016/j.cell.2005.06.028

Fujihara, Y., Kondo, H., Noguchi, T., and Togari, A. (2014). Glucocorticoids mediate circadian timing in peripheral osteoclasts resulting in the circadian expression rhythm of osteoclast-related genes. *Bone* 61, 1–9. doi: 10.1016/j.bone.2013.12.026

Gardinier, J. D., Mohamed, F., and Kohn, D. H. (2015). PTH signaling during exercise contributes to bone adaptation. *J. Bone Miner. Res.* 30, 1053–1063. doi: 10.1002/jbmr.2432

Gekakis, N., Staknis, D., Nguyen, H. B., Davis, F. C., Wilsbacher, L. D., King, D. P., et al. (1998). Role of the CLOCK protein in the mammalian circadian mechanism. *Science* 280, 1564–1569. doi: 10.1126/science.280.5369.1564

Gertz, B. J., Clemens, J. D., Holland, S. D., Yuan, W., and Greenspan, S. (1998). Application of a new serum assay for type I collagen cross-linked N-telopeptides: assessment of diurnal changes in bone turnover with and without alendronate treatment. *Calcif. Tissue Int.* 63, 102–106. doi: 10.1007/s002239900497

Greenspan, S. L., Dresner-Pollak, R., Parker, R. A., London, D., and Ferguson, L. (1997). Diurnal variation of bone mineral turnover in elderly men and women. *Calcif. Tissue Int.* 60, 419–423. doi: 10.1007/s002239900256

Guo, H., Brewer, J. M., Champhekar, A., Harris, R. B., and Bittman, E. L. (2005). Differential control of peripheral circadian rhythms by suprachiasmatic-dependent neural signals. *Proc. Natl. Acad. Sci. U.S.A.* 102, 3111–3116. doi: 10.1073/pnas.0409734102

Halloran, B. P., Bikle, D. D., Cone, C. M., and Morey-Holton, E. (1988). Glucocorticoids and inhibition of bone formation induced by skeletal unloading. *Am. J. Physiol.* 255, E875–E879.

Hamaguchi, Y., Tahara, Y., Hitosugi, M., and Shibata, S. (2015). Impairment of circadian rhythms in peripheral clocks by constant light is partially reversed by scheduled feeding or exercise. *J. Biol. Rhythms* 30, 533–542. doi: 10.1177/0748730415609727

Hansen, D., Meeusen, R., Mullens, A., and Dendale, P. (2012). Effect of acute endurance and resistance exercise on endocrine hormones directly related to lipolysis and skeletal muscle protein synthesis in adult individuals with obesity. *Sports Med.* 42, 415–431. doi: 10.2165/11599590-000000000-00000

Hara, R., Wan, K., Wakamatsu, H., Aida, R., Moriya, T., Akiyama, M., et al. (2001). Restricted feeding entrains liver clock without participation of the suprachiasmatic nucleus. *Genes Cells* 6, 269–278. doi: 10.1046/j.1365-2443.2001.00419.x

Harfmann, B. D., Schroder, E. A., Kachman, M. T., Hodge, B. A., Zhang, X., and Esser, K. A. (2016). Muscle-specific loss of Bmal1 leads to disrupted tissue glucose metabolism and systemic glucose homeostasis. *Skelet. Muscle* 6:12. doi: 10.1186/s13395-016-0082-x

Hayasaka, N., Yaita, T., Kuwaki, T., Honma, S., Honma, K., Kudo, T., et al. (2007). Optimization of dosing schedule of daily inhalant dexamethasone to minimize phase shifting of clock gene expression rhythm in the lungs of the asthma mouse model. *Endocrinology* 148, 3316–3326. doi: 10.1210/en.2007-0010

Hodge, B. A., Wen, Y., Riley, L. A., Zhang, X., England, J. H., Harfmann, B. D., et al. (2015). The endogenous molecular clock orchestrates the temporal separation of substrate metabolism in skeletal muscle. *Skelet. Muscle* 5:17. doi: 10.1186/s13395-015-0039-5

Hughes, S. M., Koishi, K., Rudnicki, M., and Maggs, A. M. (1997). MyoD protein is differentially accumulated in fast and slow skeletal muscle fibres and required for normal fibre type balance in rodents. *Mech. Dev.* 61, 151–163. doi: 10.1016/s0925-4773(96)00631-4

Iwayama, K., Kurihara, R., Nabekura, Y., Kawabuchi, R., Park, I., Kobayashi, M., et al. (2015). Exercise increases 24-h fat oxidation only when it is performed before breakfast. *EBioMedicine* 2, 2003–2009. doi: 10.1016/j.ebiom.2015.10.029

Karsenty, G., and Olson, E. N. (2016). Bone and muscle endocrine functions: unexpected paradigms of inter-organ communication. *Cell* 164, 1248–1256. doi: 10.1016/j.cell.2016.02.043

Kim, C. S., Maekawa, Y., Fujita, M., Sato, N., Nishimuta, M., Ishizaki, Y., et al. (2000). Immobilization on the day 14th does not disrupts the basic diurnal rhythm of bone resorption. *J. Gravit. physiol.* 7, P125–P126.

King, D. P., Zhao, Y., Sangoram, A. M., Wilsbacher, L. D., Tanaka, M., Antoch, M. P., et al. (1997). Positional cloning of the mouse circadian clock gene. *Cell* 89, 641–653. doi: 10.1016/s0092-8674(00)80245-7

Komoto, S., Kondo, H., Fukuta, O., and Togari, A. (2012). Comparison of beta-adrenergic and glucocorticoid signaling on clock gene and osteoblast-related gene expressions in human osteoblast. *Chronobiol. Int.* 29, 66–74. doi: 10.3109/07420528.2011.636496

Kondratov, R. V., Kondratova, A. A., Gorbacheva, V. Y., Vykhovanets, O. V., and Antoch, M. P. (2006). Early aging and age-related pathologies in mice deficient in BMAL1, the core componentof the circadian clock. *Genes Dev.* 20, 1868–1873. doi: 10.1101/gad.1432206

Kuriyama, K., Sasahara, K., Kudo, T., and Shibata, S. (2004). Daily injection of insulin attenuated impairment of liver circadian clock oscillation in the streptozotocin-treated diabetic mouse. *FEBS Lett.* 572, 206–210. doi: 10.1016/j.febslet.2004.07.036

Lau, P., Nixon, S. J., Parton, R. G., and Muscat, G. E. (2004). RORα regulates the expression of genes involved in lipid homeostasis in skeletal muscle cells: caveolin-3 and CPT-1 are direct targets of ROR. *J. Biol. Chem.* 279, 36828–36840. doi: 10.1074/jbc.M404927200

Lee, S. J., Huynh, T. V., Lee, Y. S., Sebald, S. M., Wilcox-Adelman, S. A., Iwamori, N., et al. (2012). Role of satellite cells versus myofibers in muscle hypertrophy induced by inhibition of the myostatin/activin signaling pathway. *Proc. Natl. Acad. Sci. U.S.A.* 109, E2353–E2360. doi: 10.1073/pnas.1206410109

Legerlotz, K., and Smith, H. K. (2008). Role of MyoD in denervated, disused, and exercised muscle. *Muscle Nerve* 38, 1087–1100. doi: 10.1002/mus.21087

Lipton, J. O., Yuan, E. D., Boyle, L. M., Ebrahimi-Fakhari, D., Kwiatkowski, E., Nathan, A., et al. (2015). The circadian protein BMAL1 regulates translation in response to S6K1-mediated phosphorylation. *Cell* 161, 1138–1151. doi: 10.1016/j.cell.2015.04.002

Liu, J., Zhou, B., Yan, M., Huang, R., Wang, Y., He, Z., et al. (2016). CLOCK and BMAL1 regulate muscle insulin sensitivity via SIRT1 in male mice. *Endocrinology* 157, 2259–2269. doi: 10.1210/en.2015-2027

Lowrey, P. L., Shimomura, K., Antoch, M. P., Yamazaki, S., Zemenides, P. D., Ralph, M. R., et al. (2000). Positional syntenic cloning and functional characterization of the mammalian circadian mutation tau. *Science* 288, 483–492. doi: 10.1126/science.288.5465.483

Lucassen, E. A., Coomans, C. P., van Putten, M., de Kreij, S. R., van Genugten, J. H., Sutorius, R. P., et al. (2016). Environmental 24-hr cycles are essential for health. *Curr. Biol.* 26, 1843–1853. doi: 10.1016/j.cub.2016.05.038

Marchant, E. G., and Mistlberger, R. E. (1996). Entrainment and phase shifting of circadian rhythms in mice by forced treadmill running. *Physiol. Behav.* 60, 657–663. doi: 10.1016/S0031-9384(96)80045-X

Maronde, E., Schilling, A. F., Seitz, S., Schinke, T., Schmutz, I., van der Horst, G., et al. (2010). The clock genes Period 2 and Cryptochrome 2 differentially balance bone formation. *PLoS ONE* 5:e11527. doi: 10.1371/journal.pone.0011527

Mayeuf-Louchart, A., Staels, B., and Duez, H. (2015). Skeletal muscle functions around the clock. *Diabetes Obes. Metab.* 17(Suppl. 1), 39–46. doi: 10.1111/dom.12517

McCarthy, J. J., Andrews, J. L., McDearmon, E. L., Campbell, K. S., Barber, B. K., Miller, B. H., et al. (2007). Identification of the circadian transcriptome in adult mouse skeletal muscle. *Physiol. Genomics* 31, 86–95. doi: 10.1152/physiolgenomics.00066.2007

McDearmon, E. L., Patel, K. N., Ko, C. H., Walisser, J. A., Schook, A. C., Chong, J. L., et al. (2006). Dissecting the functions of the mammalian clock protein BMAL1 by tissue-specific rescue in mice. *Science* 314, 1304–1308. doi: 10.1126/science.1132430

Miller, B. H., McDearmon, E. L., Panda, S., Hayes, K. R., Zhang, J., Andrews, J. L., et al. (2007). Circadian and CLOCK-controlled regulation of the mouse transcriptome and cell proliferation. *Proc. Natl. Acad. Sci. U.S.A.* 104, 3342–3347. doi: 10.1073/pnas.0611724104

Miyazaki, T., Hashimoto, S., Masubuchi, S., Honma, S., and Honma, K. I. (2001). Phase-advance shifts of human circadian pacemaker are accelerated by daytime physical exercise. *Am. J. Physiol. Regul. Integr. Comp. Physiol.* 281, R197–R205.

Nakao, R., Yamamoto, S., Horikawa, K., Yasumoto, Y., Nikawa, T., Mukai, C., et al. (2015). Atypical expression of circadian clock genes in denervated mouse skeletal muscle. *Chronobiol. Int.* 32, 486–496. doi: 10.3109/07420528.2014.1003350

Pastore, S., and Hood, D. A. (2013). Endurance training ameliorates the metabolic and performance characteristics of circadian Clock mutant mice. *J. Appl. Physiol.* 14, 1076–1084.

Pedersen, B. J., Schlemmer, A., Hassager, C., and Christiansen, C. (1995). Changes in the carboxyl-terminal propeptide of type I procollagen and other markers of bone formation upon five days of bed rest. *Bone* 17, 91–95. doi: 10.1016/8756-3282(95)00149-8

Pietroiusti, A., Neri, A., Somma, G., Coppeta, L., Iavicoli, I., Bergamaschi, A., et al. (2010). Incidence of metabolic syndrome among night-shift healthcare workers. *Occup. Environ. Med.* 67, 54–57. doi: 10.1136/oem.2009.0 46797

Pircher, P., Chomez, P., Yu, F., Vennstrom, B., and Larsson, L. (2005). Aberrant expression of myosin isoforms in skeletal muscles from mice lacking the rev-erbAα orphan receptor gene. *Am. J. Physiol. Regul. Integr. Comp. Physiol.* 288, R482–R490. doi: 10.1152/ajpregu.00690.2003

Powers, S. K., Kavazis, A. N., and DeRuisseau, K. C. (2005). Mechanisms of disuse muscle atrophy: role of oxidative stress. *Am. J. Physiol. Regul. Integr. Comp. Physiol.* 288, R337–R344. doi: 10.1152/ajpregu.00469.2004

Preitner, N., Damiola, F., Lopez-Molina, L., Zakany, J., Duboule, D., Albrecht, U., et al. (2002). The orphan nuclear receptor REV-ERBα controls circadian transcription within the positive limb of the mammalian circadian oscillator. *Cell* 110, 251–260. doi: 10.1016/S0092-8674(02)00825-5

Prideaux, M., Findlay, D. M., and Atkins, G. J. (2016). Osteocytes: the master cells in bone remodelling. *Curr. Opin. Pharmacol.* 28, 24–30. doi: 10.1016/j.coph.2016.02.003

Qi, Z., Liu, W., and Lu, J. (2016). The mechanisms underlying the beneficial effects of exercise on bone remodeling: roles of bone-derived cytokines and microRNAs. *Prog. Biophys. Mol. Biol.* 122, 131–139. doi: 10.1016/j.pbiomolbio.2016.05.010

Quevedo, I., and Zuniga, A. M. (2010). Low bone mineral density in rotating-shift workers. *J. Clin. Densitom.* 13, 467–469. doi: 10.1016/j.jocd.2010.07.004

Qvist, P., Christgau, S., Pedersen, B. J., Schlemmer, A., and Christiansen, C. (2002). Circadian variation in the serum concentration of C-terminal telopeptide of type I collagen (serum CTx): effects of gender, age, menopausal status, posture, daylight, serum cortisol, and fasting. *Bone* 31, 57–61. doi: 10.1016/s8756-3282(02)00791-3

Reebs, S. G., and Mrosovsky, N. (1989). Effects of induced wheel running on the circadian activity rhythms of Syrian hamsters: entrainment and phase response curve. *J. Biol. Rhythms* 4, 39–48. doi: 10.1177/074873048900400103

Reznick, J., Preston, E., Wilks, D. L., Beale, S. M., Turner, N., and Cooney, G. J. (2013). Altered feeding differentially regulates circadian rhythms and energy metabolism in liver and muscle of rats. *Biochim. Biophys. Acta* 1832, 228–238. doi: 10.1016/j.bbadis.2012.08.010

Rodan, G. A., and Martin, T. J. (2000). Therapeutic approaches to bone diseases. *Science* 289, 1508–1514. doi: 10.1126/science.289.5484.1508

Samsa, W. E., Vasanji, A., Midura, R. J., and Kondratov, R. V. (2016). Deficiency of circadian clock protein BMAL1 in mice results in a low bone mass phenotype. *Bone* 84, 194–203. doi: 10.1016/j.bone.2016.01.006

Sasaki, H., Hattori, Y., Ikeda, Y., Kamagata, M., Iwami, S., Yasuda, S., et al. (2016). Forced rather than voluntary exercise entrains peripheral clocks via a corticosterone/noradrenaline increase in PER2::LUC mice. *Sci. Rep.* 6:27607. doi: 10.1038/srep27607

Sasaki, H., Ohtsu, T., Ikeda, Y., Tsubosaka, M., and Shibata, S. (2014). Combination of meal and exercise timing with a high-fat diet influences energy expenditure and obesity in mice. *Chronobiol. Int.* 31, 959–975. doi: 10.3109/07420528.2014.935785

Sato, T. K., Panda, S., Miraglia, L. J., Reyes, T. M., Rudic, R. D., McNamara, P., et al. (2004). A functional genomics strategy reveals Rora as a component of the mammalian circadian clock. *Neuron* 43, 527–537. doi: 10.1016/j.neuron.2004.07.018

Schiaffino, S., Blaauw, B., and Dyar, K. A. (2016). The functional significance of the skeletal muscle clock: lessons from Bmal1 knockout models. *Skelet. Muscle* 6:33. doi: 10.1186/s13395-016-0107-5

Schiaffino, S., and Reggiani, C. (1996). Molecular diversity of myofibrillar proteins: gene regulation and functional significance. *Physiol. Rev.* 76, 371–423.

Schibler, U., Ripperger, J., and Brown, S. A. (2003). Peripheral circadian oscillators in mammals: time and food. *J. Biol. Rhythms* 18, 250–260. doi: 10.1177/0748730403018003007

Schroder, E. A., Harfmann, B. D., Zhang, X., Srikuea, R., England, J. H., Hodge, B. A., et al. (2015). Intrinsic muscle clock is necessary for musculoskeletal health. *J. Physiol.* 593, 5387–5404. doi: 10.1113/jp271436

Schroeder, A. M., Truong, D., Loh, D. H., Jordan, M. C., Roos, K. P., and Colwell, C. S. (2012). Voluntary scheduled exercise alters diurnal rhythms of behaviour, physiology and gene expression in wild-type and vasoactive intestinal peptide-deficient mice. *J. Physiol.* 590, 6213–6226. doi: 10.1113/jphysiol.2012.233676

Shao, P., Ohtsuka-Isoya, M., and Shinoda, H. (2003). Circadian rhythms in serum bone markers and their relation to the effect of etidronate in rats. *Chronobiol. Int.* 20, 325–336. doi: 10.1081/cbi-120019343

Shavlakadze, T., Anwari, T., Soffe, Z., Cozens, G., Mark, P. J., Gondro, C., et al. (2013). Impact of fasting on the rhythmic expression of myogenic and metabolic factors in skeletal muscle of adult mice. *Am. J. Physiol., Cell Physiol.* 305, C26–C35. doi: 10.1152/ajpcell.00027.2013

Shibata, S. (2004). Neural regulation of the hepatic circadian rhythm. *Anat. Rec. A Discov. Mol. Cell. Evol. Biol.* 280, 901–909. doi: 10.1002/ar.a.20095

Srivastava, A. K., Bhattacharyya, S., Li, X., Mohan, S., and Baylink, D. J. (2001). Circadian and longitudinal variation of serum C-telopeptide, osteocalcin, and skeletal alkaline phosphatase in C3H/HeJ mice. *Bone* 29, 361–367. doi: 10.1016/s8756-3282(01)00581-6

Stokkan, K. A., Yamazaki, S., Tei, H., Sakaki, Y., and Menaker, M. (2001). Entrainment of the circadian clock in the liver by feeding. *Science* 291, 490–493. doi: 10.1126/science.291.5503.490

Stranahan, A. M., Lee, K., and Mattson, M. P. (2008). Central mechanisms of HPA axis regulation by voluntary exercise. *Neuromolecular Med.* 10, 118–127. doi: 10.1007/s12017-008-8027-0

Sujino, M., Furukawa, K., Koinuma, S., Fujioka, A., Nagano, M., Iigo, M., et al. (2012). Differential entrainment of peripheral clocks in the rat by glucocorticoid and feeding. *Endocrinology* 153, 2277–2286. doi: 10.1210/en.2011-1794

Tahara, Y., Aoyama, S., and Shibata, S. (2017). The mammalian circadian clock and its entrainment by stress and exercise. *J. Physiol. Sci.* 67, 1–10. doi: 10.1007/s12576-016-0450-7

Tahara, Y., Otsuka, M., Fuse, Y., Hirao, A., and Shibata, S. (2011). Refeeding after fasting elicits insulin-dependent regulation of Per2 and Rev-erbalpha with shifts in the liver clock. *J. Biol. Rhythms* 26, 230–240. doi: 10.1177/0748730411405958

Tahara, Y., and Shibata, S. (2013). Chronobiology and nutrition. *Neuroscience* 253, 78–88. doi: 10.1016/j.neuroscience.2013.08.049

Tahara, Y., and Shibata, S. (2014). Chrono-biology, chrono-pharmacology, and chrono-nutrition. *J. Pharmacol. Sci.* 124, 320–335. doi: 10.1254/jphs.13r06cr

Tahara, Y., and Shibata, S. (2016). Circadian rhythms of liver physiology and disease: experimental and clinical evidence. *Nat. Rev. Gastroenterol. Hepatol.* 13, 217–226. doi: 10.1038/nrgastro.2016.8

Tahara, Y., Shiraishi, T., Kikuchi, Y., Haraguchi, A., Kuriki, D., Sasaki, H., et al. (2015). Entrainment of the mouse circadian clock by sub-acute physical and psychological stress. *Sci. Rep.* 5:11417. doi: 10.1038/srep11417

Takeda, S., Elefteriou, F., Levasseur, R., Liu, X., Zhao, L., Parker, K. L., et al. (2002). Leptin regulates bone formation via the sympathetic nervous system. *Cell* 111, 305–317. doi: 10.1016/s0092-8674(02)01049-8

Terazono, H., Mutoh, T., Yamaguchi, S., Kobayashi, M., Akiyama, M., Udo, R., et al. (2003). Adrenergic regulation of clock gene expression in mouse liver. *Proc. Natl. Acad. Sci. U.S.A.* 100, 6795–6800. doi: 10.1073/pnas.0936797100

Van Reeth, O., Sturis, J., Byrne, M. M., Blackman, J. D., L'Hermite-Baleriaux, M., Leproult, R., et al. (1994). Nocturnal exercise phase delays circadian rhythms of melatonin and thyrotropin secretion in normal men. *Am. J. Physiol.* 266, E964–E974.

Voytik, S. L., Przyborski, M., Badylak, S. F., and Konieczny, S. F. (1993). Differential expression of muscle regulatory factor genes in normal and denervated adult rat hindlimb muscles. *Dev. Dyn.* 198, 214–224. doi: 10.1002/aja.1001980307

Woldt, E., Sebti, Y., Solt, L. A., Duhem, C., Lancel, S., Eeckhoute, J., et al. (2013). Rev-erb- α modulates skeletal muscle oxidative capacity by regulating mitochondrial biogenesis and autophagy. *Nat. Med.* 19, 1039–1046. doi: 10.1038/nm.3213

Wolff, G., and Esser, K. A. (2012). Scheduled exercise phase shifts the circadian clock in skeletal muscle. *Med. Sci. Sports Exerc.* 44, 1663–1670. doi: 10.1249/mss.0b013e318255cf4c

Xu, C., Ochi, H., Fukuda, T., Sato, S., Sunamura, S., Takarada, T., et al. (2016). Circadian clock regulates bone resorption in mice. *J. Bone Miner. Res.* 31, 1344–1355. doi: 10.1002/jbmr.2803

Yamanaka, Y., Hashimoto, S., Tanahashi, Y., Nishide, S. Y., Honma, S., and Honma, K. (2010). Physical exercise accelerates reentrainment of human sleep-wake cycle but not of plasma melatonin rhythm to 8-h phase-advanced sleep schedule. *Am. J. Physiol. Regul. Integr. Comp. Physiol.* 298, R681–R691. doi: 10.1152/ajpregu.00345.2009

Yamanaka, Y., Honma, S., and Honma, K. (2008). Scheduled exposures to a novel environment with a running-wheel differentially accelerate re-entrainment of mice peripheral clocks to new light-dark cycles. *Genes Cells* 13, 497–507. doi: 10.1111/j.1365-2443.2008.01183.x

Yamanaka, Y., Honma, S., and Honma, K. (2016). Mistimed wheel running interferes with re-entrainment of circadian Per1 rhythms in the mouse skeletal muscle and lung. *Genes Cells* 21, 264–274. doi: 10.1111/gtc.12336

Yang, G., Chen, L., Grant, G. R., Paschos, G., Song, W. L., Musiek, E. S., et al. (2016). Timing of expression of the core clock gene Bmal1 influences its effects on aging and survival. *Sci. Transl. Med.* 8:324ra16. doi: 10.1126/scitranslmed.aad3305

Yang, N., and Meng, Q. J. (2016). Circadian clocks in articular cartilage and bone: a compass in the sea of matrices. *J. Biol. Rhythms* 31, 15–27. doi: 10.1177/0748730416662748

Yasumoto, Y., Hashimoto, C., Nakao, R., Yamazaki, H., Hiroyama, H., Nemoto, T., et al. (2016). Short-term feeding at the wrong time is sufficient to desynchronize peripheral clocks and induce obesity with hyperphagia, physical inactivity and metabolic disorders in mice. *Metab. Clin. Exp.* 65, 714–727. doi: 10.1016/j.metabol.2016.02.003

Zambon, A. C., McDearmon, E. L., Salomonis, N., Vranizan, K. M., Johansen, K. L., Adey, D., et al. (2003). Time- and exercise-dependent gene regulation in human skeletal muscle. *Genome Biol.* 4:R61. doi: 10.1186/gb-2003-4-10-r61

Zhang, R., Lahens, N. F., Ballance, H. I., Hughes, M. E., and Hogenesch, J. B. (2014). A circadian gene expression atlas in mammals: implications for biology and medicine. *Proc. Natl. Acad. Sci. U.S.A.* 111, 16219–16224. doi: 10.1073/pnas.1408886111

Zhang, X., Patel, S. P., McCarthy, J. J., Rabchevsky, A. G., Goldhamer, D. J., and Esser, K. A. (2012). A non-canonical E-box within the MyoD core enhancer is necessary for circadian expression in skeletal muscle. *Nucleic Acids Res.* 40, 3419–3430. doi: 10.1093/nar/gkr1297

Zouhal, H., Jacob, C., Delamarche, P., and Gratas-Delamarche, A. (2008). Catecholamines and the effects of exercise, training and gender. *Sports Med.* 38, 401–423. doi: 10.2165/00007256-200838050-00004

Zvonic, S., Ptitsyn, A. A., Kilroy, G., Wu, X., Conrad, S. A., Scott, L. K., et al. (2007). Circadian oscillation of gene expression in murine calvarial bone. *J. Bone Miner. Res.* 22, 357–365. doi: 10.1359/jbmr.061114

Permissions

All chapters in this book were first published in CRM, by Frontiers; hereby published with permission under the Creative Commons Attribution License or equivalent. Every chapter published in this book has been scrutinized by our experts. Their significance has been extensively debated. The topics covered herein carry significant findings which will fuel the growth of the discipline. They may even be implemented as practical applications or may be referred to as a beginning point for another development.

The contributors of this book come from diverse backgrounds, making this book a truly international effort. This book will bring forth new frontiers with its revolutionizing research information and detailed analysis of the nascent developments around the world.

We would like to thank all the contributing authors for lending their expertise to make the book truly unique.

They have played a crucial role in the development of this book. Without their invaluable contributions this book wouldn't have been possible. They have made vital efforts to compile up to date information on the varied aspects of this subject to make this book a valuable addition to the collection of many professionals and students.

This book was conceptualized with the vision of imparting up-to-date information and advanced data in this field. To ensure the same, a matchless editorial board was set up. Every individual on the board went through rigorous rounds of assessment to prove their worth. After which they invested a large part of their time researching and compiling the most relevant data for our readers.

The editorial board has been involved in producing this book since its inception. They have spent rigorous hours researching and exploring the diverse topics which have resulted in the successful publishing of this book. They have passed on their knowledge of decades through this book. To expedite this challenging task, the publisher supported the team at every step. A small team of assistant editors was also appointed to further simplify the editing procedure and attain best results for the readers.

Apart from the editorial board, the designing team has also invested a significant amount of their time in understanding the subject and creating the most relevant covers. They scrutinized every image to scout for the most suitable representation of the subject and create an appropriate cover for the book.

The publishing team has been an ardent support to the editorial, designing and production team. Their endless efforts to recruit the best for this project, has resulted in the accomplishment of this book. They are a veteran in the field of academics and their pool of knowledge is as vast as their experience in printing. Their expertise and guidance has proved useful at every step. Their uncompromising quality standards have made this book an exceptional effort. Their encouragement from time to time has been an inspiration for everyone.

The publisher and the editorial board hope that this book will prove to be a valuable piece of knowledge for researchers, students, practitioners and scholars across the globe.

List of Contributors

Barry Thomas Pritchard and Warren Stanton
School of Physiotherapy, Australian Catholic University, Brisbane, QLD, Australia

Roger Lord
School of Science, Australian Catholic University, Brisbane, QLD, Australia

Peter Petocz
Department of Statistics, Macquarie University, Sydney, NSW, Australia

Gert-Jan Pepping
School of Exercise Science, Australian Catholic University, Brisbane, QLD, Australia

Paola Cusumano, Elena Carbognin, Laura Caccin, Rodolfo Costa and Gabriella M. Mazzotta
Department of Biology, University of Padua, Padua, Italy

Milena Damulewicz
Department of Cell Biology and Imaging, Jagiellonian University, Kraków, Poland

Antonietta Puricella, Valeria Specchia and Maria Pia Bozzetti
Department of Biological and Environmental Sciences and Technologies, University of Salento, Lecce, Italy

Michihiro Mieda, Emi Hasegawa and Takeshi Sakurai
Department of Molecular Neuroscience and Integrative Physiology, Graduate School of Medical Sciences, Kanazawa University, Kanazawa, Japan

Nicoletta Kessaris
Department of Cell and Developmental Biology, Wolfson Institute for Biomedical Research, University College London, London, UK

Kiran Padmanabhan
"Molecular and Epigenetic Regulation of Biological Clocks", Université de Lyon, Institut de Génomique Fonctionnelle de Lyon, CNRS UMR 5242, École Normale Supérieure de Lyon, Université Claude Bernard Lyon 1, Lyon, France
INSERM, Paris, France

Marc Billaud
"Clinical and Experimental Model of Lymphomagenesis", Université de Lyon, Université Claude Bernard Lyon 1, INSERM 1052, CNRS 5286, Centre Léon Bérard, Centre de recherche en cancérologie de Lyon, Lyon, France

Donají Chi-Castañeda
Laboratorio de Neurotoxicología, Departamento de Toxicología, Centro de Investigación y de Estudios Avanzados del Instituto Politécnico Nacional, Ciudad de Mexico, Mexico
Soluciones para un México Verde S.A. de C.V., Ciudad de Mexico, Mexico

Arturo Ortega
Laboratorio de Neurotoxicología, Departamento de Toxicología, Centro de Investigación y de Estudios Avanzados del Instituto Politécnico Nacional, Ciudad de Mexico, Mexico

Aurea Blancas-Velazquez
Institute of Cellular and Integrative Neurosciences, Centre National de la Recherche Scientifique UPR-3212, University of Strasbourg, Strasbourg, France
Department of Endocrinology and Metabolism, Academic Medical Center, University of Amsterdam, Amsterdam, Netherlands
Metabolism and Reward Group, Netherlands Institute for Neuroscience, Amsterdam, Netherlands

Jorge Mendoza
Institute of Cellular and Integrative Neurosciences, Centre National de la Recherche Scientifique UPR-3212, University of Strasbourg, Strasbourg, France

Alexandra N. Garcia and Susanne E. la Fleur
Department of Endocrinology and Metabolism, Academic Medical Center, University of Amsterdam, Amsterdam, Netherlands
Metabolism and Reward Group, Netherlands Institute for Neuroscience, Amsterdam, Netherlands

Anna Blasiak and Marian H. Lewandowski
Department of Neurophysiology and Chronobiology, Institute of Zoology, Jagiellonian University, Krakow, Poland

Andrew L. Gundlach
Neuropeptides Division, The Florey Institute of Neuroscience and Mental Health, Parkville, VIC, Australia
Florey Department of Neuroscience and Mental Health, The University of Melbourne, Parkville, VIC, Australia

Grzegorz Hess
Department of Neurophysiology and Chronobiology, Institute of Zoology, Jagiellonian University, Krakow, Poland
Institute of Pharmacology, Polish Academy of Sciences, Krakow, Poland

Anthony H. Tsang
Chronophysiology Group, Medical Department I, University of Lübeck, Lübeck, Germany
Department of Clinical Biochemistry, Institute of Metabolic Science, University of Cambridge, Cambridge, UK

Mariana Astiz, Brinja Leinweber and Henrik Oster
Chronophysiology Group, Medical Department I, University of Lübeck, Lübeck, Germany

Leonardo D. De Araujo, Ernane T. Uchoa, Jose Antunes-Rodrigues and Lucila L. Elias
Department of Physiology, University of Sao Paulo, Ribeirao Preto, Brazil

Ana C. Bueno
Department of Pediatrics of the Ribeirao Preto Medical School, University of Sao Paulo, Ribeirao Preto, Brazil

Fernanda B. Coeli-Lacchini, Silvia L. Roa, Clarissa S. Martins, Paula C. Elias, Ayrton C. Moreira and Margaret De Castro
Department of Internal Medicine, University of Sao Paulo, Ribeirao Preto, Brazil

Karen Schmitt, Amandine Grimm and Anne Eckert
Neurobiology Lab for Brain Aging and Mental Health, Transfaculty Research Platform, Molecular and Cognitive Neuroscience, University of Basel, Basel, Switzerland
Psychiatric University Clinics, University of Basel, Basel, Switzerland

William Bechtel
Department of Philosophy and Center for Circadian Biology, University of California San Diego, San Diego, CA, USA

Ceyda Cubuk, Julia Kemmling, Andrej Fabrizius and Annika Herwig
Zoologisches Institut, Universität Hamburg, Hamburg, Germany

Florian Atger
Department of Diabetes and Circadian Rhythms, Nestlé Institute of Health Sciences, Lausanne, Switzerland
Department of Pharmacology and Toxicology, University of Lausanne, Lausanne, Switzerland

Daniel Mauvoisin and Cédric Gobet
School of Life Sciences, Institute of Bioengineering, Ecole Polytechnique Fédérale de Lausanne, Lausanne, Switzerland
Department of Diabetes and Circadian Rhythms, Nestlé Institute of Health Sciences, Lausanne, Switzerland

Benjamin Weger
Department of Diabetes and Circadian Rhythms, Nestlé Institute of Health Sciences, Lausanne, Switzerland

Frédéric Gachon
Department of Diabetes and Circadian Rhythms, Nestlé Institute of Health Sciences, Lausanne, Switzerland
School of Life Sciences, Ecole Polytechnique Fédérale de Lausanne, Lausanne, Switzerland

Marietou Daou and M. Elizabeth Wilcox
Interdepartment Division of Critical Care Medicine, University of Toronto, Toronto, ON, Canada
Department of Medicine (Respirology), University Health Network, Toronto, ON, Canada

Irene Telias
Interdepartment Division of Critical Care Medicine, University of Toronto, Toronto, ON, Canada
Department of Medicine (Respirology), University Health Network, Toronto, ON, Canada
Department of Medicine (Critical Care Medicine), St. Michael's Hospital, Toronto, ON, Canada
Keenan Research Centre, Li Ka Shing Knowledge Institute, Toronto, ON, Canada

Magdy Younes
Sleep Disorders Centre, Winnipeg, MB, Canada

Laurent Brochard
Interdepartment Division of Critical Care Medicine, University of Toronto, Toronto, ON, Canada
Department of Medicine (Critical Care Medicine), St. Michael's Hospital, Toronto, ON, Canada
Keenan Research Centre, Li Ka Shing Knowledge Institute, Toronto, ON, Canada

Volodymyr Petrenko and Charna Dibner
Endocrinology, Diabetes, Hypertension and Nutrition Division, Department of Specialties of Medicine, University Hospital of Geneva, Geneva, Switzerland
Faculty of Medicine, Department of Cell Physiology and Metabolism, University of Geneva, Geneva, Switzerland
Institute of Genetics and Genomics in Geneva (iGE3), Geneva, Switzerland
Diabetes Center of the Faculty of Medicine, University of Geneva, Geneva, Switzerland

Yvan Gosmain
Diabetes Center of the Faculty of Medicine, University of Geneva, Geneva, Switzerland
Molecular Diabetes Laboratory, Endocrinology, Diabetes, Hypertension and Nutrition Division, Faculty of Medicine, Department of Specialties of Medicine, University Hospital of Geneva, University of Geneva, Geneva, Switzerland

Pei-Lin Yang, Teresa M. Ward, Susan M. McCurry and Robert L. Burr
School of Nursing, University of Washington, Seattle, WA, United States

Michael V. Vitiello
Department of Psychiatry and Behavioral Sciences, University of Washington, Seattle, WA, United States

Catherine L. Hough and Vishesh K. Kapur
Division of Pulmonary, Critical Care and Sleep Medicine, University of Washington, Seattle, WA, United States

Elizabeth C. Parsons
Division of Pulmonary, Critical Care and Sleep Medicine, University of Washington, Seattle, WA, United States
VA Puget Sound Health Care System, Seattle, WA, United States

Gal Manella and Gad Asher
Department of Biomolecular Sciences, Weizmann Institute of Science, Rehovot, Israel

Dalia Luz De Ita-Pérez and Mauricio Díaz-Muñoz
Departamento de Neurobiología Celular y Molecular, Instituto de Neurobiología, Universidad Nacional Autónoma de México, Querétaro, Querétaro, México

Kenneth A. Dyar
Molecular Endocrinology, Institute for Diabetes and Obesity, Helmholtz Diabetes Center (HMGU) and German Center for Diabetes Research (DZD), Munich, Germany

Kristin L. Eckel-Mahan
Brown Foundation of Molecular Medicine for the Prevention of Human Diseases of McGovern Medical School, University of Texas Health Science Center at Houston, Houston, TX, United States

Brian T. Palmisano
Department of Molecular Physiology and Biophysics, Vanderbilt University School of Medicine, Nashville, TN, USA

John M. Stafford
Department of Molecular Physiology and Biophysics, Vanderbilt University School of Medicine, Nashville, TN, USA
VA Tennessee Valley Healthcare System, Nashville, TN, USA
Division of Diabetes, Endocrinology, and Metabolism, Department of Medicine, Vanderbilt University School of Medicine, Nashville, TN, USA

Julie S. Pendergast
Division of Diabetes, Endocrinology, and Metabolism, Department of Medicine, Vanderbilt University School of Medicine, Nashville, TN, USA
Department of Biology, University of Kentucky, Lexington, KY, USA

Andrew A. Butler, Clemence Girardet, Maria Mavrikaki and Heather Macarthur
Department of Pharmacology and Physiology, Saint Louis University School of Medicine, St. Louis, MO, USA

James L. Trevaskis
In vivo Pharmacology, Cardiovascular and Metabolic Disease, Medimmune, Gaithersburg, MD, USA

Daniel L. Marks
Papé Family Pediatric Research Institute, Oregon Health and Science University, Portland, OR, USA

Susan A. Farr
Department of Internal Medicine, Division of Geriatrics, Saint Louis University School of Medicine, St. Louis, MO, USA
VA Medical Center, St. Louis, MO, USA

Salvatore De Cosmo and Gianluigi Mazzoccoli
Department of Medical Sciences, Division of Internal Medicine and Chronobiology Unit, IRCCS "Ospedale Casa Sollievo della Sofferenza", San Giovanni Rotondo, Italy

Shinya Aoyama
Organization for University Research Initiatives, Waseda University, Tokyo, Japan
Laboratory of Physiology and Pharmacology, School of Advanced Science and Engineering, Waseda University, Tokyo, Japan

Shigenobu Shibata
Laboratory of Physiology and Pharmacology, School of Advanced Science and Engineering, Waseda University, Tokyo, Japan

Index

www.ingramcontent.com/pod-product-compliance
Lightning Source LLC
LaVergne TN
LVHW081021210926
848485LV00004B/922